From Online Platforms to Digital Monopolies

Studies in Critical Social Sciences

Series Editor
David Fasenfest
(*Wayne State University*)

VOLUME 199

New Scholarship in Political Economy

Series Editors
David Fasenfest
(*Wayne State University*)
Alfredo Saad-Filho
(*King's College London*)

Editorial Board
Kevin B. Anderson (*University of California, Santa Barbara*)
Tom Brass (*formerly of SPS, University of Cambridge*)
Raju Das (*York University*)
Ben Fine ((*emeritus*) SOAS *University of London*)
Jayati Ghosh (*Jawaharlal Nehru University*)
Elizabeth Hill (*University of Sydney*)
Dan Krier (*Iowa State University*)
Lauren Langman (*Loyola University Chicago*)
Valentine Moghadam (*Northeastern University*)
David N. Smith (*University of Kansas*)
Susanne Soederberg (*Queen's University*)
Aylin Topal (*Middle East Technical University*)
Fiona Tregenna (*University of Johannesburg*)
Matt Vidal (*Loughborough University London*)
Michelle Williams (*University of the Witwatersrand*)

VOLUME 10

The titles published in this series are listed at *brill.com/nspe*

From Online Platforms to Digital Monopolies

Technology, Information and Power

By

Jonas C.L. Valente

BRILL

LEIDEN | BOSTON

Cover illustration: Bust of Karl Marx, 1939, by S.D. Merkurov, at the Fallen Monument Park (Muzeon Park of Arts) in Moscow, Russia. Photo courtesy of Alfredo Saad-Filho.

The Library of Congress Cataloging-in-Publication Data is available online at http://catalog.loc.gov
LC record available at http://lccn.loc.gov/2021034214

Typeface for the Latin, Greek, and Cyrillic scripts: "Brill". See and download: brill.com/brill-typeface.

ISSN 2666-2205
ISBN 978-90-04-46601-2 (hardback)
ISBN 978-90-04-46614-2 (e-book)

Copyright 2021 by Koninklijke Brill NV, Leiden, The Netherlands.
Koninklijke Brill NV incorporates the imprints Brill, Brill Nijhoff, Brill Hotei, Brill Schöningh, Brill Fink, Brill mentis, Vandenhoeck & Ruprecht, Böhlau Verlag and V&R Unipress.
All rights reserved. No part of this publication may be reproduced, translated, stored in a retrieval system, or transmitted in any form or by any means, electronic, mechanical, photocopying, recording or otherwise, without prior written permission from the publisher.
Authorization to photocopy items for internal or personal use is granted by Koninklijke Brill NV provided that the appropriate fees are paid directly to The Copyright Clearance Center, 222 Rosewood Drive, Suite 910, Danvers, MA 01923, USA. Fees are subject to change.

This book is printed on acid-free paper and produced in a sustainable manner.

Contents

Acknowledgments IX
List of Figures and Tables X

Introduction 1

1 **About Technology** 11
    1 Artefact and Technological Systems 13
    2 Developing Artefacts and Technological Systems 21
    3 Society and Technology 26
    4 Technology and Society 32
    5 Summary: The Technological Regulation Approach 40
    6 Values Base to Analyse Technology under Capitalism 47

2 **Technology and Capitalist Development** 56
    1 Technology and the Economic Sphere 70
    2 Technology and the Political–Institutional Sphere 75
    3 Technology and the Cultural Sphere 83

3 **Information and Communication Technologies and Neoliberalism** 91
    1 Context: The 1970s Crisis, Neoliberalism and ICTs 94
    2 Technology and the Economic Sphere: ICTs and Their Impacts on the Economy 99
    3 Impacts on Labour Relations 104
    4 Impacts on Competition Dynamics 111

4 **The Technological Paradigm of Information and Communications Technologies** 121
    1 Structural Technologies: The Internet 126
    2 Infrastructure: High-Speed Data Networks (Broadband) 128
    3 Core Input: Microprocessors 132
    4 Carrier Branch: Computers 134
    5 Emerging Technologies: Big Data, Algorithms and Artificial Intelligence 139

5 **Digital Platforms** 152
    1 Definitions 152
    2 Characteristics 158

3   Typology of Digital Platforms   163
  4   Production Process and Labour Relations   164
  5   Competition on Platforms   170
      5.1   *Business Models*   171
      5.2   *Market Structure*   173
      5.3   *Competitive Strategies*   178
  6   Digital Monopolies   181
  7   Legislation and the Debate on Legal Regulation   184

6 **Google**   193
  1   General Technological Trajectory   196
  2   Rules   200
  3   Ownership, Control and Management Structure   205
  4   Production Process   207
  5   Competitive Performance   211
  6   System Components and Technical Resources   218
      6.1   *Other Bets*   226
  7   Dissemination   227
  8   Appropriation   231
  9   Relationship with the Values Base   238
      9.1   *Rights Promotion and Guarantees*   239
      9.2   *Damages and Violation of Rights*   240
  10 The Technological System's Impact on Society   246
  11 Analytical Overview: Google and the Fight For Online Information Control   252

7 **Facebook**   259
  1   General Technological Trajectory   261
  2   Rules   265
  3   Ownership, Control and Management Structure   269
  4   Production Process   271
  5   Competitive Performance   275
  6   System Components and Technical Resources   280
      6.1   *Primary Technological System: Facebook*   280
           6.1.1   Information (Newsfeed and Timeline)   280
           6.1.2   Connections (Friends, Groups, Pages and Events)   282
           6.1.3   Transactions   285
           6.1.4   Platform   286
      6.2   *Secondary Subsystems*   286

7   Dissemination   290
8   Appropriation   294
9   Relationship with the Values Base   302
       9.1   *Rights, Promotion and Guarantees*   302
       9.2   *Damages and Violation of Rights*   302
10   The Technological System's Impact on Society   310
11   Analytical Overview: Facebook and the Fight for Online Information Control   316

8 Final Considerations   324

References   341
Index   391

Acknowledgments

This book is based in my doctoral thesis, presented in Sociology Department of University of Brasília, Brazil. I would like to thank my thesis advisor, Michelangelo Trigueiro, and all the department colleagues for the discussions that contributed to this research. Thanks, also, to the professors who participated in the dissertation defence: Cesar Bolaño, Fernanda Sobral and Christiana Freitas. I thank Professor Francisco Louçã, who worked as an advisor during my visiting researcher period in 2017 in the Superior Institute of Economy and Management in Lisbon, Portugal. I thank the Sociology Department for nominating the thesis for the Capes Award, the main post-graduate prize for Brazilian scholarly works, and for the University of Brasília thesis award.

I would like to thank Professor Alfredo Saad-Filho for the invitation to publish in this book series. I would also like to thank Professor David Fasenfest for all the support and orientation during the preparation process. Finally, I would like to thank my partner, Raisa Pina, my family, Katia, Flavio and Leo, and all the friends who helped me get here. Special thanks go to my intellectual and lifelong friend, Helena Martins, for all the dialogue about the present and future of capitalism, information and communication, and to Bia Barbosa, Marcos Urupá and Renata Maffezoli for their friendship and support during our mutual intellectual and political journeys.

Figures and Tables

Figures

1. Information and communication technologies trajectory   123
2. Business dynamism in ICT   124
3. Wired technologies share by continent   130

Tables

1. Google – Financial data overview   214
2. Facebook – Financial data overview   277
3. Facebook – User base historical evolution   291

Introduction

The digital economy has been identified as a critical element in the development process of the capitalist system. Its implementation directly affects the productive performance of nations. Such a theory – widely disseminated by international organizations, governments, companies, and researchers – emerged in the 2010s as a mantra and, at the same time, as a beacon to project paths to success in different areas, from productivity to social development, and the rationalization of state management. Reaching these goals and unleashing the potential of these new technologies would configure a 'digital transformation.' According to the World Economic Forum (2018), this process could 'release' $100 trillion over the next decade. Regardless of segment or size, digitalization will not only yield benefits but will also be necessary for organizations to survive in a new, stronger, and different competitive environment. Following this argument, adapting becomes even more urgent in an economic scenario of considerable uncertainty after the last economic crisis, known as the 2007–8 crash.[1] This created the setting in which the theory and concrete changes of the digital economy flourished. Without a political solution or a way to deal with the logic of accumulation established up to then by the capitalist system in its neoliberal phase, at the turn of the 2020s, the 'digital transformation' became a lure to the system, even though its horizons were unclear. It was proclaimed at the G20 that "as digitalization is transforming every aspect of our economies and societies, we recognize the critical role played by effective use of data, as an enabler of economic growth, development and social well-being" (G20, 2019).

This trend indicates issues central to technology. Do digital devices make use of the best possible technologies for a particular end, or are these devices designed based on the interests of their manufacturers? If so, what are the factors involved in these decisions, other than selecting the most appropriate means or the most suitable components for a given purpose (higher durability,

---

1 Even though statistics indicate a recovery, it has been erratic, marked by a slowdown in productivity, a re-establishment of employment levels below the pre-crisis levels, and by modest growth. Additionally, the crisis still reverberates in the periphery of the system, as in Latin American countries. Political disputes have also escalated, whether within countries or between different states, disturbing geopolitical balance of the 1990s and 2000s. Within this framework of disputes, political forces seek solutions to the crisis and new expansion cycles, but through a spread of fascist or ultra-right regimes, supported by xenophobia, hate speech, and disinformation.

resistance)? How does this affect the technological development process? To what extent is it driven by external forces? Does it have autonomy regarding this kind of pressure? Would this be a linear manifestation of progress? How can we think about similar artefacts in terms of success and failure? Are there different paths and different styles of objects in dispute (just as car models)? How is development conditioned by the system's general determinants and impacted by its performance under capitalism? How do people perceive these objects, and how do they use them?

If, on the one hand, these problems do not often emerge in public debate forums, on the other hand, they have given rise to a variety of discussions in different areas, from engineering to sociology, economics, and philosophy. Technology emerges as a central aspect in understanding contemporary societies. Its specific manifestations, operational logic, and historical development are complex themes. It is also a broad theme in terms of the possible approaches to understanding it. Beyond the optimistic theory that prevails in the public debate regarding a new 'digital' paradigm for technology and information, some critical approaches question such issues, indicating the risks of using such technologies. These approaches seek to understand which interests these technologies serve and how they benefit or harm welfare, human rights, social justice, and democracy. These alternative interpretations are quite useful to go beyond the 'digital transformation' speech, which appears both among international organizations and scholars.

According to them, in its latest period, neoliberalism has suffered a mutation characterized by productive restructuring and financial dominance. In this recent evolution, information, communication, culture, and technologies have gained importance, responding to the needs of the capital to find a new accumulation regime after the 1970s crisis. In doing so, they also experienced a transformation, as their markets were reconfigured, as has been often discussed over the past two decades. Such movement, which outlined new growth waves in central capitalist nations and in the so-called emerging countries, was interrupted by the 2007–2008 crisis, which highlighted the accumulation regime's instability. This crisis of the financial and the overall system posed new challenges to capital reproduction, which sought a more profound productive restructuring and prevalence of financialization.

In a second stage, it sought the support of a new technological paradigm, based on the development of information and communication technologies (ICTs) on three fronts. The first is the massive collection of data, referred to in the literature as 'Big Data' or 'datafication.' Usually referred to as the 'new oil,' data are much more complex and valuable assets to capital, since they are not finite. Their accumulation involves an economic dimension, but, also, one of social control, behaviour modulation, and surveillance. The second front relates to the smart processing of this information, of goods and services, not only in the virtual environment, but in society as a whole. This processing is done through algorithms and artificial intelligence systems. The third front involves services and applications expanding to all types of social activities in the form of apps, automating decisions and modulating behaviour.

Digital platforms are critical actors in the evolution of this new paradigm and its spread to other social spheres. They can pervade all three fronts, and are leading actors in all of them, whether collecting data on a massive scale, creating intelligent processing systems, or offering applications and services to a broad user base. Their business models are based on gathering information from their users to distribute segmented advertising or to present customized content and services. When competing in the so-called 'attention economy,' collecting and processing data are essential. This operational logic is a response to the demands of capitalism, in its 10-year long search to recover from a systemic crisis, since it is still struggling with weak productivity rates, minimal growth rates, and increased inequality. If, on the one hand, the top of the social pyramid was successful in its strategy of recovering profits, on the other, the accumulation regime failed to create a general expansion cycle or ensure a distribution dynamic that was similar to the pre-crisis period. Amid fiercer competition, the new paradigm is seen as a way for individual capital to create value and to promote nations' growth. Digital platforms optimize the coordination between supply and demand, whether during circulation, to complete commodities cycles, or during production, to buy and sell the labour force.

These actors have become a concern for economic actors, governments, and international bodies. The recognition of their importance has led to their centrality in contemporary society, in categorizations of society and its spheres, using terms such as 'platform capitalism' (Srnicek, 2017; Vallas, 2019), 'platform economy' (Lehdonvirta et al., 2019), or the like, such as 'online platform economy' (Farrell and Greig, 2017). Other authors describe platforms not only as actors but as an adaptation process of social activities to their logic, the so-called 'platformization' (Van Dijck, 2020; Helmond, 2015). Digital platforms are active mediation spaces that connect different actors interested in purchasing goods or services (such as buying a product on Amazon or downloading an application from the Apple Store), social interaction (such as Facebook or Snapchat), or specific activities (such as hiring an Uber driver for a trip). As a technological system (Hughes, 1993), the role of users is even more central and integrated into the artefacts that are part of the system. Increasingly, offering services over the internet using the platform format is becoming a viable option, with its own various activities, objectives, operational logics, and business models.

A reference survey on this universe (Evans and Gawer, 2016) analysed 176 platforms, with a total market value of US$4.3 trillion, employing 1.3 million people. Another survey (Accenture, 2018) outlined that the top 15 public platform companies represented US$2.6 trillion in market capitalization. These actors have become fundamental elements of the digital ecosystem for several reasons, such as the development of efficient technological resources, questionable competitive strategies, and the exploitation of network effects that are characteristic of the digital economy and, more specifically, of this segment's economic logic. However, their success is also related to offering solutions that are welcomed by users. A public consultation conducted by the European Union with 10,000 respondents (European Union, 2016) identified what were later referred to as the "main perceived benefits" of using digital platforms. Access to information was the most indicated aspect (53%), followed by communication and interaction (51%), new market and business opportunities (46%), increased choice (43%), and price comparison (36%). From the standpoint of representation in the world economy, these platforms have assumed prominent positions on the list of the world's most valuable companies. According to Forbes Magazine's "World's Most Valuable Brands," the five most valuable companies are platforms: Apple, Alphabet/Google, Microsoft, Facebook, and Amazon.[2] These companies became the favourite bets of the market through an investment boom. Between 2009 and 2015, more than $23 billion was invested in the sector. By 2013, this amount was below US$2 billion (Fairview Capital, 2015).

However, although these platforms are currently seen as a dynamic segment of digital transformation, they have been questioned in several spheres of society, such as in the media, governments, civil society organizations, and the judicial branch of many governments. Google has been criticized for giving visibility to hate speech or discriminatory content in searches. YouTube was pointed out by experts as a driver for radicalization, providing visibility to conspiracy theories (such as flat-Earth theories) (Tufecki, 2018; Ribeiro et al., 2020). Uber was sued for labour rights violations (Conger, 2020). Studies (Ferré-Sarudrní, 2018) have pointed out that Airbnb contributed to the increase in rental prices. WhatsApp was accused of being responsible for lynch mob-related deaths in India, motivated by rumours spread on the network (Safi, 2018). The social network was also identified as the main channel for the illegal dissemination

---

[2] Information available at: https://www.forbes.com/powerful-brands/list/.

of mass content in the 2018 Brazilian elections (including fake news) (Borges, 2018). In 2019, new accusations of that sort came to light in the election campaign in India. Facebook was pointed out as the main platform for the distribution of disinformation in several political disputes and processes, such as the US elections, the Colombian peace agreement plebiscite, and the referendum on the withdrawal of the United Kingdom from the European Union, all in 2016. In 2019, an attack on two mosques that left 50 dead in New Zealand was broadcast live on Facebook. The platform was intensely criticized for not bringing down the broadcast in time and for not being able to prevent the episode's videos from being posted afterward (Whittaker, 2019).

Digital platforms have become central not only to the internet and digital economy, but to society as a whole. Such relevance relates not only to their size (reaching billions of people around the world) and market value, but, also, to the risks they bring to society in several areas – in politics, mediating the public debate and allowing the propagation of misinformation; in culture, being appropriated to disseminate hate speech and positions against minorities, or simply against different individuals and groups; in society, with the impacts of their excessive use (with studies relating the excess of time spent on these platforms to the decline of well-being and to disorders); and to the economy as a whole, and specifically to the internet, considering the abuse of its dominant market conditions.

Platforms are multidisciplinary objects. The literature offers analyses in several areas, from law to economics, communications, administration, and sociology. The success and scope of the platforms are related to the technological solutions developed. The services these companies offer are directly related to the tools and systems created by them. Likewise, the problems resulting from these platforms' performance also relate to their technical resources (such as the algorithm that selects Google search results or that defines the propagation of posts on Facebook). Thus, investigating these platforms' technological basis is crucial to understanding their evolution and the importance they have acquired in society as a whole.

However, such investigation does not assume a deterministic view. On the contrary, the analysis of these platforms can only succeed by considering their dynamic relationship with society, within the social context of which they are a part. The examples shown demonstrate how platforms must not be evaluated on their own, but as part of a broader digital ecosystem. This ecosystem must be seen as integrating a digital transformation effort, a project to respond to economic challenges, and spreading to other spheres of society. Similarly, examples of problems that have gained attention show that their impact is significant to several aspects of contemporary sociability. Therefore, a contextualized approach seeks to respond to the challenges imposed on these actors. As stated by different authors, technology both shapes and is shaped by society simultaneously.

It is necessary to contextualize the micro–macro relationship, and, also, the historical dimension of platforms. The society's view on platforms often idealizes instantly successful projects started by lonely and brilliant developers (or even students, as in the case of Facebook's CEO, Mark Zuckerberg, or the founders of Google, Larry Page and Sergey Brin). Compared to other companies, these platforms' exponential growth generates questions as to how these actors have achieved such progress within such short periods of time. Beyond a simple explanation for their success, their historical development can be seen either as a linear process, as previously pointed out, or as the result of successive choices and decisions resulting from disputes and influenced by several factors. These include broader factors (such as the willingness to invest in technology companies, or an economic crisis) and factors that are specific to the technological segment where the platform operates (the evolution of microprocessors' processing capacity or the sophistication of data analysis systems). Thus, a historical perspective allows us to identify trajectories and how objects change, avoiding an ahistorical view that generalizes a particular manifestation in time. On the other hand, it may create a limitation for such investigation, since it risks becoming dated, considering these companies' dynamism.

Based on these premises, we are interested in understanding Google and Facebook's technological trajectories, considering the social and internal factors that have influenced their development, as well as how these platforms impact the experience of their users and society in several spheres. In such an effort, we aim to identify the social drivers that have influenced the development of both platforms, characterize the technological paradigm of their segment (ICT), which is the basis for their technological trajectory, understand their economic dimensions, such as their control structure, production process and their competitive performance, map their components, as well as the technical resources associated with them, understand how their technical resources are appropriated by their users, and point out their impacts on the rights and safeguards of users, as well as on the social (scientific–technological, political–institutional, cultural, and economic) spheres of activity.

Having pointed out the importance of the technological element, the analysis of these platforms' evolution will be based on a critical approach we refer to as 'technological regulation.' This approach is designed to investigate these technological systems as a process whose development is marked by social (economic, political, cultural) drivers and by particular drivers resulting from the technological paradigm. Since these platforms are, fundamentally, companies, the analysis of such factors is complemented by these platforms' characteristics as providers of goods and services acting in the competitive capitalist environment. Also, the result of the choices made by the systems' controllers based on these factors and features is manifested by the components and their respective technical resources. These factors and the systems' operational logics guide how these platforms are appropriated, which is how their components (and the platforms' services as a whole) are realized. Finally, considering technology as a process implies observing these platforms' impact on their users and on society.

For such, we selected two examples: Google and Facebook. Google was born as a search engine and dominated this market, reaching more than 90% of participation in most countries (except for China, where it is prohibited). However, from an early stage, it worked to expand its operations. It entered the mobile applications market by acquiring the Android operating system, which is currently used in more than 2.3 billion devices. It acquired YouTube, a video streaming service that has become the largest on the planet, with almost 2 billion users. It entered the browser segment with Chrome, used by more than 1 billion people. It launched a suite of communication and document production tools, headed by Gmail, with over 1.5 billion users. The company also decided to operate in the equipment sector and institutionalized its multi-service strategy by establishing the Alphabet conglomerate in 2015. Under this umbrella, it has incorporated subsidiaries ranging from the development of autonomous vehicles to longevity research, as well as internet connection projects through the use of balloons.

Facebook is the largest social network in the world, reaching 2.3 billion people. The company controls not only the app of the same name but the other three main social networks (Facebook Messenger, WhatsApp, and Instagram). In the international ranking are also Tencent's digital social networks, which operate mainly in China (WeChat, QQ, and Qzone).[3] Thus, while Facebook does not control all the information in the world, it has created high-intensity online experience spaces with high daily usage rates. By allowing connections with friends and acquaintances (including from other locations), Facebook has built the largest social map on the planet, allowing people not only to interact with acquaintances but with other individuals through tools such as groups and events. Facebook also created resources for different types of users (from people to businesses) to have their own space there. Their presence on Facebook often replaces their presence on the Web as a whole (i.e.

---

3 They have many users in absolute numbers, but little penetration in most countries.

organizations that choose not to have websites and only maintain fan pages on the platform).

This book is organized into seven chapters. The argumentation begins with a debate on technology. It is investigated using a method based on its unit of analysis, the artefact. It then proceeds to a contextualization within society and its concrete historical manifestations. Finally, it focuses on the relationship between technological development and society. Such construction involves both problems related to the neutrality and autonomy of technology and an example of its concrete historical manifestation under capitalism. The approach we call technological regulation is drawn from the critical theory of technology. Chapter 2 discusses technology from the emergence and development of the capitalist system. Chapter 3 discusses the information and communication technologies (ICT) sector, examining these technologies in articulation with the development of the capitalist system, tracing its recent historical evolution, how the regulation social factors have influenced them, and how they have affected the most recent period of the system.

Chapter 4 focuses on understanding the factors that regulate technological development. The elements that constitute the information and communication technological paradigm are shown, pointing to the recent evolution of ICTs, their current stage, and their development, considering some specific technologies. The first is the internet, approached as a structural technology. The second, broadband networks, are currently considered as ICTs' underlying infrastructure. The third element is microprocessors, seen here as central products, the key artefact in most ICTs. Next, the text discusses the recent evolution of computers, considered here as the driving force of this sector. Finally, some emerging technologies are examined, especially data collection (Big Data), algorithms, and artificial intelligence.

Chapter 5 attempts to describe the phenomenon of digital platforms and identify its characteristics and operational logics. Our typology approach is presented to identify the specificities and diversity of this universe, including modalities with specific aspects. Finally, considering that these platforms (except for only a few, such as Wikipedia) are companies operating within capitalism, the chapter reflects on labour relations under this system and their performance in the sphere of capitalist circulation, articulating an analysis of the technological dimension and a critical perspective on the political economy of these actors.

Chapters 6 and 7 analyse the case studies of Google and Facebook. Based on the technological regulation approach, the analysis covers a range of platform development aspects, seeking a broader understanding, combining technical, economic, social, and political dimensions for these systems' production and their appropriation by different citizens and organizations. The journey begins by delineating a "general" technological trajectory, with an evolutionary timeline of both platforms. Recognizing these platforms' corporate nature and the relevance of understanding how this operates as a regulating factor, we examine their control and management structures, production processes (including the actors and goals, labour relations, and production procedures that affect them), and competitive performances (business models, financial performance, market positions, and competitive strategies). Then, the analysis focuses on the technological core, with its components and technical resources. Technical resources are considered regarding their functionalities and operational logic, as well as how their architecture impacts the user experience. We also examine the dissemination of these components through access numbers and legitimation processes. The appropriation of these components by users is then examined. To evaluate this phenomenon, we use interviews conducted with different audiences, considering the technological systems' set of factors and operating dynamics. Finally, the chapters briefly map the positive and negative impacts on the users' rights and on the social (scientific–technological, political–institutional, economic, and cultural) spheres of activity.

These analyses intend to contribute to technology studies and a more accurate understanding of digital platforms, especially Google and Facebook. The research sheds light on essential categories to analyse technological systems. We intend to emphasize the relevance of considering economic, political, and cultural structural aspects to understand the recent development of information and communication technologies, especially in the shaping of their technological paradigms (according to a particular interpretation of categories). We theorize about digital platforms and offer a description of their characteristics and operational logic. In the discussion, we suggest the concept of a phenomenon we refer to as 'digital monopolies.' Although the term is not original, it is associated with a particular understanding of the recent movement of these digital ecosystem actors.

Finally, an attempt is made to trace back the technological trajectory of the two most popular platforms in the world: Google and Facebook. For this, we articulate several technological regulating factors to map their concrete development. The aim is to show how various factors intersect during the life of each of these platforms, how these elements are reflected in the social content of these technological systems, and how they affect society, whether related to rights or different activities. We conclude by acknowledging both platforms as examples of digital monopolies. They emerged from different niches and now have a multifaceted reach. Their technological base and economic capacity offer enormous power and ability to influence not only the digital ecosystem but the whole of society, both now and in the future.

CHAPTER 1

About Technology

The promise of the benefits of digital devices manifested during the last decades after centuries of placing technology as a relevant element in the development of societies. Under the historical form of capitalism, the material basis was stated as evolution's driving force, and the driver of welfare through ideas such as 'progress,' 'modernity,' and 'development.' However, technology stretches far beyond a myriad of objects used within the realm of nature, as a simplistic view might suggest. To get to the explanation suggested here, we started from a basic unit – the artefact – and moved towards a general understanding of technology, to point out its dialectic relationship with society. In the first part of the discussion, in a movement we call 'deconstruction of the technological dimension,' our reflection is based on the concept of the artefact as a unit of analysis. Still in a more abstract sphere, we analyse its constitutive aspects, content (including its material basis and components), functionalities, implementation goals, inherent production process, dissemination as a product, and access by users, as well as its appropriation. Then, the technology is examined as more than merely individual artefacts, but as an articulated whole under the concept of technological systems. These systems have complex properties. Different actors come into play, establishing relationships among them (including the definition of the operating rules). As systems invested with materiality and existing in concrete social reality, they are organized according to property and control regimes, operate under certain business models, are manufactured from specific social relations of production, and circulate for consumption in the market.

These systems, however, are not static, but dynamic. Therefore, any attempt at an explanation needs to encompass their development logic, including the forms of production, dissemination, and appropriation of technology. In addition to recognizing their dynamic dimension, it is essential to take a step further and look at their context. Thus, the analysis moves on to situate technological systems in society as a whole and to consider its specific spheres (politics, economy, and culture). Technological systems are understood not as isolated social phenomena, but, on the contrary, as actors immersed in social and power relations. They are controlled, managed, planned, and produced by collectively and socially organized people in specific historical contexts. Likewise, the users of artefacts and systems are people and associations inserted into different contexts, with different characteristics and their own social markers in society's evolutionary dynamics. Such social factors are part of technology, of its constitution, development, and of the conditions for its use and appropriation. We refer to this shift in the argumentation as a 'contextualized reconstruction of the technological dimension.' Society is seen as a complex and manifested totality according to specific concrete historical formations. However, which society are we talking about, and how do individuals and communities relate within it? To provide the reader with some context, it is necessary to quickly discuss how the relationships between processes and society as a whole are structured.[1] From there, we move towards a general overview of the interactions between technology and society, discussing aspects such as the controversy on technology's autonomy and how social factors and the developmental dynamics of artefacts and technological systems emerge.

The path from the artefact to a contextualized reconstruction of technological systems is articulated under the technological regulation model. It places technology in the realm of social relations under capitalism, providing instruments to understand objects from their constitutive social factors,[2] according to the relationship they establish with the internal developmental dynamics of artefacts and systems, and the impacts they promote in the different spheres of society in their dialectic movement. Regulation is seen as how these articulations and interactions among social structures and factors – also considering those specific to each system – occur and evolve within the structure and scope of concrete processes and social formations, to guide or restrain the subject's choices (either directly or indirectly) and the conflicting power relations. Based on the critical theory of technology, the analysis is not restricted to a descriptive or purely analytical effort. Instead, it counts on value bases to question the capitalist model of technology and points to alternatives associated with social justice, the fight against oppression, and political and economic democracy. These references indicate the importance of not only understanding the technological phenomenon but ensuring that its purposes are advantageous to society, seeking to describe what benefits and impacts can be considered as drivers of welfare, freedom, and dignity of individuals and their organization in society.

---

1 Despite the complexity and risk of reductionism of any debate that refers to the very object of sociology and social sciences, the debate above is essential in establishing the referential bases used in this work to pursue the argumentation.
2 The term 'factors' will be used here to designate factors that influence some processes, especially technological development.

1 Artefact and Technological Systems

The term 'artefact' generically and adequately designates the individual technological object. We consider this concept to be most appropriate, since others present some limitations. Such is the case of 'tool,' which is currently used in production, although it can also be employed more broadly. It seems more appropriate to us than 'object,' since the range of meanings this word has extrapolates our debate, as is the case with 'device.' As for 'instrument,' its meaning already implies a certain perspective as to the concept to be explored, suggesting neutrality in different applications. The word 'machine,' which we use according to its ordinary meaning, designates a specific type of artefact, generally made of metal and with a mechanical (or electronic) operational logic, not including less-complex elements.[3]

Winner (1986: 22) suggested a similar definition to the one we offer here, referring to artefacts as "smaller or larger pieces of hardware of a specific kind." The artefact has a series of more immediate and apparent features, which we call 'functional properties.' First of all, it has content – or 'design.' The first element of its design is its material basis. Knives only cut because they are made of a particular material that exerts pressure on objects. This material basis permeates all artefacts, regardless of the raw material and the production process.[4] Other properties depend on this, such as durability, weight (essential to handling), ease of handling, and even, to a certain extent, the price (one of the elements related to this property may be the scarcity of the material the artefact is made of).

Artefacts are made up of components and vary according to their number. An artefact's complexity increases as different parts are introduced. These parts may simply perform the object's inherent purpose differently or qualify it in terms of efficiency, speed, volume, or cost. Artefacts have functionalities. Functionalities are a crucial property, since artefacts are objects created to perform a certain action. The artefact's resources are, therefore, its identity, its raison d'être, since they correspond to its performance as a material means to carry out an activity. From the perspective of the evolution of artefacts in the search for efficiency, functionalities are the essence of the object. Functionality,

---

3   Even though all these terms are used as synonyms at a given point in the text, we will start with 'artefact' for the reasons given.
4   This is the first level that Feenberg (2005) talks about in his theory of double instrumentalization, where a functional relationship of society with reality occurs and where artefacts manifest their most immediate utility. This is equivalent to "physical property," in the words of Kroes (2010).

however, may not be an absolute value. A specific functionality may be planned (or intended) by the manufacturers; another might be expected by the users, and a third may emerge from the involved actors' practice in their appropriation of a certain artefact.[5]

We classify content, physical basis, form, and functionality as 'functional properties.' They do not exist outside of concrete reality. Just as the artefact has materiality, it is inserted in concrete reality, constituted by the natural world, actors, and institutions. Such individuals assume different forms of organization to meet their material needs and to confer meaning to existence at the level of consciousness, establishing coexistence and collective management rules, and setting social markers that indicate places, functions, and limits to interactions. Artefacts are, thus, immersed in contexts of social relations, and their creation responds to specific purposes formulated based on certain interests.

The components related to such interests and their insertion in artefacts are called 'contextual properties.' This aspect is related to the debate on one of the major controversies in theoretical approaches to technology, and it deserves a more detailed analysis: how neutral, or not, artefacts would be concerning the objectives and motivations existing in society and the production process. Authors such as Weber (1991) see the use of technique and technology as optimized means to achieve specific purposes. 'Minimum effort' and 'optimal result' would be the criteria guiding technology. Therefore, an artefact would be neutral based on effectiveness and efficiency criteria, and not due to a 'metaphysical postulate' referring to qualities such as 'true' or 'right.' The author situates the artefact within the perspective of technique and rational action, such as choosing the adequate means to achieve a particular purpose. When the relationship between means and ends is unequivocal, "it is legitimate to assert that insofar as the action was rigorously rational it could not have taken any other course" (Weber, 1991: 12). Artefacts can only be understood according to the meaning attributed to them by human action. In the case of technology, objectives are at the centre of this relationship, with the use of instruments setting the tone for its choice and adoption.

In Habermas (1997), also from the perspective of neutrality, artefacts are seen as an evolution, a "gradual objectification" of rational teleological action controlled by success and related to labour. The author attributes to this and to technology a universal nature that is not historically or socially determined,

---

5 Books used as bookends may be a simple but concrete example. The microwave oven emerged from experiments using magnetrons by US engineer Percy Spenser who was focused on military technology.

assuming a neutral perspective. The author argues that "technology, if based at all on a project, can only be traced back to a 'project' of the human species as a whole, and not to one that could be historically surpassed" (Habermas, 1997: 51). To Habermas the machinery of the technological universe is "*as such* [author's emphasis] indifferent towards political ends" (Habermas, 1997: 54). Bunge (2012), for example, states the ambivalent nature of artefacts regarding their purposes. They can be intrinsically beneficial (electronic calculator), intrinsically harmful (electric chair), or ambivalent (car, television). This analysis should incorporate the social context. In the central city areas, for example, cars can be more of a problem than a convenience. Bunge believes "all technical innovation is ambivalent because it is both destructive and creative" (Bunge, 2012: 32).

Within science, technology and society studies (STS), more radical theories about the nature of artefacts have emerged. For Latour (2000), these instruments are not under human control, but they are equivalent actors in socio-technical networks. The author separates his perspective from what he calls the 'diffusion model.' In the alternative 'translation model,' the distinction between society and techno-science does not make sense, and there are only heterogeneous chains of associations that, at some points, create 'mandatory passage points.': "[...] any division we make between society on the one hand and scientific or technical content on the other is necessarily arbitrary" (Latour, 1990: 106). The author argues that understanding what machines are is the same as understanding who people are. Therefore, it is not about identifying the influences or relationships of social factors in the technological production or the opposite, but about mapping out the weakest and strongest associations and how they emerge, change, and linger over time, and through which mechanisms. Other approaches, such as the social construction of technology (SCOT) theory and the critical theory of technology (CTT), question the idea of functionalities established a priori to maximize success and point to the inclusion of interests in the very content of artefacts.

According to Bijker and Pinch (1993), technological devices would be the result of disputes and political choices made based on specific interests. This perspective analyses which variables were successful, which were neglected, and why. It highlights the 'sociotechnical' dimension of technology, its condition as a product of people's actions and conflicts, social groups, and institutions. From this perspective, artefacts would be socially built from the dispute among groups of interest that act based on problems identified and meanings created regarding the need for a given technological solution to be developed in a certain way. Each device is the result of several possible paths, and the chosen path is the product of the actors' interactions based on different interests and settlements achieved through disputes solved by power relations. In this perspective, each group or social actor builds its own meaning systems related to the artefact.

Marcuse (1973) sees artefacts as domination instruments in modern societies, embedded with what he calls 'technological rationality.' This way of looking at the world takes the 'technical' logic to other spheres of life, in an effort to eliminate or disqualify the existing disputes and inequalities in society and these specific fields of human action. Today "domination perpetuates and extends itself not only through technology but as technology, and the latter provides the great legitimation of the expanding political power, which absorbs all spheres of culture." (Marcuse, 1973: 154).

The interests and objectives are part of the device's design, thus, rejecting its merely instrumental nature. Such a perspective is also supported by authors of the critical theory of technology, having non-neutrality as one of the central aspects of their approach. Winner (1986) states that these devices 'have politics,' while Noble (2011) and Feenberg (1999, 2002) emphasize this aspect of technical objects within power disputes. Technology is defined as the result of multiple social factors within dispute processes and the resulting solutions, or "the sum of all the major determinations it exhibits in its various stages of development" (Feenberg, 1996. n.p.). Technology is a "political construct and, hence, subject to fundamental reconfiguration given changes in the relative power of the parties involved in its design and deployment" (Noble, 2011: IX). Trigueiro (2009) refers to such a concept as 'technological social content.'

Despite disagreements, the different currents do not deny the understanding of another central feature of the artefact: in a capitalist system, it assumes the form of commodity, like many goods. Therefore, among its 'contextual properties' is its nature in a given concrete social formation. Artefacts, thus, need to become 'innovations,' generating money and profits. Hence, they are manufactured to be sold on the market. Their realization as commodity also involves their circulation to reach the purpose of consumption. There is a 'business model'[6] connected to the artefact, from which its owner gets a return on the investment made.[7] Besides the commercialization method, the artefact–commodity is offered on the market, where it competes with other

---

6 This "describes the design or architecture of the value creation, delivery, and capture mechanisms the business enterprise employs" (Teece, 2010: 172).

7 This may occur simply by its commercialization, but there are other methods, such as obtaining payments for temporary use (rent). Or, as we discuss later on, there are some ways of offering artefacts for free, financed by other sources, such as advertising (as is the case, in part, with Google and Facebook).

artefacts that can be similar or different. Reaching its realization as a commodity depends on its success in this competition. This is why the strategies for introducing an artefact into the competition are an essential element for its realization.[8] The primary purpose of the artefact-commodity is its market realization and not maximizing its use or the eventual benefits to the user. As a result, its functional properties may be inferior to what they could or should be to reduce the commodity's cost or to intentionally shorten its life cycle to speed up the capital turnover cycle and increase the volume of products sold – a process that is now known as planned obsolescence.

The culmination of the artefact's life cycle is its consumption, which can occur through different actors. The artefact's purpose might be its application in other production processes, or it may be an asset for the consumer. If it is the result of economic processes, consumption is also part of social relations, including their political or cultural dimensions and different systems of meaning. Owners and other actors who are interested in these artefacts' consumption work to create systems of meaning to encourage people to consume them. However, a mediation process occurs, where other factors can influence disputes involving these perceptions and other factors. Here, the phenomenon of appropriation occurs. Appropriation designates how the consumer or user of a given artefact perceives it (such as its functional and contextual properties) and employs it in concrete situations.[9]

Under capitalism, artefacts are also employed throughout the production and circulation process to manufacture commodities, as a means to assign value to them by exploiting labour power. According to Marx (1980), in this mode of production, the use of artefacts concentrated as a machine is part of the work process' reorganization. The author sees machinery as part of the "means of labour" set in motion by living labour, referred to by the author (2014) as "constant capital," which is divided as fixed and circulating capital, that is, two points in the organic composition of the capital. As stated by

---

8 Such strategies can influence the product itself, its functionalities, form, presentation, price, and the way it is offered on the market. They work as feedback. The result of a product's rotation cycle shows the profit rates and, from this and from the reality of the market, a new production process can be restarted or adjusted.

9 The appropriation includes the technology users' view on it including the owners' promotions and evaluations of different social actors, whether individuals or reference institutions. Appropriation also includes the user's position in the social context, his or her interests, and the purposes intended and practiced towards the artefact. Appropriation is not necessarily an individual process. Since the artefact can be an instrument of production, for example, appropriation can take place in different ways among different workers and give rise even to conflicting views among the actors involved or interested in such a process.

Marx (1982: 77), under capitalism, the purpose of machinery is "to shorten the labour-time necessary for the production of a commodity," but not the time employed by the worker.

More than just reducing time and intensity, the use of machinery changes work effort qualitatively, replacing "qualified work" with "simple work." More importantly, it is directly related to the shift in the social division of labour. The latter is part of the very creation of the machine in its manufacturing process. From the new division of labour in mechanized industries, labour is objectified, it loses its content. It becomes part of a reversed relationship, in which machines rise to the condition of subjects. Thus, machinery assumes its condition of "material mode of existence of capital" (Marx, 2013: 609). The participation of machinery in capitalism's "appreciation of value" mission also occurs by higher labour productivity, related to an expansion of the means of labour employed. When Marx highlights the role of transportation and communications, he indicates another fundamental function that technology plays (as an inherent element of these areas) – contributing to reducing circulation time, accelerating the reproduction cycle's onset and, enabling the capital's mission of value appreciation to succeed.

So, far, we have analysed the artefact to identify its functional and contextual properties, with its various aspects. A first assumption has been introduced, and it states that the artefact is not an isolated, abstract, and universal entity, but manifests itself in concrete contexts from the concrete relationships it has with individuals and institutions. Different aspects of the artefact (such as its purpose and production, circulation, and consumption process) have come to depend on how such relations are constituted, rooted in society's material basis. Its dimensions are, thus, inserted into different paths according to different configurations of society, with a multiplicity of problems as well as emphases and solutions. In capitalism, it usually takes the form of commodity, as a financing model, placed on the market by its owner in a competitive context. This takes place within an environment of projected appropriations, subject to other mediation factors. At this point, we could establish a first preliminary (and insufficient) definition of the artefact: an object with a material basis and functional and contextual properties created, disseminated, and consumed on a structured market made up of heterogeneous actors and institutions, within a competitive dynamic.

However, artefacts are not only constituted as individual objects but, in many cases, are combined. Individuals are present not only in consumption, but, also, in this system's production, circulation, and operation (as owners, administrators, and workers). Different objects are articulated as combinations of elements, procedures, and actors, assuming the condition of technological systems.[10] For Hughes (1993), these are "problem-solving" structures formed by physical components (such as transformers, poles and power lines in a power distribution system), organizations (such as insurance companies, maintenance companies or investment banks), scientific knowledge (such as pre-established theories, laboratory tests, and research instruments) and legal norms (such as laws, regulatory agency guidelines and other requirements). It would be fundamental to state here that, besides these elements, the systems include workers and consumers, with different forms of incidence, as already mentioned. An artefact – either physical or nonphysical – "functioning as a component in a system interacts within other artefacts, all of which contribute directly or through other components to the common system goal" (Hughes, 1993: 51).

Therefore, the system dimension includes the modes of interaction among the parts, as well as their relationships, regardless of their different natures (such as cooperation or dispute). The whole would be the sum of these elements, as it is a synthesis created from an articulation of its components. Nevertheless, this whole is dynamic according to the reproduction logics and the limitations and adjustments imposed by each actor affecting the system. In Hughes' (1993) perspective, the technological system assumes a more complex configuration than that of artefacts. It has all the properties already mentioned. However, these properties' variables are enhanced, considering their combination possibilities. Organizational and "environmental" components are progressively incorporated. Therefore, its balance is unstable, given the arrangement's configuration in concrete situations and its dynamic movement. Such an interaction implies relationships between the parts and the whole, but, also, in the opposite direction. These parts may develop harmonic or conflicting relationships (as in employer–employee or company–regulator relationships). This approach assumes a flexible perspective as to the limits of the technological system and its environment, relativizing static views that separate technology and society. Within this framework, technological systems assume expanded properties compared to artefacts.[11]

The (functional and contextual) properties already mentioned are maintained, including each component, but human and organizational actors are introduced. The control and ownership that usually affected the artefact directly may take more complex forms, involving other actors and organizations (investors and shareholders of a given technological system, such as a

---

10   Adopting the nomenclature used by several authors, such as Hughes (1993) and Trigueiro (2009).
11   Hughes even uses the term 'large technological systems.'

satellite, or even citizens in public systems, such as a research laboratory). This network of factors also affects the objectives. These may incorporate a myriad of expectations from shareholders in the case of a publicly traded technological system, or different perspectives of high-level decision-makers and those in the management spheres of the system. In neoliberalism, marked by financial domination, the presence of financial capital actors assume an essential role in most corporations, as in the examples of Google and Facebook analysed here. If the objectives were already permeated by interests and pressures from social spheres, power disputes and different arrangements may be more pronounced in the case of technological systems (TS).

The production process is another aspect that may become more multifaceted. It may even give rise to different manufacturing operations within a TS, or to entire or partial production chains within a system. As mentioned before, a diversified manufacturing process that is intrinsically conflictive also increases the possibilities of tension and instability. Realization in commodity circulation, based on business models and competition strategies, follows the same track. The market performance then includes different market areas in which the technological system is offered. Since economic success and appreciation are the central objectives of the TS-commodity under capitalism, coordinating these different market introductions and their respective competition is essential for that end. Likewise, it may relate to different organizational actors within each of these markets. TSs also open up new possibilities in terms of access and appropriation by users. Different groups of users can influence appropriation according to their needs and different preception regarding the system. On the other hand, the technological system's gain of scale may also be used to condition the forms of appropriation. For example, a particular innovation (such as a smartphone) can be advertised as being supposedly more efficient, due to its growing popularity.

Technological systems cannot be considered as fixed structures or as detached from changes in time.[12] In that sense, understanding them involves assimilating their dynamic nature and development, including the problems formulated that resulted in their conception, the parameters that guide their construction, the production process itself, their market circulation and consumption, as well as the different interactions related to this entire movement, and the multiple relationships among its parts. But, before addressing that, we

---

12 Hughes (1993: 56) calls this dynamic movement an "evolution parameter." He lists what he refers to as the phases of this movement, such as invention, development, innovation, transfer, growth, competition, and consolidation. According to the author, these phases are not linear and can overlap.

provide here a (rather insufficient) definition of TSs: technological systems are heterogeneous arrangements, a synthesis of the combination of their parts, constituted by artefacts, individuals and institutions with functional and contextual properties, created as a result of interests and objectives which they include, operating in markets also formed by heterogeneous actors and institutions in concrete historical situations.

2   Developing Artefacts and Technological Systems

Up until now, technological systems have been assumed to be dynamic objects. At this point, we can identify some of their development dynamics.[13] For the evolutionary economics approach, these processes are an evolution of dynamic adjustments of innovations, operating within technological systems, but, also, influenced by institutions, which can fast-track or delay them. An artefact's, or system's, production is based on the previously established knowledge and solutions, on the available knowledge stock[14] – or the 'state of the art' – related to the companies' and organizations' capacity to build on this stock (Dosi, 1984). Thus, artefacts and technological systems would be objects that incorporate the technological development's achievements based on problems' solutions. The market potential depends on what is already accepted by the economic actors – the previous knowledge base – and the accumulated practical experiences. Changes occur within specific degrees of appropriation and levels of opportunities in each sector, in uncertain environments, affected by endogenous market structure dynamics and marked by irregularities and variations across companies and countries (Dosi and Orsenigo, 1988: 15–16).

---

13   The term is repeatedly used here, avoiding the use of 'progress,' due to its conceptual notion that refers to linear movements.

14   The actor–network theory examines a unity between the two, with the construction of facts and artefacts as part of the same process, ending with the use of "techno-science" (Latour, 2000). Bunge differentiates the two, pointing out that technology is the practical knowledge established and science is the theoretical knowledge established. Heidegger, on the other hand, refutes both concepts, which he calls anthropological conceptions, in the first case, and an instrumental conception of technology. From a materialistic standpoint within his phenomenological perspective, he reverses this perspective by placing technology at the centre, as an unveiling method, with science at its service. He takes technology from the ontic to the ontological sphere (Trigueiro, 2009). Trigueiro (2009: 90), by suggesting a "structure of technological practice," identifies as one of its poles the "stock of scientific and technological knowledge," which includes knowledge about nature and the needs for new insights, transformed into more in-depth analyses of reality, within the theories and research previously constructed.

When this knowledge stock, the artefacts, and methods to solve problems are combined into a set of stable artefacts and broadly socialized models, what authors call a 'technological paradigm' emerges. The term, borrowed from Thomas Kuhn's 'scientific paradigms,' characterizes "a model and a pattern of solution of selected technological problems, based on selected principles derived from natural sciences and on selected material technologies" (Dosi, 1984: 14). Paradigms include addressing problems and representing the evolving needs of the technological state of the art at a given time. They influence the visions of the various actors involved in the process, from financiers to consumers, to the different production actors. Thus, they create acceptance and exclusion principles and reproduce value systems on artefacts and systems.

Based on this knowledge, which may be sparse or consolidated into paradigms, objects are developed and complete their life cycles or "technological trajectories." While, for neutral approaches (as in Weber, Bunge, and Habermas), this development would mean choosing the most appropriate means to achieve a given technical solution's goals, for Nelson and Winter (1982), the trajectories are not linear:[15] they are a result of the tension between the previous models, the field of possibilities, and the decisions made during the development process.[16] This cumulative dimension is not only incremental, however. It can also take on a qualitative aspect. These trajectories are asymmetrical, and the higher their power, the harder it is to reverse or alter their course. The competition also occurs not only between old and new approaches but between different ones. When a paradigm shift occurs, problem-solving efforts are renewed, breaking or strongly affecting the cumulative dynamic. Companies make use of strategies to introduce pioneering innovations and to mimic outstanding and profitable technologies.

Freeman and Louçã (2004: 155–6), in their analysis within the evolutionary field, detail the technology trajectories according to these operational logics and divide them into phases:

(1) Laboratory/invention, with the first prototypes, small scale demonstrations, and early applications;

---

15   Although the paradigm shift patterns exert pressure to standardize solutions, it is possible to go beyond non-incremental but qualitatively different innovations. This warning from the authors is essential because it reduces a deterministic and closed aspect that the paradigm's framework can show.

16   An important addition should be included in this part of the explanation. Paradigms are not unified within a huge universe of diverse social and technological ramifications. Therefore, not only can the trajectories be different within each paradigm, but, also, in separate references.

(2) Decisive demonstrations of technical and commercial feasibility, with widespread potential applications;
(3) Explosive onset and growth during the turbulent phase of the structural crisis in the economy and a political crisis of coordination, while a new regulatory regime is established;
(4) Ongoing high growth, with the system accepted as common sense and as the prevailing technological regime in the major countries of the world economy; application in an even more extensive range of industries and services;
(5) Slowing down and decreasing profitability as the system matures and is challenged by new technologies, leading to a new structural adjustment crisis;
(6) Maturity, with some possible 'rebirth' effects from profitable coexistence with more recent technologies, but, also, the possibility of gradually disappearing.

Hughes (1993) suggests what he calls "phases" in the evolution of technological systems. They emerge during the stages the author classifies as "invention" and "development," in which the solution of the identified problems would occur based on social interests. After the first two stages, there would next be a stage of "innovation," when decisions involve not only engineers but, also, those responsible for the production and circulation strategies of the TS as a commodity. The author adds a "technology transfer" phase, in which a given product must have its manufacturing process replicated in other environments, such as subsidiary companies. The technological system's development and manufacturing in concrete reality constitute what the author refers to as "technological style." The next phase is called "growth, competition, and consolidation." On the market, TSs operate in competition, as previously indicated. If successful, they may not only generate profits but may also expand. The system enters a consolidation phase, in which it is established in a particular environment where it is inserted. During its maturity phase, the TS gains what the author calls "momentum" (Hughes, 1993: 76), as the persistence of the acquired characteristics.

Based on his analysis of technology under the capital (which we will discuss later on), Marx (2013) argues that the emergence of the machinery aims at monopoly systems, obtaining "extraordinary" profits (Marx, 2013: 588). They are a source of accelerated accumulation and "attract into the favoured sphere of production a large part of the additional social capital that is being constantly created and is ever on the look-out for new investments" (Marx, 2013: 637). During this initial period, in which the machinery is introduced, rapid and intense progress is observed. When these artefacts are disseminated and are then built by other machines, when the development establishes a technical basis and becomes mature, it experiences an expansion whose only obstacles are the lack of raw material or the market's capacity to absorb its production. Conquering the global market is a decisive factor for opening external trade borders for the products. Then comes "a new and international division of labour, a division suited to the requirements of the chief centres of modern industry springs up and converts one part of the globe into a chiefly agricultural field of production, for supplying the other part which remains a chiefly industrial field" (Marx, 2013: 638).

So far, we have seen the systems as dynamic entities, since they are immersed in processes of creation, development, growth, maturity, adjustments that make up the universe of these devices' trajectories. The stock of scientific knowledge is not offered freely, but within concrete institutional structures in the field of science, whose decisions also observe specific criteria with endogenous and exogenous factors within these social organizations. The basis from which new devices are conceived is not only a matter of collections of established technologies but ways of validating them, where 'meaning systems' are produced and reproduced among the actors of the process. These processes occur with actors presenting problems and demands to be solved through development, within the field of purposes. But, at this point, the actors are blurred and indeterminate. They are essential (to a greater or lesser degree, as we have seen in the discussion so far) in choosing and imposing the purposes that will guide the manufacturing of objects. Therefore, the analysis needs to consider these limitations, being socially contextualized and historically located. As the argument advances, it is necessary to underline the contextual properties more effectively. The nature of technical objects or systems is directly related to the purposes for which they were created, how their production and circulation are organized, and how their consumption and appropriation occur. By understanding the object as a system, rather than as an isolated artefact, the actors who participate in such a system and its relationships gain importance. Their analysis, as a result, must incorporate these dimensions. During the investigations, important questions arise, like: who establishes these objectives? Who works in the production? Who works in circulation? Who consumes these devices and appropriates them? And finally: under which conditions? Such manufacturing and reproduction mechanisms do not occur separately from the concrete historical context. They are included in the knowledge's logic of creation and application set by capitalism during its various periods, including neoliberalism.

The technological system's creation occurs as a production process, which, as Marx (2014) warns, is fundamental to explaining the capitalist system and its phenomena. Both evolutionists and other authors, such as Hughes, point out that, after an invention is made, a fundamental phase takes place for the transformation of this product on the market, when it becomes, or does not become, an innovation. The success of this progress and its consolidation depends on its realization as a TS-commodity. But if the success that ensures the reproduction of artefacts occurs in the sphere of the market, and especially of competition, it is not possible to understand the technological development without considering what type of market and how technical devices relate to it. What is the logic of this mode of production and circulation? How may an artefact be successful or not to star its cycle again and gain 'momentum'? What are the dynamics of the competitions where artefacts and TS s are inserted to search for survival? In what sense, as commodities in this environment, do technical objects meet their purposes or not? All these gaps and questions demand the search for these missing pieces, adopting a proper perspective of the critique of the political economy. They point to the fact that understanding technology also includes understanding society within its 'broader context.' Therefore, the indeterminate actors of the relevant groups, association networks, or social actions guided by success need to be qualified. Even in a more critical sense, this unclear nature may emerge, as in Marcuse's notion of 'impersonal domination.' Domination relations occur, and they are linked to technology, now under the condition of rationality.

The critical theory of technology considers this problem as a relevant component in its analyses. When asked if artefacts include politics, Winner (1986) points out not only to an affirmative or negative answer but to understand how it emerges and who imposes it. As Noble (2011) emphasizes, technological practice is influenced not only by "interests" but, also, by ideological conceptions according to the concrete position of the actors in society. Feenberg (2005) uses the concept of "technical code" to establish a link between technical and social demands. This code is "the realization of an interest or ideology in a technically coherent solution for a problem" (Feenberg, 2005: 52). The objectives are "codified" by establishing definitions as to what is desirable and what is not, what is allowed and what is prohibited, what is ethical and what is unethical, as well as the hierarchical parameters of these aspects. From this perspective, Feenberg affirms technology as a field of conflicts of interest, since it "favours specific ends and obstruct others" (Feenberg, 2005: 54). In a more recent work, the author (2017) differentiates the technical codes of specific artefacts and "technical domains." These interests translate into guidelines associated with technological development. But which groups are these, and how do they exercise their domination? Although the authors advance in such direction in their empirical investigations,[17] the unveiling of subjects and power relations still needs to be further developed.

So far, we have approached what we called the 'deconstruction of the technological dimension' by setting the most basic unit of technology – the artefact – as the starting point. We then proceeded to qualify it as a technological, complex, and dynamic system. Now, it is necessary to shift the discussion, once again, into what we call the 'contextualized reconstruction of the technological dimension.' Next, we reflect on the society into which technology is inserted, and, building upon this notion, we offer an understanding of technology within a social and historical context.

3   Society and Technology

Similar to the controversy over the neutrality of technology, the controversy involving its autonomy is another matter of intense debate in the field. In this controversy, quite different approaches emerge from those who adhere to the understanding of the autonomous nature of these systems to the various opposing schools of thought. But, before approaching this issue, we believe it is necessary to explore the environment into which the systems are inserted.[18] Technology, just like other human activities, is part not only of a context, but, also, of a totality, and it establishes relationships with it. Situating technology in such a context demands incorporating the notion of totality, to investigate the ways TSs articulate with this whole, of which human life is a part.

This totality currently manifests itself historically as what has come to be known as the capitalist system. Marx (2013, 2014, 2017) promoted a sophisticated analysis of the system bases and operational logic. Its historical advent is based on a new mode of established production, within which the organization of material conditions of existence emerges due to the exploitation of labour, aiming at the valorization of capital. In sum, labour is subsumed in the capital (first formally and, then, effectively) by converting the labour force into commodities to be sold on the market to obtain money for the reproduction of material demands. The distinctive feature of this

---

17   As in Noble's (2011) study on the development of automation in the United States, or Winner's famous (1986) article on the bridges to Long Island.

18   Since this is somewhat related to social theory, it carries a dangerous component. In this sense, we would like to warn that, obviously, we do not intend to solve a problem of this magnitude, but to present and discuss, in a moderate way, a range of approaches and point out the references used in this work.

commodity is its value-generating property when employed in the production process. The labour paid to the worker is no longer the products made by him, but the labour necessary to reproduction of labour force, socially defined by means of negotiations, clashes, or legislations and expressed as wages and/or benefits. In the capital rotation cycle, business owners invest capital to acquire means of production and labour force to create products. These products are put into circulation and sold, obtaining an additional surplus, known as profit, generating capital accumulation, according to the M–C–M' formula (a simplified formula that the author builds upon as his work evolves).

From a historical point of view, this organization is established with the introduction of large-scale industry, setting a structural difference in comparison to cooperation and manufacturing. In cooperation, salaried labour was introduced, as well as the commodification of social relations and the separation between a group of owners of the means of production and another group that, although no longer subject to an imposition regime (such as servitude) is now subject to compulsory labour (despite the fact that slavery lingers formally and informally). Marx identifies the historical breakthrough of capitalism and its disruptive advance over previous modes of production within his theory of the historical movement, in which he confronts two opposing extremes: productive forces and the social relations of production. The former involves the stock of technologies developed by humankind at a given moment in time, while the latter refers to the ways in which individuals organize themselves in order to produce.

Along its historical course, society also creates forms of social organization and socialization, with political and cultural institutional structures, such as the state and associations (such as trade unions and churches). Without exhausting the author's social theory, we are interested in approaching the determination relations within capitalist society in a synthetic manner (without elaborating on the historical debate from its different interpretations). In the preface to *A Contribution to the Critique of Political Economy* (2008: 47), Marx, opposing Hegel, states that legal entities and the state "cannot be explained alone" but are rooted in the "material conditions of existence." However, in the introduction to the same work, when discussing production as an abstraction and as a concrete social manifestation, the author indicates an understanding of totality as an organic and dialectic relationship with its parts. The analysis of determinations cannot disregard an understanding of the common and distinguishing traits of the historical development of each era.

Mentioning technology in one of the excerpts from *Capital* (2013), Marx suggests a more integrated notion of human activities, from their material basis to their understanding in the field of ideas.[19] In an excerpt from another historical analysis work, *The Eighteenth Brumaire of Louis Bonaparte* (2011b), he affirms historical circumstances as the limit of man's history.[20] Engels (1982: 557) mentions as a point that has not been "sufficiently highlighted" in his and Marx's works the location of ideological representations "based on fundamental economic facts." But the author endeavours to make a corrective adjustment and affirms a reciprocal action in the course of history: "Once an historic element has been brought into the world by other elements, ultimately, by economic facts, it also reacts in its turn and may react on its environment and even on its own causes" (Engels, 1982, p. 558).[21]

Gramsci (1978) discussed this issue by approaching ideological forms and their institutions in a well-known (and highly debated) schematic framework, in which he delineated what he referred to as "superstructure" – constituted by a "political society," such as the state systems, and by "civil society," including associations and other institutions that the author called private apparatus of hegemony. Gramsci offers a dialectic explanation presenting the concept of "historical bloc" as the "unity between nature and spirit (structure and superstructure), unity of opposites" (Gramsci, 1978: 12). If, on the one hand, he affirms this unity, in which "politics meets economy" (p. 14), on the other, the author stresses the specificity of politics as a different activity. Portelli (2002) sees this notion as an analysis in which it is not a question of determining which moment is more decisive, but of understanding that there is an organic link between them. Thus, structure and superstructure would constitute a

---

19   "The technology shows the active attitude of man to nature, the immediate process of production of his life and, therefore, their social living conditions and spiritual representations derived from that place" (Marx, 2013: 1294).

20   The author says: "Men make their own history, but they do not make it as they please; they do not make it under self-selected circumstances, but under circumstances existing already, given and transmitted from the past. The tradition of all dead generations weighs like a nightmare on the brains of the living." (2011b:25).

21   Given the long debate about the degree of determinism in Marx's and Engels' work and how it influences a Marxian theory of politics, law, and culture, which is impossible to reproduce here, for the purpose of this debate we can only consider that Marx's work, taken in its entirety, points to social relations that are much more complex than a mechanistic interpretation of excerpts such as those from the preface might suggest. But, at the same time, it presents boundaries that must be recognized. These, however, do not invalidate either the perception of the centrality of the material basis or the operating logic of the capital revealed by the authors. Appreciating this sophisticated scrutiny of the capitalist society, other authors have tried to provide solutions to the insufficiencies of the political, legal, and cultural spheres as they gained complexity in the historical course.

dialectic relation of factors that may be influential or conditioning, depending on how this relationship manifests itself historically, but always within a mutual logic of determination.[22]

Althusser (2015) suggests a solution to the debate focused on understanding structures, by discussing what he calls the law of "uneven development of contradictions." In the author's perspective, formulated from an analysis of the Marxist framework, "the complex whole possesses the unity of an articulated structure in dominance" (Althusser, 2015: 163), formed by dominance relations among its contradictions and by instances or levels. Dominance would be not an essence or core, but a concrete manifestation of the hierarchy among the different instances of the structure (the mode of production, in a historical analysis). The set of contradictions is essential to the structure, since the parts are "each expressing others, and each expressing the social totality that contains them, because each in itself contains in the immediate form of its expression the essence of the social totality itself" (Althusser et al. 1980: 33). In the structure, they are manifested as primary and secondary contradictions, and are not reduced to being effects or phenomena related to the primary contraction. These different positions do not affect unity. They express the dominance relations within what the author calls the "hierarchical organic whole" (Althusser et al., 1980: 38). By detailing the structural unit as being constituted by instances, the author states their distinctive nature, but underlines the centrality of the material basis. These levels establish relationships of "relative autonomy that coexist in a complex structural unit, articulating with each other according to specific modes of determination, determined in the last instance by the economy" (Althusser et al., 1980: 36–7).

Different practices are related to the instances within the complex whole. The instances of a social formation are a specific practice "articulated with all others" (Althusser and Badiou, 1979: 20). Far from being a simplistic notion opposed to theory, this includes activities carried out in the articulation of these two dimensions in specific manifestations. Althusser et al. (1979: 61) stresses that we must "recognize that there is no practice in general, but only distinct practices".[23] Among them, there are relative dependence and

---

22 Therefore, a movement's progress on the superstructure can never create changes beyond the material possibilities that are given in a particular society. Also, the organization and evolution of the "economic element" does not occur without acting on the consciousness level. In Gramsci's words, "the material forces are the content and the ideologies the form" (Gramsci, 1978: 56).

23 Among these, repeatedly mentioned in the author's works, are economic, political, ideological, technical and scientific (or theoretical) practices. Each practice has its own

autonomy relations, considering the economic practice as "determining in the last instance" (Althusser et al., 1979: 62). In society's structured complexity, production relations are not a "pure phenomena of the forces of production," and "the superstructure is not the pure phenomenon of the structure," but "its condition of existence" (Althusser, 2015: 165). This consideration on the articulated structure and the interactions among its contradictions of existing conditions is what the author calls "overdetermination."

Harvey (2010) also draws from the Marxist framework and seeks to update it to analyse contemporary capitalism. As capital revolves, it moves through what the author calls "activity spheres," organized into seven categories: (1) technologies and organizational forms, (2) social relations, (3) institutional and administrative arrangements, (4) production and labour processes, (5) relations to nature, (6) the reproduction of the daily life of the species, and (7) mental conceptions of the world. These are interrelated, influencing one another. They are organized as a set of institutional arrangements (such as property regimes and market agreements) and administrative structures (state and other forms of governance and control by authorities).

Harvey (2010) indicates a dialectical aspect by pointing out particular and, at the same time, interdependent logics: "No one of the spheres dominates even as none of them are independent of the others. But nor is any one of them determined even collectively by all of the others" (Harvey, 2010: 123). The spheres and their constitutive elements present specific dynamics when reacting to the crisis conditions in the system or to changes in social relations of production. Thus, they evolve on their own but, at the same time, in a "dynamic interaction" with others. In the constitution of institutional and administrative arrangements, decision-makers communicate with specialized sources of information (such as experts) and refer to ethical parameters. The belief systems that make up the mental conceptions of the world are "strongly present." Still, they do not exist independently of social relations, which are unstable but governed by class arrangements. All these factors, as the author notes, have played essential roles in capitalism's evolution.

By reserving to technology its own sphere (unlike Althusser), Harvey highlights its influence in contemporary societies. He characterizes the sphere of technologies and organizational forms as "crucial," impacting social relations and individuals' relations with nature, although these are not the central or determining factor. An example of this activity's effects is the creation of new

---

distinct structure which is, at the end of the day, that of a production, with objects, means of production and relationships from which they materialize.

needs, as it became a business of its own, from the nineteenth century onwards, in what the author calls the "fetish of technology" (Harvey, 2010: 129). Such configuration and dissemination into the sphere of production and labour processes did not occur without tensions, which is typical of these dynamic interactions. Since the onset of capitalism, new technologies have had disruptive effects on factories, as in the various historical manifestations of automation processes.[24]

Freeman and Louçã (2004) base their approach on certain assumptions, including 1) the denial of a totalizing quantification of the universe, moving away from positivism; 2) the focus on concrete historical manifestations instead of abstract models; and 3) the consideration of social, political and institutional factors in economic development, in a multi-causality relationship that determines society's dynamic evolution and cohesive processes. Society is constituted by five subsystems, science, technology, economy, politics, and culture (2004: 137–8), which are defined as follows:

1) Science – institutions and processes that provide knowledge about the natural world as well as the ideas and the knowledge formulated by them;
2) Technology – the conception, development, and dissemination of artefacts and techniques by individuals, groups, and institutions;
3) Economy – the production, distribution, and consumption of goods and services and the individuals, groups, and institutions involved and that affect these processes;
4) Politics – the government and society regulation processes and instances, including military action;
5) Culture – ideas, values, traditions, habits, artistic creations, and beliefs of individuals, groups, and institutions.

The authors see autonomous and interdependent relationships. At the same time that each subsystem has its own history and relative autonomy, this occurs from the interaction with the other subsystems. As in Harvey, their analysis involves understanding the integration phenomena and the mismatch among these distinct and related parts. These are characterized by what the authors call "irregular fluctuations" and "cyclical and wave-like movements with different approximate periodicities" (Freeman and Louçã, 2004:131–2), caused by the subsystems' own movements as well as by the interaction among them. Such flows are combined by "specific coordination processes that emerge after structural crises," the actual historical manifestation of the long waves of capitalism's development.[25]

---

24 This will be discussed in more detail in the next chapter.
25 Referencing to Kondratiev's work on long waves.

The authors justify the choice for this model for three reasons. First, it offers an analysis focused on the perception of subsystems overlapping, rather than their operation in isolation. Secondly, it examines phases and crises, taking into account the "inefficient adjustment" phenomena among the subsystems. Social conflicts are seen as part of the coordination processes, which create and handle them under power relations in different forms, from legitimation to the use of force. Coordination is not a harmonious phenomenon at the level of economic actors or political forces. Such coordination, as the authors add, occurs at different levels. The first would be the level of economic relations, including conventions and institutions. The second is that of what they call "power, strategy, and domination." Complexity and structural change can be explained "only as historical developments, as coevolutionary processes" (Freeman and Louçã, 2004: 132).

4   Technology and Society

In an effort to conduct a contextualized reconstruction of the technological dimension, this explanation of technology will situate technology socially and historically. This is the purpose of the following debate, whose contributions will also be analysed considering the perspectives on its autonomy and influence on social practices. Ellul (1964) is the foremost exponent of the perspective of technology's autonomy. In his historical work, he affirms such autonomy as a result of the development process of machines: "Autonomy is the essential condition for the development of technique" (Ellul, 1964: 133). Thus, such a universe responds to its own laws, and it must be understood within this analytical delimitation. The technique moves in an "omnivorous world which obeys its own laws and which has renounced all tradition" (Ellul, 1964: 14). The form assumed by machines in capitalism is so powerful that they have become the driving force of the modern world, a thesis that the author affirms when he says that "capitalism did not create our world: the machine did" (Ellul, 1964: 5). By looking at what he calls the major sociological determinants, technology is listed as one of them, gaining a central relevance to modern societies. The author recognizes the importance of human action but points out that, if the latter does not oppose these forces, they have high a chance of exercising their full impact. By historically contextualizing the debate, the Ellul sees the technological phenomenon as the most important fact and, at the same time, the "most dangerous form of determinism" in the modern world. In the context analysed, the technique would have extrapolated its corporeality as machines, leaving the industrial plants and advancing to other social activities, no longer being restricted to production and gaining autonomy.

Also from a determinist perspective, Heilbronner (1994: 59) focuses his analyses on how technology determines the nature of the "socio-economic order." He states that "the technology of a society imposes a determinate pattern of social relations on that society." Answering the question of if and how this occurs, almost 30 years later (his seminal work dates from 1964), the author summarizes: "Machines make history by changing the material conditions of human existence" (Heilbronner, 1994a: 69). The author points to the manifestation of this force combined with the influence of the economic field – which would impose its orientation towards maximization on the socio-economic order, just as a gravitational field attracts matter. Heilbronner (1994) highlights that technology plays a "mediating role" in modern societies. The phenomenon of technological determinism would not be universal but historically situated in the context of the twentieth century. He lists two types of influence of technical devices in society. The first relates to the workforce's composition. Certain frameworks of technical resources demand skills and operating capacities, which need to be met and influence what kind of worker will be able to operate them. The second impact is on the hierarchical organization of work. With different machines, different forms of supervision and coordination arise.

Another group of authors – such as Weber, Habermas, Veblen, and Heilbronner – also advocates (although within their own perspectives) the autonomous nature of technology.[26] These authors move away from influences from social factors, such as Weber (2005: 27), by stating that a theory of technology "would exclude property relations." Veblen (2001) suggests a close link between technical progress and the development of modern economics. This strategic relevance appears in the relationship he established between industrial machinery and economic management. While the former is "disorderly productive" (Veblen, 2001: 8), the latter needs to have control over production to ensure a return in the form of profit for business owners. The action of business owners leads to a "conscious withdrawal of efficiency." The author highlights the role of technological development in increasing the industry's efficiency: "The efficient enlargement of industrial capacity has, of course,

---

26 Weber, for example, indicates a particular logic of these spheres. Such an approach is related to the understanding of technology as something neutral. Being involved in the selection of the most adequate means for a certain purpose, its development would promote the elaboration and qualification of these means in the form of instruments, as in Veblen or Bunge. The scientific–technological progress would be autonomous as a "project for mankind" or as a "historical totality," in the words of Habermas.

been due to a continued advance in technology, to a continued increase of the available natural resources, and to a continued increase of population" (Veben, 2001: 21). Although the author recognizes the incidence of multiple causal factors in economic development, he stresses the primacy of experts in relation to industrial machinery as central actors in controlling the production process and optimizing its results.

Beyond the centrality of technology, the author also recognizes its autonomy and development as an evolutive process. For him (2017), technological knowledge is a common stock carried further collectively. He sees this knowledge set, which he refers to as "industrial arts," as a collective work, inherited from the past, continuously changing and counting on the contribution of insights and new capabilities offered by the current generation to the stock built historically. Individuals promote these innovations, but within community life, and according to the technological knowledge previously acquired and shared, subject to the rules of this collectivity.

At the other end are approaches linked to social studies of science and technology. The most radical view is presented by the actor–network theory (ANT), according to which the "society–technology" relationship is a poorly formulated issue. The actors' social practices are so strictly related that there are no dominant structures or instances (in reference to Althusser's framework). The production of facts and instruments (considered according to their connection, as already discussed) does not involve spheres or subsystems, using the terminologies presented in the previous section. The understanding of artefacts can only take place within social aggregates. Since ANT does not embrace this issue, as proposed by the title of this section, it is difficult to categorize it in relation to the other approaches. However, it is undeniable that its framework elevates technology to a central condition, not as a determinant factor, but as coexisting with the idea of actors.

To a lesser extent, the perspective of the social construction of technology (SCOT) offers a theoretical–conceptual framework in which society is seen as a dominant pole, since not only the application, but, also, the content of the artefact is socially built. Hughes endorses this notion in his theory of technological systems. Nevertheless, as previously pointed out, both ANT and SCOT introduce social factors more abstractly (although in different ways), dismissing in their theoretical schemes (but not in their concrete analyses) the characterization as to how the 'social' enters the 'technological' in the given historical reality. Theoretical–conceptual frameworks are considered as milestones whose dimensions are shown only upon their application, unlike other currents previously discussed. Thus, such epistemological bases have an ahistorical nature that does not appear by chance and is related to an ontological turn, from theories of the sociology of scientific knowledge (such as the strong programme) to approaches of the social studies of science and technology from the 1990s onwards (Jasanoff, 2004; Woolgar and Lezaum, 2013).

Between the two extremes of the debate, there are several 'shades of grey' where the relationship does not seem to have been extensively considered. Such cases are pointed out by the work of evolutionary economists, who see a reasonable degree of autonomy of technology in their analyses. As previously noted, this current was clearly concerned in discussing the specific aspects of technology. The theoretical input of evolutionary biological approaches shows this technological content and its progress. On the other hand, as researchers in the field of economics, its exponents have an evident concern to arrange the perspective on technology within the controversies of the economic field, of innovation theory and its concrete analysis into branches, nations, and contexts. According to one of its main references, Schumpeter, technical progress is part of the economy and, consequently, of the success of nations in achieving 'success' goals in a capitalist system.[27]

This approximation between technology and economy is also present in Marx, whose contributions cannot be easily categorized as being at one of the two 'ends' of this debate. Such fact is reflected in the different views about its more or less deterministic nature.[28] The author bases his historical development model in a relationship between productive forces and social relations of production. Its analysis should not be a simplistic one, since isolated excerpts may justify the emphasis on each of the poles. As in the basis–legal entities controversy, regarding reproductive forces and social relations of production, different points may indicate nuances as to the importance of each. At certain times, Marx suggests an almost evolutionary trend of the productive forces as a characteristic of capitalism and points out that the contradiction between these two poles is not only a parameter for the historical development but, under capitalism, the intensification of such opposition may give rise to revolutions in this mode of production. At other times, Marx is more cautious in analysing that the evolution of productive forces is not only mediated, but, also, regulated by the social relations of production.

---

27   This relationship shows, at certain times, a certain agreement with more deterministic approaches. This is the case, as already mentioned, of Freeman and Louçã (2004), who suggest a periodical categorization according to "successive industrial revolutions." Although the authors propose a synthesis that they call "techno-economic paradigms," the role of technological progress is revealed in the analysis.

28   As discussed in the references below or in other works such as Balibar (1980) and Elster (1983).

Such flexibility in Marx's works has given rise to different interpretations. Currents from the Second International (Kautsky, Bernstein) and dominant groups in the Soviet Union have emphasized the productive forces, as in "scientific–technical revolution" (Bernal, 1946). Other authors, alongside Marxist tradition, stressed the primacy of social relations of production. Poulantzas (1981) and Katz (1997) are examples that recognize the predominance of social relations of production as an engine for social reproduction:

> The productive forces do, indeed, have materiality of their own that can by no means be ignored; but they are always organized under given relations of production. Thus, while the two may enter into contradiction with each other and undergo forms of uneven development, they always do so within a process that stems from the primacy of the relations of production.
> POULANTZAS, 1981: 31

Katz notes:

> The development of the productive forces can only be accepted as a very general principle, which frames certain historical conditions and possibilities, without pre-determining the results. There is no rule for the historical change, teleologically oriented, and overcoming the 'dysfunctionalities' interposed by the successive modes of production. What can be studied are the contradictions that appear between the productive forces and the relations of production in each circumstance and that give rise to varied results.
> KATZ, 1997:7–8

Beyond a more general debate between productive forces and social relations of production, throughout the author's work, this debate reappears, whether in the machinery's role in the workers' subordination to these devices, or in the role that technological systems assume in capitalism, not only by expropriating the workers' knowledge, but, also, guiding the productive process, especially as the degree of automation increases.

Among Marxist-inspired authors who seek to complement the author's work at subsequent historical periods, Marcuse (1973) emphasizes the role of technology in advanced industrial societies, as previously discussed. Mandel (1979, 1986), on the other hand, employs an economic view on the relationship between technology and society, concerned with the central issues of Marx's theory of capitalist development which evolutionary economics resumed by discussing the role of apparatuses in the reproduction of the system, seen as unstable and structured in long waves. His approach provides an appropriate explanation for how innovation is linked to the economic process and why it does not depend solely on the creative element. Inventions, no matter how much potential they have, face a greater difficulty of receiving support in times of stagnation (due to the retraction of investments and consumer markets) and a greater likelihood of thriving during expansion cycles, where investment is promoted by improving profit and rates of return. The author includes, in the context of the cycles, an element that is fundamental in Marx: class struggles. For him, class struggles go through cycles but are especially important in solving moments of stagnation and dispute in order to reach new cycles of expansion.

Dussel (1988) stresses that the understanding of capitalist development and the role of technology cannot be based on a single model of capitalism (usually seen in central countries). There is a risk of incurring a "historical ideal model" that obscures the concrete diversity of development in time and space. In this sense, from his Latin American perspective, Dussel proposes a systematization of the Marxist view of technology, filling the gaps of these different development conditions and emphasizing the need to perceive the uneven nature of development and how technology takes shape in the international division of labour. From the historical point of view, such disparity was even more accentuated considering that important portions of the territory were maintained as colonies of central capitalist nations until the liberation processes that occurred from the first half of the nineteenth to the second half of the twentieth century.

In this sense, Dussel's views relate to more recent approaches to decolonial and post-colonial perspectives[29] applied to social studies of science and technology (Harding, 2011). This approach reveals how Western rationality has been presented as a hegemonic model within a project of historical domination, especially in the post-war period. The entire historical framework of technical progress (at least in the mainstream literature) is based on the tradition revived by the Enlightenment, and which extends to so-called modernity. This way of looking at science and social progress "is grounded in modernization theory, which is itself rooted in the Enlightenment belief in the beneficial powers of scientific rationality" (Harding, 2011: 2). This statement implies that, consequently, there are also technological development patterns specific

---

29 A very comprehensive approach, with the work of several authors, such as Fanon, Said, Spivak and Quijano.

to regions. However, the parameters for the economic model, understanding and representation of the world, and for historical development have been self-asserted as those of the West, or, more accurately, of the central capitalist nations of the West. This conceptual system has been 'exported' and imposed on the other parts of the world, overlapping models of rationality proper to each location. The rationality of scientific neutrality, which can be extrapolated to technological neutrality, is promoted under this paradigm.

The historical subjugation and control of peoples throughout the world, with different ways and conceptions of living, was justified by the notion of technological progress, while the latter was never constituted as a linear model to be followed by each nation, but as an interdependent relation, in which the 'success rates' of certain countries were obtained at the expense of those where such 'progress' occurred in a more fragile way. The linear model of progress promoted a 'dangling carrot' logic, in which success formulas were unrealistically propagated, while their realization depended on the international division of labour, in which central nations benefit from countries that export raw materials and expand their balance of payments by trading manufactured products with these and other peripheral regions, considering their technological supremacy.

The critical theory of technology provides an interesting synthesis of the relationship between technology and society. This perspective assumes a dialectical nature and relative autonomy of technology (in the words of Trigueiro [2009]), but is located among the currents that contradict the concepts of neutrality and autonomy of artefacts, including social factors at the core of their content and development. Artefacts are permeated by politics (Winner, 1986) and by social interests (Feenberg, 2002; Noble, 2011), including the devices' design. But, unlike ANT, they do not break down society into a kaleidoscope of actors and associations. On the contrary, they base the presence of social factors in technological production on concrete power and the social (economic, political, cultural) relations of society. However, such reasoning is still excessively generic (an issue that will be examined later on).

Based on the debate presented here,[30] we propose a synthesis of the references used throughout this debate on technology:

1) The analysis of society involves considering its structured whole, within which human activities, practices, and spheres articulate and develop dynamically;

---

30 As will be possible to see, the references presented are drawn from several sources, such as the Marxist theories, Althusser's structural causality, Gramsci's organic analysis, Harvey's spheres, and Freeman and Louçã's subsystems.

2) The structured whole is not a theoretical construct, but the manifestation of the historical totality in the form of the corresponding mode of production, in this case, the capitalist system;[31]

3) The historical dimension is not only a prerequisite for characterizing the mode of production, but a fundamental element of any analysis, from general theories to concrete cases. Concreteness always carries a historical attribute, which, however, should not be seen as a casual description, but as part of a complex totality;

4) Within the historical totality of the capitalist system, specific forms of social spheres emerge, constituted by practices and defined by their identity and the roles they perform for the system's reproduction;

5) These forms are characterized by relative autonomy, but cannot be perceived in isolation from the whole, assuming prominence in certain historical contexts;

6) The totality – the capitalist system – given its logic of organizing production for value appreciation, emphasizes the relevance of the material basis and confers centrality to it. However, this does not mean that it is necessarily prominent, but sets conditions from an organic link with the other spheres of activity of the system;

7) To provide a schematic view, we identify the following specific spheres of the capitalist system: economic, political–institutional, cultural, and scientific–technological. Such terminology, as a schematic representation, presumes groupings within each sphere, such as considering the specificities of science and technology within the fourth sphere, or of politics, the legal environment and the institutional forms in the second sphere;

8) Such spheres develop dialectic interdependent relationships, influencing and being affected in their concrete manifestations and development. Although each has a specific weight at a given conjuncture, the material basis does not lose its centrality.[32]

---

31 For the purposes of this synthesis, we are not interested in entering into the controversy of how theoretical–methodological frameworks approach the analysis of different modes of production.

32 We have avoided using expressions such as "in the last instance" or similar expressions, since the material basis is our basis, but it also contains part of the spheres. The scientific–technological sphere is part of the material basis, but it has relative autonomy. The example already mentioned of the clash between workers and employers also configures an intersection of the political and economic spheres with the material basis. The conceptions of the world present in consumption relations are elements present in the production–circulation unit that permeates the material basis.

9) Technology – the object of this theoretical–methodological model – is not in a 'position' to reflect on the limits of the spatial metaphor of spheres. It is, at the same time, characterized by relative autonomy, but permeates other spheres.

5   Summary: The Technological Regulation Approach

Concluding the argument developed in this chapter, we make an effort to present a contribution to a critical understanding of technology. Based on the method adopted here, two movements were employed. The first, deconstructing the technological dimension, was based on its unit of analysis, the artefact. The latter was then further elaborated as technological systems. They were contextualized within their development process, identifying stages, from production to consumption and appropriation. At that point in the analysis, the need to situate the phenomenon within the social context emerged, demanding a reflection on the relationships between technology and society. This led to a contextualized reconstruction of the technological dimension. After a brief digression on references that explain the relationship between society and specific spheres and practices, the debate moved forward to discuss technology's degree of autonomy and its relationship with society. Emphasis was given to the need to understand technology as an activity sphere combined with science and in dialectic interaction with the social structure and the other spheres.

Making such an analysis disconnected from historical reality (such as interpretations of systems theory or what structuralists might dangerously suggest) would be insufficient. Technology should be examined within its concrete historical manifestation under capitalism. Along the way, technology was characterized according to temporary definitions. Their limitations and the need to further develop and adjust such definitions were duly recorded. At this point, we can finally reach a more definitive characterization that will serve as a basis for the present work. In the debate about the artefact, we underline how technology has materiality. It permeates different historical periods, although its meaning, perception, and appropriation are historically built.[33] Those characteristics related to immediate functionality are called 'functional properties.' However, as in any human activity, technological practice materializes

---

33   Some material can be seen as more efficient and resistant in a certain historical formation and as undesirable because it is polluting in another, for example.

within concrete socio-historical models, and its development and application are forged within social relations, especially power relations, assuming one of the premises of the critical theory of technology (CTT). Thus, a second set of properties inherent to artefacts and technological systems (such as objectives, productive process, circulation, access, and forms of appropriation) has been called 'contextual properties.'

More than artefacts, technical development has evolved to the point of elaborating more sophisticated forms of constructs, constituted by different artefacts. Its concrete evolution has led to different arrangements among machines, (individual and collective) human actors, as well as operating methods (from market organizations to legal standards). Such broader configurations demand a more qualified understanding, which we assume by incorporating the designation of technological systems. This designation suggests the challenge of concrete analyses to go beyond the manufacturing of products and to understand these inter-relationships. However, technology cannot be reduced to artefacts and systems that contain these two groups of properties. Such an understanding would imply a decontextualized and ahistorical view of the phenomenon. As a human activity, technology is impacted by forms of human organizations and social activities. The allegory of the spheres, as mentioned before, should not be interpreted in 'spatial' terms, since economic, political and cultural dimensions are part of these spheres (from artefacts as products in the market to meaning systems underlying their use).

Such caution, on the other hand, does not imply the dilution of socially and historically built spheres, activities, and practices, looking at society as a myriad of successive arrangements or indeterminate networks (or associations, according to the actor–network theory). These spheres exist as such because they constitute dimensions and sets of social practices with relative autonomy in constant interaction. At the same time, society is not a sum of these spheres in unique situations seen by phenomenological combinatory analyses. Just as political, economic, cultural, and technological practices and institutions have emerged, society as a whole has 'leagues' that ensure the regularity and durability of social reproduction patterns. These make up the structure along the lines of previously discussed references. In addition, the reflection showed how such structure is seen here, not as a mechanical social determinant, but as a set of parameters that guide and limit actions, based on which human action operates and which can lead even to a shift in these logics and in the social space as a whole.

A second assumption explored is that there is more than just a relationship between a specific phenomenon and a structure according to the terms set out here. Human activity is built throughout history and as a concrete result of times, stages, and phases in which the dialectic relationship between structure and action is manifested. In that sense, our intention is not to present a "general theory" of technology. The perspective of the present work is explicitly and historically situated in relation to capitalism. The outlined framework is, therefore, a contribution to explaining technology under this system. Located in this concrete social formation, the structure ceases to be an abstract concept and takes on the forms of the system, marked by the appreciation of value, exploitation of human labour, and in the clash derived from oppressive relations, such as among classes, genders and races, and ethnicities. Such power relations promote inequalities, with the material basis as a last and central currency in an organic link with the spaces of representation and significance of experience in this system. Technology is manifested in this historical and social formation as capital in specific applications, from means of production to consumer goods or the object of political and cultural practices. Technology, thus, is a material configuration of social relations under capitalism, especially power relations. More than just a production force (Marx, 2013), it is also a socialization force, assuming an important role in various social activities. However, the capitalist form of the technical object is not omnipresent, as in any other social practice. There are initiatives for alternative arrangements and resistance that cannot be ignored (such as open-source software, for example).

Technology is not only impacted by historically situated social relationships. Artefacts and technological systems also shape social practices in their various manifestations, from the goods and services production to the operation of political and cultural institutions. But, as previously discussed, our approach does not assume a deterministic perspective, which confers to technology the prime cause of the evolution of the capitalist system. On the other hand, one of our purposes is to shed light on the relevance of technology and the need to understand its specificity to enhance the analyses in an attempt to offer a more sophisticated view of the historical movement of the capitalist system. By being forged by social practices and by shaping them in return, technology shows a dialectic relationship with the whole and the spheres of society in its historically determined manifestation and can only be explained as such.

The approach dialogues with the critical theory of technology, as we believe that it relates to the latter's theoretical–methodological precepts and guidelines. However, the present approach seeks an original articulation of its theoretical insights. If technology cannot be summarized as a thing (or set of things), but involves a dynamic sphere of objects, practices, and interactions, the value of its historical manifestation can be better apprehended by observing it as a process. Its materialization within the realm of relationships with the social totality and its other spheres occurs dynamically. Technology can, thus, be better understood within this continuous dialectic movement from other social activities that influence it, and from its influence on these spheres of activity and on the structure itself. More than an abstract relation, such manifestation occurs and constitutes systems under development, with functional and contextual properties, with rules, actors, operational logics, and, in general, as commodities in competition, given their specificity under capitalism. That is how technology manifests itself and how each artefact and system is built.

However, to understand concrete artefacts and technological systems, it is necessary to move to a deeper level of abstraction regarding the concept of the scientific–technological sphere. This movement, on the other hand, does not mean the simplification of technology to an artefact or to a group of artefacts. The parts of a TS cannot be apprehended only from the point of view of production. An electronic device is not only the sum of its chips, memory, batteries, and casing. Similarly, a ship is not only engines, hulls, and housings. The analysis of the TS must go beyond this most elementary perspective. TS s involve a complex list of items, which may include the legislation focused on it, the complex appropriation by users, and adjustments from their insertion in the competition. However, asserting technology as a system of complex parts is also insufficient to identify how these components are built within this system and how their interactions evolve.

Technology and its units and systems are not just a product, but a process involving factors, conditions, interests, disputes, materials, and procedures. Therefore, knowing the phenomenon in its complexity cannot be limited to observing its final form, but must encompass the whole constitutive movement, the influencing factors, the context in which it took place and how the components and actors operate to reproduce a technological system. Thus, technology and technological systems are not merely produced. As a process, they are 'regulated' in the formation and reproduction of this set of elements articulated and stabilized under concrete logics and conditions. Regulation here is understood as the dynamics articulated among parts, mechanisms, and factors of adjustment and transformation into processes to coordinate social activities. Coriat (2011:7–8) understands regulation as "different parts or processes that under certain conditions reciprocally adjust yielding some orderly dynamics." Regulation, the author adds, involves a relatively coherent socio-economic "tuning" within a given social context.

This regulation, however, is not only a reflection of social demands, as a radical constructivist view might suggest. The scientific–technological sphere, as a materialization in concrete historical reality, has developed, under capitalism, specific reproduction dynamics, from its institutions to its logic of creation, evolution, and appropriation by individuals and collectivities. Here we avoid using an external–internal distinction, since economic, political, and cultural factors assume both the form of dimensions of the manufacturing process and the role of institutions and phenomena of their own (such as a regulating state authority, an economic crisis, or a change in social values). Identifying the problems and demands that lead to the need to build a technological system, its creation, adjustments, its introduction into the market, reactions to it and forms of appropriation, all of which are permeated by the power relations materialized in the activity spheres, make up the regulation process of technological systems.

This approach to understanding the phenomenon is designated here as technological regulation. Technological regulation is the framework that sees technology as a sphere of social activities under capitalism in which artefacts and systems are created with functional and contextual properties, built from social factors, forged by their own dynamics for defining problems and pointing out solutions and with effects on their reproduction and on the rest of society, from a constant process of dynamic regulation, usually resulting in commodities competing on the market.[34]

Technological regulation covers three dimensions. The first, which we call 'regulation over technology,' involves the incidence of the social factors of regulation, understood here as the factors originating from the economic, political–institutional, and cultural spheres that affect the concrete development of a technological artefact or system. Examples of these factors are the market structures, the demands from segments, manufacturers and consumers, product availability, the stages of evolution of capitalist cycles, the concrete competition in the segment of the technological system, the government regime, the general and specific legislation, the performance of regulatory authorities, a state's scientific and technological policies, the action of political forces, rules and customs, the population's view about social activities, the forms of building identities and the markers that are part of the inequalities in society.

The second dimension, which we call 'regulation of technology,' concerns the internal factors of technological development. It is based on the technological paradigms, considered here as a set of stable references of normalization of technological solutions for certain demands. It focuses on how artefacts and TSs are constructed in their functional and contextual properties from a

---

[34] We refer to technology as a sphere, and we understand it as such. But, in the scheme presented here, it is situated together with science in what we call the 'scientific–technological sphere.'

set of elements of the scientific–technological sphere. Among these elements is the use of the knowledge stock available and its reproduction, the specific hierarchical structure of the technological system (as well as its control and management modes, and the actors and interests that affect it), the production processes (as well as the labour relations in the segments and manufacturers), the composition and functionalities of TS s, the financing models of each TS and its performance in the markets under competition, as well as the access and forms of appropriation in its consumption.

The third dimension is called 'regulation by technology.' If the creation of artefacts and systems is not only permeated by the factors of other spheres, but, also, impacts them, the analysis must also consider these effects and how these interactions return in the scope of dialectic reproduction. After all, as stated, technology is not only a receptacle of social factors, by itself, it is a factor that creates change. The analysis of technology cannot be limited only to the moment when the product emerges as such. Its circulation on the market, its relationship with other products in competition and how it is apprehended and appropriated by its consumers and other audiences (from state authorities to social groups) also affect its reproduction. And this, in the context of its concrete application and fruition, plays a role in other spheres, as a fundamental aspect to explain its 'existence.'

According to the Marxist tradition and the critical theory of technology, it is necessary to incorporate one last dimension, cross-sectional to the others: the assessment according to value bases and the analysis of the impacts on social activities from these references. In addition to a critical examination of technology under capitalism, this approach includes, in its reference framework, value precepts that define a horizon of what the phenomenon 'should be.' Critical theory considers the importance of valuing the elements that make up the technological regulation in question, based on a series of parameters. In order to include these parameters in the model, a quick debate is held, proposing some reflections marked by the fact that their analysis considers value elements.

Technological regulation is an effort to articulate a set of formulations and references and offer ways to contribute to them. If technology is the result and is crossed by social and power relations, neutral approaches and those based on an ideal of technology as an expression of a technique to optimize means and maximize the expected results, according to Weber, Habermas, and Bunge, may be insufficient. If this impact is not one-directional, but dialectical (if the technology is forged by society and shapes it, as claimed in several approaches), deterministic perspectives (as in Ellul, Heilbronner and Veblen) or partially deterministic perspectives (as in the case of some evolutionists), as well as those that overly emphasize social factors (such as SCOT) become limited alternatives. If such a dialectic relationship occurs in a historically concrete reality, under the capitalist system with its social relations of production and institutions, relativistic views that reduce the structure and these calcified force relations to fluid contingencies (such as ANT) do not meet the needs of the model.

If it is necessary to look at technology under the prism of capitalism as a historical phenomenon, it is necessary to understand its foundations and structural dynamics. In that sense, Marx's contributions offer valuable explanations. However, if technology has evolved into more historically complex roles beyond a productive force, assuming the condition of a socialization force, these formulations must not be disregarded, but taken as a conceptual basis to be further developed in the debate. In such an effort, CTT offers valuable elaborations by also recognizing the social factors and their incidence in the content of artefacts and TS. If, on the one hand, CTT assumes that the general principle that technology is impacted by society and influences it, it recognizes that technology has material and social dimensions. On the other hand, theoretical–methodological references to materialize such assumptions into an analysis framework with the necessary tools to investigate this process can complement this approach's efforts.

In this sense, the technological regulation approach is presented as a set of conceptual–analytical resources for examining artefacts and technological systems according to their nature as a process that took place on capitalism. Firstly, it suggests an order of analysis. However, it is not restricted to recording the groups of interest (as in SCOT) or of objectives and power relations (as in some CTT formulations). Secondly, it suggests a detailed analysis of technological development incorporating some categories into the measurement of the factors. It includes the formulations of evolutionists in its technological paradigm as a necessary reference base for the investigation. In addition, it introduces a series of categories derived from the assumption of artefacts as commodities in a competition (considered here, according to Marx, as where a concrete dispute between capital is manifested), incorporating aspects of what could be referred to as a 'political economy of technology;. This economic view of the artefact is still poorly developed in CTT, and it is a vital component of the model presented here. Finally, a commodity cannot complete its cycle, nor can an artefact accomplish its functionality, without their consumption and use, which is also an aspect that is poorly developed in CTT. We add here a category that seems central to us: that of appropriation, through which use occurs under a mediation, with the social factors affecting the users and their relationship with the artefact or technological system.

Finally, the second part of the dialectic movement, the effects of technology on society, is recognized not only by CTT, but by several approaches. However, this notion should be incorporated more systematically into a model that aims to evaluate the whole process involving technical objects. Thus, we do not deny that such perspective is present in the approaches or that it is part of the repertoire of these authors (as shown by the notorious analyses by Marx, Weber, Ellul, and Marcuse, among others). However, it seems to be less integrated than what would be necessary into the theoretical and conceptual–analytical schemes, which is why the third dimension was added as a phase of the process. Hence, we do not wish to suggest that such investigations and analyses are a novelty. From the philosophy of technology to the economics of innovation, several fields have discussed and produced a wealth of qualified research which has unveiled the dynamics of technology in many areas and contexts. We merely present here an effort to reorganize the theoretical references. But it is still necessary to discuss the value bases of the approach. This brief debate seeks to systematize the authors' contribution in their more prescriptive manifestations, in which they offered only a description to judge and suggest paths from their understanding of the effects of technology in society. The formulations of authors already discussed, which have produced reflections in this sense, will also be reviewed.

The critical theory of technology, along the lines of the critical approach to society and its spheres, does not focus only on describing and interpreting the phenomena. Beyond the idea of totality and the dialectic relationship between the society as a whole – according to its current mode of production and its sectors, as well as the action of organizations and individuals that constitute them – one key aspect is the inclusion of a value and prescriptive basis on the directions of the collectivity, following the famous Thesis Eleven of Karl Marx's Theses on Feuerbach. In this sense, we also adopt such dimensions here, presenting a brief debate on notions regarding what technology ought to be, according to values connected to social justice, economic and political democracy, and the end of oppression. Such value bases, more than just a theoretical analysis, will guide the present reflections, especially regarding the analysis of both platforms presented at the end of this volume.

6   Values Base to Analyse Technology under Capitalism

Throughout the chapter, the various interpretations of technology were presented in view of different issues, such as the neutrality or autonomy of artefacts. Finally, we discuss the value dimension of technology as a component of the critical perspective on which the theoretical–methodological model proposed here is based. The evaluation grounded on references or values for technological development does not disregard other controversies already mentioned. The critical historical approach to technology on capitalist society ranges from determinists, such as Ellul, to constructivist approaches, such as SCOT, or essentialists, such as Heidegger, to relativists, such as Callon and Latour. In their own ways, as already discussed here, a considerable number of authors and theories have pointed out different issues related to technology in modern societies, from the concentration of power to the use of technology for the expropriation of labour and creating a greater gap between business owners and workers. Faced with the countless issues presented, what would be the values and posture necessary in the technical making?

Some philosophical approaches have emerged focused on applying ethical principles to technology. Besides Heidegger (1977a) and his defence of understanding the essence of technology, other authors have dedicated themselves to the subject. Swiestra and Rip (2007) discuss the negative impacts of technology on legal, social, and economic aspects (ELSA). Jonas (1974) argues that the modern technical complex has given rise to a new discussion of ethical standards: "Technology, apart from its objective works, assumes ethical significance by the central place it now occupies in human purpose" (p. 210). Based on their self-image, human beings become makers, enjoying their present and future realization capacities. In this undefined movement of building the future, the "relevant horizon of responsibility" is constituted. Bunge (2013) advocates an "ethical code" for technology. According to the author, this code should contain: 1) an individual ethical code that should include the ethics of science and involve the researcher's responsibility not to take part in anti-social objectives; and 2) a social, ethical code for technological policies, not allowing "undesirable objectives" and inspired by society's general needs, rather than being dictated by privileged groups of society.

Another value perspective is the one that proposes an analysis based on political theory and relates technology and democracy. Based on the approach of a "strong democracy" (inspired by Benjamin Barber), Sclove (1995; 2009) argues that democracy is the guarantee of equal participation of citizens in decisions concerning their lives, based on the principle of freedom, organized within the framework of morality (inspired by the Kantian approach). Such freedom should apply to technology: "If citizens ought to be empowered to participate in determining their society's basic structure, and technologies are an important species of social structure, it follows that technological design and practice should be democratized" (Sclove, 2009: 322). According to this perspective, technological development must observe democratic principles, rather than economic interests or specific political groups. If it does not incorporate these guidelines, the artefacts undermine and limit the full realization of strong democracies more than they support it. In addition to processes, democratic preferences must be part of the very content of technologies.

The concern for participating in the formulation of artefacts also appears in debates in areas related to design (especially in Scandinavian countries), technical development, and to certain technologies (such as human/computer interaction). Vines et al. (2013) list three objectives of participating in building an artefact. The first would be to share control with users, empowering the users of such devices that are usually excluded from their elaboration. The second would be to consider users as actors with relevant expertise for the construction process, incorporating their knowledge, impressions, and feedback into the configuration of technical objects. The third is the change of the technical development processes, with new perspectives and interventions that help in the evolution of production procedures and the very content of the machines, with the objective of improving people's lives. According to the authors, the value principle of participation should even extend beyond design, including the entire decision-making processes, as well as the application and use of technologies, such as in social networks.

The approach, known as the "Scandinavian School of Participatory Design" has developed an extensive debate on the subject. According to Torpel et al. (2009: 14), this approach involves "those whose (working) lives will change as a consequence of the introduction of a computer application." Considering especially the implementation of innovations in the workplace, participation is viewed as a sign of quality in all phases of the process, from conception to implementation. Among the concerns are acknowledging the workers' expertise, searching for benefits as a result of innovations, their sustainable features, considering multiple points of view throughout the process, respecting established production and organizational practices, authentic experience, searching for solutions for the "real world," empowering marginalized social groups, and promoting reflection practices in the areas where the technical solution will be implemented.

Several authors also discuss the relationship between the scientific–technological sphere and democracy in the field of social studies of science and technology (STS). According to Jasanoff (2007), this relationship is marked by how the intersection between scientific and technological knowledge and the search for promoting democratic values in the field of politics occurs, or how each sphere influences the other. Within the modern context, the specialization of scientific–technological production and the configuration of the states, as well as the industrial model, have resulted in the accumulation of power in the hands of a few people and groups and have affected society's capacity for self-government. From the 1990s onwards, the state's authority began to be undermined in favour of the concentration of power and knowledge in multinational corporations. An old question in political theory also became part of the concerns of science and technology studies: how can a few (experts) speak for so many? Both forms of 'representation' show power and authority relations, institutions and legitimation conflicts. The approach of STS, and of the author, points towards seeing such authorities of representation of reality as social constructions (according to different perspectives, as already discussed here). The co-production of knowledge and of the world (Jasanoff, 2004) ceased to be only an analytical tool of the approach and rose to the normative condition, from which the scientific–technological production must incorporate aspects of the construction of social norms. The development of knowledge and artefacts, therefore, must incorporate public demands (and the analysis of this process must identify how the experts embrace such interests).[35]

Still within STS, several formulations seek to qualify this debate, incorporating the element of concrete power inequalities. Klein and Kleinmann (2002), proposing a new look at SCOT's method by Bijker and Pinch (1993), defend that unequal power relations should be considered. Hess et al. (2016) discuss the problems in what they call "structural inequalities" in science and technology policies, such as persistent inequities in knowledge and technical resources. These are manifested both among social groups and in areas of the world. The authors highlight the limits of the ANT method and of other branches of STS, due to their emphasis on phenomena from the microsocial perspective. The authors highlight these aspects in the oppression relations regarding race and gender. These two categories also appear in several TS studies (Wajcman, 2010; Harding, 2011). Wajcman (2010: 447) highlights the historical construction of a male profile in technology: "technology is identified as masculine, and masculinity is defined in terms of technical competence." The normative dimension

---

35 However, the contribution of the constructivist approaches of STS (from ANT to SCOT, as well as authors in the 'epistemic' and 'ontological' turns, including those of ANT and Jasanoff) set two limits to the normative debate. The first is the principle of symmetry applied by so many contributions in the area. In the search to observe the differences and controversies in the production of facts and artefacts, this principle implies a relativism even of the structures presented, of the inequalities that characterize them and of a framework of purposes to overcome or mitigate them. The second is that the important problematization of scientific authority posed by these authors advances in defence of more participatory processes, but the 'people' or the 'the laymen' still appear as an abstract category or one that is not situated historically.

would, therefore, involve considering and overcoming these inequalities, understood both according to their structural aspect and their specific social relations.

But, if such perspectives represent advances by not assuming technology as a neutral and aseptic phenomenon, but one endowed with problems and that creates iniquities, it is still necessary to move further and qualify its value base. A first challenge is to situate it historically, but without succumbing to a static resigned criticism. Marcuse (1973), in his analysis of technology as rationality in late capitalism, presents interesting reflections. The author, unlike some critics of technology, such as Heidegger, does not see the domination of technological rationality as an inexorable reality, enabled by a qualitative change. Technological transformation is, at the same time, political transformation. However, the political change would only become a qualitative social change as long as it changed the direction of technical progress – that is, developing new technology, since the established technology has become an instrument of destructive politics (Marcuse, 1973: 211). For the author, this new direction would consist of a "catastrophe" in the established order, a new reason, and not an evolution of its rationality. However, this does not mean a "resurrection of values," but their radical reorientation, which would translate into the devices themselves.

By pointing to the limitations in Marcuse's formulations, Feenberg (1996) stands out from approaches such as that of Heidegger and the Frankfurt School, that are "too indiscriminate in their condemnation of technology to guide efforts to reform it" (n.p.). The solutions offered tend to shift towards art, religion, and nature. In contrast, the approach he calls "technology reform," or "projection of critique," understands the technical arrangement as a result of political and cultural values, as well as other spheres of society, such as law or education. The author's "technology reform" approach is resumed and complemented in other works (Feenberg, 2005). To see alternatives, it is necessary to put into perspective the role of interests, rather than efficiency, as an indicator of the success of a certain technology, as well as the choices of hegemonic groups and the dominant ideology, which operate to select one or more options among the various alternatives available. The impact of interests, in a broad sense and not restricted to the dominant interests, does not reduce efficiency but establishes alternative parameters for measuring success. To address these concerns and demands, it would be necessary to change the devices' design. A "democratic transformation from below," in Feenberg's evaluation, could substantially alter the technical sphere. The prospect of qualitative traces goes back to Marcuse. In another work (Feenberg, 2002), he elaborates on the reasoning of reform to expand the interests contemplated in the design of technical devices. Seeking a critical interpretation of the idea of "rationalization" in Weber, the author suggests a "subversive rationalization" as a political project for technology, based on the democratization of this sphere and the concrete resistance in several episodes (such as the environmental movement).

Before introducing a systematization, one last reference should be introduced. If the technological regulation approach emphasizes artefacts and systems as competing commodities, the conditions of market structures must be considered, also as the idea of mitigating relations of economic domination. In this concern, the idea of competition is central. However, there is no consensual or at least commonly accepted definition of competition in the literature. This can be manifested in different ways: in sectors, relevant markets, product markets, or geographic markets. In the neoclassical economic view, in more competitive markets, the pressure of competition puts pressure on prices and, consequently, on profit margins, forcing companies to be more efficient and allocate resources more efficiently. Polder et al. (2009: 7) argue that "under stronger competition, profits are more sensitive to managerial efforts, and managerial efforts can be better monitored. In this way, competition is good for performance".

The competition scenario may also be related to the promotion of economic welfare, which is understood as the maximization of consumer and producer surplus in the economy's general context (Motta, 2004:17–18). Competition may not be an end in itself, but a way to achieve public interests and welfare (Bucirossi, 2008: xiii). Less orthodox variations previously discussed, more open to market regulation, assume that appropriate structural conditions – associated with less concentrated markets and the absence of entry and exit barriers – create incentives for companies to compete. As a result, allocation and production efficiencies and the technical progress in the economy are promoted. In such a scenario, consumer welfare would be maximized (Oliveira, 2014: 7). Ezrachi and Stucke (2020) claim that competition can be toxic to social actors or, if appropriately shaped, beneficial to workers, players and society as a whole. Competition must serve society, and not the contrary. What authors call "noble competition" can help rivals reach their full potential. As Ezrachi and Stucke (Chapter 10) say, "players compete fiercely, but do so with deep societal and moral awareness. Each player, while seeking to prevail, is aware of her wider community and recognizes how her competitiveness can help her rivals be their best selves."

More critical approaches draw attention to what they call the illusion of the manifestation of competition in capitalism by taking markets as an intrinsic locus of power relations and the system's logic as inherently concentrating and centralizing (Marx, 2013: 257). Thus, according to the author's formulation, and which we acknowledge as the most appropriate here, markets cannot be seen as places of perfect competition and balance, but, rather, as the opposite (as evolutionists and other authors in the long-wave debate, such as Mandel, point out). Herscovici (2013) stresses the importance of recognizing the specificities of electronic information networks (a concept that is close to the object of this research) in addition to traditional models for the provision of goods and services, such as the multifaceted nature of platforms and models marked by the sale of audiences to different advertisers, making the externality of the demand endogenous and creating social utility. To contemplate these arrangements, he suggests the concept of "qualitative competition." In this modality, a reduction of the price variable occurs due to other elements, such as the quality of the services offered. The debate cannot be exhausted here, but for the effects of this analysis, our view is summarized as follows: competition is considered as the quality of the scenario in which there are low entry barriers, no monopolistic or oligopolistic forms, no companies with significant market power, diversity of choice for users and maximization of the welfare of citizens participating in the market in its broadest sense, and not its strictly economic sense. This competition, however, is not an ideal point whose non-manifestation is the result of 'failures' or 'deviations,' but a countertrend which, in general, depends on an action of the legal regulation of the state.

Moving towards a synthesis of the value bases, it is worth pointing out a fundamental aspect: the inequality of nations around the world, which also includes the competition aspects referred to, since Marx (2013) indicates the global capitalist market as the locus of the concrete manifestation of the operating logic of the system. This is an issue considered by Dussel (1988) in his debate on technology under capitalism. In the international competition in the capitalist system (organized, therefore, according to its operating logic and materialized among individual capital and among nations), stronger capital (and stronger nations) influence weaker capital, appropriating the exploited labour.[36] From a Latin American perspective, his normative response is presented in general terms, but it is worth mentioning it, since it may have an

---

36 "Competition not only plays its role in the leveling or distribution of the surplus value produced, *post festum* (in the circulation of commodities), it also interferes in the process of reproduction (*ante festum*). The question of dependency, therefore, is not merely a circulatory moment, but, also, a reproductive moment, always within the sphere of 'total world capital' to which the less developed 'total national capital' turns, not only with export and import but through multiple other mechanisms that articulate it as a 'part' of a 'whole' that includes that 'total national capital' in all its moments." (Dussel, 1988: 337).

impact on alternative technological projects. Beyond the clash between classes in capitalism, the author argues, from his analysis of international competition, that a "national and popular liberation" is important to stop the transfer of appropriate overwork. The term "liberation" is used as a way out of a domination relationship.

Based on the references and reflections developed so far, we have reached the conclusion of the present debate, proposing a systematization of the value basis adopted as a framework for this study.

1) Technological regulation must be based on principles that promote a political and effectively democratic social order, without exploitation of labour, without oppression in any form, with equitable production and distribution of wealth and with adequate and sustainable management of the environment in which communities are inserted, taken not as abstract value elements but in the context of concrete social constitution, in this case, the capitalist system;

2) These values represent both a horizon for a social model in general and the parameters that guide the projected progress in the capitalist system;

3) These values must be incorporated into the technological development regarding the factors related to regulation over technology, internal factors and those related to regulation by technology, so that the technological practice may contribute to their materialization in the capitalist system or to create the transformations necessary for its effective constitution;

4) These values should be detailed according to concrete conditions for their attainment and effective realization as guarantees to individuals and collectivities, or rights, recognized as a construction based on socially mapped demands and needs, aiming at the full materialization of the value basis;

5) In the scientific–technological sphere, the value basis must materialize considering the specificities of its inherent practices. Such manifestations should occur throughout the process, from the organization of policies and instances defining the technological policies and actions of the state authorities to the consumption and advancement of development cycles of artefacts and technological systems. Here, in the debate involving content circulation platforms (our object of study), this realization is carried out assuming certain rights, such as freedom of expression, right to information, and data privacy and protection;

6) The concretization of the value basis involves prioritizing the demands and interests of marginalized, oppressed, or subordinate groups, especially those within the scope of class, gender, and race relations of

oppression. The development processes and its phases (conception, definition, testing, manufacture, and implementation, among others) must incorporate the participation of social segments related to the artefact, or that may be impacted by its fruition;

7) In addition to prior scrutiny and participation throughout the process, the creation of artefacts and systems should be subject to public evaluation and debate, in competent forums and instances and concretely affecting incremental or structural adjustments in the development of the objects in question;

8) The value basis should apply not only to the manufacturing of objects but, also, to the process of producing knowledge related to it.

Based on the technological regulation model presented here, the analysis framework will also be outlined as follows, in addition to the derivative reference framework, including detailed categories and methodological strategies relevant to examine concrete artefacts or systems, their articulation in understanding the macro sphere and the procedures to investigate specific objects in the micro sphere, and their application to digital platforms, specifically Google and Facebook.

CHAPTER 2

Technology and Capitalist Development

This chapter furthers the debate in line with the previously discussed approach to technology, which sees it not as artefacts detached from a historical and social context but immersed in it and dialectically shaped by it. Thus, we seek to point out some interrelated aspects between technology and capitalist development, assuming the spheres framework discussed in the previous chapter. Far from attempting to offer an exhaustive analysis, the following argument provides examples that help characterize technological systems under capitalism. They are understood as processes characterized by technological regulation, permeated by the social mobility needs of this new mode of production, and, also, built from the development of successive technological paradigms that help shape capitalist development. Thus, our aim is to address this process considering technological regulation's three dimensions: regulation over technology, regulation of technology, and regulation by technology.

Technological evolution has gained relevance in several dimensions according to the system progress ideology, which is widely dominant. Under this ideology, capitalism represents the spearhead of human creation's material expression, opposing other systems, which represent delay. Its advocates have, thus, promoted the ideology of civilization, as opposed to the ideology of 'barbaric' or 'savage' peoples. This ideal is very much present in sociology, when comparing capitalism to other systems (as in Weber), in anthropology's evolutionist current (Morgan, Tyler), and in the economic orthodoxy that points to development as a 'ladder' that must be reached by respecting market balance. Despite the critical role of increased productivity in the central capitalist nations, the system's rise did not occur without intense military action, wars, and complete territorial domination, such as with the colonization of significant areas of several continents in the world. Economic supremacy was firmly connected to these relations of subordination, whether by labour overexploitation in the colonies or by unbalanced economic arrangements favouring hegemonic nations in peripheral capitalism (as in Latin America) (as Dussel [1988] observes).

This perspective focused on material progress is related to the Enlightenment project and its notion of rationality. The rational action that distinguishes this project and its concrete socio-historical manifestation in capitalism would be guided not by religious inclinations, but by unveiling reality based on the scientific method and controlling nature through systematic knowledge production and technological development. Weber is one of the authors who supports this connection. Despite his famous analysis of Protestant ethics' impact on capitalism, according to the author, rational, goal-oriented action is capitalism's most characteristic development method, overcoming others, such as those guided by values or affections. When the relationship between means and ends is unequivocal, "it is legitimate to assert that insofar as the action was rigorously rational, it could not have taken any other course" (Weber, 1991: 12). Rationality is related to the reasons why the most appropriate means are chosen to promote a particular action. Here is where the neutral notion of technique and technology emerges: "Among others, the standard of efficiency for a technique may be the famous principle of 'least action,' the achievement of the optimum result with the least expenditure of resources" (Weber, 1991: 38). The properties Weber mentions are "perfection," "safety," "durability," and "efficiency" in terms of efforts, including labour efforts. Using rationality to make such a choice – in comparison with other possibilities – is what would ensure these properties. Here, the notion of efficacy emerges as an ideal point in relation to different combinations of available means and intended purposes.

Habermas, an advocate of a neutral perspective on technology, also observes the rational actions connected to the technique. This would be an evolution, a "gradual objectification" of the teleological rational action controlled by success and related to labour. The author bases his analysis on the difference between labour and interaction. The former consists of a teleological rational action that includes an instrumental action, a rational choice, or a combination of both. The use of technique and technology in material practices relate to labour in general, to meeting material demands, and to the manifestation of the teleological rational action. Their development is associated with society's dependency on managing material demands and their solutions, and by establishing new ways to meet these needs based on labour and success-oriented rational action. Habermas (2011: 513) emphasizes that "the greater our control over natural and social processes, the greater the range of action within which we can, under given circumstances, safely achieve certain ends without failing to predict their side effects." Thus, rational options for alternative means also expand. Habermas relates the rise of rational action and technique to the advent of capitalism, or the transition from traditional to modern society, as he calls it. It is during the latter that productivity grows, from which technological innovations are institutionalized. This process occurs simultaneously with the development of self-regulated economic growth. Here, the link between apparatuses and social context is formed according to his perspective.

In this relationship, political domination is legitimated "from below," in apparent reciprocity in commodity exchanges, especially in relation to the labour force. Although political domination was at the top of class society during other historical configurations, in capitalism, "the legitimization of the institutional framework [can] be linked immediately with the system of social labour. Only then can the property order change from a 'political relation' to a 'production relation'" (Habermas, 1997: 64). Rationalization manifests from below and from the top. In the first case, it emerges with a new mode of production, a new social labour organization, and the production forces' development. Modernization pervades different spheres of life. Legitimating values for teleological rational action systems and subsystems are established, such as subjective ethical convictions and the legal system. Ideologies emerge when traditional legitimations are replaced. In this scenario, modern science creates a "reference methodological framework that reveals the transcendental point of view of the possible technical arrangement" (Habermas, 1997:66–7). It creates knowledge that applies to practice, in an interdependent relationship that has become stronger since its emergence at the end of the nineteenth century.

Ellul (1964) points out that the central factor of social transformations in the advent of capitalism was the rise of technology, which demanded that the different spheres of life adjusted to the introduction of machines. This occurred in the abstract domain, while machines carried out this process in the labour sphere. Such apparatuses are efficient and bring efficiency into different social spaces. Ellul sees the emergence of capitalism from the sixteenth century and the advent of the industrial revolution as a "technical revolution," characterized as "the emergence of a state that was truly conscious of itself and was autonomous in relation to anything that did not serve its interest" (Ellul, 1964: 43). It did not manifest itself only in the technical apparatuses, but in management and the police, as a period of rationalized systems, the unification of hierarchies, systematization of rules, also changing the legal system.

By differentiating the modern stage from the previous ones, the author points out that its internal movement is no longer guided by tradition, but by previous technical procedures. Since the search for efficiency guides the technical phenomenon, this internal evolution, through the action of experts, calculation, and qualification of the use of means assumes a central role in this "progressively elaborated" movement. However, this does not occur without leaps and bounds. Ellul identifies a certain mystery in the qualitative transformation of apparatuses within what he calls technical revolution, for which he has some answers.[1] Would it be the advent of capitalism? This seems to us to

---

1   Ellul lists five possible factors: the fruition of long technical experience, population expansion, the adequacy of an economic environment, a more plastic social environment, and the emergence of a clear technical intention.

be a fruitful path of inquiry, which will be further discussed later on. As Ellul recapitulates, the nineteenth century led to a chain reaction that is easier to explain. New technologies were made feasible by the standards that had been established up to then, as well as by the scientific bases created.

For these and other authors, technical progress is directly related to the system's superiority over previous modes of production. From the military capacity of the emerging capitalist powers to their trade potential, by the use of fuels and vehicles (such as trains and ships), the system's spread throughout the world was intimately related to how its material framework allowed the expansion of production and wider distribution of commodities through transport and communications. From technological determinists (such as Ellul, Heilbronner and Veblen) to an important part of the Marxist tradition,[2] the technical devices' improvement was indicated as a critical explanation for the capitalist system's evolution, concerning the idea of "industrial revolutions" adopted by different schools of thought.

Marx begins a critical analysis tradition on the creation and development of capitalism that incorporates aspects related to technology. By examining capital's dynamics, he placed these issues at the heart of the capital development process, in its "accumulation" dynamics, based on the extraction of surplus labour by exploiting the labour force in a process that involves production and circulation.[3] Thus, he sees it both as a productive force and as specific forms of capital. These forces are at the centre of the historical development in contradiction with the social relations of production concretely established.[4]

In one of his works (1980), Marx describes the machine as a metamorphosis of the labour process, gathering the instruments used in labour processes. The artefacts concentration and the division of labour are inseparable components of this process. The machine, therefore, is different from the individual

---

2   The one that emphasizes the productive forces as an engine of development.
3   The accumulation process begins as a stage in the circulation sphere, when money buys labour force and means of production. The second stage is manifested in production, when the means of production are converted into commodities that exceed the value of their constituent parts, containing more value. Once the commodity is ready, it is brought into circulation to be traded for money. The capitalist then puts money back into the market to buy the production factors once again to continue the cycle. But he only puts the money back at a higher level due to the surplus value produced and converted into money (M'). Then, it completes the cycle as capital, because it has been "realized as a value which has created value" (Marx, 2014: 2887).
4   In doing so, even without referring to himself as a technology theorist, Marx provides a valuable approach to its operation logic under capitalism, serving as a reference for perspectives in different fields of knowledge on the subject.

instrument. While the latter is the worker's tool, the former governs the process, with the worker as a "guardian" of its proper operation.[5] The worker's action then becomes an abstraction, an accessory, a means determined by the machines. Created by science, the machinery works as a "useful automaton," reducing the necessary labour force. According to Marx (1980), machinery is the most finished form of the capital in general, as "capital's form, means, and power," hostile to labour, a "negative influx." (Marx, 1982: 163).

The machinery, says the author (1982), differs from the traditional instruments it replaces. In labour's division in the manufacturing industry,[6] instruments are created and employed according to a logic of specialization (focused on using them for a given operation or objective), differentiation (distinction of forms) and simplification (its affirmation as a means for a simple and uniform task). These are technological premises of production's development, using machines as elements that have revolutionized production relationships. Firstly, the machine gathers many instruments, "set in motion simultaneously by a single mechanism" (Marx, 1982: 146). A second way of combining instruments is when several machines are combined to operate in successive processes or phases of the production processes, being triggered by the same driving force. A third type involves adding several machines in the same plant, still set in motion by the same driving force. A first improvement would be production's continuous nature.[7] A second aspect would be that of simultaneous operations. The third would be the production speed, intensified beyond the physical limits.

In his most finished work, *Capital* (2013), Marx details the machine's constituting elements, dividing them into three parts: 1) the prime mover (the mechanism's driving force, self-generated or triggered from the outside), 2) the transmission mechanism (which modifies the form where necessary and distributes the movement to the following part), and 3) the machine-tool (which takes hold of the object and modifies it according to a purpose). Marx distinguishes between the "cooperation of many machines" and a "machinery system." In the former, the product is entirely manufactured on each machine, as in a revival of simple cooperation, albeit with a technical component (such as in weaving). In the machine system, the object goes through "a connected

---

5 As mentioned before, the labour process' protagonism is reversed, from the subject to the machine, with the latter assuming the condition of an opposing force.
6 Marx defines manufacturing as the company where the production of goods is made by hand or, when not so, by machines.
7 Unlike living labour, which requires rest for reproduction, the machines allow uninterrupted operation.

series of graduated processes carried out by a chain of mutually complementary machines of various kinds" (2013: 557). It, thus, constitutes what the author calls "a great automaton."[8]

In analysing the machinery's functions and examples in capitalism, the author discusses technology as a productive force, as a means of labour, as constant capital, and as fixed capital. Questioning Proudhon, Marx (2017) affirms machines as a productive force. The modern workshop, on the other hand, is a social relation of production. Machines play a central role in the division of labour, since the latter is organized based on the "instruments available." In another work (1982), he qualifies this understanding, characterizing the machinery as the "produced productive force" (Marx, 1982: 81). Labour, objectified under these structures as diverse work (1980), is assumed as a productive force due to the accumulation of knowledge, skills, and the "productive forces of the social brain." This force evolves as a result of the accumulated social work, and it is driven by scientific progress.[9] The means of labour (or means of production) is the genus where the technology species are found. The author defines means of labour as: "a thing, or a complex of things, which the labourer interposes between himself and the subject of his labour, and which serves as the conductor of his activity" (Marx, 2013: 328). This category involves using the physical properties of materials in other objects, "according to their purpose." This is a characteristic of human beings and of labour processes and it is a sign of different times.[10] The means of labour indicates the development degree of the productive forces and the social conditions under which the production process occurs. When producing a commodity with the aid of the means, humans materialize their labour as the product. Therefore, the means of production is a key element to set living labour in motion, but it

---

[8] "In the place of the isolated machine, a mechanical monster whose body fills whole factories, and whose demon power, at first veiled under the slow and measured motions of his giant limbs, at length breaks out into the fast and furious whirl of his countless working organs" (Marx, 2013: 560).

[9] "Such a development of productive power is again traceable in the final analysis to the social nature of the labour engaged in production; to the division of labour in society; and to the development of intellectual labour, especially in the natural sciences." (Marx, 2017, online: 2188).

[10] "What differentiates economic times is not 'what' is produced, but 'how,' 'with what means of labour' " (Marx, 2013: 329). However, in a later passage, the author establishes as a distinguishing feature the relationship of surplus appropriation: "What distinguishes the various economic formations of society – the distinction between, for example, a society based on slave-labor and a society based on wage-labor – is the form in which this surplus labour is in each case extorted from the immediate producer, the worker." (p. 374).

seems, to the worker, to be an "alien property" (Marx, 2014: 2622), like any other commodity.[11]

Since they do not affect the value, the means of labour are referred to by Marx (2013) as "constant capital." The author considers that both the raw material and the means of production, such as machinery, may have changes in value. But this does not change their condition as constant capital. Due to the need for living labour, not making use of the means seems to the capital as a loss, and there is constant pressure to extend the workday and occupy the means of production for the longest period as possible, including at night. Constant capital has such a nature because it remains in the production process (until it is worn out), but this does not mean that it does not add value to the product. This part of constant capital "yields up value to the product in proportion as it loses its own exchange-value together with its own use-value" (Marx, 2014: 5139). The parameter for this value transfer is the average time between the moment the apparatus enters into production until it is worn out and needs to be replaced. In his theoretical scheme on the production process, Marx makes a second distinction in addition to constant capital and variable capital. He differentiates constant capital as fixed capital and circulating capital, two moments in the organic composition of capital. The term also derives from the movement of "fixing" the capital invested in these production factors. It takes the form of "fixed" capital while the rest of the production factors acquire the form of "circulating" capital (Marx, 2014: 5164).[12] Such division occurs only within productive capital, and not in the forms of capital-commodity and capital-money. Machinery is one of the immovable means of labour in the production process (Marx, 2014: 5236), but immobility is not the determining element, since fixed capital can be movable (such as a vehicle or tool) and circulating capital can be immovable (such as a plantation's raw material). This fixed form has a "peculiar" rotation, according to the author's words. The value has a double existence, partly in the original object, and partly in the product placed on the market and converted into money (Marx, 2014: 5248).

When consumed, the use-value of fixed capital is its acting as the raw material's "transforming actor" to transform it into a product. It includes both the

---

11   Marx (2014) warns, however, that the means of production are not capital by nature, nor is the human labour force. "They acquire this specific social character only under definite, historically developed conditions, just as only under such conditions the character of money is stamped upon precious metals, or that of money-capital upon money" (2014: 2746).

12   Fixed capital, therefore, does not include auxiliary materials consumed during the production process, as well as raw materials.

"technological condition" where the process takes place (such as the facilities) and the "immediate condition" (the instruments and labour materials).[13] The development of fixed capital, at the general level, involves controlling the "conditions of the vital process of society" by what the author calls the "general intellect" (Marx, 2011a:943–944). From his analysis of machines to their position in the production process, Marx bases his investigation on the intimate relationship between technology and society. As explained above, he still recognizes that these social forms (from instruments to the labour force) are elements of different periods, but his description covers the dynamics assumed under capitalism. Understanding the phenomenon, therefore, entails understanding the functions and forms assumed in this concrete social context. According to Marx (1982: 77),[14] the purpose of the machinery is "to reduce the working time required for the production of a commodity," but not the time employed by the worker. The objective of introducing these artefacts is exactly to increase the proportion of the worker's unpaid labour for the reproduction of needs, that is, to increase the proportion of overwork. On the contrary, says the author, the workday extends beyond its natural limits, increasing not only the relative surplus-value, the intensity, but, also, the labour time in general. By employing machinery, the capitalist reduces the socially necessary labour time of commodities. Although it may be sold at a higher individual value, the social value of each unit falls, as the socially necessary labour also decreases. Ultimately, and not uncommonly, machinery not only reduces socially necessary labour time but replaces some of the workers,[15] which has been a controversy since the beginning of the so-called 'Industrial Revolution.' Thus, it creates a surplus of workers in the labour market.

The means of labour adds value to the product manufactured through their use, as does the labour force. While the former retains part of the value

---

13 These two are 'material preconditions' of the production process in general and the preservation of the labour instrument.
14 We refer here to the compilation organized by Mauro de Lisa under the name "Progreso técnico y desarrollo capitalista" (Cuadernos de pasado y presente), in which Books 10, 19 and 20 of the manuscripts were translated.
15 When talking about the transition from textile production to mechanization, Marx (1851 apud: Dussel, 1988) finds an example of the tensions upon the introduction of new technologies. The several operations related to textile labour were highly valued, so the craftsmen were recognized for such skills. In England, fabric handling machines that did not require manual labour were implemented. In 1758, Evert discovered a mill that performed operations related to the activity, such as a press, moved by water. One hundred thousand people who were out of work burned the mill. Evert was given compensation by the English state, which built a machine with even better features.

and transfers another small part to the product, the latter adds value.[16] The machinery's participation in capitalism's mission of "enhancing value" also occurs by increasing labour productivity, which relates to an expansion of the means of labour employed. Part of these means of labour is an effect of this movement, such as the increase of the raw material demanded. Others are conditions, especially the machinery used in this productivity gain.[17] However, the increased proportion of constant capital in relation to variable capital further enhances a contradiction at the core of the historical course of capitalism through the general trend of decreasing profit rates, as we will see at the end of this section. In terms of competition among capital in specific sectors, one of the effects of such dynamics is concentration and centralization,[18] which accelerate revolutions in the capital's technical composition, in a quantitative and qualitative change that reduces demand for labour. Thus, they become more a powerful accumulation of reproduction forces. Although not explicitly, Marx (1982) indicates that the social relations of production influence not only the use of the artefacts, but their own constitution, a topic that was resumed by the authors of the critical theory of technology referenced here. The same goes for the dialectic relationship between technology and society. Just as the division of labour is part of the machine's construction, the machine enhances it within society. Not only that, but it also transforms this division qualitatively, differently from how it was manifested in simple cooperation and manufacturing.[19]

The machinery's development occurs through the capital's appropriation of progress in general, including scientific knowledge.[20] A certain development

---

16 "By the simple addition of a certain quantity of labour, new value is added, and by the quality of this added labour, the original values of the means of production are preserved in the product." (Marx, 2013: 355).

17 "With the increasing productivity of labour, not only does the mass of the means of production consumed by it increase, but their value compared with their mass diminishes" (Marx, 2013: 846).

18 In this process of accumulation, there is a concentration of capital in the hands of each individual capital, but, also, a concentration by their suppression in favour of the emergence of larger capital. The contradiction between competition and concentration is manifested as centralization (Marx, 2013: 851).

19 In another work, he suggests a more neutral character of industrial machinery. "The contradictions and antagonisms inseparable from the capitalist employment of machinery, do not exist, they say, since they do not arise out of machinery, as such, but out of its capitalist employment" (Marx, 2013: 626).

20 "The full development of capital, therefore, takes place – or capital has posited the mode of production corresponding to it – only when the means of labour has not only taken the economic form of fixed capital, but has also been suspended in its immediate form, and

of productive forces is a condition for the transformation of value into capital, which, consequently, also drives their development. Fixed capital grows in proportion to productive forces and can materialize them. Its most advanced expression is what he calls "the automatic system of machines" (Marx, 1980: 37). This is moved by an "automaton," perceived as a driving force that sets itself in motion. The "automatic" dimension of the machine is its "most finished" form and it is an expression as a system.[21] However, Marx warns that, from the point of view of his analysis, although they manifest themselves as capital and obey its logic, machines are not limited to that: "This in no way means that this use-value – machinery, as such, – is capital, or that its existence as machinery is identical with its existence as capital" (Marx, 1980: 42)

The proliferation of machines and machine systems, according to Marx (2013), occurred as a response to concrete market demands. From a technical point of view, the challenge was to catalyse increasing driving forces while maintaining control. In terms of production organization, a fragmentation occurred in the machines' construction process into separate segments, as well as a division of labour to manufacture these artefacts. If, on the one hand, a new knowledge and expertise in machine construction took place, on the other hand, the revolution of each segment impacted others.[22]

Marx also observes the contradictory nature of technical progress: "The instruments of labour are largely modified all the time by the progress of industry. Hence, they are not replaced in their original, but in their modified form" (Marx, 2014: 5397). Such movement is pervaded by a conservative tension. On the one hand, the investment in machinery discourages the capitalist from quickly replacing it, since it is necessary to amortize the investments. On the other hand, the competition forces the capitalist to exchange the means of labour before their exhaustion to account for the productivity advances of other capital. This large-scale renewal occurs, above all, in times of crisis. The author highlights another very relevant, though not surprising, point – the type and success of machinery improvements depend on their nature and on the machine's structure. This repair and renewal movement also involves

---

when fixed capital appears as a machine within the production process, opposite labour" (Marx, 1980: 41).

21   "The automaton consists of a number of mechanical and intellectual organs, so that the workers themselves can be no more than the conscious limbs of the automaton." (Marx, 1980: 38).

22   Mechanized weaving created the demand for the production of pieces, which led to new industrial segments. This phenomenon also boosted scientific and applied knowledge, such as discoveries in the area of chemistry (such as bleaching or dyeing).

human labour, which is necessary to guarantee that machines operate (Marx, 2014: 5455).

By analysing Poppe's work, Marx (1984)[23] discusses a concrete example of a very illustrative technical advance: the use of mills. Based on the author, he states that this invention has been adopted at least since the twelfth century, but that its development and use progressed in the eighteenth century. In such qualitative progress, Marx highlights the invention's internal dynamics, such as the use of better components (such as the rotating mechanism), its architecture (the distribution of internal parts), and new theories for its installation. An example of an improvement in the first case was the incorporation of handwheels to rotate the mills, which allowed a constant speed, in contrast with levers, which irregularly transferred the driving force. An example of the second factor was the use of mutually interacting wheels that maintained the rotation movement and could duplicate it if two of these pieces were used together. One example of the third factor was mastering the water movement laws and the laws of friction. Then, another factor was the introduction of steam-based structures as a driving force.

The contradictory relationship developed between productive forces and social relations of production is perceived by Marx, as already indicated, as the driving force of a given historical course, including capitalist development. As already seen, the author offers more insightful perspectives for each of the poles on this relationship in different passages. But it is clear, from his point of view, that, under capitalism, the productive forces develop, as demanded and strengthened by the social relations of production also under transformation. However, such development occurs in a turbulent manner, through the tension between moments of expanded accumulation and crises. Expansions also cause saturations, stagnation, and periods of crisis. The life of modern industry "becomes a series of periods of moderate activity, prosperity, over-production, crisis and stagnation" (Marx, 2013: 640). Marx calls this "periodic oscillations of the industrial cycle," formed by periods of highs and lows. These appear in the concrete plan of competition between capital in the specific economic branches. In their actual movement "capitals confront each other in such concrete shape, for which the form of capital in the immediate process of production, just as its form in the process of circulation, appear only as special instances." (Marx, 2017: 993–995).

---

23   The work referred to here is Book B 56 of the 1961–1963 manuscripts, recovered in a work organized by Dussel (1984). Here, we refer to Marx (1851), and not to Dussel (1984). We only refer to Dussel when the excerpt in question consists of the opening writings of the work.

In discussing capital turnover, Marx indicates a joint development cycle between the mode of production and the industrial capital, based on a special investment over a 10-year period (Marx, 2014: 5742). In these cycles, the previously mentioned maintenance–revolution tension of the means of production is also present. However, as the author points out, the time matters less than understanding the dynamics of the cycles: "However we are not concerned here with the exact figure. This much is evident: the cycle of interconnected turnovers embracing a number of years, in which capital is held fast by its fixed constituent part, furnishes a material basis for the periodic crises. During this cycle business undergoes successive periods of depression, medium activity, precipitancy, crisis" (Marx, 2014: 5749).[24] Another characteristic is what the author (2017) calls the "tendency of the rate of profit to fall." As the profit rate is the rate of surplus-value by constant capital, then as it increases, the profit rate decreases. Then the gradual growth of constant capital in relation to variable capital "must necessarily lead to a gradual fall of the general rate of profit, so long as the rate of surplus-value, or the intensity of exploitation of labour by capital, remain the same" (Marx, 2017: 5084). As capitalism develops, the proportion of variable capital decreases in relation to constant capital. Due to the development of productive forces, its adoption tends to grow, reducing the proportion of variable capital and increasing the organic composition of capital in general. This progress makes it possible to produce the same quantity of products with less labour, which allows for a fall in product prices:

> [With] a progressive relative decrease of the variable capital as compared to the constant capital, and, consequently, a continuously rising organic composition of the total capital. The immediate result of this is that the rate of surplus-value, at the same, or even a rising, degree of labour exploitation, is represented by a continually falling general rate of profit.
> MARX, 2017: 5100

The author warns that the two production factors may grow in absolute terms, but there is a negative variation of their relationship in favour of constant capital. And this is an effect of the increase in labour productivity. The trend, he adds, does not exclude situations in which the mass of labour – and, therefore, of surplus-value – appropriated by the capital grows. Likewise, it does not avoid scenarios in which there is an increase in the mass of workers, and

---

24   One of the alternatives to such disturbances and crises is the immobilization or destruction of the capital's value. This can occur with currency devaluation, destabilization of the credit system or in a general reduction of prices.

of available labour.[25] Marx identifies an apparent contradiction here. Just as the development of productive forces elevates the organic composition of the capital, capitalism tends to increase the available working population. That is, on the one hand, there is an increase in the mass of labour (and, consequently, more labour appropriated). On the other hand, the capital's value also grows steadily, but at a higher proportion and faster than its variable counterpart. Hence, the same laws "produce for the social capital a growing absolute mass of profit, and a falling rate of profit" (Marx, 2017: 5222).

In capitalism's evolution, there is a second and fundamental contradiction. Marx (1980) indicates that, at the same time that "it awakens all the forces of science and nature as well as those of social cooperation and circulation with the aim of creating wealth in a (relatively) independent fashion of the labour time contained within them" (1980: 51), capitalism establishes labour time as a central indicator of wealth production and promotes the exploitation of surplus value. However, if labour ceases to be the main source of wealth, and time ceases to be the valuation marker, the exploitation of this effort ceases to be the condition for developing the general forces. The consequence is a collapse of production based on exchange values. In its place, the "free development of individualities" would occur (Marx, 1980: 51) by reducing labour to a minimum. Forces of production and social relations "appear to capital as mere means, and are merely means for it to produce on its limited foundation. In fact, however, they are the material conditions to blow this foundation sky-high" (Marx, 1980: 52). For the author, it is in the contradictions between productive forces and social relations of production that lies the potential to end this mode of production. These contradictions, as Marx points out, would lead the way to its end: "But, the historical development of the antagonisms, immanent in a given form of production, is the only way in which that form of production can be dissolved and a new form established" (Marx, 2013: 682).

> At a certain stage of their development, the material productive forces of society enter into contradiction with the existing relations of production,

---

25   The author also includes what he calls "counteracting influences." The first of these would be the increased exploitation of labour, which occurs by lengthening or intensifying the working day. Such change may balance, or overcome, the variation in the organic composition of capital in favour of its constant form. Inhibition may also occur when a capitalist amplifies the surplus-value due to the exploitation of inventions before they are generalized. Depression of wages is a limiting element of the downward trend in the profit rate, since it makes it possible to increase the surplus-value of variable capital. The balance of the organic composition can be given by the constant cheapening of the capital elements or by their devaluation.

or – what is but a legal expression for the same thing – with the property relations within which they have been at work hereto. From forms of development of the productive forces these relations turn into their fetters. Then begins an epoch of social revolution. With the change of the economic foundations the entire immense superstructure is more or less rapidly transformed.
    MARX, 2008:47–48

By analysing capitalism's working dynamics and its key evolution periods, Marx was able to establish a strong analytical basis for understanding this mode of production. Despite its transformations, these assumptions and categories serve as foundations for capitalism's analysis until today. The effort to look at this mode of production in its concrete configuration and the changes it had along its historical course is a task to which we adhere, conducting this brief exercise of thinking about a relevant object in the contemporary world. But, to do so, such analytical bases remain fruitful and necessary. Marx elevates technology to a central position in capitalist development. And he does so from the discussion of the machine as an analytical unit up to the forms it acquires in the reproduction process (from means of work and constant capital to fixed capital, as well as means of circulation). Thus, he provides a valuable instrument for understanding the phenomenon. Despite the fact that his historical context is already distant, he has managed to comprehend the specificities of machines and the labour objectification process they promote (especially in the separation between labour conception and execution) and the different arrangements that the apparatuses assume, including those that are more complex and systemic, based on automated control procedures.

In discussing the role of machinery in activating living labour, Marx offers a set of fundamental insights about capitalist technology, from the reduction in jobs to the simplification and specialization of activities by workers. The way he sees the potential and limits of value generation by fixed capital (especially in Volume II of *Capital*) is especially valuable in facing the debate on the extent of capitalism's transformation in current times – from the theories regarding the "end of labour" to those that advocate an optimistic role of technology as a factor for autonomous economic advancement, according to optimistic deterministic perspectives. From technology's performance at the centre of the system's production and reproduction, the author extends its role into the various aspects of the system's operation. And he makes a special contribution by considering the productive forces as a pole in the historical development, in their contradiction with the social relations of production.

On this point, there has been a debate to qualify whether or not one is prominent over the other in Marx's thought. As demonstrated, several parts of his work offer a position on this. A general analysis, however, allows us to deem it more appropriate to consider that Marxian thought viewed this relation dialectically, acknowledging that technical advancementwas anchored on the social relations of production, both in terms of its origin and regarding its effects.

These social relations of production are the reason for the contradictory nature of the increase in the global mass of value and the exploitation of surplus-value, on the one hand, and the tendency for the rate of profit to fall, on the other. Despite this theory's fatalism, its contextualization – according to these paradoxical elements, the counteracting influences, and the expansion and crisis movements – points to a more sophisticated perspective on capitalism's historical course. Such perspective, in our opinion, should balance the admitted explosive potential of the productive forces/social relations of production contradiction without, however, entering into a teleological projection of its ending and the overcoming of the current mode of production.

Next, we discuss in detail the dialectic relationship established among technology and other spheres of activity at the rise and evolution of capitalism. Although the argument is not intended to be extensive, it aims at listing examples that contributed to the historical perception of the notion of technology formulated in the previous chapter. The references seek to illustrate the technical systems' participation, going all the way to the end of the cycle of capitalism's golden years, which we will approach in the following chapter by focusing on information and communication technologies (ICTs).

1   Technology and the Economic Sphere

Despite the different approaches, the interrelationship between technology and economics appears to be a major concern in all of them. The capitalist system's development is directly related to emerging innovations in the transition period (especially from the seventeenth century onwards). This influence is the background for the debate on technology's autonomy. However, it is appropriate to further this discussion by incorporating its historic features, in line with the movement indicated above. While some currents look at the major transformations of capitalism as successive technological revolutions (as evolutionary economics), it seems more appropriate to understand its historical contribution dialectically and recognize the driving force of the material basis's form of organization anchored in labour exploitation and 'capital accumulation.'[26]

Although they were fundamental, the technological solutions were not the cause for the emergence of this mode of production or its development (as determinists like Heilbronner indicate). New forms of organization were established, with the transition from formal to actual subsuming of labour under capital. These new forms of organization have established a historical dialectic relationship with the productive forces by creating the need for their development, and by being impacted by the effects of their evolution. The problems were the basis for technical progress, but, at this moment in history, they represented mainly a form of emergence for a new mode of production based on a certain way of producing wealth from human labour. While the productive arrangement paved the way for profit at the expense of the surplus-value taken by business owners, machines contributed in several ways.

Freeman and Louçã (2004) and Mandel (1986) offer a periodization where they point out the contribution of specific segments and technological systems in different cycles of capitalism until the last quarter of the twentieth century. In the first cycles, based on Kondratiev's scheme, for example, the system's rise at the end of the eighteenth century involved cotton spinning, iron products, and hydraulic wheels. It lasted as far as the golden years after World War II, with cars, gasoline engines, oil refineries, and aviation systems. In Mandel, capitalism's emergence at the end of the eighteenth century had steam machines used in manufacturing; while the post-war period is distinguished by "the widespread control of machines by means of electronic devices (as well as by the gradual introduction of atomic energy)" (Mandel, 1979: 118). We do not intend to analyse their periodizations here. Still, we agree with the authors in acknowledging the capitalist system's cyclical dynamics (including its crises), and we mention here an example of how several innovations affected the expansive phases throughout history.

As previously mentioned, gathered at a certain location under the control of the business owner (and not of the workers themselves as in previous times), the equipment was transformed into a means of production and "assumed" a leading role in manufacturing processes (Marx, 2013). The control of production (due to its essential condition of generating value) was reversed, as if dictated by the machine. With the system's evolution,

---

26 The steam engine invented in the seventeenth century, during the manufacturing phase, "did not give rise to any industrial revolution" (Marx, 2013: 553).

such application took on different forms (providing order to the "disorderly production" nature of industrial machinery, in Veblen's words), focusing at all times on maximizing the value extraction. Coriat (2011) indicates the Taylorist model (with the standardization and reduction of repetitive procedures) and the Fordist model (with organization by the assembly line focused on mass production) as the main models.[27] Automation was a key element in the Fordist revolution and allowed a new production organization with the aim of operating in an increasingly internationalized competition (Noble, 2011). Throughout the twentieth century, the machinery expands within the companies' concentration and centralization movements, which has caused some authors, such as Braverman (1981), to refer to this phase as "monopolistic capitalism." In monopolistic or oligopolistic firms, machinery gains even more prominence, since it increasingly becomes a competitive edge, especially with the intensification of the applied research war, manifested by the elaboration and registration of patents. Thus, companies can launch products with little competition and make extraordinary profits from it. Perez (2005) mentions the petrochemical industry, household appliances, and refrigerated foods as examples of new successful technological segments from the twentieth century onwards.

A second effect of the use of machinery in capitalism is simplified tasks, which increased the owner's power over the employees by facilitating the employment and management of the labour force, expanding its potential target. Such simplification is not a unique trend. Another consequence was the diversification and specialization of functions over the following centuries. This is the case of economic segments that emerged as the system and its productive chains became more complex and increasingly internationalized, due to the multinational dimension acquired by companies from the development of an imperialist phase based on colonial exploitation. Braverman (1981) highlights that, in the twentieth century, in the form of monopolistic capitalism, a complexification of productive procedures occurs, expanding functions and enabling companies' managerial and administrative levels to grow, following the scientific administration of processes. Even so, simplification was still the main logic in the introduction of innovations.

---

27 Some authors analyse the differences of capitalism from the post-war period using the term "Late Capitalism," such as Habermas and Mandel. Others have preferred to use the term "monopolistic capitalism," such as Baran and Sweezy and Braverman. The 'regulationists,' such as Coriat, Aglietta and Boyer, have chosen to use the terminology proposed by Fordism.

The third result was a reduction in "costs," due to the replacement of human labour.[28] By taking on functions that were previously assigned to workers, the machinery made it possible to reduce the number of workers employed, which generated intense conflicts when attempts were made to deploy new artefacts (Marx, 2013). In this historical movement, several other factors must be considered, such as the aforementioned creation of new productive segments, the populational expansion, the multiple incentive effects that expansion stages of the system generate, as well as greater employability with lower wages. This is a historical controversy which extends up to today, as we will see in the next chapter. At the same time, it brings changes with labour intensification and the increase of working hours instead of reducing them (as a naive notion of human energy replacement might suggest). The reduced labour force in the specific industry generates productivity as already mentioned, but such effect is contradictory, since, in general, it can imply the reduction of profit rates in the long run.

Machinery's introduction also led, within the context of the capitalist system's emergence, to a separation between labour conception and execution. In the establishment of a production relationship, by hiring and controlling the means of production and the labour force, the wealth production concentrates on this movement's controlling parties and not on those who carry it out. With the need for expanded and rationalized production administration, conception itself became an integral part of professional production, with workers hired for such an end. The scientific–technological sphere was fundamental for such, due to the role that science assumed in the production of knowledge applied to manufacturing and the fact that the apparatuses, as driving forces central to the production process, incorporated not only the conception of labour, but, also, its performance along the assembly lines. Throughout the twentieth century, such separation has led to a complexification of the entire product development area (Braverman, 1981) and machine design. Machines acquire an even more important component from the dissemination of computer devices.

In the commodities circulation sphere, the contribution of technology was just as important. Technological evolution made it possible to tackle one of the central obstacles to capital appreciation: the realization of commodities into money to restart the production cycle. Thus, the faster it is traded, the more intense its appreciation and, consequently, the greater the accumulation

---

28 "The self-expansion of capital by means of machinery is thenceforward directly proportional to the number of the workpeople, whose means of livelihood have been destroyed by that machinery" (Marx, 2013: 612).

rate. Marx (2014: 4500) notes that "the more the metamorphoses of circulation of a certain capital are only ideal, i.e. the more the time of circulation is equal to zero, or approaches zero, the more does capital function, the more does its productivity and the self-expansion of its value increase." Several technologies have been employed to overcome this barrier. From the perspective of transportation, the cycle's duration depended on the entire transportation system. Progress was pushed in order to develop both vehicles and infrastructures (road, rail, water, and air). This effort also covered the logistics aspect as a whole, including, for example, storage and distribution structures for commodities (such as ports). Therefore, investments in infrastructure have always been key policies, from the modernization of states to their expansion of programs of 'social welfare.'

Freeman and Louçã (2004), in their periodization of capitalist cycles, highlight the evolution of these technological frameworks. In the transition from the eighteenth to the nineteenth century, the main transportation devices were boats and vehicles pulled by animals. In the second half of the nineteenth century, railroads and steamships appeared, which allowed international trade to expand. In the first half of the twentieth century, cars were created, and the naval industry became complex, with steel and large-capacity ships. The airplane was also invented, a major innovation in transportation. In the post-war period, automobiles increased in sophistication (with trucks allowing faster transportation of cargo and buses and cars giving greater mobility to workers/consumers to speed up the processes of both commuting to work and buying goods in their spare time).

Another impact of innovations on capitalism relates to communications. Firstly, they were functional to trade by allowing remote operations (Wu, 2012). The telegraph's introduction in the nineteenth century, and telephony in the twentieth century, allowed a much faster interaction within companies (from their production units), facilitating the administration of both production processes and the products' trade logistics outside the headquarters (Mattelart, 2000). Another benefit for the system's reproduction was an increasingly faster interaction at longer distances among companies, allowing greater trade integration, both domestically and internationally. The technologies also contributed to promoting products and encouraging lifestyles, as will be discussed later (Bolaño, 2000). Finally, in terms of circulation, technical objects were a fundamental part of consumer goods, in addition to being a means of production. If production is the founding basis to extract overwork in the system's reproduction, consumption is the other end where the manufactured products are realized and the cycle begins (Marx, 2014). In this sense, the history of capitalism is the history of expanding production capacities and commodity specialization, meeting demands and creating new ones. On the one hand, general-use technologies were central to the system's evolution, such as steam engines and electric power or transportation and communication systems (Perez, 2003). On the other hand, technical objects were a fundamental part of the commodities for value appreciation and market expansion.

This was the case, as we will see below, of the creation of equipment oriented to cultural practices such as photography (Benjamin, 2012) or gramophones, radio devices, and, later, television sets (Wu, 2012; Bolaño, 2000). In the United States, in 1930, 39% of homes had TV sets, a penetration that reached 99% in 1970 (US Census Bureau, 1999). The commodities' proliferation has also been leveraged by all sorts of electronic machines. In the United States, for example, in 1929, 35% of homes had telephones, an index that reached 91% in 1970 (US Census Bureau, 1999). In the second half of the twentieth century, the global production of articles based on information and communication technologies expanded considerably. Between 1965 and 1974, for example, the number of TV receivers rose from 29.9 million to 49.1 million; that of radio receivers rose from 72.8 million to 122.5 million; and that of records jumped from 447 million to 963.3 million (UNESCO, 1983).

2   Technology and the Political–Institutional Sphere

Just like economics, politics is a central sphere that interacts with the scientific–technological sphere. The emergence of capitalism has given rise to a series of innovations in firms and labour coordination, but it has also spread to the modern states that are required for this new system and the functions and strategies adopted by them. Among these, three stand out: public debate and legitimization of the current system; processes and population control; and military forces and conflicts. Each of these dimensions plays a fundamental role in capitalism's emergence as a social formation. Starting from the dialectic perspective of the social spheres pointed out above, the following debate is full of examples in which the machine building progress is intrinsically linked to social processes.

As in several aspects already discussed, the technologies involved in the public debate are creations of capitalism. The use of ink to write on surfaces is an ancient technology among people from different parts of the globe. Between the years 618 and 906, the paper ink press was a technology applied to wooden blocks. This technology was also implemented in Korea.[29] In Europe, this

---

29   https://visual.ly/community/infographic/history/printing-history-timeline

practice developed from 1300 until the so-called 'Gutenberg revolution,' with the advent of the printing press. This technical resource would be used by both absolutist regimes and the emerging bourgeois revolutionary class. The press would be a central element for the expression of opinion. This technology supports both the state's actions (and its institutional communications) and society's collectives (institutionalized or not) that were seeking to communicate. Lima (2010) highlights the importance of differentiating both concepts. While freedom of expression is an individual right related to the person, freedom of the press began, initially, as respect for the act of printing (different opinions) and then became the basis for reporting as an institution and a business, which is what we know of as 'the press' today.

Thus, if the press was already a basic resource of the pre-capitalist phase,[30] under capitalism, it gained unprecedented momentum. In 1665, *The Oxford Gazette* became the first regular newspaper published in the United Kingdom.[31] In 1690, *Publick Occurrences, Both Forreign and Domestick* was issued in Boston. In the early eighteenth century, the *Daily Courant* was the first daily newspaper in the United Kingdom (Sutherland, 1934). Between 1830 and 1850, the major agencies were created (Mattelart, 2000). These resources contributed to an emerging class seeking legitimacy in the collapse of the prevailing power structure, as Habermas portrays in his work, *The Structural Transformation of the Public Sphere*. The press was taken as the technology of the revolutionary classes for disseminating their ideas. Habermas points to a transformation of these processes in spaces (like cafés) of the central economies. However, there is some controversy here regarding the author's proposition that such historical processes would be characterized by parameters of rational debate. The end of the nineteenth century saw inventions such as the telegraph, the telephone and others that would provide the basis for developing the "information empires" (Wu, 2012). These technologies were the foundation for internationalizing information flows, an example of which was the creation of the International Telegraph Union (Mattelart, 2000).

From a Marxist perspective, from the emergence of capitalism in the eighteenth century to its consolidation in the twentieth century, the system developed legitimation mechanisms with a technical basis (Gramsci, 1978). Among these is the mass press that emerged in the nineteenth century and developed in the twentieth century. The development of information and communication technologies at the turn of the twentieth century was central to this purpose (Dantas, 1996). In the context of trade internationalization (which

---

30   The act of printing began at Oxford University in 1478.
31   https://printinghistory.org/timeline/.

already existed centuries before, but which was then organized), communications assumed three roles. The first was promoting trade and product realization, through advertising and other forms of promotion. The second was transporting the products, accelerating their realization, as previously indicated. The third was the system's promotion itself.

The ideological promotion of capitalism, which existed since its beginning, assumed an even more central role from the moment it was questioned by the Soviet offensive in the twentieth century. In this process, the media's development, especially radio and TV, gained a central role in the twentieth century in turning the means of communication from peer-to-peer to peer-to-public (Dahlgreen, 1995). Williams (2004) shows how TV is an example of a technology whose application is determined in the most varied spheres but whose technical development is based on different innovations. Such demand offers an example of technological development's social dimension. The telephone was initially designed for point-mass communication, while the radio was designed for individual interaction. Amid tests, the business models of both these innovations reversed the logic initially conceived (since it was feasible to charge the phone by pulse and the radio by advertising). From this, the radio developed as a central means of ideological diffusion. In the United States, this occurred as part of a model based on commercial exploitation[32] (McChesney, 1995). In Europe's wealthiest countries, electronic communications were built as public services, like energy and water[33] (Valente, 2009a, 2009b). Broadcasting services were a combination of political, ideological, and cultural reproduction, whether in the British BBC, in France's Télévisions, in Italy's RAI, or in similar systems. In dictatorial states, communication was used in a more authoritarian manner for ideological reproduction, such as Salazar's RTP in Portugal, or Franco's TVE in Spain. The importance of electronic communications in the ideological dispute became explicit by their use by the Nazi regime. Hitler became known for his use of radio to mobilize the masses. Such success was acknowledged by the winning allies in the war, who established that the post-war broadcasting system would have to be decentralized, with the creation of ARD (Valente, 2009b).

---

32   In the US, radio legislation was passed in 1927, while broadcasting legislation was passed in 1934. The country defined the model based on the commercial operation of large networks connecting affiliates throughout the country, such as ABC, CBS and NBC.

33   In the UK, broadcasting initially emerged from a funding model similar to other public services and an elitist conception that linked ideological reproduction with cultural dissemination. The British example was followed by other nations on the continent, such as France, Germany, Portugal, Spain and Italy.

In the central and peripheral capitalist nations, broadcasting emerged as a central instrument to disseminate the capitalist ideology (Garnham, 1990; Bolaño, 2000). In the case of dictatorial regimes, as in South America, this role was extended and gained totalitarian aspects. Meanwhile, in the Soviet world, communication systems also served for the political legitimation of the communist system. In the United States' case, the means of communication were a support structure to develop the consumer society. In the evolution of the system, they contributed to legitimize late capitalism (in Habermas's words) or technocratic rationality (in Marcuse's perspective).

Another challenge of the political systems was identifying, registering, classifying and monitoring populations.[34] In other words, controlling them within the territorial boundaries of political–institutional units. In order for individuals to be incorporated into the production and circulation process (both as expropriated producers and as consumers), to be taxed and/or to exercise political rights, they must also be identified, classified and monitored within the territorial boundaries established in administration units of collective life defined within the process of capitalism's emergence: the so-called modern states.[35] The creation of personal information systems (Rule, 2007) allowed authorities to know citizens, their resources and circumstances and to frame them within the contemporary obligations and sociability standards. In other words, it promoted the control of the populations and demanded the necessary vigilance. The issue has been subject to a long analysis tradition in the humanities. In Weberian terms, this would take place from the intensification of rationalization (and the use of technology, as we saw in the previous chapter), also penetrating the sphere of public administration into modern forms of bureaucracy. In Marx's view, the disciplining of social activities was 'qualified' in labour relations within the plants, and such action by the state would be directly linked to the need to ensure the reproduction of the system and its bases.[36] In Gramsci's perspective, it would be related to the exercise of hegemony. In Marcuse's own perspective (already examining capitalism in the twentieth century), control would be part of technological rationality itself,

---

34 Which, it should be noted, existed in much older civilizations, from the Roman Empire to ancient Egypt.

35 As in other cases already mentioned, such as that of technology itself, these social manifestations are not a capitalist invention, however their form, function and operational logic are reconfigured from their subsumption to this system.

36 Such an analysis goes from more mechanical interpretations of the state as a class instrument to others that reserve relative autonomy for the State, as in Poulantzas (1981), which conceives the capitalist state as a material condensation of class relations and class fractions.

aiming at undermining resistance and potentializing domination relations. Foucault (1976) elevates this process of disciplining society to a defining status in his idea of a disciplinary society characterized by the exercise of biopower.[37] He coined the term "technopolitics" within his approach, proposing an intimate articulation between both spheres. Lyon (1994) defines surveillance as a central feature of modern societies. He affirms this process of deeper control as the result of the combined need for state administration, military strategy and the close monitoring of economic activities.[38]

Technology has contributed to a greater data collection from an increasingly mobile population (such as with the advent of passports) and has acquired more functions (such as documenting occupations) and specialized activities. Modern states emerged after the Gutenberg revolution and have benefited from the 'development of the press, both to organize its information and to disseminate its rules and decisions through publications, which has allowed a greater reach and uniformity compared to other techniques, such as messenger announcements. A first development axis was identification, a process even more necessary considering the labour force's mobility triggered by the expansion in the market economy. Another axis was uniformly monitoring these contingents' evolution and different configurations,[39] apprehending their specificities and categories – which would be referred to in the following century as 'profiling.' In this case, technical apparatuses have also been involved in the development of government programs and statistical institutions, such as censuses. In the nineteenth century, the technical basis for these procedures was still the press, with archive records of these surveys. In the United Kingdom, the hegemonic nation during capitalism's first phase, the first regular census was conducted in 1801 (although the first census took place in 1086, albeit in a more rudimentary manner), with qualitative changes and sectorial surveys, especially to monitor economic activity (such as the Annual

---

37 "The historical moment of the disciplines is the moment in which an art of the human body is born. It seeks not only to increase bodily abilities, nor deepen subjection, but fundamentally to form a new relationship within which the same mechanism makes the body more obedient as it becomes more useful, and vice versa. This breeds a politics of coercion that works on the body, a calculated manipulation of its elements, its gestures and its behaviours. The human body becomes part of a machinery of power that ransacks it, disarticulates it and re-composes it." (Foucault, 1976:134–135).

38 "Systematic surveillance, on a broad scale as we shall understand it here, came with the growth of military organization, industrial towns and cities, government administration, and the capitalistic business enterprise within European nation-states. It was, and is, a means of power" (Lyon, 1994: 24).

39 Which led authors to coin the term "dossier society," such as in Laudon (1986).

Trade Statistics in 1855) over the next decades. Identity cards were only established in 1939. In 1903, the United States passed a law determining the establishment of a uniform system to register births and deaths (Rule, 2007).

Especially since the twentieth century, this control process has expanded as the state itself has become more complex in its size, functions and influence in society. In 1880, relatively early by comparison, Germany established its pension system and social benefits (Weller, 2012). Identification was applied to the most diverse interactions with the authorities, from voting to services access. The establishment of social security services, for example, led to the identification of its beneficiaries (in the USA's example, the service's implementation in 1936 included tens of millions of people during the first year). At the same time, the two wars that defined the first half of the century promoted this phenomenon by social, political and economic controls in exceptional situations (such as the deployment of individuals to fight in them). Mechanical calculators were fundamental tools for data processing. From the second half of the century, the race for development in what came to be known as computers and telecommunications infrastructure would begin. Lyon (1994) argues that computers did not initiate surveillance processes, but raised them to a new level of speed, range and invisibility. Chun (2006), grounded on the social construction of technology and the critical theory of technology approaches, affirms these as "ideological machines" (p. 19). This involved both economic and military demands (as will be indicated in the following section), whose example is Turing's research on the processing of numbers and commands, indicating the basis for what would be modern information technology, from studies in the World War II context. This demand for control stimulated practices, mechanisms and devices to monitor the masses of workers in urban centres and rural areas.

Control and discipline have also demanded technologies to exercise their repressive side. This includes the entire repressive apparatus, whose technological trajectories dates back from the long history of using weapons in conflicts. In this case (technology in defence forces will be addressed below), repression was aided by technology, either through weapons development (from the simplest weapons to the most sophisticated firearms) or by containment structures for convicted populations, such as prisons. Foucault (1976) describes the historical development of prisons within a process of control and exercise of biopower. And he seeks in the architectural technology of prisons and in Bentham's panopticon (elaborated in 1791) the metaphor for disciplining actions in the society he analyses. Goffman (2001) sees prisons as part of a larger set, which he calls "total institutions" with control functions, including also hospices and convents. The control and repression of internal enemies, with spying techniques and "intelligence" (so present in real life and in the vision of the population especially from the First World War to the end of the Cold War) defines the meeting between control and vigilance practices by the state and defence strategies, which will be discussed from now on.

Military forces have been important for scientific research and technological developments, since the use of technical artefacts has always been part of both defence and war strategies. Since the rise of capitalism, wars have continued to be a central strategy for territory control and have also imposed relations of political, commercial or even productive subordination (as in the case of the colonies). In the eighteenth and nineteenth centuries, the focus of development was the improvement of ships, the main means of long-distance travel (and transport of troops), land vehicles and firearms. Driven by the Industrial Revolution, technical progress was also manifested in the military area. In 1775, the first submarine was used in battle by the Americans in their dispute against the British forces. Throughout the 1800s, advancements in firearms were made, such as the creation of the machine gun (adopted by Belgians in the middle of that century, which gave its owners an advantage by allowing continuous firing). Buzan (1987) situates in the middle of the nineteenth century what he calls the "revolution in military technology." This, as the author highlights, did not happen autonomously, but in constant interaction with the movements in the "civilian" field. The development of these technologies was important for the imperialist expansion of European nations, especially the subjugation of areas of the world as colonies, such as Africa and Asia.[40]

Since the twentieth century, wars have gained a new powerful medium with tanks (introduced by the British in the First World War) and aircrafts, the main resources in the First and Second World Wars. In the First World War, the aerial dispute was characterized by zeppelins,[41] while in the Second Word War, it was distinguished by more sophisticated aircrafts.[42] Associated with them were projectiles, such as missiles and bombs, and monitoring and interception systems, such as radars and decryption machines (Copeland, 2004), or communication devices, such as radios and mobile devices. The success of communications and message interception also had consequences for data processing and encryption techniques (such as the German Enigma). The milestone of technological advancement in the first half of the century was

---

40   Colonization had occurred previously in Latin America, with independence processes still in the nineteenth century. Also, in these domination processes, the use of arms from military forces by Portugal and Spain was fundamental.
41   The LZ-70 model measured 220 meters and flew at 5,000 meters.
42   Such as the German BF 109, the Japanese Mitsubishi A6M and the US Bell P-39.

the atomic bomb, which devastated Japanese cities. Despite all these contributions to the allies in the conflict,[43] Perry (2004: 238) warns against crediting technology with the determining element of war: "Notwithstanding the creative and often brilliant efforts of the American and British scientists, the Allied victory, ultimately, rested more on American industrial strength than it did on technology." Here, politics, economics, science and technology are interrelated, in another example of the non-exclusive or hermetic nature of social spheres. This was not only a key innovation for military technology, but it guided the debate on the impacts of adopting certain technologies in the twentieth century.

In a new context, from the Cold War, defence technologies continued to be a parameter that demonstrated strength and power. Firearms continued to be developed, always seeking to expand the destruction and range capacity over the territory, as with intercontinental ballistic missiles. Under Stalin, the Soviet Union produced warfare equipment three times faster than NATO (Perry, 2004). Nuclear technology became the determining element of the Cold War arms race, acting as a "potential power" (that indicates strength by the possibility of use). In 1949, the Soviet Union tested its first atomic bomb and began developing a hydrogen bomb. This dispute was extended to space technology (Buzan, 1987), which gave rise to a new race to launch satellites, probes and aircrafts, whose new milestone was the landing of the US mission on the moon after Russian missions reached space. In the case of satellites, for example, the race to develop reconnaissance and monitoring systems – such as the CORONA and WS 117L programs conducted by the US in the 1950s (Taubman, 2003) – led to the various uses for this technology nowadays, from communications to geographic area analysis (such as for examining the evolution of deforestation). Recognizing the supremacy of Soviet military forces, the United States invested in the development of sensor 'systems' (such as radars), weapons and smart aircraft in the 1970s but eventually, with the end of the USSR, they were applied in Operation Desert Storm, the country's offensive against Iraq in 1991 (Perry, 2004). These resources, however, were not used only in these two countries, but in areas under dispute, such as in the Middle East at the turn of the 1970s to the 1980s, or also, in dictatorial regimes in the West, such as in Portugal and Spain over long periods throughout the twentieth century, and in South America during the second half of this century.

---

43 It is estimated that Turing's efforts to decipher German codes shortened the war by two years (Copeland, 2004).

3   Technology and the Cultural Sphere

The notion of culture was reconfigured with the rise of capitalism, gaining new meanings, from the arts as a whole, from states of intellectual development to even "a whole way of life, material, intellectual and spiritual" (Williams, 1960: XIV) as well as "a mode of interpreting all our common experience, and, in this new interpretation, changing." Williams adds that art – a term which was previously used to designate a human quality, a skill – has become an institution within which certain capacities related to creation and imagination are developed, in activities such as literature, music, painting, and sculpture. The changes in this sphere responded, according to the author, to others in the economic, political, and social fields, and, we would add, also in the technological sphere.

Benjamin (2012) highlights technology's role in this historical materialization by highlighting the promotion of capitalism's "technical reproducibility" as a cultural characteristic. Although the capacity to reproduce already existed before, it was under capitalism that it became the basis of mechanized systems and industrialized logic. The press has given writing a new level of dissemination. Lithography has made it possible to bring images to the market as tradable commodities. As Benjamin (2012: 284) says, "the technology of reproduction detaches the reproduced object from the sphere of tradition. By replicating the work many times over, it substitutes a mass existence for a unique existence." In doing so, it can even provide new frames, highlight certain aspects and constitute new relations of fruition, since it "updates what is reproduced." Thus, despite a series of works presented as originals (especially paintings and sculptures), art and culture under capitalism involve reproduction and reconstitution of the perception about the works in this process. This reproduction, however, is not a simple process of multiplication of copies, but is inserted in the context of the massive commercialization of culture. The work, therefore, ceases to be considered for its value of use and is now considered for its price in the market.

The technical basis of cultural activities during the rise of capitalism was the press (considered here as the technological practice of printing, not as an institution of news production). Paper had already been introduced in Europe in the twelfth century by the Arab peoples (Martin, 1992). In the following centuries, important equipment for writing on paper and text and image displays were developed. The reproduction of images and characters was improved until it reached the model established in history developed by Johan Gansefleisch, known as Gutenberg, in the fifteenth century. His experiments were only possible due to the partnership established with a banker by the surname of Fust, highlighting the need for the economic dimension for technical progress. The innovation spread throughout Europe in the following decades. In the sixteenth century, even before the emergence of capitalism, this technological system continued to evolve, as in the introduction of the high relief image technique in wood and then in metallic structures.

But it was with the emergence of capitalism that the press developed and progress accelerated. At the same time, the dissemination of printed products (books, pamphlets and, later, newspapers) affected the system's implementation in the dispute of the then-revolutionary bourgeoisie against decadent absolutism, especially in the last quarter of the eighteenth century, with its revolutions (such as in France and the United States). Martin (1992: 27) concludes that "the access to books has contributed to the structure of the social order in modern times." But it has also contributed to creating conceptions and representations of the changing world.[44] Diderot's encyclopaedia was launched in 1750, while the British encyclopaedia, a reference in terms of organization of the knowledge produced, was made available in 1768.

This extended to the arts. Part of it had already been included in the repertoire of human sociability for centuries, such as painting, sculpture and writing. However, the advent of capitalism had a profound impact on it. Williams (1977) argues that the modern sense of literature emerged in the eighteenth century and only fully developed in the nineteenth century, although the conditions for its appearance have matured since the Renaissance. Before that, the term (registered in the English language in the fourteenth century) was associated with the ability to read. This new meaning covered other fields of linguistic expression (such as poetry) and is directly related to the technical basis for the press. Literature as a new category was then a "specialization of the area formerly categorized as rhetoric and grammar: a specialization to reading and, in the material context of de development of printing, to the printed word and especially the book" (Williams, 1977: 47). This initial meaning included all books, not just fictional works or imaginative works, still containing remaining traces of the idea of educational ability. The term would then take on a connotation closer to creative written work, whose quality was derived from taste or sensitivity, "characteristically bourgeois categories."

As in other segments where technology became a mass production commodity for consumption, this subsumption by capitalist logic also occurs in culture. In the nineteenth century, the industrialization of printed publications

---

44 Berman (1982) mentions Rosseau's *New Heloise* as an example in his portrait of the migration of a young man, Saint-Preux, from the countryside to the city and the challenges facing the social turmoil.

demanded the expanded and constant consumption of periodical publications. This paved the way for consolidating the feuilleton genre, disseminated in France between the years 1820–30 (Mattelart, 2000). At the end of the century, the comic strip format emerged in the United States, amid the dispute for commercial control of the segment between Pulitzer and Hearst. Mattelart identifies in this period a complex industrial structure, with the maturing of the copyright system[45] and the trading of such rights by intermediaries, known as 'syndicates' in the United States. This system worked for the internationalization of industrialized culture, organizing its distribution across increasingly distant borders. For such, several developments in press technology were necessary. At the turn of the century, lithography was created by Alois Senenfelder. In 1810, ink cylinders were adopted, replacing the ink balls previously used and improving efficiency. Years later, steam-powered machines of this type were developed. In 1837, colour printing emerged. In the middle of the century, the first automatic lithographic cylinder was created (Kipphan, 2001) in France. The machine was used for printing large posters. At the end of the century, Ira Rubel and Caspar Hermann created offset printing in the United States. Such advances combined with lower costs paved the way for this industry's expansion. In the United States, while, in 1800, there were 235 companies producing newspapers, by 1890, this number had risen to 12,652. In the same country, between 1850 and 1900, newspaper circulation increased from 0.8 million to 15.1 million. The number of books tripled between 1800 and 1900, from 2,000 to 6,300 (Brown, 2004).

The nineteenth century laid the foundations for the information and communication technologies that would dominate the following century. These innovations would configure essentially capitalist ways of producing image and sound through records, photography, cinema, radio and television. The disc, film and photography already appeared focused on mass production (Flichy, 1980). And their technical dimension is essential, since what sets them apart is exactly the mechanization of the cultural and artistic production, as well as the representation of reality itself. The machine becomes a condition for production and circulation (in some cases for distribution, as with broadcasting, or for consumption, such as with cinema). At the same time, the technology rises as part of the cultural market in the form of means of production (such as cameras, gramophones, recorders and others) and means of consumption (such as record players, radio equipment and, later on, TV sets).

---

45 Its regulation in the UK had already been promoted in the early eighteenth century.

The commodification of culture was central to creating one of the great technological markets of the twentieth century.

In 1877, Thomas Edison launched the phonograph. Companies dedicated to the commercial exploitation of music (such as the Gramophone Company of the United Kingdom and Deutsche Gramfon of Germany) were founded even before the turn of the century (Mattelart, 2002). In 1839, the first images were captured by scientists working simultaneously: the French Louis Daguerre did so with a copper plate (which did not allow copies), while the British physicist William Talbot used a paper with silver salts that allowed the image to be recorded in negative (Rosenblum, 1997), creating the photograph and meeting the demands of that time. The next step was to look for ways to capture moving images. Thomas Edison developed, in 1876, a piece of equipment that showed moving images, however, he did not see any economic potential in the invention. The last decade of the nineteenth century was defined by different initiatives to present this new technology: W. Dickson and William Heise produced 20-minute films; Max and Emil Skladanowsky displayed films in Germany using their own technology (Bioskop); in 1895, the Lumiére brothers made the first projection of a film (Briggs and Burke, 2004).

In the following century, the US film industry was organized in the first two decades, with its major companies (Paramount, MGM, Fox and Warner), which would lead the US audiovisual empire to expand its business across the globe. The cinema business model caused it to have high production costs and lower distribution costs, creating room for centralized production structures to appear in the market, due to its investment amortization logic. In the case of the United States, as this process was still occurring internally, the films reached the other countries at low cost, configuring a tough competition with national productions. This sector's articulation with television after the first decades of the twentieth century would further empower the Hollywood empire, now not only in movie theaters, but, also, in broadcasters around the planet, in a strong transnationalization process (UNESCO, 1983). Less subject to this, the press and broadcasting industries have also been defined by concentrations at the national level, either in mercantile groups (as in the Americas) or in the hands of the state (such as broadcasting in Western Europe and all sectors in the Soviet bloc). In the Americas, this process took place through the combined control of technological development and opposition voices with a strong state participation (Wu, 2012). This was the case with McCarthyism in the United States during the Cold War or the Latin American dictatorships of the second half of the century.

Going back to the beginning of the twentieth century, if, on the one hand, the gramophone created space for the music industry, and the cinema made room for the audiovisual, these would only gain relevance thanks to two other inventions. At the end of the nineteenth century, Guglielmo Marconi introduced the radio. It was initially used for communication between people or groups, the so-called amateur radio. The history of radio is an illustration of how the economic dimension shapes an innovation. The radio was used for interpersonal communication, while the phone was used for messages directed to collective audiences. It was the consolidation of both different business models (advertising in the radio and the charging by metering pulse for phone calls) that sealed their fate. The radio was, thus, the telegraph's technical successor, but it changed the press' reference due to its ads-oriented content and sustainability (McChesney, 1995). In addition, it allowed the audience to expand, since it overcame the obstacle of literacy. In the European model, this medium emerged as a state monopoly and worked like any other public service, with fees paid by citizens (Valente, 2009b). In the UK, John Reith's pioneering project for the BBC was to promote an elite culture. The radio industry's development and the cheapening of receiver devices has allowed the cultural industry to spread. In the United States, for example, in 1930, this medium was in 39% of homes. By 1940, the penetration had reached 73%, and, in 1950, 91% (US Census Bureau, 1999). In the country, in 1922, 30 licenses for stations were granted. In the following year, they were 556 (Brown, 2004).

The television appeared shortly after that. As with the previous developments, experiments and patents emerged in different parts of the globe. In this case, Campbell Swinton discussed, in 1908, the developments involving cathodic radio beams for transmitting and receiving, while Boris Rosing, from Russia, carried out his experiments to build a TV set in St Petersburg in 1907 (Briggs and Burke, 2004). Broadcasting in the United Kingdom would only begin in 1929 after tests in 1926, when TV sets would be marketed in the country and in other nations. In the United States, experiments were conducted at the same time with similar structures, such as Charles Jenkins in Washington and Philo Farnsworth in San Francisco. This period was defined by the dispute between independent inventors and large companies, such as General Electric and AT&T (Wu, 2012). From a technical point of view, the challenges were to increase the resolution and overcome the limits of the broadcasted image and to cheapen the devices' cost to offer the service to the masses. The author shows how radio conglomerates operated together with the country's regulatory agency (the Federal Communications Commission), so the latter would grant licenses to them, rather than to new entrants, seeking control over the market and to prevent this new artefact from entering the market and having a disruptive effect over the radio industry. The Commission guaranteed the licenses' distribution until the 1940s (Wu, 2012).[46]

Adorno and Horkheimer (1985), founders of the Frankfurt School, presented a famous (and debated) approach coining the term "cultural industry" to designate culture under capitalism, especially in the twentieth century. Under this model, the standardization of cultural goods and the mastery of technique prevail over the spirit and ideas. However, such rise was not a result from the inexorable development of technological advancement, but, rather, from its appropriation, due to its functionality assumed by culture, to the system's accumulation objectives, especially in the appreciation of another sociability practice and the "control of consciences" necessary for the system's ideological legitimization. An orientation of artistic and creative activities by the shackles of profitability imposes on them the rigidity of homogeneity and undifferentiation.[47] In the search for the average taste of a mass society, homogenization seeks maximum efficiency in the realization of the commodities and the control of the uncertainty inherent to the natural randomness of the cultural product. The business model based on advertising was an expression of this social function. In the United States, the broadcasting of commercials emerged in 1922, almost at the same time as the radio service (which started in 1920), with WEAF, in New York (Brown, 2004). In the 1930s, sponsored programs, such as Texaco Star Theater, were created. In Brazil, one of the first news services was also sponsored by an oil company, Reporter Esso.

Another characteristic of the cultural industry, according to Adorno and Horkheimer, is the dissemination of entertainment as a hegemonic genre and the creation of passive and pre-arranged consumption relations for this type of content that fill the workers' free time. For the authors, culture, previously conceived as art and the abstract and creative apprehension of the world, becomes only the construction of symbols alienated from the perspective of their producers and intended to be seen as an inversion of this potentiality, as a means of objectification, rather than a means of expression. Standardization based on technique would not be an isolated movement, but an expression of the capitalist rationality that transformed "enlightenment" into "mystification of the masses." This impact is materialized in the various segments, such as

---

46   This and other examples show, according to Wu (2012), that "the conditions facing entrepreneurs determine how much innovation happens" (n.p.).

47   The emphasis on the cultural industry's functionality in relation to the reproduction of capitalism does not, however, dismiss an understanding about the role of the culture-consuming audience, which will be further developed below when we address the mediation role of this sphere.

cinema, music and broadcasting, driven by these media's expansion in society. Between 1950 and 1975, the devices in the various segments of the cultural industry presented the following growth rate in world data: press (newspapers, number of copies), 77%; radio (number of receivers), 417%; TV (number of devices), 3,235%; books (number of titles per year), 111% (UNESCO, 1983).

Bolaño (2000) presents his own formulation of the cultural industry. According to him, this would be "a new way of manifesting the contradictions of information in the historical situation of monopoly capitalism" (p. 19), as opposed to the bourgeois public sphere of competitive capitalism. Within the logic of information so as to meet the system's reproduction demands, information would assume the forms of advertising and publicity. One would work for the realization of goods in the consumption mass market and to build a consumption logic, and the other would be necessary to legitimize the general interests of the system. These functions cannot be fully operated vertically, which is why they are manifested from an appropriation of the users' cultural patterns, or their "lifeworld," using the Habermasian terminology. In this sense, while meeting the functions of advertising and publicity, this sphere has another function that the author refers to as a "program," understood as "a need that the Culture Industry has to respond to the demands of the audience itself" (Bolaño, 2000: 120). Thus, the cultural industry is a mediating element between the capital, the state and the audience. According to the author, this movement depends on the expropriation of the cultural worker's labour force. It is "special" because it creates two commodities: (1) a program that has use value to the spectators due to the empathy established and by meeting their symbolic demands; and (2) some content with exchange value to the advertisers, since it offers audience measurements obtained by the attention given by the audience in enjoying that cultural product. The author's approach relates with that of Marcuse when he discusses the role of technological rationality in late capitalism also in relation to culture, in the sense of promoting a "happy conscience" aimed at undermining reactions and resistance against domination relations.

Culture has, thus, assumed a materiality of its own. Despite its essential features in the historical manifestation, it was bestowed with specificities in its various segments, already mentioned here, which caused one of these currents to add a plural form to this term, reclassifying it as cultural industries.[48] Zallo (1988), one of the advocates of this perspective, divides the analysis of

---

48   Such as the so-called French School of Political Economy of Communication, formed by names like Huet, Salaun and Flichy, among others.

the cultural industry into the following areas: (1) pre-industrial activities (mass cultural shows), (2) discontinuous publishing (print publishing, phonographic publishing, film publishing and its videographic variant), (3) continuous publishing (print), (4) continuous broadcasting (radio, television without its hertzian, cable and satellite variants), and (5) cultural segments of the new editions and computer and telematic consumer services. Despite these specificities, US production was largely hegemonic throughout the twentieth century (with the exception of the Soviet Bloc), spreading either through music in the record and radio markets or through audiovisuals in cinema and television.

Ianni (1976) points out how these products' dissemination served to maintain a political and cultural hegemony, especially over the peripheral nations of the globe. According to the author, capitalism reproduces "its relations, processes and structures in the dominant and dependent countries. This implies generalizing and replacing ways of thinking and acting determined by the capital's reproduction demands" (p 19). More than an ideological reproduction aimed at securing the general interests of the system, from the point of view of the technological development of the cultural sector, the peripheral nations have always been in a condition of inequality compared to the wealthier nations. In 1960, for example, the number of television sets in use in Africa amounted to 122,000, while, in North America, it reached 60.7 million. The number of radio receivers was 4 million in Africa against 184 million in North America (UNESCO, 1983). This inequality extended to other areas of the cultural industry. However, the increased penetration of these technologies in the following decades did not mean a growth in their participation in the global cultural industry, since it was more an expansion of the market for electronic consumer goods than an appropriation of the means of cultural production and, as importantly, of the reach of their works, both internally and externally[49].

---

49 The cultural imperialist approach was criticized by several scholars, like Bolaño (2000).

CHAPTER 3

Information and Communication Technologies and Neoliberalism

This chapter highlights the context in which the digital platforms are situated. Based on the notion that technology should be seen from its dialectic relationship with the capitalist system – a process which we have called technological regulation –, the following approach seeks to identify such relation within a specific sector, the information and communication technologies (ICT). We took its relationship with the system's contemporary period, starting from the 1970s crisis, and presenting the general features of the theoretical model's first dimension, which we have referred to as 'regulation over technology.' Then, we will proceed in the opposite direction, addressing the impact of ICTs in reconfiguring contemporary capitalism and its spheres, taking the third dimension of the framework, 'regulation by technology.' The second dimension, 'regulation of technology,' will be addressed in the following chapter.[1] From this perspective, ICTs are viewed as information-based solutions and as a specific segment produced from the convergence among the computing, telecommunications, and media industries. The information must be understood according to its specificities, as a non-rival commodity (that is not depleted when consumed) and, also, in its concrete form under capitalism. Bolaño (2000) points out how, under this system, information is manifested in a verticalized manner in closed circuits (such as in factories) and in its own ways in open circuits, as propaganda (meeting the role of ideological reproduction of the system), advertising (to respond to the commodity realization demands) and program (to meet the lifeworld's cultural demands).

The 1970s denoted the exhaustion of the model established after the Second World War in the group of countries hegemonized by capitalism, based on the production of durable goods, the role of the state in the economic sphere and in distributive policies, the international regulation of capital flows and the overexploitation of the labour force and natural resources in the colonies. The

---

1 Although the model has been structured in a certain order so as to capture the procedural nature of technology, from its general determinants to its impacts, for the purposes of organizing the discussion, we have chosen to address the first and third dimensions at this point to allow the debate to evolve from the second dimension, which will be explored in the following two chapters.

need to overcome this crisis led to general demands from the system. These impacts also affected the area of ICTs, contributing to their qualitative change from the 1980s onwards, as monopolies were broken (telecommunications monopolies around the world and broadcasting monopolies in places such as the European countries), digitalization emerged, and information technology flourished, especially the computer industry.

This effort was manifested in the capitalist evolution stage known as neoliberalism. Saad-Filho (2015) warns about different views in the definition and characterization of this phenomenon among currents aligned with neoliberalism and more critical approaches. Assuming a Marxist approach, he four strands of analysis regarding the phenomenon: a group of ideas based on the Austrian and Chicago schools; policies, practices, and institutions inspired by these conceptions; a state-led class offensive against workers; and a "material structure of social, economic and political reproduction" that characterizes neoliberalism as the "mode of existence of contemporary capitalism." The fundamental trait pointed out by the author is the prominence of finance.[2]

Harvey (2007) sees neoliberalism as a process of restoring the dominant classes' power (or as a process that creates these classes, as in the case of countries from the former Soviet bloc) based on an ethic characterized by the affirmation of the free market. Duménil and Lévy (2014) understand this phenomenon as a new social order in which the capitalist class recovers its profits through labour exploitation in relation to the post-war decades, which can be defined as financial hegemony (for the authors, finance corresponds to the upper fractions of the capitalist classes and their financial institutions). Chesnais et al. (2014: 67) define the accumulation regime as "financial dominance." This phase is distinguished by an unprecedented accumulation of financial capital in relation to real accumulation.

Among the different approaches of this process, several definitions are presented, which are generally related to finance's centrality. Husson and Louçã (2013) characterize neoliberalism as a "productive order," using the definition by Dockés and Rosier (1983). It is an expression of capitalism's capacity to adjust its working methods to overcome the limits imposed by its contradictions. Guttmann (2008) defines this stage as finance-led capitalism. Bellofiore (2014: 8) coins the term "money manager capitalism," marked by

---

2 "In transnationally integrated neoliberal economies, finance controls the allocation of resources, including the volume and composition of output and investment, the structure of demand, the level and structure of employment, the financing of the state, the exchange rate and the pattern of international specialization, and it restructures capital, labour, society and the State accordingly" (Saad Filho, 2015: 65).

financialization and seen as the actual subsumption of labour to finance. For Saad-Filho (2019: 242–243), "in essence, neoliberalism is based on the systematic use of state power, under the ideological guise of 'non-intervention,' to impose a hegemonic project of recomposition of the rule of capital at five levels: domestic resource allocation, international economic integration, the reproduction of the state, ideology, and the reproduction of the working class." From the contribution of these authors, who adopt a critical approach, neoliberalism is assumed here to be a new social order that shapes the capitalist system's development cycle, and which is distinguished by financial dominance,[3] productive restructuring based on a flexible accumulation dynamic, and the capitalist class' movement to recover its power and share in the distribution of wealth.

Pressed by these social factors of regulation, ICTs were configured and applied as strategies to try to overcome the crisis and establish a new system expansion cycle – in the words of Mandel (1986). These technological systems were fundamental to new ways of organizing production, with the fragmentation of production plants, new labour exploitation strategies (with new ways of controlling procedures, intellectualized activities and new forms of precarious labour), expanded distribution and trading of commodities and services on a global scale, and by creating the grounds for financial capital's boom through information exchange networks connecting stock exchanges and investors all around the world. Freeman and Louçã (2004) find, in ICTs, the specificity of a new techno-economic paradigm that has emerged since this period.

The information and communication technologies will be discussed below according to their recent development and current structure, considering the social factors of regulation over technology and the factors related to the regulation of technology in dialectic interaction, according to the model presented in the previous chapter. Then, in opposition to the dialectic relationship, we advance the analysis to detail these solutions' impacts on the system's development, defined as regulation by technology. This effort will be based on the axes of the system's organization. The first one is the markets' organization, taken as the core of the productive arrangements under capitalism, even though the industrial sector is not the only one and coexists with others (such as primary industry and alternative forms). This is complemented by a quick debate about the structure of the financial markets, a sphere that has gained prominence in the system's current phase of evolution. The second category relates to the

---

3 Understood as the subsumption of labour to interest-bearing capital, especially in its fictitious form (Bellofiore, 2014; Saad-Filho, 2015).

production process, assuming the social relations of production as a structural contradiction of the system, as discussed in the previous chapter (as in Marx [2013; 2014]). Since human labour is the basis for wealth producing, both for employers and to maintain the markets through consumption, these transformations are relevant to understand the system's trends. The last category relates to the competition dynamics, considered here as the market structures, which set the limits and the specific conditions within which economic actors operate and which affect the structural inequalities among capitals, sectors, and nations.

1 Context: The 1970s Crisis, Neoliberalism and ICTs

The 1970s signaled the exhaustion of the system's accumulation regime in central capitalist economies in the decades after World War II. This was triggered by the so-called "OPEC (Organization of Petroleum Exporting Countries) oil crisis" in 1973 and 1979. But the structural change relates to the accumulation regime's limits for that period and was expressed by a decline in economic indicators at the centre of capitalism.[4] Overcoming the crisis implied defeating the obstacles to accumulation and wealth generation through labour exploitation. For such, several strategies were adopted, among which are: (1) reorganizing production by the flexibilization of labour relations, (2) enhancing financial capital's reproduction and migrating to a central position in the system's organization, (3) liberalizing finances, international trade and foreign direct investments (FDI), and (4) privatizing most of the state structure, opening new market niches (services such as education, health, broadcasting, telecommunications) and flooding the market with several assets obtained by the states from the sale of these companies.

After the fall in the rate of profits in the 1970s, these movements managed to trigger their recovery – in capitalism's central nations in the 1980s, 1990s, and 2000s and in emerging economies in the 2000s (Husson and Louçã, 2013). Such a reestablishment, however, was not sustainable. In the 2000s, financial capital expanded the diversification started during the 1980s. Global financial assets rose from US$12 trillion in 1980 to US$206 trillion in 2007 (Lund et al.,

---

4 Between 1965 and 1985, the unemployment rate went from 2% to over 10%. In the United States, between 1969 and 1980, the rate went from 3.5% to 10%. The inflation rate rose from 3.8% to 13% in Europe between 1965 and 1975, while, in the USA, it went from 2% to 9% in the same period (Harvey, 2007: 14).

2013).[5] The expansion of the financial circuit was characterized by growing fictitious capital – a concept used here in line with Marx's perspective (2017) and the interpretations of several authors – through an autonomization of the sphere of circulation in relation to that of production (Mollo, 2015). In this context, mortgage-secured debts were included in the stock market context and intensified in the banks' indebtedness processes, with the issuance of a series of financial products connected to this collateral.

Financial deregulation led to a change in banks' dynamics, which shifted from money holders to money distributors, expanding circulation. Following the logic of the increasingly complex financing and valuation cycle, a series of financial assets and products was created. At the turn of the 1980s, the decline in the commercial banks' share and the rise of other financial institutions such as mutual funds, money market mutual funds, issuers of asset-backed securities and security brokers and dealers. Two central elements contributed to further developing this model and expanding this circuit.

The hegemony of financial logic and the obstacles to productivity and growth associated with it have triggered income inequality through a new distributive dynamic. Growing profit shares were passed on as dividends to shareholders. However, a basic profit rate needed to be maintained in order to survive in an increasingly fierce, globally articulated competition. This has put pressure on business owners to maintain profits through wage reductions or stagnation (Guttmann, 2008: 14). Ostry, Loungani and Furceri (2016) prepared a survey that corroborates with this thesis regarding the impact of speculation on inequality. The authors have mapped 150 episodes of significant outbreaks of foreign capital inflows in 50 emerging economies since the 1980s. In 20% of the cases, these phenomena resulted in economic crises and increased inequality by up to 3.5%. Another cornerstone of neoliberalism, the ideology of state weakening (which conceals a reorganization of the state in favour of the system's new configuration), is also deconstructed in a study by the International Monetary Fund itself. The survey, based on 17 OECD countries, showed that, after austerity measures were adopted, inequality increased by 0.9% in the short term and 3.4% in the medium term; the wages' share in GDP fell 0.8%; and the unemployment rate increased by 0.5% (Ball et al., 2013: 4).

Chesnais (2014) identifies, over these two decades, a combination of financial capital's centralized development, its accumulation and production dynamics separation, new products creation and profitability methods with

---

5   The relationship between these assets and GDP went from 120% to 355% in the same period. Non-securitized loans increased 260%, securitized loans 650%, corporate bonds 360%, financial bonds 525%, government bonds 522% and equity assets 454%.

diminishing guarantee in terms of real wealth.[6] On the other hand, Saad-Filho (2015) questions the opposition between the finance and production spheres, conferring on the former the role of organizing the entire system's reproduction. Changes in global legislation have reinforced the rise of financial capital. In the USA, one of the (most visible) grounds for such was an increase in these products' trading based on mortgages. One element of the real estate boom was house price inflation. This affected the poor, who were unable to profit from this situation, reinforcing inequality. This relationship between inequality and asset valuation was reproduced in the financial market as a whole, in a circular reinforcement mechanism. This dynamic's evolution led to the 2007 crisis, which became known as the '2007 crash.'

According to Chesnais (2014), the crisis highlights two facts: (1) the unsustainability of the financial illusion that money reproduces itself without the complete accumulation cycle, especially regarding production; and (2) that the oligopolistic competition at the global level forged within the framework of capitalism demands some control over value generation and investments (this reasoning is in accordance with some cries for reindustrialization observed in Europe). The author classifies the crisis as an economic – and not only financial – crisis of over-accumulation and over-production. In industrialized countries, the phenomenon took place in specific industries, such as the automotive industry, and some sectors (real estate and construction). In the economy as a whole, it occurred in Asia, especially in India and China. In China, sector I, which includes capital goods, experienced higher growth than the consumption sector, whose proportion in the gross domestic product was reduced. Steel production was twice as large as the four competitors in the world ranking; in the aluminium industry, 60% of the industry has negative cash flow, and, in the cement sector, the country manufactured in 2011 and 2012 more than the United States did in the entire twentieth century (Berger, 2016: 1).

Duménil and Lévy (2014: 30) describe the crisis as a "crisis of neoliberalism" and not just a financial crisis. The authors disagree that this is a profit rate issue. They argue that, as in 1929, this is a financial-hegemony crisis in which the financial mechanisms inflate, in this case, with the rise in stock market indices, the unsustainable indebtedness level, and the rise in speculation (Duménil and Lévy, 2014: 47). With the liquidity injection by governments, wage freezes, the flow of resources from developing economies (through public and private debt, for example), and the re-emergence of speculative activity,

---

6   In 1975, 80% of transactions among countries were related to real economy, while 20% related to financial speculation. By the early 1990s, the former had been reduced to 3%, while the latter reached 97% (Chesnais, 2016: 50).

the United States and Europe's economies have shown signs of recovery during this decade. However, instability remains. Husson and Louçã (2013: 133) list the current contradictions. The first one relates to distribution: the profit margin has recovered without a corresponding increase in jobs and wages, configuring it as a "jobless recovery." The second concerns globalization: central economies contain the reaction while emerging countries have been increasing their participation in world trade.[7] The third contradiction regards national deficit management. The remedies adopted have been to reduce expenses (as in Greece and Portugal, in Europe, and Brazil and Argentina, in South America), making it challenging to promote growth and solve the demand problem, reinforcing the vicious circle.

The 1970s crisis posed several challenges by bringing about a recessive phase in the cyclical dynamics of capitalism – refer to Freeman and Louçã (2004) and Mandel (1986). Overcoming these obstacles led to the formulation of problems that would guide the technical development options. Powerful interest groups, economic elites, and supporting state regimes would influence the non-linear course of ICT development. In coordination with such orientations and the incidence of such forces, these technological systems responded to such pressures. Through faster or even immediate communications, information and transaction flows in business and finance, ICTs have contributed to defeating one of capitalism's historical obstacles: overcoming space and time constraints. These technologies "have compressed the rising density of market transactions in both space and time. They have produced a particularly intensive burst of what I have elsewhere called 'time-space compression' " (Harvey, 2007: 3). The emergence of digital platforms is a key phenomenon in this sense. The ICTs' dissemination has given rise to a series of theories on how to overcome or radically transform capitalism, both at the political level (as in the speeches of governments and international organizations) and in the literature in the most varied fields (especially in sociology and economics).[8]

Reorganizing production through the flexibility of production chains and labour relations – a capitalist class demand in central nations – could not occur without new telecommunications structures. Increasingly internationalized production chains needed to be coordinated with more efficient contact methods among units as a whole (especially between headquarters

---

[7] Between 1991 and 2011, industrial production in central countries grew by 24%, while that in developing nations increased by 240% (Harvey, 2007: 3).

[8] Among numerous works we can mention Bell's *The Coming of Post-Industrial Society* (1977), Castells' *The Network Society* (2005) and the indiscriminate use of terms like "Information Society" (Webster, 2014).

and affiliates) and between them and suppliers and customers. Information flows were central to speeding up production, ensure the units' functionality in peripheral areas and cut costs. At the same time, they allowed rationalizing transnational assembly lines with maximum profit against minimum resources spent on new flexible models, such as what has become known as 'Toyotism.'[9] Through telephony, fax, and, later, the internet, conglomerates were able to build complex production chains not only for their activities, but, also, for subcontracting, outsourcing and other resources. Operations were decentralized while strategic decisions, financial control and marketing efforts became more centralized. Real-time communications "allowed investors and executives to accelerate profit rates, cross profit rates, and shrink profit measurement parameters" (Hope, 2011: 526).

In the 1980s, the expansion of national infrastructures (through telephone networks, cable TV, and satellite television) was driven by new private operators. This effort was also manifested in international data networks, such as with submarine cables. This expectation put pressure on state-owned telecommunications systems in several regions (such as Europe, Latin America, and the Soviet bloc) towards privatization to allow a greater diversity of communication channels and, at the same time, lower costs through competition among different service providers (Dantas, 1996). The social regulating factors affected not only the content, but, also, these technological systems' disciplinary rules, underlining how these changes could reconfigure their purpose and application (highlighting the system's nature beyond artefacts).

ICTs have assumed an even more fundamental aspect with the widespread use of personal computers. These have become central to several data processing operations within companies and, at the same time, they have become the technological essence of workstations.[10] Solutions under development at the end of the 1970s and beginning of the 1980s were promoted as part of the expansion cycle from the 1990s onwards, reaffirming the relationship suggested by Freeman and Louçã (2004) and Mandel (1986). Using these machines offered a series of advantages, due to their functional properties. These were enabled by the digital support of information, which translated different types of information into bits. The first advantage was the high capacity to store information. The second was the capacity to process data in different ways.

---

9   The impacts on labour organization will be discussed in more detail below.
10 While, in the 1970s, investment in information technology was at the same level as that in production and physical infrastructure, in 2000, the proportion had increased dramatically, to 45%, while participation in physical production networks and structures had fallen (Harvey, 2007: 157).

The third was that these different activities converged in a single terminal, optimizing the worker's time, increasing the intensity and, thus, increasing the labour exploitation. The fourth was the capacity to organize and monitor the results of labour by systematizing the information produced, increasing the rationalization efforts and 'scientific' control over the work. All these functionalities were strongly enhanced with the advent of the internet.

2 Technology and the Economic Sphere: ICTs and Their Impacts on the Economy

This section attempts to discuss the relationship between ICTs and the economic sphere considering the regulating social factors resulting from the context outlined in the previous section. A survey by the Organization for Economic Cooperation and Development (OECD, 2019) establishes a direct relationship between the use of ICTs and economic development. The presence of telecommunications services, especially the internet, directly impacts the industry, especially electronics. Estimates suggest that "an increase in telecoms density of 10% is associated with between 2% and 4% higher export prices in the electronics sector, and an increase in intra-industry trade in the sector by between 7% and 9%, depending on the initial density" (OECD, 2019: 37). A study by the World Bank (Qiang, Rossotto and Kimura, 2009) also points out such relationship in the expansion of broadband internet access.[11] Analysing a ten-year period (2007–2016), Bahrini and Qaffas (2019) found that internet usage increased growth in MENA countries by 4.87% and in SSA countries by 2.17%.

While these technologies may create benefits, their unequal access poses important challenges. As the *Global Information Technology Report* (Baller et al., 2016) shows, the gap between richer and poorer nations in internet use is striking. In the index used by the authors (on a scale of 1 to 7), while Sub-Saharan Africa reached 2.4, advanced economies (such as North America and Europe) exceeded 6. According to ITU (2019), internet usage was 29.1% in the least developed countries and 86.6% in developed countries.

---

11   According to the survey, a 10% increase in this technology's penetration would result in a 1.21% increase in the wealthy countries' gross domestic product, and a 1.38% in that of developing countries (Qiang, Rossotto and Kimura, 2009). However, quantitative and qualitative analyses on the impact of internet access and ICT use on the economy are still far from reaching a consensus and are the subject of major controversy (Katz, 2012).

While wealthier nations were consolidated as the leading markets for ICT production and use, this development has been much slower in developing countries, especially in poorer nations, highlighting the 'digital divide.' Such inequality in access and ownership of technology indicates the system's class and geographical structural disparities, according to Dussel (1988). The differences are not restricted to the general picture and manifest themselves in different ways with different technologies. Internet access is the leading resource in this process, but the same indices are not observed regarding other important technologies. An OECD survey with the 31 member economies shows that broadband is the main resource, followed by websites, e-commerce, and social networks. Other mechanisms, such as resource planning programs, cloud computing and supply chain management programs, still have rates below 30%, highlighting a challenge in terms of ICT use within large-scale production processes (OECD, 2019: 36). This access is also unequal in terms of company size, illustrating the technological development's unequal dynamics indicated by evolutionists, such as Dosi (1984). In small and medium-sized companies, digital technology is implemented more modestly than in larger companies (OECD, 2019: 41).

Such inequality is more disturbing if we consider that economic actors have promoted the introduction of these technologies as the new paradigm of industrial organization. International organizations indicate the companies' transformation into 'Industries 4.0' (or digital enterprises) as a radical adaptation process involving new digital business models, operational models, skills and competencies, measurement indicators of economic activities and results, as well as an understanding of how to use and manage data, recognize the importance of electronic security, combine automation and on-demand teams and coordinate these processes with investments and investors. The Industry 4.0 expression "involves adopting industrial automation systems that assist in managing the value and supply chains, and more widely manage all their related processes" (Buchi et al., 2020: 3). This is pointed out by companies and international organizations as the 'face' of the production forces' meaning systems (using Marx's concept [2013]) under contemporary capitalism. However, such a perspective can and should be questioned from several points of view, as we intend to do here.

The new ICTs paradigm[12] is based on data collection and processing in digital media and expands to the convergence of all these new machines into processes that are increasingly controlled in real-time, with high accuracy and

---

12   This will be further discussed in the next chapter.

the ability to analyse the market's operating patterns and consumer behaviour to define strategies, prices and products and service offerings. One concern of traditional enterprises is the supposed 'threat of digital companies,' reinforced by the visibility gained by these industries in recent years. One example is the lists with the most valuable brands in the world. In Forbes "Most Valuable Brands" ranking (2020), all five top brands belong to this sector. The growth rates reveal the segment's growing relevance compared to the previous year. The main companies are Amazon (54%) and Facebook (40%) (Ronald Berger, 2017a). In addition, medium-sized companies, the so-called 'unicorns,' have also quickly gained in value. Considering the 20 main brands, the average growth was 15.4%, with negative performance only from IBM. Among companies from other areas, the average valuation was 6.1%.[13]

However, we must watch out for the idea suggested by companies, governments, and advocates of this notion of a new market 'democratized by technology,' open to opportunities and in which success depends only on a good idea that meets a demand in a way that has not yet been done or that is better than other initiatives. While recognizing the visibility of firms that did not exist up to recently – or at least that were not as prominent as they are now (such as Facebook, Amazon, and Google) – perceiving the system's and the new markets' evolution requires understanding the characteristics of concrete historical forms and strategies that the capitalist system employs to enhance the accumulation dynamics and labour exploitation. Although the impacts of ICTs on competition should be the subject of a further detailed analysis, it is worthwhile to include here some issues in the scenario presented.

For small technology-based companies called 'startups,' it is also reasonable to consider the failure rate to understand the phenomenon properly. Amid the companies in this category, 25% close during the first year, 36% during the second, 44% during the third, 50% during the fourth, 55% during the fifth, 60% during the sixth, and 71% during the tenth. That is, seven out of every ten companies in the segment do not make it past their tenth anniversary, and half do not make it past their fifth anniversary (Statistic Brain, n.d.). Considering industries, in the fourth year, the failure rate is higher in the information industry (63%), followed by transportation and communication (55%), retail and construction (53%), manufacturing (51%), and mining (49%). The areas where startups show the highest survival rates are finances (58% still in operation in the fourth year) and education (56%) (Statistic Brain, n.d.). These data

---

13   It is worth mentioning here that the brand equity calculation is not uniform or consensus-based and may vary depending on the list's author.

illustrate the complex movement from formulating technological solutions to their maturation and consolidation (Hughes, 1993). This market is dominated by uncertainties and by different and dynamic technological trajectories, as evolutionary economic states.

Moreover, in the arguments presented here, the care to avoid deterministic or superficial analyses does not imply denying the transformations operated by technology. On the contrary, our aim is precisely to go beyond exaggerated or naive perspectives and to explore how (in terms of forms and processes) the dialectic relationship between technology and society takes place during this stage of capitalism, where social forces establish problems and demand the development of new technological systems. The latter is one of the factors in the contradiction between the system's reproduction or change.

Beyond these transforming factors that affect the industrial organization, one of the ways in which ICTs have been influential in encouraging flexible accumulation (Harvey, 1992) and internationalized market liberalization is electronic commerce. The share of e-commerce in total retail sales rose from 7.4% in 2015 to 15.5% in 2021.[14] By 2021, the sales volume should reach US$4.5 trillion, 300% more than the US$1.33 trillion registered in 2014.[15] In 2016, the largest market was China (US$975 billion), followed by the United States (US$650 billion), the United Kingdom (US$192 billion), Japan (US$124 billion), France (US$79 billion) and Germany (US$74 billion).[16]

E-commerce is an important segment in the market liberalization strategy and the flexible accumulation of neoliberal capitalism. By making use of it, brands expand their reach and their logistics networks through the internet, since sales are only completed upon delivery (and herein lies one of the challenges of this modality). This direct transaction between seller and consumer enhances the commodities' realization by streamlining the distribution cycle, avoiding intermediary importers and the need for local points of sale. It also facilitates production plants' fragmentation, since it reduces the need to ensure that the product has to be distributed to all points of sale and allows it to be sent directly to the buyer's house, reducing costs and optimizing resources.

---

14 E-commerce share of total global retail sales from 2015 to 2021. Disponível em: https://www.statista.com/statisTIC/534123/e-commerce-share-of-retail-sales-worldwide/.

15 Retail e-commerce sales worldwide from 2014 to 2021 (in billion US dollars). Disponível em: https://www.statista.com/statisTIC/379046/worldwide-retail-e-commerce-sales/.

16 Countries with the largest B2C e-commerce markets in 2015 and 2016 (in billion US dollars). Disponível em: https://www.statista.com/statisTIC/274493/worldwide-largest-e-commerce-markets-forecast/.

The influence of ICTs in commerce occurs not only through direct sales over the internet. The web is a field of dispute for commodities' realization in several ways. The first and most traditional is advertising, which is increasingly personalized and ubiquitous in users' lives. Another role is the search for prices and product information. This type of search is increasingly common, even when the purchase occurs in the physical environment. Price comparison sites have grown and, also, have become marketing channels themselves (Ronayne, 2018). But, to ensure such reach, relevant investments are required for the system (especially in terms of payment methods and safety), data storage and processing capacity, control of product flows, and delivery organization. This dynamic is an additional factor that stimulates capital concentration and centralization, since it increases the requirements to maintain competitive conditions both nationally and globally.

In finance, information and communication technologies have played an even more central role. The establishment of the financial capital hegemony was directly related to accelerated transactions between markets and stock exchanges on an international scale. The relentless pace of a global financial market 'that never sleeps' (and that annihilates space and time, as one of capital's goals identified by Marx) was only consolidated, as the actors in this space were able to communicate in real-time, regardless of where they were. The telecommunications networks, the dissemination of computers (in companies and among people) and the internet formed the basis for the proliferation of this new business circuit. The use of technical resources in the sector became known as "Fintech," which comprises "initiatives, with an innovative and disruptive business model, which leverage on ICT in the area of financial services" (Nicoletti, 2017: 12).

According to Paraná (2016), one of the milestones of large-scale data processing, which evolved strongly between 1980 and 2000, was the development of algorithms, which started to be used as a technology to operate transactions. These became known as 'algorithmic trading.' One of the practices derived from it was the use of these solutions for trading at very high speed, referred to as 'high-frequency trading.' High-frequency trading (HFT) "generally refers to trading in financial instruments, such as securities and derivatives, transacted through supercomputers executing trades within microseconds or milliseconds (or, in the technical jargon, with extremely low latency)" (Miller and Shorter, 2016: 2). According to Miller and Shorter, surveys show that these transactions can be profitable nearly 100% of the time. This type of trading, which corresponded to 20% of the equity trading market in the United States, reached more than 60% in 2009 and stabilized at about 50% from 2012 onwards (Chaparro, 2017).[17] Revenues from HFT companies in the US peaked at US$7 billion and dropped back to US$1.4 billion in 2014. According to Paraná (2016), the principles for adopting this model involve the labour economy, the reduction of the 'human factor' risk, the increase in the negotiation speed, which, consequently, increases the gains, and an 'omnipresence' in the negotiations due to the monitoring capacity from the large data sets analysed:

> This increase in algorithmic trading brings with it both benefits and risks to our capital markets, including new and emerging risks. This means that continued vigilance in monitoring these advances in technology and trading, and updating of systems and expertise will be necessary in order to help ensure that our capital markets remain fair, deep, and liquid.
> STAFF OF SEC, 2020: 83

Time, always a central element of capitalist development and competition, has taken on an increasingly valuable condition, now with competitive advantages amounting to milliseconds or nanoseconds. And this difference depends directly on the telecommunications infrastructure and the connection speed through its various supports (copper cables, coaxial cables, submarine cables, satellites). Latency has become a key differential element. The data traffic speed has become a fundamental aspect and object of individual attention and investment in the financial markets. The search for overcoming time limits ranges from the network through which the transaction takes place to the terminals in which they operate. Even space is an obstacle to be overcome, which is why many investors install server extensions in the stock exchange's region or in its surroundings.

3 Impacts on Labour Relations

At the end of the 2010s, the discussion on the impact of new technologies on labour organization gained momentum through several innovations, with relevant repercussions for labour organization as a whole. The advance of automation and the rise of data collection and processing (Big Data or datafication), artificial intelligence, network computing, and 3D printing led to uncertainties, mainly due to the economic recovery challenges after the 2007–2008 crisis.

---

17 In international futures market transactions, HFT is responsible for 80% of transactions (Miller and Shorter, Op. Cit.: 2).

The period indicates the consolidation of a turnaround, which had begun in the 1970s, towards a more significant proportion of the service sector in relation to the others (Antunes, 2018). The positions in this area represent 49% of the total, while those in agriculture represent 29%, and those in industry, 22%. In the United States (as seen in the graphic below), an increase in the number of positions in the services sector occurred between 1970 and 2010 (from 45% to 70%), while there was a more representative decline in the industry, going from 30% to less than 10% (*The Economist*, 2014).[18] According to the US Bureau of labour Statistics (2020), in 2019, services providing represented 80.3% of jobs, goods-producing, 12.9% of jobs and agriculture, 1.4% of jobs.

Another change that also shaped this recent period was internationalization through growing global supply chains,[19] company networks from different countries created to trade goods and services. In 1995, the number of jobs was just under 300 million. It reached almost 500 million in 2006 in the pre-crisis period and fell to 450 million in 2013 (Kizu et al., 2016: 7). These two trends cross. When GSCs are considered, services were the fastest growing area in the so-called 'advanced' economies, but also in emerging countries (Kizu et al., 2016:11).

Faced with these changes, the world economy has been unable to recover the employment level before the 2007–8 crash.[20] This picture is fostered by the global economy's difficulties, especially the deceleration of the total productivity factor and the reduction of investments and global trade. The world needs to create 600 million jobs by 2030 simply to return to pre-crisis levels. Despite a recovery in economic indicators close to the period prior to 2007, there is a concern regarding what has been called a jobless recovery, i.e. that

---

18 However, Huws (2014) believes that this change does not diminish the industry's importance. Much of the service activities are based on infrastructure (roads, railways, cables), products (petrochemicals, clothing, cars, household appliances), and devices (computers, smartphones, televisions). The author recalls that 80% of the largest transnational companies are not in the services sector and that studies show that the industry has performed well in expanding its investments.

19 Kizu et al. (2016: 2) define GSC as "demand-supply relationships that arise from the fragmentation of production across borders, where different tasks of a production process are performed in two or more countries."

20 The world unemployment rate had reached 197 million people (ILO, 2016: 3). This amount is 30 million above the rate recorded before 2007. There is a risk of this number growing, as the demographic dynamic causes 40 million people to enter the labour market every year and the economy continues to struggle. The International Labor Organization's (ILO, 2016) estimate was that the rate could be increased by 3.4 million if the growth projections for the economy were maintained.

this does not lead to a recovery of previous employment rates. This situation puts pressure on demand, highlighting the system's contradictions and the intensification of labour exploitation at a time of uncertainty regarding the possibility of a new expansive cycle of the accumulation regime.

The introduction of technological solutions is considered essential by governments and international organizations, since the underlying premise points to a direct relationship between digitalization and productivity increase in several industrial segments (OECD, 2019). This impact did not occur homogeneously in the past, but at different paces. In the 2000s, the sectors with more intensive technology use had an annual increase of 3.5% in productivity, against 0.5% in the other sectors (OECD, 2019). The expectation is that these resources contribute to face the slow pace of productivity expansion – which is referred to as a 'productivity slowdown' in international studies. According to the Organization, the phenomenon can be explained by several factors, such as the large income capture by leading companies (as in the ICT sector), these companies' ability to attract highly qualified workers, and the difficulties of worse-performing companies, which operate under a less productive logic. In addition, the OECD stresses the role of structural limitations, hindering the entry of new companies: "Turning digitalization into productivity growth will, therefore, require a comprehensive approach that considers these elements in turn" (OECD, 2019: 15).

The challenge of creating jobs sees in new technologies a clear, albeit controversial, factor for change. Optimists claim that introducing new technologies, including at the current stage, may eliminate jobs and create other jobs in compensation. Among the new roles would be architects and data analysts, digital marketing professionals, software developers, risk analysts, social media curators, etc (O'Halooran, 2015: 32). There is a belief that technological solutions stimulate a virtuous cycle by increasing productivity and reducing product prices. The problem would be the lack of skilled workers to master these new technological solutions and enjoy the rewards (World Bank, 2017: 2). Some approaches assume the elimination of jobs but point out that it will take place on a more modest scale and without compromising the overall employability framework (Arntz et al., 2016). Baller et al. (2016: 13) warn of the negative impacts of introducing ICTs. Since automation and digitalization allow devices to operate tasks, this has a direct consequence for 'middle-skilled' workers[21].

---

21   Many of these workers have seen their jobs 'evaporate.' This phenomenon is known and discussed in the literature as job polarization.

However, several studies go in the opposite direction and present data related to the replacement of job positions by introducing new technical systems and productive arrangements. Frey and Osborne (2013) evaluated the impact of adopting new technologies and the consequent task automation on jobs, taking, as a reference, 702 occupations in the United States. They (Frey and Osborne, 2013: 37) concluded that 47% of the jobs are at high risk of undergoing a 'computerization' in the next 10 or 20 years, 19% are under medium risk, and 33% are under low risk. Other studies have indicated negative impacts, as in Chang and Huynh (2016). The assessment that recent advances (the Internet of Things, Big Data, AI and automation) can lead to the elimination and reduction of jobs is also addressed in the official documents of international organizations (OECD, 2019). One of the central factors in replacing jobs is automation. These perspectives seem to us to present more consistent prognoses and more rigorous evaluations regarding the risks of introducing ICTs and their impacts on jobs.

The consequences of ICTs did not occur only from a quantitative point of view, but, also, from a qualitative one. The 'flexible' dynamics meant the end of the model that required the full-time presence at a specific location (the company), symbolized by the punch clock. Communication through mobile devices and the internet facilitated teams' coordination without the need for full or partial physical presence. This has stimulated the already-mentioned phenomena of reduced contracts and working hours. An example is the expansion of work from home, referred to as teleworking (homeworking or telecommuting). In the United States, this practice increased by 79% between 2005 and 2012, although it still reaches 2.6% of the country's labour force (Tugend, 2014). With the COVID-19 pandemic, theere was an increase from 18% to 37% (Moss, 2020). A World Economic Forum study with thousands of company directors supports this trend. The most commonly mentioned factor for change (44%) is the adoption of ICTs to reorganize the work environment and build flexible arrangements. Managers see new teams with an ever-smaller core of full-time workers with fixed duties and the use of external people, teams or organizations (not only from outside the company but from outside the territory where it operates) to carry out specific projects (World Economic Forum, 2016: 6). Huws (2014) highlights the intensification of this process, especially among young people from the 2010s, many of whom are already fully inserted in the culture of using connected devices. Outsourcing was one of the central factors for the fragmentation of productive plants. In the United States, the proportion of outsourced jobs in multinational companies (MNE) went from 28% in

1999 to 37% in 2014.[22] The global outsourced services market has grown from US$45.6 billion in 2000 to US$92.5 billion in 2019.[23]

Antunes (2009) highlights the direct relationship between the use of ICTs and the precariousness of labour relations through fragmentation, outsourcing, informality and the rise of new actors, in what he refers to as the "new morphology of labour," marked by the rise of services and a "process of structural labour precariousness.": "In other words, in an era of labour digitalization, of a machine and digital world, we are getting to know the era of intensification in labour informality, with outsourced, precarious, subcontracted, flexible, part-time workers" (Antunes, 2009: 55). Changes resulting from these innovations manifest in the production processes. Braga (2006) characterizes this process as "info-Taylorism." Working time is still the central element that confers value. Still, in the services sector, this model configures an attempt to narrow the worker's understanding of the interaction with the client as something instrumental, an automatic exchange of signs (Braga, 2006: 9). Controlling the time and the worker is maintained as a relevant characteristic of capitalism, according to Marx's analysis (2013), and technology is a facilitating factor.[24]

These changes have consequences for workers' identity and their awareness of their occupations and the labour world. The violent offensive towards precariousness and its ideological basis (directly within the companies or through education or the media) pressures workers to accept these constructions as an 'unavoidable reality.' Technology has often assumed the role of a justifying element for a 'new era,' that is, the transformation of labour organization would not be a conscious initiative of the employer to force the exploitation of labour, but an imperative of the 'digital era,' or the 'information society.' The meaning systems' part of the appropriation process does not concern technology only during its consumption, but, also, during production. The problems and interests involved in the production process and in the social content of the artefacts, derived from the capitalist classes, are internalized, as in the resistance elimination process underlined by Marcuse (1973). The dismantling of bonds, guarantees, and protection networks and the increasingly intense control of the labour process regulate behaviour through various mechanisms

---

22   Statistics available at: https://www.bls.gov/oes/.
23   Statista. Global market size of outsourced services from 2000 to 2019 (in billion US dollars). Published in 15 jan 2020. At: https://www.statista.com/statistics/189788/global-outsourcing-market-size/.
24   Staab and Nachtwey (2016: 469) use the term "digital Taylorism" to define these new forms of control from computer systems.

(from subtle ones, with retaliations or rewards, to violent ones, such as threats of dismissal).

The introduction of new technologies is one of the factors for change in labour relations, in dialectic cause–effect phenomena including other factors, such as (1) changes in the proportion of jobs in segments with clear service hegemony; (2) quantitative changes in jobs; (3) fragmentation in disseminated and decentralized production sites; (4) precariousness of contracts, remuneration, and guarantees; (5) intensified control over the labour process, (6) elimination or reduction of protection mechanisms established directly (by subsidies or social policies) or indirectly (by corporate duties, such as fines for dismissal or social security); (7) internationalization (with the advance of global value chains and the intensified inequality through variations in the international division of labour); and (8) unequal distribution of wages (especially concerning gender, region, and qualification).

Regarding the expansion of the services area, using connected systems and terminals allows a transition from sectors previously based on manual activities to those structured around activities aimed at meeting some demand through the increasing use of information flows that rely on connected systems and devices whose lack of territorial constraints enables less face-to-face experiences (such as customer service, medical diagnoses, sales or share trading). Such changes help to spread an intellectualization of occupations and, consequently, increase the subsumption of intellectual labour by capital and accelerate economic transactions. The quantitative impact is subject to a fierce debate among perspectives aligned with maintaining the status quo, technophile approaches, favouring the replacement and expansion of jobs, and more concerned and critical approaches. It is undeniable that, in the labour market as a whole, or even when looking at industries in general, new occupations and vacancies will be created to meet the new demands of companies and activities. However, this does not take away the fact that the nature of technological advance includes the necessary labour force suppression. Within the essence of economic actors under capitalism, one way to seek increased profits involves reducing costs. The studies mentioned indicate consistent and disturbing worker replacement estimates that can already be observed. The claim of increased employment, even with technical changes in the twentieth century, cannot disregard the fact that the post-war accumulation regime, as a whole, created the economic conditions for this expansion. It is possible that a new expansionary cycle could compensate for these losses, but the difficulty in triggering it further aggravates the problem of job reductions.

In this context, the fragmentation of production plants should continue to be a trend. It contributes to reducing costs with the implementation of units in locations with lower wages and less demanding and more flexible regulations. Setting up telemarketing centres (such as customer support centres) in countries on the periphery of capitalism without any loss to the service operation is a striking example. Such deterritorialization does not occur only within conglomerates, involving fragmentation into various forms of control or partnership – through affiliates, subsidiaries, or partners (both with minority and majority shareholdings) or several types of contracts (exclusive, fixed or variable contracts). An increasing number of companies create their own value chains with complex input and labour flows, as well as production processes and distribution stages, including marketing, maintenance, and other support activities. To implement these changes in an increasingly internationalized competition scenario, flexible accumulation (Harvey, 1992) demands flexible working relationships, including eliminating barriers, obstacles, or obligations, hence the trend observed during recent decades, which has intensified since the 2007–2008 crash and the deceleration of productivity growth, leading to a process of increasing precariousness. This process involves changes in organizational cultures with the use of increasingly partial and informal positions (either by making use of resources such as freelancers or by different forms of fraud in labour requirements) or through pressure on governments to implement reforms in legislation, as in the cases of France in 2016 and Brazil in 2017.

The production restructuring based on models no longer based on workers in a workplace requires more sophisticated and radical forms of process control. These include expanding the use of digital devices in processes, from automated robots to smartphones or sensors. These resources would monitor all worker activity, recording performance, and intensifying productivity requirements in real-time. In the subsumption of intellectual labour, intelligent systems use machine learning to extract unprecedented 'learning' from the workers' activity and appropriate it as databases and industrial activity analyses. They also use it to reconfigure the execution methods according to automated indications from algorithms. Such control is also manifested in resistance. Punch clocks, internal communication software, surveillance of communication applications, and restrictions on the use of alternative mechanisms (such as social media websites) undermine the organized resistance of workers, who, paradoxically, see an increase in communication methods alongside increasing difficulties in their management.

Finally, the so-called digital transformation intensifies the economic globalization and a new international division of labour that deepens inequalities. The complexity and high research and development costs for building one's own systems or acquiring high-performance ones facilitate the competitive advantages of the largest groups, as already seen, and reduce the chances of smaller ones. Despite the recognized increase in developing economies' participation in global wealth, in terms of cutting-edge technological sectors, the system's periphery is increasingly restricted to the production of commodities, primary products, and less complex industrial sectors, as occurs in their history under capitalism (Dussel, 1988). The renewal of the liberal myth of equal chances through startups and unicorn companies is confronted with a highly concentrated scenario among ICT companies (which will be further discussed in general terms below and in the next chapter specifically regarding online platforms), among which the larger companies stand out by using their control over these technical resources to expand their operations to other spheres, absorbing new and smaller companies through different mergers, acquisitions, and stock control.

4 Impacts on Competition Dynamics

The economy's digitalization and the spread of ICTs have had a major effect on market structures and competition dynamics. From the point of view of technology advocates and economic optimists, these effects would be beneficial. The new phase of digital innovations would lower entrance barriers for smaller companies, since it would allow cost reductions (Ezrachi and Stucke, 2016). They would no longer need to have points of sale, decentralized storage, and warehousing spaces or large distribution networks, and could adopt e-commerce and direct consumer sales strategies, with only the delivery logistics left. Popular websites like eBay allow the direct selling of products and services online. Platforms such as Shopify.com offer e-commerce spaces, support, and services. Social networking websites, such as Facebook, have changed in recent years, offering commercial transactions within the platform.

Advertising would also be less costly to operate in a manner that would be more customized (with ads directed to the intended audience instead of an indiscriminate audience), widespread (the ad can reach any intended country without the need to hire an agency), and controlled (monitoring the performance of ads on digital platforms offers more details, reducing waste). Even simple requirements, such as a commodity's location, could be mitigated by using the website as the primary sales space. The emergence of disruptive models and initiatives would be facilitated, as symbolized by startups. A second effect would be the mitigation of product search needs and costs. Instead of face-to-face visits to stores, whether distributed locally or concentrated in sales centres such as malls, users could benefit from websites and price comparison systems.25 An additional benefit would be the market's increased transparency, providing more information for consumers to make their choices. This includes not only the official product data, but, also, the reviews written by the consumers themselves, whether or not these areas are associated with each website or platform, according to various requirements (scores or comments on previous experiences).

However, technology is immersed in social production relations (Marx, 2013; Marcuse, 1973). The capitalist competition dynamics and the need to accelerate accumulation articulate the new technical resources based on the system's reproduction needs. The global-scale concentration tendency of capitalist markets that has been promoted since the 1990s finds in digitalization a strong encouragement and intensification according to specific characteristics. The real impacts of digitalization on competition indicate different paths from the promises outlined above. These consequences are more severe in the ICT sector and its cutting-edge segments (such as digital platforms) but gradually affect the entire economy, which can no longer do without these resources for all its activities (from production to the realization of commodities).

The demand for the use of ICTs in production (such as automation, management and planning programs), distribution (logistics and product shipment management) and sales (advertising and product presentation through e-commerce platforms) underlines the difference between leading firms (frontier firms) and the base of the production pyramid (laggard firms).26 The OECD (2019) has revealed a historic decline in the economy's dynamism in several G20 countries, especially in the ICT sector or those that use these technologies. The use of a suite of ICT resources requires investments that are often inaccessible to small and medium-sized enterprises. This choice has an integrated dimension, since implementing one service requires others to be implemented as well. The use of network computing or payment systems raises the need for more effective digital security measures, for example. On average, in OECD countries, 78% of large firms (over 250 employees) use enterprise resource planning (ERP) programs, while in small companies (up to 50 employees), the rate drops to 27% (Peña-Lopez, 2015). On average, taking 2012 data also for OECD economies, 67% of large companies used data management programs while, for smaller firms, the percentage was 41% (OECD, 2019: 118). These

---

25 Such as Google Shopping, Shopping.com, PriceGrabber and Buscapé for general products. There are also specific systems for certain services, such as the Trivago website for hotels.

26 The term is used by Andrews, Criscuolo and Gal (2016) to refer to the worst performing firms in the economy.

obstacles illustrate the manifestation in the competition of the inequalities assumed by evolutionists, as in Dosi (1984). Moreover, they show how the clash between different interests also occurs among firms, which may lead to different formulations of problems and interests in terms of technological development in the business field in relation to the economic sphere.

Besides service integration, a complexification phenomenon occurs. If, during the first phase of the internet, it was enough for a company to have a website and an e-mail account, the digital environment's competition requirements have now increased. Although not compulsory, adopting these resources is essential for medium or small firms to compete with those on the frontier. More recently, the advent of Big Data and algorithms has demanded new solutions from companies not specialized in technology and information, with algorithmic pricing as one such example, which will be discussed later. The next frontier, already under development, is artificial intelligence, even more complex and costly in terms of research and development.

A second dimension that impacts competition and consumers is the use of algorithms, machine learning, and artificial intelligence for price setting. Large-scale data collection and processing (Big Data) offers companies excellent possibilities to solve this challenge by increasing the scale and scope of the data processed. As discussed at the beginning of this chapter, using these resources allows for an unprecedented understanding and estimate of behaviours and trends. Whereas previously, companies relied on quantitative and qualitative research with consumer samples, now they cannot only use data from their customer base, but, also, from third parties (intermediaries that sell data analysis, social networks that customize ads, etc.). The data scale increases the possibilities of mapping behaviours and trends. A consequence of this is the adoption of the so-called 'dynamic price,' whose variation would respond to supply and demand fluctuations.

The high processing capacity makes it possible to customize consumer monitoring further to establish prices in real-time. This is referred to as pricing discrimination, which implies that the pricing is set based on information about consumers and how much they can pay. This practice is seriously questionable because it harms sectors and people, usually those in a less favourable situation. A report by a consumer protection organization in the US revealed that car insurance companies charged higher prices in neighbourhoods with a higher incidence of black people (Angwin et al., 2017).

Custom pricing goes deeper. It gets to the very core of the individual, who is not a purely rational being with pre-established purchasing decisions and resource availability. Kahneman (2011) deconstructs the pillars of the neoclassical economy by pointing out precisely the absence of such rationality, the uncertainty with which decisions are made, the role of intuition, biases, the importance attributed to certain characteristics and to perspective in decision-making, as well as conflicts between internal systems that work quickly and automatically (System 1) and "allocate attention to the effortful mental activities that demand it, including complex computation" (Kahneman, 2011: 19). A second dimension where decision-making occurs is in creating and reproducing meaning systems in the cultural sphere. If, on the one hand, according to these perspectives, exploring biases, tastes and worldviews is a historical phenomenon that follows capitalism (with the cultural industry as a milestone in the twentieth century), on the other hand, the presence of algorithms and customization takes this process to a new level. Through these resources, companies have given rise to a new type of discrimination based on behaviour. Ezrachi and Stucke (2016: 106) note "we base our choices on the product's relative advantage or disadvantage to other things." Another strategy is to present products in different ways to different segments, known in the antitrust field as 'steering,' or to present different products to different population groups. In the online environment, such a case occurs when a website changes search results based on a person's characteristics (Executive Office of the President of the United States, 2015: 11).[27] Hannak et al. (2014) studied 16 popular e-commerce, hotel booking, and car-rental price comparison websites and showed how they manipulate suggested products in searches (steering) and make use of price discrimination based on individual information (profiling).[28]

Implementing these strategies is detrimental to citizens. It amplifies the asymmetry of information and power between companies and clients. It enhances profits and reduces the 'consumer surplus' by violating privacy and exploiting consumers' biases, characteristics, and conditions, reducing their autonomy to operate in the market. It increases the cost of living for the most vulnerable, who are subject to discrimination due to their socioeconomic conditions or characteristics related to class, ethnicity, gender, sexual orientation, generation, or geography, among others. The idea of an exchange relationship between equals hides a strongly unequal structure, in which the buyer is increasingly subject to a situation of control by companies. The search for the

---

27   A notorious case was the discovery that the Orbitz ticket price comparison website displayed more expensive results for people using the OS operating system used in Apple computers.
28   The study (Hannak et al., 2014: 306) discovered a list of different discrimination strategies, such as showing lower prices for members (Orbitz and Cheaptickets), customization in case of mobile devices (Home Depot and Travelocity) and customization based on the click and purchase history (Priceline).

'ideal' value of the reserve price also has a broader deleterious effect on users in general. By becoming a central competitive advantage in the market, it puts pressure on all actors to adopt similar resources, which demands increasingly intense, complex, and widespread forms of data collection. No wonder a central theme of the contemporary debate on ICTs is the so-called 'Internet of Things.' It includes technologies that are in citizens' daily lives (such as cars, clothes, accessories, household appliances, and others) in the internet ecosystem (by connecting these devices). In a spiral process, economic actors demand increasingly more data, processing, forecasts, and customized offers. Data-intensive segments (social networks, terminals, applications) enhance the collection and processing methods, creating new solutions that increase market demands, and so on.

From the point of view of competition, algorithmic pricing and the various forms of discrimination also pose problems. The former is associated with an expansion of entry barriers and the 'winner-takes-all' dynamic. The greater the capacity to use resources such as algorithms and customization, the greater the competitive edge and possibility of growing in the market, increasing the gap in relation to actors with fewer resources and less capacity to make use of these technological solutions. Ezrachi and Stucke (2016) identify scenarios in which the adoption of intelligent algorithms and systems could result in different forms of anti-competitive practices and raise entrance barriers, even in automated and not necessarily combined processes.

Another impact of ICTs on competition is the logic of the 'network effect,' which is characteristic of businesses in the ICT sector, in particular, digital platforms. This feature involves a feedback dynamic according to which the higher the number of users of a provider (one-sided in typical businesses or multi-sided in the case of platforms, as explained above), the greater its expansion and the better its performance. This phenomenon is intrinsically concentrating, since it promotes a more significant difference between frontier firms and others. The network effect can be 'direct,' when the inclusion of people in a network makes it more valuable to its members. The addition of a person is seen as a 'positive externality.' There can, however, be a negative externality. A particular service can be considered more valuable by its members due to its reduced basis, considering the trust and safety it brings.[29] Regarding indirect effects, the value of a business or platform will be higher

---

29   This could be the case, for example, with Couchsurfing or even a dating application. Regarding auction sites, the higher the number of buyers, the more successful a transaction becomes.

the broader the presence of users on the other side.[30] This is what Hagiu and Wright (2015: 5) call "cross-group network effects." Indirect effects can also be negative.[31]

Two characteristics discussed in the economic literature are the time-related advantage and the user base advantage. In the first case, the oldest actor would tend to attract more users, triggering the network effect cycle first. In the second case, regardless of who started to operate first, the one with the largest base (even if it emerged later than competitors) would tend to maintain and expand its leadership. Ezrachi and Stucke (2016: 133) add other modalities. The so-called 'trial and error' assumes that the larger the user or customer base, the greater the ability to employ machine learning resources. The so-called 'scope of data' implies a more intense effect as the variety of data collected from users increases (Yahoo only offers search information, while Google offers search information, email exchange, calendar, document archiving, and other applications). The 'snowball' format involves one side of the platform supporting the other and creating a chain effect. This is the case with social networks whose increased profile base enhances advertisers' alternatives (as in Facebook, as we will see in Chapter 7).

One feature of these markets, in addition to network effects, is the 'mass scale.' Platforms can add new users at no extra cost with raw materials, facilities, call centres, and new employees. Another feature is the 'lock-in' effect. It is a result of the network effect but goes a step further. The larger the user base of a given platform or service, the greater the user's pressure to be part of it. This limitation is amplified by data control, the accumulated network of friends, contacts, and content, the threats to privacy, and the established trust and reputation. Such obstacles increase when it comes to structured ecosystems beyond a single device, operating system, application, or platform, as seen below.

The transformations triggered by digital technologies pose significant challenges in investigating, monitoring, and fighting concentrated markets and anti-competitive practices. The paradigm focused on prices is not enough to analyse complex markets characterized not only by their network effects, but,

---

30   This is the case with credit card operators (Mastercard or Visa), hotel search websites (Booking.com or Hostelworld), or food delivery applications (iFood). When the basis on one side means offering goods and services, the increase of this offer makes the platform a more attractive space for potential consumers.

31   In media services, where advertisers seek to showcase their products to users attracted by the content, the growth of this basis may be, and is likely to be, poorly received by viewers. One way to regulate this in the case of television was to set defined time slots.

also, by their multilayered nature and the combination of transactions among different sides. When there is no clarity regarding the price to be measured, since these are multilayered platforms, which methods should be used more appropriately? Researchers and multilateral organizations are beginning to recognize the problem, as well as the OECD. But there are still no concrete proposals for recommendations, let alone the adoption of new indicators to address this situation by national competition bodies.

Becerra and Mastrini (2019) question the insufficiency of competition law paradigms and regulatory and antitrust instruments to deal with the new reality of the digital economy and the communications ecosystem. The authors criticize the hegemonic concept of "consumer welfare," established especially since the last quarter of the twentieth century in the United States, and which, in agreement with the neoliberal program, allowed for large info-communication and technology conglomerates to consolidate all over the world, especially in the US. The parameters in competitive analysis, as in mergers, cannot be restricted to prices when such an economy complexifies the commodities and services supply methods, including those provided free of charge for certain audiences (such as platforms supported by advertising). A critical approach is offered by Newman (2019: 1502): "Unfortunately, the antitrust enterprise has thus far chosen to maintain a hands-off approach to digital markets. Digital defendants have received, and continue to receive, a free pass in the form of de jure and de facto immunity and leniency."

In this scenario, one of the first challenges is defining the market, the relevant market, and the market power. With the use of data to operate in several markets, narrowing down the universe and its actors becomes increasingly more complex. Is Amazon an e-commerce company only? Increasingly, data collection and processing are becoming a market, with ramifications and different services offered to the user. As a consequence of the decreasing clarity, it is increasingly difficult to identify relevant markets and significant market power. When market share is not easily calculated, it becomes more complicated to frame a conglomerate under this condition, allowing for increased concentration due to the lack of action of regulatory institutions.

A second challenge involves addressing the nature of these markets and their operating logics by competitive assessment, which implies considering aspects such as network effects, the importance of data control and processing, the 'lock in' of segments, the domain of 'control points' of the ecosystem and the importance of the technological base. Such aspects go far beyond traditional indicators, especially those based on prices and the ability to control them within a market. Assessing competition levels implies considering the constitutive elements of this new paradigm and the new competition modalities, as well as how these can be managed in order to build entrance barriers to the different markets.

Another problem for applying antitrust measures in this sector is its internationalized nature. Authorities face difficulties in such a task. A third challenge is the classification of antitrust measures for automated decisions. The lack of explicit agreements among actors, which is now a requirement to characterize a cartel situation or anti-competitive practice, is no longer a condition. When pricing is defined by an algorithm, how can enforcement be carried out? How much transparency is offered and required? How can distortions and abuses be verified? In other words, the use of algorithms, artificial intelligence, and other resources can produce anti-competitive practices and form cartels in much more efficient ways than humans did before.

This chapter presented an overview of the development of information and communication technologies and their relation to the evolution of the capitalist system as a whole in the last historical period. Taking the analytical framework of the long waves employed by evolutionists and Mandel alike, we choose to the last systemic crisis, in the 1970s, as the beginning of the historical period studied here. In the debate reviewed so far, we showed the problems the entire system faced, as well as how its need to reproduce and overcome the obstacles impacted its operation and logic. By understanding and explaining these phenomena, we can identify the structural regulating factors that help us to examine the present study and the specific objects analysed. To summarize the arguments presented here, the main social factors of regulation whose impact must be taken into account are presented below:

1) The capitalist system still seeks to recover from the 2007–8 crash. In terms of statistical improvements, the productivity deceleration phenomenon and the insufficient restoration of jobs are indicators of this recovery's fragility. On the other hand, the triggers that led to the crash, especially the massification of fictitious capital circulation, have reached alarming levels again, increasing the risks of new crises. In this sense, the system is still searching for a new expansive cycle;

2) Companies are going through a transformation of their productive organization, with an increasingly hegemonic system that sees ICTs as a fundamental factor for change in what is referred to as a 'digital transformation.' This project refletcts the system's difficulties in finding a configuration that supports a new expansion cycle. At the same time, they push for the accelerated development of digital solutions, especially in intelligent data collection and processing;

3) Such 'digitalization' of the economy occurs in an unequal manner, from the point of view of company size and areas of the world, with the central

nations of capitalism advancing at a more intense pace when compared to peripheral areas. As solutions become more complex (going from websites, e-mails and payment systems to process management software or price control algorithms), the difficulty in leveling their use also increases;

4) The system's challenges require cost reductions. Automation has gained maturity and spread to meet this demand more extensively. The phenomenon is still heavily concentrated in capitalism's central nations, and it is modest in comparison to the global labour mass, but it is assumed as a central component of the digitalization project of production lines, risking the maintenance of jobs at a time when unemployment rates are still significant;

5) Amid a macroeconomic scenario of uncertainty, the pressure for labour force exploitation increases. This is expressed both in more intense control, facilitated by ICTs, and by changes in the political–institutional sphere (such as legal changes) as well as in the cultural sphere (changes in meaning systems regarding the workers' identity and their conditions). The 'servicification' and use of ICTs are functional to these movements since the intellectualization and computerization of labour activities, monitoring and managing activities can be accurately apprehended, as well as allow increasingly flexible labour arrangements, such as through the increasing fragmentation of contracted and performed tasks;

6) The use of ICTs and digitalization has also entered the financial market's sphere, the main pillar of the system's development dynamics. The automation of share trading reduces human action (or even removes it) in one of the current bases of capital appreciation, to which various spheres of the economy are linked, such as public finances, pension funds, and workers' savings. The inherent risks of fictitious capital expansion are increased;

7) In the circulation sphere, companies' market performance depends more and more on ICTs, either through the emergence of online advertising in its increasingly segmented form or through direct internet sales in e-commerce mechanisms. Just as automation reduces costs, so does online marketing by optimizing the meeting between demand and supply and the commodities' distribution logistics;

8) Still regarding circulation, an increasingly fierce competition in a regressive cycle with difficulties in terms of demand and more restricted incentives than during expansive cycles (such as credit) also creates the need for more accurate competitive strategies. The economy's digitalization takes concentrating logics to new sectors and entrance barriers that were previously restricted to the information economy, such as the network

effect and the costs of implementing technological solutions. But the current stage implies new competitive techniques, such as algorithmic pricing. In this scenario, companies that are 'native' to the ICT segment and have adapted to these competitive dynamics may gain space, as has already been happening.

Next, the analysis shifts the focus from the context and definition of the social factors related to regulation over technology, moving to the second dimension of our model: the regulation of technology. The discussion on the regulatory factors of the technological sphere will define its paradigm. Focusing on the ICT segment, the paradigm presented relates to that sector. Once the technological production parameters have been defined in the ICT segment, Chapter 5 will further characterize the regulation of digital platforms.

CHAPTER 4

The Technological Paradigm of Information and Communications Technologies

Having indicated the structural social factors that influence the regulation over technology, we will move forward in this chapter to the factors that are specific to the second dimension of the technological regulation model: the regulation of technology. When analysing the internal factors (always based on their dialectic relationship), the first step is to establish the technological paradigm as a reference framework and a standard for establishing and solving problems. As we have focused on ICTs, the technological paradigm discussed will consider such a technological system segment based on the categories already described in the analysis.

Contemporary innovations in ICTs involve a significant change in hegemonic technological systems by the end of the twentieth century. The search to reduce production costs in the 1970s constituted a social factor of regulation to the expansion of telecommunication networks. These networks offered central technical support for decentralizing production sites and expanding financial market operations. These factors caused the rupture of the telecommunications monopolies at the core of capitalism. This evolution was possible thanks to the development of a technological basis stimulated by the capital accumulation demands.

The rise of ICTs from the 1980s onwards was technically based on digitalization, which allowed any type of information or content to be transformed into bits. Negroponte (1995: 19) observes that "a bit has no colour, size, or weight, and it can travel at the speed of light. It is the smallest atomic element of the DNA of (digital) information. It is a state of being: on or off, true or false." This new support allowed a better understanding of information and more plasticity in data manipulation. The storage units, for example, moved from the old 5"1/4 floppy disks (with a capacity of up to 320 Kb) to the current flash drives, with a memory of up several terabytes. Information digitalization allowed the applications, also structured in such a language, to interact more deeply with text, image, and sound. Unlike the physical world, digital support production can occur almost indefinitely (even if subjected to the storage capacity of servers). There is no exclusion principle, and products can be reproduced at very low marginal costs and consumed, at the same time, by a large number of people. The logic of excess, not lack, prevails (Santos and Cypriano, 2014).

However, based on the understanding of technology as the manifestation of the social relations of production, under capitalism, digital technical systems are usually characterized by the logic of private appropriation and the creation of artificial scarcity.

With the digitalization of different types of information, services that were once separated started to be offered together, in what is now known as technological convergence. This phenomenon goes far beyond the simple technological aspect and involves changes in organization dynamics and performance of companies, in the forms of production, dissemination and consumption of the most varied contents, and in the transformations in human interactions. We can list seven levels in which this convergence occurs: (1) actors, with the relentless merging of the sector's capital; (2) production, with contents increasingly designed for the most different display windows or consumption methods; (3) distribution, with the growing possibility of platforms to disseminate sound, image and data at the same time; (4) service offering, by the same economic group, even from different distribution channels; (5) terminals, increasingly interconnected with different platforms; (6) policies and regulations, with legislation reforms and changes in the liberalization of borders across services and in the limits to foreign capital participation in order to make previous processes legally feasible; (7) integration with other spheres of technological production.

Mobile devices spearheaded this process. Smartphones became the most widespread technology in the world (98% range), surpassing television (92%) (World Bank, n.d.). They benefited from the expansion cycle (according to Mandel [1986]) of the 1990s and 2000s, which stimulated investments in the sector and the critical mass of consumers that allowed their expansion. From the most modest phones to complex terminals capable of performing all types of information and communication activities, mobile phones have become an important market niche and the space in which a convergence occurs among content and application providers, infrastructure operators and connection services and the end-user. The data processing–large-scale connection–mobile devices triad formed the basis for the emergence of a new wave of inventions whose transformation into innovations has not been stablized.

In the field of ICTs, the cutting-edge technologies of this new wave are based on massive data collection (also called Big Data or datafication), the processing of this information by intelligent systems (algorithms and artificial intelligence systems) and applications based on customization, automated decisions and behaviour modulation. This whole new paradigm is built on a high-speed data traffic infrastructure (fixed broadband and 4G and 5G) and with remote access servers (cloud computing). Individuals and organizations operate through a

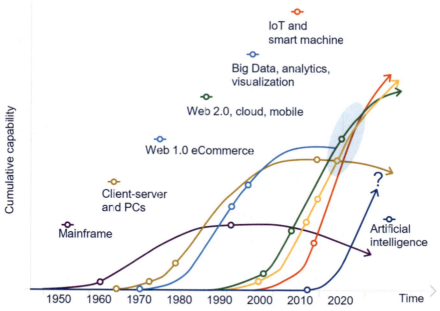

FIGURE 1   Information and communication technologies trajectory
SOURCE: WEF, 2018

series of connected devices, whether smartphones or sensors that communicate (the so-called Internet of Things), with an upward trend of "wearable" devices. This new paradigm, which starts with ICT but extends far beyond it, represents the current spearhead of technological development that began with the advancement of computing in the 1950s (as seen in Figure 1).

All sorts of expectations are generated with this paradigm, pointed out as an essential element for the recovery of the capitalist system after the 2007 crisis, in a new manifestation of technological solutionism and techno-triumphalism, as questioned by authors of the critical theory of technology (such as Feenberg and Winner). The idea of a Fourth Industrial Revolution (Schwab, 2019) is just one example, as is the Digital Transformation Initiative of the World Economic Forum. However, these promises contrast with an unstable industry dynamic. Between 2001 and 2011, there was a decline in dynamism in the ICT sector (OECD, 2019), as seen in Figure 2. The already mentioned network effects that characterize competition in contemporary capitalism and, specifically, in the ICT sector impact how this market is shaped (Andrews, Criscuolo and Gal, 2016).

The network effects hit the ICT sector hard (Andrews, Criscuolo and Gal, 2016), with the emergence of the "winner-takes-all" dynamics. The productivity

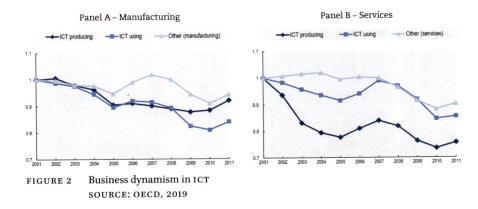

FIGURE 2   Business dynamism in ICT
SOURCE: OECD, 2019

gap between firms at the top (frontier) and others (laggards) increases progressively over the years, revealing a trend in which the leadership would reinforce top performance. The smaller the universe considered (2% or 5%), the greater the difference. The multi-factor productivity rate in elite firms (2%) is almost 10 times higher than in non-frontier firms. Even when considering the top 10%, the difference is still very representative: about six times more. This inequality is greater than in the financial sector, also characterized by the winner-takes-all logic due to the central role of assets in this business.

Another important indicator on the presence of ICTs in the economy is the ratio of patents in this segment, which suggests the capacity to use the stock of available knowledge and its transformation into new knowledge (remembering the importance of this path-dependent dynamics highlighted by authors such as Pérez [2002] and Bunge [2013]). However, there is an increase of patents related to new technologies, called next-generation ICTs, that is also characterized by concentration and inequality. Inventions related to the Internet of Things, Big Data and quantum computing have seen a rapid rise since 2010. That year, the IoT presented a growth rate of 40%, while, in 2012, it was 78%, and in 2012, 120% (OECD, 2019). With regard to patents related to Big Data, the rate was 20% in 2010, 25% in 2011, and 30% in 2012. The research, however, varies from country to country. For example, in the IoT sector, the US has a 30% share of total patents, compared to 24% among the entire European Union and only 7% among central economies such as Japan and China (OECD, 2019). In Big Data inventions, this unequal distribution increases: the US accounts for 50% of the number of patents, compared to 15% for the European Union, 11% for Japan and 6% for China. The exception among the cutting-edge sectors is quantum computing, where the European Union holds 30% of the total number of patents, Japan 26%, and the United States 25%.

The following is a more detailed analysis of the recent development of ICTs and possible trends, seeking to characterize this segment's technological paradigm. The basis is the categorization employed by Freeman and Louçã (2004) based on Pérez (1986) when the former described what they call the new techno-economic paradigm of information and communication technologies.[1] We will look at three categories established by the authors. The first consists of the infrastructure, fundamental for the operation of the paradigm technologies. In it, we will discuss the data traffic networks that support the internet, especially the high-speed or broadband ones, as they are popularly known. The second involves the core input, an artefact whose use is disseminated and that plays the role of a fundamental element (input) for other technologies and for economic activity as a whole. For this category, microprocessors were chosen due to their widespread use in ICT devices. The third one highlights the carrier branch of the paradigm, a sector that is already stable both in the technical and economic spheres and which drives the set of innovations, from which we selected the computers, as the main devices currently marketed. Besides these, two new categories are proposed. The first we will call structural technologies.[2] Just as in the twentieth century, it was possible to say that the electrical system occupied such a position, in the twenty-first century, the internet assumes this place. The second category will be called 'emerging technologies,' including, in the general picture, those inventions with disruptive potential and with the potential to assume prominent positions in the new paradigm. We will examine the data collection and processing in more detail in what has become known as Big Data, or the processing through algorithms and artificial intelligence systems. As already pointed out in the previous chapter, these emerge as bets amid the uncertain economic context and amid pressures to recover productivity and jobs, key social factors to understand the present paradigm.

---

1   As seen before, Freeman and Louçã work on the concept of a techno-economic paradigm for a more general analysis of capitalism cycles. But the categorization used can, in our opinion, be applied to examine the technological paradigm.
2   They are not necessarily configured as a core input, since they are not included in several other products. Nor are they a specific technology for general purposes (a concept sometimes adopted among evolutionists). But they assume a fundamental role for the technological paradigm, although they are not necessarily available to the population as a whole. In addition to serving as a basis, they offer environments, means and drivers for the operation of a representative portion of the paradigm's existing set of resources. Exactly because of this dimension, they are not only reduced to the condition of artefact, assuming more complex features of socio-technical systems.

1   Structural Technologies: The Internet

One of the characteristics of the beginning of the twenty-first century is that the spread of the internet has created a new locus for carrying out a wide range of human activities, from business to social interactions, including the production and dissemination of widely different content. About 59% of the world population was connected in 2020 (We Are Social, 2020). Mobile connections reached 4.18 billion in 2020 (We Are Social, 2020). This is a cutting-edge segment for possible expansion. In 2020, there were about 5.19 billion mobile phones in the world (We Are Social, 2020). The internet goes far beyond computers, mobile phones, modems and cables. Several authors have worked on conceptualizing the web from a systemic perspective (such as the debate on technological systems).

Dutton (2013) defines the internet as a network of networks that involves artefacts, but, also, people who are part of it and are affected by it. Lievrow (2012) defines the internet as a constellation of emerging and interconnected platforms, uses, devices and resources, and social and cultural relations. Sandvig (2013) describes it as an "ecosystem of technical and social innovations." Fuchs (2008) describes the internet as a "socio-technical system" (dialoguing with approaches from the social studies of science and technology). Feenberg (2019: 3) treats it "first as a network containing systems, second as a host to virtual worlds, third as a developmental dynamic affecting users and technology, and, finally, as the basis of a new mode of governance." The internet is constituted as a technological system from a diverse set of relationships. Human beings constantly create and recreate knowledge and the forms in which it is stored and circulated and, at the same time, do so through technologies, infrastructures, services and protocols defined by various interest groups (companies, institutions, organizations), which set their own social content, modes of action, possibilities and limits, with dynamic choices, emphases and exclusions. This is governed by a code (Lessig, 2006), a set of rules governing the network and its devices, which would constitute the internet 'law': "the instructions embedded in the software or hardware that makes cyberspace what it is." The code, thus, would be the social content, the result of political choices materialized in command lines, which not only expresses previous definitions but, also, fixes modes and limits of action, illustrating the dynamics of technological regulation.

Just as the internet is constituted as a system of technologies, services and actions by individuals, groups and institutions, this environment's regulation is also a complex and dynamic process that encompasses several spheres. Both in technical circles and in discussion circles on internet regulation and governance, this debate has been conducted mostly based on how the internet is structured, or what has been called in the literature as its "architecture." Historically, this architecture has been seen and analysed based on what is known as "layers." Benkler (2006) suggests a division into three major layers. The first is called "physical" and includes the elements as explained above. The second is referred to as "logical" by the author and covers the protocols, algorithms, standards and other procedures able of "translating human meaning into something that machines can transmit, store, or compute, and something that machines process into communications meaningful to human beings." (Benkler, 2006: 392). On top of this is what Benkler defines as the "content" layer, related to what, in the TCP/IP scheme, is identified as the application layer. Each of these layers plays an important role and is the object of disputes for internet regulation, which, ultimately, means the clash among actors to define who can say what, in which way and under which conditions in the online environment.

In many debates, the internet is pointed out as a central element for economic development and the promotion of society's well-being by governments, companies, civil society organizations and scholars. The promise endorsed by actors in these different fields is that access to these and other information and communication technologies can generate economic gains, expand the available knowledge, promote the freedom of expression, and strengthen democracy. Castells (2003) argues that the Web provides a superior organizational form for human action. Benkler (2006) believes that the changes generated are "profound" and "structural," creating new opportunities for the development and exchange of culture and knowledge, expanding the citizens' involvement and non-commercial and non-proprietary forms of social production, with successful results. However, other researchers warn of the importance of observing the internet's real dynamics in order to understand how it can or cannot meet the noble desires and objectives conceived for it, in a closer orientation to critical postures towards technology, as in Marcuse (1973) and CTT. McChesney (2013) sees the internet as mostly, though not exclusively, formed by economic agents in search of profit. This capitalist logic is manifested in inequality and exclusion dynamics. Still, 41% of the world's population is excluded from the internet. While in Western Europe, 92% of citizens have access to it, in Middle Africa, the rate is 23% (We Are Social, 2020).

In this new scenario, the information of billions of users has become a fundamental input. Personal data, referred to as economy's "new oil" (*The Economist*, 2017a), ensures the grounds for business to occur, whether with personalized advertising from Google and Facebook or with Amazon's purchase recommendations. This scenario is stimulated by large-scale collection (Big

Data) and intelligent processing through the use of algorithms and artificial intelligence. In this scenario, two new challenges emerge: privacy violation and the increasing control of users' personal and collective experiences. Shoshana Zuboff (2019) points out that the dissemination of Big Data generates such an impact that it would be possible to refer to it as "surveillance capitalism," in which such massive collection would be a condition for and the rising of this new social system and, at the same time, its expression. The author makes a sophisticated analysis of the current scenario in which she warns about the problem not only of collecting data, but, also, using them to predict behaviours and modulate people's behaviour.

Amid this scenario, the market movement points to a new ultra-connected environment that is being called the 'Internet of Things' (IoT). This expression indicates a change in connection, as an individual's asset made through a device to something operated across machines (Machine-to-Machine or M2M), sensors and systems. This model has been assumed by the major actors in the industry and international organizations to be the "future of the internet." The World Economic Forum (World Economic Forum, 2018) places IoT among the main technologies responsible for "accelerating change." In addition, IoT itself represents a shift in the power relationship between subject and object (in the words of Feenberg [2002 and 2005]) in the online world. It goes beyond the instrumental ideology of technology to assume a perspective in which the artefact is positioned as subject, to the detriment of its users.

2 Infrastructure: High-Speed Data Networks (Broadband)

High-speed data traffic networks, also called 'broadband,' are the central infrastructure of the ICT technological paradigm, as well as for the entire information and data flow that supports various other social, economic and political activities (Broadband Comission, 2020). By 'infrastructure,' we refer to the definition by the European Commission which states that (European Commission, 2015: 2): "Infrastructure refers to a physical medium over which information can be transmitted." These networks are central to the contemporary economy's operation, such as in payments using credit cards or in transactions on stock exchanges or payments over the internet or electronic terminals. They support all interactions based on digital information. Understanding their operational logic and organization is central to understanding how availability and access occur and the barriers to billions of people participating in these communications, as discussed in the previous section.

The concept of "broadband" is defined by international organizations such as the International Telecommunication Union (ITU) and the OECD as a capacity of at least 256 kbps in both incoming and outgoing data (Broadband Commission, 2014: 16). This speed is related to several notions, such as access speed, connection continuity and the ability to enjoy several services simultaneously. This is the minimum level, but the advanced technologies used in networks aim at achieving a speed of multiple Gbps.[3]

In terms of architecture, broadband networks may assume different arrangements, but they have a common topology. Continents are connected by fibre optic cables, known as 'submarine cables,' since, as the name suggests, they are lain under the water. Currently, there are almost 400 cables in operation (Telegeography, n.d.).[4] The connection within countries or regions is made by robust networks called backbones. Connected to these are other networks that connect cities or localities, also known as backhaul. The connection to the households or users is operated by what has been internationally referred to as the 'last mile.' This ecosystem is completed by servers that store the information accessed on websites and other applications[5]. These grow in importance as 'direct' internet operations increase, in what has come to be known as 'cloud computing': a form of access and fruition in which applications do not process data that are present on the individual's computer or device but are stored on the application or storage providers' servers.

High-speed networks can adopt different technologies, whether physical (such as ADSL, coaxial cables and fibre optics) or using the radio frequency spectrum (4G, Wimax or satellite broadband). The twisted-pair cabling (used to support the connection known as ADSL) is the oldest and has the lowest capacity. Then come the coaxial cables, which started to be used for so-called 'cable TV' and were gradually applied also in data offering, in data packets that became known as 'triple play.' The constant evolution of these networks stimulated the adoption by the ITU of the concept of new generation networks, defined as technologies based on packets capable of guaranteeing high-speed transmission, with 'quality of service' and in which the services offered

---

3 Silva (2012) evaluates that speed is taken as a central indicator for the definition, because it directly impacts the network experience. The slower it is, the more difficult it becomes to upload websites and content, such as audio and videos. With the rise of synchronous services, such as video and audio streaming and video and audio links, the speed dimension becomes even more central.
4 The Telegeography organization provides an interactive map: https://www.submarinecable-map.com/.
5 Despite its unrivalled nature, the information has a concrete materiality, and these servers are a necessary infrastructure for storage.

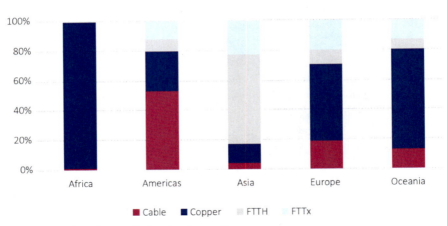

FIGURE 3   Wired technologies share by continent
SOURCE: BROADBAND COMMISSION, 2017

are independent from this technological base (Broadband Commission, 2017: 33). The problem with this infrastructure is its cost, which is still very high and higher than the other options, since it is still in a consolidation phase (Hughes, 1993).

In the 'wireless' category, another set of technologies is based on the use of radio frequencies on the electromagnetic spectrum. In comparison with the previous group, Fox and Hao (2018) point out to their functional property based on the electromagnetic spectrum as a limited means, but one which offers some advantages. The 'wireless' group has some of the main technologies. Wi-Fi has an average speed of 300 Mbps for downstream and upstream, with a 300-meter range. The main current mobile broadband 'generation,' 4G, offers speeds of 100 Mbps for downstream and 30 for upstream, ranging from three to six kilometers (European Commission, 2015). Another modality is satellite broadband, whose range is its strength, and speed its limitation, once it reaches 22 Mbps. The 'next-generation' network in the wireless group is 5G. Internet exchange points (IXP) interconnect these networks.[6] Wired technology around the world (Figure 3) are more widely used in central and weaker areas on the periphery of the system (Broadband Commission, 2017).

There are major obstacles in accessing broadband networks. In the case of fixed networks, penetration is low, at around 14% (Itu, 2019), and it varies globally. The infrastructure with the highest reach is mobile broadband, with

---

6   In 2016, there were 464 IXPs in operation, with 275 in the G20 economies (OECD, 2019).

a rate of 83% (ITU, 2019).[7] In Africa, the rate is 0.4%, while in Europe, it is 31.9%. Accesses using this network exceed the number of inhabitants in five countries: Japan (139%), United States (117%), Australia (115%), Saudi Arabia (114%) and South Korea (112%), but remain at 40% in Indonesia and 20% in India (OECD, 2019).

This infrastructure model poses several challenges. It is the entry point, or the first barrier, for users to be part of the connected world. Access to these networks is directly linked to infrastructure availability, service costs, and competition in markets, and these three elements are interrelated. As these networks are the successors of telephone models that were seen as natural monopolies, there are obstacles to implement various networks, especially as countries are larger. In this sense, unbundling rules are fundamental. Unbundling consists in establishing a regulation subjecting the network owner to non-discriminatory treatment, thus preventing the latter's position as owner of the infrastructure from being used to their own benefit and to hinder the performance of competitors. As the costs of building their own networks are high, new market players depend on access to these networks in order to offer services to end users. This model, which we have called 'services competition' (SC) (Valente, 2012), was used in successful experiences involving internet penetration among the population, such as in Europe and South Korea. Other countries have preferred to privilege operators and bet on competition between different infrastructures such as ADSL, coaxial cable and satellite. This model, used in Brazil, is called 'networks competition' (NC) (Valente, 2012). In the Brazilian case, even with limited subsidies, the maintenance of the NC model has shown to be insufficient, with the expansion of mobile broadband, which is also subject to disputes.

Mobile broadband is influenced by its operation based on the radio frequency spectrum. It presents an important difference from the wired infrastructure: it is a scarce resource and, in general, a public good controlled by states. This brings about two relevant issues: (1) its finite nature places the problem of allocation at the centre of the debate on this infrastructure's management, (2) its public nature implies state management resulting from public policies built (at least in theory) from democratic processes involving the different actors, and not just decisions by economic actors. The growth of mobile broadband, Wi-Fi networks and the Internet of Things (with

---

7   Even among wealthier countries, the rates are still less than 50%. France is the country with the highest penetration (40%), followed by South Korea (39%), the United Kingdom (37%), Germany (37%), Canada (36%) and the United States (32%) (OECD, 2019).

communication between sensors and devices) has indicated an increase in the spectrum usage demand and pushed changes in its allocation. In terms of legal regulation, there is a dispute over spectrum management models. In recent decades, the private sector has pressured governments for a more liberalized model in which an actor that controls a portion of the spectrum could trade it in different ways, the so-called "secondary spectrum market." Having become an increasingly essential resource for a strongly wireless infrastructure, this clash directly impacts the network's organizational capacity and management.

3 Core Input: Microprocessors

The microprocessor (or MP, as we will call it from now on) is considered the computer's 'brain.' It consists of a small 'chip' with the ability to perform calculations and operations on demand, providing results.[8] The microprocessor[9] is an integrated circuit modality. This is a circuit formed by components gathered in a small semiconductor (chip), usually made of silicon, through a chemical process (Collin, 2004: 175). The arithmetic logic unit is the area where logic operations occur (Hexsel, 2006). The control unit decodes and organizes the execution of instructions. The registers are resources for storing different information. These components are structured in a computer around the central processing unit (CPU).

In 2010, a diversification process occurred, with the entry of new companies manufacturing chips for mobile devices and with new demands, which made room, for example, for the introduction of Nvidia, originally a company that produced graphic processing units (GPU) aimed at strengthening the ability of CPUs to run complex games. The MPU and GPU market was valued at US$74 billion in 2017 and should reach US$83.7 billion in 2022 (Markets and Markets, 2017: 2). In 2020, 47% of the market was dominated by MP sales for computers,

---

8 The microprocessor is the equipment ultimately responsible for ensuring the processing from the mode of operation of the program (software) that structures the data collection, the receipt of the requests and the responses offered.

9 MPs were created out of the need to carry out ever-increasing operations at an accelerated pace, driven by various social regulatory factors: control of production processes in the private sector and information on market subjects and actors and policies in the public sector served as demand elements for the growing processing capacity throughout the twentieth century.

servers and mainframes. The second most used applications are smartphones (26%).[10]

Since the 1990s, competition on CPUs has focused on the Intel and AMD dispute. The former has taken the lead throughout this technology's history. However, in 2006, AMD reached a similar share; however, after this period, the difference has increased again, reaching high levels in 2017, when considering the desktop, server, and mainframe hardware market (AMD, 2017). In 2020, Intel had a 65% market share and AMD, 35%.[11] Other competitors are IBM (USA), Texas Instruments (USA), Qualcomm (USA), Nvidia (USA), NXP Semiconductors (Netherlands), and Samsung (South Korea).

In the processors market for mobile devices, new actors have emerged. The major market player in this segment is Qualcomm, whose share reached more than half of the market in 2014 and has settled at around 40% since then. Apple has a similar share as in the smartphone market, since its production is focused on its own devices. Media Tek is the new player that has emerged to disrupt the dominance of US firms. The Taiwanese company has stabilized with about 20% of the market. In 2018, Qualcomm tried to buy another major MP manufacturer: Broadcom. The operation caused controversy, sparking resistance from the United States government. Considering the whole MPUs market, in 2019, Intel had a 19.7% share, followed by TSMC (9.7%), Qualcomm (9.7%) and SK Hynx (9.6%).[12] One of the market's dynamic elements was the growth in sales of graphic processing units (GPUs).[13]

The industry's development faces two types of challenges: from social and internal factors (maintaining the dialectical understanding of the two dimensions). Internally, chip development faces some important obstacles, such as

---

10   Statista (2020) Market share projection of microprocessor unit (MPU) sales worldwide in 2020, by application. At: https://www.statista.com/statistics/553450/worldwide-microprocessor-unit-sales-distribution-by-application/.

11   Statista (2020) Distribution of Intel and AMD x86 computer central processing units (CPUs) worldwide from 2012 to 2020, by quarter. At: https://www.statista.com/statistics/735904/worldwide-x86-intel-amd-market-share/.

12   Statista (2020) Share of the microprocessor market worldwide from 2018 to 2019, by vendor. At: https://www.statista.com/statistics/883715/microprocessor-market-share-worldwide-by-vendor/.

13   The sale of these components skyrocketed in 2016, with a growth of almost 40% over the previous year. This performance contrasts with the results of the sale of CPUs, which has shown a negative percentage evolution since 2012, with the exception of 2014. Nvidia is the main actor in this segment. The company went from an annual revenue with these processors of $US3.5 billion in 2013 to US$8.5 billion in 2017 (Trefis, 2018).

clock frequency limits[14] and high power consumption. At the level of social factors, the diversification of demands for new devices and their qualitative change (with quantum computing[15] and artificial intelligence,[16] for example) poses new problems and puts pressure on the sector to incorporate new demands and interests. At the same time, the spread of portable devices (such as mobile phones, tablets and the like) makes room for new products and large-scale reproduction, but, at the same time, reduces profit margins by cheapening the average price of units.

All these factors, however, still include artefacts in early stages of their respective technological, invention and development trajectories (Hughes, 1993). As in any trajectory, stabilization will depend on the arrangements that will be made from the consolidation of social demands, technical capacities and market configuration. Quantum processors do not yet have a well-defined business model, but they come up as a possible new system for emerging technologies in the near future. Understanding these demands and these directions requires a perspective on computers, which will be discussed in the following.

4   Carrier Branch: Computers

A computer is an electronic device that can process, store and retrieve data according to a set of instructions (O'Regan, 2016: 2). The machine consists of two 'parts.' The hardware comprises physical resources such as the microprocessor (including the arithmetic and logic unit and the control unit), a short-term storage memory (RAM), an information storage memory (commonly known as a 'hard disk' or HD) and peripherals that help to handle the instructions and produce results (such as computer mouses, keyboards or video boards). These are basic definitions of their functional properties. The software is a set of instructions, whose operation is organized from programming prepared

---

14 To overcome this, one of the outputs still in the 2000s was the institution of multi-core processors (Pangrle, 2011). However, even with the use of this resource, there are controversies about the ability to maintain the pace of performance acceleration of these chips.

15 Using quantum bits (qubits) allows the storage of a larger amount of data and reduces power consumption. This requires processors that keep pace with this new reality.

16 MPs no longer keep pace with the demand for increasingly sophisticated applications, and with the strong advancement of artificial intelligence and machine learning. Two types of specialized chips are the 'application specific integrated circuits' (ASIC) and 'field programmable gate array' (FPGA). As a result, technology giants such as Google and Microsoft have been betting on specialized processor manufacturers and invested in the development of their own parts (*The Economist*, 2017b).

through codes and that receive data and demands, perform the operations requested and present results, or products. They are known as 'programs' or 'applications.' The coordinated action of the programs and their interaction with the hardware occurs through what has historically been called an 'operating system.' The approach called critical computing studies highlights the central role of contextual properties, social content, and power relations incorporated when affirming computers as "ideological machines" (Chun, 2006).

Computers were stimulated by the structural factors of the large-scale operation processing system, whether for economic transactions or for different state actions, such as storing bureaucratic information, controlling statistics on citizens or even making war.[17] Simultaneously, the information technology industry has become the driving force behind the current technological paradigm of information and communication technologies and, to some extent, the set of contemporary technologies. This phenomenon was part of the opening of new market expansion fronts from the 1980s onwards as a way of reinventing the system and recovering the accumulation volumes and profit margins of the whole capital.[18]

To get established, the computer industry relied, as did other sectors, on the private appropriation of knowledge, developing patents for hardware, components and software. In this area, however, a radical opposing movement has emerged, called 'free software.' Its proponents support open source programs, which could be known, improved, changed and used by anyone with the capacity to do so, free of charge. But its definition is not restricted to this latter dimension. The meaning of "free" is related to freedom of expression and is an important example, in concrete reality and in the capitalist social model, of the possibility of bringing an alternative and free model to the core of a technological solution, and not only to its use system (as in whether or not it is charged) or its application (as in copyright licenses).

---

17   These systems allowed not only processing, but, also, two new features. The first was speed, meeting the system's need to accelerate productive dynamics and capital flows (the greatest example of which is stock trading by algorithms, as presented in the previous chapter). A second novelty of digitalization is the centralization of activities, whether in the processing spaces (mainframes, servers) or, especially, in the workstations, expanding the capacity to obtain greater productivity in the same or shorter time, as seen in the previous chapter. This change was a fundamental basis for reorganizing the labour relations operated as part of the strategies to overcome the crisis during the post-war years, illustrating the dialectic return movement in regulation by technology.

18   However, this segment illustrates the power relations and disputes for the design conformation. The free software movement offered programs, distributions, and operating systems operating within other logics, such as open source and improvement capabilities.

> By free software we mean the users' freedom to run, copy, distribute, study, change, and improve the software. We especially refer to four kinds of freedom for software users: Freedom 0: the freedom to run the program as you wish, for any purpose. Freedom 1: the freedom to study how the program works, and change it so it does your computing as you wish – access to the source code is a precondition for this. Freedom 2: the freedom to redistribute copies so you can help your neighbour. Freedom 3: the freedom to distribute copies of your modified versions to others. By doing this you can give the whole community a chance to benefit from your changes – access to the source code is a precondition for this.[19]
>
> STALLMAN, 2004: 45

In recent years, two general trends in technology regulation factors put pressure on the computer segment in contemporary times: (1) a replacement of the dynamic segment between desktops and mobile devices, with the former having a strong growth curve in the 2000s and a drop from 2011 onwards, while smartphones also grew in the 2000s and exploded in 2010; and (2) a market re-accommodation with new manufacturers, but concentrating on four competitors in the desktop market and a slightly larger number in the mobile device market. Although desktop penetration is still far from the process that occurred with television sets, the spread of smartphones has boosted this sector as a driver of ICTs.

Desktops were the central electronic device for digitalization and media convergence triggered from the 1980s onwards. During this and the following decades, they would become the wish item of families throughout the world. But, even in 2005, the percentage of homes with this technology was 27.6%. In a little less than 15 years, between 2005 and 2019, the penetration rate rose to 49.7%, reaching almost half of the population.[20] If, on the one hand, the processing capacity of smartphones is increasing, they do not replace desktops in terms of functionalities, whose penetration rate is still a major obstacle. The reduction in the sales expansion pace also affects smartphones. The evolution over the previous year reached almost 30% in 2014 for this device and stabilized at almost zero. The commercialization of desktops declined as of 2011, but stabilized in 2017 (IDC apud Ovide, 2018). The market share of computer sales shows a loss of dominance of firms with the highest market share in the

---

19   Stallmann, Richard. *Software libre para una sociedad libre*. Madrid: Traficantes de Sueños, 2004.
20   Statista (2020) Share of households with a computer at home worldwide from 2005 to 2019. At: https://www.statista.com/statistics/748551/worldwide-households-with-computer/.

1980s and 1990s, such as IBM and Apple, in favour of the rise of the HP, Dell, and Lenovo.

While, until the last decade, the key market segment was the desktop segment, the last few years have seen the spread of mobile devices. In 2020, there were 8 billion mobile connections (GSMA, 2020). However, access statistics add up the number of working lines (numbers of chips, often used simultaneously by the same user). Therefore, the number of people using mobile phones should be considered: 4.7 billion in 2016, and 5.19 billion in 2019 (We Are Social, 2020).[21] However, these accesses are extremely unequal. While the average penetration in 2020 was 80% in Europe, it dropped to 45% in Sub-Saharan Africa (GSMA, 2020). Data exchange on these devices has grown 18-fold in five years. Speed is also an important aspect of this scenario as it relates to the use of the service and the applications. In 2016, the average speed of mobile devices increased from 6 to 6.8 Mbps (Cisco, 2017).[22].

The mobile device market is characterized by a predominance of Asian manufacturers. Samsung is the leader, with a participation of 21%. Then comes Apple, with 14 per cent. Besides the presence of Apple, the pioneer in the market and the only American company, the following competitors are all Chinese: Huawei (10%), Xiaomi (7%) and Oppo (6.8%) (Statista, 2018a). Note that there is a higher competition level in this market, with the 'Other' category covering 40% of global sales. The historical movement shows the rise of Samsung from 2009 and the decline of Nokia, which went through a turbulent history, involving the sale of its mobile division to Microsoft in 2014, instability in the smartphone market and a partnership with the company HMD. The mobile access market is controlled by operators in wealthy countries and with large population, as well as by groups of consolidated leadership in their countries and with international operations. The ranking of operators by annual revenue (Johnston, 2020) is led by AT&T (USA), Verizon (USA), Nippon Telegraph & Telephone Company (Japan), China Mobile (China) and Deutsche Telekom (Germany). If accesses are considered, the ranking changes as follows: China Mobile (China), Vodafone (UK), Telefónica (Spain), China Unicorn (China) and

---

21 According to GSMA (2020), 56% were based on 4G technology, 20% on 5G and 18% on 3G. While wealthier countries occupy the top of 3G and 4G penetration statistics, the poorest have the worst performances (Opensignal, 2016), highlighting the inequality between the centre and periphery of capitalism highlighted by Dussel (1988).

22 As in the previous parameters, the inequalities are striking. While the ranking of countries with the highest average speed in mobile internet is occupied by wealthier countries (South Korea, Singapore, Hungary, Australia and Denmark), the base is formed by poor nations (Afghanistan, Costa Rica, Ethiopia and Iraq) (Opensignal, 2016).

América Móvil (Mexico). Three main conclusions can be drawn from this survey: (1) Operators in wealthier markets have better financial performance by combining a large customer base with more expensive products and, therefore, higher revenues; (2) the mobile operator market is less internationalized than others (such as content or platforms) due to its infrastructure-based nature, although those conglomerates that have advanced their operations in other countries have gained important positions, which occurs with the European companies Vodafone and Telefónica (which operate in both Europe and Latin America) and the Mexican América Móvil, with strong growth in Latin America.

When the operational systems are analysed, the concentration reaches a new level. Google's Android has a 74.25% market share in mobile platform, followed by Apple's IOS with 25.15%.[23] Only these two companies dominate almost 100% of the market. The leadership of Android is leveraged by its use by more manufacturers: Samsung, Huawei, LG, ZTE and Motorola. The comparison between the three markets (access providers, devices and operating systems) brings elements to question the argument that more information-based activities would provide an environment of greater competition for lower entry barriers. In this case, it is exactly the most information-intensive service, whose market has very high degrees of concentration, in a clear duopoly on a global scale between Android and IOS.

As far as usage is concerned, the mobile internet has grown as well. In the United States, in 2016, the average use time for each mobile phone exceeded 3 hours and 22 minutes daily, reaching, in 2019, half of total internet time (We Are Social, 2020). A survey in the United States, the United Kingdom and South Korea measured the main activities carried out using mobile devices: e-mail (82%), web browsing (81%), voice calls (80%), news reading (70%), messages (66%), and social networks (64%). The same study, taking a sample in the UK, revealed that, among the younger age groups (18–34), the usage habit changes, with time being dedicated to social networks, IP messaging (such as WhatsApp) and video streaming (GSMA, 2016).

Rising to the status of the most widespread household appliance in the world, mobile phones are gaining centrality in the digital ecosystem and its operating logic sets its own central factors for the regulation of technology, operating on digital platforms (as we will see in the following chapter), especially Google and Facebook (as seen in Chapters 6 and 7). Regarding desktops, their greater processing capacity can set the stage for developing a solution

---

[23] Statcounter Global Stats (2020) Mobile Operating System Market Share Worldwide. Available (consulted 22 Semptember 2020) at: https://gs.statcounter.com/os-market-share/mobile/worldwide.

that could reconfigure this branch within the paradigm, knowingly quantum computing. However, it is still in a very early phase, according to Hughes' (1993) invention and development stage.

5 Emerging Technologies: Big Data, Algorithms and Artificial Intelligence

So far, the chapter's argument has discussed the foundations of the ICT technological paradigm. We started with a brief overview of the internet, taken as a structural technology, and worked on a perspective on other components of this universe: the infrastructure, the core input and the carrier branch. In this section, we also present a general characterization and the challenges of three emerging technologies: massive data collection (Big Data), algorithms and artificial intelligence. The analysis will be a little more restrained, since these groups of technical solutions are strongly embedded in Google and Facebook's technological systems, with their operating logics and derived issues (including questions and risks) that directly affect the two digital platforms chosen as case studies of the present work.

The search for data has become an essential economic input to guide business strategies and service delivery. In the context of global dissemination of ICTs, these data are gathered on a new scale and involve individuals' experiences through computerized systems. The use of various types of devices, such as smartphones, generates 'traces' or digital 'footprints' captured as data, including both information about the individuals and their interests and activities in the digital environment, a phenomenon that Newell and Marabelli (2015: 4) call the "digitalization of everyday life." The process of producing and capturing data on a large scale for processing and applying it in the most varied spheres of social life (economy, politics, and culture) has been referred to as Big Data. Bulger et al. (2014) list four characteristics of this concept: (1) high volume, from the expansion of production and storage conditions, (2) diversification, which goes from structured statistics to information on different aspects of people's daily lives, (3) higher speed in generation and analysis, and (4) integrity, which remains a central challenge, since the other three dimensions have greatly amplified data collection and processing. Schroeder and Cowls (2014: 1) point to Big Data as "a knowledge advance that represents a step change in the scale and scope of knowledge about a given phenomenon."[24] Favaretto et al. (2020) claim that Big Data is a shifting and evolving

---

24 However, the authors point out ethical limits involved in this new reality. One of them is the depersonalization and reduction of the role of the individual's will in favour of a culture determined by the data.

phenomenon, with no consensus on its content. Other authors work with the term "datafication" (Micheli et al., 2020; Van Dijck, 2014). Van Dijck (2014) warns about the normalization of "datafication," in a process that is actually configured as data surveillance, according to Clarke (1988). This is enhanced by the presence of people in services such as digital social networks which, in turn, collect and process data. Micheli et al. (2020) see this context of data-governance dominant models established by few corporate big techs, but with the presence of practices of societal actors.

This is enhanced by the presence of people in services such as digital social networks who, in turn, collect and process data (as will be discussed in the chapters on Google and Facebook). Andrejevic (2013) locates Big Data in a context of excessive information (infoglut) in which the control and management of this wealth of records play a central role in human activities, not only in technology, but, also, in politics and power relations. This phenomenon is characterized by an inequality between those who can collect, store, access and process data and those who cannot. Associated with this inequality is the capacity of the holders of the databases to extract information, predictions and trends from the analysis of this large amount of information. "Big Data factories" operate by "putting data into action," "generating correlations and patterns, shaping decisions and sorting people into categories for marketers, employers, intelligence agencies, healthcare providers, financial institutions, the police, and so on." (Andrejevic, 2013: 42). Pasquale (2015) also warns about this process.[25] It is expressed by the numbers of its economic dimension, which is already manifest as a market of its own. The Big Data global market is estimated to grow from US$138.9 billion in 2020 to US$229.4 billion in 2025 (Markets and markets, 2020).

Raley (2013: 123) sees this collection massification as a "data bubble" in which data brokers make predictions about the "speculative future of the data" (betting on unknown uses for them), driving new technological systems both to collect and process data, analyses and speculations from them. Tene and Polinetsky (2012) raise concerns about ensuring the users' privacy in this context. Supporters of Big Data advocate that large-scale processing would not involve this type of risk, since the users' identity would be preserved

---

25   "As technology advances, market pressures raise the stakes on personal data. Surveillance cameras become cheaper every year; sensors are incorporated into more places. Mobile phones track our movements; programs record keystrokes. New hardware and software promise to 'profile' us all, whether we like it or not. The resulting information – a large amount of data that has not been recorded until recently – is fed into databases and assembled in profiles with unprecedented depth and specificity" (Pasquale, 2015: 4).

through anonymity. However, for the authors, this promise has not been confirmed: "Over the past few years, however, computer scientists have repeatedly shown that even anonymized data can often be re-identified and attributed to specific individuals" (Tene and Polinetsky, 2012: 65).

Such concerns should take into account that privacy is an internationally recognized human right.[26] Diggelmann and Cleis (2014) define it as a "key right" that emanates from a sometimes-paradoxical relationship between the right to stay away from society (privacy as freedom from society) and the right to standards of living in society related to the protection of intimate relationships and honour (privacy as dignity). This large-scale collection and the risks associated with it are normalized and institutionalized through a logic of compulsory consent. Although the use of data without consent is common practice, another part of handling personal information occurs legally by the authorization granted at the time of accepting the conditions imposed upon the installation of applications, called 'terms of use' or 'terms and conditions.' This leads to a dangerous transfer of rights over the data and its use that encourages further mining for various purposes, such as in digital advertising.

To handle such a large amount of data, high processing capacity is required. Such demand has led to the creation of mechanisms to read and process information to meet certain purposes: the algorithms. Domingos (2015: 1) briefly defines the term as "a sequence of instructions telling a computer what to do." But, beyond instructions, they must be "precise" and "unambiguous" to be executed appropriately.[27] For Gillespie (2014), algorithms are assuming an increasingly central role in the selection of information relevant to individuals, affecting a fundamental dimension in shaping world views and engagement in collective life.[28] The author defines algorithms as "encoded procedures for transforming input data into the desired output, based on specified

---

26 Article XII of the Universal Declaration of Human Rights states: "No one shall be subjected to arbitrary interference with his privacy, family, home or correspondence, nor to attacks upon his honour and reputation. Everyone has the right to the protection of the law against such interference or attacks" (UN Organization, 1948).

27 They represent a 'knowledge logic' based on what should be considered most relevant, a definition that is implemented by the institution of filters. Thus, the algorithms favour certain interests and limit others.

28 Algorithms designed to calculate what is "hot" or a "trend" or a "tending topic" distinguish what is relevant from the existing chatter. Together, these algorithms not only help to find information, they also provide a means for knowing what one should know and how to do it, to participate in public and social debate, and to get familiarized with the population we are part of (Gillespie, 2014: 267).

calculations" (Gillespie, 2014: 267). They use a "sequence of well-defined steps and instructions to create categories to filter information based on a combination of reasons for the desired output" (Rosenblat et al. 2014: 1). Starting from the social studies of science and technology, Seaver (2019) defines the object as "social constructions from which we, as outsiders and critics, contribute to their operation and development."

These mechanisms are assuming an important role in the new ICT paradigm. Beer (2017), for example, declares the "social power of algorithms" as their influence on decisions made in society increases. Striphas (2015) discusses an "algorithmic culture." Analysing the action of algorithms in communication and finance, Pasquale (2015) sees the emergence of a "black box society," in which actions in key areas are taken in a non-transparent way by these systems. Aneesh (2009) and Danaher (2016) claim the existence of an "algocracy," in which structures based on algorithms limit and determine human beings' participation and, consequently, public decisions about society.

Algorithms are fundamental to the intelligent processing of new computer systems and the so-called 'digital economy.' They transform masses of data into analyses, recommendations, responses, commands, indications, and the most different forecasts. Their operating logics have come to influence different aspects of social activities – from targeted advertising to the organization of production routines; from the evaluation of employee performance to the coordination of fleets and product distribution; from learning content in virtual educational environments to patient monitoring; from the definition of which content appears in social network feeds to what is shown in search engines; from video recommendations to product suggestions in e-commerce environments.

A relevant issue regarding algorithms is their 'autonomous' processing logic. "If software code is directly executable, then it means these algorithmic systems can operate 'automatically' (in the background) without the need of human intervention" (Introna, 2015: 26). Barocas, Hood and Ziewitz (2013) highlight automation as one characteristic of algorithms, which occurs on two levels. In the first level, the data are analysed according to form parameters, which would not be possible to perform manually. In the second level, this processing indicates trends and guides or determines the decision-making. Newell and Marabelli (2015) highlight two characteristics of automated choices: (1) decision-makers rely on suggestions made by algorithms from large-scale data processing, and (2) decision-makers do not consider what is behind or has been instrumental in making such recommendations.

The agency process, previously operated by human beings based on knowledge and choice, now relies on a relevant component: a processor of associations and multi-determining factors that are not clear to whom, ultimately, makes the choice for a particular action. Would this understanding be restricted, therefore, to programmers or developers? Rosenblat et al. (2014: 2) argue that the level of obscurity also reaches the authors of these instruments: "The logic of an algorithm is not immediately visible, nor would that logic be available if one had the source code. Many algorithms are too complex for any one developer to understand the mechanisms at play." This obscurity leads to two correlated concerns: the understanding of operating systems and the possible correction of rules, procedures and processes that are considered partial, biased or inadequate. Regarding the first concern, Ananny et al. (2015) highlight two difficulties. The first is the elaboration of the algorithm as a collective development. Such characteristic involves some complexity so that each individual on the team can know the whole. The second concern relates to the relationship between the algorithm and the processed data (inputs). Understanding this resource would require knowing the activity's raw material.

A paradox then emerges; at the same time that the algorithm allows human beings to be somewhat autonomous from that operation, eliminating the need for presence or even controlmakes the activity depend on the operation and on the instrument that carries it out. The issue of autonomization is intensified in the case of algorithms that learn from the activities developed (machine learning algorithms). These modalities develop the processing and selection parameters from the data reading, and not a priori, and have, in their own architecture, operating logics that cannot necessarily be reconstituted from the decisions. Thus, the algorithm is not limited only to a set of criteria and rules, generating products, suggestions, answers and indications. The elements that define the processing and the recommended choices are forged during the historical course of the algorithm. Such dynamics enhance the obscurity of the operating logics of these programs and the potential for discrimination from the most different perspectives. At the same time, adopting or not the suggestions and changes in programming, combined with this automated dimension, produces complex circuits of processing, results and decision-making between algorithmic systems and their operators. Andrejevic (2014) considers that even if there are interactions between subjects and machines, these constitute an "algorithm alienation,"[29] with these systems acting without an understanding

---

29 "In the age of Big Data, correlation threatens to eclipse the explanation: even if I have the right to question why a decision was made there may not be an explanation available. One of the beauties or horrors of data mining, depending on how you look at it, is that it is designed to uncover unanticipated and undetectable patterns – that is, patterns that may

and appropriation by the users on their reasons, as well as an effective control over them.

Pasquale's remarkable work (2015) points to the problem of a lack of transparency and how inputs become outputs, an aspect which is criticized in several other works (Introna, 2015; Beer, 2017; Diakopoulos, 2015; Cech, 2020). Kaminski (2020: 2–3) highlight that "transparency is necessary, if not sufficient, for building and governing accountable algorithms. But, for transparency to be effective, it has to be designed. It can't be sprinkled on like seasoning; it has to be built into a regulatory system from the onset." The lack of transparency can be perceived at different levels: (1) data collection, including its nature and the universe of subjects and objects; (2) the ways of collecting these data; (3) the definition of which data are used; (4) the purposes for which they are used; (5) the criteria and parameters of valuation for each specific use and processing; (6) the development of the algorithm and its functionalities and potentialities; (7) the data processing; (8) the results and eventual indications; (9) the application of these results; (10) the impact of this application; and (11) the evaluations and eventual corrections at each of these levels.

Such automation can reinforce injustices. One example is how it classifies people in order for organizations to provide services, such as insurance and loans, where the possibility of discrimination has a direct detrimental effect on certain segments of the population. In analysing the actions of algorithms in the ranking of people when granting loans, Zarsky (2016) lists three types of injustices involving algorithms: (1) the transfer of wealth from people with fewer resources to those with more resources, especially companies and service providers; (2) discriminatory treatment of similar individuals; and (3) damage to individual autonomy. In the study, the author identified how algorithms can, in certain situations, produce results (such as debt renegotiation calculations) detrimental to loan applicants in favour of the profitability of the financial companies providing the service. The discrimination and biases in these solutions have been an object of special attention, with studies pointing to this differentiated treatment with damages to poorer people and black people, for example (Noble, 2018; Eubanks, 2018).

The concerns with the development of algorithms and with their 'learning capacity' increase greatly with the emergence of even more complex systems and with the capacity to produce results according to their own logics, contained within the term that came to be consolidated as 'artificial intelligence.'

---

have no clear or immediate explanation but emerge when different variables are taken into account in a large enough data set" (Andrejevic, 2013: 179).

Frankish and Ramsey (2014: 1) define this as a "cross-disciplinary approach to understanding, modeling, and replicating intelligence and cognitive processes by invoking various computational, mathematical, logical, mechanical, and even biological principles and devices." This area, the authors add, involves strongly theoretical debates about the understanding of cognition, decision-making and the limits to its replication in computer systems and, also, more pragmatic research on intelligent programs and applications with different functionalities and purposes.

Russell and Norvig (2016) consider that there are several approaches within this field, which the authors classify into four major groups according to the types of behaviour of these systems and devices: (1) think like humans, (2) act like humans, (3) think rationally, and (4) act rationally. The notion of intelligence, thus, can be related to a similar understanding of human mind or behaviour or be more tied to a normative dimension of rationality as doing what is "right" or "giving the best answer" to a stimulus, demand or problem solution. One of the approaches that has gained prominence in the field is that of "intelligent agents." On the internet, their presence has become something common, earning the popular nickname of "bot." Russell and Norvig point out that the Web has been a fertile land for the proliferation of these agents since the 2000s. Systems with varying degrees of intelligence (including algorithms) are now adopted in the most different applications, such as search engines, personal assistants, social network websites and e-commerce platforms, among others.

In 2003, the MIT, an already traditional research centre on the subject, created the Laboratory for Computer Science and Artificial Intelligence. In 2000, an important subfield created was Artificial General Intelligence, which advocates the focus on the search for a universal system that can learn and react to any task, rather than specific applications (Goertzel, 2007). The US government is beginning to invest in the development of intelligent war robots. Speech recognition systems are becoming a widespread reality with their introduction into smartphones. In recent years, artificial intelligence has become part of the agenda of economic sectors, governments and international organizations as a central technology in the attempt to recover productivity rates. Within the scope of a data-based economy, intelligent applications are the most important products in collecting this raw material, triggering their escalation due to the creation and adoption of technologies based on AI. From the middle of the 2010s onwards, this appears in the technological trends forecasts of agencies such as the World Economic Forum, the OECD, the G20 and the main consultancies in the sector such as Accenture, McKinsey and others.

As a consequence, the market associated with these technologies has gained strength (McKinsey, 2017).

McKinsey estimates that, in 2016, companies invested between 26 and US$39 billion in these systems. Of this total, between US$20 and US$30 billion would have been spent by "technology giants" and the rest by startups. Since 2013, foreign investment has tripled. But the widespread deployment of these technical resources, despite the favourable discourse, is still modest. Among firms interviewed in McKinsey's study, 20% said they were already employing some type of AI-based technology, while 40% said they were experimenting or partially using it, and 40% were uncertain about the need to incorporate these types of applications (McKinsey, 2017: 5). According to a survey with companies in the United States (LeGassick, 2017), the number of startups developing AI systems went from 0 in 1995 to over 600 in 2015. In the same period, the annual investment of venture capital funds went from 0 to more than US$3 billion. In both cases, the evolution shows upward curves from 2011 and 2012, highlighting the emergence of AI as a targeted technology in the process of speculation and financing of the financial market geared to the sector.

In the geographic perspective, the centralization of AI research and development is clear. The industry's race is basically divided between the United States and China, the former with its technology giants, Google, Amazon and Microsoft, and China with Baidu and Alibaba. A second group of companies includes Oracle and Salesforce in the US and the German SAP. Google launched its cloud AI platform called Tensor Flow. In November 2017, the conglomerate announced another, the AutoML Cloud project, a system into which companies can feed data and receive suggestions on how to improve their business. Microsoft has brought its Azure platform to market. Although it does not yet have large commercially feasible systems, Amazon has invested heavily in the acquisition of AI startups. Two of the company's flagship projects are its assistant, Alexa, and the application of AI in its cloud computing services, which dominate 40% of this market.

The segments that are most open to AI are technology, telecommunications, automotive and finance. The large platforms are the leading companies in this sector, with heavy investments in research and development, which represent 90% of the expenditures in this category (the remaining 10% was directed to acquisitions). Vehicle manufacturers, on the other hand, have been investing in the automation of their assembly lines for decades. And the financial market, as discussed in the previous chapter, is increasingly betting on algorithms and intelligent systems for tasks such as stock trading. The segments with average permeability are retail and media. On the other hand, the areas where the use is still incipient are education, health and tourism. The consulting company pointed out a large difference between the firms at the top and bottom of the ranking. In general, the former are larger companies, with a more mature stage of digitalization. Such disparity may suggest that artificial intelligence may widen the gap between the top companies in the world economy and those with lower performance, soon becoming a barrier to entry and an element that reinforces or deepens leadership positions, evincing a spread of the network effect in the general economy, as previously discussed.

In technology, most interest has been directed to machine learning. The central idea of this approach is to apply the learning process to machines, enabling them to draw general inferences from concrete experiences (Oliveira, 2017: 97). Besides this, other applications have been gaining attention, such as speech recognition, translation, image recognition and processing, decision management, virtual agents, biometrics and semantic technology. According to a survey by Forrester, the most successful technologies are decision management, AI-optimized equipment, machine learning platforms and virtual agents. Those areas with more moderate success are text analysis and the robot automation process (Forrester, 2017). Much of these resources have been provided by the leading economic players in the industry for cloud computing services. Google's expectation is that the use of AI has the power to double the cloud computing market, currently valued at US$260 billion (Burrows, 2018).

If, on the one hand, it is not possible to talk about the stabilization of these technologies in their economic dimension, in terms of performance compared to humans, in the last years there has been a strong development of these systems' capabilities. The Artificial Intelligence Progress Measurement project (Electronic Frontier Foundation, n.d.) suggests evolution in several indicators. In image recognition, the error rate of the tested systems went from 5x that of a human in 2011 to less than this limit in 2015. In several video games (the study uses examples from the Atari console) the same occurred, as in Assault (best performance achieved in 2013), Beam Rider (2015) and Chopper Command (2015). The AI Index (LeGassick, 2017) also mapped these breakthrough moments, which occurred in 2014 in the case of object detection, and in 2016 in the case of speech recognition. However, the supremacy of machines is far from being absolute and still does not occur in indicators such as translation, and answers to textual and visual questions. The AI Index study provides interesting data that reveals the spiral involvement of the promotion of AI as a cutting-edge technology among companies, governments and financiers. The media are also part of this movement. The number of articles with a positive approach to technology expanded between 2015 and 2016, from 10% to 30% of published texts. But if, on the one hand, there is a frenzy around the subject, on the other hand, the advance of these systems has been causing alerts and concerns in various specialists and segments.

Webb (2019) calls AI "the third era of computing." Sometimes it is hard to see where it will lead, just as during the process of the Industrial Revolution. Webb rejects utopian or catastrophic views about the impacts of this new technology. She points to the lack of state projects on the subject in the United States, with an "outsourcing" of its development to six "technology giants" in the country: Google, Facebook, Amazon, Apple, Microsoft, and IBM. On the other side of the world, in China, three other companies complete the leadership team in this area, but with strategies that are strongly encouraged by their government: Alibaba, Tencent and Baidu. She sees AI as a positive force with the potential to create benefits. But it is subject to problematic uses or unforeseen or unintended consequences. These may constitute risks, as humanity transfers activities and decisions to AI and its role becomes less and less visible to us. The central question that should be broadly discussed is: "What happens to society when we transfer power to a system built by a small group of people that is designed to make decisions for everyone?" (Webb, 2019, n.p.). According to her, AI should be treated as a "public asset," in contrast to the current scenario of concentration in the hands of the "Big Nine."

Floridi et al. (2018) and his expert group on the initiative, called AI4People, follow a similar direction, seeing AI both as an opportunity and a risk. In the first group are ways to promote the self-fulfilment of humans, stimulate human agency, increase human capabilities[30] and deepen social cohesion. The risks involve the devaluation of human skills, the elimination of human responsibility, the loss of human control and the erosion of self-determination. In order to maximize gains and mitigate risks, the authors defend an ethical approach to the subject based on other recommendations from authorities and researchers, involving six groups of principles. The first is prioritizing people's well-being. The second is the non-violation of privacy. The third is affirming the autonomy of individuals to make decisions, balancing agency and the ability of machines. The fourth is promoting justice without discrimination. The fifth is ensuring that the decisions made by intelligent systems are explained. The sixth involves transparency and oversight of the agents that create and manage intelligent agents.

In 2015, more than a thousand AI researchers and experts, such as the late physicist Stephen Hawking, Apple's co-founder, Steve Wozniak, and the brain behind Tesla and SpaceX, Elon Musk, signed an open letter calling on

---

30   Such as preventing disease or optimizing urban mobility.

the United Nations to ban the use of autonomous weapons, such as drones (Russell et al., 2015). These were described as the "third war revolution" after gunpowder and nuclear weapons. The signatories strongly advocate avoiding a race to create these machines, whose development will be easier than that of missiles and nuclear bombs, since they do not demand rare materials, such as uranium. This characteristic, the document warns, will allow this resource to be appropriated by criminal and terrorist forces in a short time.[31]

Musk has been one of the main voices alerting the world about the risks of AI and the need to seek regulation for it. He has classified this technology as "humanity's greatest existential threat" (Gibbs, 2014). Tesla's CEO said (Musk, 2015) that, in the near future, robots will be able to do everything better than humans. "I am not sure exactly what to do about this. This is really the scariest problem to me," he said in a speech to authorities in the United States. Musk was the co-founder of a research centre on the subject, called Open AI. A group of scholars from Oxford and Cambridge universities in the United Kingdom, as well as organizations such as the Electronic Frontier Foundation and Open AI, published a paper on the risks of what they called "Malicious AI"[32] (Brundage et al., 2018).

In the field of cyber security, the use of AI can raise the possibility of attacks on systems to a new level. Just as AI enables automation, the processing of stimuli and learning how to perform a task better, this can also occur in the case of malicious systems, through automated hacking. At the political level, the authors point to the risk of using AI to enhance surveillance by states and companies, as well as to control behaviours from the processing of collected information. Facial recognition and the analysis of texts and speeches greatly facilitate this type of data record, episodes and experiences. These resources, on the other hand, can confer a more realistic nature to messages, facilitating, for example, disinformation, popularly known as 'fake news.' The use of AI can also deepen personalized analysis and advertising (microtargeting), as in Cambridge Analytica's role in the 2016 elections in the United States. Through AI systems, platforms can manipulate public debates and the cultural consumption of millions of users, using content curatorship algorithms. Brundage

---

31 Autonomous weapons are ideal for tasks such as murder, destabilizing nations, subjugating populations and selectively killing an ethnic group. We believe that a military race of artificial intelligence will not benefit humanity. There are many ways that AI can make battlefields safer for humans, especially civilians, without creating new tools to kill people (Russell et al., 2015).

32 The authors work with the concept of 'malicious' as something that can bring risks to the safety of individuals, groups or society.

et al. (2018) present four central recommendations based on the risks identified: (1) authorities should engage with researchers to map and mitigate possible harmful effects of the use of AI; (2) researchers should be sensitive to the nature of their work, incorporating possible malicious uses into research priorities and warning relevant actors when identifying risks; (3) good practices should be adopted more effectively in research, with more effective methods to identify possible problems; and (4) actors should seek to expand those involved in the discussion about these challenges and possible risks of using AI.

Villani (2018), author of a report discussing policies for France on the subject, argued that AI should not be used to reinforce processes of exclusion and concentration of wealth and resources, nor should it contribute to stimulate the government of society by "black box" algorithms, fighting the risks of discrimination (such as in insurance prices or in credit granting). With regard to changes in the labour market, the author advocates the need to anticipate harmful changes, such as the elimination of jobs through the use of intelligent automation and working with a logic of complementarity, not alienation, ensuring training of the workforce. The author advocates an ethical perspective for these technological systems that would open the "black boxes" and ensure transparency in the modes of operation, facilitating audit modes of these artefacts. As AI can reproduce prejudices and biases existing in society, an analysis is fundamental to assess whether such problems are occurring. It is also necessary that the diversity of society is also represented among the developers of intelligent solutions. These ethical dimensions must be inscribed in the design of the artefacts, a proposal that dialogues with the denaturalization of the content of systems, as discussed by the proponents of SCOT and CTT.

Frischmann and Selinger (2018) also highlight the risks of intelligent machines and hold companies responsible for their design and for controlling the "techno-social engineering." In this field, however, the object that is being "engineered" is humanity itself. As in the narratives of technological progress, the promise involves benefits and advantages. But this is not "the whole picture," since this phenomenon becomes more and more pervasive and incorporated into systems and devices scattered throughout the environments and our activities, warn the authors, raising questions about the "techno-triumphalism" detected by Winner (2016). As we collectively race down the path towards smart techno-social systems that efficiently govern more and more of our lives, "we run the risk of losing ourselves along the way. We risk becoming increasingly predictable, and, worse, programmable, like mere cogs in a machine." (Frischmann and Selinger, 2018: I).

Jin (2018) highlights the privacy risks of AI. Observing the ecosystem based on data, the author highlights that the centrality of the collection, treatment and applications (especially those of AI) based on personal information make these the fundamental assets of this model, resulting in them becoming increasingly widespread in economic activities. This demand increases the value of data, causing a race for its collection and treatment, which is manifested both in activities focused on this (such as social networking websites) and those to do not include data management among their main tasks but that begin to incorporate it, such as the example of retail chains that create loyalty programs to compile their customers' consumption habits. The intelligent nature of the systems demands an increasing amount of personal information and situations so that you can learn from them and develop more "qualified" responses. This aspect makes AI a central element of "inflation" in the value of data, since it is strongly based on it. At the same time, intelligent systems perform increasingly sophisticated cross-matching, which makes monitoring by the user and authorities or regulatory agencies difficult. In addition, there is the risk of discrimination, injustice and other harm caused to users, due to the decidion making process and obscurity of AI systems.

Introducing the technological paradigm of information and communication technologies and its factors for regulation of technology, the present approach has attempted to narrow down the type of ICT group under analysis, i.e.: digital platforms. The previous chapter has already contextualized the specificity of this branch of the technological sphere within a historical perspective and identified the social factors of regulation over technology, and this chapter has presented the concrete reference bases within which the development of technological systems occurs. The next chapter will discuss the platforms, punctuating their definitions, characteristics, distinctive features, typologies and how they are manifested within the capitalist system, that is, as agents in the market in competition.

CHAPTER 5

Digital Platforms

This chapter aims at, defining digital platforms, listing their specific characteristics and types and analysing their rise. Since they are generally systems operating in the capitalist market, their economic dimension assumes a central role. For this reason, the chapter also covers aspects related to production within the platforms, highlighting their labour relations and their distinguishing competition dynamics. After presenting these characteristics, we underline how digital platforms assume a special condition, becoming what we call 'digital monopolies,' a crucial phenomenon for this analysis. Finally, we briefly discuss legal and regulatory initiatives regarding these economic agents.

1   Definitions

In the literature, the definitions regarding platforms or even the terms used to name them are not consistent. MacKinnon, Hickok, Bar and Lim (2014) call these agents "internet intermediaries," the most popular term in the academic works of the 2000s. They have the ability to gather and facilitate transactions among third parties on the web. They host, make available, allow access to, and organize information created by individuals and collectivities other than themselves, just as hosting providers or website creation services (such as blog platforms) have done throughout the history of the development of the World Wide Web. Van Gorp and Batura (2015:7–8) define platforms as one of the main assets in the digital economy: "A platform provides a (technological) basis for delivering or aggregating services/content and mediates between service/content providers and end-users." The central role of the platforms is to aggregate services and content.[1] Jin (2015: 5) also uses the name "platforms" and defines them as "digital intermediaries." These are constituted not only of certain hardware architecture, but, also, of a software model that allows other programs to operate. Also, they enable people to interact, communicate, and perform

---

1   Another distinctive feature is the network effects inherent in them, according to which they have become more appealing, as their user base and service providers, content and goods grow. Another feature would be their competition for the users' attention.

transactions. Finally, these companies have their values embedded in their design and architecture.[2]

'Matchmakers' is the definition coined by Evans and Schmalensee (2016) to designate companies whose business is to connect people with a desire to sell or offer a good or service to others with such a demand or willingness to consume. This new category sells access from one group to another. The demand from one side to the other becomes the distinguishing factor and an essential indicator of market position and price structure. This characteristic is leveraged in markets or agents when network effects occur.[3] Criticizing an exaggerated emphasis on the economic or technical dimension, Gawer (2014) suggests an "integrated" perspective, "grounded on an organizational base." Absorbing elements of both approaches, Gawer (2014: 1240) then defines "technological platforms" as organizations or meta-organizations that: "(1) federate and coordinate constitutive agents who can innovate and compete; (2) create value by generating and harnessing economies of scope in supply or/and in demand; and (3) entail a modular technological architecture composed of a core and a periphery."

Allen and Flores (2013: 31) base their definition on a separation between two types of agents. The first, called "aggregation platforms," is configured as "services whose role is to allow end-users to access another provider (a content provider) that is located upstream in the value chain" (such as internet connection providers, connected TVs or websites). The "inter-communication platforms" would be "players whose role is to allow end-users to interact with each other" (this group includes messaging systems, such as WhatsApp, voice-over IP services, such as Skype, and social networking sites, such as Facebook). The European Commission (European Commission, 2016: 2) adopts the designation "online platforms," but does not provide a comprehensive definition. Instead, it points out common characteristics of several types of platform.[4]

---

2 The author highlights the platforms' geographic centralization in the United States and indicates that the phenomenon cannot be perceived separately from its imperialist dimension, applying the concept of "platform imperialism."
3 This operation is different from that of traditional firms. While a traditional industry acquires raw material, transforms it into products and sells it to consumers, matchmakers' business is to establish the connections between the two or more sides and monetize this action. The main resources are the users of the service or platform.
4 Among them are: (1) the ability to facilitate and earn income from interactions between people; (2) the collection of personal and non-personal data to be used to model the services offered, resulting in an information asymmetry about the users; (3) the ability to form networks, increasing the benefits to each member for their participation – the network effect; (4) the possibility of creating new markets and affecting the already existing ones; (5) promoting engagement by collecting, processing, editing, and collectively posting information.

This term is also used by Helberg, Pierson and Poell (2018: 1). These authors see them as "socio-technical architectures that enable and steer interaction and communication between users through the collection, processing, and circulation of user data." These (usually private) agents develop architectures by means of which people communicate and through which producers and consumers trade goods. Such activities occur based on the platforms' internal rules, regulating the interactions, engagement, permissions, denials, resolving possible conflicts and establishing limits for what can or cannot be done. These spaces facilitate "public activities" and pledge to "empower users" as information producers and goods and services providers.

Ejik et al. (2015: 2) use the term "digital platforms." According to them, these are the basis for the platform economy, characterized by an offering and exchange of services and content across agents in a point-to-point relationship focusing on the intermediation role played by the platforms, catalysing the interaction and transaction channels in a relationship hub. This is also endorsed by Andersson Schwarz (2017), Herscovici (2019) and Cammaerts and Mansell (2020). This concept is defined by the author as systems that enable control, interaction and accumulation. They solidify markets, act as social exchange networks, and establish material arrangements of "trackable activity." Digital platforms constitute infrastructures that serve as a basis for operations in proprietary systems, partly customizable by the user and allowing multi-layered market exchanges. These agents measure, or even "dictate" social actions and economic relationships and cannot be understood merely as neutral intermediaries. They, thus, assume not only the role of social utilities, but, also, of knowledge operators. Couldry and Mejias (2019: 51) also use digital platforms and discuss these agents as key to a new process they call data colonialism: "Digital platforms give gatekeeping power to their owners, much as the navigation routes of historical colonialism empowered the towns near where goods had to land. But, because of the connected nature of the online environment, today's gatekeeping power has consequences on a vast global scale, not just a local or national one."

Gillespie (2010) criticizes the use of the term 'platform' as a discursive and economic positioning strategy of large companies in this segment that provide internet services and act as intermediaries. This definition is specific enough to convey an idea but vague enough to include a large number of activities and audiences. These industries, the author adds, are characterized not by the traditional computational sense, by which they allow a code to be operated on them, but by the ability to allow people to interact, communicate or trade goods and services.⁵ Hands (2013), within an approach he classifies as "platform politics," defines platforms as software structures running on the World Wide Web as social network interfaces that connect users to one another, to the Web and to the internet itself.

Van Dijck (2013) also stresses that these agents cannot be seen merely as facilitators, since their construction and social practices are mutually constitutive. They are "dynamic objects" whose evolution responds to their owners' objectives, the competition with other platforms, and the technological and economic infrastructure on which they are based. Focusing on social networks, she describes these services as "autonomous systems that engineer and manipulate connections" (Van Dijck, 2013: 12).⁶ DeGryse (2016) sees digital platforms as a new type of company arising as one of the three pillars of n the contemporary economy, along with Big Data and the dissemination of connected infrastructures and mobile devices. Platforms are a new business model characterized by the exploitation of massive data, whose collection and services offered are be possible due to the technological basis of networks and connected devices. More than their most visible facets, such as digital social networks or e-commerce, platforms are characterized as catalysing elements of the digital transformation operating in several industries.⁷ Focusing on the so-called "sharing economy" and its synonyms (gig economy, peer economy), Scholz (2016: 2) classifies the economic activities made possible by digital platforms as an "on-demand service economy that set out to monetize services that were previously private".⁸ Slee (2015) also compares the promises of the so-called "sharing economy" with reality. It extends a deregulated market into the protected areas of our lives. The main companies are now giants that establish new control, surveillance and exploitation logics instead of security.⁹

Pasquale (2016) sees the term as a systemic adjective when dealing with the concept of "platform capitalism," also used by Srnicek (2017) and Seidl

---

5   However, the widespread use of the term 'platform' by these industries aims at conveying a sense of openness, neutrality, egalitarianism and accessibility to users.
6   In the rhetoric of companies, the aspect of human connections is emphasized to relegate the automatic logics of operation and business models.
7   Part of these platforms not only exploit data, but, also, labour. On an international scale, these companies make use of a mass of low-income workers already existing and incorporated from the economic crisis in their specific manifestations in different parts of the world.
8   These industries articulate, from this concrete basis, new forms of exploitation, reaching new spheres of work often unpaid and invisible, advancing to a sphere of commodification of activities previously settled in more private domains of society.
9   Instead of freeing individuals and allowing greater control over their lives, these companies increase the income of their shareholders by removing labour protections.

(2020). Unlike a hegemonic narrative promoted by companies describing the latter as promoters of new opportunities, Pasquale (2016) advocates a counter-hegemonic discourse that specifies another dimension of these agents, indicating practices such as the reinforcement of existing inequalities, the promotion of precariousness by hindering the bargaining power of workers, broadening discrimination by adopting profile-based interactions, realigning operation conditions through strong lobbying strategies funded by billionaire revenues, and gaining market share by exploiting network effects and low operating costs and impacts on growth by reducing the gains of the workers connected to them. Some authors extrapolate this definition to qualify more radical transformations. Seidl (2020: 2) highlights the key societal factor, arguing that the "nature of platform capitalism is not preordained by technology itself but depends on how societies decide to regulate it."

Van Dijck et al. (2018) suggest the existence of a "platform society." In it, these agents are inextricably linked to social structures, infiltrating institutions and producing new arrangements. But they are also non-neutral constructs, whose architectures are constituted by values and norms. The term 'platform society' "emphasizes that platforms are an integral part of society, where conflicts of interest are currently played out at various levels" (Van Dijck et al., 2018: 2). These disputes involve the pursuit of profit by companies on the one hand and public values on the other. The ways to equalize these disputes include thinking about the search for complex solutions. This platform society is formed at the micro-level by "online platforms," digital architectures aimed at organizing interactions among users. At the intermediate level, a combination of these structures composes what the authors call "platform ecosystems," responsible for a core infrastructure for data flows. Analysing the sector where most of them originate, Mosco (2017) states that these companies, especially the five largest ones (Apple, Google, Amazon, Microsoft, and Facebook), command what he calls the "next internet," characterized by the commodification of institutions, bodies, and minds.

By analysing such references, the definition should describe the object by searching for what limits its universe and what its members have in common. Digital platforms can be understood as technological systems in which activities are developed on a technological basis, commanded by owners (a company, such as Google, or cooperatives, such as the European trade platform Fairmondo) but in which other agents participate (producers, intermediaries, users), whose control and management play a key organizing role and in which economic logics, cultural practices and different (regulatory and internal) norms operate, from which the TS s promote active mediation in the activities in which they are inserted.

Their main asset is to facilitate access across different parties, connecting users, vendors, advertisers, and workers in different arrangements.[10] A second constitutive element is an active mediation role among the different sides. As authors have emphasized, despite the fact that the platforms claim to be disinterested facilitation spaces, these companies establish the rules of the game, the logic through which the interactions and transactions take place, and their limits. Thus, digital platforms are not neutral systems.[11] Instead, they seek to expand their active mediation into more and more spheres to control the flows of information, interactions and transactions operated by the different user modalities that participate in the ecosystem they model. Thus, they assume the role of central mediation structures in the sociability of contemporary capitalism.

Based on the features and characteristics discussed, we opted to use the term 'digital platforms'. The modifier seems adequate to describe the phenomenon, circumscribing the object and differentiating it from the generic term 'platforms'. At the same time, the term 'digital' does not imply a deterministic view of technology. It includes the technological basis, the data input (collected and processed through this medium) and encompasses different elements of the technological systems, being the informational basis of the current technological paradigm of ICTs. This classification seems more comprehensive than "online platforms," which reduces the technological dimension to the internet.[12] Based on the initial observations, developed below, it seems possible to us to propose our own definition: digital platforms are technological systems that work as active mediators of interactions, communications and transactions among individuals and organizations operating on a connected digital technological basis, especially through the Internet, providing services grounded on these connections, strongly based on data collection and processing, and characterized by network effects.

Platforms are central agents in the evolution of the new ICTs paradigm and its spread to other social spheres. They are able to cross the three fronts (massive data collection, intelligent processing and customized modulating applications), and are leading agents in all of them, whether in massive data

---

10   Facebook, for example, allows users to interact with each other and, at the same time, with advertisers and application developers from outside the platform. Uber connects drivers and passengers; Google connects websites and people searching for information.
11   This mediation dimension is valid for the algorithms that define the content presented (such as those used by YouTube), the forms of marketing (such as Amazon or EBay) or practices accepted or not to be part of the community (such as CouchSurfing).
12   But, for the purposes of simplicity, it will be used as a synonym.

collection, in building intelligent processing systems, or in offering applications and services to a broad user base. Their business models depend on these activities' intensification, since they need information from users to either deliver targeted advertising or provide customized content and services. Within the dispute of the so-called "attention economy," data collection and processing are essential to competing under this new model. Below, we will examine in detail the characteristics outlined in the argument developed.

2   Characteristics

One of the digital platforms' characteristics is their ability to promote access among the different parties involved in supply and demand, as one of their essential features in the technological system dimension. Thus, these agents optimize the coordination between supply and demand, whether in the circulation sphere, regarding the realization of goods and finance, or in the production sphere, regarding the labour force's purchase and sale. This potential is greater in sectors where demand and supply have a higher fluctuation (thus creating greater uncertainty and making its reduction an important asset), where the connection capacity is reduced and the supply optimization side is deficient (McKinsey, 2016: 57). In the economic literature, these have become known as "multisided markets." Rochet and Tirole (2003: 990) stress that "many if not most markets with network externalities are characterized by the presence of two distinct sides whose ultimate bene. It stems from interacting through a common platform." The connection between individuals and organizations on different 'sides' distinguishes them from traditional companies that acquire raw materials and use the workforce to process them as products to be sold on the market.[13] The main business is to offer this connection across the various sides, whether voluntarily (a buyer looking for a product from a company in Alibaba) or involuntarily (a Twitter user exposed to advertising).

The first characteristic derived from this nature is the need to define a price structure for both sides, and not simply fixing the price per unit for the consumer. Rochet and Tirole (2003) identify one side as "profit centre" and the other as "loss leader" or at least "neutral" from a profit point of view. The characteristic of multisided markets is precisely the capacity of one side to

---

13   Airbnb connects room owners with people interested in renting them. Google Store makes developer applications available to users who demand solutions on their devices. LinkedIn shows professionals' profiles to firms or hiring agencies. Bandcamp offers music and band information to interested listeners.

subsidize the other involved in the transaction (which takes place according to the specificities of each case). Profit is not only the result of price but of its structure and decomposition. From the point of view of market conformation, it is possible that the platforms' actions are not exclusive.[14] Rochet and Tirole point out the platform's central role: the exchange between both sides is only possible because the platform exists and mediates it. The platforms establish the prices to put both sides "on board." An increase in simultaneous consumption (multi-homing) on the buyers' side makes it easier to control the sellers' side and creates a more favourable price structure for them.

One aspect derived from the multisided nature of platforms is the importance of the network effects, as already discussed. As seen in Chapter 3, they can be direct or indirect, with positive and negative impacts. On auction sites, the higher the number of buyers, the more competitive a transaction becomes. By allowing different sides to get in contact, platforms benefit from these effects to expand their base and attract more users from various sides.[15] The concomitant use (multi-homing) element must also be integrated into the analyses. There are several activities in which users (regardless of sides) can use several platforms simultaneously. These are cases such as in the credit card industry, browsers, real estate rental services, and several others.

The distinctive feature of digital platforms is their technological basis, specifically ICT. As evident as it may be, it is important to highlight this as one of their distinguishing features that sets them apart from so many other forms of intermediation in society, such as credit cards or real estate. As such, the quality of the functional properties of these TS s' technical architecture and the services and activities made possible by them is an important competitive and survival strategy, highlighting the qualitative dimension of competition underlined by Herscovici (2013). This search for differentiation can take place in the product and/or service provided (such as Google's search engine or Apple's operating system) or it can be a feature or condition that guarantees a service that is similar to another with better performance or that is more qualified.[16]

The technological nature and differentiation as a competitive advantage cause these companies to work within a logic of constant search for innovation as a key factor in the regulation of technology. This is in the company's

---

14 This is the case of digital social networks, for example.
15 The large number of Facebook users, for example, is appealing to new service providers from all walks of life, whether they are marketplace vendors or application developers in the company's ecosystem.
16 Such as Linux's operating systems' invulnerability to viruses, the privacy guarantee of Mozilla browsers, or the 'Stickers' feature or the lack of limitations for groups in Telegram.

foundation and in its strategy of attracting investments, which can be evidenced by the myriad of startups offering solutions to the most diverse problems. Once the service is established and attention is drawn to it, this vanguard movement draws attention to a previously unnoticed or underused demand and stimulates the entry of new players into the same market.[17] When it is possible to establish a position, but leadership has not yet been reached, innovation becomes a central element, since it includes the ability to offer something unique compared to other competitors. When this is newly established, the company takes advantage of the bumper profits resulting from this condition (Freeman and Louçã, 2004; Mandel, 1979). Even in consolidated leadership situations (such as Google, Facebook, Amazon and Microsoft), innovation and the testing of new features or improvements is constant. In the cases where the platforms are free, they work to expand their user base and not lose users. In both cases, they can even work to advance into other market niches (as will be detailed below).[18] However, not all new technological resources or products turn into innovation or appeal to users. In addition to developing, disseminating and establishing technologies, exclusive control is one of these firms' strategies, creating barriers to competitors to be able to make use of the same or similar resources. One of these strategies is the use of patents.[19]

The platforms are also agents operating through the internet. This has allowed easier access for members on each side[20] and access from one side to the other.[21] For a person with access to the web (it is worth mentioning that about half of the world population does not yet have access to this resource), this capacity makes room for an increasing number of agents to operate on an international scale, not only restricted to their home market. This, however,

---

17 One example was the platforms offering private transport services. After Uber's success, other companies, like Lyft, entered the market to compete in the same activity.
18 At the same time, they can also serve as a way to prevent competitors from ascending by absorbing previously non-existent features (such as the introduction of the story format by Facebook after it emerged as a Snapchat feature).
19 The main platforms (Amazon, Apple, Facebook, Google and Microsoft) applied more than 52,000 patent orders between 2009 and 2016 (CB Insights, 2016). Some of these companies control not only product patents, but standard patents (Standard Essential Patents – SEPs). Due to their importance and their character as a means for the development of other technological solutions, a non-discriminatory concession culture was established, a non-regulated market arrangement (Van Gorp and Batura, 2015: 27). Knowledge control can be one of the barriers to competition in the platform market.
20 Airbnb doesn't have to go into a new city or open an office there for a person to sign up for the service.
21 A buyer finds an item on eBay from someone in another city without having to leave home.

does not necessarily mean greater competition.[22] As many of these platforms are based on information services and products, the internet's intercommunication capacity has enhanced these services and product offerings, the exchange of content and interactions among people. Although part of these platforms' activities occurs offline,[23] their central operations depend on contact, actions and relationships built through the internet (either in the application's direct interface or the interface through browsers).

An important internal factor of the regulation of technology was the dissemination of mobile telephony and the internet in these devices. This allowed greater control of users, reducing the risk of fraud and problems. Since the DPs' central asset is the user, such control becomes a fundamental aspect. At the same time, the use of mobile broadband has enhanced the monitoring of users' actions and preferences by collecting and processing personal data. The requirement to use GPS, for example, allows the monitoring of movements made. There are cases where even activities performed outside the service are monitored, such as Facebook's use of navigation data to identify preferences. This modus operandi raises serious debates about users' privacy, as will be discussed later in this work.

A final and perhaps most important feature of these platforms is the intensive use of data in all their activities. If the main business of digital platforms is the connection between individuals and organizations on the various sides, one challenge is to identify each user's demands and how the other (on a different or the same side) can best respond to it. In order to do this, these websites collect massive amounts of data and use their analysis systems to identify behaviours, preferences and interests that can be translated into goods and services offered (suggestions of books, movies and other Amazon products, for example). Similarly, they use this information basis to make it available to public service providers who are more susceptible and can become potential customers (such as Google and Facebook's custom advertising mechanisms). In this type of economy, "the collection and processing of personal and other data are regarded in much of the technology and business literature as constituting the quintessential 'resource' input that enables the financialization of data through the provision of services to consumers and citizens" (Cammaerts and Mansell, 2020: 136). As previously discussed, since these are agents that mediate among several parties, the data are configured as central inputs so

---

22 As will be discussed later in the "Challenges to competition" subsection.
23 The car shared in ZipCar or the product purchased through Etsy.

that these multiple relationships occur as directly and accurately as possible.[24] The fundamental basis for this collection is the customization of individuals or organizations' participation in these spaces. An increasing number of activities are conditioned not only by the users' identification but, also, by their registration. Several levels of identification and control over data and activities are created there. Authors have referred to this as "dataveillance" (Clarke, 1988; Andrejevic, 2013).

Customization meets a series of demands for the platforms' operation. First, they allow individuals and different parties to make contact, which implies identifying the connection that can best meet the needs of each side and, consequently, generate more revenue for the intermediary. Advertising in companies such as Facebook and Google has the potential to reduce the circumscription of a potential audience as much as possible by combining different interests and digital tracks collected and analysed. Secondly, these agents are strongly focused on data collection and processing and have a competitive advantage. both among themselves and in relation to other traditional competitors.[25] Thirdly, data dominance means the anticipation of consumption desires and the possibility of adjusting or even changing substantially (in a disruptive manner, to use a fashionable term) portions or even the core of the platform's own business model in order to maximize the search for profit, reducing the uncertainties of competition and achievement as a whole in the circulation sphere. Silveira (2020) discusses how digital platforms act to modulate user behaviour, like when Facebook decides what content can be seen or not, based on an individual's profile. Castelluccia (2020: 9) argues that dataveillance can turn into "datapulation," using cognitive attacks in several ways. Cognitive attacks affect the confidentiality, integrity and availability of cognitive systems. They are often very powerful because, as shown by the Cambridge Analytica case, they rely on AI and are dynamic, highly targeted, can be performed at scale and are, most of time, fully automated. Next, we will present a typology of digital platforms, since this type of technological system is quite comprehensive and its understanding goes through recognizing such diversity.

---

24 This can mean providing an address for the delivery of an item purchased on Amazon, providing a mobile phone number to request a ride on Uber, or a photo or name for the Twitter or Snapchat interaction.

25 The use of data analysis (Andrejevic, 2013), algorithms (Gillespie, 2014), machine learning (Domingos, 2015), artificial intelligence (Webb, 2019) and other resources raises the capacity of these agents not only to analyse and cross-reference information, as in the official discourse about the safe nature of Big Data, but, also, allow total individualization, violating the supposed anonymization of users in these processes purportedly offered by companies.

3 Typology of Digital Platforms

Since digital platforms are systems operating in a multitude of activities, a typology can be useful to organize analyses on specific fields within this complex universe. In this section, some classifications will be discussed in order to present the framework for the analyses that will be carried out in the next stages of the analytical journey. Ejik et al. (2015: 18) propose a classification of the different modalities: (1) resellers, which offer content or products elaborated by them or acquired from suppliers (example: Netflix); (2) marketplaces, which facilitate transactions between users and user groups, exchanges which involve products or services (for example, eBay); (3) social networks, which allow interactions and content exchange among users (for example, Facebook, Qzone); and (4) platforms of platforms, which are ecosystems where other platforms operate (for example, Apple, Microsoft, Google/Android). The European Commission (2016) applies a classification similar to that of Ejik et al: (1) E-commerce platforms (marketplace or e-commerce), which are spaces where direct transactions between buyers and sellers take place; (2) application distribution platforms, which offer application spaces, paid or free, for mobile devices and desktops; (3) search services, which services that help users find answers to demands, whether these are specific websites, answers to questions, images, videos or news; (4) content and social networking platforms; and (5) online advertising platforms, which are spaces that intermediate the purchase and sale of advertisements on the internet, such as on websites or applications.

Evans and Gawer (2016), based on a global survey, present a different classification from the previous two: (1) trading platforms, which are technologies, products or services that act as conductors or intermediaries of transactions between sellers, buyers, users and offerors; (2) innovation platforms, which are technologies, products or services that serve as a foundation upon which other firms develop complementary technologies or services; (3) integrated platforms, which are technologies, products or services that act both as trading and innovation platforms; and (4) investment platforms, which act as holdings, as platform investors or as both. Of the three typologies, the latter has a different logic from the other two. The classification by type of activity seems more interesting to us. The model adopted here, therefore, is based on the contributions by Ejik et al. (2015) and the European Commission (2016).[26]

---

26 However, some adjustments are necessary. The category of 'resellers' would be far from the platform concept, since there is no simultaneous intermediation, but a traditional logic of acquiring a good for subsequent sale. Moreover, in the second classification, the

In the proposed typology, the platforms will be classified into five groups:

1) Trade/retail – The main activity of these is the intermediation of transactions of third-party products which they do not own.[27] Examples of these are Mercado Livre, eBay, Amazon.
2) Digital social networks – The main activity of these is the interaction among people and groups, allowing profiles to be created, lists of friends or "followers" and offering different features for posting and circulating messages. Examples of these are Snapchat, WeChat.
3) Application systems – The main activity of these is to organize access to a set of applications for use on personal devices such as operating systems and application stores. Examples of these are Windows, Linux, Android/Play Store, iOS/Apple Store.
4) Sharing of goods, services and activities – The main activity of these is the exchange and sharing of services, goods, time and physical or intellectual work. Examples of these are Uber, Airbnb, Craigslist, TaskRabbit.
5) Content circulation – The main activity of these is the circulation of cultural, informative and scientific content. The search engines that do not host content but make it easier to find it are also included here. Examples of these are YouTube, Google, iTunes, Spotify, Soundcloud, Vimeo, Wikipedia, ResearchGate, Academia.edu.

4 Production Process and Labour Relations

Just as the platforms are heterogeneous, the labour relationships within them are also diverse. In those platforms focused on e-commerce, digital social networks, application systems and content circulation, the basic logic is to manage the work to assemble teams of developers who build the platforms and their various technical resources. Here, the subsumption of these creators' intellectual labour is manifested (Bolaño, 2007)[28] as the development of software, algorithms, smart solutions and any other products derived from the

---

choice of search engines and online advertising agents as specific modalities does not seem to us the best arrangement either.

27 Another form of action is the reseller platform. This is what large departmental firms that buy and stock products do, for example. There are hybrid cases, such as Amazon, in which it connects buyers and sellers, but, also, performs resale from acquired products.

28 The author explains: "Thus, my own hypothesis on the subsumption of intellectual labour follows the same line of thought, defining the Third Industrial Revolution, in the wake of the sociological transformations brought about by the development of Monopoly Capitalism throughout the twentieth century, which will lead to the constitution of a

programming and processing of commands from inputs in order to generate outputs. The platforms create ways to enhance the subsumption of intellectual labour, characteristic of scientific and technological segments, through their ability to articulate demand and supply, in this case, the workforce.

The control ability of both ends of the chain, customized to the interests and characteristics of both buyers and sellers, and the territorial mapping in real-time of these connections in an increasingly connected environment offer possibilities to optimize the supply of goods and services, accelerating the realization and eliminating space and time (Marx, 2014). At the same time, it provides ways for such an offer to take place in an increasingly fragmented manner, through activities and tasks, and not through traditional hiring models. These new arrangements modify the forms of labour organization established throughout the nineteenth and twentieth centuries, creating room to deconstruct the fixed form of employability, the identity of workers and their collective organization. Defining the platforms' labour world is still an initial and fragmented effort, based more on surveys than official data, due to the absence of these forms in the censuses and records promoted by the national states in their labour markets. However, it is possible to identify some characteristics and trends. In general, the teams are organized around highly specialized groups of employees, such as engineers, programmers, data scientists and mathematicians. These are the central foundations of the intellectual labour that is to be subsumed into programs and artefacts that are integral parts of computerized systems for data collection and processing (such as algorithms), and applications offered to customers, be they end users or companies.

Associated with this group, there is a second technological support group, which allows the production infrastructure on which the digital production line is based. These are network engineers, computer scientists, electronics engineers and others. A third support group involves activities that are not directly related to the platform's business, but that are essential to the business model and to promote the activities, such as management, human resources, sales support, marketing and communication. There are also a number of general and accessory activities, such as drivers, cleaning personnel, security, secretaries, receptionists. This division is not intended to be schematic, and certainly varies according to the size of the platform and its organization mode. But it does allow a preliminary view.

---

middle class of intellectual workers with an important relative autonomy in the work process, within the large company" (Bolaño, 2007: 4).

There is a lack of studies and literature analysing the work force of all platforms. As we will see below, the literature includes analyses of specific cases and segments. Statistics on the technology industry in the United States, and on the Silicon Valley region in particular, may provide relevant clues for analysing this issue regarding the main platforms. One study (Silicon Valley Rising, 2016) states that, in the last 24 years, the number of jobs has increased by 31%, an average of 1.1% per year. Part of this low rate, in the authors' evaluation, is due to the growth of outsourcing, which increased 54% over the same period. In 2016, the average salary of workers at these firms was US$113,000 per year. In the so-called 'blue collar' category (security guards, cleaning staff, drivers), it was US$19,900 per year. Benner and Neering (2016) indicated the existence of between 19,000 and 39,000 outsourced workers in the region. The authors highlight a major inequality between direct workers and subcontractors. The wages of the latter are, on average, 70% lower than those of the former. As for colour, race and origin, while in the direct hires of these companies, black people and Latinos represent 10%, in the outsourced functions – referred to as "white collars" by Benner and Neering (sales representatives, for example) – this rate rises to 26%, and in the blue collar category, it reaches 58%. In 2015, several technology companies, such as Google and Apple, closed a deal in court worth US$415 million. They were accused of colluding to keep wages down from an articulation to prevent one company from hiring workers from another (*Los Angeles Times*, 2015).

Another survey (McCandless, 2018) mapped the gender and race inequalities in major technology companies in the United States. The study recorded a gap in the distribution by gender, with fewer women employed than the general representation. The platforms with more women employed were Groupon (47%), Pinterest (44%) and LinkedIn (42%). In the last few years, this insertion has increased, albeit modestly. The presence rate rose by 2% on average. Inequality is also manifested in the distribution by race in the case of black people and Latinos. The presence of white people sometimes occurs at a lower proportion than the average demographic framework of the United States, due to a large presence of Asians, including people from Japan, China, Korea, as well as India, the country of origin of many workers in this industry.

The network of workers mobilized is increasingly fragmented. And the variety of people involved in these platforms raises questions among researchers about the possible role of those who benefit from these services. In digital social networks, a controversy has emerged in recent years about how much the activities allowed by the platforms involve the work of users from sides connected through them or not. Terranova (2013) argues that the value of digital social network giants has been boosted by the mass of users, and that would have become "common sense." According to her, a double exploitation of labour occurs on these platforms. The first concerns the exploitation based on wage dynamics, characterized in the digital economy by the loss of autonomy and the reduction of wages due to the productivity crisis. The second would involve the appropriation and accumulation from the exploitation of interactions within the platforms – such as publications, sharing, appraisals ('likes'), dissemination of links, comments and the like. Fuchs (2014) analyses what he calls "informational labour."[29] Within its scope, more specifically, in "digital cognitive labour," human beings make use of their brains, mouth, discourse, ears, the internet and platforms such as Facebook as instruments to translate experiences that are transformed into content posted on these spaces, giving rise to new experiences and social interactions.[30]

Bolaño and Vieira (2014), in response to Fuchs, defend the need to understand the audience commodity in order to correctly apprehend the processes operating in the context of social networks, a development that can be extrapolated to other platforms for the circulation of free content and content based on advertising.[31] As in cultural industry, the audience commodity has a dual aspect (Bolaño, 2000). However, the authors do not compare both logics. Taking digital social networks as their object of analysis (as did Fuchs), they claim they sell ads to advertisers, just like TV stations, but the audience is active, not passive. The productive labour would not occur on the part of social network users or website producers used by Google in their searches, but on the part of the teams responsible for development and for all activities related to providing these online services, such as engineers, researchers and other

---

29   "Information is a work process, in which cognitive work creates ideas, communicative work creates meanings and cooperative work co-creates information products that have shared and co-created meaning" (Fuchs, 2014: 249).

30   Digital labour employs all these tools in order to create new products: online information, meanings, social relations, artefacts and social systems. Information no longer has only an indirect role in production relations (such as knowledge stock, skills, techniques, etc.), but it now plays a role in the form of informational labour that generates informational products.

31   Just as in the case of TV, where programs were offered to attract viewers' attention, which was sold to advertisers as advertisement price lists, several online services (such as websites, digital social networks, news, games) are offered to users in order to get their attention. The buyers of this commodity are the people who need to communicate with this audience, whether these are companies, governments, or civil society organizations that serve ads seeking to reach these people. Therefore, these services and products on the internet have two characteristics: first, they are goods produced by informational companies; second, although they are free, they reproduce the advertiser's capital in the circulation process.

employees of these companies who develop the tools responsible for generating the audience commodity, which is marketed to advertisers.[32]

This approach seems more appropriate to us. If, on the one hand, it is possible to perceive an intellectualization of labour under ICTs (including its spread to other economic spheres, as previously discussed), on the other hand, care must be taken not to equate people's involvement and attention to labour. Taking as a reference ICTs in which users produce and disseminate content (such as digital social networks), when these are transformed into strategies to create attention and to spend time on the platform, as well as to generate data for advertisement customization, this resembles, in some ways, the audience commodity 'consumed' by advertisers. There is no exploitation of labour there, but the agency of attention to generate revenue from advertising. The productive labour would not be that of the users who post a photo, despite their position as an active audience member, but of the chain of workers who engender the systems responsible for this agency.

In goods and services sharing platforms, an important specificity of labour relationships must be highlighted. In this segment, which has grown in the last few years, a set of conceptual approaches has emerged, ranging from a focus on consumption (collaborative consumption or the 'on demand economy') to an emphasis on labour (the gig economy, the sharing economy, and peer-to-peer markets). The term 'gig economy' was chosen by the economics publication *The Financial Times* as one of 2015's key terms (in the article "A Year in a Word") and is defined as: "the freelance economy, in which workers support themselves with a variety of part-time jobs that do not provide traditional benefits such as healthcare" (Hook, 2015, n.p.). The new aspect would be the scale achieved to bring people together through the use of technology, especially the internet. At its core is the coordination of different tasks and workers through application-based platforms. Donovan, Bradley and Shimabukuro (2016: 1) define the gig economy as "the collection of markets that match service providers to consumers of on-demand services on a gig (or job) basis."

The Oxford Internet Institute maintains a mapping of the gig economy segment called the Online Labour Index.[33] Between May 2016, when our analysis began, and May 2018, a 30% growth was recorded for this type of activities organized by platform. Forde et al. (2017) estimate that 33% of the people in

---

32 The content published by users, as well as their interactions, are raw materials, and not productive labour, since they do not generate use-value. However, they have free access to the service, because it is paid for by advertisers, in an indirect commodification.

33 The mapping is available at: http://ilabour.oii.ox.ac.uk/online-labour-index/. Data mentioned refer to the access on June 13, 2018.

the US and the European Union have already participated in the platform economy (the authors identify the sector by relating the terms "collaborative," "platform," and "gig" economy). Interviewees stated that their participation was due to reasons such as increased income and flexible arrangements. On the other hand, they complained that these forms imposed on them a 24/7 availability logic, even when the request occurred in different time zones.[34] A study by the consulting company McKinsey (2016) found that 15% of self-employed people in the United States are already on some job or service intermediation platform. The TaskRabbit platform operates in 18 cities in the United States, gathering 30,000 freelance workers. IBM maintains a more restricted platform for freelance work, Liquid, and another that is more open, TopCoder. The members of the latter are only paid if the work is analysed and approved. Workers are evaluated by time and performance, participating, as in the other platforms, in a rating system (Wobbe, Bova and Gaina, 2016: 20). After a review of studies and reports aimed at estimating the number of platform workers O'Farrel and Montagnier (2020) found out the exampels in which rates varies from 0.5% (Norway) to 3% (like Great Britain and Germany). Analysing European Union countries, Pesole et al. (2018) estimated an average of 10% of adults who has ever engaged in provision of services mediated by some kind of platform.

The survey by Forde et al. (2017) listed several problems and concerns of workers involved in the "gig economy." The first is the lack of control over the tasks performed, generating an acute sense of autonomy loss over the realized product. The second is the absence of a career perspective, since it is completely fragmented in the tasks, which also guides the remuneration structure. Also, there is no longer the notion of length of service, relevance development (such as junior, full and senior positions used in some workplaces) or a clear hierarchy in command chains (different levels of management are a way of conferring movement to careers). The third is the payment level. As shown above, the average hourly wage is much below even the country's minimum wages. Finally, workers have shown concern for job security and the protection guarantees in fixed contracts. More than 70% of respondents said they were not entitled to maternity, child and housing benefits.[35]

---

34 As for earnings, the authors' survey respondents worked an average of 23 hours on these tasks, with an average pay of US$6 per hour. This level was much lower than the minimum wages of the countries, with a lag of 54% in France's case.

35 One problem, the authors point out, would be in the identification by the states of these people as workers.

Fontes (2017) sees the labour mediated by platforms within a process of concentration of social production resources in the scope of the capitalist system's transformations. At the same time as there is an extreme concentration and centralization of capital and ownership of social resources of production, an intense labour decentralization occurs. The platforms connect large conglomerates, seeking ways to increase revenues and a mass of workers seeking to ensure their subsistence. These agents articulate capital, means of production, labour force and consumer markets, holding the social resources of production. They do not put an end to labour but accelerate the transformation of the contractual employment relationship into a diffuse type of labour that undermines rights and guarantees.

Graham et al. (2017) interviewed task agency platform workers in African and Asian countries, such as the Philippines, Malaysia, Vietnam, Nigeria, Kenya, and South Africa on the problems experienced in these activities. A first concern expressed was the loss of bargaining power. As platforms seek to escape formal labour relations regulations, workers are treated as individual service providers. Moreover, by operating internationally, platforms can perform an "arbitration," seeking the cheapest workforce wherever it is, at no additional cost, which can lead to a spiral of reduced remuneration and working conditions. This imposed relationship creates fragmentation, attacking the recognition of other individuals in the same position and making it difficult for them to organize themselves to demand better conditions in these areas. A key element for such is these platforms' transnationalization, which makes it complicated to define the rules when dealing with different jurisdictions.

Just as the general analysis of these platforms must consider their diversity, the same goes for discussions on labour relations. Terms that aim to reduce this entire universe to a single arrangement, such as the so-called "uberization of labour" (Fontes [2017], Abilio [2017]), are reductionist. A term that encompasses the worker's relationship with the platform is necessary. The labour of the platforms is that performed directly during their construction and operation, while the labour mediated by these agents takes the labour performed by the participants of the platforms' ecosystems and facilitated by them, but that is not directly related to their development.

5   Competition on Platforms

Since the platforms constitute different economic arrangements from those typical of the twentieth century, based on linear production chains, changes also occur in competition. Although the services and goods offered and the subscription models listed involve the commercialization of products, there are several other forms of revenue generation, including some free-of-charge for the agents (as with the advertising model) or charged through the taxation of transactions and interactions (as in the access model). A central competitive advantage of the platforms is the ability to provide the infrastructure and resources to facilitate these actions. In addressing what he calls electronic information networks, Herscovici (2013) stresses the importance of recognizing specificities beyond traditional models of goods and services provision, such as the multi-sided nature of platforms and models characterized by the sale of audiences to different advertisers, creating an endogenous demand and social utility. To contemplate these arrangements, he proposes the concept of "qualitative competition." In this modality, a reduction of the price variable occurs according to other elements, such as the proposed services' quality.

These differences led to a notion regarding the platforms, as in the digital economy, according to which they would offer ways to increase competition and reduce entry barriers (Ezrachi and Stucke, 2016). In the universe of the digital economy, and especially of digital platforms, some of their aspects impact the dynamics of the agents' dispute, characterized by factors that reinforce dominant positions and make the entry of new agents difficult. The network effects that characterize the platforms, the data control and their ability to establish connections between agents lead to a concentration trend, without eliminating possibilities of countertrends.

5.1   *Business Models*

According to Zhao et al. (2020: 2), the platform business model "identifies transaction partners, establishes the value proposition(s) for each partner, and describes how a focal firm connects to them" and, also, "defines how value is delivered, monetized, and shared among transaction partners." Van Gorp and Batura (2015) list three types of platform business model: subscription, advertising and access. In the subscription model, the user must pay to have access to the service. This can be a general precondition (one can only access the service by hiring it),[36] but it is also possible to combine this model with the free-of-charge model in a hierarchy of ways of providing functionality, rights and content. In these cases, the user can have free access to the service, but on a limited basis and under certain conditions (such as excessive exposure to

---

36   As in the case of pornographic audiovisual content platforms.

ads).[37] To have access to more content and better conditions, the user needs to subscribe to the service.

In the advertising model, platforms generally do not charge for users' access, but they serve ads. This form of advertising has the ability to accurately define a message's target audience, giving the advertiser the ability to filter recipients by a set of criteria, characteristics, interests and behaviours. The large-scale, near-real-time data collection and processing dynamics and the means employed to do so allow websites to identify, in great detail, segments and groups[38] that are susceptible to a certain message, product, or service. Facebook offers all of these possibilities in what they call "personalized audiences."[39] A second difference is the way of capturing the users' attention and engagement.[40]

In the access model, platforms charge a fee or percentage from a provider of a good or service so that it can be offered. In sharing modalities, these agents may be on an equal level (such as in car sharing services, skills exchange or selling a used product), but, in several other cases, professional providers of goods and services (whose main activity is their commercialization) operate, and see in these spaces important sales channels. Aware of this, platforms charge fees or percentages from these providers to serve as virtual shopping malls. In the access model, the focus of monetization is the transaction, more so than the agent's participation (as in the subscription) or the attention of users to product promotion strategies (as in advertising).[41] Increasingly, platforms have been building hybrid models in which they serve as intermediaries and supply channels or offer pre-purchased products (Amazon has migrated from the latter model to include the former).

---

37 Such as the Chinese social networking site Qzone subscription forms, or the premium packages of Spotify or YouTube.

38 However, the platform can go much further under the argument of seeking the effectiveness of its advertising strategies. In 2017, a report revealed that the website offered to advertisers segments of young people in states of emotional fragility (Machkovech, 2017).

39 The platform offers several variables for the targeting of messages. See more at: https://www.facebook.com/business/a/online-sales/ad-targeting-details.

40 In advertising, attention is key, because the business model of this segment works exactly under the logic of marketing customer attention to advertisers (Bolaño, 2000). More than attention, advertising seeks the effectiveness of its messages and the reaction of the audience that translates into sales. On the platforms, the chance of the successful targeting of ads increases with the loss of clear boundaries between advertising and non-advertising content.

41 This is the case, for example, with markets such as eBay or Amazon or application stores such as Apple's App Store or Google's Play App Store.

5.2 Market Structure

The trading and resale platform market represents 10% of the over US$5 trillion retail market, showing that it is still far from replacing the circulation and consumption of goods in physical spaces. However, Nielsen's (2017) projection is for an average growth rate of 20% by 2020, five times higher than the projected pace of sales in general, which should be 4% in the same period. According to Statista's projection, between 2014 and 2021, the amount mobilized by electronic commerce increased from US$1.3 trillion and should reach US$4.48 trillion, a growth of 3.4 times (Statista, 2018b). According to a survey from the same source, in 2016, China's Taobao and the United States' Amazon ruled the market, both with 16% of the market share. Then came the Chinese Tmall (11%), JD (5%) and eBay (4%) (Statista, 2018b). In the study, the category called "rest of the Web" is responsible for 39% of sales. Although the market structure is not as concentrated as in the following modalities, the top five competitors account for more than half of the market (52%). It is worth noting that this is an extremely complex sector, due to the variety of products (often marketed by the e-commerce brands' own services) and their delivery logistics, which increases the costs of a globalized operation.

Although the growth rate is higher, there are still major obstacles to the consumers' purchasing habits. A survey (Nielsen, 2017) indicated that the main resistance factors for adopting online channels were the preference for inspecting the product (69%), concerns as to whether the merchandise is "fresh" (64%) and regarding its quality (62%). If, on the one hand, online commerce represents cost reductions and optimized realization of goods for companies, on the other hand, despite the "advantages" to the consumer (such as no commuting), there are certain products that still require closer contact, such as food and clothing.

In digital social networks, Facebook is the market leader (2.6 billion users), followed by WhatsApp (2 billion), Facebook Messenger (1.3 billion), WeChat (1.2 billion), Instagram (1, 1 billion), TikTok (800 million), QQ (694 million), Sina Weibo (550 million), QZone (517 million), and Reddit (430 million).[42] Considering the advertising market of DSN s, although platforms do not reveal the numbers of advertisers, secondary sources may show evidence of differences in the market. A survey (Bain, 2019) revealed that Facebook is the preferred leader in marketing (more than 1,200 firms were consulted).

---

42 Statista (2020) Most popular social networks worldwide as of July 2020, ranked by number of active users (in millions). Available (consulted 23 September 2020) at: https://www.statista.com/statistics/272014/global-social-networks-ranked-by-number-of-users/.

Considering revenues, it is necessary to use control groups as a comparison unit, which sometimes own more than one DSN. Facebook's dominant position is even more prominent when compared to DSN revenues. In 2016, the company's revenues amounted to US$27.6 billion (from Facebook.com, Facebook Messenger, WhatsApp and Instagram), compared to US$11 billion from Tencent (from Qzone, QQ and WeChat), US$2.5 billion from Twitter, and US$70 million from Tumblr. Facebook's revenue represents 67% of the total among the controllers of the 10 largest SNS (US$27.6 billion of US$41.17 billion).

The operational systems market is quite concentrated. Considering the OSs on desktops in 2020, Microsoft controlled more than 77.21% of share, with Windows, while Apple accounts for 17%, with OSX.[43] In mobile systems, Android has absolute control. Considering web access, connections made through Google's Android OS represent 74.25%; those operating through Apple's iOS amount to 25.15%.[44] In the applications segment, there has been an increase in supply in the last few years. According to the statistics website Statista, the number of apps in Apple's store went from 201,000 in 2010 to 3.1 million in 2017.[45] In the Android operating system's store (Google Play Store), the number of offers increased from 70,000 in 2010 to 3.3 million in 2017.[46] After 150 billion downloads in 2016, the number is estimated to reach 352 billion in 2021.[47] In general, among free apps, the most downloaded are social networks (including messengers): WhatsApp, Facebook, Instagram, Snapchat, and UC Browser (Sensor Tower, 2017).

A ComScore (2017) survey of the US market concluded that half the time spent on digital media is on mobile applications. Of that, half the time is spent on the user's favourite application, and the top 10 apps consume 95% of users' time. In other words, despite the multiplicity of offerings, users concentrate

---

43 Statcounter (2020) Desktop Operating System Market Share Worldwide: aug 2019-aug 2020. Statcounter. Available (consulted by 23 September 2020) at: https://gs.statcounter.com/os-market-share/desktop/worldwide.

44 Statcounter (2020) Mobile Operating System Market Share Worldwide: aug 2019-aug 2020. Statcounter. Available (consulted by 23 September 2020) at: https://gs.statcounter.com/os-market-share/mobile/worldwide.

45 Number of available apps in the iTunes App Store from 2008 to 2017 (in 1,000s). Statistics available at:https://www.statista.com/statistic/268251/number-of-apps-in-the-itunes-app-store-since-2008/.

46 Number of available applications in the Google Play Store from December 2009 to September 2017. Statistics available at: https://www.statista.com/statisTIC/266210/number-of-available-applications-in-the-google-play-store/.

47 Number of mobile app downloads worldwide in 2016, 2017 and 2021 (in billions). Statistics available at: https://www.statista.com/statisTIC/271644/worldwide-free-and-paid-mobile-app-store-downloads/.

their consumption on only a few applications. Considering the economic groups, Facebook is responsible for the top three apps (WhatsApp, Facebook, and Instagram), showing an important position in this market. On platforms for sharing goods, services and activities, there is a more fragmented picture, given its diversity. A study conducted in the United States with more than 50,000 people (Owyang and Samuel, 2015) estimated that 105 million US citizens carried out transactions or collaborative services, representing 51% of the population.[48]

In the private paid transportation sector, Uber, Lyft and other initiatives have taken advantage of the inadequacies of taxi services (such as occasional poor supply, price and access). However, these experiences vary. There are services in which full-time dedication characterizes informal employment, as in Uber, and those announced as rides (BlaBlaCar). The service providers supposedly only monetize on a trip they would already take. Uber operated in 2019 in 69 cities and has reached the milestone of more than 7 billion trips (Uber, 2020). In Q1 2020, it realized 1.6 billion trips (Iqbal, 2020a). In 2020, the US ride-sharing market share was 71% for Uber and 29% for Lyft. The Chinese equivalent, Didi Chuxing, provided, in 2019, more than 10 billion trips and operated in 1,000 cities around the world (Business Wire, 2019).

In the personal services segment, the most used service is Craigslist (65%), followed by Kijiji (22%) and TaskRabbit (6%). In the transport segment, the main one is Uber (86%), followed by Lyft (10%) and Sidecar (3%). In used goods, the first position is occupied by eBay (41%), followed by Kijiji (22%) and Craigslist (20%). For professional services, Craigslist ranks first (38%), followed by Kijiji (20%). In accommodation, the first is Airbnb (55%), followed by VRBO (29%) and Couchsurfing (5%). For learning, Khan Academy (55%) controls the segment. In custom goods, the Etsy platform (91%) has established a monopoly, while, in the crowdfunding segment, Kickstarter (57%) shares the market with Indiegogo (20%) (Owyang and Samuel, 2015).

In content circulation, according to the Alexa internet database,[49] from the Amazon conglomerate, the world's most visited website ranking is dominated by Google, YouTube, TMall, Baidu, QQ, Facebook, Sohu, Taobao, 360.cn and

---

48   The percentage indicates an important growth in relation to the previous year, when people's participation in this form of economy was 39%. In Canada, the rate was higher, 58% in 2015.
49   Information available at: https://www.alexa.com/topsites. Consulted by 23 september 2020.

Yahoo.[50] If we consider the 20 most accessed sites, all of them are platforms except Netflix: two (10%) are from Google/Alphabet (Google.com, YouTube), nine (45%) are American, eleven (55%) are Chinese, two are search engine-centred platforms (Google.com and Baidu), four are e-commerce platforms (Amazon and the Chinese Taobao, Tmall and JD), two are social networks (Facebook, and SinaWeibo), three are content circulation platforms (YouTube, Reddit and Wikipedia), four are multi-service platforms and portals (the Chinese QQ.com, Sohu, 360.ch and Live.com, from Microsoft), one is a news portal (Xinhuanet.com) and one is a video streaming service (Netflix).

The online video market is growing in a substantive manner. According to a study with data from 10 developed countries, the video on-demand market total revenue grew from US$45.7 billion in 2017 to US$60.9 billion in 2020, with a forecast of reaching US$95.9 billion in 2025. In the same period, the number of users increased from 1.18 billion to 1.59 billion and are estimated to reach 1.9 billion by 2025. From 2017 to 2020, penetration rate rose from 16.44 to 20.05. The geographical distribution of market revenue in 2020 was: United States (US$56.67 billion), China (US$35.83 billion), Japan (US$15.77 billion), United Kingdom (US$7.88 billion), and South Korea (US$5.56 billion).[51] In a report showing the video streaming market share of audience demand for digital originals in 2019 worldwide, Netflix was responsible for 61%, followed by Amazon Prime Video (12,4%), Hulu (7,6%), DC Universe (4,9%), and CBS All Access (3,8%).[52]

The absolute leader in number of users is YouTube, with 2 billion users (Spangler, 2019). In 2019, it was the app with the fifth-largest gross revenue (App Annie, 2019). However, this number does not necessarily represent a diversity within the platform. A survey by Tubular (2017) revealed that 24% of content creators are responsible for 71% of views. On Facebook, the percentage is even higher: 26% of producers earn 77% of views. On both platforms, the companies with the highest number of views are Buzzfeed (4.2 billion on Facebook and 703 million on YouTube), LADbible (4.2 million on Facebook and 2.3 million on YouTube), Unilad (4 million on Facebook and 2.7 million on YouTube), Jungle Creations (4 million on Facebook and 9 thousand on YouTube) and Time Warner (1.9 million on Facebook and 1.3 million on YouTube) (Tubular, 2017). If we consider the number of subscribers, the most

---

50   Platforms that are perhaps less known, such as Baidu and QQ, have a large access volume because they serve the market of the most populated country in the world, China (also including migrant communities living in foreign countries).
51   Statista (2020, July) Digital Market Outlook.
52   Statist (2020) Neflix Dossier.

popular channels on YouTube are PewDiePie (58 million), YouTube Movies (54.1 million), HolaSoyGerman (32.6 million), JustinBieberVevo (32 million) and T-Series (28.7 million).[53] In paid video streaming, Netflix is the specialized paid service that stands out.

Between 2011 and 2016, while the number of program minutes fell on the main stations in the United States (such as NBC Universal, Disney, 21st Century Fox and Time Warner), on Netflix, it increased by 669% (Meeker, 2017). In a survey by TIVO (2017) with viewers in the United States and Canada, Netflix was the most popular subscription on demand video service (53.6%), followed by Amazon Video (21.6%), Hulu (15.7%) and HBO Now (5.6%). Among the reasons for this are the possibility of creating individual profiles (58.9%), the price (56%), the autoplay feature, which produces the following episodes automatically (46.4%) and the search engine (44.5%). The survey also revealed the high penetration of this type of service in this region: 94% said they were subscribers of one of the companies in the market. Netflix is the main paid streaming video service. In the US, the number of subscribers rose from 20 million in 2011 to 72 million in 2020.[54]

In audio, the rise of digital music had an even more devastating effect. In 2006, revenue from CD sales and other physical units totalled US$16.3 billion, against US$2.1 billion from digital formats (IFPI, 2017). Ten years later, revenues from physical media had fallen to US$5.4 billion and those from the digital segment had reached US$7.8 billion, representing 50% of the sector's total turnover. In 2016, these revenues increased 5.9% over the previous year. At first, in the 2000s, music downloading sites prevailed. More recently, as in video, streaming has gained popularity. In 2016, the segment's income growth was 60%, ten times greater than the average performance of the recording industry (IFPI, 2017). In 2019, the device share was: 29% for radio, 27% for smartphones, 19% for desktops and laptops, 8% for turntables and 4% for other mobile devices (IFPI, 2019). The music purchasing was reported by 29% of interviewees.

According to the IFPI report, 89% of listeners used on-demand streaming services, with 64% in the month before the interviews spending four hours each week (IFPI, 2019). The main reasons to opt for this type of platform is access to a diversity of songs (62%), the possibility to listen to what the user wants, when they want to (61%) and convenience (47%). Spotify appears as the main platform specialized in paid audio streaming. Between 2010 and

---

53 Information available at: <https://socialblade.com/youtube/>.
54 Statista (2020) Number of Netflix paying streaming subscribers in the United States from 3rd quarter 2011 to 2nd quarter 2020 (in millions). Statista.

2016, the company went from 0 to 60 million subscribers, reaching 130 million premium subscribers in 2020 (Iqbal, 2020b). In 2019, the companies with the largest music streaming shares were Spotify, with 35%, Apple Music, with 19%, Amazon Prime Music, with 15%, Tencent, with 11%, YouTube, with 6% and others, with 14%.[55] When considering free music streaming, YouTube was the most popular, with 77% of listeners using the platform that year (IFPI, 2019).

5.3 Competitive Strategies

If analysing levels is important in all economic sectors, it is even more relevant concerning platforms, given the argument that these agents would configure a way to increase competition and reduce entry barriers. In Chapter 1, we reviewed some literature on the positive nature of a competitive economic environment. In the digital economy, and especially among digital platforms, some of these aspects impact the competition dynamics, characterized by factors that reinforce dominant positions and make the entry of new agents difficult. Van Gorp and Batura (2015) highlight two phenomena in this sector: the network effects characteristic of digital services lead to a trend towards concentration, but the possibilities of using different routes to offer services create countertrends to challenge the market powers of certain agents. In this universe, value networks are constituted.[56] These would be an interconnected set companies hat make up a network of services and assets (which can include content, applications, portals), each one being a node. The different combinations of these nodes make room for the different routes to offer digital services. Van Gorp and Batura (2015) identify problems arising from concentration of ownership. The user base's growth may lead to a platform's dominant market position, raising it to the condition of "gatekeeper" in the segment. They occupy the decision-making and organization position of network flows in key "locations" that constitute "control points" of the web: as search engines for information (Google, Bing, DuckDuckGo), digital social networks for monitoring events (Facebook, WeChat, Twitter), operating systems as a technological basis (Android, iOS), browsers as a gateway to websites (Chrome, Safari), application stores as spaces for accessing apps (Play Store, Apple Store), and portals as page aggregators (MSN.com, Yahoo.com). Under this condition, in the absence of interoperability, users are unlikely to leave or exchange the platform for another. The more indispensable it becomes, the greater its ability

---

55 Statista (2020 Share of music streaming subscribers worldwide in 2019, by company. Statista. Available (Consulted by 26 September) at: https://www.statista.com/statistics/653926/music-streaming-service-subscriber-share/.

56 A term used to the detriment of the well-known value chain concept.

to influence the market as a whole and the greater the risks to competition. In other words, the active condition of their mediation, as discussed earlier, impacts not only the mediated activities but the market structure itself.

One competitive practice is 'defensive leveraging,' which consists of ensuring an attained monopoly. This can happen through acquisitions or by establishing barriers or obstacles.[57] Another strategy is to take advantage of dominant positions to advance in other markets through various mechanisms, such as those mentioned above.[58] These movements are manifested in what we call here "expansion strategies," a key element in the competitive performance of digital platforms. Horizontal expansion, for example, is a phenomenon not restricted to platforms, but quite common in this environment. It can happen in several ways. Amazon began as an e-business space for books and has embraced new products and services. Twitter originally did not have its own image and video posting services and acquired them to expand the content circulation possibilities on the timelines. Google may be the greatest example, in its journey from originally being a search engine to becoming a platform with email, calendar, file storage, chat, group messaging and other features. The platform can expand its reach through partnerships, such as the one between Facebook and Microsoft for online advertising in the early years of Mark Zuckerberg's company.

A second strategy is incorporation, in which the company acquires other players in the same market. This can be done horizontally (acquiring another agent operating in the same market) but it can also be done vertically (acquiring an agent from another stage of the production chain, such as infrastructure or input manufacturer). It can also be a crossed strategy (a combination of both properties).[59] This type of initiative may be either motivated to expand the original product or to contain possible competitors. Facebook's acquisition of Instagram and WhatsApp, as we will see in Chapter 7, is a classic examples, as is Snapchat's refusal to follow the same path and become another arm of this digital social network. However, the incorporation methods are not always

---

57 An already-mentioned example is Facebook's acquisition of Instagram and WhatsApp. Another was the purchase of the online advertising company Double Click by Google in 2007. Both cases will be detailed in Chapters 6 and 7.
58 Microsoft has done this to try to introduce its own software in several segments. In 2000, the European Commission opened an investigation to examine whether the company promoted anti-competitive practices by pre-installing Windows Media Player on all Windows operating systems.
59 Here, we refer to the typological framework in the literature on mergers and acquisitions, which defines these two strategies as horizontal and vertical acquisition modalities (Abbas et al., 2014).

the same. In WhatsApp's acquisition, Facebook opened a channel to listen to the users on whether or not the two applications' data should be combined, without imposing a more obvious synergy. Facebook Messenger, on the other hand, remains an independent application, but its operation takes place inside the Facebook interface.

A third strategy involves forms of integration among companies, products and services of the same group, beyond the mere horizontal or vertical expansion described in the first strategy. In the horizontal mode, the platform owner benefits from controlling the goods and services offered on one side. This is the case of Microsoft with the Windows operating system and with programs it produces, such as Office. A vertical integration occurs when a controller owns different sides and integrates them, as well as steps in the production chain. This process occurs with Apple. The company is responsible for the iOS operating system, for a significant part of the applications, and it also manufactures devices (iMac, iPhone). The integration does not occur only by controlling several stages of the product chain, but by an 'enclosure' and exclusive connection among these stages. In this example, iOS can only be run on an Apple device and Apple devices can only have iOS as an operating system. The same goes for a set of the company's applications, such as iTunes. Apple's competitors, such as Samsung, also use this strategy by providing a set of mandatory applications that cannot be handled or uninstalled (such as music, voice recording, file management, and other applications). Vertical integration can occur by combining the online and offline worlds. The Dutch e-commerce platform Bol.com now uses Albert Heijn supermarkets as its distribution network. Amazon has partnered with several logistics companies for its deliveries, such as UPS, FedEX and the US Post Office. The company has also partnered with the British supermarket chain Morrisons to offer its premium users products available in the chain's stores.

However, the largest digital platforms now employ a fourth strategy, which we call here diversification of activities. This happens when an agent includes in its operations activities different from the one that first defined its creation and growth. This movement is related to what is called product extension mergers or conglomerates in the literature on mergers and acquisitions (Abbas et al., 2014). However, this strategy does not happen only in mergers and acquisitions. It can also happen in situations such as when Facebook acquired Oculus to enter the virtual and augmented reality market. But it goes beyond that, since these platforms can develop new activities from their technological production capacity, from the user base (and the inputs extracted from it) and from their reach from the connected sides and their performance in the online environment.

6 Digital Monopolies

These combined strategies and the influence in making use of the diversification of activities gave rise to a phenomenon referred to here as digital monopolies. These are conglomerates that have acquired a strongly dominant presence in a sector, but who have started to operate beyond it, based on the exercise of power from their technological basis, which we refer to as "technological power." The term "monopolies" is not used here as a market structure, as commonly applied in the economic and antitrust literature. The object of this debate is rooted in the sociological perspective, but with an intense interdisciplinary debate that characterizes this work. However, it refers to a phenomenon whose protagonists are large digital platforms based on their more recent moves.

They are digital, as their business is strongly focused on ICTs and this informational support. The use of the adjective 'digital' is always risky, given its exhausting use, in examples as digital world, digital economy, digital work forces. The digital, as already seen, is a base for information flows in the twenty-first century's capitalism. However, despite this risk and the lack of rigor in using this term, the adjective is used here as a necessary and adequate element of the proposed concept. It is a phenomenon not only restricted to the internet, although the latter is its main stage. It is also not only a process in the information and communication iechnology industries, although these provide its technical basis and the basis from which it exerts its power. The dissemination of digital monopolies involves exactly their capacity, intention or attempt to reach more diverse branches of the economy and human experiences. The digital is becoming[60] more and more intricate and assuming a supporting position regarding how our activities are digitalized and computerized, combining the online and offline environments.

A set of characteristics denotes the phenomenon of digital monopolies. The first is the strong dominance of a niche market. These large corporations are based on solid foundations in a previously dominated segment in which they assume a monopolistic position. This is the case with Google in search engines, Microsoft in desktop operating systems, Facebook in digital social networks, and Amazon in book e-commerce. The exception is Apple. Although it has no market share above 50 per cent, it has a strong influence, due to its global

---

60   It is always essential to remember that there are still considerable portions of the world population without access to these technologies. More than 2 billion people do not have a smartphone and more than 3 billion people do not have access to the Web (We Are Social, 2019).

weight and market valuation. This market dominance is fundamental for the companie's expansion. It provided revenues for a robust expansion and essential inputs, such as personal data managed by Google and Facebook or computers whose entry port is commanded by Microsoft and a giant buyer registry from Amazon.

Associated with this, a second feature is their large user base. These conglomerates operate with hundreds of millions or billions of users. Facebook counts 2.6 billion users of its FB platform and 2 billion of WhatsApp. Amazon has 310 million customers (51% of US households were Prime subscribers in 2018). Apple's customer base amounts to 1.3 billion (Nellis, 2018). Considering volume, the major Chinese platforms also stand out, despite these numbers being related to that country's large population. Tencent has more than 1 billion users with its WeChat digital social network. The e-commerce platform Alibaba has almost 500 million customers. Google has more than 2.3 billion smartphones with Android (Van Der Wielen, 2018).

A fourth feature is the global scale operation. Despite a slower pace in some platforms' internationalization, such as Amazon, others already have services worldwide. The user bases that account for billions of users are the central indicator in this sense. For platforms that trade goods (such as Amazon, Apple, and Microsoft), the global reach is more complex, but even so, these platforms succeed. In addition to resellers, Apple had its own stores in 25 countries in 2018 (Farfan, 2018). Even for those offering services directly over the internet, there are important demands for a global reach, such as language. For example, Facebook was already available in more than 100 languages in 2016 (Guynn, 2016). Google has its own domains in more than 200 countries.[61]

A fourth feature is a spread to other segments besides the original niche. This aspect is at the phenomenon's core, since it distinguishes these agents precisely by their capacity to perform, with quality and speed, the strategy of the diversification of activities. Microsoft, initially a software company (including the Windows operating system), now offers electronic game consoles (Xbox), intelligent lenses (Hololens), computers (Surface), and services for companies (such as the Azure artificial intelligence-based development platform or the Intune management platform). Amazon sells a wide range of products, owns a work agency platform (Mechanical Turk), recently launched automated convenience stores, and entered the food market by purchasing the Wholefoods network. Apple has entered the audiovisual content production segment and

---

61   Information available at: <http://www.genealogyintime.com/articles/country-guide-to-google-search-engines-page1.html>.

the payment media market with Apple Pay. Facebook and Google also operate beyond their original niche, as will be discussed in the following chapters.

A fifth feature is the development of data-intensive activities. The large user base, technology-based services, the growing logic of customization and the importance of using data to anticipate demands and reduce uncertainties in the realization of products and services has caused these groups to expand their collection and to develop new solutions and products that would intensify such monitoring, in a dataveillance spiral regarding their users. This is because the control of these large databases is a distinguishing feature of these agents, compared to their competitors. The more data about the user, the higher the ability to recommend products that can be acquired, which makes the platforms more successful in their markets (such as Amazon in selling products or Google and Facebook in advertising sales). Also, record control operates not only on the logic of knowledge but, also, on prediction and modulation of behaviour, giving these platforms enormous power over their customers. Thus, they can anticipate demands and launch new services.

A sixth characteristic is the control of an ecosystem of agents that develop services and goods mediated by their platforms and activities. If a platform's distinctive feature means controlling the intermediation of communications, interactions, and transactions, this is not only an important feature for the power of digital monopolies, but for the control and conditioning of relationships, a clear example of the active mediation mentioned above. Historically, Microsoft has operated under this logic through its pre-installed software on Windows. The Google Play Store and the Apple App Store also do it with applications for mobile devices. By offering the means to connect with consumers, these platforms impose the rules of these transactions, as they do in the interactions between producers and content consumers (such as Amazon Prime Video or YouTube).

A seventh and final feature involves the acquisition or equity control strategies of competitors or market players. This is a traditional feature in capitalist competition, where mergers may occur within markets themselves (horizontal), at different stages of the production chain (vertical), among companies that produce similar products but in different markets, or among companies in the product extension line (Abbas et al., 2014), which we refer to here as the diversification of activities strategy. Microsoft has a long list of acquisitions, such as GitHub in 2018, LinkedIn in 2016, and Skype in 2011. Apple purchased the Shazam app in 2018 or the Siri virtual assistant in 2010. Amazon acquired the Whole Foods supermarket chain in 2018 (for US$13 billion) and the Twitch sports streaming service in 2014. The Google and Facebook cases will be discussed in the following chapters.

In digital monopolies, these characteristics are combined in different ways. The phenomenon highlighted here implies a new form of technology development and logic to implement innovations in the market, with a much more agile ability to identify demands, to reach a critical mass during the growth phases (Hughes, 1993), to reinforce success conditions by exercising technological power through the articulation of other services of the platform and the capacity to employ data and a technological basis in a cumulative and scalable manner. The importance of the economic dimension given by the technological regulation model is shown here not only in this production logic, but, also, in the importance of the position and strategies in the competition of these agents according to the success conditions or solutions or even new technological systems launched in the market.

More than merely an effect of these competitive strategies, the digital monopolies phenomenon is characterized, as already explained, by the spread of these conglomerates to new segments and markets. |Due to the centrality they have gained in various social activities, they expand their mediation logics through the exercise of technological power. Apple, which mediated an ecosystem of applications around its operating system and its store, expanded its active mediation to the content universe with Apple TV and with the launch of its own news aggregation service. Amazon also expanded its mediating action into the labour sphere with Amazon Mechanical Turk. Thus, more than an active mediation, digital monopolies operate an expansion to new branches of the social spheres of activity.

Now we offer synthesis of the concept presented here, according to which digital monopolies could be understood as a phenomenon by which large digital platforms start from a market power conquered in certain niches, take advantage of certain conditions (such as a large number of users, global performance, and their technological basis), and employ certain strategies (such as control of an ecosystem of agents and businesses, incorporation of competitors) to diversify their activities into new segments, operating an expansive mediation over new social practices and amplifying their market power in both original and new segments.

7 Legislation and the Debate on Legal Regulation

This section does not attempt to make an extensive presentation about global legislation,[62] which would not even be possible within the limits of this work,

---

62 A fairly complete and comprehensive mapping can be found at: <https://wilmap.law.stanford.edu>.

especially considering the diversity of the conglomerate's operating areas and the number of countries where it provides services. Our intention here is to provide central points to indicate the scenario where the objects of the investigation operate, as well as the emerging debate on the need for legal regulation (understood as its ordinary meaning, related to laws and administrative rules). We identify the following as the main areas and objects of legislation concerning digital platforms (and Google): (1) data protection and privacy, (2) copyright, and (3) management, monitoring and removal of content.[63] At the international level, platform regulation has become an agenda for governments, business sectors, scholars, and civil society. Telecom operators, dissatisfied with platform competition for similar services (such as voice-over IP or streaming), demand the regulation of what they called OTT (over-the-top) services or the deregulation of traditional sectors to balance competition. They have promoted an offensive in countries and international bodies, such as the International Telecommunications Union. At the 2018 ITU conference, a resolution was passed, affirming these agents' interdependence and a breakthrough in the debate.

Governments have already begun to see the centrality of this agenda.[64] At the 2018 Global Internet Governance Forum, the President of France, Emanuel Macron, launched a joint document with governments and civil society organizations entitled the "Call of Paris" (French Republic, 2018). In it, he presented a complex plan for disciplining services as an alternative to what he calls the bipolar division of geopolitics between two internet models, one linked to the United States (with total freedom for large private conglomerates) and the other to China (strongly controlled by the government). The document highlights the need for open, secure, stable, and accessible cyberspace. It points out that international and national legislation in the offline world should apply to online environments, including human rights guarantees. The text states the following: "We recognize the responsibilities of key private sector actors in improving trust, security and stability in cyberspace" (French Republic, 2018: 2). Such guarantees involve fighting threats, cyber offensives, and malicious practices, such as attempts to interfere in electoral processes.

The United Nations rapporteur for freedom of expression has released a report on the regulation of third-party content on internet platforms (Kaye, 2018). He raised concerns about exaggerated demands, censorship, or the

---

63   A fourth item would be competition rules, but these are still in the early stages of national legislation and will, therefore, not be addressed here.
64   As they have already done with the digital economy as a whole, as indicated in the Introduction.

criminalization of legislation and governments in monitoring and removing publications under justifications such as fighting extreme messages, violence, abuse, or fake news. There are several types of posts, monitoring methods, and accountability modes. The rapporteur pointed out that several ordinances have exempted intermediaries from punishment for third-party statements, as shown below. He stressed the complex challenge of balancing fair motivations (such as privacy and national security) with non-interference with the freedom of expression of those posting on these platforms. On the other hand, the excessive power of private actors to decide what may or may not be published (whether by legal or administrative mandate or by the companies' own decision, based on their terms of use) also brings risks. In the second case, the lack of transparency in internal rules and in content management and removal methods, vague prohibitions (such as extreme content, harassment, abuse), limits on automated systems, the lack of explanation and remedies after the overthrow, the challenge of context in content analysis, and the difficulty of identifying disinformation, among other factors, may result in censorship and various forms of reducing the freedom of expression (such as silencing dissenting groups and minorities). Kaye (2018) advocates adopting human rights parameters in content moderation to avoid state abuse and the negative impacts of private regulation.

Moving towards international legislation focused on data protection and privacy, the main innovation was the entry into force in 2018 of the European Union's General Data Protection Regulation (GDPR). It updated the previous directive establishing a set of new obligations for those who collect and process data on the continent and from European citizens outside it, such as getting consent to obtain data from a specific holder through requests in a clear and accessible manner, ensuring the right to cancellation. Other requirements include notifying users in cases of leaks, communicating when data are processed, the purpose and how this occurs, and implementing measures in technical design to promote the protection of information (privacy by design). In its 2017 report, Alphabet (Google conglomerate) recorded that these new requirements "could cause us to change our business practices and will increase financial penalties for non-compliance significantly" (2018: 7). The prediction quickly came true. In January 2019, the French data protection authority (CNIL) imposed the maximum fine of 50 million euro on Google for not respecting the stipulations to obtain users' consent for the use of their data in the ad customization, as well as for failing to provide clear information on how the records are handled, the purposes and the scope.

In Latin America, Brazil was the nation with the most recent legislation passed in 2018, which came into force in 2020. The Brazilian General Data

Protection Law (LGPD) was inspired by elements of European legislation, but with its own wording. In addition to defining personal data as including the identifiable records of a person and instituting the category of sensitive data (such as racial and ethnic origin, religious beliefs, or political opinion), it set out the possibilities for data processing by companies and public institutions. The latter have gained greater flexibility. The former imposed obligations, such as ensuring data security, informing the purpose of processing and obtaining consent from the data subject, among others. The loopholes for abuse lie in exceptions, such as the figure of "legitimate interest" (when the controller uses the data for a purpose other than that for which it was collected). According to a Google executive at the time the law was formulated, in Europe, before the GDPR, 80% of the legal basis for treatment was derived from "legitimate interests," with consent being a tiny fraction (Microfocus, 2018). The law also established users' rights, such as that to require a company to disclose the data that it possesses on them, as well as to whom they were passed and for what purpose. It is also possible to request adjustments if any registration is incorrect, and to oppose certain types of treatment. The law has ensured the right to portability and specific rules for children, such as the need to obtain consent from parents or tutors. The application of sanctions, such as fines, was delegated to the version approved by Congress. A data protection authority was established, but in a later provisional measure, it was undermined due to its independent nature and submitted to the federal government.

Other countries in the region also have laws on this issue. Chile was one of the first countries to pass data protection legislation, which it did in 1999. This legislation also includes the personal and sensitive data categories, in addition to establishing the need for consent to the processing, but, also, makes exceptions, as in the case of collection from sources accessible to the public, by private legal entities for their own use or by public bodies. Rights are also listed, such as the right to correct incorrect information. The law provides for penalties, such as indemnification, but does not provide an authority to inspect and apply them (Viollier, 2017). The United States is a reference model, but differs from European and Latin American experiences in its fragmented regulatory framework, with specific legislation for segments or audiences, such as health (Health Insurance Portability and Accountability Act, 1996), financial services (Right to Financial Privacy Act), electronic communications (Electronic Communications Privacy Act, 1986), or children (Children's Online Privacy Protection Act). The first establishes security obligations in medical records, as well as reporting requirements in the event of a leak, and sets situations where consent is required and where it is not. The second protects citizens from unreported access by authorities to bank records, for example. The third prohibits the interception of telephone or electronic communications. The fourth works with a co-regulatory logic, in which companies can submit codes of conduct to the country's trade authority (FTC) that become binding. The Privacy Act of 1974, on the other hand, regulates the performance of federal agencies in the collection, storage, and processing of personal data. There is no data protection authority, and supervision and sanctions are carried out by the authorities in each area (Guidi, 2018).

Copyright laws are a second important set of rules, as they involve holding platforms accountable for the content of third parties circulating within them. These were seen as a gateway to piracy, but the combination of stricter regulations and content removal mechanisms from large content producers has reduced criticism somewhat. In the United States, the Communications Decency Act of 1996 created a paradigm not only for copyright, but, also, for third-party content in general by stating that platforms (then called intermediaries) were not responsible for them. In the field of copyright specifically, the primary law on the subject in the country (Digital Millennium Copyright Act – DMCA), from 1998, works in the same direction by exempting some types of intermediaries (among these, the search engines) from liability for copyright infringement if they meet some conditions. Among these are the non-receipt of revenues arising from illegal content and the implementation of ways of receiving notices to overturn content framed in this type of violation (a model that came to be known in the sector as 'notice and take down'). This model has inspired other legal frameworks, such as is the case of South Korea.[65] However, the law of that country provides a mechanism for notifying the author of the content indicated as infringing and a reposting mechanism if the author proves that the content was in accordance with the legislation. The rule also establishes obligations to provide information about the alleged violator to the complainant.

The European Union approved, between 2018 and 2019, a reform of its copyrights directive with important impacts on digital platforms and achievements for media companies and content producers (publishers). In its Article 13, the new rule established the responsibility of intermediaries for published content and the obligation to implement mechanisms to monitor and overturn publications that infringe copyrights, which includes both cultural works and journalistic texts by media outlets. Platforms (called information society service providers) can purchase work licenses, thus avoiding accountability. According to Reda (2019), the measure will result in the implementation of filtering in the

---

65   Information available at: <https://wilmap.law.stanford.edu/topics/copyright-0>.

publication of content, making room for the censorship of texts, images, and videos. In Article 11, taxation by links for materials protected by copyrights was established. To publish "more than a few words or a short extract" of a piece of news, the intermediary or website must acquire a license. This obligation is not graded by company size, affecting sites and personal profiles. During the proposal elaboration, the changes were criticized by scholars and civil society organizations[66] (Civil Liberties Union for Europe et al., 2017).

The controversy surrounding the European copyright directive highlights a third set of standards related to message management, monitoring, and removal. The directive already points in this direction but includes only those publications protected by copyright. However, regarding the set of messages circulating within digital platforms, the last years of the 2010s were characterized by intense controversy. The power of digital platforms was at the heart of these controversies, as well as their role in the dissemination of disinformation, which affected several countries in the world. In Brazil, the Brazilian Civil Rights Framework for the Internet established a mixed regime. The platform or website can be held responsible if it does not obey a judicial order. Thus, neither a private agent nor an authority can request the exclusion of a publication (except for any case of disclosure of sexual content without the consent of the victim). However, the law does not prohibit application providers from excluding content according to their terms of use.

One law that generated international debate was the German Network Enforcement Act (also known as NetzDG). It imposed several obligations on application providers (telemedia service providers), especially the monitoring of illegal content (including fake news and hate speech) and its removal in up to 24 hours for more blatant violations and a week for less obvious violations. The rule brings a set of transparency requirements from service providers regarding the publication of moderation and content withdrawal reports. It also creates mechanisms for notification and for authors to appeal to overturn the censorship of communications. Fines can reach up to 20 million euros. Journalists' and freedom of expression organizations have criticized the rule (Reporters Without Borders, 2018). Within Macron's agenda of regulating the internet, France passed legislation in November 2018 that allows judges to order the immediate removal of posts considered fake news in elections. Also, platforms and other content must account

---

66   "Article 13 appears to provoke such legal uncertainty that online services will have no other option than to monitor, filter and block EU citizens' communications if they are to have any chance of staying in business." (Civil Liberties Union for Europe et al., 2017, n.p.).

for resources received to promote information. Opponents criticized the approval, pointing out that it gives the state the power of being "thought police" (Florentino, 2018).

Russia passed an amendment to the Information, Information Technology and Protection of Information Act in 2018 that allowed court officials to block access to sites that failed to delete information after a court has identified such information as having discredited the honour of an individual or the reputation of a public institution. In 2014, another amendment to the aforementioned act established that owners with sites with more than 3,000 visitors per day should refrain from using the site for illegal activity, should maintain correct information, provide contacts, as well as empower the national authority in the area to request information about those responsible for these sites. In China, the Cybersecurity Law, passed in 2016, criminalizes content that undermines the socialist system or spreads false information that disturbs the social or economic order, also holding platforms and application providers responsible (Conger, 2016). Malaysia gained notoriety for passing a law that imposed up to six years in prison, in addition to a fine, for people convicted of disseminating false information, including foreigners in the country. The law covered both media outlets and digital social networks.

This chapter aimed at narrowing down the discussion on the factors regarding the regulation of technology by establishing an overview of digital platforms, introducing the relevance of the phenomenon, discussing its definitions in the literature and presenting our own contribution, developing the central characteristics, establishing a typology to understand the specificities of this complex and heterogeneous object, mapping the market(s) of each of these specific manifestations and addressing the dynamics of competition and labour relations within it. Thus, we have defined the universe that motivates the discussion of this work. We have established elements for its understanding and have delimited the scope from which we will proceed by observing case studies on Google and Facebook.

So far, this work has discussed the issue of technology, contextualized the recent development of the capitalist system, and its relationship with the sector addressed here – information and communication technologies. We have listed its dialectic relationship and the structural factors of regulation over technology, mapped the technological paradigm of this area with its factors of regulation of technology, and included the general characterization of our object – digital platforms – showing its distinctive features and pointing out its constitutive elements as commodities under capitalism. In the next two chapters, the concrete cases of Google and Facebook and their historical development will be examined. The discussion of these two examples is based on the references used throughout the work regarding technology and digital platforms.

We will outline the general technological background of these platforms, presenting a periodization. We will identify representative examples of the external and internal rules that govern them. Since they are conglomerates, we will enter their control and management structure, identifying the groups (and individuals) of interest that define the system's destination. Also in this economic dimension, their production process will be examined (along with the consequent labour relations and the manufacturing procedures of the design of products and services) as well as their performance in the market, focusing on the system's performance in the competition, either from their business model, their financial performance, or participation in competition and competitive strategies. Then, their components and technical resources will be mapped as a way to understand the anatomy of these technological systems and their relationship with their other aspects and regulatory factors.

The understanding must also include these technological systems' reach in society (considering not only their scope, but, also, how the various meaning systems conform to their legitimacy with regard to different interest groups). More than a quantitative phenomenon, their objectives and content are mediated by the forms of appropriation, which will be debated based on interviews with different types of users. Representatives of different types of audiences that relate to the analysed platforms were interviewed:

1) Public entities: a network publisher of the National Council of Justice (Respondent 1) and a social network coordinator of TV Câmara (Respondent 2);
2) Political and party associations and campaigns: a specialist in political marketing with majority and proportional campaigns (Respondent 3) and a communications coordinator of a large political party (Respondent 4);
3) Advertising agencies with digital operations: a planning director of a large digital agency (Respondent 5) and a vice president of media of a large digital agency (Respondent 6);
4) Researchers: A researcher in a research institute on data analysis with national operations (Respondent 7) and a researcher in a research institute on technology and society with national operations (Respondent 8);
5) Developers: a developer of solutions for campaigns and entities (Respondent 9) and a developer working on a mobility app (Respondent 10);
6) Media: a senior executive of one of the main media groups in the country (Respondent 11) and a coordinator of web media in a country town (Respondent 12);

7) Civil Society Organizations: a technology analyst dealing with privacy in an international organization (Respondent 13) and a coordinator of an NGO with national and international operations in the subject (Respondent 14);
8) Leaders in governments and parliaments: a former senior federal government official (Respondent 15) and a congressman with a strong background in data protection legislation (Respondent 16);
9) Non-professional users: a student from Curitiba (PR) (Respondent 17), a university student from Pelotas (RS) (Respondent 18), a commercial representative from São Paulo (SP) (Respondent 19), an independent seller from Paracatu (MG) (Respondent 20), a teacher from Crateús (CE) (Respondent 21), a student from Salvador (BA) (Respondent 22), a cultural producer from Belém (PA) (Respondent 23), a legal advisor from a public entity from Macapá (AP) (Respondent 24), a professional musician from Goiânia (GO) (Respondent 25), and a student from Barra do Garças (MT) (Respondent 26).

After considering the social and specific regulating factors, as well as the content and these implementation methods, we conclude with the third dimension of technological regulation, underlining the impacts of the technological system according to the value base and in the social spheres of activity listed in Chapter 2: scientific–technological, economic, political–institutional and cultural.

CHAPTER 6

Google

Google emerged as a search engine in 1998. Introna and Nissenbaum (2000) described it as a "powerful source of web access and accessibility."[1] Trielli and Diakopoulos (2019: 1) define it as a "powerful intermediary, both in exposing audiences to news information and assisting them in making sense of it." The complex work of organizing massive volumes of information was seen since the beginning by Google's founders as a quest that would demand sophisticated solutions. Search "is a really hard problem. To do a perfect job, you would need to understand all the world's information, and the precise meaning of every query. With all that understanding, you would then have to produce the perfect answer instantly" (Page, 2007, n.p.). These systiems have generally been structured into four artefacts, or features. The first is the network data search, which can be done by scanning the available pages. The second involves storing this information in a database. The third is the mechanism for selecting the results from the presented demand. The fourth is the interface from which users send their request (Ippolita, 2007). By being able to track and offer information to users' demands, these search engines have assumed a key position on the internet, since they have become the organizing locus for information traffic on the web. Therefore, they are intermediaries as platforms. Search engines, especially Google, promote active mediation, mentioning one of the distinctive features of the platform concept adopted here. Diaz (2008) defines them as "gatekeepers" of cyberspace. By understanding such systems as intermediaries, he characterizes them as the web's main "general interest intermediary."

Pasquale (2015) highlights that the search affects not only our perception of the internet, but of the real world. More than just offering answers, search engines evaluate and rank information, organizing it according to relevance and presenting it hierarchically to users. They are "guides" that influence the formation of world views, decisions, and attitudes, such as shopping, voting,

---

[1] Introna and Nissenbaum indicated the policy behind these engines and how they organized information flows as the "broader fight" concerning the level of democracy on the internet. Indexing and ranking were already essential filters for visibility and access by audiences. Under the internet's logic, it was not enough to create and post content. It was also necessary to reach audiences, to be seen, to get attention.

and the like. These technological systems are spaces not only for offering answers and knowledge, but, also, for uniquely modulating the world's perception, based on customized results. The ability to manage such information leads to power concentration, as Pasquale (2015: 61) states: "The power to include, exclude, and rank is the power to ensure which public impressions become permanent and which remain fleeting." Mager (2016) states that search engines often assume the condition of web access points. They operate according to a logic of "algorithmic ideology," incorporating the capitalist ideology (Mager, 2017). In the previous chapter, we presented the concept of a 'control point,' which seems more appropriate, since Google is not only an access point, but it also controls online information flows and experiences. Haider and Sundin (2019) observe that search became widely used and people have stopped noticing it. Search engines became key infrastructures for knowing and obtaining all sorts of information. They are, at the same time, dispersed in a variety of social activities and centralised commercially and technically. Google is the centre of this centralized system.

Google has established itself based on this logic. The company's mission was defined as "to organize the world's information and make it available to everyone,"[2] based on the principle that "information serves everyone, not just a few" (Alphabet, 2018: 9). To "organize the world's information," one had first to have access to "the world's information" and then be able to order it. The first obstacle was faced with a system browsing the entire internet. Through it, information is compressed and stored in servers (Brin and Page, 1998), which gather it in a repository.[3] In an effort to try to provide as much information as possible, some information is not available. Therefore, it must be produced (Page, 2007).

The second challenge was its organization. A concept promoted by the company's directors is that of 'relevance.': "Our search team also works very hard on relevance – getting you exactly what you want, even when you aren't sure what you need" (Page, 2005, n.p.). This was sought by a series of strategies in the TS architecture.[4] Founders Brin and Page (1998) highlighted two attributes of Google. The first was reading the link structure to calculate a "quality ranking."

---

2 Information available at: <https://www.google.com/search/howsearchworks/mission/>.
3 Each one gets an ID. From them, an index is created which is decoded using different resources (such as anchors) to provide answers to the searches made and offer the pages according to the ranking. The company's trackers collect information from "hundreds of billions" of pages.
4 As will be presented later, as in the example of customization mechanisms.

This was called "PageRank,"[5] an algorithm characterized by the company as one of its "most valuable assets" (*SearchKing vs. Google*, 2003).[6] However, throughout history, such computing has become sophisticated, incorporating several other factors. In 2007 alone, 359 changes were implemented in the system, almost one per day (Brin, 2008). At the end of the day, Batelle (2011) notes, the "holy grail" of search is to decipher the real intention of the user asking the questions. It is more about understanding than about quick answers to the demands made. Former Google Vice President Marissa Meyer (2011), in a US Senate hearing, said that search engineers "mathematically compute, with more than 200 signals, a whole bunch of insights of how to rank things" (n.p.), which became more complex by the end of the 2010s. In 2019, Google summarized the choice criteria as follows:

> to find the best information from across the web, these algorithms analyse hundreds of different factors, such as the date the content was created, the number of times your search terms appear, and the user experience on the pages. To evaluate whether the content is reliable and informative on the subject, we look for sites that stand out among users with similar queries. If other important websites on the subject also have links to the page, that's a good sign that the information is of high quality.[7]

Vaidhyanathan (2011: 3) describes Google as a catalogue of "our and collective judgments, opinions, and (most important) desires," and, therefore, considers it both the most important internet company and one of the most relevant institutions in the world. Batelle (2006) has referred to Google as a "database of intentions," which registers culture as a whole and "is holding the world by its thoughts;" because of that, he concludes, it has immense power. Miconi (2014) defines Google as "the most powerful company in the history of cultural industries." It is structured according to a dialectical framework: maximum degrees of standardization and individualization coexist in its operating logic. Mager (2011), in turn, sees this technological system as a manifestation of capitalism's new spirit (Chiapello and Boltanski, 2009), of a system organized in flexible networks, as well as in an informational expression (Fuchs, 2014).

---

5 This work did not aim at proposing a technical analysis of the technological systems. However, this would not be possible since the algorithm is a trade secret (*SearchKing vs. Google*, 2003).
6 This type of content organization took the hyperlinks "map" as a reference as an objective measure of a page's "importance."
7 Information available at: <https://www.google.com/search/howsearchworks/algorithms/>.

Thus, the company would be a manifestation of contemporary capitalism, of the "connectionist world" in connection with "techno-fundamentalism." Van Couvering (2008) classifies Google as a "media company." Although it does not create texts, images, or videos, it is a relevant actor in this market, due to its business model, based on online advertising. In this sense, the author considers that the company should be seen within the new media ecosystem, with traffic as its main asset.

Contrary to what its executive director says (Pichai, 2015), Google is much more than an information company, as we will detail in this chapter. In addition to launches and incorporations of several units, products, and services, its expansion was institutionally solidified with the company's transmutation to a conglomerate under the name Alphabet in 2015. The group refers to itself as a "collection of businesses" (Alphabet, 2020: 1), the largest of which is Google. All those outside Google are classified as "other bets": "Our Other Bets include earlier stage technologies that are further afield from our core Google business. We take a long term view and manage the portfolio of Other Bets with the discipline and rigor needed to deliver long-term returns." (Alphabet, 2019: 1) At the same time, the conglomerate is an "incubator" for new solutions and new businesses. One area has been singled out to serve as an innovation centre, entitled Xlab. It gave rise to Wing, a delivery business using drones. The balance between core business (search and online advertising services) and other applications and segments is a historical concern of the company. Page (2004) informed that, faced with the challenge of diversification, he and Brin evaluated that a strategy based on "70–20–10" was a possible way forward.[8]

1 General Technological Trajectory

In 1998, the first phase of periodization begins, which we will refer to as 'birth and implementation'. Google was presented in an academic paper submitted by the founders at Stanford, entitled "The Anatomy of a Large-Scale Hypertextual Web Search Engine." It was characterized as "a large-scale search engine which makes heavy use of the structure present in hypertext" (Brin and Page, 1998: 107). The system's goal was to index the internet, offering "more satisfactory" search results than those available at the time. Thus, they wanted a mechanism that could handle the magnitude of information available on the

---

8 Of all the company's activities, 70% of the energy and investments would go to the core business. Another 20% would be dedicated to "adjacent areas," such as Gmail. The remaining 10% would be dedicated to the "freedom to innovate."

web, update it and provide quick responses to searches, offering quality results. When they decided to market the system, they were confronted with the problem faced by any innovator: resources.

In 2000, AdWords was launched, starting with 350 advertisers (Brin, 2008). It originated a revenue inflow that removed the need for third-party capital search. Then, Google announced the self-proclaimed "world's largest search engine," covering more than 1 billion pages, then about 2/3 of the content available on the Web (Wired, 2000). In 2001, the company was making progress in terms of visibility and market position. Google entered the list of the main PC Magazine sites in 2001 in the 11th position (Jensen, 2016).[9] In addition to the tool itself, the company increased its possibilities by acquiring the firm DejaNews. During the same year, Google closed a deal with AOL, the online arm of the Time Warner conglomerate. The following year, the company continued to introduce new products into the market, such as AdSense. Google Print was also launched, later rebranded as Google Books, one of the company's most important internal expansions, since it allowed it to expand its search base and allowed to compete in a new market sector, then dominated by Amazon.

The year 2004 represents the beginning of the second phase of our periodization, which we will refer to as 'initial public offering (IPO) and incorporation'. The first term is due to the company's going public on the stock exchange. Share prices doubled in just over four months (Batelle, 2006). This decision was an important change in the technological system's trajectory. Even though control was maintained by the founders and with a prominent role of Eric Schmidt as CEO, but not necessarily as a shareholder, the company, responding to a structural factor of regulation over the technology, due to the system's financialization and its economic actors, began to respond to the financial market through its shareholders, which raised the pressure of quarterly results and growth targets.

The year was fruitful in terms of new products made available. The social network Orkut, Google Scholar, Video, Maps, an SMS response and tips service, and the beta version of Gmail, offering one gigabyte of storage to each user, were launched.[10] The company also launched Google Desktop Search, which works as an "internal" search engine, reading and accessing the user's hard drive content. With this, the platform advanced even further into people's

---

9   The image search was launched in this year. The company began to introduce other services into the market, with the promotion of Google Groups.
10 The launch raised questions due to the positioning of ads close to the messages and with content related to the content of texts sent between users. The platform related terms and keywords with its segmented advertising system, AdWords.

information. The integration feature is due to the acquisitions during this period. In 2004, the company bought Picasa, an image editing, storing and posting service, and Blogger, a personal page posting service. In the same year, Google tried to buy Friendster, then a digital social network with a satisfactory market share (Facebook was still in its development phase and with limited availability). The merger movement continued in the following years. In 2005, the major acquisition was Android, and, in 2006, YouTube. By that time, the application already had the largest video audience and accumulated more than a thousand partnerships with content producers, such as Universal, CBS, BBC, Sony, and Warner (Brin, 2006). These two companies would become its two main arms after the search engine, strengthening its strategies to expand its operations. In 2005, Google signed a deal with T-Mobile to insert its application into smartphones. In 2007, it entered the mobile market with the launch of the Android platform. The goal was to make the smartphone a better device than the computer (Page, 2007). Another important acquisition that year was Doubleclick, a marketing agency specialized in electronic media, which added key technology to advertising services.

In 2008, on its 10th anniversary, Google took the lead, initiating a new phase, which we will call 'leadership consolidation'. In 2008, the company launched what would become one of the group's key products, the browser Chrome. The company operated its range of activities vertically while searching for other links in the production chain. The following year, it launched Google+, a new attempt to enter the digital social networking market, then already dominated by Facebook. But these launches were not the whole picture. Some projects were shut down. In 2010, after starting operations in China in 2006, Google closed its search engine in the country, redirecting users to the Hong Kong-based site. The decision arose from the fact that the results were censored. The company claimed to no longer accept those conditions (Google, 2010).

The year 2012 opened a new phase in the company's technological trajectory with the change of its privacy policy, which we refer to as integration through data exploration. More than an internal normative aspect, the change related to a relevant reconfiguration: from that moment on, data from all applications and services would be combined. The new policy made it clear that "if you're signed in, we may combine information you've provided from one service with information from other services. In short, we'll treat you as a single user across all our products, which will mean a simpler, more intuitive Google experience" (Brodkin, 2012). Through the change, Google has transformed its activities diversification in several markets into a great engine of integrated data production and processing, strengthening one of the features pointed as a basis for the platforms' operation. Besides the new privacy policy, in 2012,

Google made an important move in the mobile apps and content segment by launching Google Play, already introduced with 700,000 apps, music, movies and books (Google, 2012). In its searches, two important new features were introduced. The first was the display of travel price results. The second was the hotel search, Hotel Finder.[11] The year 2013 highlighted Google's progress to intensify its activities diversification strategies, as in connection provision.

The year 2015 is the beginning of the final phase of the company's technological trajectory (at least until the conclusion of this work), with the 'institutionalization of its multi-market activity' represented by the launch of Alphabet. Its 'other bets' started to be structured. This was a milestone, and the conglomerate now maintains the development of its core business but encourages the diversification sector. One of the expansion fronts involves equipment. As such, in 2016 the company launched a family of devices, called Pixel, including laptops, tablets and smartphones. With this move, the group took an important step to verticalize its chain, ensuring its status as a standard operating system in most smartphone manufacturers, with the exception of Apple with its iOS. Another expansion front was the connection and coordination of connected devices, following the regulation of technology factor of the 'Internet of Things' paradigm. To manage home devices, Google Home was launched. In 2017, Project Loon (of subsidiary X) deployed a network using balloons to provide the internet to 100 people in Puerto Rico after Hurricane Maria. In 2018, it unified payment applications (Android Pay and Google Wallet) in the new Google Pay service. Another important front in 2018 was YouTube. The service had already started providing original content in 2016 with YouTube Originals.

In 2018, the Red paid service was replaced by Premium, in one of the group's "freemium" business models. And a service specific to music, YouTube Music, was launched. Google took a bit step of not only acting as a information gatekeeper, but, also, providing information: "This drive to make information more accessible and helpful has led us over the years to improve the discovery and creation of digital content, on the web and through platforms like Google Play and YouTube." (Alphabet, 2019: 2). In June 2019, Google announced its game platform, Stadia. With this decision, the conglomerate extended its business to a profitable media sector (Rubin, 2019). The Google research team published a paper claiming to achieve quantum supremacy (Arute et al., 2019). The term is used when a computer performs an operation no other machines have performed before (Preskill, 2019).

---

11   With this, the company showed that its strategy went far beyond making information available, but fundamentally in the sense of trading access to it (indirectly until now).

In 2020, with the COVID-19 pandemic, Alphabet announced a series of actions and projects. According to Alphabet's CEO (Pichai, 2020), it worked with authorities offering data (with a community mobility report), settled a partnership with Apple for offering a infrastructure for contact tracing apps, started to disclose authoritative information in search results and in YouTube and made available US$800 million for small business. Also according to Pichai, the demand for the company's digital services increased. In the US, coronavirus-related search were four times larger than searches related to the Superbowl, the country's main sporting event. Android app downloads rose 30 per cent between February and March 2020. Google classroom, the conglomerate's educational platform, reached 100 million users.

2   Rules

An overview of the legislation governing digital platforms was presented in Chapter 5. That legislation reached Google. In addition, the search engine also imposed a specific rule, which came to be known as the "right to be forgotten." Cavalcante (2014) defines it as "the right a person has to not allow a fact, even if true, that occurred at a certain moment in life to be exposed to the general public, causing suffering or inconvenience." Ferraz and Viola (2017) characterize it as "an instrument of effective protection of the personality rights, with regard to potential injuries caused by continuous and permanent accessibility to data and information that, even true, eternalize the damage and suffering already historically caused to their respective protagonists." During the discussion of the data protection regulation in the European Union, the new law was included in the debate and, finally, incorporated into the directive.[12] In the same sense, Russia approved, in 2015, an amendment to the Law on Information, Information Technology and Information Protection on the issue.[13]

But the regulating factors of the political–institutional sphere go beyond the legal sphere and, also, cover the aforementioned decisions of courts and regulatory bodies in various areas, such as information, data protection and

---

12   According to the regulations (EU General Data Protection Regulation, 2016), holders have the right to have their information deleted in cases where the information is no longer necessary for the purposes for which it was collected. They can do it also if holders withdraw consent, if the data were processed illegally, or to comply with a legal obligation.

13   The subject has given rise to intense controversy. Critics considered the forecast "the greatest threat to freedom of expression on the internet" (Rosen, 2012).

competition.[14] In the last decade, the platform's growing importance, including in the economic environment, has been accompanied by discussions about its practices and related processes. In 2011, the company paid US$500 million in a settlement with the US Department of Justice for allowing the sale of over-the-counter drugs by Canadian pharmacies (Department of Justice, 2011). In 2013, Google signed an agreement with the Federal Trade Commission (FTC) to change some practices upon the authority's investigation. In 2015, the Federal Antimonopoly Service in India initiated an investigation to uncover anti-competitive practices, since Google was preventing competitors' applications from being installed through agreements with smartphone manufacturers that wanted to use the Android operating system. The regulatory authority found that there was a violation of the country's competition law (Pita and Valente, 2018).

In 2017, the company received a 2.4 billion euro fine from the European Union for favouring its own products and services (Bercito, 2017).[15] In March 2019, another fine for 1.49 billion euros was applied for anti-competitive practices.[16] In terms of copyrights, in June 2017, the High Court of Canada ordered the removal of Google search results that, according to the complaining company, violated copyright because they consisted of a copy made by a rival company. In 2019, the French Information Authority (CNIL) imposed a fine of 50 million euros for irregularities found in data processing.[17]

In 2019, 50 state attorney generals began an investigation on possible Google anti-competitive practices and dominant market power over the advertising sector (Newton and Schiffer, 2019). In December 2019, Google and YouTube paid US$170 million to the FTC and New York State for violations of US children's privacy law (COPPA). The complainant argued that YouTube used a variety of methods of data collection of children's activities on the internet,

---

14 The history of disputes in this field is extensive, so we will only mention a few examples that illustrate different legal aspects involving the conglomerate.

15 The investigation identified that competitors were only shown in search results from the fourth page on. The company's own services, such as Google Shopping, appeared at the top of the results.

16 According to the decision, Google was harming sites that adopted advertising services other than its own AdSense. In the "partners" clauses of the AdSense platform company network, some requirements impacted the competition by affecting other competitors, such as exclusivity clauses (Lomas, 2019).

17 Among them, the inadequacy in making information available to platform users about data collection and treatment was pointed out. Sometimes a person needed to take up to six steps to get relevant information. Another problem found in the verification was the failure to obtain consent in a valid, clear and expressed way for the use of data with the objective of advertising segmentation.

violating legal rules (FTC, 2019). That same month, the European Commission announced an investigation about Google and Facebook activities aiming to identify problems in data gathering and processing for its advertising services (Riely, 2019). Also, in December 2019, Google was fined US$166 million by France's Antitrust Board for unfair practices in online advertising markets, like imposing discriminatory and non-transparent rules on advertisers (Keslassy, 2019). In February 2020, FTC issued a special order to investigate prior acquisitions of large tech companies, including Alphabet (FTC, 2020). In France, the competition regulator ordered Google, in 2020, to negotiate with publishers the ways in which the tech giant would pay fees for using their content, so that they could get compensation when Google showed their news in search results (Bonnard, 2020).

Google, on the other hand, also intervenes to influence institutions in the political–institutional sphere. The independent Google Transparency Project survey monitored employees and executives that left the company and associated firms (such as Eric Schmidt's Groundwork) to assume positions in the government and vice versa, a movement called the "revolving door" and reported 218 occurrences[18] up to April 2016.[19] Taplin (2017: 125) sees this as a central element for the company's success vis-à-vis regulatory authorities in the United States: "How have monopolies escaped regulation? Like its two peers, Facebook e Amazon, Google has used the tools of political lobbying and public relations to cement its unique market power" (Taplin, 2017: 215).

Another set of rules is defined by Google itself. Among its internal rules, the main one is the Terms of Service (ToS), last updated in October 2017[20] (hereinafter referred to as Terms). The rule begins by expressing the authoritative aspect regarding user acceptance, by saying that "by using our Services, you are agreeing to these terms." The text initially stresses that the user has no ownership rights to what he/she publishes or shares.[21] However, in the case of

---

18 Google Transparency Project. Google's Revolving Door Explorer US. Available on: <https://www.googletransparencyproject.org/googles-revolving-door-explorer-us>.
19 Apart from subsequent years, the initiative mapped 218 migrations of this type, with 58 former employees of the technology giant taking up positions in government, regulatory agencies or Congress and 160 managers of these institutions going in the opposite direction.
20 The terms of service are not a dated document, but are available on: <https://policies.google.com/terms?hl=pt-BR>. The following citations are taken from this source.
21 By publishing or storing on the platform services, you "give Google (and those we work with) a worldwide license to use, host, store, reproduce, modify, create derivative works [...] communicate, publish, publicly perform, publicly display and distribute such content."

content originating from third parties, the company waives responsibility for it, but informs that it can review or remove it according to its compliance analysis regarding a certain location's current legislation or the platform's internal rules. The text also highlights that the company may refuse to display publications that they "reasonably believe violate our policies or the law" (Terms, n.d.). Copyright compliance is monitored in accordance with United States law (the Digital Millennium Copyright Act). Like copyright infringements, all content deemed by a complainant to be illegal may be reported to Google, which will review the request.[22] A request submission tool has been created by the group.[23]

The terms are quite explicit as to the company's total disclaimer of liability for any warranties, losses and other forms of questioning, subject to specific legal provisions. There is no user warranty in the document regarding the services or their functionality. The 'agreement' set forth in the ToS includes Google's ability to change or terminate services at any time. Users have the right to terminate their accounts or abandon the product[24] but their data will still be processed. The document highlights that additional terms for artefacts may be changed at any time, whether as a result of a legal requirement or an internal decision. Google assumes no responsibility for notifying users, and users are required to "regularly check the terms" of the company. The most the company is willing to do is announce changes to the terms page or to specific service pages. What if the user disagrees with them? "If you don't agree to the new terms, you should remove your content and stop using the services," the conglomerate informs.

One central point is the user data handing. There are two important issues in the Terms. The first one concerns the use of content for customized services: "Our automated systems analyse your content (including emails) to provide you personally relevant product features."[25] The second concerns the effect of user activities when you are "logged in" with your Google account.[26] The

---

22 Information available at: <https://support.google.com/legal/answer/3110420?visit_id=636886943368116112–2469908920andhl=pt-BRandrd=2>.
23 Information available at: <https://support.google.com/legal/troubleshooter/1114905>.
24 The document states that "when reasonably possible," users will be informed of a service's termination so that they can withdraw their data (which will not cease to be used).
25 Although the company has stated that it no longer carries out email scanning (Valente, 2019), the practice is in the Terms.
26 Activities performed on the group's applications as well as others linked to a Google account "may appear on our Services, including for display in ads and other business contexts" (Terms, n.d., n.p.). There are some types of settings, though restricted, such as preventing name and photo from appearing in ads.

Privacy Policies (which we will call "Policies") are a separate document among the company's internal rules. This rule (updated in January 2019)[27] states that, when a person is not connected, information is still collected through "unique identifiers" in browsers (such as cookies or pixel tags), applications or devices. When the user is logged in, activities are collected and stored as "personal information." In addition, all content exchanged, published or stored in the user's activities and experiences in the artefacts of the technological system is collected.[28] In addition, data about applications, browsers and devices the person uses to access the services are recorded.[29] In case of the Android operating system, it periodically contacts the platform's servers "to provide information about the device and the connection to our services," such as device type, operator, error report and installed apps (including those not related to Google).

When a person uses Google services, data are collected related to their activities, including searches, videos watched, voice and audio information when they use the services (i.e. the content of personal communications), purchases, people they communicate with, Chrome's browsing history, purchases and activities on any third-party websites or apps that use Google services. Websites often use Google Analytics also track activity on these sites, and this information is 'embedded' into Google. An important aspect of the collected records relates to the user's geolocation[30]. In addition to users, activities and apps or devices, Google also collects information from public sources (such as databases of available workplaces or a university's registration number) or from 'partners.' The latter include 'marketing partners', who hold data about the individuals and see them as potential customers. It is not specified, however, whether Google verifies or subjects these bases to the condition of the

---

27 Available at: <https://policies.google.com/privacy?hl=pt-BR>.
28 "We also collect the content you create, upload, or receive from others when using our services. This includes things like email you write and receive, photos and videos you save, docs and spreadsheets you create, and comments you make on YouTube videos." (Policies, n.d.).
29 "The information we collect includes *unique identifiers*, browser type and settings, device type and settings, operating system, mobile network information including carrier name and phone number, and application version number. We also collect information about the interaction of your apps, browsers, and devices with our services, including *IP address*, crash reports, system activity, and the date, time, and referrer URL of your request." (Policies, n.d., n.p.).
30 Several elements are used to send this information, such as GPSs, device sensors (accelerometer), IP addresses and nearby points (such as base stations or wi-fi routers). These can be collected from the device in cases of Android smartphones or Google services used. You can disable the location setting on your phone. However, the company can still perform an approximate location based on IP number.

users' consent. Thus, the use of databases obtained without permission, in a dubious or even illegal way, could be a means of circumventing and amplifying the wealth of information with which the company works.

All these forms and sources are combined in data processing. Fundamentally, the collection aims to offer customized services. Among these, the main motivation, as we will see below, is the customized advertising service.[31] Google shares user data in a number of situations. The first is through the person's authorization. Policies state that permissions will be required before sharing "sensitive" information, but do not detail what they are. The second is in the event that the account is linked to an administrator (such as a business or educational institution). The third is to transfer it to affiliates "or other trusted companies or persons to process information for us." Finally, and something which is highly concerning, Google may share browser or device information from people to "specific partners" for "advertising and measurement" purposes.[32] Three specific information control pages were also created: My Activity,[33] Google Dashboard[34] and Your Personal Information.[35] The Terms and Policies highlight the asymmetry in the subject–object power relationship, to resume the analysis by Feenberg (2002), with the company having all the prerogatives, and the user having almost none.

3 Ownership, Control and Management Structure

Alphabet is a private conglomerate, but it is considered "public" according to the financial market, for having offered its shares in stock market in 2004. Nevertheless, the two founders own less than 13% of the shares but are

---

31 In the ad settings, you can disable customization. However, since the collection for customization is performed by a set of partner site mechanisms, Google provides a link to handle these authorizations. At the time this feature was accessed, there were 136 different tools for collecting data to customize ads.
32 "For example, we allow YouTube creators and advertisers to work with measurement companies to learn about the audience of their YouTube videos or ads, using cookies or similar technologies. Another example is merchants on our shopping pages who use cookies to understand how many different people see their product listings" (Policies, n.d., n.p.).
33 Information available at: <https://myactivity.google.com/myactivity?utm_source=p-pandhl=pt_BR>.
34 Information available at: <https://myaccount.google.com/dashboard?utm_source=p-pandhl=pt_BR>.
35 Information available at: <https://myaccount.google.com/?utm_source=ppandhl=pt_BR#personalinfo>.

guaranteed more than 50% of the voting power, 25.9% for Larry Page and 25.1% for Sergey Brin. Thus, they ensure their control over decisions and the future of the group. Besides them, the largest shareholder is Eric Schmidt, with 5.6% (Alphabet, 2018).[36] What we see is that the board has been kept under the command of its founders and the other member of the triumvirate, Eric Schmidt, since the beginning. Page and Brin have been in charge of the business since they founded it in 1998. But their search for financing at the beginning led to changes in management.[37]

Page and Brin have alternated between positions throughout the company's history and its transformation into a conglomerate. With a degree in computer engineering from the University of Michigan and a master's degree in computer science from Stanford, Page served as chief executive officer from 1998 to 2001 and from 2011 to 2015, when he became chief executive officer of Alphabet. Between 1998 and 2002, he also held the position of chief financial officer. Between 2001 and 2011, he assumed the role of president of Google products. He holds a bachelor's degree in mathematics and computer science from the University of Maryland and a master's degree in computer science from Stanford University. Brin served as president of the company and chairman of the board of directors from 1998 to 2001. In 2015, the founders made room for a new person in charge of Google: Sundar Pichai, who joined the company in 2004 and became vice president, responsible for Android, Chrome and applications in 2013 and products between 2014 and 2015. A graduate of the Kharagpur Institute of Technology in India, he earned his master's degree in engineering from Stanford University. The financial arm was taken over by Ruth M. Porat, who had held several management positions at Morgan Stanley Bank since 2003, including investment management and chief financial officer.

In January 2018, Eric decided to step down from the Alphabet board of directors, a position that was assumed by an independent member: John Henessy. Alphabet has four committees: one for auditing, one for leadership development and compensation, one for nomination and corporate governance, and an executive committee. In 2019, the year in which this study was

---

36   However, Dantas (2018) highlights that, like other large digital conglomerates, there is a representative participation of investment funds and other financial market groups, which together control 27.69% of the shares (but not the voting power, as can be seen below). They are: Vanguard Group (10.66%), FMR (4.11%), State Street (3.49%), Price (T. Rowe) Associations (5.76%), Capital Research (1.29%), Bank of New York Mellon (1.17%) and Fidelity (1.21%).

37   Upon obtaining US$25 million from investment firms Kleiner Perkins and Sequoia Capital in 1999, a condition was imposed to hire someone with industry experience to help turn the idea into business. Eric Schmidt would only be hired in 2001 (Sánchez-Ocaña, 2012).

completed, the board of directors was formed by: Brin (president), Page (executive board), Amie O'Toole (accounts board), Ruth Porat (financial board), and David Drummond (legal board). The board incorporates individuals such as John Henessy (former president of Stanford University), Roger Fergusson (with experience in pension fund administration), Alan Mulally (former director of Ford Motors) and Ann Mather (former chief financial officer of Pixar). In December 2019, Larry Page and Sergei Brinn stepped down from the conglomerate's leadership, staying in the company's board, nominating Sundar Pichai as Alphabet's new CEO (Matsakis, 2019).

4 Production Process

In the production process, a key point identified by the social construction of technology and critical theory of technology approaches is identifying interest groups and their objectives. Due to its size and the diversity of its artefacts and services, Alphabet establishes relationships with a series of agents. The conglomerate publicly expresses what it calls "its interests" in its mission and institutional statements. The mission is to "organize the world's information and make it accessible to all." According to the company, the most effective – and profitable – way to fulfil this mission is "to put the needs of our users first" (Google, 2009, n.p.). There are three commitments associated with the mission (Google, 2009): (1) to make available the most relevant and useful search results, which are displayed objectively and without any room for trading; (2) to provide the most relevant and useful advertising, making it clear when it appears on the search results pages; and (3) to work to improve the user experience, search technology and other areas. The conglomerate indicates its vision is to use technology to answer to "big problems"[38] and affirms in several documents a self-image that sees technology with much potential, especially in its interaction with information, as mentioned in Page (2013, n.p.): "We're motivated by a profound belief that access to knowledge will improve humankind." However, there may be gaps between the declared intentions and the objectives and interests. The company was born with the initial intention of offering a better search engine than those available until then, with the ambition of making all the information on the web available. As a result, the following are the conglomerate's objectives: (1) controlling an increasing amount and

---

38 "Our vision is to remain a place of incredible creativity and innovation that uses our technical expertise to tackle big problems" (Alphabet, 2018: 1).

scale of all kinds of information, (2) collecting personal data and its integrated exploitation, and (3) developing various solutions based on this data, especially from the customization logic as a competitive edge. Within the limits of this work, it is not possible to map all interest groups related to the conglomerate's artefacts and services, so we will focus on the interests of the most representative groups and "platform sides":

(1) Advertisers – These see Google as a central tool to reach the intended audiences. That's why they not only support its business model, but, also, contribute to how it explores data by integrating records into databases.

(2) Advertising network partner sites and apps – Google is a source of income from them through the partner network, in which ads of all kinds are displayed.[39]

(3) Websites in general – They depend on Google to gain higher access, since the search engine is one of the main "gatekeepers" of the internet. They struggle with SEO tactics to gain prominence in the results.

(4) Applications in general – They see on Google a key "gatekeeper," since Play Store is an important trading locus, although it is less exclusive than in the previous case (due to the existence of a competitor like Apple Store).

(5) Professional producers of cultural and informational content – They also depend on Google services to reach their audiences, such as search results, the Play Store or appearing on YouTube.

(6) Non-professional users – These are mass of individuals and collectivities that use services other than Alphabet and have different interests. But, in short, they could be reduced to using the service in its various modalities, optimizing purposes (such as getting informed through the search, communicating with friends through Gmail, accessing sites through Chrome or consuming video and music on YouTube).

(7) Companies – In addition to using free Google services or having their websites displayed in search results, companies are an important part of this technology system in the consumption of cutting-edge services, especially G Suite, Google Business and Google Cloud corporate solutions.

(8) State institutions and regulatory authorities – Also varying because of different political understandings and projects, governments and regulatory authorities can either support and drive forward projects or demands of the group (such as expanding access to the web in countries or regions,

---

39 Such as banners or videos.

or entering into partnerships with some group), or impose obstacles to its activity through legislation, government decisions or administrative measures (as seen in the rules section).
(9) Researchers – Despite their indirect participation in the system, they are key players to support or not Google's intended legitimization with the public or to unveil its operating logic. Due to their established authority (as shown in several works of the social studies of science and technology), researchers can influence the meaning systems of different audiences about the company and its services.
(10) Civil society organizations – Also varying according to their conceptions and political projects, they can legitimate the conglomerate (supporting or participating in its promotion initiatives) or question it, making criticisms and accusations or presenting claims.
(11) Competitors – As will be seen later on, Alphabet has several competitors, which seek to gain positions in the market and decrease Alphabet's participation and its specific artefacts or services.

Besides the external agents, there are also the internal ones. In this complex ecosystem, Google organizes the development of its technological system's artefacts with unique labour relations. The company's workforce can be divided into three groups: (1) middle managers, (2) formally hired workers, and (3) subcontracted workers. Over the past decade, the conglomerate has seen an increase of its formally hired employee base from around 20,000 in 2009 to 100,000 in 2018, a 500% growth, which represents an average total expansion of 50% per year in the period.[40] Between 2017 and 2018, the expansion was the strongest in nominal terms, with almost 20,000 people added to the work environment. The company's worker base is much larger than Facebook's,[41] giving it a competitive edge. This advantage can be verified in the important research and development sector, which is specifically responsible for proposing new technological solutions materialized in several products and services. Despite the fact that, in the last two years of the survey, the workforce breakdown by area was not available, in 2016 Alphabet, already had more people in this sector than the entire current Facebook base.

Regarding remuneration, the disparity is striking. Eric Schmidt, for example, received a salary of US$1.25 million in 2017, which, with other payments, amounted to US$4.7 million (Alphabet, 2018). Unfortunately, the company does not provide data on its salaries for a more accurate analysis of the

---

40 The data comes from the company's annual reports, compiled by us.
41 Whose number is given in Chapter 7.

remuneration breakdown within groups. A survey by Equilar (Molla, 2018) showed average salaries in large companies in the US economy. Alphabet appears almost at the top of the list, behind Facebook only. However, the data should be considered carefully, as the compensations for positions at the top of the labour pyramid are high, which pulls the average up. According to the same survey, CEO compensation at these companies is 40 times the average salary paid in the United States.

In addition to the remuneration structure, in terms of workforce composition, it is important to keep in mind who these employees are. Recently, Alphabet has become the target of criticism, due to its lack of diversity. Like Facebook, the conglomerate created an area for the topic and started producing reports to offer transparency regarding the gender and ethnic-racial composition of its workforce (Google, 2018). The results showed no diversity: men predominate over women, with 69.1% against 30.9%. In terms of distribution by race and ethnicity, whites make up more than half of employees (53%), followed by a large presence of Asians (36.3%). The participation of Latinos (3.6%) and blacks (2.5%) is quite low. There is also a part of the workforce made up of outsourced workers that is not even considered in the official figures.[42] The company hired such people for a controversial partnership project between Google and the US Department of State for analysis using artificial intelligence for that institution's drone activities (Fang, 2019).

Since 2019, Google has started to be criticized by its own employees. Google's workers released an open letter requesting the company to cancel the Dragonfly Project, which would create a censored search engine in China (Google Employees Against Dragonfly, 2019). Google's workers staged a walkout on November 1st, 2019 against the company's lack of action against sexual harassment and other workplace issues. The protest was motivated by multi-millionaire settlements with executives accused of sexual harassment (Tiku, 2018). In 2019, it was reported that walkout organizers faced retaliation by Google managers (Tiku, 2019a). In December, the Labor Relations Board opened an investigation about possible labour laws violations when firing four employees and when acting to discourage workers from unionizing (Elias, 2019).

---

42   Like other platforms, such as Amazon, the company benefits from 'on-demand' and precarious forms, such as the testing of software and other activities susceptible to 'outsourced' hiring. Irani (2015), a former Google employee, highlights, in the evaluation of algorithms and software, the role of "judges": workers who analyse the search results as a way to feed their "calibration." The author calls this modality "digital microwork."

5 Competitive Performance

Google is apparently a technology company, but its business model is based on advertising, which supports the search engine, Gmail, Maps, Calendar, Translator, as well as other resources. Other models combine free and paid solutions, like Google Play and YouTube. In the commercialized services segment, there are products aimed mainly at companies, such as G Suite and Google Cloud. In the company's other bets, each unit develops its business model.[43] These specificities impact the very nature of the technological system artefacts, since the business model is a crucial element in TSs in capitalism, connecting the production process to its manifestation in competition.[44]

In the case shown, despite variations, it is possible to see, and Google itself states, that its business model is based on the sale of advertising.[45] That is how Google fulfils a vital function under capitalism, supporting the realization of goods (Marx, 2014), however, bringing this classic area of cultural industries (Bolaño, 2000) to a new level.[46] The system is headed by services renamed as Google Ads, Google Marketing Platform, and Google Ads Manager in 2018. The revenues come mainly from the marketing of 'performance advertising' and 'brand advertising.' 'Performance advertising' involves features on which users click and are directly forwarded to spaces indicated by advertisers, such as websites.[47] This is based on AdWords (whose name was then changed to Google Ads), an advertising system organized around 'auctions' that manages the ads' content and their distribution on Google and to company partners. The big difference was its cost-per-click (CPC) logic, according to which the investment is considered to have a return not due to ads being simply displayed, but to the user clicking on them. In the cost per acquisition mode of commercial products, the advertiser only pays when the purchase is actually accomplished.

---

43 The sale of autonomous cars and hardware, for example, is structured around traditional goods marketing logics.
44 They articulate social factors (based on the economic scenario and forms of insertion into it) and their own factors. They appear especially from the economic scenario, which impacts both the capacity of companies to advertise and of citizens to consume.
45 Kang and McAllister (2011) classify search engines as "the most important technological development for advertisers" for their ability to map user interests from the searches and then direct ads from them.
46 At this point, the first and second dimensions of technological regulation intersect in their dialectic process.
47 The system provides tools to define the objectives (such as generating clicks or visits), plan the campaign, fix the budget and create the advertising messages. "Most" advertisers pay when engagement with the ad occurs (Alphabet, 2018: 2).

One of the measurement methods is the click through-rate, a measure that is based on the probability of clicks on a particular ad. The display network uses another system, called AdSense, which manages the insertion of ads and remunerates sites when users click on them. YouTube is based on a freemium model (part free, part by subscription), ads and fees charged from creators. In 2020, YouTube kept 45 per cent of revenue from ads. In membership systems, it takes 30 per cent of the amount gained by the creator (Alexander, 2020).

The company's economic strategy, characterized by Fuchs (2013), is based on collecting data from its users in different applications. The greater the forms, time and intensity of use, the larger the data set available to analyse the users' behaviour and to direct the services. Similarly, Vaidhyanathan (2011) defines Google's core business model as based not on selling ads, but on profiling people, creating "dossiers" on individuals. With Android, such surveillance has become more profound in terms of recording what users do on mobile devices. The platform's surveillance goes far beyond the notorious Panopticon model, the author adds. Mager (2011) points out that the company backs away from traditional models of information services, such as audience-related services, as portals, and works with traffic as a commodity, conversing with Van Couvering (2008).

Google's financial performance charted an explosive rise. At the beginning of the chosen time frame (2009 to 2018), the company was already a mature company, inserted in the logic of financialization and having recently become the leader of the search market. The period also begins right after the 2008 economic crisis. In ten years, Alphabet's total annual revenues have risen more than fivefold, from US$23.6 billion to US$136.8 billion. The accumulated increase in the period reached 579%, corresponding almost to a sixfold expansion, with an average of 60% per year. Even so, by analysing the table below, it is possible to see that this was a substantial increase in the company's positive results. Despite significant annual growth rates at the beginning of the decade, especially in 2012, from its transformation into a conglomerate, in 2015, the group's annual growth rate was above 20 points, showing a sustainable evolution. During this period, the largest nominal increases also occurred, with the company adding US$15 billion to its outcomes in 2016, US$20 billion in 2017, and US$26 billion in 2018. The graph below shows revenue and expense items.[48] Even in the COVID-19 pandemic period, revenues kept coming into the conglomerate:

---

48   It starts from the general revenues to detail them in some categories. "Google Revenues" includes both search engine advertising and advertising linked to different products such as Gmail, Maps, Play and YouTube. Other bets are Alphabet's independent businesses,

> That ad business has become increasingly complex, and Google has been maintaining its substantial share of overall online advertising because its vast trove of data and searches lets advertisers more precisely target users. So, while online ad prices generally are falling, Google has increased revenue by selling more ads and helping advertisers obtain higher response rates.
>
> KARABELL, 2020

With the impact of COVID-19 pandemic, the company released its Q1 results showing losses, but with better performance than expected (see Table 1): "The results came as a surprise to analysts, who had feared they would sound a death knell for the digital marketing ecosystem." (Martineu, 2020).

This growth has resulted in successful positions vis-à-vis the competition.[49] The search engine market has been stable for 10 years. In the 1990s and 2000s, there was still some competition (as seen in the general technological trajectory section). Since the turn of the 2010s, the market share has stabilized, with Google at around 92%.[50] Then came Bing, from Microsoft (2.83%), Yahoo (1.65%), and the Russian Yandex (0.65%). Regarding the operating systems market, Android reached a historic milestone by surpassing the market leader, Windows (considering operating systems on all devices, not only on desktops). In January 2009, Windows ruled the market, with a share of over 90%. In 2020, Android managed to reach 39.2% of the market, against 35.4% for Microsoft's operating system. Combined, they form a duopoly, with almost 75% of the market. They were followed by Apple's iOS, with 14.5% and OSX, with 7.7%.[51]

---

such as Nest, X and Waymo. Other Google revenues consist basically of app rentals, digital content on the Play Store, cloud service and hardware, or Motorola mobile business while it was under Google's control in 2012 and 2013. Network members include revenues from Google's "agency" ads on partner sites and apps. Revenue costs mainly involve TAC, the funds passed on to network partners (network members) for advertising inserted in their sites and apps. In addition, they include costs of content acquisition (such as YouTube and Play Store), and infrastructure such as data centres. The group's annual reports contained some discrepancies; they were selected using data from certain reports to the detriment of others.

49 Since it operates in several markets, mapping Alphabet's competitive position is a complex task. For illustration purposes, we will work with the technological system's main services: (1) the search engine under the same name, (2) the Android operating system, (3) the YouTube video platform, (4) the Chrome browser, and (5) the cloud service.

50 Statcounter (2020) Search engine Market share worldwide Aug 2019 Aug 2020. Availale (consulted 29 September 2020) at: https://gs.statcounter.com/search-engine-market-share.

51 Statcounter (2020) Operating Systems market worldwide aug 2019 aug 2020. Available (consulted 29 September 2020) at: https://gs.statcounter.com/os-market-share.

TABLE 1   Google – Financial data overview

	2009	2010	2011	2012	2013	2014	2015	2016	2017	2018
nET Income	23.6	29.3	37.9	50.1	59.8	66	75	90.2	110.8	136.8
Google	23.6	29.3	37.9	46	55.5	65.6	74.5	89.9	110.3	136.2
Growth over previous year (%)	24%	24%	29%	32%	19%	10.3%	14%	20%	24%	23%
Other bets	-	-	-	-	0.01	0.3	0.4	0.2	0.5	0.6
Revenues with advertising	22.8	28.2	36.5	43.6	51	59.6	67.4	79.4	95.3	116.3
Advertising share (%)	96.6%	96.2%	96%	87%	85.2%	90%	89.8%	88%	86%	85%
Other Google revenues	0.7	1	1.3	2.3	4.4	6	7.1	10.6	15	19.9
Other Google revenues (%)	2.9%	3.4%	3.4%	5%	8%	9.3%	9.6%	11.8%	13.6%	14.6%
Partner network	7.1	8.7	10.3	12.4	13.1	14.5	15	15.6	17.5	19.8
NET Income	6.5	8.5	9.7	10.7	12.9	14.1	16.3	19.4	12.6	30.7
Expenses	15.3	18.9	26.1	37.4	45.8	25.7	28.1	66.5	84.7	110.4
Revenue costs	8.8	10.4	13.2	17.2	21.9	9.8	10.2	35.1	45.5	59.5
Transfer to network members	n/a	n/a	n/a	n/a	9.3	9.8	10.2	16.7	21.6	26.7
R&D	2.8 (12%)	3.7 (12.8%)	5.1 (13.6%)	6.8 (18.2%)	7.1 (12.9%)	9.8 (14.9%)	12.2 (16.3%)	13.9 (15.5%)	16.6 (15%)	21.4 (15.7%)
Marketing and sales	2 (8.4%)	2.8 (9.5%)	4.5 (12%)	6.1 (16%)	6.5 (11.8%)	8.1 (12.3%)	9 (12%)	10.4 (11.6%)	12.8 (11.6%)	16.3 (11.9%)
General and administrative	1.7 (7%)	1.9 (6.8%)	2.7 (7.2%)	3.8 (10%)	4.4 (8%)	5.8 (8.9%)	6.1 (8.2%)	6.9 (7.7%)	6.8 (6.2%)	8.1 (5.9%)
Fines								0.4	1	8.5

SOURCE: AUTHOR, FROM INFORMATION IN THE COMPANY'S ANNUAL REPORTS

This performance was achieved by the size of the mobile device market, where Android dominates.[52] In 2018, it was 'embedded' into 87.7% of the devices, while iOS was present in 12.1% (Statista, 2018c).

The video platform market is more complex to analyse.[53] Covering free streaming services, the company Tivo (2019) indicated, in a survey based in the United States and Canada, that YouTube was the preferred service, with 57.9% of the mentions. Then came Facebook (43.9%), Twitch (19.9%), Snapchat (18%), Pluto TV (17.7%), Crackle (14.7%), and Vevo (14.3%). According to World Economic Forum (WEF, 2021) the largest video on demand services were Netflix (204m), Prime Video (150m), Tencent Video (120m), iQiyi (119m) and Disney+ (95m), all with less users thand YouTube. .

In the browser market, Chrome achieved a rise over the decade, becoming the absolute leader in 2018, with 65.9%. Its competitors were in much lower positions in that year, with Safari with 16.8%, Firefox with 4%, Samsung Internet with 3.4% and Edge with 2.3%.[54] The evolution since 2015 shows Chrome's growth and the fall of Microsoft's Internet Explorer, which was discontinued in favour of a new browser, Edge. In cloud services, Google ranked fourth in 2018 (Novet and Levy, 2018), behind IBM, Microsoft and Amazon.

Such positions are the result of successful strategies, enhancing its edge in "qualitative competition" (Herscovici, 2013). The initial strategy, typical of the concentrating and centralizing trend of capitalism (Marx, 2013), was the incorporation of other companies.[55] The incorporation strategy gave Google advantages in its business model, as in the cases of DoubleClick and AdMob, because it removed potential competitors (such as Waze) (Reynolds, 2017), allowed the expansion of activities to the segment of operating systems and mobile applications (Android), ensured the company's entry into the video market

---

52 The strategy of opening the operating system to several manufacturers, not just verticalizing it on its own hardware (as Apple does with iOS), has made Android the standard OS in almost the entire smartphone market, showing the strength of a vertical expansion without any enclosure strategies.

53 Several rankings, such as that of the Statista consultancy, place YouTube within the digital social networking market, which we don't consider the best way to understand the market. The platform can be seen in the free streaming market (competing with Vimeo) or in the general streaming platform market, competing with Netflix and other services such as Amazon Prime Video.

54 Statcounter (2020) Browser market worldwide aug 2019 aug 2020. Available (consulted 29 September 2020) at: https://gs.statcounter.com/browser-market-share.

55 If this practice is common in large groups, in information industries and on platforms, it is even more important, because, to take advantage of the network effects (and prevent or mitigate the impacts of the network effects of competitors), the pursuit of leadership is fierce (Ezrachi and Stucke, 2016).

(YouTube), and signaled unsuccessful experiences in the hardware market (Motorola) or ongoing experiences (Nest). Google's list of acquisitions is extensive (CB Insights Consulting lists 246 operations of this type), with a higher volume at the beginning of 2010, when the group launched its most aggressive strategy of constituting a conglomerate. In June 2019, Google acquired Looker, a business intelligence company, for US$2.6 billion (Finley, 2019). In November 2019, Google announced the acquisition of smartwatch and fitness device company Fitbit for US$2.1 billion (Gartenberg, 2019). The process continued through 2020. European antitrust regulators started to assess the competition impact on the digital health sector (Vincent, 2020).

Through these incorporation movements, Google has promoted an aggressive strategy of activity diversification. We highlight here five pillars of this movement. The first is towards the video and streaming segment. The turn of the 2000s to the 2010s saw the emergence of online video, favoured by its own factors of regulation of technology to increase the bandwidth and cheapen packages. Google took advantage of this trend and moved forward to incorporate a fast-growing agent in this segment. However, the streaming market is driven not only by personal videos posted, but by quality content. The group has not missed out and launched, in 2012, its paid on-demand video service on Google Play Store (Google Play, Movies and TV). The second was its breakthrough in the "mobile world."[56] The growth of the mobile device base was a phenomenon perceived and discussed throughout the 2000s, and Google operated a strategy of acquiring several companies in this area. Unlike other important acquisitions, Android was not yet a major player (having been bought for US$50 million) (Callahan, 2018). The investment was successful, and the system grew from 2008 onwards, filling a gap left by Windows Mobile's limitations and Apple system's hermetic nature (and its iOS system), not only due to its functional properties, but, also, due to a tactic of agreements with manufacturers that allowed its presence in the devices.[57]

The third front was the entry into e-commerce and financial services. The group launched several products for advertising and sales (such as Google

---

56 This mobilization considered social factors of regulation of both the economic spheres (greater consumption power and expansion of these devices' basis) and the cultural spheres (portability meeting a growing individualist trend).
57 Furthermore, the purchase of AdMob was another example of the company's effort to adapt the functional properties of its technological system's artefacts to this universe of services and devices.

Shopping, Google Flights and Google Business). A second group of innovations in this field included payment tools. In 2011, Google launched the Wallet feature, a way to process payments without going through an external financial operator. Its Android platform also included another product, Android Pay. In 2018, they were brought together under a new brand, called Google Pay (Guilherme, 2018).[58] The fourth front involved the company's entry into telecommunications infrastructure services and connection provision. In 2013, it launched the Loon project to provide balloon access. One of its other bets, Access, is a renewal of the access provisioning project effort. The fifth front is a meeting point between the extension of activities and the group's third strategy of vertical integration. The main movement in this sense was in the area of hardware. The most daring initiative was the purchase of Motorola Mobile in 2011. The company put the Nexus, Pixel and Chromebook lines on the market. With this, it approached models of what has been called 'experience enclosure' (Quintarelli, 2015) and 'walled gardens' (Dantas, 2010), which imprison the user's experience in the scope of "converging" architectures.

This last strategy, together with the activity extension pillar, gave rise to a new specific strategy, which we will call 'application ecosystem control'. It includes aspects of activity extension and horizontal and vertical integration. When buying and then launching Android, Google sought to reproduce in the mobile app environment its logic of asserting itself as a regulating agent[59] of the information and money flows in each segment of online markets. According to Pon et al. (2014), Android constituted an "operating system-based power" in which the system operates as a "bottleneck," establishing "control points" in this technological subsystem. A second bottleneck operated is its application store. It is the control point of both offer and technological parameters employed.[60] The company used Android to "pre-install" its own applications, such as search, YouTube, Chrome, Maps, Documents and other artefacts.

---

58 This was an example of how the extension of activities benefits from the previously constituted technological system's basis, since one of the functional properties of the artefact is its interconnection with other services of the group, using, for example, saved data from purchases made in Chrome or through some Android app.

59 We will use this denomination instead of 'gatekeeper', since we consider that Google's actions seek to regulate how its platform and the Web work as a whole.

60 As a mandatory intermediary, it removes the user's autonomy in defining the sources of apps (as in the culture of loading programs on desktops), also promoting the market control.

6 System Components and Technical Resources

We now come to a crucial point in the analysis. In this section, we seek to articulate social and technical factors, characteristics and constitutive elements in the examination of the components, including technical resources.[61] Given the extent and variety of the subsystems and artefacts that make up the technological system, this discussion will establish a prioritization based on our own relevance criteria, giving each part a different emphasis, influencing the extent and depth of the debate about each part. The components will be divided between Google and "other bets," as Alphabet proposes. In the first group, in order of priority, the analysis will focus primarily on the following components:[62] search, Chrome, Android and Play Store, YouTube, Gmail and personal work suite, equipment (Pixel, Chromebooks, wearables, connected home appliances), and business services (G Suite, Google Business, AnalyTIC, Cloud). The second group includes the other bets, without detailing their technical resources.

As stated throughout the chapter, the search was the conglomerate's original product and is, to this day, the focus of the group's operations (Alphabet, 2018). The search is based on algorithms that scan and index the results, classify them according the search conducted and present the contents developed from the original PageRank model. Over the years, new functionalities have been introduced, such as custom search (based on user profile), the "autocomplete" feature while typing, direct answers to questions (Page, 2013) and voice search. In 2018, the company promoted a set of algorithm updates (Hutchinson, 2019), such as: greater visibility for mobile versions of the pages in the results, including a "carousel" of videos in the results page and displaying direct (and unique) answers to certain questions (such as time, conversions, calculations). The search is the "gateway" of the technological system, having in its architecture the aggregation vertex of several other artefacts. The interface is the area shown to users so that they can access a program or website. In Google's case, it is its home page, whose central element is the field where the questions are entered in order to get the results. Integrated into the

---

61 This work does not aim at or use analytical instruments of technical disciplines (such as engineering and computer science). This study, therefore, will take as a basis the methodological strategies of the technological regulation model, seeking to articulate the various dimensions that integrate it and a discussion on how the architecture reflects and interacts dialectically with them.

62 These can be considered specifically, like YouTube, or in groups, like equipment. Such grouping has been adopted arbitrarily to facilitate the examination.

search are other artefacts of the technological system (such as Google Maps, Gmail, Drive, and YouTube).

Among the search's technical resources, the central functionality is the insertion of a word, term or question to search for related content. The answer page offers results (according to the classification logic discussed above), divided into several categories (all, images, shopping, videos, news, maps, books, flights, finances). At the top of the results, ads are displayed. When a term refers to a video content, links to that type of content are displayed. When a word is related to a product, indications of stores may appear. When a word suggests an establishment, information about the company, such as location, address, telephone number, prices, websites, comments and times are displayed separately.[63] In the cases mentioned, investigations and experience show that Google's own services (such as Google Shopping, Google Business and Google Flights) are displayed.[64] Millions of results are shown, but they are distributed ten per page. In addition to its ability to mediate access to knowledge on the web, Google's search is structured based on a contradiction. In the subject–object technical relationship outlined by Feenberg (2002), the system gives users a feeling of control, since they define the demand for information, but the former regains its power in the relationship by defining the purpose of the search, by presenting the "options" menu. This does not determine what the user should know, but it delimits the scope of possibilities of its meaning in the world. Thus, a factor of technology regulation (the structured format of Google search) imposes a regulation by technology on individuals, affecting society in a collective dimension in its different spheres. An example is the common practice of users to remain on the first page.[65] Although the search engine customizes the results (as already discussed), this targeting can be further enhanced by accessing the site while logged in. In 2019, BERT (Bidirectional Encoder Representations from Transformers) software was launched, with higher text reading and understanding capacity (Wired, 2020).

Chrome is the company's browser.[66] One of the intentions with its release was to create a space that could maintain the user's online searches and

---

63   In case of a band or song, there is an indication of how to find it on a streaming platform. In the test performed with the band Pato Fu, the first indication was for YouTube.
64   The only way for a competitor to try to overcome this obstacle is through an ad, as tests confirmed in a ticket simulation for the Brasília–Fortaleza stretch on March 12, 2019. The flight platform Decolar.com appeared in sponsored content, while Google Flights was the first organic result, with the fields already available without the need to click on the link.
65   A study (Brafton, 2013) found that 95% of web traffic comes from the first page.
66   Its release in 2008 represented Google's entry into Microsoft's traditional territory with its Explorer, together with other agents, such as Mozilla with Firefox.

activities through multiple screens (Page, 2013). Likewise, it also represented an advance and mitigation of browser dependency, which could accomplish what Google understood as a key strategy: to favour its own applications by default. This was the case, for example, with Microsoft. The interface, in line with the search engine, was built to be simple and, consequently, fast. Unlike other browsers with portals as home page (such as MSN.com from Explorer, and now Edge, from Microsoft), Chrome was designed so that Google's search page (which already offered access to other services, such as the recapitulation of interface changes in the previous section showed) assumed the condition of a home page.

The browser's main technical feature is navigation on the World Wide Web (WWW). The search field is integrated with the search engine and can either have the complete URL or search words typed. This integration with Google makes the user's access to a specific URL increasingly less direct, depending on this operating logic, which is similar to that of the search engine, by typing the keyword with the response already directed to the results page.[67] Just as the search engine has adapted to Google's search, the latter has made the opposite move, assuming features of a homepage with functionalities such as including shortcuts to bookmarked sites. Chrome itself includes suggested sites on its top bar, supposedly from the user's navigation.

Less complex than mobile apps, Chrome, like other browsers, is also a platform that aggregates simpler artefacts, the extensions. These can have different purposes, including fighting tracking by users. As an aggregator, it reinforces its strategy of creating and reproducing application ecosystems. Chrome also allows the user to "login." This option, as previously indicated, implies another level of submission to Google's systems control and customization. Once the user is logged in, Google offers features such as "contact synchronization" and photo and name indication, so that browsing is identified for both Google and its extensive partner network. In general, with Chrome, the conglomerate has taken a step forward in the various "control points" (Pon et al., 2014), going from the already powerful search engine to the web-entry feature in various devices, whether desktops or smartphones.

Android is a widely used operating system across mobile devices and based on which developers can create apps for these devices. With the expansion of smartphones, especially, which reached more than five billion people in 2019, 3.6 billion of them with mobile internet (GSMA, 2019), the operating system

---

67   With this architecture, Chrome has become almost like a second version of the search engine, more direct since it does not require accessing the website www.google.com.

gained importance as a "regulatory agent" not only in international flows, but in the very use of applications in this environment, totaling US$194 billion and increasing to US$101 billion in 2018 (We Are Social, 2019). This regulation is carried out either by making available pre-installed applications (which also reinforces the power of Google's apps) or through its application store, the Play Store. In 2020, it charged a 30 per cent comission when an app made a sale of digital goods, including subscription. The fee drops to 15 per cent to the subscription transactions after the first year (Alexander, 2020).

A key aspect of Google's technology basis for Android was the choice for an open architecture. This decision was driven by political options (referring to Winner [1986]), since it allowed an expansion of the platform for three fundamental parties. The first party was manufacturers, who could adapt and have an alternative for an operating system without the need to develop it (as in Apple's case) or which was more easily available, making one of the key elements of smartphones feasible at a lower cost. The second party is developers, who were able to increase the apps' creation in the open architecture, giving the platform plenty of alternatives, even if the focus of its core apps is on Google products. The third party is users, who saw in the operating system an environment for more possibilities, unlike Apple's more hermetic system or those with a small base of technological solutions, such as Windows Phone.

Android meant a successful acquisition in terms of its impact, despite the initial amount paid (US$50 million). If, on the one hand, Google sought to find room for Chrome as an OS, it was with Android and the bet on the mobile segment that the company was catapulted to control the market of "application system platforms" (according to the typology established in Chapter 5), having surpassed Windows in general figures and reached more than 80% in the mobile market. As Pon et al. (2014) pointed out, such system was configured as a "bottleneck" in this market, imposing "control points." Among these are the technical standards for the development and operation of these applications. Another fundamental point is the application distribution and trading centre, the app store. As related "control points" of these platforms, the breakthrough in this segment was a consequence of Google's vertical integration, with the creation of Play Store, also incorporating other products such as books, music and movies (Lee, 2014). Thus, the Android ecosystem and the app store are not only the technical basis for these programs, but, also, assumed the condition of agents for Google's entry into other sectors of communications, such as the online cultural goods market, characterized by its editorial nature, since they provide audiovisual works, music and books.

YouTube is Google's main video platform. A subsystem of the conglomerate's technological system, it was acquiredas a result of the incorporation strategy to be powered as the largest video publication and consumption space on the planet. Created with the motto "broadcast yourself," YouTube currently represents the conglomerate's largest audiovisual content circulation locus, but, also, a representative subsystem both from the point of view of revenue growth (as shown in the financial performance section) and the development of new business models combining free and paid services. The platform is gaining more and more space as an alternative to traditional media for information and cultural consumption on a global scale (as will be seen in the Appropriation section).

YouTube allows two central modes of experience: consumption and publication. In the first, users have a video catalogue to watch. Videos are organized by channels and authors. The first category is "Recommended" – despite the name, all categories are suggested. These include popular themes (such as breaking news) and combine several forms of indications. The user can also follow "channels" (profiles of video publishers). New content placed in these spaces is communicated through notifications. The platform also provides features for organizing the viewing processes in addition to following the channels, such as creating their own lists (playlist), selecting a video to watch later, a history of videos already watched, the possibility to "like" content and purchase access to it.[68]

Thus, YouTube clearly assumes the role of "editor" of the content availability, a position that used to be typical of traditional media agents. More than just the "initial menu," the platform has several "targeting layers" (or curatorship, a term more associated with a techno-triumphalist view of the platform, reclaiming a concept by Winner [2016]). The first consists of the initial menu already approached. The second involves the creation of "video lists," the "mixes." The third, and perhaps more fundamental, organizes the recommended works after viewing a video, in an infinite sequence of works, assuming something of a "flow" logic characteristic of broadcast television (Williams, 2017).

Acquired from an internal factor of regulation of the technological system related to the business model, YouTube is the central locus of the strategy of taking Google's customized advertising also to videos, which has been gaining space, due to factors such as the time spent by users (greater than that spent on searches, for example). Like other products, it follows this main objective, as a subsystem subsumed by the capitalist logic. The resource with the greatest adjustment potential in its specific technological trajectory is not technical,

---

68 All these tools contribute to generating more digital tracks and data points (increasing data surveillance, according to Clarke [1988] and "datafication," as Van Dijck (2014) points out).

but, rather, relates to its purpose: the realization of original productions, in the digital integration strategy.

Gmail is a subsystem that assumes the condition of Google's main interpersonal communication service. Despite the spread of instant messaging apps (a segment dominated by Facebook, as we will see in the next chapter), it remains a widely used artefact and maintains a set of important functional properties that allow it to manage the flow and content of messages. In addition, it is an important surveillance tool, as it has allowed the company to access various message exchanges from its users. Gmail also served as an integration interface among a set of Google artefacts. It has been integrated with features such as messaging (like chat and Hangouts) and others, which can be included in the form of add-ons. The tool works as a "gateway" to a set of Google artefacts, such as the suite of applications for personal work (Drive, Documents, Spreadsheet and Presentation).

In its technical features, Gmail has a simple initial interface, basically for logging in. Once you've "signed in," you see your messages in chronological order. These are received in the inbox automatically, organized into categories, or "tabs." Available in five categories, these can be reconfigured by the user. The tabs organize the flow of incoming messages. But the artefact also allows its storage to be sorted by "manually" defined filters (saved messages from a sender or group in a certain folder) and by "markers" (visual identifiers that can be applied to messages either manually or using some signals, such as senders). The suite basically works as a virtual editor of the document production modalities defined within Microsoft's Office packages: texts, spreadsheets and presentations. Google Drive operates as a locus for storing and organizing any kind of user documents.

The evolution of Gmail's resources has shown a trend, like other artefacts and subsystems, of increasing its influence on the subjects in terms of information organization. If, on the one hand, it offers tools for the manual management of messages, on the other hand, it has advanced in its automated ordering, especially with the tabs. By adopting functional justifications for this (such as the removal of "spam" in the inbox), it has, in practice, mitigated against the progress strategies of competitors, such as digital social networks, whose competition for attention involves notifications sent by e-mail (as most of them do, including Facebook). With the recommendations, it sought to assume a mediator role in the valuation of user conversations. With automatic responses using artificial intelligence, Gmail is moving forward in an alarming manner in replacing human agency (as Webb warned [2019]). Moreover, in a scenario of increasing flexibility of labour relations (as discussed in Chapter 5), it assumes an increasing role of a work tool with a personal aspect.

Within its vertical integration strategy and extension of activities also vertically, Google started to produce an equipment line, either through partnerships with manufacturers or on its own. The first modality is more frequent, from agreements with several brands, such as HP, Dell, Samsung, Lenovo, Acer and Asus. The conglomerate entered this market in 2010 and started to launch tablets, desktops and smartphones in the Chromebook, Nexus and Pixel lines. This insertion did not happen through the acquisition of an equipment manufacturing structure, but through product control in the specification definitions and, mainly, through the Chrome operating system and the applications that would be "embedded" in it. These lines were developed from a logic of artefacts based on the "cloud" (or used in connection with the company's servers).

For the mobile devices market, especially smartphones (since Chromebooks were also launched as tablets), Google initially developed the Nexus line and then Pixel, following Motorola's frustrated experience. As in Chromebook, the lines consisted basically of a brand manufactured by an electronic equipment company with a Google operating system, in the case of Android. It was a response to the adaptations that hardware firms made when launching their embedded models with Android (Chokkattu, 2016). Nexus was a way for Google to take control of the Android interface and application packages (like Samsung's Galaxy Nexus). Pixel appeared for the first time as a Chromebook model, in 2013, with a new version in 2015, until the change to the Pixelbook line, in 2017, with the 2-in-1 version (laptop and tablet) (Hardawar, 2017). The line of mobile devices was introduced on the market (evolving to Pixel 2 and 3 models) in the following two years.

In addition to the traditional ICT devices of the 2000s, Google has invested in "wearables," such as lenses and watches. The model was the same as for Android, making available a specific OS, Android Wear, from 2014, for companies to manufacture prototypes. The company's significance system for these devices, due to the small screen dimensions, was mainly a tool for notifications. In the wake of the Internet of Things, Android was also adapted as an OS for cars, relating to the boundaries of the company's "new bets" (as we will see below). Another important front is that of personal assistants and their integration with home devices. A third front is that of augmented and virtual reality, in which equipment plays a central role (*The Economist*, 2017).

Google's investment in hardware is an important arm of its competitive strategy and its expansion into the internet and ICT segments. It has shown how the nature of this industry and the competition dynamics specific to it create specific demands. Although it already dominated the mobile market with Android, the company still saw in laptops and desktops an important area to be conquered within its logic of increasingly offering and controlling the user experience, regardless of the devices. One barrier was Microsoft's presence in the personal computer segment. Just as it was impacted by its own factors of technology regulation and by the complexity of the competition, it responded with strategies based on its platform nature. Its ability to be the conversion point among manufacturers, developers and users allowed it to forge a model of partnerships with hardware companies in which Google assumed fundamental control of the business as an operating system and the definition of the software layer.

The conglomerate has also entered corporate services, based on Cloud solutions. The most famous and widespread is advertising, already discussed in the business model section. In this section we will deal with other segments, ranging from applications for labour management, such as G Suite, to infrastructure for the most diverse online services, from website hosting to analytics for monitoring and production management (Cloud Platform).

G Suite is one of the main business services. It gathers a series of resources for internal information and communication (Gmail, Calendar, Hangouts), document creation (Documents, Spreadsheets, Slides, Forms, Sites and Apps), content access (Drive and Cloud Search) and process control (Admin, Mobile Management and Vault). The package integrates the functionalities of the personal Suite and adds others aimed at organizing work and facilitating activities and tasks for companies. Google Drive, for example, has solutions for both quick access to files and artificial intelligence systems that monitor the employee's work routine (including actions, interactions, meetings and projects), in order to seek to anticipate information or the availability of documents before the worker demands them (Meyer, 2016).

G Suite is a suite of services that runs on the cloud, along with another important product of the company, the Google Cloud platform.[69] The latter has an extensive set of services, these include: unified, scalable, secure and fast access data storage; personalized virtual machines; workflow orchestration; data analysis and visualization, and solutions for the Internet of Things. One of the relevant product groups is that of artificial intelligence applications. Functionalities listed include: hiring support; unstructured text and image analysis; voice to text conversion and vice versa; machine translation; custom insights and forecasts of customer behaviour; creation of specific applications and deep learning solutions.

Although they have not yet grown in revenue share, these services have gained importance by placing Alphabet at the heart of the management of

---

69 More information at: <https://cloud.google.com/>.

millions of companies using them. It responds to "problems" (using SCOT's terminology) related to production control and optimization, a demand for which technology has been a central element throughout the history of capitalism. With the Suite solutions for companies, Google offers much more sophisticated forms of control than those existing in the competitive (Marx, 2013) and monopolistic (Braverman, 1981) stages of the capitalist system. Such tools deal with the most basic aspect of production time reduction, one of the great indicators of value generation in capitalism, by automating and speeding up procedures, as in the case of Drive, as it operates in the Suite. In addition, they contribute to intensify the exploitation of intellectual labour through a series of processes.[70] The Cloud Platform allows the management of this exploration on a global scale, providing conditions for the fragmentation of plants and production processes necessary for the accumulation of capital in its current stage of globalization. In the scenario of an increasingly fragmented workforce with different relationships (in growing subcontracting modalities, as discussed in Chapter 3), the "management integration" of the work process is gaining new possibilities and tools.[71]

6.1   *Other Bets*

The so-called "other bets" cover several areas less related to core businesses, which make up Alphabet's new format as a conglomerate. The group's management classifies them as "early stage," with a view to generating gains and success in the medium term (Alphabet, 2018: 3). Access is Alphabet's division of infrastructure services and internet access. Within it are units such as Fiber, which deals with fibreoptic access, and Webpass, also focused on internet connection using satellites. Currently, Fiber covers eleven cities in the USA, and Webpass, seven others. Google Fiber offers a web connection with speeds of

---

70   Firstly, by the visibility placed on work activities, which can occur in shared reports whose smallest changes are recorded and identified. This can occur by the control operated over the browsers and apps used by workers. Each work instrument is monitored and generates information for analysis. By means of remote communication instruments (or even used in the same workplace), interactions become less private, intensifying inspection over the workforce, which has cultural and political reverberations in terms of identity and the organizational capacity of the working class.

71   More than just managing workers' activity, the cloud computing capability processes the work itself as information produced and exchanged in documents, tasks and other actions within computerized work dynamics. Artificial intelligence and machine learning tools allow companies, as discussed in Chapter 6, to go beyond simple analysis to prediction and even behaviour modulation. The cloud platform hiring tool is an example of this type of impact.

up to one thousand Mbps. Calico is a research unit on the use of digital technologies in health, focused on longevity. It brings together scientists from fields such as medicine, pharmaceutics, molecular biology, genetics, and computational biology. In 2014, it announced a partnership with the company AbbVie to promote research to develop therapies to combat ageing-related diseases. The total amount of investments reached US$1.5 billion. Verily is also a company in the health sector, focused on developing research and solutions to find ways to apply data collection and analysis in a broad sense. It undertakes projects under development, adding big data, microsensors and treatments.

CapitalG is Alphabet's "growing" investment fund. It is focused on the disruptive business potential of companies in the technology sector in areas identified with industry trends. The focus is on firms with some structure. GV is focused on startups in the early stages of development, having already invested in more than 300 companies. The scope of action of the beneficiaries is broader, starting from segments of the technology industry (such as artificial intelligence and cyber security) and reaching businesses in more distant areas, such as agriculture and transportation. Waymo works with research for the development of autonomous vehicles. This involves self-driving vehicles for various purposes (such as transportation services for people as well as for commodities transportation and delivery). The challenge is huge, since this area is one of the most controversial and sensitive in automation using, due to the risks to human lives involved (Lin, 2016). In 2017, the unit started operating with vehicles on highways (Brin, 2017). In 2018, Waymo One started to run in Phoenix (USA). X is the conglomerate's main technological creation laboratory. Also known as "Moonshot Factory," its goal is to develop technological solutions that have tenfold impacts on the main problems of mankind. One action front is the development of drones for various services, which was named the Wing project. The Malta project develops forms of energy storage with renewable sources in salt.

7 Dissemination

As we've seen so far, Google's operation is quite comprehensive. Despite its significant presence, there is little transparency. Many of its subsystems and artefacts are not even objects of public information regarding penetration and the access numbers. Nevertheless, available data indicate the robustness of the conglomerate's means of access in various markets where it operates, on an internationalized scale that few digital platforms have. For example, Google does not disclose the number of users who resort to search, mainly because part of the access can occur without using an account. But related information can provide an idea of the platform's size. In a scenario where more than 4.3 billion Internet users conduct searches every day (We Are Social, 2019), Google reached 92% of the market[72] in 2020.[73] Although without a systematic disclosure of its user base, an important report on the mobile market (Van Der Wielen, 2018) indicated that Android is installed in 2.3 billion devices. This means 62.8% of all connected mobile devices on the planet.[74] It is the most popular operating system in the world, having exceeded Windows in 2017 and reached 37.93% of devices connected worldwide. On the "side" of the manufacturers, in 2015, there were 24,000 devices with the OS, from 1,294 brands (Tung, 2015). Google Play is a "pre-installed" platform on Android. It is possible to infer that its range is the same as the operating system's, reaching 2.3 billion people. Regarding the "side" of the developers on the platform, in December 2018, there were 2.6 billion applications in Play Store.[75] From these, 2.47 billion were free and 0.12 billion were paid.

Unlike other Google products, considering YouTube, the number of users is counted and disclosed regularly. In 2019, the platform reached 1.9 billion monthly users.[76] As for geographical reach, it has already made specific versions available for 91 countries, in 80 different languages. In 2016, at its Developer Summit, Google announced that there were already more than 2 billion devices with Chrome installed (Lardinois, 2016). This represented a market share of 70.9%.[77] Gmail had 1.5 billion users in 2018 (Google Cloud, 2018). According to a survey (Campaign Monitor, 2018), it was the second most popular email tool, behind only Apple's iPhone.[78] Regarding linked applications, such as G Suite, in 2018 Drive surpassed 1 billion users (Google Cloud, 2018). It is difficult to make an "overall" comparison between Google and Facebook,

---

72 Statcounter (2020) Search engine Market share worldwide aug 2019 aug 2020. Available (consulted 28 September) at: https://gs.statcounter.com/search-engine-market-share.

73 A survey showed the existence of Google sites (domains) in 192 countries. Information available at: <http://www.genealogyintime.com/articles/country-guide-to-google-search-engines-page3.html.

74 Information for May 2016 to March 2017. Available at <https://www.netmarketshare.com/operating-system-market-share.aspx?qprid=10andqpcustomd=1andqpcd=130>. Accessed on April 15, 2017.

75 Information available at: <https://www.appbrain.com/stats>.

76 Information available at: <https://www.youtube.com/intl/en-GB/yt/about/press/>.

77 STATISTA. Global market share held by leading desktop internet browsers from January 2015 to December 2018, Statista, 2019.

78 In the sample, the latter was responsible for 28%, while the Google tool reached 27%. Then came Apple iPad (9%), Outlook (9%), Apple Mail (8%), Yahoo Mail (6%) and Samsung (3%).

given the fact that their services and subsystems do not necessarily compete in the same markets. However, a comparison released by Parse.ly (Lee, 2017) is worth mentioning here. The consultancy monitored the traffic generated by the two companies and found that, until 2015, Google generated the most information on the web, when it was surpassed by Facebook. However, in 2017, it beat the competitor again, according to the analysis.

This wide reach of Google in several market sectors had, as its driving force, the company's need to legitimize itself in society. Two years after its launch, in 2000, Google won an important award in the internet community, the Webby Awards in the technical category (Brin, 2008). In 2003, it reached the top again in the news category with Google News and in the technical achievement category. In the following years, it won awards in several categories, such as best practices (2004), navigation structure (2005), visual design, for Google Earth (2006), art, for Google Art Project (2012), corporate responsibility (2014), and others.[79]

Google has become a common verb. More than a synonym for searches in general, it means a very prosaic and recurring form of searching for information and meanings in the place where all (or almost all) of the records are available in the modern world. To "google" something has become a synonym for "to search on the internet." In 2002, the word was chosen as the "most useful" of the year by the American Dialect Society. In 2006, the term was included in the *Oxford English Dictionary* as a verb, defined as: "search for information about (someone or something) on the internet using the search engine Google." Such semantic identification reinforced a meaning system, aligning or relating the specific technological system to a digital platform modality. Or, more importantly, to the very act of searching for information on the internet. To Google something, therefore, is "to accept the fiction that Google is both the whole information world – and the only path through it." (Heffernan, 2017).

Another aspect that became part of the TS's imaginary was the idea of a space for new unconventional labour relations, in which the production coexisted with structures and leisure spaces, such as courts, sports equipment, massage areas and others (Henderson, 2017). Google has been featured eight times, in the first place, of Fortune magazine's "Best Companies to Work For" ranking, six times in a row in the 2010s.[80] Its headquarters, called "Googleplex," has become part of the system of meaning and representation that supports

---

79   Information available at: <https://www.webbyawards.com/winners/2003/web/general-website/news/>.
80   Information available at: <http://fortune.com/best-companies/>.

the company's legitimization, suggesting a space in which both work and fun are combined. The group's management has worked hard to build this image. The company's evolution was permeated by a discursive strategy of associating it and its services to the "democratizing power" of technology, the possibilities of access to information created by the internet and how Google itself and its products facilitated raising society's knowledge level.

In this sense, promoting its image with the aim of legitimating it takes into account the entire ideology of progress and techno-triumphalism analysed and criticized by authors such as Marcuse (1973), Noble (2011), Feenberg (2002, 2005) and Winner (2016). For each new product, the associated discourse highlighted its benefits based on this ideology and linked that new artefact to the conglomerate's technical capacity and the new experiences enabled. These strategies' goal is not only to promote its commodities, as one of capitalism's historical characteristics, but, also, to deal with the challenge of how to promote, or even create, needs in consumers through artefacts endowed with functionalities that, until then, were not part of the individual's daily life. Why does one need to have a connected household appliance or a smart watch? The stimulus to such consumption benefits from Google's image and contributes to reproduce it, increasing its legitimacy.

However, legitimation is not only a result of the agent's construction, it also involves the influence of other interest groups (Bijker and Pinch, 1993). In this sense, throughout its history, Google has faced criticism from citizens and regulatory bodies (Geissler, 2011). In the UK, people gathered in a chain to try to prevent the vehicle responsible for taking the mapping photos from continuing its course. As seen in the "Rules" section, in several countries, authorities have opened investigations, prosecuted or convicted the group for various reasons, such as anti-competitive practices or data violation. In Greece and the Czech Republic, data protection authorities have initiated investigations to verify possible privacy violations. In Germany, politicians have accused the group of violating privacy rules. Residents' associations have advocated approving regulations instituting the need to obtain Google's authorization from each household for their audiovisual recordings. In Edward Snowden's reports of a government-coordinated surveillance program, the company's image was associated with this initiative. In 2018, Google was in the firing line of US Congress, which called on company executives to testify, as it did with leaders of other technology giants, like Mark Zuckerberg. Google has also entered the process of public debate regarding the risks of digital monopolies in contemporary capitalism. Reports from various vehicles began to question the power of these agents, especially the group analysed.

8 Appropriation

After discussing the system components and their technical resources, this section will evaluate how the appropriation of various agents takes place from interviews conducted with several types of users.[81] Without any intention to propose a generalizing view, the reports in the present section offer elements from actual cases as a way to underline the subjects' importance in technological regulation through the several forms of appropriation.[82] Google's importance has been highlighted both by individuals who use its artefacts on a daily basis and by people who relate to the technology system in their professional practices. "At Google, the purpose is to be the information company. And, in fact, they are," was how a senior director of a large Brazilian media group characterized them (R11). In comparison with Facebook, the technological system was better evaluated. One interviewee saw Google as "more serious:" "Considering what we look for there, its results are more serious, and they are established. And it offers a more direct use. On Facebook, even if I don't want to see something, it's there" (R21). For a marketing professional specialized in digital media with long experience in political campaigns (R3), Google is fundamental for users and, also, for electoral disputes. For the first audience, the TS has become the main locus for obtaining information: "They access Google, type their search, and that magical engine offers them an endless list of things. It offers everything, videos, recipes, where to buy things." In politics, unlike the interaction with other networks, which he refers to as a "summer fling," with Google, the relationship has to be permanent.

When talking about the relevance of the search engine, the network publisher of the main institution of one of the judiciary branches (R1) pointed out to its role as the main "channel" for targeting access to the institution's website: "It is essential. The largest number of accesses to our portal comes from the search. It reaches 80% through the search" (R1). The social network coordinator of a federal legislative institution (R2) feels the same, and reports

---

81   The discussion will take into account the various modalities of agents involved with the technological system, such as (1) public institutions, (2) political associations and those responsible for their communication strategies, (3) media outlets, (4) researchers, (5) developers, (6) civil society organizations and (7) non-professional users. The testimonies and dialogues will contribute to give examples of ways of using different types of agents involved, forming interest groups in line with SCOT and "sides" of the platform, according to the conceptual debate conducted in Chapter 7.

82   For indication purposes, interviewees will be identified by their numbers from the list presented in the section that explained the analysis framework. "R" means "respondent." We will refrain from including the date, since all the interviews occurred in 2019.

that this is a central channel for people to reach the institution's website: "Most people reach us not because they access the [institutional] portal." Among the respondents who were non-professional users, the significance system generally included an insight into the system's functionality for day-to-day activities. Several people interviewed claimed to use the search daily, such as an agronomy student in the city of Pelotas (RS) (R18). "I use it to search for different things, both for school and culture, also, to find reviews on series," commented a student with regular performance in digital social networks, from Curitiba (PR) (R17). A commercial representative from the city of São Paulo (SP) (R19) reported using the search "mainly for clients that I will seek." An independent saleswoman living in Paracatu (MG) (R20) reported to use Google "a lot, for college research, any doubts I have I go straight to Google. I find it very useful in my life." A teacher from Crateús (CE) (R21) also said she accesses it for information when preparing classes. "I use Google many times a day to look for information," said the professional musician from Goiânia (R25). The legal advisor from Macapá (AP) (R24) highlighted its functional properties: "I think it's faster than other search engines."[83]

A young student from Salvador (R22) mentioned the features that make searching easier, such as auto-complete, as an advantage of the platform. The freelance saleswoman and student from Paracatu (R20) also pointed to the auto-complete feature as a convenience. Both reports meet the company's strategy of including this type of functionality to speed up the search. A cultural producer from Belém (PA) listed integration with other services as a positive functional property: "I use it every day, every time. I don't use any other search engines. It's all there, Gmail, YouTube" (R23).[84] When questioning respondents about Google's offering of its own services in the results, virtually none of them reported realizing that this happened. Thus, the company takes advantage of this lack of perception to promote its own subsystems and artefacts.

The perception as to the results' relevance (one of the key concepts of the model built by the TS's management) varied. The agronomy student from Pelotas (R18) stated that, although sometimes he does not get the best search

---

83 The use and the corresponding system of meaning associated with the platform, at least among those interviewed, highlighted its scope and legitimacy. However, despite this role, when asked if they knew the internal rules of the Terms of Use, none of the respondents had ever read them.

84 This statement reinforces the logic of the strategies of incorporation, expansion, integration and extension of activities operated by Alphabet, in the combined offer of services. This "integration," as discussed, favours the services, "bundling" the products (Edelman, 2015), with alarming competitive impacts.

results, he "usually finds" what he is looking for. The teacher from Crateús (CE) (R21) also stated that the links listed are not always the best but considers that the results "are relevant." And how well do these people know how the results are processed and displayed? The vast majority did not know how the process was carried out or what criteria were used. An interviewee (R21) admitted the lack of information about it: "I don't know how they are selected" (R20). "I don't know how they define the results for me." In a few cases, the respondents offered some hypothesis related to their activity and/or conditions. "I think it displays the links that are most searched for by people and by me. It shows me everything that I usually search for. Based on this, it can show me what I want," answered a teenager from Salvador (BA), who seemed to be unsure about the information. "I think it shows me the most accessed links," reported the student from Barra do Garças (MT) (R26).

Most of the respondents also did not go beyond the first results page. Respondent 18 said: "I do not look beyond the first page." Interviewee 20 as another example: "I almost never look beyond it." The student from Salvador reported that it is easier to make another search than to "go to the second page" (R22). The teenager from Curitiba (R17) commented that he has "never noticed" whether he goes beyond the first page. These responses suggest a crystallization of the experience modulated by the platform to naturalize the search itself, such as entering the term, checking the first results and choosing the link, without a culture of checking a broader list of results, indicating an example of regulation by technology.

However, there are exceptions. The commercial representative from São Paulo (R19) reported that he goes beyond the first page "when I see that I didn't find what I wanted." The teacher from Crateús (CE) (R21) said it was more common to go to the second or third pages and compare results "out of curiosity." Articulating Google's importance as a channel to reach websites with the practice of sticking to the first page, the 'achievement' of being placed the first results becomes a measure of survival and success for pages on the internet. This reaffirms the power of the ranking algorithm and its criteria, regulating an important part of content production on the web.

For people who work with website creation, such regulation is expressed in techniques to improve ranking called "search engine optimization" (or SEO). In the main institution of the Federal Judiciary Branch, the social network editor (R1) reported such measures: "When journalists write a story, they have to mention other related news so that we can make the 'link' [include links]. Give suggestions for titles. The press editorial office now has to pay attention to the keywords in the titles." According to her, such practices have improved the website's ranking: "We always appear on the first page" (R1). The social network coordinator of an important legislative house (R2) said that these issues "end up being largely taken into account in the portal's own tools."

Virtually all respondents also reported using Chrome. Interviewee 18 said "the interface is simple, it's easy and fast" (R18). Although there is no need to login to the browser to conduct the activities, there were reports showing that this feature is used. Respondent 19 also use the software: "Most of the time I use Chrome. I access it and I remain logged in to work." The logic of promoting Google's own products was mentioned as a reason. Respondent 22 saw this integration as a positive feature: "Because it's on Google. It all comes together; we really use it." One respondent (R20) also confirmed using Chrome in her everyday life. When asked about the reason, she answered: "I don't know." The lack of understanding about why a certain artefact is accessed, its social content and what it represents is one of the crystallization aspects of the appropriation modes promoted by Google, configuring a technological rationality for these relations, according to Marcuse (1973). With YouTube, the reference suggested a period of lower "maturity," according to Hughes [1993], but a representative reach, having become a consumer space for virtually all respondents. This was seen in the communication strategies of public agencies. The coordinator of an important legislative house (R2) reported that YouTube became the "online version" of the institutional TV station.

Among the non-professional users interviewed, there were several reports of how the platform was configured as a source of information, as reported by Respondent 20: "Nowadays, I use YouTube more." Respondent 22 was another example: "I use it all the time, mainly for entertainment. I play whatever I want to watch" (R22). According to this model where any user is able to post content, YouTube has promoted people with visibility, known as "youtubers," which attract audience. "I use it to watch some youtubers. Mainly from the United States," said Respondent 17. For artists, the business model is still limited compared to other streaming platforms (R25). It has been recognized both by genres (less informative and more entertaining) and by formats (shorter videos). The notifications sent upon these channels' updates were also pointed out as a tool that facilitates consumption. "YouTube sends a notification, and it is more convenient," noted Respondent 20. Regarding the recommendation system, an adolescent from Barra do Garças (MT) (R26) complained about the suggestions. "YouTube recommends things I have never searched for. Related to makeup, gossiping, things I never looked for," she said.

With the platform's rise and growing participation in the dispute for the audience's attention, Brazilian media groups have been devising different positioning strategies. Analysing the market, the director of a large national television network (R11) shows how there are cases in which national networks have bet on the platform as a space for online broadcasting, such as the channel SBT. For others, the number of posts is more limited, prioritizing their own platform, such as Grupo Globo with GloboPlay. He claims that the platform has not yet entered the competition for quality content (such as services like Netflix or Amazon Prime Video), sticking to the logic of short videos, which can be successful, but do not assume mass communication, in his opinion.

Another important conglomerate's subsystem discussed in the interviews was Android. Most respondents commented they had a smartphone with this operating system. But none said it was a specific choice, the acquisition being more related to the device purchased. "I bought a Motorola phone, and it comes with Android. It doesn't matter to me" (R18), said one of the respondents. The strategy of working with several manufacturers allowed a wide base of diverse offers, including more affordable devices, which is not the case with its main competitor, Apple. This is part of the respondents' perception, as commented by Respondent 19. "I bought an Android due to its cost-benefit, because Apple's devices are very expensive." "I didn't even choose much. What mattered to me is that I had access to Facebook, WhatsApp and to take pictures, in addition to the low price. It was good enough," said Respondent 21. The teenager from Salvador reproduced the "Googlization of everything" discourse, using a term from Vaydhjanathan (2011): "Are there non-Android phones?" (R22).

When asked about the role of Play Store and pre-installed applications, most respondents reported making use of the tools already embedded in the operating system. "I usually use what's in it. I only download banking applications and Waze. But I basically use what is in it" (R19). A developer working on a major transport application pointed out that the operating system performs well: "Android works. After 25 minutes, you're using it for everything you need. The ease of use is a distinguishing feature in that sense" (R10). However, some respondents expressed a preference for Apple, as Respondent 23 said: "I've used Android a lot. The smartphone allowed us not to waste time on activities. Android crashed a lot and was subject to viruses. So, I migrated to iPhone and I've been using it until today. The system doesn't crash, I don't waste time."

With respect to Android, another side of the platform, that of developers, comes into play. A researcher and developer from an institute of technology and society in Rio de Janeiro (R8) commented that the operating system and app dissemination store are less bureaucratic for those who create apps. The technological requirements are not overwhelming, and the approval process is fast. "It requires an app signature key, to ensure the authenticity of that compilation to run on mobile phones. You sign up, pay a developer fee and you can register the apps," the respondent said. Other advantages are the analysis tools, which offers data about who downloaded the application, such as demographic data. Another developer, an employee of a mobility app (R10), also mentioned the simple procedures and few requirements. He stressed, as an important concern, the availability of information for the program presentation in the platform and the updates from new versions. However, none of the developers interviewed said they knew the criteria used by the store to sort the apps presented and the main ones, called "top apps."

A lesser number of respondents reported using Google's work product suite. After trying free solutions, the developer who worked for the transportation application (R10) reported he was not able to "get rid of" the suite, "partly because the tool is good. The email tool has a good volume limit, the usability is ok. That's what the service is, it's easy to use. It hardly suffers any downtime," he added. The most commonly mentioned artefact was Gmail. As with Chrome and the search, the leading product image (derived from the platform's network effect, its functional properties and its built legitimization) contributed to its use in relation to other services. Respondent 18 could not explain the preference for the software: "I don't know why I chose Gmail. I chose it because it's the most used one."

All of these services are backed by the conglomerate's online advertising tools. They have suffered changes in this area, both in the professional field and in the users' perception. For the planning director of a large digital agency (R5), the segmentation enabled by Google "completely changes the way you advertise," allowing the advertiser to "target" an audience with accuracy: "Targeting helps to send what makes sense to the user and increases the level of interest." The respondent mentioned as an example the use of information from a credit service (Serasa) to find out when the user would draw a benefit payment (Severance Pay Indemnity Fund) and, thus, send a real estate ad to that person, since the payments from this benefit can be used in such acquisition.

The media vice president of a major digital agency (R6) pointed out that this way of advertising offers new logics. One of them is that of relevance, since the ad is built from the profile of the target audience to offer them what has meaning based on these characteristics. The second is the "stalking" of the internet user by the advertisements. With the AdSense feature, the production of promotional messages must seek relevance "regardless of the journey." On YouTube, the platform also works by providing services that would be typical of an ad agency to advertisers and content producers.[85] One of them is by

---

85   One of them is youtuber influencers. "Let's say an influencer charged 40,000 BRL as payment. You pay 80,000 BRL to YouTube, 40,000 BRL to the influencer and 40,000 BRL goes to the media. The influencer talks about the brand and then the media piece is shown" (R5).

offering tools and knowledge to "support" advertisers to use the platform and spend more.[86]

Respondents were not consistent in assessing whether this new way of advertising delivered relevant ads in practice. Part of the respondents complained about the messages. Respondent 18 thought that "they are pushing too hard. It pollutes the search page. Windows pop up everywhere". Respondent 22 expressed rage about it: "It's too much. It makes me angry sometimes. You go to a page, and ads pop up." The freelance saleswoman from Paracatu (R20) considered that ads on Google are shown less frequently than on Facebook and YouTube.[87] The student from Barra do Garças (MT) especially criticized the ads in the middle of YouTube videos. "I find it very annoying" (R26).

In the interviews, we also asked if the respondent had clicked on an ad thinking it was an organic result. "I've been misled. It took me a while to realize that the first results were ads. Then when I realized I started to ignore them," reported the student from Curitiba (R17). "Once I wanted to know how much I was going to pay as IPVA [Brazilian motor vehicle property tax]. I typed the term 'IPVA' and then clicked on a result. But it was an ad and it took me to a dispatcher's website. Then I had to search all over again," said a commercial representative from São Paulo (R19).

Regarding the understanding as to data usage in targeting, the same respondent said he was aware of the role of geolocation in targeting ads. But, in a few cases, questions were raised, even if intuitively, regarding advertisements. Respondent 22 said it is "very strange:" There are things I don't even search for, and an ad for something that my sister searched for on her computer pops up. She searches for a book and it shows up here. I don't even know how that happens." They were also asked if they knew the ad preferences and if they ever changed the settings. Almost all of them responded negatively. Only the agronomy student from Pelotas (R18) reported using advertising blockers. "It was a hint from a friend of mine who was already using it. Now that you've mentioned that, I remember. I've already been misled. In the beginning, we always click on the first search results" (R18).

---

86 "The point is that this kind of service is available in general for big advertisers, privileging them over medium and small ones. Google today already has a format that takes the audience from main channels and sells it to advertisers. This was in beta version and only larger advertisers could use it" (R6).

87 In assessing the relevance or not of the advertisements, some respondents saw these ads as a 'compromise' for the service's gratuity and content remuneration. Two respondents talked about this: "I understand the need for an ad in order to pay youtubers" (R17). "I think it's free remuneration. It's not a big deal. You can live with them" (R26).

Finally, the interviews addressed the users' perception of the use of their data and their privacy. When asked if they knew how Google used these data, most responded negatively. Some said they had heard about certain types of uses. "I've read reports. I have a remote idea, but I don't know exactly how it works," (R25), said the respondent. The commercial representative from São Paulo was one of the few to express some knowledge, although generically: "Using the geolocation system, it shows you what you like in that region" (R19). Similarly, they were asked whether they had ever read the privacy policy, a question to which almost all of the respondents replied negatively. The degree of concern about Google's use of personal data was also asked about. In this case, most of them showed that it was not a compelling problem. "It doesn't worry me. From the moment I use a platform whose terms I don't even read, I know I'm subject to privacy invasion," said Respondent 17. "I don't make a big deal out of it. I use it as a work tool," commented Respondent 23. In some cases, the granting of personal data was understood as a necessity to obtain some features, as stated by Respondent 22: "I don't like to keep some things in there, I don't know how it will be used. Other things I do, like school passwords, enrolment number, since I use it all the time." When given information about some application, such as the cross-use of data across services and the reading of emails, the reactions changed: "I didn't know they did that. It seems they know more about you than other people," said Respondent 18. "Do they read Gmail's messages? Wow, total invasion of privacy," complained Respondent 20.

Such behaviours suggest that awareness regarding the exploitation of personal information is directly influenced by people's knowledge of these practices and operating logic. As in the discussion proposed in Chapters 2 and 3, companies seek to impart a "neutrality aura" to their artefacts and systems to prevent or hinder an understanding of their social content (Trigueiro, 2009) and their technical code (Feenberg, 2005).

9   Relationship with the Values Base

This section assumes the value basis discussed in Chapter 1 and details it from the analysis of the chapter's case study, given the categories concerning the rights "promotion" and "damage." To this end, Google's activities and its artefacts or subsystems will be detailed, such as data protection and privacy, public debate, and the right to communication, discrimination, transparency, and competition. More than carrying out an extensive discussion on these impacts, whose relevance demands separate research, our intention here is to highlight this dimension of technological systems and incorporate the third dimension of the technological regulation model – the impacts on society.

9.1 Rights Promotion and Guarantees

By making relevant parts of the web available to users through two trillion searches a year, it can be said that Google contributes to promoting the right to information.[88] Lev-On (2008) highlights search engines as "vital tools" for information searching, especially in the vast database that the internet has become. Concerning systems based on link mapping, such as the one we analysed here, Lev-On sees several advantages over the previous forms, organized from selections by people, as well as in relation to response services by experts. These systems are able to cover a much larger number of sources and present the information in less time. An interesting aspect of the engines, he adds, is that "they occasionally generate unplanned and unpredictable exposures to diverse views, even to information that runs counter to searchers' prior beliefs" (Lev-On, 2008: 138). The difficulties in a "perfect search" according to the user's intention and profile would, thus, be positive aspects for promoting diversity.

Felten (2004, n.p.) takes a similar approach. In his opinion, Google is a "voting scheme": "Google is not a mysterious Oracle of Truth but a numerical scheme for aggregating the preferences expressed by web authors. It's a form of democracy – call it Googleocracy." In this model, content creators "vote" by adding links on their pages, and Google counts the votes. This democracy, in the author's opinion, would be an element of Google's nature, rather than a problem. As in democracy, he adds, the results are not always the best, but the system, including the moves of its members to compete for the highest-ranking positions, is part of its manifestation.

The YouTube subsystem is seen by authors as a locus not only of promoting the right to information, but of exercising freedom of expression. The first right would be related to the possibility of accessing the most different sources of information through the platform, within the more than one billion hours consumed. Although they recognize the subsystem's metamorphoses, Burgess and Green (2018) identified in it a phenomenon of participative culture, facilitating the production and posting of video content. Wall and Zahed (2011) underline YouTube and Facebook's role in Egypt's popular mobilizations in 2011, part of the wave of uprisings that would become known as the "Arab Spring."

---

88   Farias (2004) breaks this down into the right to inform oneself and to be informed, in an understanding that intersects with freedom of expression. Analysing the traditional media, Sousa Júnior et al. (2016: 14) point out that "the media constitute a public sphere and must realize the democratic values that ensure the right to free information."

9.2 *Damages and Violation of Rights*

One of the most critical aspects of Google's loss of warranties and rights involves data protection and privacy. Westin (1967: 7) defines privacy as "the claim of individuals, groups, or institutions to determine for themselves when, how, and to what extent information about them is communicated to others." Other authors have also worked with this concept.[89] By intending to "organize all the information in the world," Google depended on massive data collection. In this sense, it came into conflict with data protection and privacy of its users. The company's understanding of the subject was summed up in a remarkable statement by its former executive director, Eric Schmidt: "If you have something that you don't want anyone to know, maybe you shouldn't be doing in the first place" (CNBC, 2009, n.p.). The statement led to repercussions from privacy and data protection organizations, as well as conceptual elaborations. Google is classified by Spinik and Zimmer (2008) as a "dataveillance infrastructure."[90] Such vigilance is part of its operating logic as a company, according to Fuchs (2013).[91]

Perhaps the most striking example is the scanning of messages exchanged through Gmail. For a long time, the content of messages sent among the millions of e-mail addresses in the application was scanned as an additional element for ad customization within the platform (Kang and McAllister, 2011). Google Street View is another application with privacy risks. First of all, due to the unauthorized collection of information in public places. In addition to the unique characteristics of each artefact, surveillance also underlies a relationship strategy among them. In 2012, Google updated its privacy policies and put an end to the separation of user records in its various applications (such as not using Gmail data for YouTube recommendations). This deeper integration has created increasingly higher surveillance, especially for the group's primary

---

89   Altman (1975: 24) defines privacy as "selective control of access to oneself." Burkert (1997: 136) raises questions about the perception of privacy as something individual and argues that the concept of privacy should be inserted in a broader perspective, in a "political" dimension, being immersed in a set of rights related to communication and democratic participation. Concealment inherent to privacy should be an option of the subject together with its opposite, the subject's exposure as a political actor who assumes positions and gets mobilized.

90   Clarke (1988) defines dataveillance as follows: "Dataveillance is the systematic use of personal data systems in the investigation or monitoring of the actions or communications of one or more persons" (apud. Spinik and Zimmer, 2008, n.p.).

91   The introduction of ever more applications "does primarily serve economic ends that are realized by large-scale user surveillance" (Fuchs, 2013: 33).

source of revenue: advertising.[92] In July 2019, Google was, again, the subject of complaints that became public: its staff were listening and reviewing users' audio recordings through virtual assistants and other devices. The German Data Protection Authorities started an investigation. In September, Google said it would maintain the staff listening and reviewing only when users opted for it (Woolaccott, 2019). In 2019, Google launched an "Incognito Mode" with some privacy features, such as not collecting some location data, but it didn't stop the application from tracing users' movements (Newman, 2019). During the COVID-19 pandemic, Maps started to show the disease prevalence in different locations to inform users about the pandemic distribution in their cities and neighbourhoods (Valinsky, 2020). That same year, it was reported that Google had a project, called Nightingale, based on the collection of tons of health data. The company made a partnership with Ascension, the second largest health company in the US (Barber and Molteni, 2019). In 2020, researchers found 500 Chrome extensions uploading private users' data, as part of an ad-fraud scheme (Goodwin, 2020). This shows the vulnerability of extensions in the navigator. In the context of the COVID-19 pandemic, Google and Apple announced a partnership for a contact tracing app. The promise and the risks were big, considering the two companies controlled nearly 3 billion smartphones in the world. But, in US, several states' health authorities opted not to use the system (Vogelstein and Knight, 2020).

In terms of public debate and the right to communication, freedom of expression and the right to information,[93] one relevant discussion was how the content presented in the results is selected, especially regarding the existence of "biases," which would affect the right to information of those making the search and, consequently, would impact the online discussion. Biases in search results have been pointed out many times throughout the history of the company and are one of its main problem areas.[94] Responding to accusations by US President Donald Trump in 2018, the company issued a statement denying political or ideological bias in the presentation of its search results (Reuters,

---

92   In 2019, several European civil society organizations filed a lawsuit against Google for using sensitive data to build profiles of citizens in that region (Blashcke, 2019).
93   Using here the UNESCO definition (1983).
94   This problem has even led to lawsuits, such as that filed by Search King in 2003 (*SearchKing vs. Google*, 2003), accusing the plaintiff of deliberately reducing its position in the ranking. In its defence, Google admitted having purposely changed the result for three reasons: because the plaintiff (and its search advertising service, a competitor of Google) was damaging the integrity of the system, the absence of an obligation to include the site in the ranking and the fact that the results are statements, thus being protected by the First Amendment.

2018). In a testimony to the United States Congress, Google's CEO, Sundar Pichai (2018), also rebutted the claim that there was bias in the results. Studies point to the effective presence of such biases in the search results,[95] undermining new websites.[96] A second bias stage involves customization strategies, which started in 2009 and ended up reinforcing the logic of "filter bubbles" (Pariser, 2011). It also was criticized by its role in disinformation diffusion. The Tech Transparency Project showed how, besides efforts declared by Google to stop misinformation about COVID-19, the company still profited from it. An investigation by the organization showed 97 websites spreading misinformation running ads with Doubleclick and AdSense tools (Tech Transparency Project, 2020). In the 2020 US Elections, Google announced it would turn off autocomplete tool about election queries, since the results could provide false information (Cohen, 2020). The company declared it would ban ads right after voting day to avoid the political use of promotional messages to influence the repercussion of the results (Fung, 2020).

However, the impact on the public debate and the internet users' right to communication does not occur only with respect to the search engine. YouTube has been criticized for its recommendation system.[97] Tufecki (2018) observed an "extremist" pattern in the recommendations. In political themes, the algorithm led to videos about both left-wing and right-wing conspiracy theories. Chaslot (2017), a former YouTube employee who worked in the area of recommendations and was fired from the company, examined the recommendation results for topics related to conspiracy theories and identified this "radicalization" trend.[98] Bloomberg (Bergen, 2019) interviewed former YouTube executives and heard from them that the company repeatedly prioritized views,

---

95   Goldmann (2008) criticizes the idea of the neutrality of the results, reminding that the algorithm analyses a section of the universe and that there are ranking criteria.
96   Cho and Roy (2004) pointed to a "huge and worrying impact" of search engines on new pages by favouring the older and more "popular" ones.
97   In 2018, the algorithm raised to the top of the "trending topics" a video with a conspiracy theory that a survivor of a shooting that left 17 teenagers dead in the United States was actually a perpetrator (Lapowsky, 2018). The logic of considering views and interactions (such as likes and comments) as indicators in recommendations creates a reinforcement method in which offensive and appealing content spreads and the algorithms drive this by recommending it to new people, which generates a circulation spiral on the platform.
98   In the search, when asking whether the Earth was flat or round, 90% of the recommendations were related to the flat Earth conspiracy theory. When asking who the Pope was, 85% of the recommendations associated Catholic authority with terms like "devil," "anti-Christ," or "Satanic." When searching for content on global warming, videos saying that it was a rumour appeared in 70% of the recommendations.

and profits originated from engagement, over combating misinformation, hate speech or toxic and extreme content.

The biases in the search results impacted not only the democratic public debate and the right to communication in its various dimensions. It includes discrimination logics on several aspects, reinforcing social classification mechanisms (Quijano, 2011). Baker and Potts (2013) analysed more than 2,600 suggestions and concluded that different population groups are treated differently.[99] Elers (2014) examined the Maori people of New Zealand and found pejorative associations, such as "fat," "poor," "lazy," or "violent." Criticism in relation to this led to the creation of an internal standard for the tool, called Autocomplete Policies.[100] It is a list of topics that is considered inadequate.[101] The feature was terminated in 2017. The company's argument involved the growth of mobile devices search and the restrictions imposed by these smaller devices and screens to adapt the search results shown in real time with every new character typed.

Gender discrimination practices have also appeared in Google technologies. One example is the translation artefact (Google Translator) which, when showing a term in another language, presented the terms in the male gender by default. In the translation of professions, for example, the term 'engineering' was associated with the male gender while 'nursing' was associated with the female gender. In 2018, the company announced that it would introduce the words in both genders. In Gmail's autocomplete tool (smart compose), the company removed the pronouns related to gender to avoid discrimination or bias in this sense. Technicians from the group found cases in which the artificial intelligence system suggested responses associating male pronouns with certain professions or conditions, such as being an investor (Dave, 2018).

All these impacts on people's lives occur, in general, without their knowledge about the operating logic processes. Pasquale (2015) gave such importance to this obscure scenario that, when analysing the operation of algorithms

---

99   Gays or blacks were related to negative stereotypes, such as, in the first case, "seropositive," "going to hell" and "talking like girls," and in the second, "lazy," "traitors" and "criminals." When the searches involved "whites" and synonyms, the complements suggested sexual behaviour (especially attraction to other ethnic groups).
100 Google. Autocomplete Policies. Google Search Help. Available at: <https://support.google.com/websearch/answer/7368877/>.
101 The first of these is sexually explicit content or vulgar language. The second is terms that reflect hate speech against people or groups based on race, ethnic origin, religion, disability, gender, age, nationality, veteran status, sexual orientation and gender identity. The third are graphic descriptions of violence. The fourth are activities that encourage harm in the offline world.

in several segments, he coined the term "Black Box Society" and listed Google as the main example. This is because, in the first place, the company does not reveal the criteria effectively used in its PageRank, although it publicly maintains that the system ranks sites by relevance and importance. Despite the secrecy justification as a business strategy, the author warns, the result is "devastating" for the understanding of how the platform represents the world to users. Another level of lack of transparency lies in the indicators used and ways of processing search results by algorithms. It also involves actions by various agents (from political campaigns to companies) to enhance their visibility on the platform, in more or less official ways. This can occur through paid content, not always so discernible from others, through SEO techniques, for a better performance in results, or even based on Google and YouTube teams' guidance concerning how to better use the tools available for those who are able to pay for this service.

Miconi (2014: 31) addresses the problem as follows: "Let's be honest: we don't know exactly how Google works. However, we all use Google to get information, probably because everybody else does." And at the heart of this is the search engine's algorithm, which the author defines as "the digital version of the Coca-Cola recipe": everyone likes it but doesn't know how it's made. For him, there is a question not only of effective transparency, that is, how much information is available or not on how PageRank works, but of perceived transparency, that is, concerning the fact that the arbitrary ranking is not even a concern for its users, due to the apparent neutrality transmitted by the platform or the lack of knowledge regarding this central aspect.

According to several examples already mentioned, Google strongly impacts competition. The figures showing the share of several subsystems and artefacts do not point to competitive market structures, but to situations of monopoly, oligopoly, and the occurrence of entrance barriers and anti-competitive practices. Among the monopolistic markets are search engines, browsers, mobile operating system, and free video streaming services. In the first case, Alphabet's share is over 90%; in the second, it is more than 70%; in the third, it is more than 60%; in the fourth, it is 60% in North America. This is especially true for the conglomerate's main entrance door, the search engine, as indicated by Pasquale (2015).[102] Quintarelli (2015) also

---

102 According to the author, a UK price comparison firm, Foundem, which, according to its directors, would have had its visibility reduced, was taken off the first result pages. From the moment it started to provide information on searched establishments, Google directly affected the performance of services, providing tips and information on locations, such as Yelp.

highlights the rise phenomenon of monopolistic platforms, such as Google and Facebook, driven by large returns, the global scale, enclosure effects on their ecosystems, the lack of interoperability, and factors that combine to strengthen dominating positions.[103]

Edelman (2015) highlights the importance of "tying" strategies among the conglomerate's several subsystems and artefacts as an anticompetitive practice. This is seen in the promotion of the conglomerate's services in the search, as discussed above. Edelman mentions, as an example, the need to create a Google+ account to comment on YouTube, implemented in 2013. He considers that such practices are subject to punishment according to antitrust rules: "There is strong evidence that Google's tie hinders competition in the markets for the tied products" (Edelman, 2015: 8).

In 2019, a former Mozilla executive claimed that Google made suspicious decisions to undermine the Firefox browser, like running ads next to Firefox search. Gmail and Google Docs started to present bugs when running on Mozilla's browser (Keiser, 2019). *The Wall Street Journal* confirmed (Schechner, et al. 2020), in an investigation, that Google prioritizes YouTube over rivals on vídeo search results. In searches conducted, YouTube got 95% of the first spots in the results carousel when compared to Facebook Watch, and 86% compared to Twitch:

> Engineers at Google have made changes that effectively preference YouTube over other video sources, according to people familiar with the matter. Google executives in recent years made decisions to prioritize YouTube on the first page of search results, in part to drive traffic to YouTube, rather, than to competitors, and, also, to give YouTube more leverage in business deals with content providers seeking traffic for their videos, one of those people said.
>
> SCHECHNER, ET AL. 2020

In 2020, *Protocol* reported that Google made agreements with tv manufacturers to licence its Android TV imposing the ban of Amazon's Fire TV streaming services (Roettgers, 2020).

---

103 As an example of this regulation in the immaterial dimension in the area of competition, in the case of Google, the author mentions the example of the change in the algorithm of the company's search engine in 2014 that cost US$200 million for eBay, its competitor in the e-commerce segment.

10 The Technological System's Impact on Society

This section discusses the third dimension of the technological regulation model developed here: that of regulation by technology.[104] There are two transversal elements in the impacts of Google, as well as Facebook and the other large technology companies, regardless of the sphere. The first is the already discussed surveillance and the relentless data collection from people and institutions in all possible ways, including those not admitted and illegal. The second, and perhaps most dangerous one, is not just storing the world's digital tracks but processing them to predict how individuals will behave next, or at different times in the future. Forget about trying to describe a world (and the various impasses this poses) "and focus on predicting it" (Andrejevic, 2013: 85–6). This movement presumes a shift in the perspective of these information industries from understanding to correlation. But, even more so, such platforms move on to a third stage, which involves modulating behaviour by organizing access to applications and user content.

In the scientific–technological sphere, the interrelationship between this and science within the sphere assumes a dialectic dimension. As well as part of previous knowledge stocks (Bunge, 2012; Heilbronner, 1994; Dosi, 1984), the very construction of systems and artefacts offers new elements both from the point of view of scientific research and the evolution of specific technology trajectories or even from the technological paradigm as a whole. If, in Google's case, this would already be a reality in key areas of the ICT paradigm[105] (such as the emerging technologies mentioned in Chapter 4), Alphabet's "other bets" highlight the attempt to develop knowledge and technologies, as well as products that enable its participation, in several markets in other areas. Both Calico and Verily have projects focused on the life sciences sector. X is a peculiar example, since it does not have a focus in terms of segment, but its goal is to create technologies that "create impact," ranging from internet access through balloons to energy storage.

In addition to the research in its R&D laboratories and its other bets, the conglomerate has been investing energy and financial resources in knowledge

---

104   This is the moment when systems and artefacts are evaluated by the impacts they generate on society and on specific spheres according to the schematic organization that is part of the model. However, as warned in the analysis framework, this section does not intend to exhaust the debate or even analyse it to the minimum degree of depth that would be necessary.

105   Among which the most important is artificial intelligence.

production. Google Transparency Project Survey[106] identified 330 scientific papers published between 2005 and 2017 on public policy topics in approaches favouring the interests of the company that funded them in some way. From these, in 179 (54%) of the cases the funding was direct, and in 151 (46%), it was indirect. In 65%, the financial support was not mentioned by the authors of the academic papers. Among the subjects addressed were issues directly related to the regulation of the platform's activities, such as antitrust, privacy, network neutrality, patents and copyright. Competition was the most recurrent theme, with 113 studies. The authors of the survey point to a coincidence of searches on the subject in years during which Google was under investigation about its monopoly power, as in 2012.[107] The authors recognize works in peer-reviewed journals with appropriate methodologies, but, also, several cases published in spaces that are not peer-reviewed and without any scientific rigor.

Google has propagated search projects around the world. In Africa, it has hosted competitions in software engineering colleges calling on students to develop compatible equipment for use in Google as an application (Tavory, 2008). It has also celebrated partnerships with educational entities, such as the Zawadi African Education Fund, focused on low-income women and people in the countryside. The company funded grants for students to complete their courses in computer engineering. On the Google Code website, the company also provides tools to develop innovations for its services. Among the tools are the graphical elements for the interfaces, which save time, on the one hand, but that homogenize and apply company parameters on the resources created, on the other.[108]

In the economic sphere, Google's performance has a significant impact. In the general sphere, it offers services that facilitate numerous activities performed by companies. The main one is advertising, which is the basis for promoting commodities in capitalism (Marx, 2014; Bolaño, 2007). With its

---

106 Google Transparency Project. Google Academics Inc. Google Transparency Project. Available at: <https://www.googletransparencyproject.org/articles/google-academics-inc>.
107 This funding involves prestigious universities in the country such as Stanford, MIT, California Berkley and Columbia. In Europe, Oxford (UK), Berlin School of Economics (Germany) and University of Edinburgh (Scotland).
108 "Libraries, therefore, allow programmers to create their own software from a set of shared elements, true and authentic de-facto programming standards. Supporting the libraries means implementing the work using a very broad and complex starting base, which optimally uses the code already available and stratifies skills. Libraries, therefore, have a strategic value both in the dynamics of spontaneous FS cooperation and in the relational economy of the OS" (Ippolita, 2017: 42).

flexible and scalable online advertising model, adapted to "any budget," it has allowed agents with lower revenues to advertise. More than just "opening up" the advertising market to more people, the company has qualitatively changed this market through customized advertising. In 2017, 1.5 million firms and institutions made use of it (Google, 2017). Google's tools allowed a level of detailing in campaigns that was previously inconceivable. The data analysis resources (analytics) provide possibilities for monitoring the results. Advertisers can accurately target the audience, reducing promotion uncertainties. Combined with e-commerce, these features allow for a reduction in the product rotation cycle and savings on circulation actions, including logistics. In 2017, 30% of the clicks on US companies' websites through Google tools came from outside the country, highlighting the internationalization potential (Google, 2017).

This customized advertising system gained momentum in a scenario of recovery after the 2007–8 crisis, with a slowdown in productivity and shortcomings in employment rates compared to the pre-crisis period. In a scenario of fierce competition at the global level, weaknesses in advertising gains, and the difficulty in creating a new expansive cycle (Freeman and Louçã, 2004), customized advertising, as previously discussed in this work, emerged as a cost rationalization element. But not only did this service meet demands related to the economic moment, the whole set of the company's "business solutions" went in that direction of offering alternatives to enterprises that needed to cut costs and increase work rationalization. The product Suite and the platform's management and monitoring solutions on the conglomerate's Cloud, on the one hand, played the role reserved to technology since the rise of capitalism: to reduce and simplify work[109] and allow greater coordination by business owners, as stated by Marx (2013) and Dussel (1988). But, by subsuming information to these exploitation dynamics, as is typical of capitalism, they also do so in new ways. Surveillance, the precise management of activities, the analysis of results by artificial intelligence, and the use of these and other technologies for prediction transform the workplace into a space of total control of the workforce, intellectual labour and its subjectivity.

The conglomerate's overall impact and its technological subsystems on the economy is difficult to quantify. But an institutional report (Google, 2017) of the company offers some data on its effects in the United States. According to the document, the conglomerate helped provide US$238 billion in revenues for companies, content producers and broadcasters, and non-profit organizations.

---

109   With forms, for example, the company claimed to have tackled a distributed data collection problem, "making it simple to collect survey data within a firm, a critical issue to obtain internal feedback" (Brin, 2008).

Each month, the group's services and infrastructure enable a billion transactions, such as calls, payments and restaurant reservations. The document indicates that small businesses using "advanced tools," such as online advertising and analytics, have been three times more likely to create jobs than those that did not make use of them.

In the political–institutional sphere, Google acts as a central mediator in the provision of information, as already discussed in the section "Compliance with the value base." By being the "regulatory agent" (or gatekeeper) of an important part of the web and the users' search for information, Google also regulates the public debate, together with digital social networks, such as Facebook. As Harris (2016) says, if "you control the menu, you control the choices." This power is also exercised through the control of the world's leading free video platform, YouTube. By influencing how people get informed, the conglomerate directly and indirectly affects the political–institutional sphere. It can determine or modulate what types of information will gain more visibility, as shown by the aforementioned case of prioritizing extreme videos.

By its logic of measuring sites according to a set of criteria, among which the "popularity" of a page considering the number of links is a central one, Google reinforces the narratives of the largest and already most visible sites on the web. On the other hand, it also conceals results. In 2004, photos of inmate abuse in Abu Ghraib prison "disappeared" from the search results for several months (Hinman, 2008). There is an effect on narratives circulation related to ads. The platform has already been criticized for banning certain promotional messages. One case that has gained notoriety is the blocking of a campaign by the civil society organization Oceana against the tour package firm Royal Caribbean Cruise Lines. The company was also an advertiser (Diaz, 2008).

A second aspect concerns surveillance. Hinman (2008) points to a shift in Google's rise from a governmental "Big Brother" to a corporate "Big Brother." Extraordinarily powerful economic forces "are pushing search engine development towards the more and more sophisticated tracking of users" (Hinman, 2008: 72). However, the company has also contributed to the surveillance within the states. The most notorious case emerged with the accusations by Edward Snowden in 2013. A former employee of the US National Security Agency, he explained to media outlets the existence of a program called PRISM to watch over the citizens of the country and other nations (such as Brazil and Germany), in order to meet the demands of the US federal intelligence agencies. At the time, Larry Page denied any involvement of the company with such a project (Rushe, 2013).

More than just through its services, Google has had a direct institutional stake in United States politics. However, in a bipartisan system, its directors have engaged in dialogues with the two major forces in the country. Eric Schmidt created a company (Groundwork) that advised Hillary Clinton's campaign in 2016. Larry Page participated in meetings of the Republican Party in that same election to discuss the digital strategy that would be crucial for Donald Trump. "My own experience in talking to legislators about internet reform has led me to understand that Google, Amazon, and Facebook are deeply embedded in both parties, and their interest will be protected no matter who in the White House," said Taplin (2017: 130).

Google also plays a strong role in the legislative arena to influence laws under debate. The company spends more than US$15 million a year on lobbying (Taplin, 2017). In 2012, the Stop Online Piracy Act (SOPA) was presented to the US Congress, which contrasted, on the one hand, the content industry eager for copyright enforcement mechanisms and, on the other, user-generated content platforms. The proposal aimed to make platforms, such as search engines and social networks, responsible for content that violated copyright. Sites such as Google and Facebook were down for 24 hours displaying messages against the project, which was eventually withdrawn. Besides trying to influence law approvals, Google also seeks to impact regulatory agencies' debates.

In 2016, the Federal Trade Commission (FTC) promoted a privacy seminar (PrivacyCon). More than half of the speakers had received some funding from Google (Google Transparency Project, 2018). The agency's own chief of technology, Lorrie Cranor, received US$350,000 (Bidle, 2016). In 2018, the Federal Trade Commission conducted a series of debates to assess whether current rules on issues such as privacy, competition and consumer protection are sufficient to monitor large technology companies.

The company also works to promote its interests in the communications sector's regulations. One example was the auction of the 700 Mhz radio spectrum band in the United States in 2007. Initially, the agency did not require network neutrality. Google announced that it would defend four principles: applications, devices, services, and open networks. According to them, consumers could download any app or use any devices with the telecom operator, and resellers could acquire traffic under non-discriminatory wholesale conditions (Schmidt, 2007). The process included opening the platforms to devices in Block C, the most desired block. With that, it favoured technology companies, such as Google, to the detriment of telecom operators, such as Verizon and AT&T. Google had informed that it would only enter the dispute if open platform conditions were ensured. In the founders' version, the company was successful in "convincing" the FCC to incorporate the principles (Page, 2007).

Its control of information not only impacts political debates and deliberative processes, but, also, the cultural sphere, which extends to all areas and dimensions, from the publishing market, through Google Books, to the cultural industry, through YouTube. Vaidhyanatan (2011) classifies this as "Googlization." He triggers the discussion around the "Googlization of everything": people, knowledge and the media. It is a "ubiquitous" brand, increasingly present in people's lives. More than a central element in online practices, the search has become a central activity in contemporary societies. In the words of Spink and Zimmer (2008: 3), it has become a "defining component of the human condition:" "Web searching can be conceptualized as a complex behaviour embedded within an individual's everyday social, cultural, political, and information-seeking activities."

Sparrow and Wegner (2011: 776) analysed how Google impacts the memory of its users: "It seems that when we are faced with a gap in our knowledge, we are primed to turn to the computer to rectify the situation." In an experiment to evaluate the memory capacity of a sample of respondents in word search situations, the authors identified that those who believed the searches would be saved remembered less than others who understood that the search would not be recorded: "People forget items they think will be available externally and remember items they think will not be available" (Sparrow, Wegner, 2011: 778). The Kaspersky Lab research centre (2017) also conducted research in this regard and found the same correlation. Among the respondents, 34% stated that their smartphones are their memory. The authors classified the phenomenon as "digital amnesia."

Hinman (2008) argues that the technological system in question is not only ensuring access to knowledge but playing a central role in its construction. Systems such as search engines were born with the potential to democratize knowledge and facilitate access to it. Paradoxically, the techniques to store and transmit knowledge were appropriated by new "regulatory agents," who began to control a significant portion of these processes, guided by profit and secret systems and criteria. This leads to what the author calls the "abuse potential" inherent to the control of such a large information base. By resting on a single company, this power to control information is manifested in an unprecedented way in human history. Never before "will so few have controlled so much with so little public oversight or regulation" (Hinman, 2008: 74).

Such knowledge control relies on Google Books and Google Scholar services as two key fronts. In Scholar, the system "delimits" the knowledge available or not, operating as a dangerous exclusion factor. Moreover, by giving visibility and quantifying academic citations, the search engine materializes a hierarchy, building relevance by presenting the main results and endowing them with "importance." In the tests we made, certain works used in this study did not appear in Google Scholar's results, even with different attempts by changing the search words or resorting the search by author. Finally, by "validating" researchers, the service works as a certifier that values certain sources of knowledge (and their formulations) to the detriment of others, directly impacting the access to academic articles and their application in the elaboration of new studies.

By addressing not only Google, but other technologies, Harris (2016) questions how the mediation of access to knowledge and of an increasing number of everyday activities puts these platforms in a position of power regarding choice and decision-making alternatives. With his motto, "If you control the menu, you control the choices," the author (2016) warns of the platforms' capacity, especially Google's capacity, to mould our action horizons. This brings impacts, therefore, to the very notion of experience and the human agency capacity. And it is not only an "unforeseen consequence," but the result of strategies, of its technological social content (Trigueiro, 2009), and of technological rationality itself (Marcuse, 1973), involving the fruition of these technological systems. They are deliberately built according to the interests of their controllers (in the words of Bijker and Pinch [1993]) with the intention of generating growing consumption.[110]

11   Analytical Overview: Google and the Fight For Online Information Control

Throughout this chapter, we have analysed Google in terms of the Technology Regulation model, presented in Chapter 1. Our intention was to evaluate its technological trajectory based on the social and technological regulating factors, corresponding, respectively, to the model's first dimension (regulation over technology) and second dimension (regulation of technology), including the aspects that constitute its commodity form(s) in competition in the capitalist market(s). The analysis also contemplated the technological system's components and its technical resources, analysing how they materialize in the interaction with the various related agents, from access and legitimization to appropriation methods. Finally, the chapter focused on the impacts of the technological system, both in relation to the value base and to other spheres of society (scientific–technological, political–institutional, economic and cultural).

---

110   Harris draws a parallel between the attention-gathering strategies of slot machines and smartphones, calling the latter "pocket slot machines."

We analysed Google's emergence as a search engine, based on the ambition to scan the entire internet and rank it for users. This objective was driven by a demand due to the growing abundance of information and the need to create aggregation and organization tools. We can say that this "problem" (using the SCOT and CTT terminology) was real. The portals were the main model to try to create aggregation structures. No wonder search engines were made available in association with them, as in Yahoo's case. To stand out from this model, an engine was born supported by PageRank, based on a hierarchization logic, by counting links that lead to each page. This architecture already posed problems, since it conferred "relevance" based on such indicator, which showed several weaknesses, as already pointed out. Besides the fact that the number of links does not necessarily imply a page's quality, this method also impacted diversity by reinforcing the leadership of those who were already at the top, deepening the network effect in searches.

Google's origin as an "invention" may suggest, in a less critical view, the notion of the myth that technical progress is possible for anyone with an innovative idea. From the very beginning, its development was subsumed into the logic of capital and technology markets. Like any business, it first needed investment. And so, its founders looked for investment firms, initially benefiting from the speculative frenzy of the ".com" bubble, in an example of a social factor of regulation of the economic sphere. As seen, the company also benefited from the crisis resulting from Nasdaq's downfall by not going public on the stock exchange, in addition to having the possibility of hiring professionals at low prices with the restructuring of the technology market in the country. The case also reveals an illusion regarding the internet's democratizing potential. It is not a question of recognizing that PageRank, and Google as a whole, have brought new functional properties that have given the technological system "problem-solving" capabilities (in an allusion to evolutionists) that have taken advantage of the paradigm's own regulatory factors (such as the spread of computing and internet connection) and have met the demands of the time. However, they did so by being "framed" under the logic of the system's reproduction. Eric Schmidt's admission to calm investors and indicate professionalization in management is one of the examples. The negotiation with other companies, like Yahoo, is another.

Google's capitalist DNA was also part of its business model. As a company, it needed to create a way to generate revenue, with results to satisfy investors. This logic intensified with its IPO in 2004. From that moment on, quarterly estimates and results exerted pressure on the company's decisions. However, it is important to note that, like Facebook, Google opened up to the financial market, while its founders maintained their control and decision-making power. Without deciding to bet on a paid service, Page and Brin found in advertising the decisive axis of their business model. In a scenario of economic crisis, especially since 2007, the optimization of advertising investments became a demand from economic agents and a regulation over technology factor, as already discussed. And Google filled this gap, along with Facebook, a few years later.

The combination of this business model and the technological capacity to index much of the internet and organize its sites to offer search results was explosive. Google has developed technology to scan increasingly massive volumes of information, index them and present answers. As it gained in market share, it was able to expand its infrastructure, in an evolutionary dynamic of its technical base. Meanwhile, competitors were struggling, especially Altavista, Yahoo!, and Microsoft. But the business model would foster a fundamental adjustment. Driven by the need to offer a competitive edge, advertising would have to be as effective as possible. Google took advantage of its database of millions of customers expressing their interests and combined these records to enable an increasingly detailed and accurate segmentation. As seen in the Appropriation section, one benefit of this model was the fact that the platform not only had users receiving information, but actively seeking it, which allowed for greater potential returns.

In order to carry out this customization, it was necessary to take it to the whole system. The ranking logic has progressively changed to incorporate new elements, especially the user experience. Other indicators were developed and adopted to value the pages for their "quality." Over time, these two axes became the reference base for the search offerings. In addition, the scope of indexable knowledge has been expanded, including books, academic papers, patents and other databases, in a clear manifestation of the network effect characteristic of the platform. By relating results to the user's interests, the perception of relevance was broadened, feeding a "vicious circle" of the technological system's search service usage, leading to an appropriation characterized by a system with a positive meaning over its performance. However, to improve the model, it was necessary to collect more and more information about the user. In addition, the gaining of market power in searches allowed new products to be launched.

As we have seen, this has occurred both through the internal development of solutions and by incorporating companies. In the first axis, several products were launched in the early 2000s, such as the social network Orkut, Scholar, Video, Maps, an SMS response and tips service, and Gmail. The latter, in particular, played an important role in putting the company in the market as the main interpersonal and group communication tool online at that time, and allowing the use of these communication networks (and message content) in their advertising tools. Its functional properties, especially the volume of data allowed in the storage and the anti-spam filters, led to the tool's popularization. With the creation of Maps (and other tools such as Earth and Street View), Google occupied a relevant field in data collection, the geolocation of users.

In the second axis, the phase between 2004 and 2008 discussed in the "general technological trajectory" section was a milestone, with the acquisitions of Android, YouTube, and Doubleclick. The first one was an initial bet, which still required years of development. In the second case, the acquisition took place when it was already a booming platform. In the third, Google promoted an expansion of its advertising services, incorporating the firm's customer base. The three acquisitions are examples of how the company articulated the scalable nature and leveraged non-rivalrous economic assets, a solid technological base, an established user base, data collection and processing capabilities, and capital to buy competitors and potential new businesses.

When it reached a position of market leader, in 2008, the company had new ways to manage this process, being able to exercise its market power over the audiences connected to the platform. As it consolidated this position, it began to have a unique ability to establish standards and guide the operating logic for much of the World Wide Web, consolidating itself as what we called the regulatory agent of information flows on the Web. With the competition for more and more attention and a huge volume of information, Google's condition as a "gatekeeper" intensified. Having visibility, which meant, in practice, to exist on the web, became directly related to one's position in Google's ranking. This power coincided with a scenario of spreading from the offline world to the online world (either from political forces, public institutions or companies that started using this space to market products). In this information pool, there was no place for everyone on the front page. Online advertising became more and more an imperative. This demand was exploited by a strongly modular system adapting to any budget, allowing the advertiser base to expand beyond companies that were able to compete for expensive minutes on TV or radio stations.

At the turn of the 2010s, the internet expanded internationally (and so does Google), access conditions (such as speed and bandwidth) improved, mobile devices spread came with the introduction of new consumption logics and the capacity to produce and disseminate data expanded with new participation tools such as YouTube and digital social networks. This context opened new frontiers for data collection and processing. The international competition was marked by large conglomerates, such as Microsoft, AOL, Time Warner, Apple, and some emerging ones, such as Facebook and Amazon. Google's network effect structure and ambition have led the company to seek new boundaries to adapt to this scenario. Google had already dominated the search market and understood it as a key bottleneck of the internet. More than the domain of an economic segment, it was about controlling the information flow on the web. But there were other fundamental niches, and the competition over them would define who would succeed in the fight for controlling the internet, or for it what was even possible to achieve.

The company then moved into the browser market, with Chrome, and mobile operating systems, with Android. These were key control points. Microsoft was prominent, with IE and Windows. And through them, it sought to impose its software. But the mobile world was a new open segment. And Google was able to provide a more effective response with Android. Looking at the company's vertical integration strategies, it conducted a failed experiment in buying Motorola Mobility, with which it recognized the complexity of entering the hardware area. Relying on the mobile frontier, its technology base and the interconnected logic of its products, it promoted Chrome's advance. However, the company implemented an important strategy with its equipment line (Nexus, Chromebook and Pixel). Also in this move, it sought to reconfigure the users' experiences, bringing desktops into "its arena," becoming ever less dependent on hardware (servers, data centres, fibre optic networks, etc.) and, increasingly, on the cloud.

This integration of its technological subsystems and artefacts, as mentioned, is part of its expansion and activity extension strategy. Google has considerably expanded its tools, offering more diverse solutions for different audiences. Expanding the available products, interconnecting them and accumulating more and more records of each user were the steps pursued. Commercially exploiting data has become an increasingly consolidated practice as the company's core business (despite the fact that this was part of its strategy since it started selling ads). This required sophisticated artefacts to be developed. The pressure of regulating factors from expanded competition (since it involved no longer only the search market, but a general market for online services) led the group to invest heavily in the research and development of algorithms, machine learning and artificial intelligence. By doing so, Google is helping to promote what we refer to here as emerging technologies as crucial tools of the present and future, not only of the ICT technological paradigm, but in the digital economy as a whole.

More than just internal factors, these artefacts' development faced new social factors of regulation, such as economic stagnation: the inability to generate a new expansion cycle and struggles with productivity. As this scenario developed, Google was already looking at the corporate market with a new expansion frontier. Services such as those offered on G Suite and the Cloud platform were now announced as "solutions to optimize resources, decrease task time and increase productivity." These tools allow a deeper subsumption of intellectual labour, extending the computerization processes started in the 1980s and whose driving forces included the digital technologies. They help to codify, quantify, analyse and modulate intellectual labour on a new level. The contradiction between customization and undifferentiation also emerges here, by fostering individualization at the performance control level, and employing undifferentiation at the intellectual effort appropriation level. Even on the economic level, Google has contributed to the expansion of e-commerce, a remarkable trend, as already seen.

The way this volume of information was controlled and exploited created directly impacts individuals and collectivities in other spheres. The problem of data protection has perhaps gained the most strength, with several controversies raised throughout the history of the platform, especially since the 2010s. As seen in the Rules section, Google basically controls everything the user does through its services under a blackmail logic: the only way not to be subject to the terms is not to make use of the services. It can read emails and other communications, know what we do in the browser or on our smartphone. In the case of mobile devices, even the withdrawal strategy bumps into limits, since there is a duopoly of operating systems, with Android and Apple, and the latter also operates under this logic. Conquering the mobile OS as a control point was a major success, as it has led to growth over a portion of the web where free solutions do not yet offer alternatives. The cases mentioned and discussions regarding privacy violations are just examples of a much more serious and widespread problem.

The impacts are also felt on the public debate and on ensuring the right to communication. By controlling the menu, Google defines the delimitation of the stock of available knowledge and the possibilities of framing reality. The controversy about the biases found in the search engine illustrates not only the company's power, but, also, the impacts it can have without the users even being aware that they exist. In a scenario of platform dependence to access any type of information, including cognitive reverberations, the ability to shape the menu extends Google's power over our way of knowing the world, pondering it, defining alternatives, and future paths. This impact is reinforced by a lack of transparency, which is deepened as its artefacts' gain in processing and decision-making complexity.

This power and control over people, their data, their experiences, and their actions puts the conglomerate in an extremely superior condition to the user in the subject–object relationship. Google has the ability not only to know what users are doing and their history but to build tools to increasingly predict how they will behave and how they can influence that according to their best interest. Regarding neutrality, the considerations and examples presented reveal that their artefacts show no trace of it, and these "social constructions" are directly shaped by the social and internal factors of regulation. The tools and resources are adjusted to collect increasingly more data and process them under the logic of control.

As for technology's autonomy, we describe here how Google's technological regulation is carried out, being forged by social and internal factors and impacting several spheres of reality, in a dialectic and historically situated movement. However, its technological power with impact on diverse social activities produces an expansion of its specific relative autonomy, by exerting technological power over the spheres in which it operates. This aims both to reproduce its dominant position and to create and conquer new frontiers. To do so, Google understood it was necessary to go beyond the "traditional" Web content services, launching its other bets, until it realized that it was no longer a company, but a conglomerate. By institutionalizing its business transformation, it became a digital monopoly.

In the next chapter, the investigation presented here focuses on another case study: Facebook. Although Facebook was originally a digital social network, it is possible to see how its platform nature and several regulatory factors have historically allowed the company to gain prominence in the digital economy and impact various social activities across the planet. Finally, we present our final considerations, articulating the two case studies with the general arguments of this work, making a comparison that illustrates the movement of digital platforms from the two main exponents of this modality of agents.

CHAPTER 7

Facebook

Facebook emerged as a digital social network, a type of content circulation platform. Such platforms enhance the articulation of online and offline interactions, the organization in groups, and the engagement in collective processes. Boyd and Ellison (2013) call these "social networking sites," composed of uniquely identifiable profiles, messages generated by users, visible and accessible connections articulated by them, and the interaction among profiles with message flows produced by members of the network. Zhang and Leung (2015) prefer to use the term "social networking services." According to the authors, these encompass more components and purposes of the daily manifestation of this phenomenon and its dynamic practices regrading social interactions: "Social networking services is not simply a static object but a fast-changing phenomenon, both in terms of technological features and usage patterns." (Zhang and Leung, 2015: 1009). Lee et al. (2020: 1) chose to use the term "social media" (as popularly adopted). These platforms "are spaces in which people can freely record and share their everyday lives to develop and strengthen their relationships. At the same time, social media facilitate the circulation of political information, enabling encounters with the political lives of other users." Also adopting "social media," Velasquez and Montgomery (2020: 1) declare these spaces "have become spaces for sociality, not only because of the social interactions that take place there, but, also, for the role they play for individuals' self-presentation and self-concept construction."

Recuero (2012) works with the concept of internet social networks or online social networks. According to her, such definition distinguishes these modalities from offline ones. She highlights the difference in mediation, where one has access not to individuals but to a representation of them. Interactions are also different, since they are mediated by these systems' tools, allowing such representations to exist.[1] Considering Boyd and Elisson's (2013) contribution, the concept of "social networking sites" is linked to the access by pages and

---

[1] This context brings some changes. The first is the control that individuals have over their representation. The second is the form of connections, which are now intermediated by these platforms. A third is the scale, with the possibility of users sustaining a larger set of interactions, since they do not face the limits of the offline world. The fourth is the change in the quality of interactions, which are now determined by the association. A fifth is its ability to enhance information circulation.

browsers. At the same time, it highlights only the site itself, disregarding the entire technological system covered by these platforms. The concept proposed by Recuero (2012) includes interesting elements, as well as the critiques by Zhang and Leung (2015). We consider these approaches appropriate, however, to highlight the platform's broader ecosystem, which goes beyond online experiences, we have chosen here to use the term "digital social networks," which will refer to digital platforms for interaction and messaging and content circulation based on digital technologies, available in online environments, constituting a technological system in which technological, economic, political, cultural, and legal frameworks interrelate within its structure.

Mark Zuckerberg defines Facebook as "one of the great economic machines of our time" (Facebook, 2012a). Throughout its development, there was a transition from a one-product company to a group with several arms. In its 2012 annual report (Facebook, 2012a), the general business presentation was structured according to products within the social network, such as the newsfeed, timeline, photos and videos and Facebook Platform. In the 2017 annual report (Facebook, 2017), such delimitation changed and was presented by business units: Facebook, Instagram, Facebook Messenger, WhatsApp, and Oculus. Within the new configuration, Facebook is defined as a system that allows people to connect, share, discover, and communicate with others. The newsfeed is the most important tool for such activities. Considering its architecture, the company offers different forms of integration and interaction among its arms, as well as regarding the nature of artefacts and integral parts of the technological system (understood here as the whole company). Some applications remained relatively independent, such as Instagram and WhatsApp, although, with recent partial integrations (as in message exchanges). Others were "elevated" to specific applications but were linked to Facebook's general operation, such as Facebook Messenger. In other cases, this movement was attempted and then interrupted.

In works about the company, there are both positive and critical definitions. Kirkpatrick (2010), a member of the first group, states that the platform can make communication more efficient, promote familiarity, and deepen intimacy. Cohen (2008) characterizes Facebook as an "online communications platform" combining email, messaging, photo sharing, posting to personal pages (blogs), and the monitoring of friends' activities. Based on Rheingold's contribution, Parks (2010) defines Facebook, as well as other DSNs, as a "social avenue" where different communities are formed. This is part of these networks' rhetoric: they justify their existence by affirming their role in theability to connect with "people in your life." Kaun and Stiernstedt (2014: 1, 154) argue that Facebook goes far beyond the interaction promoted by its users. It organizes their external experience and their relationship with time "in terms of managing social contacts, reminding them of birthdays and events, and serving as an archival repository, providing access to past memories" (Kaun and Stiernstedt, 2014: 1154). Marichal (2016) sees Facebook as part of an era of "hyper-connection" built around a "disclosure architecture," pressuring users to share more and more about themselves. Andrejevic (2013) points to the need to understand Facebook in terms beyond that of a digital social network. It is the largest "focus group," generating more data than any advertiser could ever imagine. What is important is not so much the content itself as what is posted, shared and commented on, but the fact that it can be registered, filed and analysed. Van Dijck (2013: 12) goes in a similar direction and sees on Facebook automated systems that program and manipulate connections: "In order to be able to recognize what people want and like, Facebook and other platforms track desires by coding relationships between people, things, and ideas into algorithms." Nieborg and Helmond (2019) see Facebook as more than a social networking site, but a data infrastructure hosting platform. It contributes to the platformization of infrastructure and the infrastructuralization of platforms. The company expands its boundaries to distinct sectors in a platformization movement, as in the mobile ecosystem, with Facebook Messenger.

In this work, we assume Facebook to be a digital platform and, at the same time, an economic agent responsible for the digital platform of same name and others, such as WhatsApp and Instagram. Facebook's platform is digital social network, a content circulation platform modality, but one that is increasingly connected to its other services and platforms, building a platform ecosystem. And, as we saw, it turned into a digital monopoly once it benefited from its usertechnological base and vast data gathering abilities to expand into distinct services and activities.

1 General Technological Trajectory

In 2003, then-Harvard student Mark Zuckerberg created Facemash, whose system featured photos of people, allowing its visitors to vote for the "most attractive" ones. He was called to the student council, where he was accused of security, copyright and privacy violations, but not expelled from the institution (Kaplan, 2003). Between 2004 and 2006, the first phase of the technological system's historical development took place, which we refer to here as 'creation and implementation: from universities to the general public'. Facebook was launched on February 4, under the ownership of Zuckerberg and two university colleagues, Dustin Moskowitz and Eduardo Saverin. After the Facemash "experiment," the site was launched for Harvard students and initially called "The Facebook." In March 2004, it was expanded to other institutions such as Columbia, Stanford and Yale. By the end of May, it already had over 100,000 users (Kirkpatrick, 2010). The company's first investment came from Peter Thiel, PayPal's founder. Months later, a new company was formed with Sean Parker, who had experience with Napster software, as president. In 2005, the name of the technological system was changed to "Facebook." In September, the digital social network was made available to higher education institutions throughout the United States.

In 2006, a new phase emerged – 'consolidation of the model: from opening to leadership'. The network was finally opened to any user (Marichal, 2016). Alongside this development, new privacy control tools were introduced. In addition, the possibility for users to share texts from other sites on the network was implemented. During the same year, an important new feature was the launch of newsfeed.[2] Also in 2006, the platform entered the world of politics by allowing candidates to create profiles in the context of that year's legislative elections. In 2007, Facebook opened its application programming interface (API) for developers, launching an application offering a platform, Facebook Platform (widgets and games).[3] In the same year, "Facebook Ads" was launched, classified as a system for companies to connect with their audiences using targeted advertising to reach the audiences they wanted.[4]

From 2008 onwards, a new phase in the technological system's evolution began, which we refer to as 'content flow reconfiguration'. In 2009, the platform released a proposal for the "Facebook Principles," a set of parameters that guide the social network's operations and rights and duties of users in the activities carried out within it and in the interaction with its various participants. In 2011, it made an important change in the newsfeed, with the "subscribe" button and the possibility of not seeing all updates from friends as well as seeing notifications from people who are not part of your network (Rait, 2011). The newsfeed started to display the "top stories," abandoning the message flow's chronological organization. Another important reconfiguration

---

2 This has meant an important change in the logic of the platform's use, as it then shared, by default, a considerable part of users' activities to their friends.
3 In addition, it announced the platform for mobile devices and applications (Facebook Mobile), which allowed developers to extend their applications to that universe as well.
4 The company suffered its first major legal challenge by the attorney general of New York, which resulted in an agreement with measures to prevent the dissemination of pornography images (NY Attorney General, 2010).

was introducing the "timeline," in which the users' posts and activities (not the content from third parties they received) were organized in chronological order (Lessin, 2011).

In 2012, Facebook entered a new phase, referred to here as 'horizontal incorporation', due to the company's acquisitions during the period. In a billion-dollar deal, Facebook purchased Instagram (Bastos, 2012). In May, the company went public, with 421,233,615 shares offered at US$38. Eight years after its creation, Facebook reached 1 billion users. In 2013, in its horizontal expansion strategy, the company tried to buy Snapchat (Shinal, 2017), identified as a dangerous competitor that was beginning to gain usership, especially among the young. Facebook acquired the Parse development platform as a way to enter the business mobile apps market (Lardinois and Constine, 2016), where it was far from obtaining a market share close to Google's, with Android, and Apple's, with iOS. In addition to its horizontal integration efforts, Facebook began to promote partnerships to expand its potential user base. In 2013, *The Guardian* published reports by former US National Security Agency (NSA) official Edward Snowden revealing a mass surveillance scheme by the US government with the help of technology giants, including Facebook (Greenwald, 2013). Among the responses, it started to present "transparency reports" in which it disclosed, for example, the balance of data requests by governments. In 2014, the company purchased WhatsApp, a new milestone in its horizontal integration strategy. In 2015, an important new feature in its movement to expand user data collection was an extension of the "like" button to the "reactions" feature, with a set of facial signals, using emoticons, to express other reactions to a posting, such as "love," "wow," or "angry" (Tosswill, 2015).

In 2016, the period of 'legitimation problems', the last phase of our periodization, began, which lasted until the end of the decade. During that year, Facebook was questioned about its role in spreading disinformation in the period leading up to the 2016 US elections. Initially, Zuckerberg minimized the criticisms, but then recognized the problem of disinformation in the plea (Valente, 2018). In the same year, he also suffered public criticism after being denounced by the ProPublica agency for discrimination in real estate advertisements (Angwin and Parris Jr., 2016). The year 2017 was marked by liability charges for problems in the United States elections and other processes, such as the referendum in the United Kingdom's resulting in the country's exit from European Union. In 2018, the US Congress investigated Facebook's responsibility in of Russian agents' interference and the platform admitted to having found Russian accounts and content driven to influence the 2016 election. A new scandal hit the worldwide headlines when *The Guardian* revealed that a British consulting firm, Cambridge Analytica, had obtained information on nearly 90 million Facebook users[5] and used this to influence the US elections in favour of Donald Trump. It became the focus of two other scandals, being accused of contributing to ethnic genocide in Myanmar and lynching-related deaths in India after messages circulated on WhatsApp. In September of that same year, it reported a large-scale data leak in which hackers would have been able to access the accounts of more than 50 million users, in what was called the biggest leak in the platform's history.

In 2019, Facebook launched Facebook News, and dedicated space inside the platform to journalism information. It started only in US (Brown, 2019). In June, it declared it would create a new cryptocurrency, called Libra, in a consortium with other tech companies like PayPal and a digital wallet called Calibra, demonstrating its digital monopoly character. In September, it announced its dating feature, which was designed to compete with Tinder (Leskin, 2019). That same year, Facebook launched a new brand identifying its control in all its products and subsidiaries, like Instagram, WhatsApp, Oculus and Workplace (Lucio, 2019). Facebook responded to the COVID-19 pandemic with new content measures, such as rolling out a notification screen with more information on this subject originating from authoritative sources, like the WHO, and creating a COVID-19 information centre (Hegeman, 2020). In May, it launched Shops for Facebook and Instagram, an interface for business to gather products for sale and show them on Facebook as a storefront (Newton, 2020).

In 2020, in the context of the pandemic, when live events and streamings grew significantly, Facebook announced a tool to watch vídeos together, called "Live With," the possibility to listen to live audio only (Facebook, 2020, April, 24). It made available paid virtual events, declaring them as a way to allow businesses to profit during the quarantine period (Simo, 2020). Another new product responding to the COVID-19 pandemic was Campus, a communication tool for educational institutions (Hung, 2020). In April 2020, Facebook launched and dedicated a gaming app with features allowing streaming. With this movement, the company aimed to compete with YouTube and Twitch (Browne, 2020). In May, the company started to roll out its new interface for Facebook.com (Bonifacic, 2020). This interface gave visibility to some features, as Watch, Groups and Marketplace. In its design and interface the platform showed its priority services and tools for the next years.

---

5   The consultancy obtained the data from a developer, Aleksandr Kogan, who would have gotten them by posting a quiz app on Facebook that collected data not only from people, but from their entire network.

2   Rules

Chapter 5 presented a summary overview of the legal regulation debate on digital platforms, listing some examples of data protection, content management and copyright legislation. In addition to being subject to national states' legislation, Facebook has also been the subject of court decisions and regulatory authorities. In 2007, the company signed an agreement with New York Attorney General Andrew Cuomo to "promote online safety for children."[6] In 2009, the Office of the Privacy Commissioner of Canada conducted an investigation into complaints from the Canadian Internet Policy and Public Interest Clinic (CIPPIC) and issued a set of recommendations (Office of the Privacy Commissioner of Canada, 2009).[7] In 2011, the US Federal Trade Commission (FTC) opened an investigation into privacy violations by Facebook (Federal Trade Commission, 2011). In its complaint, the institution pointed out problematic measures and initiatives regarding the privacy of its users. After the investigation, the agency concluded that the social network violated the FTC law and signed an agreement with the social network (Federal Trade Commission, 2012) establishing a series of obligations.[8]

In 2016, the Competition Directorate-General of the European Commission opened an investigation to assess whether the firm had committed any irregularities in presenting the information during the review of the WhatsApp acquisition (Fioretti, 2016). The European Commission (2017) concluded that there were irregularities in the information provided and fined Facebook

---

6   Faced with an assessment that the platform had become a space for the dissemination of offensive content, the agreement provided a set of measures to mitigate this phenomenon. Facebook is committed to responding quickly and effectively to complaints regarding obscene content, sexual predators and harassment practices (NY Attorney General, 2010).

7   The agency made several recommendations, some of which were addressed by Facebook and others, ignored, including "limiting application developers' access to user information not required for a particular application" and "prohibiting the provision of personal information from users other than those who have added the application."

8   To "(1) adequately represent the privacy and security of its users, as well as the ways of controlling the availability of information (2) obtain express consent before changing users' privacy preferences, (3) prevent someone from accessing a user's material more than 30 days after the person's account is terminated, (4) maintain a user privacy protection program; (5) conduct independent audits every two years for the next 20 years." (Federal Trade Comission, 2012). The agreement was finalized the following year (Federal Trade Commission, 2012), adding the obligation to obtain express consent to share user data with third parties, and separately from general rules (such as privacy policy), make available explanations of third-party data use, such as what non-public information would be made available, the identity and category of these third parties, and how this would exceed the restrictions set by the user in their privacy settings."

in US\$110 million. The decision, according to European Commissioner for Competition Margarethe Vestager, signalled to companies that "they must comply with all aspects of EU merger rules, including the obligation to provide correct information" (European Commission, 2017, n.p.). In 2017, the French information regulatory authority (CNIL) imposed a fine for several violations of national data protection legislation. The punishment was the result of a verification and mandated several changes in the privacy policy. In 2018, the company was fined in 500,000 EUR in the UK, the maximum amount allowed in the country, for the Cambridge Analytica scandal. However, as Novak (2018) recalled, considering the annual revenue of 2017, the amount corresponded to what the company earned in 9 minutes. In Italy, the digital social network had to pay a bigger fine in the same year, of 10 million Euros, for misleading its users regarding data usage. The first problem related to encouraging users to enter the network without properly explaining how their data were used by third parties. The second was the pressure to discourage users from trying to limit how the company uses their personal data.

In 2020, Facebook agreed to pay US\$650 million in a class-action lawsuit questioning the use of facial recognition in the photo tag feature in the state of Illinois. The state has a rule requiring companies to obtain the consent of the user before gathering biometric data from citizens (Morrisson, 2020). In June 2020, German top court considered Facebook violate user's privacy rights abusing its social media dominant position to gather and process personal information across its different platforms, such as Instagram and WhatsApp. It confirmed a decision from the national antitrust authority condemning the tech company. The court ordered Facebook to allow people to block the joint use of the data collected from them in the Facebook app with those collected in other applications (Satariano, 2020).

Internally, Facebook has developed several standards to regulate activities within the platform. The main one, like Google, are the Terms of Service (ToS).[9] The document[10] indicates, as the company's main service, the provision of a "customized experience," built by leveraging user data, "about the connections you make, the choices and settings you select, and what you share and do on and off our Products."[11] When "the improper use of our

---

[9] FACEBOOK. Terms of Use. Facebook, n.d. Available at: < https://pt-br.facebook.com/terms>. Access on: 12 Jan. 2019. We will refer to them from now on as "Terms."

[10] There are additional terms for some products (such as the Business Terms for Profitability Tools or Music Guidelines). The latter even prevail over the General Terms.

[11] These records can also be analysed to "understand how people use our Products" and to "improve our Products." Such information is also processed in other company artefacts.

Products" or "harmful conduct against other persons" are identified, according to its Terms, the company takes steps such as to "offer help, remove content, block access to certain features, disable an account, or contact authorities." The Terms list commitments users (compulsorily) make. Such conduct may result in shared content removal or sanctions against the account, such as suspension or deactivation.[12] The latter may also occur in the event of recurring copyright infringements. To identify these violations, the system provides tools for reporting postings.[13]

In addition to listing commitments and prohibitions, the terms include the permissions that the platform user grants, simply by using it. The first is to use texts and images produced and shared by the user.[14] Another permission "granted" is the use of profile and activity information for the purposes of targeted advertisement and publications. When the Terms are updated, it is anticipated that notifications will be sent to the user, so that they have access to them.[15] As with Google, Facebook gives "no guarantee" that the products will be safe, free from errors, or uninterrupted. The platform also disclaims any liability for what "third parties do or say," as well as their conduct or content they share, "including offensive, inappropriate, obscene, illegal or objectionable content."[16] One of the important points of the Terms are the procedures for questioning and appealing the measures adopted.[17] The Terms are a manifestation of how the "agreement" in the subject–object relationship (in this case, the technological system) is characterized by a colossal asymmetry. Showing the non-neutral nature of the TS, they institutionalize the exercise of the system's technological power over its users, in articulation with the social content of its design (including the default settings and operating logics).

---

12 It is also liable to termination of the account "if you create risks or legal exposure to us, or when we are authorized or required by law to do so" (Terms).
13 The feature has specific ways to report various types of content and conduct, such as photos, pages, groups, ads or profiles. More information at: <https://www.facebook.com/help/181495968648557?ref=tos>.
14 "If you share a photo on Facebook, you give us permission to store, copy and share it with others (again, consistent with your settings) such as service providers that support our service or other Facebook Products you use." (Terms).
15 However, the acceptance of the changes is compulsory, having, as an alternative, only to stop using the service.
16 These guidelines make it clear that beyond its discourses of concern and responsibility, in the term of its (internal) laws, Facebook assumes rights but not responsibilities.
17 The company recognizes that in the field of consumer relations, the national laws in this area govern complaints. If not, the resolution will have to be made in a court in the United States appointed by the company (Northern District of California).

The company's many privacy policies[18] go in the same direction. According to them, Facebook collects what is accessed through features made available, such as images recorded by the platform's camera. Certain information, such as religious choice, political preference, health, and who the user is interested in, may or may not be included in the user's profile. These and others, such as racial and ethnic origin, philosophical beliefs or trade union affiliations "*may* [emphasis added] be subject to special protections according to the laws of your country." Another category of registration involves the person's usage practices, such as content viewed or shared, engagements with messages, profiles and groups, actions taken. When an individual makes purchases, Facebook retains all related information, such as credit card numbers and transaction amounts. Third-party information about users, such as photos in which the users appear or in posts in which the users are mentioned, are also added to their related database. In addition to the services themselves and the users' activities within the platform, data are collected about the users' devices that "integrate" with Facebook.

One controversial aspect, highlighted after the Cambridge Analytica scandal, was the exchange of data with third parties, such as application developers. Data policies allow these third parties handing data to Facebook, such as sites using users' Facebook account to allow the users to log in and that have a Facebook "like" button in webpages. These records, however, are unrelated to the use of resources linked to Facebook and involve any activity on these pages or applications. The digital platform, on the other hand, transmits data about its users "when you access or use their services or through third parties with whom they work." Which third parties? That is unclear. The user's location is tracked as well, regardless of whether this feature is enabled on the device. In other words, the data controlled by Facebook about individuals exceeds what users generate when using their products, involving an entire network of "partners" who, by various types of agreements, hand over records about their lives, including in the "offline" world (such as shopping in stores). Facebook's vigilance goes far beyond just data collected to improve services or just targeting ads. Similarly, the monitoring of users and their activities across Facebook's "partner" network generates subsidies for data analysis tools regarding the ads and services the platform sells to businesses and institutions. The data collected is used for "security" purposes and to "conduct and support research and innovation on topics of general social welfare, technological advancement,

---

18   Facebook. Privacy Policy. n.d. Available at: <https://www.facebook.com/about/privacy/update>. Accessed on: 12 Jan. 2019. We will refer to them as Policies.

public interest, health and well-being." In addition to the artefacts of the technological system, this information is used to customize resources and content (such as newsfeed) and to make suggestions *"inside and outside our Products"* (emphasis added).

In order to regulate practices regarding the content posted and disseminated on the platform, a specific internal standard has been created, called Community Standards[19] (hereafter referred to as Standards). Structured on some principles,[20] it lists an extensive set of prohibited behaviours within the platform. For example, posts that pose a threat of violence and risks to public safety, profiles of organizations considered "dangerous" (such as terrorist associations, "organized hate" collectives, "mass murderers" or "criminal activity"), promotion and dissemination of violent crimes, and negotiations of controlled products (non-medical drugs, medications and marijuana) are not permitted. The document lists what it calls "questionable content." Despite of the importance of fighting these practices on the platform, at this point (as in the discourse evaluation as a whole) there is a fine line between mitigating abuses in the public debate on digital social networks and violating the right of its members to communicate.

3   Ownership, Control and Management Structure

After contextualizing Facebook's trajectory and its external and internal rules, this and the next two sections dwell on its dimension as a technological system of an economic nature under capitalism. According to the technological regulation model and the categories exposed in the analysis framework, we will present its institutional nature as a company, the production process and its performance in competition. Facebook is a publicly traded company. Its founder and main leader, Mark Zuckerberg, opted for a model similar to Google's, maintaining control through its percentage of voting shares, but trading shares to capitalize the company. Facebook doesn't include its composition in its annual reports. According to the investment website Investopedia (Maverick, 2019), the main shareholders are Zuckerberg, other co-founders and current directors, such as the chief operating officer, Sheryl Sandberg, and

---

19   Facebook. Community Standards. Facebook, n.d. Available at: <https://www.facebook.com/communitystandards/>. Access on: 12 Jan. 2019.
20   These include security (removing content posing risks in the real world, such as physical harm), voice (embracing plural perspectives), equality (applying standards equally, but considering contexts).

the technology director, Michael Schroepfer. Dantas (2018) highlights a strong presence in the shareholding composition of typical financial market institutions, such as investment funds and banks.[21] One important social regulating factor today is the action of these groups and shareholders on companies. In digital platforms, where the growth pace is strong, such pressure is even more evident and impacts the value of the shares and, consequently, the company's valuation. The evolution of Facebook's share value is an example of such (see chart below). It has risen in the last few years, even with the scandals and questions about the company. However, a cut-off point was the release of quarterly results in July 2018, when the company's management reported that there would be a reduction in the growth pace. In one day, it lost US$120 billion in market value (Charney, 2018).

The board of directors is the company's executive body. Headed by Zuckerberg, its task is to ensure the company's growth and worldwide expansion. Besides him, Sheryl Sandberg, his right-hand person, is responsible for the Chief Operating Office, David Wehner for the Finance Office, and Michael Schroepfer for the Technology Office. The changes at the end of the 2010s also led to losses. Chris Cox, product director for many years, announced his removal from the board of directors due to disagreements with where the company was heading, specifically regarding the decision to integrate Facebook Messenger, Instagram and WhatsApp message exchange (Estadão, 2019). The board of directors is a body with the prerogative of advising the company's officers on various topics, such as activities in general, acquisitions and governance development, and performance standards. The board also monitors the company's management and its periodic results (Facebook, 2018b). Its composition is headed by Mark Zuckerberg, and it is also integrated by Sheryl Sandberg. Facebook has sought to surround itself with experienced people in the industry. An example was choosing Marc Andreessen for the board of directors in 2008. In his long career in technology, Andreessen had been technical director of AOL and was co-founder of Netscape, a company responsible for one of the main browsers of the 1990s (Facebook, 2008b). During that same year, Donald Graham, CEO of the Washington Post, was also elevated to the same position. In 2011, Reed Hastings, Netflix's CEO, was hired (Facebook, 2011b). The company also sought members with governmental experience. In the same year, Erskine Bowles, a scholar who had headed a commission on tax reform and responsibility for Barack Obama's government, was chosen for the

---

21   Eight of these institutions control 29.43% of the company: Vanguard Group (9.98%), FMR (5.65%), State Street (3.9%), Price Associations (3.81%), Fidelity (2.74%), Morgan Stanley (1.18%), Northern Trust Corp (1.11%), and Bank of New York Mellon (1.06%).

board. Another Facebook strategy was to incorporate the integrated business leaders into its management structure. This was the case with Jan Koum, CEO of WhatsApp, who, in addition to continuing to run the application, was elevated to the board of directors.[22] In 2019, Facebook created an oversight board. The entity will assess content moderation cases and help to establish guidelines for content governance inside the platform. In May 2020, the company announced its first 20 members, after a period of consultation with scholars, civil society organizations and other institutions. Facebook declared that the board will be fully autonomous to make its decisions (Clegg, 2020).

4 Production Process

The production process is a central stage to develop technological systems. As discussed in the technological regulation model (and emphasized in the approaches of the social construction of technology and critical technology theory), it involves the action of interest groups and their objectives, especially the technological system's controllers. As a digital platform, Facebook operates by connecting various audiences, which assume the condition of interest groups, such as professional users (companies, public institutions, civil society organizations), non-professional users, developers and journalistic and cultural vehicles. This interaction is organized based on the company's objectives, which guide the production process. The company has established, as its mission, "to give people the power to share and make the world more open and connected" (Zuckerberg apud: Facebook, 2012b, n.p.). This institutional statement has changed over the years. In its 2017 annual report (Facebook, 2017: 5), the mission was defined as "giving people the power to build communities and bring the world closer together." However, despite the textual adjustments in the mission, in its historical evolution, Facebook has kept as its focus solutions aimed at posting and sharing posts by its users. The recent years' scandals (such as Snowden's report and the use of data by Cambridge Analytica) have shown that the real purposes are different. As the technological regulation[23] approach shows, it is necessary to take these systems in their condition as commodities (or commodities providers) in competition under capitalism.

---

22 Amid the turmoil of scandals in 2018, he left the collegiate. In his profile, Koum announced his departure. without detailing the reasons.
23 Adopting, in practice, a "political economy of technology" by recognizing the role of this material condition of technology for its understanding.

In this case, Facebook's goals involve leveraging its economic performance from its business model (which will be detailed below). Since this is basically based on advertising, the main goal of the TS is to provide a service that regulates advertisers. This mission involves capturing the attention of users (so that they are available to be "reached" by the ads), the ability to build their profiles to sophisticated targeting and expand the results (such as click rates or conversion). Next, we will very briefly present what we understand as the objectives and interests of the platform's other audiences:

(1) Advertisers and associated providers – These see Facebook as a key channel to reach their audiences and build their brands (with customer relationship actions). The associated providers mentioned above count on Facebook as one of the main regulatory agents in the online advertising market.

(2) Non-professional users – These access Facebook and its products for various motivations, such as connecting with friends or acquaintances, seeking information or engaging in discussions on topics of interest (as will be discussed in the Dissemination and Appropriation sections).

(3) Content producers and broadcasters – The actions of these agents in creating and disseminating information or cultural assets is intended to obtain profit, being able to use Facebook both as a channel of dissemination (using advertising tools such as content promotion) or promotion of their works and media financed by other mechanisms (such as advertising or subscriptions).

(4) Business, public and social organizations – Despite their different missions (whether to make a profit from a product or to promote public policies in a certain area), these organizations see the ST as a place to build and reproduce their reputations. Thus, Facebook represents a space where their activities are promoted and the ramifications of these activities monitored in order to avoid damage to their image. These organizations can, within this objective, assume the condition of advertisers.

(5) Developers – These count on the platform as an agent regulating an ecosystem of applications with billions of potential users, which opens a market of large proportions on the one hand, but determines the conditions of access to it.

(6) Regulatory bodies and authorities – Unlike business, public and social organizations, these are public institutions that relate to the company directly as an object of regulation or indirectly (as a controller of information for an investigation, for example).

(7) Researchers – These focus on the firm as an object of study (such as the present work), as sources of information for research (as in the case of an analysis of public debates on a topic) or as a method and tool for conducting a study (using Facebook Messenger to conduct interviews, for example).

(8) Civil society organizations – These have different interests related to Facebook, in general regarding their view on the platform's impacts on a given audience or social activity (which may vary from those working in the ICT area to others where the effect is more incidental, such as movements concerned with the dissemination of a certain content).

(9) Competitors – By acting in several markets, the digital social network competes with several agents, as will be discussed in Section 8.

Despite the relations with these interest groups, the technological system's design has, as a central constitutive element, the working relations existing in its production. Analysing these relations on Facebook is an extremely difficult job, since little information is made available by the company. As with Google, it is possible to divide the workforce into three major groups: at the top of the pyramid are (1) managers, responsible for coordinating processes and teams and with higher compensation; next come (2) employees with formal contracts, divided into several areas such as research and development (R&D), sales and marketing and administrative functions; and, finally (3) a (non-reported and non-public) mass of subcontracted workers for various functions such as tool testing or content moderation. The workforce of the expanded significantly, by more than 11 times, during the period analysed (2011–2018).[24] Still, it is way behind Google's numbers.

As for compensation, an Equilar survey (Molla, 2018) indicated Facebook as the technology company with the highest average salary among those surveyed. The figure contrasts with other sources, pointing to an average annual salary at the company of about US$117,000.[25] The lack of information on the pay distribution prevents a more appropriate analysis of the inequality dynamics. Another point discussed in labour relations within the platform was the degree of diversity. In the year 2014, ten years after the company's emergence, Facebook released, for the first time, statistics on the composition of the workforce by gender and ethnicity (Williams, 2014, Facebook, 2018a). Since that year, the company has periodically released such information. In the comparison between 2014 and 2018 elaborated in the research, it is possible to note a

---

24 Data compiled by us from the company's annual reports.
25 Information available at: <https://www.payscale.com/research/US/Employer=Facebook_Inc/Salary.

reduction in male participation, but it is still above 60%. In the composition by ethnicity, whites are no longer more than half, but are still close to it. While Asians have a significant share, blacks and Hispanics do not exceed 5%. Such disparity directly influences the design of artefacts, since the perspective of the developer is one of the regulating factors affecting the production process.[26]

An important part of the workforce does not appear in official figures. The company outsources part of its activities to subcontracting companies. This is the case, for example, with "content moderators:" workers who evaluate whether or not posts meet the Community Standards. Faced with the scandals of spreading fake news, Russian agents' participation in the US elections and data leaks, the company announced, in 2017, that it would double its workforce from 10,000 to 20,000 people, mostly outsourced for moderation or security functions (Balakrishnan, 2017).[27] Scholz (2017) also identifies in this activity unpaid labour initiatives, such as free software testing (through beta versions) and user surveys. In digital social networks analyses, a debate has emerged about the role of users in production social relations, as discussed in Chapter 5. Fuchs (2014) argues that the work performed on the platform is basically informational, and that it would, therefore, be exploited by companies.

As discussed in Chapter 5, Bolaño and Vieira (2015) question Fuchs' argument. According to the authors, digital social networks (they use the concept of social network sites) differ (including from previous media, such as broadcasting) in how they mobilize the "commodity audience." Internet companies such as DSNs "refine information collected from an active audience when users spontaneously provide data about their personal tastes, preferences, desires, and pathways through their browsers" (Bolaño and Veira, 2015: 5). They argue that one should not talk about users as a commodity or as labour to be exploited, when this would, in fact, relate to workers who develop the systems to capture the volume of data necessary to the advertising services (through the free access model).[28]

---

26 As shown by the feminist approaches to social studies in science and technology, as in Wajcman (2010).

27 Solon (2017) documented reports from moderators classifying the function as underpaid and undervalued. "Every day watching videos of people's heads being cut off," one moderator reported. "Every day people needed to see psychologists. Some couldn't sleep because of the nightmares," said another. "The training to endure this was insufficient," evaluated a third moderator.

28 Figueiredo (2019) goes in a similar direction, highlighting the phenomenon inside the DSNs as that of "a brutal colonization of daily life of users accompanied by surveillance and control" (Figueiredo, 2019: 164) and placing the exploitation of labour in its employees.

5 Competitive Performance

Performance in competition is part of an economic agent's business model (as discussed in Chapter 3). The Facebook model is mostly based on advertising services. In addition to this source, the technological system generates revenues from two sources: the taxation of transactions occurring on the application platform and the marketing of virtual and augmented reality devices after the purchase of the subsidiary Oculus. The ads allow advertisers to "reach people based on a variety of factors including age, gender, location, interest, and behaviours" (Facebook, 2017: 5). The promotional pieces are distributed to an extensive network formed by the company, its own applications (Facebook, Instagram, WhatsApp and Messenger) and even applications from third party members of the audience network. On Facebook, the main distribution channel, ads are displayed in newsfeed in different formats and positions. These can include texts, images (individual or carousel), links, videos and lead to purchases or actions such as registration. After the campaigns have chosen their objectives, the platform provides several types of formats for the campaign's execution. The most important resource is audience segmentation, which can occur from demographic (age) or geographic (locations) characteristics, interests (activities, artist preferences or practices) or connections (individuals who like the campaign author's page, or who went to an event). This tool is the ultimate example of a social construction artefact of large-scale data collection and processing. It shows the goals of economic maximization over its business model, expressing the "technical code" (Feenberg, 2005) of the TS.[29]

By creating the audience network, Facebook has become an advertising channel, not only within the platform and the applications it controls, but in other applications. The digital social network blurred the boundaries between traditional advertisers and users by instituting the paid content logic (especially for pages) through "drive posting" (a mechanism through which a message reaches more people on the network itself, since the platform does not guarantee that the content will reach all friends or followers), or beyond the network itself. The platform has also created a channel for users to directly sell products, earning revenues by charging fees and percentages on these transactions. The same is true for transactions related to applications made available through the platform, such as Candy Crush. With the acquisition of Oculus,

---

[29] Feenberg (2005) highlights the "technical code" as the articulation of social and technical demands within the artefact, as in this case.

Facebook has also earned revenue from the sale of technology (virtual reality glasses) and audiovisual VR products (games and movies).

Based on this business model, the company has experienced robust financial performance since its inception. In the evolution analysed, between 2009 and 2018 (see Table 2), total revenues went from US$777 million to US$55.8 billion, a growth of more than 700%. However, regarding the growth rate over the previous year, it is possible to see a fluctuation in the middle of the 2010s towards a reduced intensity from 2016, with increases over 2015 of 54%, 57% and 37%, respectively. When it announced, in 2018, a shift in this percentage, the company was already warning investors of the current movement (which generated a significant loss in market value). Advertising revenues grew from 85% of all revenues in 2011 to 98.5% in 2018.[30] The data also highlights two important factors in the growth of advertising revenues: the increase in the number of ads and their value.[31]

This performance caused Facebook to take the lead as the main DSN (2.6 billion users), followed by WhatsApp (2 billion), Facebook Messenger (1.3 billion), WeChat (1.2 billion), Instagram (1.1 billion), TikTok (800 million), QQ (694 million), Sina Weibo (550 million), QZone (517 million), and Reddit (430 million).[32] Facebook (with Facebook.com, Facebook Messenger, WhatsApp and Instagram) has 57% of the users on the top 10 largest digital social networks. However, one important consideration must be made. Tencent – the second in the ranking – has 28% of the profiles, due to its popularity in China, but is restricted to this country and the Chinese community outside it. Thus, Facebook's dominance is even more effective at the global level.

However, because these are informational markets (and, therefore, an unrivalled asset) and permeated by simultaneous consumption dynamics (a person can access Facebook, WhatsApp and Instagram), it is not possible to use

---

30 The remainder, still almost US$1 billion, comes from transactions in applications (such as online games), the Marketplace and sales of virtual and augmented reality devices.

31 In its duopolistic condition in online advertising (together with Google) Facebook operated an aggressive policy. In 2014 and 2015, for example, the average value of ads was increased by 173% and 140%, respectively. But, in these two years, the number of pieces displayed fell, in a policy in which quantity and price are balanced. In 2016, the relationship was reversed, with an adjustment of 5% in the prices of advertisements, but a 50% increase in the number of pieces shown. But, between 2011 and 2018, Facebook doubled (103%) the number of ads posted and more than quadrupled (417%) the average price of ads.

32 Statista (2020) Most popular social networks worldwide as of July 2020, ranked by number of active users (in millions). Available (consulted 23 September 2020) at: https://www.statista.com/statistics/272014/global-social-networks-ranked-by-number-of-users/.

TABLE 2 Facebook – Financial data overview

	2009	2010	2011	2012	2013	2014	2015	2016	2017	2018
Revenues ($ million USD)	777	1974	3711	5089	7872	12466	17928	27638	40653	55838
Revenues with advertising	n/a	1868	3154	4279	6986	11492	17079	26885	39942	55013
Advertising share	n/a	n/a	85%	84%	89%	92%	95%	97%	98%	
Mobile advertising	n/a	n/a		11%	45%	65%	77%	83%	88%	92%
Other sources	n/a	106	557	810	886	974	849	753	711	825
Advertisement average price increase	n/a	n/a	18%	3%	36%	173%	140%	5%	29%	13%
Increase in the number of ads made available	n/a	n/a	42%	32%	20%	-40%	-38%	50%	15%	22%
ARPU	n/a	n/a	5.01	5.32	6.81	9.45	11.96	15.98	20.21	24.96
Earnings by operations	262	1032	1756	2804	2804	4994	6225	12427	20203	24913
Profit (NET income)	229	606	1000	53	1500	2940	3688	10217	15934	22112
Growth over previous year	n/a	n/a	88.0%	37%	55%	58%	44%	54%	47%	37%
Costs and expenses (% of revenue)	515	942 (48%)	1955 (53%)	4551 (89%)	5068 (64%)	7472 (60%)	11703 (65%)	15211 (55%)	20450 (50%)	30925 (55%)
Revenue costs	n/a	493 (25%)	860 (23%)	1364 (27%)	1875 (24%)	2153 (17%)	2867 (16%)	3789 (14%)	5454 (13%)	9355 (17%)
R&D	n/a	144 (7%)	388 (10%)	1399 (27%)	1415 (18%)	2666 (21%)	4816 (27%)	5919 (21%)	7754 (19%)	10273 (18%)
Marketing and sales	n/a	167 (8%)	393 (11%)	896 (18%)	997 (13%)	1680 (13%)	2725 (15%)	3772 (14%)	4725 (12%)	7846 (14%)
General and administrative	n/a	138 (7%)	314 (8%)	892 (18%)	781 (10%)	973 (8%)	1295 (7%)	1731 (6%)	2517 (6%)	3451 (6%)

SOURCE: AUTHOR, FROM INFORMATION IN THE COMPANY'S ANNUAL REPORTS

a simple sum to reach the total Facebook base or work exclusively with the base of other DSNs. Despite these observations, the technological system's prevalence becomes evident, showing how the trend towards concentration and centralization (Marx, 2013) is manifested in its specificities in the digital social network market, stimulated by several factors involved in the competition dynamics among platforms (as discussed in Chapter 5). Although the annual reports and official sources from the parent companies do not provide detailed information on the countries of each platform's users, the volume of users and secondary sources indicate that the most consolidated global reach is that of Facebook.[33]

According to a survey[34] on the most popular DSNs in each country, Facebook is the most used network in 153 of 167 countries. Only China, Russia, Kazakhstan and Iran have other dominant local digital social networks: Qzone in China, VKontakte in Russia, Odnoklassniki in Kazakhstan, and Instagram in Iran. An important feature of Facebook's competitive position is its network nature. As discussed in Chapters 3 and 5, this gives rise to several features that enhance expansion, the agent, and its leadership position, as its participant base grows (Ezrachi and Stucke, 2016). According to Herscovici (2013), in the electronic information network business, when the costs for exchanging a network for a competitor exceed the social utility of the latter network, it forces users to remain where they are.

This dominance in the DSN market was built by successful competitive strategies. The first one was incorporation. The company started targeting its competitors and did not measure efforts to acquire them. In 2012, this was the case of Instagram, a content circulation social network focused on photos with great growth potential. In 2014, Facebook acquired WhatsApp, a social network focused on messaging, for US$19 billion. At the time, WhatsApp was growing strongly, but had not yet found a business model, since its founders had decided to keep it ad-free. Also in 2014, the company purchased the Oculus VR virtual reality devices and services startup for US$2 billion. In 2019, the company bought Beat Games, the enterprise responsible for the popular VR game "Beat Saber." The deal was an attempt to strengthen its VR subsidiary, Oculus (Rodriguez, 2019). In 2020, Facebook acquired Giphy for US$400

---

33   Taking June 2016 as a reference, 33.3% of users were from Asia, 19.5% from Latin America, 19.5% from Europe, 13.3% from North America, 8.7% from Africa, 4.5% from the Middle East and 1.2% from Oceania. Available at: <http://www.internetworldstats.com/facebook.htm>.

34   World Map of Social Networks. Available at: <http://vincos.it/world-map-of-social-networks/>. Access on: 20 Mar. 2019.

milllion (Brown, 2020). The company provided a search engine for gifs, a name used to refer to quick animations largely used in the social media ecosystem (Romm and Lerman, 2020). Giphy was incorporated as part of Instagram's business unit.

The technological system also undertook a horizontal and vertical integration strategy by introducing new artefacts and technical solutions. Among these are Facebook Chat (later converted into Messenger), Groups, Pages, Newsfeed, Timeline and video applications (Video and Watch). A specific integration modality was the introduction of new features mirroring technological resources from competitors.[35] In 2011, the company incorporated the "subscribe" feature into newsfeed, much like the Twitter "follow" dynamic. Also in 2013, Facebook introduced its search feature, Graph Search (Geron, 2013). One notorious move by Facebook was its offensive against Snapchat. After trying to buy the application for US$3 billion in 2013, the company started to develop its main feature: the stories format, through which content is gathered in a daily "summary" of the user's activities. The video was an increasingly important area for the company. In 2016, the firm launched Facebook Video for TV feature. It then launched Watch, its own service for channel content and edited programs (not from third parties, such as YouTube).

In addition to integration, the company has pursued a strategy of both horizontal and vertical expansion. The company sought to spread the resources of "social engagement" to the whole Web. The first step in this direction was the provision of action buttons (such as sharing) for websites, in 2006. A second initiative in this direction was Facebook Connect, which was launched in 2008. A third action occurred in 2013, by introducing embedded posts (Capra and He, 2013). This tool allowed users to post on their blogs and websites, as well as to allow interaction with them, with reactions such as sharing or liking pages. Facebook's growth, as with any digital platform, depended on people being connected to be able to reach them. That's why the company fostered a strategy to promote easier access. Facebook sought to facilitate access in packages hired through partnerships with operators so that users were not charged for traffic generated by the social network, allowing them to use the platform without worrying about data consumption, or even after their packages had ended. The other was that the company itself engaged in actions to promote connectivity. In 2013, together with six other technology companies such as

---

35 The very initial nature of the platform as a social network was not really Zuckerberg's invention. According to the former president and one of the company's first executives, Sean Parker, the person responsible for "defining the basic structure of social networks" was Jonathan Abrams, former CEO of Friendster (Kirkpatrick, 2010).

Samsung and Sony Ericsson, the company launched an initiative to promote connection called "Internet.org," whose goal was to take the web to two-thirds of the population still outside of its reach at the time (Curtis, 2013). The project was subject to strong reactions from civil society organizations.[36] In 2015, Facebook announced the name change for the project's app and website, which were renamed "Free Basics," while the project was kept under the name Internet.org.

6   System Components and Technical Resources

Facebook's investigation as a company will be divided between the primary technological system (Facebook itself) and secondary subsystems, following the cut-off introduced in the analytical framework. The primary TS will be examined in subsections according to their internal function. In section 6.1.1, Information, two information flow areas – newsfeed and timeline – will be examined. In section 6.1.2, Connections, we will discuss components that facilitate these interactions, such as pages, groups and events. In section 6.1.3, Transactions, the focus will be on the components that allow monetary transactions, such as the Marketplace. In section 6.1.4, Platform, the application access service will be considered. The secondary subsystems will be discussed in a less detailed manner, taking those products and subsidiaries organized with some degree of independence from the primary technological system: Messenger, WhatsApp, Instagram, Workplace and Oculus.

6.1   *Primary Technological System: Facebook*
6.1.1   Information (Newsfeed and Timeline)

Newsfeed and timeline make up the core of the technological system. They are the network user's two sides of information flow: on the one hand, users set up their "page" with the information they want to make available on the network (timeline) and, on the other hand, they receive messages posted and shared, in addition to notifications related to their network members (newsfeed). These

---

36   A letter signed by over 60 organizations (18 MillionsRising et al., 2015) addressed to Mark Zuckerberg expressed concern about the impact of the initiative on the open nature of the internet, marked by non-discriminatory treatment of content and services. According to the authors, the project violated network neutrality and threatened freedom of expression, equal opportunities, security and privacy. The Internet.org represented a "walled garden" in which its "beneficiaries" could only access a limited set of applications, unlike its promotional discourse of "internet access."

two artefacts structure Facebook's information architecture, organizing the information flow across network nodes, whether they're individuals or page profiles. It is also through them that other platform tools and user activities gain visibility. The timeline is the user's 'virtual identity' on the platform. Newsfeed is "the core solution of a user's page" (Facebook, 2012b: 6). As such, the tool edits what it makes available to each user, not only mechanically mirroring each posting or interaction with text and images (such as reactions) from network points. This defining feature is decisive in Facebook's relevance and the impacts it can generate. The tool is also the preferred location for the company's main revenue source: ads. Over the years, its operating logic and criteria have been adjusted several times. In a most recent statement on these parameters (Mosseri, 2018), the company explained the ranking dynamics.[37]

The most important technical resource is the basic algorithm for selecting available content. Its operation is quite unclear, except for some explanations, such as the ones presented above. Despite the fact that Facebook releases its changes more frequently than Google, the logic is still not transparent. At most, the platform superficially states its criteria.[38] Despite the lack of transparency, an algorithmic change was clearly understood by all users: the drop in the posts' organic reach. Several studies have indicated this trend. One of them pointed to a 50% drop in page engagement between 2017 and 2018 (Peters, 2019). On the other hand, ads have gained much more room, with a general increase of 400% over the last seven years (see section "Financial Performance").[39] In addition, the change in 2018 promoting closer circles created a drawback on diverse perspectives from "weaker" nodes on the network, with the potential to reinforce the user's bubble. At the end of the 2010s, the combination between these two

---

37   First, the inventory, or set of posts of friends and pages that the person has decided to follow, is taken. These are prioritized based on what the company calls "signals," information about the user, including their preferences, the content (the age of a page), and the fruition conditions (such as connection speed). These signals include content identifiers defined by the company as "problematic" in its internal rules or in decisions, such as posts with violent content, hate speech or "click-bait." The third step is to proceed with the "predictions" of what the probability of a user commenting, sharing, hiding or reporting a story is. These elements are weighed in a "score" of how "interesting" a publication is to a person.

38   Such as types of posts that will lose visibility (such as click-bait) or types of connections that will become privileged (such as the last change in favour of interactions with nearby people and family members, or local news). Still, the company uses generic terms in this disclosure, such as "low quality" pages.

39   Thus, the problem of the hegemonic interest group (to use terms related to SCOT and CTT), the platform's controllers, was the expansion of internal advertisements to enhance their reach compared to the displays shown in less visible areas.

trends shaped the newsfeed's social content (Trigueiro, 2009): a space where content increasingly depended on commercialization (whether professionally through ads or small-scale through driving) and was limited to circles closest to the user. In this sense, the mission of "bringing the world closer together" does not apply much in this case. In June 2020 the feed got a new update to, according to Facebook (Brown, 2020), prioritizing original reporting and stories with transparent authorship: "We do this by looking at groups of articles on a particular story topic and identifying the ones most often cited as the original source." Transparent authorship will be assessed by searching for staff page on the publisher's website.

In terms of technical resources, the timeline, as said, allows a number of settings. By default, it includes all user activities in the main column, showing, in the left column, a general presentation, photos, and the individual network's friends. The timeline is constituted from profile information and actions performed. In addition, you can add interests, political preferences and religious options and events (such as having started a new job or graduated from college). This profile data are a key element for Facebook to build a profile on the person, complemented by the individual's actions and interactions within the network. Thus, they are a pillar of the platform's surveillance. With these resources, the timeline becomes a mix between personal repository and a constructed virtual identity. In this last feature, the possibility of following someone indicated Facebook's efforts to expand people's exposure range using an architecture that allows different levels of regulation of their virtual presence.[40]

6.1.2   Connections (Friends, Groups, Pages and Events)

"Friendships" are the default form of connection on Facebook. This link structures the platform's interconnection architecture, establishing the basis upon which interactions occur, including the information flows discussed in the previous section. The technological system allows both bilateral (friendships) and unilateral ("following" someone) connections.[41] According to the technological system's design, interaction gradually became less proactive (with the user accessing a "friend") and acquired "passive" features, in which the feed

---

40   With this, the characteristic regarding representations more than individuals that Recuero (2012) speaks about becomes even clearer.

41   Connections with friends are the main reason for entering the platform, especially in the case of distance relationships in which the platform's resources allow closer contact, whether in monitoring people's lives in the newsfeed or through "virtual dialogs" in the feed or message artefacts.

organized the monitoring of the user's actions on the network. Thus, the system gained even more centrality as an active mediator and regulating agent managing these associations, in three ways: 1) by defining what appears in the feed or in other points of the interface, and at what intensity; 2) by establishing the interaction resources (first sharing, then liking, then reactions, among others); and 3) by establishing interaction modalities. This mediation intensification is linked to a sophisticated collection and user data processing for directing advertising. The changes in the platform's interface and functionalities resulted in increasing stimuli for interaction and expression (indicating tastes, preferences and the like) within the social network. Its technical resources allow sending invitations, which must be accepted. There is a limit of 5,000 friends. Many users create "additional profiles" to account for a larger group of friends. In each friendship, it is possible to adjust some forms of interaction. There are default categories in which the person can be "fitted," such as best friends or acquaintances. In the feed, new friendships are often "suggested" from people the user "may know."[42]

Another form of connection is establishing connections with "Pages." They were created so that companies could present themselves and their products on the social network (Facebook, 2012b). However, pages are now also "imposed" on any form of legal entity, such as public bodies or civil society organizations. In practice, they seek to replace the role of websites. Such a tactic indicates Facebook's strategy to "confine the experience" of its users, aiming at reproducing experiences from the entire web. As part of the technical features, the user can connect as a page's author or as a "follower." In the first case, the page is associated with a user's profile and the user can include description information and post on the page. In addition, there are features such as posting services, offers, selling products in a store, linking to a group, offering jobs and receiving messages. Facebook establishes a validating role for these pages with the verified pages feature. While this prevents fraud, it also hands more control to the platform regarding the information to be made available to enhance a user's reputation and posting reach. There are features related to interactions in the page's posts, such as comment moderation.

Groups are another form of connection, but with different attributes. They can also be created according to interests or characteristics (a group for fans

---

42 This tool is an example of two characteristics of the system: the mediation it exercises when "recommending" all kinds of interactions and messages to the user and the recurring stimulus to establish connections so that these are used as reading points in the data analysis to build profiles.

of a team, or graduates from a certain college), and their architecture is more similar to a forum, but with relevant control mechanisms for administrators. With the possibility of having "official groups," the platform aims, as in the case of pages, for their features to be used as priority and institutionalized spaces of connection between members of various collectivities. By seeking to assume the condition of official virtual communities, in some cases, the DSN creates a control point over relationships pressuring people to make part of it (such as students who create accounts in the platform due to the demands of the educational institution). In terms of technical resources, the groups are basically organized around the discussion feed of their members. Administrators have some tools both for the information flow (such as making a permanent post) and the members' management (such as banning people or approving the entry of members). Thus, the creation initiative has a relevant impact on the interactions within these spaces. Facebook has even started to hold events with administrators of large groups,[43] establishing relationships with them, although it is still unclear how such relationships can influence these connection spaces.

Finally, events are connection resources organized from a specific situation: a meeting, a concert, a birthday party or a campaign. As they are not permanent, they constitute an intermediate connection modality between groups and profiles, offering more flexibility. This artefact's purpose is to mobilize a target audience around initiatives. Often these are not only in the physical environment, but, also, situations organized by Facebook itself, such as a celebratory event or a virtual action. As with groups, events can involve users as organizers or as participants. In the first case, the event provides tools to facilitate mobilization, such as inviting people from your network. In the fruition mode, the artefact was designed to bring together two other tools that already existed before (and in which Google held market predominance). These are an event manager and calendar, including all events to which the user was invited. In the different forms of connection it offers, Facebook operates a series of joint strategies. The company expands its network effect by creating various types of connections between people and institutions, including encouraging their expansion. As a result, all these technological solutions converge towards its main goal of large-scale data collection and processing.

---

43 Called the Facebook Community Summit, the events occur periodically. More information at: <https://www.facebook.com/community/summit/>.

6.1.3 Transactions

Transactions on Facebook are primarily conducted through the Marketplace service. Introduced in 2016, this is an e-commerce platform where users can buy and sell goods and services (Ku, 2016). The user can access the platform as a seller or buyer. In the first case, through an easy-to-use interface, the user posts an item, setting its price, location, category and including photos. Without charging fees, the tool offers some benefits, due to the integration with other Facebook products. It allows the seller to communicate through Facebook Messenger, posting the product in the timeline (already counting on the user's network reach) and offering advertising services for the product with its features (such as segmentation alternatives, especially from the person's own network).

For buying, the Marketplace is configured as a search engine for products. You can search by location, category or price. The person can "save" items, allowing a kind of search management for completing the purchases later. You can also share goods or talk directly with the seller through Facebook Messenger. Another integration is the participation in "buying groups," which use the Marketplace tool but includes people more willing to sell and buy goods. Just as Google took advantage of its control points and promoted its shopping service by leveraging its assets by directing search results, Facebook sought to enter this marketplace from its huge user base and the ability to aggregate and segment data related to them to offer specific functional properties over other competitors, in yet another example of a strategy to diversify activities made possible by its condition as a digital monopoly.

In 2018, Facebook (Liu, 2018) announced updates to the platform's design, introducing artificial intelligence tools. These make recommendations based on category and price to speed up the sale. Another feature is the identification of products on the Marketplace from images (like taking a picture of a product on the street). The estimation by the responsible team is that AI can help in the home-made design of a product from raw materials purchased through the Marketplace. Such technological solutions pose potential risks in economic transactions between people, with the platform advancing from controlling the availability of offers to their own content or controlling the goods purchased.

In 2019, the company launched another way to conduct transactions inside of its activities. The feature called Stars was made available. The tool was a new form of monetization in which users buy "stars" to send to creators, as a kind of tip. The company also introduced fan subscriptions, with a fixed amount payed monthly (Lee, 2019). In 2020, Watch got new features, like music vídeos and collective video watching chats (Hrivnak and Raji, 2020).

6.1.4 Platform

The platform is Facebook's application intermediation space (Facebook, 2012b). According to the company, it offers developers scale from their user base, engagement (segmented, customized and "social" products) and monetization alternatives. It performs three main functions: 1) it offers diverse services within the platform, preventing users from seeking them outside the platform, 2) it constitutes a source of revenue, since the DSN charges the transactions performed by these applications, and 3) it expands the audience network, giving greater reach to ads conveyed by the advertising services. For such, the platform has a set of "key elements." The first is open graph.[44] The second are social plugins. The third are payment methods, through which developers can be paid through transactions based on secure infrastructures.

As creators, users must create a specific account. Within the platform, they have a number of tools available (such as a graph API explorer, an access token generator, and an app comment moderation mechanism). As consumers, the platform operates as an app store (like Play Store). Despite its low representativeness in revenues, the application platform is an important subsystem within the technological system. Just as the Marketplace aims at taking advantage of the user base to occupy an important market of the online ecosystem, the apps platform also targets a market strongly dominated by Google through Android and Play Store, and, to a lesser extent, by Apple, with iOS and Apple Store. In addition, it accumulates more records to analyse users' activities, across a greater diversity of actions than those available by digital social network services. In the struggle for hegemony in data collection and processing technologies, especially artificial intelligence, the apps platform is an important control and contact point, with more than 100,000 developers related to it. In the fight for control for dominance in ICT paradigm, this field of competition is increasingly assuming a central position.

6.2 *Secondary Subsystems*

Facebook Messenger is Facebook's messaging application. Unlike other secondary subsystems, it has a 'hybrid' nature, being perhaps the best example of the technological system's integration strategy. Having replaced the messaging functionality, it is an application of its own, albeit connected to Facebook's interface. Its technical features serve its hybrid nature and partial connection to Facebook. When you log in to your home screen, you can access the app

---

44 System through which apps and websites are connected to each other and to Facebook, making their functionality available to users so that they appear in the newsfeed.

directly. For such, a preview screen shows the incoming messages. Clicking on them opens the specific dialog box in another area of the Facebook interface, where the user can chat without leaving Facebook. The tool also allows video and audio calls. In 2018, 400 million people used video and voice chat each month. In addition to sending messages, people shared over 17 billion photos (FacebookIQ, 2018). With this, it assumes the position of a personal communication tool almost similar to an e-mail server.

The investment in Messenger (as well as WhatsApp) is gaining strength within Facebook's overall strategy, as these applications have grown within the digital platform industry. By including tools that allow any type of interpersonal communication (such as audio and video), Facebook also offers Messenger as an alternative to traditional telecom operators' calls, fuelling the OTT's regulatory debate, as seen in Chapter 5. With the integration movement among Facebook Messenger, WhatsApp and Instagram messaging systems, announced in 2018, Facebook promotes a bold integration across different applications, an example of what digital monopolies can do by incorporating services with interoperable functionalities. In 2020, Facebook introduced new tools for Messenger. One was Rooms, a vídeo chat (Facebook, 2020), that lately could go live (Stoy, 2020). Other was Whatch Together, allowing users to see vídeos in room chats (Micheva, 2020). As was done in WhatsApp, the enterprise limited forwarding messages in the app to five contacts (Sullivan, 2020).

Also, a digital social messaging network, WhatsApp has become the world's most popular service in this category. With a point-to-point cryptography architecture, the app boomed in accesses during this decade, becoming the main source of information consumption in several countries. It allows not only conversations, but audio and video calls and sending files in interpersonal and group communications. As in the technological style of messaging apps (mentioning a concept by Hughes [1993]), the artefact allows sending messages to a group of recipients. Its design and interface are considered simple and usable, guaranteeing reception and rapid ascension at a time when there were not so many options available only for this purpose.

Its acquisition in 2014 was the result of the most exemplary case of Facebook's incorporation strategy, being the largest operation in this sense in the platform's history. In 2018, there were 65 billion daily messages and 2 billion minutes of audio calls (Al-Heeti, 2018). By the end of the 2010s, Facebook had not yet turned WhatsApp into one of its ad-serving arms, maintaining only one service for businesses (WhatsApp Business) that included customer communication management tools (such as message labels and others). Amid the emergence of messaging, and with Facebook looking at how to monetize this, WhatsApp was still the last frontier of resistance. In 2020, new features were introduced, like group calls (Facebook, 2020). It was a response of the growth of apps like Zoom during the COVID-19 pandemic. In April, the app got new forwarding restrictions. Highly shared messages could only be forwarded one chat at a time. The company declared the decision was an attempt to curb spread of misinformation inside of it (Singh, 2020).

As with WhatsApp, Instagram was a result of Facebook's embedding strategy. But it emerged as the main competitor to the primary technology system. The tool is organized according to a general profile but privileges a specific format: images.[45] In addition, the interface, also simple and organized in a feed, enhanced the experience of "continuous scrolling," stimulated by the logic of constant search for posts. What might seem like a strange situation is perhaps the most concrete example of Facebook's digital monopoly condition. The technological system did not acquire a company focused on one of its functionalities (like WhatsApp with messaging), but a digital social network that competed directly with it.

Over the years, the network introduced new tools such as filters, the "hyperlapse" (which accelerated videos), and the "layout," an app that allowed photo editing and montages (Instagram, 2015). The social network started displaying ads (Facebook, 2015) and counting on an edited feed, not a chronological one (Greenberg, 2016). Its most important resource was the stories format. The stories went from 0 to 400 million users between 2016 and 2018 (Read, 2018). In 2018, the social network, which already broadcasted videos, launched a specific application to compete with YouTube: IGTV. Instagram was Facebook's most successful competition control bet. With it, Facebook controls the main alternative to its main TS, in a "false competition," showing that Facebook should be seen beyond merely as an application, but as a company and a regulatory agent of digital social networks. At the same time, Instagram has been a place to test tactics to fight competitors, as in the adoption of the stories format, which was, until then, the main competitive advantage of Snapchat. With IGTV, the company is also seeking to test an alternative to YouTube. But the largest bet was the messaging integration, which can create a new architecture for the Facebook technology system as a whole. In August 2020, Instagram introduced Reels, a tool imitating TikTok resources to video editing (Perez, 2020). Also on Instagram, Facebook incorporated new resources related to live streamings, like allowing comments using the app on a desktop and save your live streamings on IGTV (Facebook, 2020).

---

45   Just as Twitter was organized around short messages and Pinterest around a preference organization, Instagram emerged as a network focused on posting images and gained projection for this kind of feature.

The company has also entered the product market for companies with Workplace, focused on tools for work process organization and internal communication. It brings together the already traditional Facebook features (such as newsfeed, groups, reactions and trending posts), taking the Facebook interface and its tools into a corporate sphere. In addition, it offers specifically designed features. One of them is the live video call, allowing people to be reached from a distance, such as in meetings. Through an automatic translation feature, it allows people to communicate without speaking the same languages. It also provides a control panel with process analysis tools (analytics), integrations with its own information technology systems and possibilities of integrated use by multiple companies. It also allows the creation of bots for various activities, such as service.

With these resources, the Workplace is the technological system's corporate services arm, a central market, due to the number of resources it handles and due to its access to major economic agents. Several business groups have already offered solutions in this sense and Facebook took advantage of this technology to apply solutions that had already been developed or adapted them to new solutions to enter this market. By deploying the 'traditional' tools in Workplace, however, it reverses the logic, providing resources for employers to perform surveillance. Communications among people and among teams are fully controllable. And this works as a direct subsidy to automated systems for analysis, prediction and recommendations. The battle for informative self-determination in the work environment, which was even more asymmetrical, given the vertical nature of information in the social relations of production under capitalism (Bolaño, 2000), is even more unbalanced. Through real-time interactions and video calls, the monitoring scale is amplified, responding to the neoliberal demand for control of more fragmented production sites and more flexible processes, to highlight a regulation over technology social factor.

Oculus is the service arm for activities employing the use of virtual reality, including a platform for access to games, programs and equipment to enjoy these types of immersive experiences. Different device formats make it possible to run applications in this type of environment. The company supplies two groups of equipment. The Oculus Rift is a complete kit, composed of a headset (a head device covering the user's eyes for the imaging perception of contents), hand drivers (for commands) and sensors (to translate the real movement into the immersive experience). In 2019, the company announced (Facebook, 2019) a new model, Rift S, with higher resolution and a mechanism for orientation in the physical environment without having to remove the kit. The Rift itself does not do the processing, requiring a computer with minimum specifications to process the applications and graphics. Gear VR is a kit used together with a smartphone (until 2019, a partnership was held with Samsung), with a headset and a general controller, with the availability of a joystick.

As seen in Chapter 4, as well as hardware, there is a need for software. Oculus provides one platform for Rift and another for Gear VR. On this platform, electronic games as well as other cultural products are offered. Video platforms have specific applications to provide 3D audiovisual works. These include Facebook Watch, the company's video service. A feature called "Arena Oculus," with an immersive experience in real events. A tool allows the user to add elements of augmented reality to their own homes. Gaining space in this market,[46] Facebook is advancing in a segment with great potential for the near future of internet services. Virtual and augmented reality technologies create new audience experiences for existing content (such as games and streaming video and audio) and new interaction services with the most diverse environments, from the home environment to meetings of friends separated by distance. The platform logic based on existing services directs the appropriation to improved experiences of already accessed services. In one of its main activity extension bets, Facebook can play an important role if this market develops.

7 Dissemination

Facebook built its upward trajectory by adopting an existing digital social networking model that already featured experiences, like Friendster and MySpace. Its 'free' offering (supported by data collection for personalized advertising) meant the removal of a fundamental access barrier. But, beyond that, the tool met the demands of an audience seeking tools to interact and maintain contact with friends, acquaintances and people belonging to various circles of their lives. Nadkarni and Hofmann (2012) wondered why people use Facebook. Examining the literature, the authors concluded that it was for two main reasons: (1) the need to belong, and (2) the need for self-representation. The two factors may coexist or be more prominent in users' motivations for joining Facebook.

Facebook ended 2018 with 2.3 billion users and reached 2.6 billion in 2020. These are calculated by those called "monthly active users" (MAU). Over the past ten years (see Table 3), the digital social network has expanded that number by 6.4 times, from 360 million users in 2009. After years of peak growth at the turn of the 2010s (with 66% in 2010 and 38% in 2011), the expansion rate

---

46 In 2017, Facebook sold 700 units, second only to Sony, which sold 1.7 million (Statista, 2019).

TABLE 3   Facebook – User base historical evolution

	2009	2010	2011	2012	2013	2014	2015	2016	2017	2018
MAU (millions)	360	608	845	1006	1228	1393	1591	1860	2129	2320
Growth	n/a	66%	38%	25%	16%	13%	14%	18%	14%	9%
DAU	185	327	483	618	757	890	1038	1227	1400	1520
Growth		76%	47%	28%	22%	18%	17%	17%	14%	9%
Mobile DAU	n/a	n/a	n/a	374	556	745	934	1146	n/a	n/a
Mobile DAU growth	n/a	n/a	n/a	57%	48%	34%	25%	22.6%	n/a	n/a
DAUs by region										
USA and Canada	64	99	126	135	147	157	169	180	184	186
Europe	63	107	142	169	195	217	240	262	277	282
Asia Pacific	23	64	105	153	200	253	309	396	499	577
Rest of the world	29	58	109	161	216	263	319	388	441	478

SOURCE: AUTHOR, BASED ON ANNUAL COMPANY REPORTS

has stabilized, until it started to decline from 2016 onwards (in a phenomenon whose repercussions are discussed in the Management and Control Structure section). The "daily active users" (DAUs) moved at a similar pace. In 2018, they represented 65% of monthly users, which expresses a significant portion of the user base constantly making use of the digital social network.

In relation to secondary systems, WhatsApp was the second largest service of the platform in 2019, also in 2nd in the global ranking, with 2 billion users. From these, 1 billion are active users. The messaging platform has already reached 180 countries around the world. WhatsApp is the most popular service in several countries, such as Canada and Mexico, all South American countries, much of Western Europe, most African nations, Russia and India (We Are Social, 2019). Facebook Messenger was the company's third service, with 1.3 billion in 2020.[47] The application, conditioned to Facebook for the use of the messaging functionality, was a hit, going from 200 million users in 2014 to 1.3 billion in 2017 (Constine, 2017). Instagram comes right after, having reached the milestone of 1 billion users in 2019. The digital social network has

---

47   Statista (2020) Most popular social networks worldwide as of July 2020, ranked by number of active users (in millions). Available (consulted 23 September 2020) at: https://www.statista.com/statistics/272014/global-social-networks-ranked-by-number-of-users/.

multiplied its base by ten in six years, going from 90 million in 2013, reaching a billion in 2019 (Statista, 2019a). The proportional dissemination of the DSN is higher in Turkey and Sweden (58%), Saudi Arabia and Malaysia (49%) and Australia and Ireland (46%) (We Are Social, 2019).

These numbers were also the result of how users see the company and its services, a relation we discuss here as legitimation. From the start, Facebook was surrounded by an aura of the example of the possibilities of technology, where a group of students could create a solution that would become one of the world's most used products and best-known brands. Mark Zuckerberg embodied the figure of an early genius, as he was only twenty when he launched the platform. He was catapulted to stardom status and was selected as "Person of the Year" by *Time* magazine in 2010 (Grossman, 2010). According to that renowned publication, what began as a "game" turned into something real, covering, that year, a considerable portion of the planet, in dozens of languages and connecting the most diverse aspects of people's daily activities.[48] Facebook's level of popularity and reach has gained such momentum that some people even mistake the digital social network for the internet itself. A study (Mirani, 2015) found high percentages of people interviewed who could not discern between the platform and the World Wide Web as a whole. In a survey on internet use in Southeast Asian countries, the percentage of people who claimed to be users of the TS was higher than those who claimed to use the internet. When asked if Facebook corresponded to the internet, 65% of the respondents in Nigeria, 61% in Indonesia, 58% in India and 55% in Brazil answered affirmatively.

Facebook's popularity is a result of its dissemination, a solid technological base, but, also, a diverse set of strategies for building systems of meaning. The main one was the attempt to foster an imagery of the platform's societal benefits. The company created an arm exclusively dedicated to developing solutions focused on education (Facebook Education). In 2017, a "disaster maps" tool was announced, employing user data to provide information to organizations working in support of disaster victims, such as the Red Cross. Among the features were "safety check," real-time movement and travel maps (post-disaster locations). In addition, the company sought to establish a dialogue with users about their changes (including voting), (Schrage, 2012) and promoted spaces

---

48   In the same year, a film was released inspired by Zuckerberg's trajectory in the creation and early years of Facebook: *The Social Network*, by director David Fincher. The film received eight Oscar nominations, in categories such as "Best Film," "Best Director" and "Best Actor."

for debate with group administrators (Deve, 2017), including with financial aid of over US$10 million.

But, despite all these initiatives, Facebook has become the most criticized technology company since 2017, with accusations of playing a prominent role in the dissemination of fake news in several processes (US elections, the referendum in the United Kingdom, withdrawal from the European Union, and the plebiscite on the peace agreement in Colombia, all in 2016); responsibility for external interference in electoral processes (such as that of Russian agents in the US presidential plebiscite in 2016); abuse in the collection and transmission of user data (such as the Cambridge Analytica scandal in 2018 and the British Parliament's complaints from a lawsuit involving the company Six4trhee in 2019); and lack of security (such as the major leak involving the data of 50 million accounts in 2018).

Facebook has been investigated in the United States Congress. Its leaders have been summoned to testify by governments and parliaments of several countries. Regulatory agencies fined the company for abusing user data (as seen in the Rules section). In 2018, the "Delete Facebook" campaign gained visibility, encouraging people to leave the platform. Well-known artists in the United States, such as Jim Carrey and Will Farrell, the singer Cher, the technology company Mozilla and the technology company director Elon Musk, among others, did so (Tuttle, 2018). These legitimation problems (as referred to in the general technological trajectory section) constituted a major inflection in the upward curve of legitimation that occurred at the turn of the 2010s. From being a role model company, a global leader and one of the most valuable in the world, Facebook has come to be intensely questioned both for its role in the deterioration of public debate (with the dissemination of fake news, hate speech and political polarization) and in the treatment of users' data (whose problems will be addressed in the Relationship with the Values Base section, below). This has been translated into the meaning systems of its users about the technological system, as can be seen in the following section in the interviews carried out.

In 2019, Facebook was strongly criticized after a shooter opened fire on two mosques in New Zealand and live-streamed its attack (Ohlheiser, 2019). The episode increased the call for more effective actions against abuses and social media use for violence promotion and content moderation regulation. Facebook faced, in 2020, a massive boycott campaign called Stop Hate for Profit that pressured big enterprises to stop running ads on the platform during some weeks (Aziz, 2020). The organizers called for efficient policies to fight hate speech, toxic content and misinformation spread in the platform.

8 Appropriation

As a digital platform, Facebook has a number of agents that it connects and among whom it promotes active mediation. In the previous chapter (the Production Process section) we listed these audiences, which involve everything from non-professional users to businesses, public institutions and non-profit associations, to advertisers and developers. In addition, it is subject to regulation by state authorities, the object of research by scholars and other types of experts and the subject of concern by civil society entities. In this section, we present an analysis of the appropriation forms under a qualitative methodological approach from the interviews conducted within the scope of the research, with various types of audiences.[49] Facebook was recognized by the respondents as a key platform in the online environment today. Users also stressed Facebook's centrality to different activities, whether in politics or the impacts it has had in areas such as freedom of expression and user data protection. The technology analyst for an internationally active civil society organization (R13) classified Facebook as "the leading social networking platform."[50]

This perception was also shown by professional users. The social networking publisher of the main federal institution of the Brazilian Judiciary Branch considered Facebook "one of the platforms that has the most tools. You can work with events, photos, videos, gifs, stories." But she reports that Facebook is no longer the most important network.[51] The social networking coordinator of the TV station of one of the Brazilian Parliament houses also pointed out a decline in Facebook's centrality after the recent changes in the algorithm: "Before, it was where we posted ads for the programs, small videos, and the articles separately. We felt a decline since the algorithm change and we started to invest in Twitter," she reports[52].

---

49 They were organized as: (1) public institutions, (2) political associations and those responsible for their communication strategies, (3) media outlets, (4) researchers, (5) developers, (6) civil society organizations, (7) public managers and (8) non-professional users.

50 Respondent 13 afirms: "They control the market; they influence the types of content that are consumed. Their decisions impact expression, privacy, and personal security. For many users, Facebook is the whole internet."

51 This is due to the fact that the newsfeed algorithm has worsened the reach of the agency's posts. Respondent 1 said: "They've changed a lot for those who produce content. Since we produce content and are not selling anything, it has been harder to distribute content." According to her, Facebook is still relevant to "older" people. "It's where they want to find the content to share" (R1).

52 But she believes the platform still has relevance: "With us there, we are opening a place of discussion, of digital presence, allowing people to share, to give visibility, and allowing us to reach people who were not paying attention to anything in the political debate" (R2).

A director of one of Brazil's largest communications groups (R11) highlighted Facebook's power, which he called "one of the great players on the internet." However, the company is no longer just an intermediary, but has established itself as a "media company," as it broadcasts content and earns money from advertising revenue. A cultural producer from Belém (R23) with an art page on the platform considered this an important dissemination channel: "I post some relevant articles or small reviews of relevant things." A professional musician from Goiânia uses Facebook to promote his band: "I do the ads, I create events. The tools contribute to promoting the group's gigs, which are an important income to maintain it." The motivation to enter the platform, once again, highlights the power of the network effect. The musician adds: "We, as an independent band, exist on the internet. We entered Facebook as a matter of practical necessity. People were all there."

A digital marketing professional (R3) underlined how the DSN and other similar networks have impacted how politics is done: "It's all about my store 24 hours a day, seven days a week. On TV, you don't have to answer to comments, monitor, attract attention, but on Facebook, you do" (R3). The nature of platforms and online fruition adds new challenges, as Respondent 3 states: "Users are not sitting in front of the TV. They are doing many things, in class, at work, at lunch, in the middle of a conversation. The voters' attention deficit when they're on Facebook is huge." The communications coordinator of a major Brazilian party highlighted that Facebook has "totally changed the way we communicate," including in politics. According to him, the platforms have undermined the mediation of public debate as it was done before. These agents' architecture and their logic of operation stimulate a new, more polarized form of political dispute, with serious risks to democracy. Respondent 4 stresses the platform's relevance "They managed to make an important part of the public debate cease to be held in the open, in a mediated way. Without it, people have no commitment to what they say, even if it is not a valid argument." The concern relates to the wave of fake news spreading in the DSN. For a developer who has worked on political campaigns (R9), despite its relevance as a dispute arena, Facebook is not a public space, but under this illusion, it works in the opposite way: "The logic of the relevance algorithm that attracts what you like operates in the opposite direction of the public space. Public space is the space for contradictory views. This logic reinforces what you already agree with and removes what you disagree with. And it makes money out of it" (R9).

In interviews with non-professional users, different attitudes towards the DSN emerged. In general, there was a recognition regarding the platform's importance as a channel to publish content and stories from people who started to access it from a very early age. However, some respondents expressed a decline in frequency and interest, especially in favour of Instagram. A legal advisor from a public institution in Macapá (AP) pointed out that she joined the network to maintain contact with her family, who live elsewhere, and that this became her main information channel. An agronomy student from the city of Pelotas (RS) (R18) reported that he made intensive use of it and gave an example of how the direct network effect works in expanding its base: "I use it every day to read content from websites and to promote activities. I joined it because I received an invitation from friends." A sales representative from São Paulo (R19) said he uses Facebook "every day, more than I should." A teacher from Crateús (CE) and a trade union member (R21) also reported making intense use of the social network: "I really like to see the news links. But I also see gossip. Facebook works to bring distant knowledge closer and faster. You're connected to the world, it's a social network that's a very good tool when you know how to use it." A teenager from Curitiba (R17) said she currently uses it less, having dedicated more time to Instagram: "It's a way to pass the time. I see memes, kitten videos."

Most respondents answered the newsfeed was an important source of information. "I like the pages. I follow sports pages [and] news" declared Respondent 18. The most common practice recorded was the constant scrolling of the feed, in the standard appropriation mode stimulated by the technological system's architecture. This conduct was manifested by other respondents. "I go through the feed. I don't seek information, it comes to me" (R19). However, some respondents identified a problem in the excessive debates and opinions in their feed. In the answers, it became clear how the tool's operational logic is configured as an internal factor for regulating the action of users (the regulation by technology phenomenon), as in the option for certain formats and not others. The social networking coordinator of a legislative house evaluates that Facebook asks for "more elaborate" content. To attract attention, they put on a mask with the theme of the video, while in other networks they publish more "raw" content.

In politics, the logic of Facebook's competition for attention to "serious" issues (and interests shown on the social network) ended up leading to a debate that the digital marketing professional with experience in several campaigns (R3) calls "histrionic.": "It's not in-depth. An agenda like social security reform will not be discussed in depth. One group shout, 'burn it' and the other shouts, 'save it'" (R3). And this discursive strategy generates engagement, resulting in visibility. According to a developer who has also worked on political campaigns (R9), the newsfeed algorithm changes and the incorporation of driving as a possibility in the Brazilian elections from 2018 onwards made the sponsored content a prominent role on the organic messages: "Paid ads took over the organic network ranking. So, when you have one algorithm overlapping the other, the one with more economic power wins the dispute" (R9). He also noticed an inequality between the agents who work professionally in the network and the users promoted by the technological system's architecture, since the former create more profiles and produce more, gaining more visibility.

Users become "hostages" of the algorithm; a relationship enhanced by a lack of understanding about its operation. "We do not know the feed" (R2). Some respondents expressed some evidence, but without a more complete understanding, as 18 commented: "I know it makes a selection. But I don't know how it's done". But, despite the lack of knowledge (resulting from the company's lack of transparency about its algorithms' content), the assessments about this newsfeed selection role were mixed. "I think it's good. As far as I know, it shows what you access most. It makes it easier. It gets to the point" said Respondent 8. "I think it's bad. I think that it should show everything that is posted. Since it's an exposure social network, it should expose everything" (R20). "I'm even a little upset because I wanted to know things that don't show up" (R22).

But, while there was support from some of the respondents for how the feed works, the complaints were widespread about receiving disinformation through it. Respondent 12 reported receiving several false messages: "I have received much 'fake news:' lately, about politics, but [also] about the most varied subjects". Respondent 17 reported: "On Facebook, I get fake news about absolutely everything". The quick consumption and sharing dynamics in the feed was a facilitator of cases where respondents said they had already passed on this kind of content. Respondent 19 admitted to share a false content: "I spread it without checking the source and I was embarrassed. But I acknowledged it. What's bad for others I don't want for myself.". The logic of the easiness of forwarding false messages was seen in some cases. "It has already happened [to pass on fake news]. Sometimes we consider the news so overwhelming that we pass it on," reported Respondent 20. For the director of a large Brazilian media group, the platform's responsibility for disseminating disinformation should be recognized: "I call that collective damage to democracy. It interferes with the democratic process. It's not just in the United States, it's been happening in electoral processes around the world." (R11). As far as reporting resources are concerned, few said they had used them. "I don't report it, but I don't interact with it," said Respondent 23. A developer who worked on campaigns in the last elections (R9) tried to make use of the mechanisms made available to stop the spreading of fake news, such as reporting. Some respondents said they received more disinformation from other DSN s: "I constantly receive fake news, more commonly through WhatsApp."

Another complaint reported was regarding the advertisements. "I don't like it. It pollutes the page a lot," complained Respondent 18. "I don't think so much advertising is necessary. It gets in the way" (R21). The commercial representative from São Paulo also pointed out such excess but related it to his behaviour on the platform: "The ads are excessive, yes. But this excess is proportional to how many things you like." "It's a lot of advertising. We don't want to see that. You download three pictures and then two ads show up." (R22). But, for representatives of other audiences with a professional relationship with the platform, its advertising system brings important possibilities. The planning director of a large agency that handles this type of advertising points out that the driving ability totally changes the way they develop their campaigns. With the amount of data collected, and the possibilities of combining people's records, this precise reach capacity is greatly enhanced. In addition to the segmented reach, the resources allow sending specific discourses to each precisely defined audience. This involves more work, which demands larger agency structures (and higher costs for advertisers) for campaigns with high reach. With the collapse of the organic reach, sponsored content and ads have gained more importance. If organic reach has dropped, the increase in the amount of content and the competition for users' attention have led to a central challenge: to deliver advertising without them looking like ads. To leverage the tools, Facebook has created a support service for large advertisers called the "creative shop." "If you advertise and spend a lot you can use them for free," reported a marketing agency executive (R5). This support also highlights how advertising on the platform is not a mitigator of entry barriers but reinforces the inequality of companies according to the size and resources available for advertising on the DSN.

A researcher at a national data analysis institute highlights how Facebook pages are fertile locations for evaluations, since they are public, and how this information can be used in profile building. Before the change of the Facebook API, says the researcher of the data analysis institute, there were many more possibilities. But, after that, access was more restricted, even though public data still allow different analysis. This type of analysis is not only useful for commercial purposes, but, also, for what Respondent 6 (R6) called "listening" to customers, for any type of purpose, including politics. "On Facebook you have metrics, you have statistics," says the communications coordinator for a political group (R4). However, these metrics are a key issue in the advertising service. Facebook covers several steps in the production chain (such as ad agency, ad serving, and outreach statistics). The researcher at the data analysis institute warned that one of the problems is that metrics are overvalued. In e-commerce site metrics, the "count" of whether a purchase was the result of an ad on Facebook includes "broad" indicators that configure "an outrageous overbilling," in the words of the researcher (R7). A developer who has worked on political campaigns (R9) mentions "reach" as another example of problematic metrics.

In addition to advertisers, another audience with an intense relationship with Facebook is developers. A researcher from a technology and society institute with experience in developing applications and posting them on Facebook (R8) reported that the procedure, like Play Store, requires a registration for posting on the app platform. He pointed out that one of the platform's major tools is the connection to an app through its login, the "social login." In a developed app, he and his team adopted this technological solution. A programmer and engineering professor at a federal university (R9) tried to use an application on Facebook, but reported that, after the API closed and the Cambridge Analytica scandal, the DSN became more restricted. In addition to the API closure already mentioned, he had to approve each application that would be made available.

A developer working in mobile applications (R10) sees the concentration of power and information on Facebook and other digital platforms with some concern, including the mediation of access to apps and the definition of internal rules that regulate the relationships within them: "We don't have any kind of control over what they do and what they stop doing. In relation to the terms of use, we can hardly do anything, and they can do almost anything" (R10). The developers, he adds, are "completely tied to how they decide things are going to happen." Also, Facebook gets access to a lot of data, like which user has which app, when and how often they access each one of them.

Such access and handling of personal data were also subject to questions in the interviews. The technology analyst of an international civil society organization (R13) highlights the rise of Facebook over the information collected, in a dynamic of invisible surveillance, often without the knowledge of users: "In Facebook, people are subject to invisible surveillance. They don't have much control over what happens to their data." According to him, Facebook is "everywhere," reaching a series of spaces on the internet through its partner site network: "About 35% of websites have some Facebook code installed. It's a giant traffic that goes through the platform. These sites aren't owned by the company, but it sees them" (R13).

In the interviews, almost all non-professional users said they don't know how Facebook uses their data. Some demonstrated some knowledge, generally intuitive knowledge. "I know they use synchronization with contacts. When I add someone to WhatsApp, they appear as a Facebook friendship suggestion," said Respondent 17. Only part of the respondents was uncomfortable with the DSN's personal information exploitation. "I don't like them using my data. I think it should be something more restricted, not so public" complained Respondent 21. According to some respondents, even knowing about the importance of being concerned with their data, people end up not considering it because they think nothing will actually happen or that it won't make a difference, as Respondent 2 commented: "We always think that we are not being watched because we are nobody". "We think we already know everything. I know it's wrong, but we think it's all very safe and that our information won't be so relevant and it's just an account" (R26).

Issues such as the ones pointed out generated an exit trend from Facebook manifested in the conversations. Some respondents reported having already suspended accounts, decreased the time spent there, or even left the network. In these behaviours, the migration to paying more attention to other networks was mentioned, especially Instagram. A commercial representative from Paracatu (MG) (R20) reported having disabled Facebook, motivated by fights in a romantic relationship as a result of surveillance between both parties on the platform. A cultural producer from Belém (R23) decided to end his personal account due to personal exposure. A student from Barra do Garças (R26) also deleted her account, as she no longer saw any advantages of being on the platform and complained about the discussions. A teenager from Curitiba (R17) reported having stopped using Facebook and currently privileges Instagram: "On Instagram, I only share photos. On Facebook, it has become a lot about politics, people are always sharing, and at this moment in the country they only post long texts, and I think that's why it has been decreasing."

In addition to users, business, social and public organizations have also been making this transition. "Facebook has stagnated a bit. In terms of reach, it has dropped a lot. The number of followers hasn't declined, it's increased timidly. On Instagram, the numbers keep growing," said a public institution's social networking editor.[53] However, the digital marketing professional with major and proportional campaigns in his curriculum warns that in elections, in a scenario where Facebook is widely disseminated, such as in Brazil, this change is still incipient. Respondent 3 pointed out that Instagram still needs to be more known in Brazil: "It is easy for Facebook there, there are operators that offer free navigation. Some parts of the country don't know Instagram. For

---

53 But she also highlights differences in the design of the two technologies, such as limitations in Instagram. "Instagram has the problem of not allowing links. When I want to promote something for the site, Facebook still offers me this function, which I still use," commented Respondent 1.

80% of municipalities, Instagram does not exist". The professional musician from Goiânia (GO) (R25) also identified the drop in engagement on Facebook and the rise of Instagram among the DSN users. And he credits this to the already-mentioned algorithm changes that have led to the drop in the postings' organic reach.

Among the representatives of the various audiences interviewed, Facebook was seen not only as a tool, but, also, as an economic and political agent and, therefore, one subject to legal regulation. The director of a large Brazilian media group (R11) argues that, if Facebook is a media company, there should be more equal treatment between it and other companies in this market: "What we demand is a minimum of equal treatment. There are some discussions about regulating these platforms. Maybe the solution is to deregulate us" (R11). A former senior manager in the Brazilian government has reported an episode that highlights one of the issues in holding Facebook accountable as a subject of legal and administrative discipline: the way it applies its internal (California-based) rules in relation to its activities in states with different laws. The agency published some content with an image that was removed by the platform. Although it was not a case of nudity (but an image of an indigenous woman), the DSN removed the post arguing that it violated its Community Standards. In the board's view, there were "violations of national identity and sovereignty" as well as "cultural uniformization as global standards are applied." The former government leader stressed the platform's power in other regulatory approval processes.

A respondent from a national and international civil society organization (R14) reports that the company adopts several tactics in Brazil to act with governments and the National Congress in order to maintain its positions in legal debates and attempts to approve rules that affect its activities. Although it does not often publicly express its positions in meetings, events and hearings, it maintains a robust policy team in Brazil, which closely follows the legislative procedures and establishes dialogues with public managers and members of Congress.[54] In addition, Facebook organizes activities such as "brunches," events, visits to headquarters, or even courses for these politicians' communications teams. "This relationship is part of a lobbying process that happens

---

54 Respondent 14 added: "Facebook operates a lot in the background, it prepares technical notes. It does not publicly expose its positions. It prefers to have someone speaking for it, or to be dispersed in an association of 30 to 40 companies." These technical notes play an important role from the point of view of the company's strategy, since there is a lack of knowledge among managers in different powers about how it works and its impacts on society.

systematically by these companies," observed Respondent 14. However, with Facebook's public scandals and the introduction of bills related to digital social networks, the respondent sees the company assuming it will have to go into a more public debate about its responsibilities and possible ways to discipline its operation.

9   Relationship with the Values Base

9.1   *Rights, Promotion and Guarantees*

Facebook has allowed new forms of connection between individuals, businesses, institutions and associations. Although no tool is specifically new – since social networks already existed, such as Friendster and MySpace, as well as messaging and interpersonal communication features, such as mail servers – Facebook has elevated the many tools available to a new condition, in what Kirkpatrick (2010) calls the "Facebook effect." Facebook has become a factor for promoting these guarantees. The company ensured forms of relationships by overcoming obstacles imposed by distance, allowing people to communicate more intensely than in traditional media. The platform also made it possible to "find" people with whom they had lost contact. In terms of freedom of expression, Facebook has facilitated alternative voices to express both within its networks and publicly. Facebook has become a privileged space for political participation, not by chance having become the target of actors seeking to influence the electorate. A survey by Vesnic-Alujevic (2012) showed the positive effects of political practice on Facebook: "This means that the more respondents were involved in online political participation through their Facebook profile pages (such as posting or forwarding political information or participating in the discussion), the more they participated in politics offline" (p. 469). Cohen (2008) highlights, as one of the advantages of social networking, its ability to conduct several information activities at the same time.

9.2   *Damages and Violation of Rights*

The scandals from 2016 onwards have put Facebook under scrutiny. The company has been questioned in several aspects, from the spread of disinformation to the lack of security that allowed data leaks affecting millions of people. Whether the consequences are intentional or unintentional, the power assumed by Facebook and how it structures the public debate has put democracy or even the physical and mental integrity of people, threatened or violated from the spirals of hate speech and disinformation, at serious risk. One of the most critical issues is the violation of data protection and privacy.[55] Facebook's surveillance potential, and the resulting abuses and violations in the use of personal data, have been built up over the historical technological system's evolution. This trajectory had, in the Terms of Use and Privacy Policies, two crucial tools for extending pervasive collection practices (as seen in the previous chapter). One crucial way of expanding users' data collection was to set more invasive modalities as "default."[56] Another strategy was expanding user data and its uses for new purposes.[57] The company has also enhanced its data collection by using records of individuals obtained from third-party partner sites of the platform. Although the platform's Terms of Service required the data to have been obtained with the consent of its owners, the company did not adequately monitor whether this requirement was met (Lomas, 2018). Mark Zuckerberg (Zuckerberg, 2011) admitted "many mistakes," referring to the Beacon case in 2007 and the transition to the new privacy model in 2009.

One of the most salient issues in the Facebook privacy debate was access to data by third-party applications. In 2018, newspaper reports from the UK and US revealed how a UK digital marketing firm, Cambridge Analytica, used data from 87 million people around the world to interfere in election processes,

---

55 Kwecka et al. (2014: 116) argue that the concept of privacy should be taken as a public good related to the guarantee of democracy and the exercise of other rights, such as free association and public participation. Allmer (2013) assumes a critique of traditional notions about privacy, which would be liberal in character and associated with a self-protective possessive individualism, locating surveillance in the state and affirming the protection of the individual against it to be part of market relations. In the place of these meanings, Allmer proposes a more critical approach that incorporates power asymmetries in society, relations of domination, class struggles, resource controls and exploitation. Surveillance on the internet would be associated with the reproduction of this framework of social relations, manifested in the spheres of production, circulation and consumption. A more critical approach should incorporate this understanding, placing the role of this practice in protecting individuals from coercion for the reproduction of the social system. This includes protection against surveillance on the internet, especially that conducted by corporations.

56 One example was the launch of Facebook Chat in 2008. The feature showed which of the friends were online by default. In order not to be seen, the user needed to opt out of the default control instead of the choice of going online so that others could start a conversation as a clear option ("opt-in").

57 The Beacon advertising service, released in 2007, monitored users even when they were not logged into Facebook. This data collection was not reported to users, but showed tests conducted by information security companies. The tests indicated that even after the introduction of share deactivation settings, the sending of purchase information to Facebook continued (Perez, 2007). A lawsuit was filed in which Facebook had to pay US$9.5 million (Lomas, 2018).

including the US presidential elections of 2016 (Cadwalladr and Graham-Harrison, 2018).[58] Overall, the Cambridge Analytica scandal was treated as a "surprise" by Facebook.[59] The company reported, in response, that controls would be implemented so that these applications would have to obtain the express consent of users and explain the purposes of the data collection, which, as seen in the scandal, did not occur. All of these actions, as said at the beginning of the section, have caused a lot of damage to Facebook's image. In one of his statements in 2018, director and founder Mark Zuckerberg admitted, at least in part, the platform's responsibilities in protecting its users' data.[60]

Apologies have been a recurring phenomenon since the time Zuckerberg developed Facemash, before Facebook. However, they do not change the central problem: the abuses stem from the very social content of the technological system, from its logic of collecting records to offer not only customized advertising, but increasingly diverse services and resources. Internal emails held by the British Parliament in an investigation that resulted in a report on disinformation and the risks of the platform showed practices of abuse, such as accessing data without permission and giving permission to access special data to some companies (Levin, 2018). The problem embedded in the technological system's own architecture has impacted other areas of the TS, such as the information flow, as we will see below.

In 2019, NBC News obtained internal Facebook documents showing that it used users' data to harm rivals and reward partners (Solon and Farivar, 2019). Amazon got access to users' data because it was running ads on Facebook to launch its Fire smartphone. According to the report, the company discussed to sell users data to developers. In July 2019, Facebook made and agreement with Federal Trade Commission ending the investigation related to Cambridge

---

[58] A former employee, Christopher Wylie, reported how the company used data obtained by a developer of an application with questions about psychological profiles to support aggressive content targeting campaigns exploiting people's fears and feelings. The firm integrated the data obtained with others (such as search histories) to reach more than five thousand data points from 230 million Americans (Isaak and Hanna, 2018). Facebook confirmed it knew about the data leak from developer Alexsandr Kogan since 2015. Faced with the scandal, Facebook suspended the social network company.

[59] However, an investigation by the Office of the Privacy Commissioner of Canada in 2009 had already pointed to problems with the transfer of data to third party applications (Office of the Commissioner of Privacy of Canada, 2009).

[60] The CEO admitted the company has not done enough: "It's clear now that we didn't do enough to prevent these tools [the platform] from being used for harm as well That goes for fake news, foreign interference in elections, and hate speech, as well as developers and data privacy. We didn't take a broad enough view of our responsibility. I'm sorry" (Valente, 2018).

Analytica scandal, approved by a federal court in April 2020. The settlement content involved a US$5 billion fine and changes in the platform, such as: creation of a new privacy committee in the board of directors, updating the privacy check-up tool, rolling out an Off-Facebook tool (a summary of apps that send information about to Facebook about the user) and report quarterly and annually to FTC about the compliance with its terms (Priotti, 2020). Also, in 2019, the company announced its intention of using end-to-end encryption on its messaging apps (Messenger, WhatsApp and Instagram). US Attorney General William Barr sent a letter with policymakers from other countries asking the company to stop these plans. Facebook denied the claim, arguing that doing so would be a gift to hackers and repressive regimes (Palmer, 2019). In 2020, Facebook announced a series of actions, allegedly to improve privacy in platform. Among them were expanding the prohibition of changing groups' privacy settings from private to public and filing lawsuits against actors bypassing Instagram fake engagement restrictions (Priotti, 2020b).

The scandals and criticisms were part of the technological system's trajectory also with regard to public debate and the right to communication.[61] With the newsfeed's creation, Facebook has increasingly taken on the role of regulatory agent for information flows, determining what each user would see. The progressive segmentation built by Facebook (such as through customized audiences or the use of third-party databases) would attract not only brands seeking to realize their merchandise by meeting the "right consumers," but, also, political forces and agencies acting in electoral competitions with new features far superior to what existed until then in electoral and political marketing strategies. One criticism against Facebook regards its role in promoting "bubble filters" and "echo chambers" (as discussed in Pariser [2011]). Quattrociocchi et al. (2016: 2) elaborated a study pointing in this direction: "We find that intentionally false claims are accepted and shared, while debunking information is mainly ignored."

One impact already mentioned was the reduced reach of its users' posts and, especially, pages. In 2018, a new change in the algorithm brought some new criteria for valuing postings in the newsfeed (Mosseri, 2018).[62] Faced with the scandals, one of its reactions was to reduce the content of news and

---

61 Already discussed within Google's analysis in Chapter 8.
62 Among them were the favouring of sources considered "reliable," news that people considered "informative" and local contents. With that, the company on the one hand favoured traditional media outlets and, on the other hand, harmed those with a national reach. In Brazil, one of the most important newspapers, Folha de S. Paulo, announced after the change that it would no longer post on the platform (Folha de S. Paulo, 2018).

politics in favour of "meaningful interactions" from close people, such as family and friends.[63] Then, in a newsfeed update, Facebook reconfigured the public debate inside (in a huge user base). To evade criticism regarding its responsibility in spreading disinformation, instead of effectively addressing the issue, it changed the priority indicators in the feed to reduce the discussion of political issues.

In 2020, an article from *The Wall Street Journal* (Horwitz and Seetharaman, 2020) reported Facebook staff admitted its algorithm stimulated divisiveness in order to gain users' attention and increase time on the platform. The company promoted studies about the subject, but, according to the newspaper, the effort and its possible application in products and internal rules were weakened inside the conglomerate. One preoccupation was that changes could affect more conservative publishers. Facebook responded (Rosen, 2020), mentioning what it called "investment to fight polarization." Among them were initiatives such as: recalibrating the newsfeed to prioritize content from friends and family (at the expense of professional news visibility), reducing the presence of click-bait headlines in the newsfeed, creating a integrity team, restricting recommendations, prohibiting hate speech and acting to reduce the circulation of misinformation.

In September 2020, a Facebook employee named Sophie Zhang said in an internal memo leaked to press outlets (Wakefield, 2020) that she had "blood on her hands" and had influenced political processes in countries without oversight:

> In the three years I've spent at Facebook, I've found multiple blatant attempts by foreign national governments to abuse our platform on vast scales to mislead their own citizenry, and caused international news on multiple occasions. I have personally made decisions that affected national presidents without oversight, and taken action to enforce against so many prominent politicians globally that I've lost count.
> WAKEFIELD, 2020

In the second half of the 2010s, Facebook was subject to questioning for its role in spreading hate speech and disinformation. As shown in Delmazzo and Valente (2018), after accusations that Facebook played a central role in

---

63 With this change, despite the company not eliminating the circulation of more political content, it has directed the public debate towards fewer discussions on topics of this nature and from a broader list of sources (people not so close) in favour of more depoliticized daily conversations.

the election of Donald Trump as president of the United States (Allcott and Gentzkow, 2017), the first reaction of the company's leader, Mark Zuckerberg, was to classify the statement as a "very crazy idea" (Solon, 2016). Shortly after that, he stated that the company took the disinformation problem "seriously" and was committed to fighting it (Zuckerberg, 2016).[64] Lyons (2018) has published a new text updating the company's strategy on the subject: (1) to remove accounts that violate community parameters and internal regulations, (2) to reduce the dissemination of fake news (the company now uses the term "false news") and "click-bait," and (3) inform people by providing more context about the posts they read and content to which they have access. In the first case, accounts are not shut down due to the posting of fake news, but for other violations, such as spamming, hate speech, fake accounts, "inauthentic behaviour" or "false engagement."[65] In the second case, the reduction in reach occurred in relation to pages considered by the company as "low quality" and in relation to posts indicated as fake by partner checking agencies. In addition, there is a reduction in the 'overall' reach of pages that repeatedly spread fake news. The

---

64   In December 2016, the company's management announced a number of intentions, including the implementation of barriers to the sponsoring of fake postings, the possibility for users to report fake news, and the establishment of partnerships with fact checkers to flag contested content on timelines. Newsfeed criteria have been changed to reduce the circulation and impact of fake news. One of the objectives was to inhibit the reach of "click-bait" (Mosseri, 2017). The term was used to classify sites that published content only to search for clicks, and, consequently, ads from this traffic. The company also said it made it more difficult to create fake accounts and said it would deactivate paid content from pages that repeatedly shared fake news (Shukla and Lyons, 2017). In March 2017, the disputed tools were deployed for part of the users (SU, 2017). In August 2017, the company announced two important measures. The first was automatic analysis to identify hoaxes, a term used in the United States to point out intentionally produced lies. The second novelty was the implementation of one of the previously announced changes to show the user whether a content is questioned by a fact checker – "disputed," according to the term used by the company (Su, 2017). In the disclosure of the measures, the company adopted the terms "hoaxes" and "false news" instead of "fake news" (Oremus, 2017). Also in the first half of 2017, an investigation was opened in the US Congress on the influence of Russia on the country's politics by digital means, especially the social networking sites (Calabresi, 2017). In September, Facebook reported that it identified and closed 470 inauthentic profiles somehow related to Russian sources that would have spent US$100,000 on ads between June 2015 and May 2017 (Stamos, 2017). The company also launched a tool that presents users with tips on how to identify fake news. In December 2017, it announced that it would replace the "disputed articles" resource with "related articles," showing information from "respected" sources (Su, 2017). In 2018, a new tool was included, now to provide "context" about a post, how to show other materials from that source, which friends shared something from that source and the age of the content's author.
65   One example was the deletion of accounts during the Brazilian elections in 2018 (G1, 2018).

third strategy involves the related articles and context tool in the feed as well as educational campaigns on the subject.

According to Reuters Digital News Report 2020 (Reuters, 2020), Facebook was seen as the main space for misinformation in the Phillipines (47%), US (35%) and Kenia (29%), among other countries. In Brazil, WhatsApp was mentioned as key false news source (35%), while Facebook was the second (24%). Solon (2020) reported Facebook reacted politically to conservative critiques about alleged bias and weakened its monitoring and moderation responses to right-wing sources contents. During the COVID-19 pandemic in 2020, Facebook kept being a platform for the spread of misinformation, undermining public health. A report from the NGO Avaaz (2020) showed that health misinformation spreading websites got 460 million views on Facebook in April, when the pandemic was rising. The content of ten main health misinformation sites got four times more views than those of official health authorities. And only 16% of health false news reports had a warning label placed on them.

Facebook's editorial role was not only questioned regarding disinformation, but, also, discrimination. In 2016, the news agency ProPublica denounced the platform for allowing certain races and ethnic groups from being excluded in the ads segmentation (Angwin and Parris Jr., 2016).[66] Facebook responded by arguing that the system included "ethnic affinity" among its categories, which would not be the same as race. The company announced that it would remove the segmentation fields claiming that discriminatory advertising was against the company's guidelines.[67] In 2019, the US government formally denounced the platform for discrimination, in violation of a national law (the US Fair Housing Act).[68]

But discrimination and the reinforcement of stereotypes do not occur only in targeting ads. Bailey et al. (2013) argues that the exposure logic, based on valuations and interactions, generates a stimulus to seek approving engagement, with 'likes,' sharing and positive comments.[69] Silva and Braga (2016) analysed

---

66 It was possible, for example, for advertisers to direct a house ad only to whites, excluding blacks and Hispanics. This practice violated US law governing the real estate market.

67 In a new article, ProPublica identified, after Facebook's announcement, that alternatives for customizing the ad's target audience were still available, allowing blacks, Jews, people looking for wheelchair ramps and Spanish speakers to be excluded (Angwin et al., 2017).

68 According to the accusation, Facebook analyses data from its users and then employs machine learning to predict people's reactions to ads in order to recreate groups like race (Paul and Rana, 2019).

69 In their study, they identified how this dynamic (built by the connection and information design and architectures) creates an environment in which the reproductive self-exposure of stereotypes (such as sexualized images) is promoted as indicators of social success and popularity. On the other hand, the survey concluded that women are the

cases of racism on Facebook. In the study, respondents expressed the opinion that Facebook facilitates racist assaults for three reasons: 1) the possibility of creating a fake profile, 2) freedom of expression on the network, and 3) the fact that the attack occurs remotely, which makes it harder for the offenders to be held accountable or to react to the attack.

This selection process that leads to the targeting of public debate, access to information and discrimination is reinforced by the lack of transparency in the content of the technological system and how it operates. Facebook's lack of transparency is evident in different areas: (1) data collection, including its nature and the universe of its subjects and objects; (2) the ways of collecting such data; (3) the definition of which data are used; (4) the purposes for which they are used; (5) the criteria and parameters of valuation for each specific use and processing (as in the newsfeed); (6) the development of the algorithm and its functionalities and potentials, (7) the ways of processing the data (not only in the newsfeed but in all algorithms); (8) the results and possible indications (as in the Marketplace products); (9) the application of these results; (10) the impact of this application; and (11) the evaluations and possible corrections at each of these levels. Such lack of transparency is disguised through the explanations and justifications regarding the existence these algorithms.

This characteristic is manifested on two levels: 1) it covers the very design of the system's artefacts and the way they are organized in its architectures, 2) it also includes the company's own strategies, its interests and the way it handles its business. This point has already been analysed in studies about the platform and the algorithms' lack of transparency, as in Eslami et al. (2015), Tufecki (2018) and Diakopoulos (2014). Doneda and Almeida (2019) advocate a "governance" for these technological systems in order to ensure transparency and oversight by users and other agents of the system.

Facebook impacts not only the technological practice, but, also, the market in which it operates. The digital platform has boosted the concentration dynamics of information and communication technologies, especially digital platforms in niche markets. In addition, it has undertaken concentration actions that are typical of capitalist agents by acquiring WhatsApp and Instagram. More than that, it has developed a specific design in order to enhance its competitive edge in "qualitative competition" (Herscovici, 2013). The result was absolute dominance of the DSN market, as discussed in the Competitive Performance section. Facebook controls the three largest players

---

focus of greater judgment, favoured by the surveillance dynamics in the digital social network. Fear ends up being a limiting factor in women's full participation in these spaces, reproducing gender inequalities in this online environment.

in this segment (Facebook, WhatsApp and Facebook Messenger) and the fastest growing player (Instagram). Facebook has created entry barriers that have made it difficult for competitors like Twitter, Snapchat and other networks, such as Tumblr, Reddit, LinkedIn and Pinterest, to emerge. The company appears as a "modern monopoly," as stated by Moazed and Johnson (2016). However, the authors recognize a competitive capacity in these markets, while we highlight here the company's movement towards its status as a "digital monopoly" (as discussed in Chapter 5).

10   The Technological System's Impact on Society

As we have just examined the positive and negative impacts of Facebook in promoting guarantees and rights, this section outlines the third dimension of the technological regulation of the object, showing its effects on the other spheres of society.[70] In the scientific–technological sphere, like Google, Facebook has been a leading agent in technological development, especially in the area of artificial intelligence and connectivity (which it calls "founding technologies"). In the former, it created a specific program (FAIR). Through FAIR, the company has been conducting research in the areas of language comprehension, computer vision and machine learning. A platform to gather solutions around these themes and make new ones possible has been created, called Facebook LearnerFlow.[71]

A second "founding technology" receiving Facebook investments is connectivity. In 2016, it launched the Telecom Infra Project to develop solutions aimed at innovations in telecommunications infrastructure (Parikh, 2016).[72] In addition to its direct research, the company has developed programs to support studies (Facebook Research). One of them is the scholarship program, which covers one year scholarship plus expenses for travel and equipment acquisition. Those selected for the program get to know the Facebook headquarters and interact with the company's team. With these scholarships, the TS both

---

70   As in the previous chapter, this is not an exhaustive examination, which, in itself, would give rise to other in-depth investigations. But we will bring some examples to illustrate these consequences as a way to exemplify the process of technological regulation according to the model presented in Chapter 3 and detailed in the analysis framework.

71   These solutions have already been adopted in several products, such as simultaneous translation, newsfeed filtering or Workplace services.

72   The initiative was based on the company's concern with the fact that the capacity of telecommunications networks was evolving at that time at a rate lower than the volume of data employed by users with the expanding universe of platforms and applications.

contributes to networking within the academic environment and is able to direct research according to its interests.[73]

In the economic sphere, as with Google, the quantitative measurement of Facebook's impacts on the economy is limited. In a study developed in 2015, Deloitte (2015) estimated a direct effect on the generation of US$227 billion and 4.5 million jobs, considering third parties linked to the platform and not its financial results. Most of these are what the consultancy called "marketing effects," totalling US$148 billion. The revenue generated by apps linked to the platform would have totalled US$29 billion. The acquisition of mobile devices and connections motivated by Facebook would have moved US$50 billion. Notwithstanding the aforementioned fragility of the report, this data indicates how the distribution of wealth associated with Facebook reproduces global parameters of inequality in the international division of labour, strengthening the capitalist core to the detriment of its periphery.

Beyond the numbers, it is possible to state that the greatest economic influence involves its advertising services and the expansion capacity of companies promoting its products and services. The broadening of the advertiser base has resulted in representative growth in recent years. Between 2016 and 2019, it more than doubled, from three million to seven million advertisers (Statista, 2019b). If, on the one hand, such a feature exacerbates capitalist competition in the markets in which it is employed, on the other hand, it supposedly lowers existing entry barriers in traditional advertising models, such as broadcasting and print media. However, this assumption is rather limited. As seen in the Appropriation section, Facebook gives greater visibility and directly supports the largest advertisers by reproducing (and even amplifying) inequalities between these economic agents and their ability to reach their target audiences on the platform. No wonder the most popular brands in 2018 on the DSN were large companies: Samsung, Coca-Cola, Instagram, Red Bull, Windows and Nike.

Another Facebook effect is on the production process itself through its corporate service, the Workplace. In 2018, it was used by 30,000 companies worldwide (Chapman, 2018). It allows an enormous flow of information on production process and workforce activity through its tools. By using the features already adopted by users, such as Facebook Messenger, it also fosters a growing erosion of boundaries between the work environment and sociability outside it. The analytics and prediction functionalities lead to automation in

---

73 Explicitly or implicitly, the supports end up becoming factors for regulating the production of knowledge by these agents, but within academic institutions, thus gaining a scientific authority linked to the internal dynamics of these environments.

the work environment, reducing the already limited agency of the workers and elevating the direction of the production process by machinery in capitalism, about which Marx (2013) spoke, to a new level.

In the political–institutional sphere, the technological system has had relevant impacts. By adopting progressive projects to promote political debate or even to encourage participation in elections, it has assumed a condition of being a key mediator in public debate and political discourse. This importance has given rise to questioning from the most varied political forces. In the 2016 US presidential election, the company was questioned for its role in spreading disinformation. The Buzzfeed website noted that, in the months before that election, the best-performing fake content generated more engagement than the most popular stories of traditional media outlets in the country: 8.7 million shares versus 7.3 million (Silverman, 2016). Gunther et al. (2018) pointed to an influence of fake news on the elections.[74] Nelson (2017) mapped sites known for spreading fake news and traditional vehicles in the United States and concluded that their audience is significantly larger than that of the former.[75]

Facebook has also been strongly criticized for its role in the possibility of interference by foreign forces in a country's elections. What triggered this was the US elections in 2016 and accusations of Russian groups taking action in the propagation of pro-Trump paid and organic content as part of the investigations into the winning candidate's relationship with Putin's government. Investigations were opened in Congress (Calabresi, 2017). The company acknowledged that Russian groups created 80,000 posts, reaching 126 million US citizens (Chakrabarti, 2018). Faced with evidence of the social network's use by Russians to interfere in the US elections (and the investigations into Facebook's responsibility for that), Mark Zuckerberg (2017) expressed regret and pointed to investments in security in the following years, as well as cooperation with the US government. The controversies also involved the role of political advertisements (content driven) and their impact on political disputes. In 2018, faced with pressures regarding new risks of the platform's harmful effects in elections in several countries (such as Brazil, Mexico and the

---

74 Through interviews focused on Barack Obama's 2012 voters, finding support for Democratic candidate Hillary Clinton at just 77%. In fake facts reported in the campaign (such as Clinton's illness or the Pope's support for Donald Trump) 25% and 10% of respondents reported believing the allegations, respectively. Other studies, however, have minimized the impact of this phenomenon on the elections.

75 In the sample analysed in November 2016 – the month of the election – 40,100 people visited traditional sites, considered by the author to be safe sources of news, while 3,100 accessed news from pages known for fake content.

United States), the company implemented mechanisms for the transparency of advertisements and pages.[76]

In 2018, criticism went beyond the effect on election results when accusations began to emerge that Myanmar's army was using the social network as a propaganda tool to justify killing and "ethnic cleansing" against the Rohingya minority (Mozur, 2018). Hate messages against Muslims and fake news of rapes of Buddhist women by Muslim men were some of the examples.[77] Facebook has also been used to monitor opponents and attack them on their accounts as a way to discredit resistance. The case illustrates an example of regulation by technology. According to the company, one problem detected was the standard for displaying text used by Facebook (Unicode). However, 90% of phones in the country used an alternative standard, Zawagi, so their users could see the messages, but not Facebook's rules and institutional content. In July of the same year, deaths were reported from lynching in India associated with fake and hate messages spread by another Facebook application, WhatsApp (Safi, 2018).[78] In response, WhatsApp reduced the limit of recipients for forwarding messages to 20 worldwide and to five in India. In Libya, after playing a major role in the mobilizations to overthrow Muammar Gaddafi, in the process that came to be known as the "Arab Spring," Facebook was an instrument adopted by armed political groups in 2018 to threaten and silence opponents (Advox, 2018).

Facebook has also been a surveillance promotion force (see the Values Base section), but not just privately. In 2013, Edward Snowden's accusations and the leak of classified documents put the company at the centre of a massive scandal surrounding the espionage conducted by the US government not only against its citizens, but against people and authorities in other countries (Greenwald, 2013).[79] Mark Zuckerberg denied participation in the program and that the

---

76 Political ads started to be labelled as such in some countries (such as the United States, Canada and Brazil). Users are now able to view active ads on a Facebook page, Instagram and Messenger, and a file has been created for each page. Information was also made available about the pages, such as their owners, age, and recent name changes. Facebook also now requires more information from page administrators in order to register pages.

77 In an official statement, a product manager acknowledged that Facebook was "very slow" to prevent disinformation and hate speech in the country. In response, it brought down the accounts of military officers and amplified the performance of their artificial intelligence systems to map out the content to be brought down (Su, 2018).

78 The government even cut off the internet to prevent rumours from spreading through the social network. At least 30 people were killed accused of kidnapping children.

79 According to the allegations of the former NSA employee and documents obtained by the British newspaper *The Guardian*, the ultra-secret PRISM program, which began in 2007, consisted of direct access by that country's intelligence agencies to the servers of the technology giants, including Facebook, which would have joined in 2009. Among the

company had given any governmental access to its servers (Zuckerberg, 2013). According to the executive director, the transfer of data to governments was only carried out if required by law. In response to the denials, *The Guardian* published a supposedly leaked slideshow detailing how the program worked (Ball, 2013). As a response to the scandal's impact, the social network published a Global Government Requests Report in which it systematized these requests by country and generically informed whether the requests were met (Strecht, 2013).

In the cultural sphere, Facebook has had impacts in several fields. Twenge et al. (2018) pointed out that young people who spent more time on social networks, computers and electronic games had lower rates of well-being, self-esteem, enthusiasm in the relationship with friends and the feeling of security. Griffiths et al. (2014) proposed the idea of a "social network addiction," which would occur through the presence of some factors: salience (strong presence in the user's life), mood changes (sensations arising from the use of social networks), tolerance (increased time on social networks to obtain sensations, stimulating the use period), withdrawal symptoms (negative feelings when the person is deprived of the use), conflict (generated due to the time spent in this space) and resumption (back to high consumption levels after moments of control).[80] Kross et al. (2013) found a relationship between the degree of use of the social network and the feeling of affective well-being of those interviewed, taken in the research as the way people felt at the time of the survey and how satisfied they were with their lives.[81]

Excessive time on the network and these effects on users' well-being are built into the design of the platform and its features. Harris (2016) indicates the "mind hijacking" techniques adopted by platforms like Facebook as variable rewards and the exploration of sensations, such as the need for social

---

material collected were the search history, e-mail messages, live chats and documents exchanged by users. The Centre for Democracy of the American Civil Liberties Union (ACLU) classified the episode as an "unprecedented militarization of domestic communications infrastructure" (Greenwald, 2012).

80 The authors warned that another phenomenon, "Facebook addiction" (Hartmann and Wanner, 2016), has taken on a condition of its own, since the platform has ceased to be strictly a social network and has incorporated other activities, such as online games and video consumption.

81 Blease (2015) indicated that the possibilities of negative impacts were related to certain conditions, such as time spent on the social network and its regularity and concluded by identifying "triggers" that could harm well-being, such as depression. However, the assessment is not consensual in the literature. Jelenchick et al. (2013) conducted a study in which they did not find this direct relationship and considered it premature to talk about this phenomenon.

approval or the "fear of missing something important" (FOMSI), in which the DSN builds a system of meaning for the user, whereby it would become the place where important information about events or friends are disclosed, and the user must keep track of it at all times, so as not to miss out on this kind of news. Fogg (2009) discusses the use of mechanisms to capture users' attention and engagement on machines and platforms such as Facebook with the use of "persuasive technologies," which he calls "captology."[82] Facebook employs all sorts of techniques in its design to modulate user behaviour inside (as discussed in the Appropriation section). Faced with the negative consequences of these impacts, Facebook announced, in 2017, a new control tool for the newsfeed (named Snooze), such as the possibility of "suspending" notifications of profile or page updates for 30 days (Muraledhraran, 2017). In 2018, the company added the keywords feature as well. In the same year, it created new tools for users to more effectively monitor and control time spent on Facebook and Instagram (Ranadive and Ginsberg, 2018).[83]

Facebook has had an impact on social relations as a whole, and has done so in the most intimate circles, such as in romantic relationships. In 2015, the social network created a set of specific tools to mediate interactions between users after relationship breakups (Winters, 2015). According to the company's report, users had informed concerns about the possibilities of interaction in these situations. Among the resources focused on these cases was the possibility of reducing the frequency with which the name and profile photos of the ex-partner were displayed, as well as their postings, such as texts, links and photos in which they appear. It is also now possible to edit posts involving users in the relationship. The platform also became a repository of memories and individual activities. With the timeline, Facebook asserted itself as a repository of the records, interactions and postings (articles, videos, links) of each user. The recording of the user's life has even gone beyond its life. The

---

82   Techniques include choosing small behaviours to change (such as generating newsfeed scrolling), finding (or producing) a receptive audience (such as Facebook users), identifying resistance (such as competing for attention from other technologies), choosing a familiar technology channel (such as smartphones), choosing successful examples of persuasive technologies (such as notifications), testing and interacting quickly (such as experiments with users, as in Kramer et al., 2014).

83   One of them was the "Your time on Facebook" feature, within the "Your activity" section. The control now provides a feature to count the time connected to the social network on that device. It allowed the user to stipulate a "limit" of use, with a notification when this was reached. Another feature was to "mute" notifications as a way to reduce the newsfeed checking triggers and other features.

company created a set of solutions for users to manage a future situation in case of their death.[84]

11 Analytical Overview: Facebook and the Fight for Online Information Control

Facebook was born as a digital social network, and it is still seen as such by many of its related audiences. Under the guise of connecting individuals and collectives, its previous experiment, Facemash, would already anticipate some of the characteristics that would define its evolution: the abuse of data collection, social classification, appropriation modulation and the resigned and unaccountable reaction when faced with the evidence of violations. In the first case, the photos used for "voting on the person that is more attractive" were obtained without authorization. In the second case, the logic of the "game" was to classify people by their looks. In the third, the application defined a very clear logic of appropriation by imposing voting as the only option. Finally, Mark Zuckerberg's apologies to the Harvard board that investigated the problems with Facemash are similar to the posture he adopted in front of a US Senate committee when questioned about his role in the damage to democracy.

Based on Zuckerberg's image as a "prodigy boy" and the recurring view of technology as an instrument of progress (as in Marcuse's [1973] critiques, or those of critical technology theorists such as Feenberg [2002], or Winner [1986]), Facebook has grown in society. Its progress (in what Hughes [1993] calls invention and development), initially, in educational institutions, and, later, in companies, would prepare the company and its infrastructure for later scalability and would already include, in its initial stage, another distinctive feature: its character as a promoter of distributed surveillance, not only of the application over its user, but susceptible to appropriation by economic agents and organizations. As seen in interviews, its presence in these environments was an expansion factor. But, beyond this, there were other factors. Facebook wasn't the first digital social network, but it was successful in outperforming its competitors by offering distinct features and, in the midst of its growth, was

---

84 In 2015, the social network implemented a "legacy contact" in which the user chose a person (a relative or loved one) who could intervene in some way in the profile in case of death, such as the inclusion of a post announcing the burial, responding to friendship requests and updating the profile photo and cover (Callisson-Burch et al., 2015). Ambrosino (2016) classified the measures as promoting "a growing and unstoppable digital graveyard."

driven by both direct networking effects (the more a user's friends used the platform, the more a user felt pressure to participate) and indirect networking effects (the more people that used the platform, the more advertisers ran ads or developers built apps), a feature highlighted by Ezrachi and Stucke (2016) or Evans and Schmalensee (2016).

As in the case of Google, the social factors of regulation (the first dimension of technological regulation) have served as fuel for such evolution. Having been "open to the public" on the eve of the 2007–2008 crash, by gaining a mass of users, Facebook has become, like Google, an agent with the ability to meet market demand for a more optimized and streamlined promotion of goods in directing advertising to precise audiences, reducing costs. It has also opened space for companies to market both directly through pages and groups and the Marketplace. On the cultural level, this growth has resulted in indirect network effects, attracting a mass of content producers and broadcasters, as one respondent reported. In doing so, its informational flow gained relevance by concentrating all the main actors in this sphere. At the political level, its scope was used as an arena of competition and attracted the attention of political forces, including those whose level of competition (and access to power) demanded a "professionalized" (and often reprehensible or illegal) performance in this social arena. In a political scenario of international and national instability (Brazil is just one example), the DSN became a space for confrontation between political forces.

In addition to the social factors, Facebook took the internal factors of technological development (the second dimension of technological regulation) and took advantage of the stock of knowledge (as in Bunge, 2013) and technological alternatives available through the technological paradigm of ICTs (according to the approach of evolutionists like Dosi [1984]) to develop its systems on top of massive data collection and processing (Big Data), algorithms for the most different functions and artificial intelligence. The expansion of internet access (emerging technology), the strengthening of broadband networks (infrastructure), the sophistication of microprocessors (core input) and the dissemination of portable computers and mobile devices (carrier branches) (categories developed from the Freeman and Louçã model [2004]) were factors which Facebook used to spread throughout the internet. At the same time, they impacted the technological system, such as in the switch to mobile applications and devices discussed in this chapter. Like Google, Facebook realized the centrality of these technologies and their present and future importance and entered the race to master their progress, positioning itself in this market, as in the case of the artificial intelligence program. In this field, one of its frontiers is to extend its activities and performance as a digital monopoly.

With these technologies, it was successful in developing a technological base for its digital social network, with important advantages. In addition to basic features for creating profiles, establishing connections among acquaintances and friends and posting information or images, Facebook offered two decisive features, although they were not original. The first was the newsfeed, which became the apex of the DSN fruition, creating a logic of continuous feeding that generated consumption time. This was central to competition over the scarcest resource in the rise of connected services and devices: the users' attention. Thus, the newsfeed has become a "bottomless soup" (in reference to Harris [2016]) of infinite scrolling, as several respondents have reported. Having implemented the user behaviour orientation and attention-capturing channel, a second resource enhanced the first: the linking of actions inside the platform and even outside it to the feed confluence. Not only the posted messages, but everything the user did (from a tagged photo or a link that received a "like") was recorded and posted on the newsfeed. Even activities outside Facebook, such as reading a text on a website, could be tossed there through social plugins.

Such structure (or social content) of the technological system created the basis for a process, which we will call the "commodified surveillance spiral": the more people, the more interactions; the more interactions, the more data collected to build profiles; the larger the database, the greater the ability to targeting advertising services; the greater the revenues earned as a result of such trading, the greater the ability to develop and implement new solutions that attracted more people and intensified the operations, and so on. The commodified surveillance spiral is a specific manifestation of Facebook's technological regulation as a result of the technological system's content articulation with its operation based on its business model and market performance. Such dialectic interaction could also be described within what Feenberg (2005) calls "technical code." However, it is important to consider that its commercial logic does not exclude the platform's participation in surveillance processes linked to governments, as Snowden's reports indicate.

This model is structured around what we'll call here 'Facebook's triple architecture.' Despite the technological system's complexity, its resources, and its internal and external articulation, we will highlight three internal architectures whose specificity is justified by the activities they organize. The first we call 'interactive architecture', which defines how the members of the network can connect, in which modalities, in which directions (uni-, bi- or multi-lateral), in which spaces (such as groups or events) and under which degrees of visibility. In addition, they establish the forms of interaction (reaction buttons, sharing, comments, subscribing to a profile, invitations to an event, etc ...). As shown in the appropriation modulation strategies, Facebook has constituted several mechanisms to direct the actions of its users, from encouraging posts by asking questions in the "status" field to building friend list categories (closest friends, acquaintances). In this interactive architecture, Facebook has lived under a constant tension of dissociation of individuals in offline world and their virtual identities (with the possibility of creating more accounts) and of different categories and forms of profiles (individual and institutional, for example). The interactions, as discussed throughout the chapter, were coordinated to deepen tracking for personalizing advertising and services.

However, as mentioned earlier, one of the DSN's distinguishing features was its ability to go beyond connections, creating informational flows not only of people's messages, but of records of their activities on the network. These are arranged around an 'informational architecture'. The latter has, as its two central channels, the timeline and the newsfeed. The former has opened the possibility for users to edit their own profile, giving them more control over their information but, on the other hand, allowing an artificialization of their presence on the network, which makes room for a proliferation of images manufactured from some phenomena, such as the need for social acceptance or engagement with social circles. This logic has repercussions for social classification and can reinforce stereotypes (as seen in the section Relationship with the Values Base). The newsfeed has triggered several considerations so far, which have shown how its algorithm actively mediates the information provided, directly affecting the information repertoire accessed by a mass of users around the world. The algorithm changes and the page reach drop demonstrate the pressure of the business model and its impact not only on the platform's functioning, but on how it is appropriated and legitimized.

This change is an example of the technological system's third key architecture, which we will call 'transactional architecture' (concerning the transactions that occur within it). The main example, and what has impacted the system's content from the beginning, are the advertising services. The offer of segmented ads, or even personalized ads, are the main transaction and source of the business model, depending on sophisticated profile building and ad positioning capabilities. This model's hegemony has resulted in the colonization of the information architecture, by creating a content-boosting alternative. This has caused the information circulating to be increasingly blended and incorporated by the transactional architecture. In addition to online advertising, other forms of trading, such as application taxing and selling products on the Marketplace, are still incipient, but constitute a model that can expand.

Through these architectures, Facebook disciplines how users behave on the platform or even outside of it (promoting a regulation by technology movement), such as in websites with social plugins, applications using Facebook login or offline spaces that make use of social networking, such as associations with groups or companies with pages on the platform. From the technological system's internal rules to the guidelines embedded in the social content and its resources (part of its design), Facebook establishes what types of conduct are allowed, acceptable or recommendable (ranging from prohibitions to stimulation), with different regulatory mechanisms. Thus, the technological system builds internal regulating factors (which we call regulation mechanisms), defining the limits and directing forms of appropriation. We will call this phenomenon "private regulation of the connected experience." Such regulation does not operate in a verticalized and unilateral manner, but in mediation with the social conditions and the actions of users inside the platform. The interviews showed how, despite general strategies, different perceptions of Facebook's role and ways of dealing with its resources are reproduced. However, such mediation is in no way symmetrical. On the contrary, as a technological system forged by and immersed in power relations (as CTT points out), Facebook reacts to those relations and exploits its power within the environment it regulates. We will call this "technological power." It operates under a domination logic (Marcuse, 1973) and establishes relations that are not at all responsible (as Jonas [1974] states), or democratic, as advocated by Sclove (1995), Jasanoff (2004) and Feenberg (2002). This does not occur only within the limits of the platform but affects society as a whole.

A first key impact is the massive surveillance of individuals (Lyon, 1994; Allmer, 2013), constituting data surveillance (Clarke, 1988). This was evidenced at several points in this case study. The Terms of Services and Privacy Policies are already quite explicit about the platform's extreme powers over its users and the tracks they leave, without much shame in exposing people's lives. Investigations by regulatory authorities and sanctions have shown several cases of violation by Facebook, including recurring ones. Analysing the components and technical resources, the development of tools for data collection is evident, from newsfeed to logins and social plugins for apps and websites. In the interviews, such issue appeared both in more intuitive reports from non-professional users and in the explanation of segmentation methods by professionals from digital agencies. The explanation given by a technology analyst of a civil society organization on data collection modalities (from social plugins to pixels) offered relevant information for characterization and, at the same time, a concerning panorama regarding the assumption of data protection and privacy as fundamental rights in the twenty-first century. As already pointed out, the interviews also showed how the surveillance promoted by Facebook does not concern only the user, but becomes a surveillance platform for other organizations and institutions, or even among individuals (as illustrated by Respondent 20 with her monitoring of her boyfriend's posts). Facebook thus assumes the status of a platform for distributed surveillance.

A second key field of impacts is on public debate. In this area, complex trends have emerged in recent years posing real risks to democracy. With the user base's expansion, there has been an increase in the volume of messages and opinions posted on the network. The quantitative increase of the debate generated a qualitative deterioration of the discussion, as evidenced in the interviews. More than merely a brutalization of the users, the excess of information (referred to as "infoglut" by Andrejevic [2013]) created a dispersed scenario, posing challenges to capturing attention. A second phenomenon involved the already mentioned "commercialization of public debate," with the pressure for post "sponsoring" to have visibility. The combination of the feed algorithm's operational logic (favouring interactions to generate visibility and fostering "bubble filters") and these various elements and factors (added to the political framework mentioned above) ended up making room for solutions based on the spread of disinformation, hate speech and political polarization. This was not only a "posture" of individual users, but operations by organized groups that made use of these resources both in a professional and paid manner and seeking remuneration (from the messages' circulation).[85]

The articulation of these factors and the appropriation made by these actors constitute what we will call here a 'double contradiction of the online debate on Facebook'. The first contradiction involves a seemingly unregulated debate environment with neutral flows of information (or flows perceived as having merely been filtered to the user's interests, as seen in the interviews), or of passive mediation (in terms of the platform conception discussed in Chapter 5), against a space organized around active mediation and with flows strongly disciplined by algorithms geared to stimulating data production and connections. This expresses what Andrejevic (2013) called "algorithmic alienation," not only with respect to algorithms, but to the social content of the technological system as a whole.

The second contradiction opposes a seeming equality among users on the network in the public debate, in which all account owners would have the same conditions to act, depending only on their content and their capacity to engage. This scenario is (as Respondent 9 stated) a "false public space." Firstly,

---

85 The case of the bunker of young people created in the city of Veles, Macedonia to create fake news during the US elections is a good example of how the combination of the algorithm's operation and the Facebook business model promotes the spread of this type of content (Delmazo and Valente, 2018).

because the networking effect is not just a phenomenon of Facebook's growth, but it is manifested within the platform. Thus, profiles with more followers gain more visibility and, thus, even more followers, reproducing a deeper inequality within the platform. If the posts' reach is related (according to the algorithm's design) to the number of interactions,[86] larger accounts should grow, and smaller accounts should remain small. This scenario is further reinforced by the debate's commercialization within Facebook, which has given centrality to the economic power in the ability to obtain reach within the platform. Since commercialization is no longer restricted to ads, since any post can be driven, public debate has been subordinated to the resources of each party (which would make Habermas shiver).

The consequences of these phenomena were felt among users. The interviews indicated Facebook's saturation, with examples of people leaving the digital social network. Curiously (and unfortunately), this was less due to the data protection violation scandals regarding its users and more due to the fatigue caused by the polarized debate and the escalation of hatred and aggressive dialogue on the platform. However, an important part of the user base has migrated to WhatsApp and Instagram. Here is Facebook's most successful strategy in its evolution: horizontal incorporation to consolidate its absolute domination of the digital social networking market. From that, "Facebook has gone beyond Facebook," and, like Google, it has become a conglomerate (though not formally) of different services, most of them DSNs. Facebook, as a company and technological system, remains hegemonic in this market. Its messaging integration movement tends to reinforce the company's market dominance, offering features to users without mischaracterizing each of the products. In terms of appropriation, this migration can indicate a risk of "depoliticization of the online experience" when it privileges spaces less dedicated to debate and more to personal exposure (Instagram) or to personal communication and intimate circles (such as WhatsApp).

But Facebook's evolution goes far beyond the boundaries of digital social networking. As a digital monopoly, the TS uses its technological base, its extensive database and the services already established to spread to other areas. In this chapter, we presented these sectors, such as connectivity projects, Workplace's corporate solutions, the virtual and augmented reality market with Oculus, and even audiovisual production with the works that will be featured in Watch. Despite a still small share in the company's revenues,

---

86   We point out that, due to the intensity of the changes in the criteria and content of the newsfeed algorithm, any statement here can be dated in face of new changes.

such services completely change the very nature of the platform, transmuting it from a DSN to a digital monopoly. The investment in research, especially in artificial intelligence, creates possibilities for new solutions by monitoring demands, which can be applied with scalability to a consolidated user base.

But, to fulfil its digital monopoly potential, Facebook needs to face the legitimacy crisis resulting from how it has exercised its power, impacted society, and reacted to other affected interest groups that have critically addressed such events. Its future is not just about seeking to rebuild its legitimacy with non-professional users, but with states and populations. In addition to the legislative scenario already outlined in Chapter 5, which impacts the platform, it has been the most questioned platform in recent years. In 2019, after yet another scandal,[87] Zuckerberg (2019) again admitted the need for more effective legislation on his company. While, in 2018, he only acknowledged that this might be possible in his statements to the US Congress, in 2019, he detailed necessary points for regulations, such as harmful content, the circulation of content during elections, data protection and data portability. The initiative may be yet another apology, like so many released throughout the history of the TS. But, at the time this thesis was completed, Facebook's assumption of power, its risks to democracy, and the need for its legal and administrative discipline (its regulation in the political–institutional sphere) was gaining ground. The future will tell whether the clash between this regulatory agent and interest groups in the political–institutional, cultural, and technological spheres (such as competitors, regulatory agencies, researchers, civil society entities, and their own users) will result in the prevalence of these social factors of regulation over the platform. By the examples and impacts shown here, this has emerged in the second half of 2010 as an urgent agenda, both from the point of view of the rights and guarantees not only of its users, but of society.

---

87   An attack on mosques in New Zealand that ended in the murder of 50 people was broadcast live for 17 minutes on the platform.

CHAPTER 8

Final Considerations

The digitalization process of several social spheres has been gaining centrality in contemporary capitalism. Companies speed up the introduction of these technologies in production processes and the circulation of goods and services. Users are ever more present on the internet, despite the barriers due to the still prohibitive access costs for the lower-income population and in the system's peripheries. These technologies increasingly mediate daily life, from interactions to political participation, from labour relations to product consumption. States have started to turn their attention to this sector, either in the digitalization of public administration or in assuming the need to establish clearer guidelines and rules for the economic agents' performance in this ecosystem. International organizations advocate a major digital transformation and emphasize the importance not only of understanding this phenomenon, but, also, of preparing for it, often portrayed as an inevitable course of history. These technical solutions are adopted affirming their neutrality, and it is up to individuals and organizations to ensure their 'correct' or 'adequate' use to avoid harmful consequences.

Recognizing this phenomenon, however, does not imply a deterministic view. On the contrary. The present discussion outlines the need for an alternative approach, based on a more structuring, dialectic and critical interpretation of the present process. On the one hand, it is necessary to 'deconstruct' the role of technology to avoid a deterministic illusion or one that is based on a linear notion of progress in society and technological development. Digitalization should not be understood as an inevitable course, resulting from efforts to search for efficiency that would generate smaller and faster devices and technical solutions with more robust processing capabilities. The 'aura' with which these artefacts are involved – from the performance capacity of artificial intelligence systems to the still fascinating experiments of quantum computing – should not work as a veil to cover up their structures, functioning logics and applications in the capitalist system, as well as their contradictions and unequal power relations. Behind the seeming neutrality lies the essence of artefacts built and realized within concrete social relations and defined by power asymmetries.

'Deconstructing' digital technologies involves identifying a procedural nature typical of these artefacts and of the entire information and communication technologies segment. Such technological systems are influenced by social factors that regulate their creation, their social content and realization as commodities in capitalism. These factors are understood here as economic, political–institutional and cultural factors that influence this process in various degrees. This impact is recognized by several theoretical approaches to technology, among which are the social construction of technology and critical theory of technology.[1] In this work, we relied on references from these academic perspectives, but found limitations in some cases. In the case of Social Construction of Technology, the interest groups in the objects' social construction seem undifferentiated and disconnected from power relations and social structure. Regarding Critical Theory of Technology, we found the need to consider both the economic dimension of the technological systems and a more detailed description of how social relations take place in technological development. In addition, it is important to have a clearer categorical framework regarding the dimensions of the technological development process to analyse, in concrete cases, how it is shaped by society, incorporates power relations and, in the same way, impacts human activities.

In an effort to suggest some additional tools for the technological phenomena analysis, we have elaborated what we call here the technological regulation model. It sees technology as a process of constant disputes, shaped by social factors of regulation, by its own factors (such as the stock of available knowledge and the general or sectorial technological paradigm) and by power disputes. Just as such factors are embedded in the social content of technological artefacts and systems, they are set in motion in concrete historical reality and impact how individuals and institutions act and relate. In this sense, just as we seek to "deconstruct" a superficial view of technology, we have also proposed its "reconstruction," recognizing its importance in historical development as part of one of the spheres of activity – the scientific–technological sphere. In assuming the concrete historical positioning, the model also emphasized, as an element to explain an artefact or technological system, the understanding of its logic under a concrete social formation – that is, capitalism. Constitutive elements of this object as a commodity or provider of goods and services under the capitalist logic were added to this theoretical model.

Starting from this conceptual basis and the view towards a "historically concrete contextualized analysis," we have identified in digitalization a crucial phenomenon of recent capitalist development. It was born from the information and communication technologies, more specifically in their development since the 1970s crisis. Having responded to this crisis and helped the rise of

---

[1] Or, in a more radical way, by the actor–network theory, as discussed in Chapters 2 and 3.

neoliberalism in several ways,[2] ICTs – now fully digitized – have again been pointed out as an alternative amid a new crisis, that of the 2007–08 crash.[3] The "digital transformation" is set by different entities[4] as a development project, from firms to governments. Faced with a scenario of decelerating productivity, fragile recovery in the employment levels, and growth data that in no way resemble the post-war era, the capitalist class seeks ways to resume a new expansion cycle and recover its profits in neoliberalism with financial dominance, in which the hypertrophy of the financial market was nothing more than a centripetal pressure element of a spiral of fictitious capital. However, considering both these goals, the second has been more successful than the first, in a movement of increasing wealth concentration.

As in other phases of capitalism, reduced production costs and labour exploitation appear as alternatives for resuming profit rates. But, in this recent neoliberal stage, increased exploitation involves a deeper subsumption of intellectual labour, a modality that is increasingly widespread. This results in conflicts over the flexibility of institutional guarantees of labour relations conquered in the past, and the search for new, more precarious arrangements. Such factors find in digital technologies ideal machines, since they allow labour to be replaced by automation and production rationalization through an increasing control of production allowed by data collection and processing.[5] In a context of fierce competition in which growing shares of value are transferred to the financial market and the demand is weakened, the realization of goods also becomes crucial, emphasizing the importance of more efficient promotion and sales strategies (such as through online advertising and e-commerce). But none of these processes happens without contradictions and conflicts. The difficulties of a new expansion cycle have revealed the lack of a new economic and political arrangement that could lead to a general effective resumption. At the competition level among capital, dominant groups and nations, the absence of this consolidated arrangement implies a political–institutional instability and a radicalization of disputes, as can be seen from the capitalist

---

2   Strategies detailed in Chapter 5.
3   Which, as we have seen, despite this historical milestone, must be understood more broadly in its dissemination across the globe, such as in the effects of this in Europe and on the periphery of the system, such as in Brazil in 2010.
4   Like the World Economic Forum, G20 and the Organization for Economic Cooperation and Development (OECD).
5   As seen in the features offered by Google and Facebook for businesses, such as G Suite, Cloud Platform and Workplace.

core (United States and United Kingdom) to its periphery (Latin America and Africa).

This scenario and the demands to overcome it impose a set of factors (as discussed throughout the work) and, at the same time, demand digitalization as a solution and services to respond to these problems. These meet other factors that are internal to the ICT segment. Among them are the internet's consolidation, the expansion of data processing infrastructures and the dissemination of computers and mobile devices with increasing data processing capacity. These technologies, whose evolution had been going on for decades, made room for others, which we call emerging technologies: massive data collection (Big Data, or datafication) and intelligent processing through algorithms and artificial intelligence systems. Driven by these factors, the internet abandoned its supposedly open and 'democratic' character to be dominated by great agents that assumed this ecosystem's spearhead: digital platforms. Its nature as a connection between various 'actors' (such as individuals, companies, public institutions, content producers and developers), its intensive data collection logic and sophisticated technological bases have allowed it to rise to this condition.

Although the platform format is not new,[6] in the digital ecosystem, information's specificity as a non-rival good and the economic logic of this environment, characterized by network effects, have allowed some operators to grow and consolidate themselves as major regulatory agents of the segment. This select group combines long-term companies (such as Microsoft and Apple) and other more recent online service providers (such as Google, Facebook and Amazon). Not by chance, Google and Facebook are the most genuine examples of faster growth and global reach. These companies have succeeded in articulating such characteristics of digital platforms but have been "successful" with their advertising-based and free business models, building databases of billions of people, creating ways to massively collect data not only from their own users, but, also, from a significant portion of internet users (such as through Facebook's social plugins or Google's AdSense) and controlling activities within them. While Google has established itself as the main written information access regulator agent (with the search feature), images (with Google Images), and videos (with YouTube), Facebook has assumed the condition of primary interactions regulator agent by controlling the main social networks on the planet.

---

6 Such as the real estate or credit card market.

Both platforms have shaped their technological systems from a business model strongly based on online advertising, which has found economic agents eager to promote goods and services more effectively. Both have operated what we call here the "commercialized surveillance spiral," deepening their data collection dynamics for an increasingly personalized advertising offer, receiving feedback with customer acceptance, launching new products and services or improving the current ones, recruiting more users, recording more user information and amplifying the spiral. Google and Facebook's technological trajectories have been shaped by offering new tools and services aimed at obtaining increasing volumes of registrations from individuals, not only within the platforms, but, also, on the Web (such as the use of Facebook Pixel or Google cookies). They have benefited from technological solutions suited to this and from the dissemination of devices, allowing this day-to-day registration of information, especially with the expansion of the internet and mobile devices. This combination of social factors, technical factors and business models has included the evolution of technological systems.[7] The result has been a social content of the technological systems' components aimed at deepening the surveillance dynamics.[8] The research made it possible to identify how, even though the two companies came from different niches (search and digital social networks), they have adopted data collection and processing for advertising as the technological and economic cores of their businesses.[9] Based on this, both progressed to introduce intelligent solutions through algorithms and artificial intelligence systems.

To further this spiral, the platforms had to face competition for the increasingly unstable attention of users and their retention. As previously pointed out, Google has worked to be the main regulator of access to information in the digital ecosystem. Facebook sought to be the central regulator of interactions by dominating the digital social networks segment. But, in both cases, an asset was fundamental: the dispute for attention and, consequently, for the user's connected experience time. To obtain it, both promoted strategies that we call "experience enclosure," as in the integration of services (such as Gmail

---

7   Whose many examples were shown in Chapters 6 and 7, from Facebook's newsfeed to the integration of data processing of various Google services.
8   Such as the newsfeed, the reactions and the social login on Facebook, geolocation, the custom search or Gmail on Google.
9   Google was born as a search engine through direct access, without the need for logging in. Facebook has had this requirement since its inception. Google understood the importance of login for customization and included this feature in Gmail, expanding it to Chrome, YouTube and Android (in the latter case to connect to the user's smartphone). Facebook has also come closer to offering the same features as Google, by including a search tool.

to G Suite on Google or the integration of Facebook's messenger services). The platforms have defined how users could behave within them, asserting themselves as active mediators and carrying out what we call "private regulation of connected experiences." Whether by stimulating newsfeed posting on Facebook or by exerting pressure to search for assistants on Google, both agents began to compete for users' activities on the internet. More than just directing the experience, the companies sought to connect it through verticalization (as in Google apps pre-installed on Android or the Internet.org project on Facebook). It was also a common strategy to implement connectivity projects to expand the user base, either through the subsidiary Access and its Google access service or through agreements with operators for free services or the free use of Facebook).

Both platforms have also formulated different incorporation strategies. Facebook has bet, above all, on a horizontal logic, dominating the digital social networking sector, with the acquisition of WhatsApp and Instagram. Google turned to new segments at an early stage, such as the purchase of Android and YouTube. Google's strategy of diversifying its activities has given rise to an institutionalization of its multi-market character as it turned into the Alphabet conglomerate by investing in subsidiaries with quite different business operations, such as Calico, Verily and, above all, X. Despite its horizontal incorporation strategy, Facebook has also diversified its business, such as in connectivity projects, the acquisition of Oculus, or an embryonic audiovisual products arm for its Watch service. In all cases, both platforms relied on their user base, their robust databases, and their technological capacity to launch new services.

These strategies of diversifying activities (which are not only acquisitions but use these different arms in an articulated offer)[10] were referred to as 'digital monopolies', as a central point of the work. As explained in Chapter 5, the term was not used in its strict sense (as a market structure), but to designate agents that are based on different niches and articulate certain assets (number of users, data collected, technological base, global scale, operation on the internet) to configure themselves as a very specific type of digital platform whose operation is anchored in a capacity to understand demands for goods and services and technological responses to them, with increasing diversification.

---

10   Some tools were developed internally, such as Gmail on Google, or improved by companies, such as Android, which took three years since its purchase to be released. Even in the case of Oculus, from Facebook, despite the company having been purchased, their services were expanded and qualified by the company's technology.

This phenomenon is not exclusive to Google and Facebook,[11] but these two platforms are the clearest examples of it, as was possible to see in the analysis of both technological systems' development (in Chapters 6 and 7). Such expansion is not yet mature, with both company's revenues coming almost entirely from advertising. However, their move towards new segments (as in the institutionalization of Google as Alphabet) seems to us irreversible as a present and future trend, not only for both platforms but, also, for other major ones (Apple, Microsoft and Amazon, as well as the Chinese Tencent and Baidu).

This phenomenon is not restricted to a manifestation of the concentrating and centralizing logic of capitalism (as Marx [2013] pointed out), but presents a specificity in the form of platforms that go beyond promoting incorporating strategies (as occurs in several sectors) to exercise what we call here 'technological power.' Understanding this adjective from a dialectic nature of the relationship among technological, economic, political and cultural practices, the use of this power is based on the ability to shape the segments in which they operate from their technological base, acting as a regulatory agent for them. The various practices to reinforce their monopolistic condition in the original niches and to advance over new areas, as well as to establish barriers to the entry for competitors,[12] are a distinctive feature of digital monopolies. Under the appearance of a false neutrality as intermediaries, extremely unequal power relations are revealed among these technological systems and their users, raising the contradiction present in the artefacts mentioned above to a new level.

Google and Facebook have been developed seeking to exercise this power, respectively, over access to online information and interactions. However, as digital monopolies both have broadened the focus to a competition over the dominance of surveillance, attention and regulation of the connected experiences in the digital ecosystem, including advancing over each other's original areas.[13] The internal development factors of the ICT sector, with the sophistication of data processing mechanisms and artificial intelligence systems, have opened the possibility of going beyond user monitoring. These systems

---

11   Amazon sells books and audiovisual works, going through operations in the offline world. Apple combines its hardware and software services with investments in the area of content, such as its own production and an online magazine subscription service.

12   Such as Facebook's attempt to favour its own video service or to overthrow the organic reach of pages as a way of controlling the information flow or Google's favouring of its own services.

13   Google launched two digital social networks, Orkut and Google+, and Facebook sought to enter the market of application platforms with the Facebook Platform.

moved to a second phase of the regulation of connected experiences to 'predict' behaviours, in order to anticipate[14] users' reactions. But the regulation of experiences, already in Google and Facebook's current scenario, has evolved to a third phase, to promote the modulation of behaviours. More than just the 'experience enclosure' defining limits, the operating logic of the technological systems technical resources is designed to direct, to a greater or lesser degree, the actions of users.[15] By using this technological power, these digital monopolies not only direct the experiences within them, but, also, have impacts on society, carrying out the dialectic movement of the third dimension of technological regulation (that of the regulation of social activities by technology). This is potentialized through the constant search for control points on the internet.[16]

But, exercising this power is not automatic. The realization of technological systems is crossed by interest groups' actions (from competitors to regulators, including researchers and civil society entities) and its use is mediated by the appropriation of those who employ it for some purpose, as shown by the interviews conducted here. The analysis of Google and Facebook's trajectories revealed intense activity by different interest groups. Workers questioned conditions and initiatives[17], regulatory authorities have imposed fines and changes in rules, governments and parliaments have approved legislation and administrative rules on various topics (such as data protection, copyright and monitoring and removal of content), media outlets have published articles that have led to scandals[18], researchers pointed out rights violations and abuses, brands and notorious users abandoned the services. Civil society entities have created

---

14   Google and Facebook ad display algorithms are examples of tools that have incorporated predictive logic. In the Google Ads (AdWords) auction, the algorithm used is based on the possibilities of a user clicking on a certain ad as one of the indicators.
15   With the use of the term 'modulation', we do not seek here to affirm an automated relationship, as this would disregard the mediations in appropriation, one of the elements of the theoretical–methodological model. However, both Google and Facebook have included forms of modulation in their features. The greater reach of videos on Facebook ends up leading users to bet more on this format, as was possible to notice in Chapter 7. The (non-transparent) criteria of page valuation for search results led to the formulation of widely used techniques for optimization of results (SEO).
16   As is the case with Google having advanced to the operating systems, browsers and equipment segments or Facebook operating services in the cloud infrastructure.
17   Like Google employees' protests against treatment for gender discrimination in 2018 or executives leaving Facebook against certain decisions, like product director Chris Cox when he announced the integration of messaging systems in 2019.
18   Like the Cambridge Analytica cases for Facebook or Google's project to create a browser in partnership with the Chinese government.

mechanisms to avoid surveillance and have even conducted campaigns questioning the platforms or defending their legal regulation. Even so, by the end of the 2010s, the impact of these actions was still small compared to the power acquired by them.

In the appropriation process, the interviews[19] offered important elements about the practical application of the platform services, constituting a fundamental material for the present study. The statements indicated a naturalization of these agents and their role in the online ecosystem, almost as if there were no alternatives. The exception was, in some cases, with Facebook, but, yet, the user migrated to another network under the company's control, Instagram. This "illusion of choice" reproduces the technological power of this digital monopoly. The answers showed a low awareness of the operating logics and mechanisms of experience regulation, with few respondents who knew the terms of use or changed "standard" settings.[20] Professional users were more concerned with the platform's directions (especially the reduction of the organic reach of pages or the dissemination of disinformation), but were more powerless than seeking alternatives. The most concerning data were that possible abuses in data collection and treatment or the modulation of behaviours, even after pointed out, caused little concern, indicating a normalization of the surveillance scenario. Offering services and solutions valued by users and with little critical awareness about the process of surveillance and private regulation of the experiences, the digital monopolies studied promote relevant impacts in the social spheres of activity.

In the economic sphere, the constitution of a duopoly of both platforms in online advertising (and the advancement of this modality in relation to other forms) has made them key locus for the realization of a representative volume of goods and services. Under the advantages of customization, services increasingly depend on these features. While claiming to broaden the base of "advertisers," these platforms use their predominance to reinforce inequalities (favouring large brands over small companies) and establish a "pattern" in which the realization of goods becomes intrinsically related to the total surveillance of potential consumers. In the production field, its corporate services (G Suite and Google Cloud Platform and Facebook's Workplace) have grown significantly, contributing through production control tools to deepen

---

19 Despite their qualitative dimension and the limitation that they cannot be extrapolated to a generalization.

20 Such as ad preferences, limitation of customization forms (such as use of searches for Google ads) and data collection (such as permission for facial recognition on Facebook) or mechanisms to limit the reach of newsfeed posts.

the subsumption of intellectual labour, reducing the boundaries between the individuals' private activities and their availability for the labour process. In terms of circulation, e-commerce services (Google Shopping and Facebook Marketplace) are still not market leaders[21], but they are relevant, especially when compared to exploiting the network effect.

In the political–institutional sphere, the rise of the monopolies led to a process of concentration of information flows. While the diversity of services allowed more people to express themselves through blogs, websites, profiles on social networks and content production tools, the sphere of circulation became even more restricted, dominated by the power of these agents[22]. In a scenario of excess of information, circulation took on an even more important role in the visibility of discourses. The result was what we call here the "online diversity paradox," with an apparent widening of diversity in production, but a limitation in its circulation. This predominance accentuated these platforms' influence on public debate, as discussed in Chapters 6 and 7. In spite of the use possibilities to foment political participation, the incidence of Facebook in electoral campaigns, the dissemination of disinformation in several political processes and the incentive to create "bubble filters" in discussions have led to what we call the "double contradiction of the online debate." If, on the one hand it has expanded, it has become more and more fragmented in circles of interest, deepening the polarization. Google has also reinforced these trends, spreading disinformation, promoting discrimination in resources, and providing an outlet to extremist opinions through YouTube. On the political level, the action of political forces using these platform tools has also evinced an indirect exercise of technological power.[23]

In the cultural sphere, the "online diversity paradox" has also impacted not only political disputes, but the very reproduction of identities and meaning systems on collectivities. The deaths in India, the attacks in Libya, and the use of digital platforms to amplify hate speech or promote discrimination against minorities and segments have contributed to a polarization not only in politics, but, also, in society. Discussions regarding the case studies have also pointed to the effects of these platforms on people's well-being (such as research on

---

21 Losing in revenues to Amazon and Chinese giants, like Alibaba.
22 In traditional media, the relationship was reversed. Global audiovisual and journalistic production was dominated by international agencies and Hollywood studios. The circulation was in charge of the national monopolies, the TV and press networks.
23 This was the case with extremist groups taking advantage of YouTube's recommendation algorithm or Russian agents who disseminated pro-Trump content in the US elections of 2016.

excessive time on digital social networks and low rates of happiness or connections to mental pathologies) or even on cognition (such as correlations between the use of Google and memory loss or difficulties). By privately regulating connected experiences, platforms affect human sociability, involving billions of people, shaping forms of interaction and perception of social bonds. The negative effects, as discussed, are not only unintended consequences, but are the result of 'persuasive' techniques to 'hook' users and keep them interacting as long as possible.

Finally, Google and Facebook forge their own centrifugal-technological sphere. In the research level, they are the spearhead (along with other platforms[24]) for the development of machine learning and artificial intelligence, the main emerging technologies, in addition to other areas.[25] In the technological sphere, as digital monopolies both dominate not only their original niches, but, also, have important participation in other segments (such as audiovisual) and potential for further expansion. Their condition of being digital monopolies and the exercise of technological power affirm these as regulatory agents of the digital ecosystem and, consequently, of digital transformation. The consolidation of this influence highlights a major limitation of the discourse, according to which the digital economy would reduce barriers to entry and allow new companies to ascend easily. While both are new firms and show that, in some cases, the technological edge in qualitative competition can generate explosive growth, the stabilization of the ICT sector around digital monopolies signals that such phenomena are more of an exception than the rule, with the reproduction of market dominance through the exploitation of network effects and their extension to other segments being the general trend.

The reference in the critical theory of technology and the model adopted by the technological regulation incorporate an analysis of the impacts also on value bases. Both in the field of philosophical prescriptions (such as Jonas' responsibility principle [1974] or Bunge's ethical codes [2013]) and in the proposals of authors in the field of sociology (such as Sclove's strengthening of democracy [1995], a change that promotes Marcuse's popular class interests [1973], or Feenberg's subversive rationalization [2002]), Google and Facebook's actions confront these guarantees, rather than comply with them. In detailing the rights promoted,[26] the performance of both platforms enables

---

24 Mainly the US Microsoft and Amazon and the Chinese Tencent, Alibaba and Baidu.
25 Like Facebook's connectivity projects or other Google bets, especially the subsidiary X.
26 In which they served as reference for data protection and privacy, right to communication, freedom of expression and right to information, non-discrimination, transparency and guarantee of competition.

the realization of some of these rights (such as access to information or freedom of expression), but in a much lower proportion than the risks brought by both the general plan of the value bases mentioned and the specific rights that served as reference for the analysis.

This scenario poses a series of challenges, part of which have already been identified and are the object of reactions and initiatives from different interest groups. The main one is in terms of legal regulation, covering both legislation and administrative rules. While China is following its own path with its own digital monopolies (Tencent, Alibaba and Baidu) and the United States is still struggling to take action in this field, Europe is the main driver, whether through the approval of the General Data Protection Regulation, the voting on the new copyright directive, the laws on the moderation and removal of illegal, harmful or non-informative content (as in Germany and France) or in recent initiatives for guidelines to discipline research and innovations in algorithms and artificial intelligence. Even in the US, recent scandals have raised concerns, but they are still insufficient. In the periphery of capitalism, several movements occur, from the approval of protective laws (as in the case of Brazil and India) to measures aimed at fighting disinformation (including of a reckless nature, as in Malaysia). Regulatory authorities are conducting investigations in several countries, especially in the field of data protection in Europe on the basis of the new general regulations and in the field of competition.

However, it is still unclear whether these reactions will be enough to meet the challenges posed. In the context of the end of the 2010s, countries were still trying to understand the impacts' dimension and ways of exercising technological power of these agents and discussing an update of legal regulation instruments for a new phase. Faced with a scenario of uncertainty in economic recovery and political radicalization, the operating logic of these digital monopolies has not shown any sign of a more effective change, pointing more to a deepening of this scenario than a reversal of it. In this sense, there are several challenges. The first is how to stop the spiral of commodified surveillance, which goes beyond the platforms and covers more and more economic segments. The imperative of data collection and control as a key element of a digital economy brings serious risks not only to privacy, but to the very autonomy of individuals and collectivities. To face these trends, data protection must be taken less as an individual liberal guarantee and more as a perspective for affirming human dignity at the collective level.

A second challenge concerns the right to communication and public debate. At the end of the 2010s, this was perhaps the greatest concern of governments and civil society organizations, especially alerted by the wave of disinformation and discursive war. Such phenomena are resulting and amplified by the customization model and the mediation forms of information flows. Without confronting these problems, it will be difficult to arrive at adequate responses. On the contrary, measures that have not been extensively thought through (such as assigning more power to platforms to bring down content) can generate more violation of rights and increase these agents' power. Another associated challenge is transparency in AI algorithms and systems. This is an agenda as urgent as the others, however still incipient. It concerns the ability to prevent or restrain discriminatory treatment, favours, the strengthening of bubbles or hate speech. But, more than that, such an effort is linked to the very battle to preserve human agency over a rampant development of a technology that is not new (since the first studies in this field occurred in the middle of the twentieth century) but seems to have assumed a phase of qualitative and quantitative advance. Confronting such matters cannot do without a look at the competitive issue. The scale of these agents challenges any notion of competition and there has been very little movement in adapting antitrust instruments to this scenario. This, however, cannot prevent us from recognizing this matter as a crucial aspect for competition authorities.

The proposed debate raises the need to recognize the growing role of digital technologies, especially digital platforms, in the current phase of neoliberalism. Platforms are making a major contribution to shaping different aspects of social practices, thus impacting the system's reproduction movements. Economic activities have been experiencing a significant migration to forms of production, circulation, and consumption based on information in its digital form, a process aggravated by the covid-19 pandemic. Human labor is exploited and encoded in bits, which allows broad socialization of work, but under the control of a few. We are not talking only about workers classified as uberized, but about an increasing range (doctors, teachers, lawyers, architects, etc.), which has an impact on the configuration and organization of the working class.

Benefiting from their large numbers of users and their ability to connect sides, digital platforms have also risen as great mediators of labor relations and processes of exploiting surplus-value, seeking to circumvent the obstacles posed by labor protection rules for their own benefit. This process has been given different names (digital work, uberization), but we prefer to call it here "platform work", comprising both the working relationships within these companies (as shown in the present work in the cases of Google and Facebook) as the one mediated by them, in applications in practically all areas, going far beyond the most visible examples of Uber and delivery apps.If, in the 1990s and 2000s, the computer gained strength as a new convergent instrument of intellectualized work, in the 2010s mobile devices spread, with software, applications, and online services increasingly used as means of production. This does not mean a praiseworthy vision of digital technologies towards "post-industrialization", "end of work", "Empire" or the transmutation of the capital-labor contradiction to something based only on knowledge. On the contrary, it is a matter of locating the expansion of the subsumption of intellectual work in the current phase of neoliberalism and understanding the agents at the edge of this process. Companies like Google, Facebook, Microsoft, and Amazon are among the main providers of corporate technological solutions for coordinating production routines, managing information about these processes "in the cloud" (which means in fact on their servers), and anticipating or producing demands through the processing of personal data. That is why they collect an ever-increasing set of data on the world population, gaining unprecedented knowledge about individuals both in their position as workers and consumers, which carries with it the second face of increased surveillance.

Digital technologies, especially platforms, also play a central role in the digitalization of the circulation of goods. With the growth of services and their encoding as digital information, platforms become increasingly essential agents to coordinate supply and demand. Thus, in informational products, these are instruments to give new impetus to the effort of capital and to overcome space over time. These agents enable trade on a worldwide scale and optimize the realization of goods by centralizing purchasing decisions and reducing product logistics costs. As mediating agents for financial transactions, they also become central to the circulation of goods by various companies, especially those of medium and small size that depend on these spaces to offer their goods beyond the limits of their physical stores.

In the scope of consumption, digital platforms have become key environments both for promoting products through advertising and in promoting the consumption habits of individuals. These agents build walled gardens that embrace different forms of sociability, from access to information to the subject's interactions with interest groups, families, and friends. In this way, they promote colonization of individuals' free time, which is not restricted to them, but turn into relevant environments in which users spend their free time and have their most diverse connected experiences regulated privately.

Considering the financial dominance of the neoliberal stage, platforms are also emerging as players in this area. Digital payment services are offered by different platforms, from the technical basis of transactions (as made possible by PayPal) to digital wallets (like Apple Pay). Here, as in the other examples, the logic of digital monopolies operates to take advantage of its big number of consumers, its technological base, the data collected, and the ability to spread its tentacles to new segments. In 2020, Facebook announced payment systems using Whatsapp and has even sought to create its currency, showing the reach that such companies may have. Thus, platforms have not only been spearheads in the digitalization of financial transactions but can disorganize the structures previously put in place. On the other hand, they use financial instruments to grow, acquiring other firms, or diversifying the markets, while they are configured as prominent tax evaders, which prevents the socially produced wealth from being shared.

As we argued throughout the book, these mutations have developed over the past few decades. Now, it is possible to point out that these are no longer trends or sectoral changes. With the coronavirus pandemic, the technologies of these companies gained momentum, being adopted in all sorts of social activities, including among public institutions and social movements. Thus, more than just corporate services, such platforms have amplified the condition of global structures for mediating social practices. They took new steps to expand their mediation to segments such as educational services and instruments for interaction and workplace management.

Perhaps the most evident impact of digital platforms is on the ideological reproduction of the capitalist system, as there is a hegemonic cultural form forged in alliance with technological configurations, which is marked by the fragmentation so typical of neoliberalism. These are the space for the consumption of information, expression, interaction and public and private debate, the construction of identities, the apprehension of social norms, and the development of degrees of autonomy and contestation against them. In a scenario of economic crisis and political instability at the turn of 2020, pressure for the repression of resistance to the system and the offensive of the ruling classes to amplify their returns increased at the expense of the participation of workers in the products of the wealth created by them.

The architectures of large digital platforms and the spiral of commercialized surveillance drive a fragmented environment that is increasingly conditioned by economic power, in new privatization of online public debate of a more complex nature and associated with the dynamics of the platforms' operation. The organization of resistance to the offensive of the dominant classes comes up against the limits imposed by the architectures of the informational and discursive flows of these environments controlled by digital monopolies.

In the Introduction, we questioned whether technological development was an unequivocal and linear path. In the case of digital platforms, the present work showed that, like other technological systems, there is no and only possibility of development. Starting from the technological regulation approach, we present here how digital platforms are driven by the structural demands of neoliberal capitalism and how they offer answers to those that, that are used by the dominant classes to keep their condition. The social vectors thus offer development of these technological systems oriented to the needs of capital in the 2010s with its economic crisis and political instability.

While digital technologies, and platforms, in particular, are seen as part of the "solution" to the structural obstacles of the system, these players promote regulation of technology on social activities, contributing greatly to reconfiguring the forms of exploitation, dynamics of managing the capital-labor contradiction, the formation of new social relations of production and the control of tensions arising from the class struggle and relations of oppression (such as gender and race) that structure capitalism. They are, therefore, agents whose advance on the dynamics of the increasingly digitalized economy must be carefully examined to understand the transformations of neoliberal capitalism at the turn of the 2010s to the 2020s and the paths for the promotion of a more socially and politically democratic society. This means that it is not a general criticism of technologies, but their current configurations and their social form. Another political project requires a thorough review of these elements.

References

18Millionrising et al. (2015) *Open letter to Mark Zuckerberg regarding Internet.Org, Net Neutrality, Privacy and Security.* Available (consulted 12 May 2018) at: https://www.accessnow.org/open-letter-mark-zuckerberg-regarding-internetorg/.

Abbas H. et al. (2014) Merger Failures & Corporate Strategy: Change Management to Solve the Query. *International Journal of Sciences: Basic and Applied Research* (IJSBAR), v. 3, n. 1.

Abílio L.C. (2017) Uberização do trabalho: subsunção real da viração. *Passa Palavra*, 19(02).

Accenture (2015) *Technology vision.* Dublin: Accenture.

Accenture (2018) *Digital platforms will define winners and losers in the digital economy.* Dublin: Accenture.

Adorno T. and Horkheimer M. (1985) A Indústria Cultural, ou o esclarecimento como mistificação das massas. In: *Dialética do Esclarecimento*. Rio de Janeiro: Zahar.

Advox (2018) Netizen report: What role does Facebook play in Lybia's civil war? *Advox Global Voices*, 6 September. Available (consulted 02 January 2019) at: https://advox.globalvoices.org/2018/09/06/netizen-report-what-role-does-facebook-play-in-libyas-civil-war/.

Alexander, J. (2020) A guide to platform fees. The Verge, 22, September. Available (consulted 28 september 2020) at: https://www.theverge.com/21445923/platform-fees-apps-games-business-marketplace-apple-google.

Al-Heeti A. (2018) WhatsApp: 65B messages sent each day, and more than 2B minutes of calls. CNET, 1 May. Available (consulted 10 February 2019) at: https://www.cnet.com/news/whatsapp-65-billion-messages-sent-each-day-and-more-than-2-billion-minutes-of-calls/.

Allcott H. and Gentzkow M. (2017) Social media and fake news in the 2016 election. *Journal of Economic Perspectives*, v. 31, n. 2, 211–236.

Allen J. and Flores N. (2013) The role of government in the Internet. *Final report for the Dutch Ministry of Economic Affairs.* Analysys Mason. Available (consulted 24 August 2017) at: http://www.analysysmason.com/About-Us/Case-Study-Content/Case-study-50-Government-role-Internet-case-study/Government-role-Internet-case-study/.

Allmer T. (2013) Critical internet surveillance studies and economic surveillance. In: *Internet and Surveillance.* New York, NY: Routledge, 144–2.

Alphabet (2018) *Annual report 2017*. San Francisco, CA: Alphabet.

Alphabet (2018) *Notice of 2018 Annual Meeting of Stockholders and Proxy Statement.* Califórina: Alphabet. Available (consulted 6 March 2018) at: https://abc.xyz/investor/static/pdf/2018_alphabet_proxy_statement.pdf?cache=582d718.

Alphabet (2020) *Annual report 2019.* San Francisco, CA: Alphabet.

Althusser L. Badiou A. (1979) *Materialismo histórico e materialismo dialético.* São Paulo: Global Editora.

Althusser L. et al. (1979) *Ler o capital.* Vol. 1. Rio de Janeiro: Zahar Editores.

Althusser L. et al. (1980) *Ler o capital.* Vol. 2. Rio de Janeiro: Zahar Editores.

Althusser L. et al. (2015) *Por Marx.* Campinas: Ed. Unicamp.

Altman I. (1975) *The environment and social behavior.* Monterey, CA: Brooks/Cole.

Ambrosino B. (2016) Facebook is growing an unstoppable digital graveyard. *BBC Future,* 14 March. Available (consulted 29 November, 2018) at: http://www.bbc.com/future/story/20160313-the-unstoppable-rise-of-the-facebook-dead.

AMD. (2017) AMD vs Intel Market Share. *AMD channel on Reddit.* Available (consulted 20 February 2019) at: https://www.reddit.com/r/Amd/comments/6koktx/amd_vs_intel_market_share_current_state/.

Ananny M. (2015) Toward an ethics of algorithms: Convening, observation, probability, and timeliness. *Science, Technology, & Human Values,* Brandeis University, USA, v. 41, n. 1: 93–2.

Andersson Schwarz J. (2017). Platform Logic: An Interdisciplinary Approach to the Platform-Based Economy. *Policy & Internet,* 9(4), 374–394.

Andrejevic M. (2013) *Infoglut: How too much information is changing the way we think and know.* New York, NY: Routledge.

Andrejevic M. (2014) Alienation's Returns. In: Fuchs C, Sandoval M. *Critique, Social Media and the Information Society.* New York: Routledge.

Andrews D., Criscuolo C. and Gal N. (2016) *The Global Productivity Slowdown, Technology Divergence and Public Policy: A Firm Level Perspective.* Paris: OECD Publishing.

Aneesh A. (2009) Global labor: Algocratic modes of organization. *Sociological Theory,* 27(4), 347-370.

Angwin J. and Parris T., Jr (2016) Facebook Lets Advertisers Exclude Users by Race. *ProPublica,* 28 October. Available (consulted 10 December 2018) at:https://www.propublica.org/article/facebook-lets-advertisers-exclude-users-by-race.

Angwin J. et al. (2017) Car Insurance Companies Charge Higher Rates in Some Minority Neighborhoods. *ProPublica,* 21 April. Available (consulted 28 November 2018) at: https://www.consumerreports.org/consumer-protection/car-insurance-companies-charge-higher-rates-in-some-minority-neighborhoods/.

Angwin J., Tobin A. and Varner M. (2017) Facebook (Still) Letting Housing Advertisers Exclude Users by Race. *ProPublica,* 21 November. Available (consulted 02 December 2018) at: https://www.propublica.org/article/facebook-advertising-discrimination-housing-race-sex-national-origin.

Antunes R. (2009) O trabalho, sua nova morfologia e a era da precarização estrutural. *Theomai Journal: Estudios sobre Sociedad y Desarrollo,* Ciudad de Buenos Aires,

n. 19:47–2, jan-jun. Available (consulted 30 March 2019) at: http://revista-theoMay unq.edu.ar/numero19/artantunes.pdf.

Antunes R. (2018). *O privilégio da servidão: o novo proletariado de serviço na era digital.* São Paulo: Boitempo editorial.

App Annie (2019) State of mobile 2019 report. San Francisco, US: App Annie.

Arntz M., Gregory T. and Zierahn U. (2016) *The Risk of Automation for Jobs in OECD Countries: A Comparative Analysis* OECD Social, Employment and Migration Working Papers. n. 189, Paris: OECD Publishing.

Arute F., Arya, K., Babbush, R., Bacon, D., Bardin, J. C., Barends, R., ... & Burkett, B. (2019). Quantum supremacy using a programmable superconducting processor. *Nature*, 574(7779), 505–510.

Aziz A. (2020) Facebook Ad Boycott Campaign 'Stop Hate For Profit' Gathers Momentum And Scale: Inside The Movement For Change. Forbes, 24, June. Available (consulted 29 September 2020) at: https://www.forbes.com/sites/afdhelaziz/2020/06/24/facebook-ad-boycott-campaign-stop-hate-for-profit-gathers-momentum-and-scale-inside-the-movement-for-change/#4167e40b1668.

Bahrini R. and Qaffas A. A. (2019). Impact of information and communication technology on economic growth: Evidence from developing countries. *Economies*, 7(1), 21.

Bailey J. et al. (2013) Negotiating with Gender Stereotypes on Social Networking Sites. *Journal of Communication Inquiry,* [s.l.], v. 37, n. 2, 91–112.

Bain P. (2019) 10 Need to Know Facebook Marketing Stats for 2019. *Social Media Today*, 5, February. Available (consulted 25 December 2018) at: https://www.socialmediatoday.com/news/10-need-to-know-facebook-marketing-stats-for-2019/547488/.

Baker P. and Potts A. (2013) Why do white people have thin lips? Google and the perpetuation of stereotypes via auto-complete search forms. *Critical Discourse Studies,* [s.l.], v. 10, n. 2, 187–204, may.

Balakrishnan A. (2017) Facebook pledges to double its 10,000-person safety and security staff by end of 2018. CNBC, 31, October. Available (consulted 09 December 2018) at: https://www.cnbc.com/2017/10/31/facebook-senate-testimony-doubling-security-group-to-20000-in-2018.html.

Balibar E. (1980) Sobre os conceitos fundamentais do materialismo histórico. In: Althusser L et al. *Ler o capital*, Vol. 2. Zahar Editores.

Ball J. (2013) NSA's Prism surveillance program: how it works and what it can do. *The Guardian*, 8, June. Available (consulted 4 November 2018) at: https://www.theguardian.com/world/2013/jun/08/nsa-prism-server-collection-facebook-google.

Baller S, Dutta S, Lanvin B. (org.). (2016) *The Global Information Technology Report 2016: Innovating in Digital Economy.* Fórum Econômico Mundial, Geneva. Available (consulted 25 March 2019) at: http://www3.weforum.org/docs/GITR2016/WEF_GITR_Full_Report.pdf.

Barabasi A. (2011) Introduction. In: Papacharissi Z. (Org.). *A networked self: Identity, community, and culture on social network sites.* New York: Routledge.

Baran K.S. and Stock W.G. (2016) Chapter 10. "Blind as a Bat": Users of Social Networking Services and Their Biased Quality Estimations in TAM-like Surveys. *Facets Of Facebook,* [s.l.], 265–284.

Barber, G and Molteni, Megan (2019) Google Is Slurping Up Health Data –and It Looks Totally Legal. Wired, 11, November. Available (consulted 26 September 2020) at: https://www.wired.com/story/google-is-slurping-up-health-dataand-it-looks-totally-legal/?itm_campaign=TechinTwo.

Barocas S., Hood S. and Ziewitz M. (2013) Governing Algorithms: A Provocation Piece. In: *Governing Algorithms Conference.* 2013, New York University, May 16–17.

Bastos R. (2012) Facebook compra Instagram por US$ 1 bilhão. *Techtudo,* 9, April. Available (consulted 08 December 2018) at: https://www.techtudo.com.br/noticias/noticia/2012/04/facebook-compra-instagram.html.

Battelle J. (2011) *The Search: How Google and Its Rivals Rewrote the Rules of Business and Transformed Our Culture.* Boston, MA: Nicholas Brearley Publishing.

BBC News. (2005) News Corp in $580m internet buy. *BBC News,* 19, July. Available (consulted 15 November 2018) at: http://news.bbc.co.uk/2/hi/business/4695495.stm.

Becerra M. Mastrini G. (2019) La convergencia de medios, telecomunicaciones e internet en la perspectiva de la competencia: Hacia un enfoque multicomprensivo. Cuadersnos de discussion de comunicación y información 13, UNESCO.

Beer D. (2017) The social power of algorithms, Information, Communication & Society, 20:1, 1–13.

Bell D. (1977) *O advento da sociedade pós-industrial: uma tentativa de previsão social.* São Paulo: Cultrix.

Bellofiore R. (2014) The Great Recession and the contradictions of contemporary capitalism. In: Bellofiore R, Vertova G. (ed.). *The Great Recession and the contradictions of contemporary capitalism.* Cheltenham, UK: Edward Elgar Publishing.

Bellofiore R. and Vertova G. (2014) *The Great Recession and the contradictions of contemporary capitalism.* Cheltenham, UK: Edward Elgar Publishing.

Benjamin W. (2012) A obra de arte na era de sua reprodutibilidade técnica. In: Duarte R. (org.). *O belo autônomo: textos clássicos de estética.* São Paulo: Autêntica.

Benkler Y. (2006) *The wealth of networks: How social production transforms markets and freedom.* New Haven, CT: Yale University Press.

Benner C. and Neering K. (2016) *Silicon Valley Technology Industries Contract Workforce Assessment.* Everett Program, University of California Santa Cruz.

Bercito D. (2017) Google é multado em quase R$ 9 bi na Europa por favorecer serviço próprio. *Folha de S. Paulo,* São Paulo, 27, jun. Available (consulted 18 January 2018) at:https://www1.folha.uol.com.br/mercado/2017/06/1896360-por-monopolio-uniao-europeia-multa-google-em-224-bilhoes-de-euros.shtml.

Bergen, M. (2019) YouTube Executives Ignored Warnings, Letting Toxic Videos Run Rampant. Bloomberg, 2, April. Available (consultede 28 September 2020)at:https://www.bloomberg.com/news/features/2019-04-02/youtube-executives-ignored-warnings-letting-toxic-videos-run-rampant

Berger R. (2016) Keep the dragon flying. Roland Berger.

Berman M. (1982) *Tudo que é sólido desmancha no ar*. São Paulo: Companhia das Letras.

Bernal J. (1946) *The social function of science*. London: George Routledge & Sons.

Bidle S. (2016) Tech money lurks behind government privacy conference. *The Intercept*, 15, September. Available (consulted 24 March 2019) at: https://theintercept.com/2016/09/15/tech-money-lurks-behind-government-privacy-conference/.

Bijker W.E. and Pinch T. (1993) The social construction of facts and artifacts: or how the sociology of science and the sociology of technology might benefit each other. In: Bijker WE, Hughes TP, Pinch T. *The social construction of technological systems: new directions in the sociology and history of technology*. 4.ed. Cambridge: MIT Press.

Bijker W.E. and Pinch T. (2012) Preface to the aniversary edition In: Bijker WE, Hughes TP, Pinch T. *The social construction of technological systems: new directions in the sociology and history of technology*. 4.ed. Cambridge: MIT Press.

Bijker W.E.(2009) How is technology made?--That is the question! *Cambridge Journal Of Economics*, [s.l.], v. 34, n. 1:63–76, 11 November Oxford University Press (OUP). Available (consulted 15 January 2019) at: http://dx.doi.org/10.1093/cje/bep068.

Blashcke Y. (2019) Google and IAB: knowingly enabling intrusive profiling. *EDRI*, 21 February. Available (consulted 30 March 2019) at: https://edri.org/google-and-iab-knowingly-enabling-intrusive-profiling/.

Blease C.R. (2105) Too many 'friends,'too few 'likes'? Evolutionary psychology and 'Facebook depression'. *Review of General Psychology*, v. 19, n. 1, 1–13. Available (consulted 22 March 2019) at: https://www.apa.org/pubs/journals/features/gpr-gpr0000030.pdf.

Blue V. (2018) More companies are chipping their workers like pets. *Engadget*, 16 November. Available (consulted 19 January 2019) at: https://www.engadget.com/2018/11/16/employee-microchip-security-orwell/.

Bobbio N. (1999) *Ensaios sobre Gramsci e o conceito de sociedade civil*. São Paulo: Paz Terra.

Bolaño C. (2000) *Indústria cultural, informação e capitalismo*. São Paulo: Hucitec.

Bolaño C. (2007) Processo de trabalho e crítica do trabalho imaterial sobre o intelecto geral, comunicação e conhecimento. In: *I Encontro Nacional de Economistas Marxistas*, 2007, Curitiba: UFPR, 1 – 13. Available at: http://www.sitiodeeconomiapolitica.ufpr.br/CesarBolano2.pdf (consulted 5 February 2019).

Bolãno C. and Vieira E. (2014) Economia política da internet e os sites de redes sociais. *Revista Eptic Online*. v.16, n. 2, 75–88.

Bolãno C. and Vieira E. (2015) The Political Economy of the Internet. *Television & New Media*, [s.l.], v. 16, n. 1, 52–61.

Boltanski L. and Chiapello E. (2009) *O novo espírito do capitalismo*. São Paulo: Martins Fontes.

Bonifacic, I. (2020) Facebook's redesigned website finally starts rolling out to everyone. Engadget, 8, May. Available (consulted 29 September 2020) at: https://www.engadget.com/new-facebook-desktop-redesign-official-160054794.html.

Bonnard, J. (2020) French regulator orders Google pay copyright fees to media groups. Yahoo Finance, 9, April. Available (consulted 26 September 2020) at: https://finance.yahoo.com/news/french-regulator-orders-google-pay-copyright-fees-media-101441515.html.

Boorstin, J. (2020) Facebook launches a new cryptocurrency called Libra. CNBC, 18, June. Available (consulted 29 September 2020) at: https://www.cnbc.com/2019/06/17/facebook-announces-libra-digital-currency-calibra-digital-wallet.html

Borges R. (2018) WhatsApp, uma arma eleitoral sem lei. *El País Brasil*, 21 October. Available (consulted 30 March 2019) at: https://brasil.elpais.com/brasil/2018/10/18/tecnologia/1539899403_489473.html.

Botsman R. and Rogers R. (2010) *What's Mine Is Yours: The Rise of Collaborative Consumption*. New York: Harper Collins e-book.

Bradley G. (2014) Social Informatics and Ethics Towards the Good Information and Communication Society. In: Fuchs C, Sandoval M (Org.). *Critique, Social Media and the Information Society*. Oxon: Routledge.

Brafton (2013) 95% of web traffic goes to sites on page 1 of Google SERPS. *Brafton*, 21 June. Available (consulted 2 March 2019) at: https://www.brafton.com/news/95-percent-of-web-traffic-goes-to-sites-on-page-1-of-google-serps-study/.

Braga R. (2006) Infotaylorismo: o trabalho do teleoperador e a degradação da relação de serviço. *Revista Eptic Online*. v. 8, n. 1. Available (consulted 1 March 2019) at: https://seer.ufs.br/index.php/eptic/article/view/291/270.

Braverman H. (1981) *Trabajo y capital monopolista*. 4ª ed. México City: Nuestro tempo.

Briggs A. and Burke P. (2004) *Uma história social da mídia: de Gutemberg à Internet*. Rio de Janeiro: Zahar.

Brin S. (2006) Founders' letter. Google. Available (consulted 14 jannuary 2019) at: https://abc.xyz/investor/founders-letters

Brin S. and Page L. (1998) The anatomy of a large-scale hypertextual WEB search engine. *Computer Networks and ISDN Systems*. Stanford, v. 30, n. 1–7, 107–117, 1 April Available at: http://snap.stanford.edu/class/cs224w-readings/Brin98Anatomy.pdf (consulted 2 February 2019).

Brin S. and Page L. (2008) *2008 Fonders´ letter*. Google. Available (consulted 25 October 2018) at: https://abc.xyz/investor/founders-letters/2008/.

Brin S. and Page L. (2010) *2010 Fonders´ letter*. Google. Available (consulted 25 October 2018) at: https://abc.xyz/investor/founders-letters/2010/.

Brin S. and Page L. (2014) *2014 Fonders' letter*. Google. Available (consulted 25 October 2018) at: https://abc.xyz/investor/founders-letters/2014/.

Brin S. and Page L. (2017) *2017 Founders' letter*. Alphabet. Available (consulted 25 October 2018) at: https://abc.xyz/investor/founders-letters/2017/.

Brittos V. and Collar M. (2008) Direito à comunicação e democratização no Brasil. In: Martins P, Pieranti O, Saravia H (org). *Democracia e regulação dos meios de comunicação de massa*. Rio de Janeiro: FGV.

Broadband Comission (2020) The State of Broadband 2020: Tackling digital inequalities – A decade of action. International Telecommunications Comission.

Broadband Commission (2014) *The state of broadband 2014: broadband for all*. International Telecommunications Union. Available (consulted 23 February 2019) at: http://www.itu.int/pub/S-POL-BROADBAND.10-2014.

Broadband Commission (2017) *The state of broadband 2016: broadband catalyzing sustainable development*. International Telecommunications Union. Available (consulted 23 February 2019) at: https://www.broadbandcommission.org/Documents/reports/bb-annualreport2016.pdf.

Brodkin J. (2012) Google privacy change taking effect today is illegal, EU officials say. *ArsTechnica*, 3 January. Available (consulted 18 November 2018) at: https://arstechnica.com/tech-policy/2012/03/google-privacy-change-taking-effect-today-is-illegal-eu-officials-say/.

Brown D. (2004) Communication technology timeline. In: *Communication technology update*, v. 9.

Brown, C. (2019) Introducing Facebook News. Facebook Newsroom, october, 25. Available (consulted 29 September 2020) at: https://about.fb.com/news/2019/10/introducing-facebook-news/.

Brown, C. (2020) Prioritizing original News reporting on Facebook. Facebook Newsroom, june, 30. Available (consulted 29 September 2020) at: https://about.fb.com/news/2020/06/prioritizing-original-news-reporting-on-facebook/.

Browne, R. (2020) Facebook launches a dedicated gaming app to take on Twitch and YouTube. CNBC, April, 20. Available (consulted 26 September 2020) at: https://www.cnbc.com/2020/04/20/facebook-launching-dedicated-gaming-app-to-take-on-twitch-and-youtube.html.

Brundage M. et al. (2018) *The Malicious Use of Artificial Intelligence: Forecasting, Prevention, and Mitigation*. Available (consulted 30 March 2019) at: https://arxiv.org/ftp/arxiv/papers/1802/1802.07228.pdf.

Buccirossi, P. (2008). *Handbook of antitrust economics* (Vol. 1). London: The MIT Press.

Büchi G., Cugno M. and Castagnoli R. (2020) Smart factory performance and Industry 4.0. *Technological Forecasting and Social Change*, *150*, 119790.

Bulger M., Taylor G. and Schroeder R. (2014) *Data-driven business models: challenges and opportunities of big data.* Oxford Internet Institute. Available (consulted 1 October 2014) at: http://www.nemode.ac.uk/wpcontent/uploads/2014/09/nemode_business_models_for_bigdata_2014_oxford.pdf.

Bunge M. (2012) *Filosofía de la tecnología y outros ensaios.* Lima: Fondo Editorial Universidad Inca Garcilaso de la Vega.

Bunge M. (2013) Philosophical inputs and outputs of technology. In: Scharff R.C. and Dusek V. (org). *Philosophy of technology: The technological condition An anthology.* New Jersey: John Wiley & Sons, e-book.

Burgess J. and Green J. (2018) *YouTube: Online video and participatory culture.* New Jersey: John Wiley & Sons.

Burkert H. (1997) Privacy-Enhancing Technologies: Typology, Critique, Vision. In: Agre E. and Rotenberg M. (eds.). *Technology and Privacy: the new landscape.* London: MIT Press.

Burrows P. (2018) How the AI cloud could produce the richest companies ever. *MIT Technology Review*, 22 March 2018. Available (consulted 20 January 2019) at: https://www.technologyreview.com/s/610554/how-the-ai-cloud-could-produce-the-richest-companies-ever/.

Business Wire (2019) DiDi Introduces New Product Upgrades in International Markets. Business Wire, 10, July. Available (consulted 26 September 2020) at: https://www.businesswire.com/news/home/20190710005884/en/DiDi-Introduces-New-Product-Upgrades-International-Markets/.

Butler S. (2018) Uber loses appeal over driver employment rights. *The Guardian*, 20 December. Available (consulted 20 February 2019) at: https://www.theguardian.com/technology/2018/dec/19/uber-loses-appeal-over-driver-employment-rights.

Buzan B. (1987) *An introduction to strategic studies: military technology and international relations.* New York: Springer.

Cadwalladr C. and Graham-Harisson E. (2018) Revealed:50 million Facebook profiles harvested for Cambridge Analytica in major data breach. *The Guardian*, 17 March. Available (consulted 02 November 2018) at: https://www.theguardian.com/news/2018/mar/17/cambridge-analytica-facebook-influence-us-election.

Calabresi M. (2017) Inside Russia's Social Media War on America. *Time*, 18 May. Available (consulted 04 January 2019) at: http://time.com/4783932/inside-russia-social-media-war-america/.

Callahan J. (2018) Google made its best acquisition 13 years ago: Can you guess what it was? *Android Authority*, 11 July. Available (consulted 10 January 2019) at: https://www.androidauthority.com/google-android-acquisition-884194/.

Callisson-Burch V., Probst J. and Govea M. (2015) Adding a Legacy Contact. *Facebook Newsroom*, 12 February. Available (consulted 10 January 2019) at: https://newsroom.fb.com/news/2015/02/adding-a-legacy-contact/.

Callon M. (1984) Some elements of a sociology of translation: domestication of the scallops and the fishermen of St Brieuc Bay. *The Sociological Review*, v. 32, n. 1, 196–233.

Callon M. (1993) Society in the making: the study of technology as a tool for sociological analysis. In: Bijker W., Hughes T. and Pinch T. *The social construction of technological systems: New directions in the sociology and history of technology*. Cambridge: The MIT Press.

Cammaerts B. and Mansell R. (2020). Digital Platform Policy and Regulation: Toward a Radical Democratic Turn. *International Journal of Communication*, 14, 20.

Campaign Monitor. (2018) *Gmail and today's popular e-mail clients*. Campaign monitor. Updated 2018. Available at: https://www.campaignmonitor.com/resources/guides/most-popular-email-clients/.

Capra D. and He R. (2013) Introducing embedded posts. *Facebook Newsroom*, 31 July. Available (consulted 25 January 2019) at: https://newsroom.fb.com/news/2013/07/introducing-embedded-posts/.

Castells M. (2003) *A galáxia da internet: reflexão sobre a internet, os negócios e a sociedade*. Rio de Janeiro: Zahar.

Castells M. (2005) *A sociedade em rede*. São Paulo: Paz e terra.

Castelluccia, C. (2020). *From Dataveillance to Datapulation: The Dark Side of Targeted Persuasive Technologies*. Hal-02904926.

Cavalcante MAL. (2014) *Principais julgados do STF e do STJ comentados*. Manaus: Dizer o Direito.

CB Insights. (2016) *The Big 5 patents report*. CB Insights.

Cech, F. (2020, January). Beyond Transparency: Exploring Algorithmic Accountability. In *Companion of the 2020 ACM International Conference on Supporting Group Work*, 11–14.

Chakrabarti S. (2018) Hard Questions: What Effect Does Social Media Have on Democracy? *Facebook Newsroom*, 22 January Available (consulted 09 January 2019) at:https://newsroom.fb.com/news/2018/01/effect-social-media-democracy/.

Chang J., Rynhart G. and Huyn H. (2016) *The future of jobs in automation*. Geneva: International Labour Organization.

Chang J.H. and Huynh P. (2016). *ASEAN in transformation the future of jobs at risk of automation* (No. 994906463402676). International Labour Organization.

Chaparro F. (2017) Credit Suisse: Here's how high-frequency trading has changed the stock market. *Business Insider*, 20 March Available (consulted 05 February 2019)at:https://www.businessinsider.com/how-high-frequency-trading-has-changed-the-stock-market-2017-3.

Chapman G. (2108) Facebook seeing growth in business network Workplace. *Phys.org*, 9 October. Available (consulted 08 March 2019) at: https://phys.org/news/2018-10-facebook-growth-business-network-workplace.html.

Charney M. (2018) Facebook stock drops roughly 20%, loses $120 billion in value after warning that revenue growth will take a hit. Market Watch, 26 July. Available (consulted 10 January 2019) at:https://www.marketwatch.com/story/facebook-stock-crushed-after-revenue-user-growth-miss-2018-07-25.

Chaslot G. (2017) How Youtube's AI boosts alternative facts. *Guillaume Chaslot Medium*, 31 March. Available (consulted 02 November 2018) at: https://medium.com/@guillaumechaslot/how-youtubes-a-i-boosts-alternative-facts-3cc276f47cf7.

Chesnais F. (2014) Fictitious capital in the context of global over-accumulation and changing international economic power relationships. In: *The great recession and the contradictions of contemporary capitalism,* chapter 4, pages 65–82, Cheltenhan, UK: Edward Elgar Publishing.

Chesnais F. (2016) *Finance capital today: corporations and banks in the lasting global slump.* Boston: Brill Academica Publishing.

Cho J. and Roy S. (2004) Impact of search engines on page popularity. In: *Proceedings of the WWW2004 Conference,* New York. Available (consulted 3 January 2019) at: https://oak.cs.ucla.edu/~cho/papers/cho-bias.pdf.

Chokkattu J. (2016) 14 devices, 6 years, 1 name: Revisiting every Google Nexus ever built. *Digital Trends,* 3 October. Available (consulted 23 January 2019) at: https://www.digitaltrends.com/mobile/history-of-google-nexus/.

Chun W. (2006) *Control and freedom.* Cambridge: MIT Press.

Cisco Visual Networking Index (2017) *Global Mobile Data. Traffic Forecast Update, 2016–2021.* CISCO, 2017. Available (consulted 10 April 2017) at: http://www.cisco.com/c/en/us/solutions/collateral/service-provider/visual-networking-index-vni/mobile-white-paper-c11-520862.pdf.

Civil Liberties Union for Europe et al. (2017) Article 13 Open letter – Monitoring and Filtering of Internet Content is Unacceptable. *Letter to European Parliament,* 16 October. Available (consulted 12 December 2018) at: https://www.liberties.eu/en/news/delete-article-thirteen-open-letter/13194

Clark J. (2016) The booming of on demand economy. In: *Encyclopedia Britannica.* The book of the year 2016. Chicago, IL: Encyclopedia Britannica.

Clarke R. (1988) Information technology and dataveillance. *Communications Of The Acm,* [s.l.], v. 31, n. 5, 498–512, 1 May. Association for Computing Machinery (ACM). Available at: http://dx.doi.org/10.1145/42411.42413 (consulted 24 March 2019).

Clegg, N. (2020) Welcoming to overight board. Facebook Newsroom, 6, May. Available (consulted 29 september 2020) at: https://about.fb.com/news/2020/05/welcoming-the-oversight-board/.

CNBC (2009) Inside mind of Google. *CNBC,* 30 November. Available (consulted 08 November 2018) at: https://www.cnbc.com/2009/11/30/Inside-the-Mind-of-Google.html.

Cnil (2017) Facebook sanctioned for several breaches of the French Data Protection Act. *CNIL*, 16 May. Available (consulted 30 December 2018) at: https://www.cnil.fr/en/facebook-sanctioned-several-breaches-french-data-protection-act.

Coberly C. (2017) Facebook is shutting down its Groups app. *Techspot*, 10 August. Available (consulted 03 January 2019) at: https://www.techspot.com/news/70512-facebook-shutting-down-groups-app.html.

Cohen N.S. (2008) The valorization of surveillance: Towards a political economy of Facebook. *Democratic Communiqué*, v. 22, n. 1. Available (consulted 30 March 2019) at: http://journals.fcla.edu/demcom/article/view/76495.

Cohen, N. (2020) Platforms' Election 'Fixes' Are Rooted in Flawed Philosophy. Wired, 14, September. Available (consulted 9 september 2020) at: https://www.wired.com/story/platforms-election-fixes-are-rooted-in-flawed-philosophy/.

Collin S. (2004) *Dictionary of Computing: Over 10,000 Terms Clearly Defined*. London: Bloomsbury.

Collins J. (2108) Google's Data Exposure Revelations Highlight The Risk Of Regulation Of Big Tech. *Forbes*, 8 October. Available (consulted 03 March 2019) at: https://www.forbes.com/sites/jimcollins/2018/10/08/googles-data-exposure-revelations-highlight-the-risk-of-regulation-of-big-tech/#3d2140021cd4.

Comscore. (2017) *The 2017 U.S. mobile app report*. Reston, US: Comscore.

Conger K. (2016) China's new cibersecurity law is bad news for business. *Techcrunch*, 6 November. Available (consulted 10 January 2019) at: https://techcrunch.com/2016/11/06/chinas-new-cybersecurity-law-is-bad-news-for-business/.

Conger, K. (2020) California Sues Uber and Lyft, Claiming Workers Are Misclassified. *The New York Times*, 5, May. Available (consulted 9 september 2020) at: https://www.nytimes.com/2020/05/05/technology/california-uber-lyft-lawsuit.html.

Constine J.(2017) Facebook Messenger hits 70M daily users as the app reaches 1,3bB monthies. *Techcrunch*, 14 September. Available (consulted 19 March 2019) at: https://techcrunch.com/2017/09/14/facebook-messenger-1-3-billion/.

Copeland J. (2004) Enigma. In: Turing A.M. *The essential Turing*. Oxford, UK: Oxford University Press.

Coriat B. (2011) *El taller y el Robot: ensaios sobre el foridsmo y la producción em masa em la era de la eletronica*. Tres Cantos, Spain: Siglo XXI.

Couldry N. and Mejias U. (2019) The Costs of Connection. Palo Alto: Stanford Press.

Curtis S. (2013) Facebook launches inernet.org to boost global web access. *The telegraph*, 21 August. Available (consulted 12 February 2019) at: https://www.telegraph.co.uk/technology/facebook/10256491/Facebook-launches-internet.org-to-boost-global-web-access.html.

Da Silva T.P. and Braga C.F. (2016) Racismo e Sexismo Sofrido por Mulheres Negras no Facebook. In: *Anais* – XXXIX Congresso Brasileiro de Ciências da Comunicação. São

Paulo: Intercom – Sociedade Brasileira de Estudos Interdisciplinares da Comunicação, 2016. 14 p. Available (consulted 27 January 2019) at: http://portalintercom.org.br/anais/nacional2016/resumos/R11-2490-1.pdf.

Dahlgren P. (1995) Television and the public sphere. *Citizenship, democracy and the media.* Vol. 10. Thousand Oaks, US: Sage.

Danaher J. (2016) The threat of algocracy: Reality, resistance and accommodation. *Philosophy & Technology*, 29(3), 245–268.

Dantas M. (1996) *A lógica do capital-informação.* Rio de Janeiro: Contraponto.

Dantas M. (2010) Convergência digital: entre os 'jardins murados' e as praças públicas. In Sel S. (Org.). *Políticas de comunicación en el capitalismo contemporâneo.* Buenos Aires, Argentina: CLACSO: 41–68.

Dantas M. (2018) *Internet: praças de mercado sob controle do capital financeiro.* VIII Forum da Internet no Brasil.

Dave (2018) Fearful of bias, Google blocks gender-based pronouns from new AI tool. *Reuters*, 27 November. Available (consulted 18 January 2019) at: https://www.reuters.com/article/us-alphabet-google-ai-gender/fearful-of-bias-google-blocks-gender-based-pronouns-from-new-ai-tool-idUSKCN1NW0EF.

Davis A. (2107) Using Technology to Protect Intimate Images and Help Build a Safe Community. *Facebook Newsroom*, 5 April. Available (consulted 09 January 2019) at: https://newsroom.fb.com/news/2017/04/using-technology-to-protect-intimate-images-and-help-build-a-safe-community/.

Degryse C. (2016) *Digitalisation of the economy and its impact on labour markets.* Brussels: European Trade Union Institute.

Delmazo C. and Valente J. (2018) Fake news nas redes sociais online: propagação e reações à desinformação em busca de cliques. *Media & Jornalismo*, v. 18, n. .32, 155–169.

Deloitte (2015) *Facebook's global economic impact: a report for Facebook.* London: Deloitte.

Department of Justice (2011) Google Forfeits $500 Million Generated by Online Ads & Prescription Drug Sales by Canadian Online Pharmacies. *Department of Justice*, 24 August. Available (consulted 06 January 2019) at: https://www.justice.gov/opa/pr/google-forfeits-500-million-generated-online-ads-prescription-drug-sales-canadian-online.

Deve A. (2017) Announcing Facebook Communities Summit. *Facebook Newsroom*, 11 April. Available (consulted 08 January 2019) at: https://newsroom.fb.com/news/2017/04/announcing-facebook-communities-summit/.

Diakopoulos N. (2014) *Algorithmic accountability reporting: On the investigation of black boxes.* New York: Columbia Journalism School.

Diaz A. (2008) Through the Google Goggles: Sociopolitical Bias in Search Engine Design. In: Spinik A., Zimmer M. (Eds.). *Websearch: Mulidisciplinary perspectives.* New York: Springer.

Diggelmann O., Cleis M.N. (2014) How the Right to Privacy Became a Human Right. *Human Rights Law Review*, [s.l.], v. 14, n. 3:441–458.

Digital McKinsey. (2018) *Creating Value with the Cloud*. New York: McKinsey.

Dockès D. and Rosier B. (1983) *Rythmes économiques: crises et changement social: une perspective historique*. Paris: La Découverte/Maspéro.

Domingo S. (2015) *The master algorithm: How the quest for the ultimate learning machine will remake our world*. New York: Basic Books.

Doneda D., Almeida V. (2019) O que é governança de algoritmos. In. Bruno F. et al. *Tecnopolíticas da vigilância: perspectivas da margem*. São Paulo: Boitempo Editorial.

Donovan S.A., Bradley D.H. and Shimabukuru J.O. (2016) *What does the gig economy mean for workers?* Congressional Research Service.

Dosi G. (1984) *Technical change and industrial transformation: the theory and an application to the semiconductor industry*. New York: Springer.

Dosi G. and Orsenigo L. (1988) Coordination and transformation: an overview of structures, behaviours and change in evolutionary environments. In. Dosi G. *Technical change and economic theory*. London, UK: Pinter Publishers.

Dulski J. and Archibong I. (2018) A New Investment in Community Leaders. *Facebook Newsroom*, 9 February. Available (consulted 14 August 2018) at: https://newsroom.fb.com/news/2018/02/investment-in-community-leaders/.

Duménil G. and Levy D. (2014) The crisis of the early 21st century: Marxian perspectives. In: Bellofiore R., Vertova G. *The Great Recession and the contradictions of contemporary capitalism*. Massachussets: Edward Elgar Publishing.

Dussel E. (1988) *Hacia un Marx desconocido*. Un comentário a los manuscritos de 1961–1963. Tres Cantos, Spain: Siglo XXI.

Dutton W.H.(Org.) (2013) *The Oxford inteternet handbook*. Oxford: Oxford University Press.

Edelman B. (2015) Does Google Leverage Market Power Through Tying and Bundling? *Journal of Competition Law And Economics*, [s.l.], v. 11, n. 2:365–400.

Edelman, G. (2020) Why don't we jut ban targeted advertising? Wired, 22, March. Available (consulted by 26 September 2020) at: https://www.wired.com/story/why-dont-we-just-ban-targeted-advertising/.

Ejik N.V., Fahy R., Til H.V.N., Stokking H. and Gelevert H.F.B.F. (2015). *Digital platforms: an analytical framework for identifying and evaluating policy options*. [pdf] Available at: https://www.tno.nl/media/7366/analytical_framework_digital_platforms_tno_eccd_18_april_2016_no_poll.pdf (consulted 16 June 2017).

Electronic Frontier Foundation. (2018) *AI Progress Measurement*. Available (consulted 25 March 2018) at: https://www.eff.org/ai/metrics.

Elers S. (2014) Maori are scum, stupid, lazy: maori according to Google. *Te Kaharoa*, v. 7, n. 1.

Elias, J. (2019) Google under investigation for 'Thanksgiving Four' firings, allegedly discouraging unions. CNBC, December, 9. Available (consulted 30 September 2020) at: https://www.cnbc.com/2019/12/09/google-under-investigation-from-nlrb.html.

Ellison N.B. and Boyd D.M. (2013) Sociality through social network sites. In: Dutton W. (ed). *The Oxford handbook of internet studies.* Oxford: Oxford University Press.

Ellul J. (1964) *The technological society.* New York: Vintage Books.

Elster J. (1983) *Explaining technical change: A case study in the philosophy of science.* Cambridge, UK: Cambridge University Press.

Embury-Denis T. (2018) Facebook fined €8,9M by Italy by misleading users over data use. *The Independent*, 7 December. Available (consulted 05 March 2019) at: https://www.independent.co.uk/life-style/gadgets-and-tech/facebook-fine-italy-user-data-scandal-privary-settings-cambridge-analytica-social-media-a8673376.html.

Engels F. (1982) Cartas a Mehring. In. Barata Moura et al. *Obras Escolhidas.* Tomo III, Editora Avante! Available (consulted 30 January 2019) at: https://edisciplinas.usp.br/pluginfile.php/4239010/mod_resource/content/2/Aula%203%20texto%202.pdf

Eslami M. et al. (2015) I always assumed that I wasn't really that close to [her]:Reasoning about invisible algorithms in news feeds. *Proceedings Of The 33rd Annual Acm Conference On Human Factors In Computing Systems – Chi '15*, [s.l.], 153–162.

Estadão. (2019) 'Número três' do Facebook e chefe do WhatsApp deixam a empresa. *Estadão*, 14 March. Available (consulted 07 January 2019) at: https://link.estadao.com.br/noticias/geral,numero-tres-do-facebook-e-chefe-do-whatsapp-deixam-a-empresa,70002755511.

Eubanks, V. (2018) *Automating inequality: How high-tech tools profile, police, and punish the poor.* St. Martin's Press.

European Commission. (2017) *Mergers: Commission fines Facebook €110 million for providing misleading information about WhatsApp takeover.* European Commission, 18 May. Available (consulted 20 July 2018) at: http://europa.eu/rapid/press-release_IP-17-1369_en.htm.

European Commission. (2015) *State and future of broadband technologies.* Brussels: European Commission.

European Parliament. (2016) *EU General Data Protection Regulation (GDPR): Regulation (EU) 2016/679 of the European Parliament and of the Council.* Brussels: European Parliament.

European Union. (2016) *Online Platforms.* European Union, Comission Staff Working Document, Communication 288. Brussels: European Commission.

Evans D. and Gawer G. (2016) *The rise of the platform enterprise: a global survey.*

Evans D. and Schmalensee R. (2016) *Matchmakers: the new economics of multisided platforms.* Boston: Harvard Business Review Press.

Executive Office of The President of United States. (2015) *Big Data and Differencial pricing.* Washington: Executive Office of the President of United States.

REFERENCES 355

Ezrachi A. and Stucke M.E. (2016) *Virtual competition: the promise and perils of the algorithm-driven society.* Boston: Harvard University Press.

Facebook IQ. (2018) Por que trocar mensagens com as empresas é o novo padrão. *Facebook IQ,* 14 June. Available (consulted 03 January 2019) at: https://www.facebook.com/business/news/insights/why-messaging-businesses-is-the-new-normal.

Facebook (2008a) Facebook Welcomes Donald E. Graham to Board of Directors. *Facebook Newsroom,* 11 December. Available (consulted 12 January 2019) at: https://newsroom.fb.com/news/2008/12/facebook-welcomes-donald-e-graham-to-board-of-directors/.

Facebook (2008b) Marc Andressen joins Facebook Board of Directors. *Facebook Newsroom,* 30 June 2008b. Available (consulted 05 March 2019) at: https://newsroom.fb.com/news/2008/06/marc-andreessen-joins-facebook-board-of-directors/

Facebook (2011a) Facebook Launches Open Compute Project. *Facebook Newsroom,* 7 April. Available (consulted 12 January 2019) at: https://newsroom.fb.com/news/2011/04/facebook-launches-open-compute-project/.

Facebook (2011b) Facebook Names Reed Hastings to Its Board of Directors. *Facebook Newsroom,* 23 June. Available (consulted 22 March 2019) at: https://newsroom.fb.com/news/2011/06/facebook-names-reed-hastings-to-its-board-of-directors/.

Facebook (2012a) A new design for messenger. *Facebook Newsroom,* 20 September. Available (consulted 12 January 2019) at: https://newsroom.fb.com/news/2012/09/a-new-design-for-messenger/.

Facebook (2012b) *Annual report 2012.* Facebook. Available (consulted 12 January 2019) at: https://s21.q4cdn.com/399680738/files/doc_financials/annual_reports/FB_2012_10K.pdf.

Facebook (2013) *Annual report 2013.* Facebook. Available (consulted 12 January 2019) at: https://s21.q4cdn.com/399680738/files/doc_financials/annual_reports/FB_AR_33501_FINAL.pdf.

Facebook (2014a) A New, Optional Way to Share and Discover Music, TV and Movies. *Facebook Newsroom,* 21 May. Available (consulted 19 December 2018) at: https://newsroom.fb.com/news/2014/05/a-new-optional-way-to-share-and-discover-music-tv-and-movies/.

Facebook (2014b) *Annual report 2014.* Facebook. Available (consulted 27 November 2018) at: https://s21.q4cdn.com/399680738/files/doc_financials/annual_reports/FB2014AR.pdf.

Facebook (2015[a]) *Annual report 2015.* Facebook. Available (consulted 27 November 2018) at: https://s21.q4cdn.com/399680738/files/doc_financials/annual_reports/2015-Annual-Report.pdf.

Facebook (2015b) Update to Internet.org Free Basic Services. *Facebook Newsroom,* 24 September. Available (consulted 27 November 2018) at: https://newsroom.fb.com/news/2015/09/update-to-internet-org-free-basic-services/.

Facebook (2016) *Annual report 2016*. Facebook. Available (consulted 27 November 2018) at: https://s21.q4cdn.com/399680738/files/doc_financials/annual_reports/FB_AR_2016_FINAL.pdf.

Facebook (2017) *Annual report 2017*. Facebook. Available (consulted 27 November 2018) at: https://s21.q4cdn.com/399680738/files/doc_financials/annual_reports/FB_AR_2017_FINAL.pdf.

Facebook (2018a) *Facebook diversity report*. Facebook. Available (consulted 27 November 2018) at: https://www.facebook.com/careers/diversity-report.

Facebook (2018b) *Annual report 2018*. Facebook. Available (consulted 27 November 2018) at:http://d18rn0p25nwr6d.cloudfront.net/CIK-0001326801/a109a501-ed16-4962-a3af-9cd16521806a.pdf.

Facebook (2018c) *Facebook economic impact report*. Facebook. Available (consulted 23 February 2019) at: https://www.facebook.com/business/news/the-connecting-benefits-report.

Facebook (2019) Introducing Oculus Rift S: A New PC VR Headset Coming This Spring. *Facebook Newsroom*, 20 March. Available (consulted 21 March 2019) at: https://developer.oculus.com/blog/introducing-oculus-rift-s/.

Facebook (2019) *Termos de Uso*. Facebook, s/d. Available (consulted 12 January 2019) at: https://pt-br.facebook.com/terms.

Facebook (2019) *Políticas de Privacidade*. Facebook, s/d. Available (consulted 12 January 2019) at: https://www.facebook.com/about/privacy/update.

Fairview Capital (2015) *The sharing economy: selling access instead of ownership*. Fairview Capital.

Fang G.L. (2019) Google Hired Gig Economy Workers to Improve Artificial Intelligence in Controversial Drone-Targeting Project. *The Intercept*, 4 February. Available (consulted 23 February 2019) at: https://theintercept.com/2019/02/04/google-ai-project-maven-figure-eight.

Farfan B. (2018) Apple's retail stores arround the world. *Small business*, 27 December. Available (consulted 10 December 2018) at: https://www.thebalancesmb.com/apple-retail-stores-global-locations-2892925.

Farias E. (2004) *Liberdade de expressão e Comunicação: teoria e proteção constitucional*. São Paulo: Revista dos Tribunais.

Farrell D. and Greig F. (2017) *The online platform economy: Has growth peaked?*

Favaretto M. De Clercq E. Schneble C. O. and Elger B. S. (2020). What is your definition of Big Data? Researchers' understanding of the phenomenon of the decade. *PloS one*, 15(2), e0228987.

Federal Trade Commission (2019) Google and YouTube Will Pay Record $170 Million for Alleged Violations of Children's Privacy Law. Federal Trade Comission, 4, September. Available (consulted 26 September 2020) at: https://www.ftc.gov/news-events/press-releases/2019/09/google-youtube-will-pay-record-170-million-alleged-violations.

Federal Trade Commission (2020) FTC to Examine Past Acquisitions by Large Technology Companies. Federal Trade Comission, February, 11. Available (consulted 26 September 2020) at: https://www.ftc.gov/news-events/press-releases/2020/02/ftc-examine-past-acquisitions-large-technology-companies.

Federal Trade Commission. (2011) *Complaint In the matter of Facebook.* Doc. 0923184. Washington, US: Federal Trade Commission.

Federal Trade Commission. (2012) *Docket No C-4365 in matter of Facebook, Inc.* Washington, US: Federal Trade Commission.

Feenberg A. (1996) Marcuse ou Habermas: duas críticas da tecnologia. Inquiry: An Interdisciplinary. *Journal of Philosophy*, v. 39. Available (consulted 5 April 2014) at: http://www.sfu.ca/~andrewf/marhabportu.htm.

Feenberg A. (1999) *Questioning Technology.* London: Routledge.

Feenberg A. (2002) *Transforming Technology: a critical theory revisited.* New York: Oxford University Press.

Feenberg A. (2005) Critical theory of technology: an overview. *Tailoring Biotechnologies*, v. I, n. I, Winter 2005, 47–64.

Feenberg A. (2017) Critical theory of technology and STS. *Thesis Eleven*, v. 138, n. 1:3–12.

Feenberg, A. (2017). *Technosystem.* Boston: Harvard University Press.

Feenberg, A. (2019). The Internet as network, world, co-construction, and mode of governance. *The Information Society, 35*(4), 229–243.

Felten E. (2004) Googlecracy in action. In. *Freedom to Tinker.* Available at: https://freedom-to-tinker.com/archives/000509.html.

Ferraz J. and Viola M. (2017) O direito ao esquecimento. *Internet e Sociedade.* Rio de Janeiro: Fundação Konrad Adenauer.

Ferré-Sarudrní L. (2018) Airbnb Drives Up Rent Costs in Manhattan and Brooklyn, Report Says. *The New York Times*, 3 May. Available (consulted 8 March 2019) at: https://www.nytimes.com/2018/05/03/nyregion/airbnb-rent-manhattan-brooklyn.html.

Figueiredo C. (2019) Algoritmos, subsunção do trabalho, vigilância e controle: novas estratégias de precarização do trabalho e colonização do mundo da vida. *Revista Eptic Online*, v. 21 n. 1, 156–172.

Finley, K. (2019) Why Google Would Drop $2.6 Billion on an Analytics Company. Wired, 6, June. Available (consulted by 26 September 2020) at: https://www.wired.com/story/google-drops-26-billion-analytics-company/.

Fioretti J. (2016) EU accuses Facebook of misleading it in WhatsApp takeover probe. *Reuters*, 20 December. Available (consulted 27 February 2019) at: https://www.reuters.com/article/us-whatsapp-m-a-facebook-eu-idUSKBN14917T.

Flichy P. (1980) *Las multinacionales del audiovisual.* Barcelona: Gustavo Gilli.

Florentino M.R. (2018) France passes controversial 'fake news' law. *Euronews*, 22 November Available (consulted 23 January 2019) at:https://www.euronews.com/2018/11/22/france-passes-controversial-fake-news-law.

Floridi L. et al. (2018) AI4People –An Ethical Framework for a Good AI Society: Opportunities, Risks, Principles, and Recommendations. *Minds and Machines,* [s.l.], v. 28, n. 4:689–707.

Fogg BJ. (2009) Creating persuasive technologies: an eight-step design process. In: *Proceedings of the 4th international conference on persuasive technology.* ACM, april, 1–6.

Folha de S. Paulo. (2018) Folha deixa de publicar conteúdo no Facebook. *Folha de S. Paulo,* 8 February. Available (consulted 09 January 2019) at: https://www1.folha.uol.com.br/poder/2018/02/folha-deixa-de-publicar-conteudo-no-facebook.shtml.

Fontes V. (2017) Capitalismo em tempos de uberização: do emprego ao trabalho. Marx e o Marxismo. *Revista do NIEP-Marx,* v. 5, n. 8.

Forbes (2020) The World's Most Valuable Brands 2020. Forbes. At: https://www.forbes.com/the-worlds-most-valuable-brands/#65a42fbc119c.

Forde C. et al. (2017) *The social protection of workers in the platform economy.* Directorate-General for Internal Policies, European Parliament. Available (consulted 05 March 2019) at: http://www.europarl.europa.eu/RegData/etudes/STUD/2017/614184/IPOL_STU(2017)614184_EN.pdf.

Forrester (2017) Tech Radar: Artificial Intelligence Technologies Q1, 2017. *Forrester,* 18 January. Available (consulted 05 March 2019) at: https://www.forrester.com/report/TechRadar+Artificial+Intelligence+Technologies+Q1+2017/-/E-RES129161.

Foucault M. (1976) *Vigilar y castigar.* Tres Cantos, Spain: Siglo XXI.

Fox R. and Hao W. (2018) *Internet infrastructure: networking, webservices and cloud computing.* Boca Raton, US: CRC Press.

Frankish K. and Ramsey WM. (ed.). (2014) *The Cambridge handbook of artificial intelligence.* Cambridge, UK: Cambridge University Press.

Freeman C. (1988) Introduction. In: Dosi G et al. *Technical Change and Economic Theory.* Londres: Pinter Publishers.

Freeman C., Louçã F. (2004) *Ciclos e crises no capitalismo global: das revoluções industriais à revolução da informação.* Porto: Afrontamento.

French Republic. (2018) *Paris call for trust and security in cyperspace.* French Republic.

Frey C.B. and Osborne M.A. (2013) *The Future of Employment: How Susceptible are Jobs to Computerization?* University of Oxford. Available (consulted 02 February 2019) at: https://www.oxfordmartin.ox.ac.uk/downloads/academic/The_Future_of_Employment.pdf.

Frischmann B. and Selinger E. (2018) *Re-engineering humanity.* Cambridge: Cambridge University Press.

Fuchs C. (2008) *Internet and Society: Social Theory in the Information Age,* Abingdon: Routledge.

Fuchs C. (2013) Critique of the political economy of web 2.0 surveillance. In: Fuchs, C. *Internet and Surveillance.* Abingdon: Routledge.

Fuchs C. (2014) *Digital Labour and Karl Marx*. Abingdon, UK: Routledge.

Fung, B. (2020) Google will temporarily stop running election ads after Election Day. CNN Business, 25, September, Available (consulted 28 September 2020) at: https://edition.cnn.com/2020/09/25/tech/google-election-day-ads/index.html.

G1. (2018) Facebook remove rede brasileira de 'engajamento falso'. *G1*, 15 August. Available (consulted 22 February 2019) at: https://g1.globo.com/economia/tecnologia/noticia/2018/08/15/facebook-remove-rede-brasileira-de-engajamento-falso.ghtml.

G20 Information Centre. (2017) *G20 Leaders' Declaration: Shaping an Interconnected World*. Hamburg, July 8.

G20. G20 Osaka Leader's Declaration. G20 Osaka meeting, 28–29 june, 2019.

Garnham N. (1990) *Capitalism and communication: Global culture and the economics of information*. Thousand Oaks, US: Sage.

Gartenberg C. (2018) Qualcomm's simulated 5G tests shows how fast real-world speeds could actually be. *The Verge*, 25 February. Available (consulted 09 January 2019) at: https://www.theverge.com/2018/2/25/17046346/qualcomm-simulated-5g-tests-san-francisco-frankfurt-mwc-2018.

Gartenberg, C. (2019) Google buys Fitbit for $2.1 billion. The Verge, 1st, November. Available (consulted 24 September 2020) at: https://www.theverge.com/2019/11/1/20943318/google-fitbit-acquisition-fitness-tracker-announcement.

Gawer A. (2014) Bridging differing perspectives on technological platforms: Toward an integrative framework. *Research Policy*, [s.l.], v. 43, n. 7:1239–1249, September.

Geissler R. (2011) Private eyes watching you: Google Street View and the right to an inviolate personality. *Hastings Law Journal*. v. 63, n. 897.

Geron T. (2013) Facebook Launches Graph Search, A Social Search Engine, With Bing Partnership. *Forbes*, 15 January. Available (consulted 02 January 2019) at: https://www.forbes.com/sites/tomiogeron/2013/01/15/live-facebook-announces-graph-search/#324d4aab216b.

Gibbs S. (2014) Elon Musk: artificial intelligence is our biggest existential threat. *The Guardian*, 27 October. Available (consulted 30 January 2019) at: https://www.theguardian.com/technology/2014/oct/27/elon-musk-artificial-intelligence-ai-biggest-existential-threat.

Giddens A. (1979) *Central Problems in Social Theory: Action, Structure and Contradictions in Social Analysis*. California: University of California Press.

Giles M. (2016) Mobile operator group ranking Q2 2016. *GSMA Intelligence*, September 2016. Available (consulted 28 August 2018) at: https://www.gsmaintelligence.com/research/2016/09/mobile-operator-group-ranking-q2-2016/573/.

Gillespie T. (2010) The politics of 'platforms'. New Media & Society, [s.l.], v. 12, n. 3:347–364.

Gillespie T. (2014) The Relevance of Algorithms. *Media Technologies*, [s.l.], 167–194.

Gleit N. and Zeng S. (2014) COTTLE: Introducing safety check. *Facebook Newsroom*, 15 October. Available (consulted 20 September 2018) at: https://newsroom.fb.com/news/2014/10/introducing-safety-check/.

Goertzel B. (2007) *Artificial general intelligence.* New York: Springer.

Goffman E. (2001) *"Manicômios, presídios e conventos."* São Paulo: Perspectiva.

Goldman, E. (2008) Search Engine Bias and the Demise of Search Engine Utopianism. In. Spink A., Zimmer M. *Web Search: Multidisciplinary Perspectives.* Berlin, Heidelberg: Springer, 121–134.

Goodwin D. (2011) Google's Timeline Search Option is History. *Search Engine Watch*, 11 November Available at: https://searchenginewatch.com/sew/news/2124563/google-s-timeline-search-option-is-history.

Goodwin, D. (2020) 500 Chrome extensions secretly uploaded private data from millions of users. Ars Technica, 13, February. Available (consulted 26 September 2020) at: https://arstechnica.com/information-technology/2020/02/500-chrome-extensions-secretly-uploaded-private-data-from-millions-of-users/.

Google Cloud. (2018) *G Suite: a journey of customer focused innovation.* Google Cloud. Available (consulted 17 January 2019) at: https://services.google.com/fh/files/blogs/g_suite_timeline.pdf.

Google Employees against Dragonfly (2019) We are Google employees. Google must drop Dragonfly. Medium, 27, November. Available (consulted 28 September 2020) at: https://medium.com/@googlersagainstdragonfly/we-are-google-employees-google-must-drop-dragonfly-4c8a30c5e5eb.

Google Transparency Project. (2018) *The lobbyst in the garage.* Google Transparency Project.

Google (2009) *Annual report 2009.* Google. Available (consulted 26 October 2018) at: https://www.sec.gov/Archives/edgar/data/1288776/000119312510030774/d10k.htm.

Google (2010) *Annual report 2010.* Google. Available (consulted 26 October 2018) at: https://www.sec.gov/Archives/edgar/data/1288776/000119312511032930/d10k.htm.

Google (2011) *Annual report 2011.* Google. Available (consulted 26 October 2018) at: https://www.sec.gov/Archives/edgar/data/1288776/000119312512025336/d260164d10k.htm.

Google (2012) *Annual report 2012.* Google. Available (consulted 26 October 2018) at: https://www.sec.gov/Archives/edgar/data/1288776/000119312513028362/d452134d10k.htm.

Google (2017) *Economic Impact Report.* Google.

Google (2018) *Google Diversity Report 2018.* Google. Available (consulted 16 January 2019) at: https://static.googleusercontent.com/media/diversity.google/pt-BR//static/pdf/Google_Diversity_annual_report_2018.pdf.

Google (2020) *Terms of use.* Google.

Graham M., Hjorth I. and Lehdonvirta V. (2017) Digital labour and development: impacts of global digital labour platforms and the gig economy on worker livelihoods. *Transfer: European Review of Labour and Research*, [s.l.], v. 23, n. 2, 135–162.

Gramsci A. (1978) *Maquiavel, a política e o Estado Moderno.* Rio de Janeiro: Civilização Brasileira.

Greenberg J. (2016) Like Facebook, Instagram Is About to Go – Gasp – Algorithmic. *Wired*, 15 March. Available (consulted 20 February 2019) at: https://www.wired.com/2016/03/instagram-will-soon-show-thinks-want-see/.

Greene, T. (2019) Report: Palantir took over Project Maven, the military AI program too unethical for Google. The Next Web, 11, December. Available (consulted 26 September 2020) at: https://thenextweb.com/artificial-intelligence/2019/12/11/report-palantir-took-over-project-maven-the-military-ai-program-too-unethical-for-google/.

Greenwald G. (2013) NSA Prism program taps in to user data of Apple, Google and others. *The Guardian*, 7 June. Available (consulted 03 January 2019) at: https://www.theguardian.com/world/2013/jun/06/us-tech-giants-nsa-data.

Griffiths M.D., Kuss D.J. and Demetrovics Z. (2014) Social Networking Addiction. *Behavioral Addictions,* [s.l.], 119–141.

Grossman L. (2010) Mark Zuckerberg. *Time*, 15 December. Available (consulted 14 January 2019) at: http://content.time.com/time/specials/packages/article/0,28804,2036683_2037183_2037185,00.html.

Gruppi L. (1978) *El concepto de hegemonía en Gramsci.* Mexico City: Ediciones de cultura popular.

GSMA (2020) *The mobile economy 2020.* London: GSMA.

GSMA. (2016) *Global Mobile Trends 2016.* London: GSMA.

GSMA. (2019) *Global Mobile Trends 2019.* London: GSMA.

Guidi G. (2018) Modelos Regulatórios para Proteção de Dados Pessoais. In: Branco S., Teffé C. (2018) *Privacidade em perspectivas.* Rio de Janeiro: Lumen Juris.

Guilherme (2018) Android Pay e Google Wallet se unem para formar Google Pay. *Techmundo*, 8 January. Available (consulted 07 February 2019) at: https://www.tecmundo.com.br/software/125875-android-pay-google-wallet-unem-formar-google-pay.htm.

Gunther R., Beck A. and Nisbet E.C. (2018) *Fake news may have contributed to Trump's 2016 victory.* Manuscrito não publicado. Available (consulted 20 January 2019) at: https://www.documentcloud.org/documents/4429952-Fake-News-May-Have-Contributed-to-Trump-s-2016.html.

Guttmann R. (2008) Uma introdução ao capitalismo dirigido pelas finanças. *Novos Estudos – Cebrap,* [s.l.], n. 82, 11–33, November.

Guynn J. (2016) Does Facebook speaks your language? *USA Today,* 29 September. Available (consulted 09 February 2019) at:https://www.usatoday.com/story/tech/news/2016/09/29/facebook-translation-new-languages-corsican-fulah-malta/91268284/.

Habermas J. (1997) *Ciência e Técnica como Ideologia.* Lisboa, Portugal: Ed. 70.

Habermas J. *Teoria e práxis: estudos de filosofia social.* São Paulo: Ed. Unesp.

Hagiu A. and Wright J. (2015) Multi-sided platform. *Working Paper 15–037*. Harvard Business School. Available (consulted 30 March 2019) at: http://www.hbs.edu/faculty/Publication%20Files/15-037_cb5afe51-6150-4be9-ace2-39c6a8ace6d4.pdf.

Haider J. and Sundin O. (2019). *Invisible Search and Online Search Engines: The ubiquity of search in everyday life*. London: Routledge.

Hands J. (2013) Platform communism. *Culture machine*. v. 14.

Hannak A. et al. (2014) Measuring Price Discrimination and Steering on E-commerce Web Sites. *Proceedings Of The 2014 Conference On Internet Measurement Conference – Imc '14*, [s.l.], 305–318. ACM Press. Available (consulted 28 February 2019) at: http://dx.doi.org/10.1145/2663716.2663744.

Hardawar D. (2017) Google's Pixelbook is a 2-in-1 premium Chromebook. *Engadget*, 4 October. Available (consulted 03 February 2019) at: https://www.engadget.com/2017/10/04/google-pixelbook-chromebook/.

Harding S. (ed.). (2011) *The postcolonial science and technology studies reader*. Durham: Duke University Press.

Harris T. (2016) How Technology is Hijacking Your Mind – from a Magician and Google Design Ethicist. *Thrive Global*, 18 May. Available (consulted 10 January 2019) at: https://medium.com/thrive-global/how-technology-hijacks-peoples-minds-from-a-magician-and-google-s-design-ethicist-56d62ef5edf3.

Hartmann S. and Wanner B. (2016) Does Facebook Cause Addiction? An Analysis of German Facebook Users. In. *Facets of Facebook: Use and Users*. Berlim: De Gruyter.

Harvey D. (1992) *Condição pós-moderna*. São Paulo: Edições Loyola.

Harvey D. (2007) *A brief history of neoliberalism*. Oxford: Oxford University Press.

Harvey D. (2010) *The Enigma of Capital and the Crises of Capitalism*. London: Profile Books.

Heffernan V. (2017) Just Google It: A Short History of a Newfound Verb. *Wired*, 5 November Available (consulted 14 January 2019) at: https://www.wired.com/story/just-google-it-a-short-history-of-a-newfound-verb/.

Hegeman, J. (2020) Providing People With Additional Context About Content They Share. Facebook Newsroom, 25, June. Available (consulted 29 September 2020) at: https://about.fb.com/news/2020/06/more-context-for-news-articles-and-other-content.

Heidegger M. (1977a) The question concerning technology. In: Heidegger M. *The question concerning technology and other essays*. New York: Harper Torchbooks.

Heidegger M. (1977b) The Turning. In: Heidegger M. *The question concerning technology and other essays*. New York: Harper Torchbooks.

Heilbronner R.L. (1994a) Do Machines Make History? In: Smith, M.R., Marx, L. (Eds). *Does technology drive history?: The dilemma of technological determinism*. Cambridge: MIT Press.

Heilbronner R.L. (1994b) Technological determinism revisited. In: Smith, M.R., Marx, L. (Eds). *Does technology drive history? The dilemma of technological determinism*. Cambridge: MIT Press.

Heilbronner, R. Do machines make history? (1994) In: Smith M.R. and Marx, L. (ed.) *Does technology drive history? The dilemma of technological determinism.* London: MIT Press.

Helberger N., Pierson J. and Poell, T. (2018) Governing online platforms: From contested to cooperative responsibility. *The information society, 34*(1), 1–14.

Helmond, A. (2015). The platformization of the web: Making web data platform ready. *Social Media+ Society, 1*(2), 2056305115603080.

Henderson F. (2017) *Software engineering at Google.* arXiv preprint arXiv:1702.01715.

Herscovici A. (2013) Economia de redes, externalidades e estruturas de mercado: o conceito de concorrência qualitativa. *Revista Brasileira de Inovação.* v. 12, n. 1.

Herscovici, A. (2019) Deus e o Diabo na terra das plataformas digitais: uma aná-lise a partir da hipótese braudeliana. *Revista Eptic Online,* v. 21, n. 1, 125–141.

Hess D.J. et al. (2016) Structural Inequality and the Politics of Science and Technology. In. Hackett E. et al. *The handbook of science and technology studies.* Cambridge: MIT Press.

Hess, D.J,. Amir, S., Frickel S., Kleinman D.L., Moore K. and Williams, L.D. (2016). Structural Inequality and the Politics of Science and Technology. In: Felt U, Rayvon F., Miller C. and Smith-Doerr, L.*The Handbook of science and technology studies,* London: MIT Press. 319–47.

Hexsel R. (2006) *Sistemas Digitais e Microprocessadores.* Curitiba: Editora UFPR.

Hinman L.M. (2008) Searching Ethics*:* The Role of Search Engines in the Construction and Distribution of Knowledge In: Spinik A., Zimmer M. (Eds.). *Websearch: Mulidisciplinary perspectives.* Switzerland: Springer.

Hook L. (2015) Year in a word: Gig Economy. *Financial Times Online,* 29 December. Available (consulted 18 July 2017) at: https://www.ft.com/content/b5a2b122-a41b-11e5-8218-6b8ff73aae15.

Hope, W. (2011). Global capitalism, temporality, and the political economy of communication. içinde, J. Wasko, G. Murdock & H. Sousa (ed.), *The Handbook of Political Economy of Communication,* London: Blackwell Pub, 521–540.

Horwitz J. and Seetharaman D. (2020) Facebook Executives Shut Down Efforts to Make the Site Less Divisive. The Wall Street Journal, may, 26. Available (consulted 24 September 2020) at: https://www.wsj.com/articles/facebook-knows-it-encourages-division-top-executives-nixed-solutions-11590507499.

Hrivnak T. and Raji V. (2020) Now playing: music vídeos on Facebook. Facebook Newsroom, 31, July. Available (consulted 24 September 2020) at: https://about.fb.com/news/2020/07/music-videos-on-facebook/.

Hughes T. (1993) The evolution of large technological systems. In. Bijiker W., Hudges T., Pinch T. *The social construction of technological systems: New directions in the sociology and history of technology.* Cambridge: MIT Press.

Hung C. (2020) Introducing Facebook Campus. Facebook Newsroom, 10, September. Available (consulted 24 September 2020) at: https://about.fb.com/news/2020/09/introducing-facebook-campus/.

Husson M. and Louça F. (2013) Capitalismo tardío y neoliberalismo: una perspectiva de la actual fase de la onda larga del desarrollo capitalista. *Sin Permiso: República y socialismo también para el siglo XXI*, 08 July.

Hutchinson A. (2019) Google's Biggest Search Algorithm Updates of 2018 [Infographic]. *Social media Today*, 31 January. Available (consulted 05 February 2019) at: https://www.socialmediatoday.com/news/googles-biggest-search-algorithm-updates-of-2018-infographic/547167/?fbclid=IwAR0K21R1ujO%E2%80%94wZguTbkIJ9nX-TAsmwq%20tGy9OHKb9dzrWSgd3onIAJZ71i8.

Huws U. (2014) *Labor in the global digital economy: The cybertariat comes of age*. New York: NYU Press.

Ianni O. (1976) *Imperialismo e Cultura*. São Paulo: Ed. Vozes.

IC INSIGHTS (2018) *The Mclean Report*. Scottsdale, US: IC Insights.

IDC (2017) *Worldwide Semiannual Big Data and Analytics Spending Guide*. Framinghan, US: IDC.

IFPI (2019) *Music listening 2019*. London: IFPI.

IFPI. (2017) *Global music report 2017*. London: IFPI.

Ingersoll M. and Kelly J. (2010) Think big with a gig: our experimental fiber network. *Google Official Blog*, 10 February. Available (consulted 10 October 2018) at: https://googleblog.blogspot.com/2010/02/think-big-with-gig-our-experimental.html.

Instagram (2015) Introducing layout from Instagram. *Instagram Blog*, 23 March. Available (consulted 20 October 2018) at:https://instagram-press.com/blog/2015/03/23/introducing-layout-from-instagram/.

International Federation of Robotics (2016) *World robotics report 2016*. Frankfurt, Germany: International Federation of Robotics.

International Labour Organization (2016) *World employment social outlook 2016*. Geneva, Switzerland: International Labour Organization.

International Telecommunications Union (2017) *ICT Facts and Figures 2017*. International Telecommunications Union, Junho. Available at: http://www.itu.int/en/ITU-D/Statistics/Pages/facts/default.aspx.

International Telecommunications Union (2019) Measuring digital development: facts and figures 2019. Geneva: ITU.

Introna L. (2015) Algorithms, Governance, and Governmentality. *Science, Technology, & Human Values*, [s.l.], v. 41, n. 1, 17–49.

Introna L. and Nissenbaum, H. (2000) Shaping the Web: Why the politics of search engines matters. *The information society*. v. 16, n. 2.

Ippolita. (2017) *The dark side of Google*. Institute of Network Cultures.

Iqbal M. (2020a) Uber revenue and usage statistics. Business of apps, 20, August. Available (consulted 24 September 2020) at: https://www.businessofapps.com/data/uber-statistics/.

Iqbal M. (2020b) Spotify usage and revenue statistics (2020). Business of apps, 4, September. Available (consulted 24 September 2020) at: https://www.businessofapps.com/data/spotify-statistics/.

Isaak J. and Hanna M.J. (2018) User Data Privacy: Facebook, Cambridge Analytica, and Privacy Protection. *Computer*, [s.l.], v. 51, n. 8, 56–59, August.

Jasanoff S. (2004) *States of knowledge: the co-production of science and the social order.* Abigdon: Routledge.

Jasanoff S. et al. (ed.). (2007) *Making order: Law and science in action.* The Handbook of Science and Technology Studies. 3rd ed. Cambridge: MIT Press.

Jelenchick L.A., Eickhoff J.C. and Moreno M.A. (2013) "Facebook Depression?" Social Networking Site Use and Depression in Older Adolescents. *Journal Of Adolescent Health,* [s.l.], v. 52, n. 1:128–130, January.

Jensen L.T. (2016) Exploring the most popular websites in 20 years. *Pc Magazine*, 8 December. Available (consulted 15 January 2019) at: https://www.pcmag.com/article/350122/exploring-the-most-popular-websites-of-the-last-20-years.

Jin D.Y. (2015) *Digital platforms, imperialism and political culture.* Abigdon: Routledge.

Jin G.Z. (2018) Artificial Intelligence and Consumer Privacy. In:Agrawal A., Gans J., Goldfarb A. (2018) *Economics of Artificial Intelligence.* Chicago: University of Chicago Press.

Johnston M. (2020) 10 Biggest Telecommunications Companies. Investopedia, 6, August. At: https://www.investopedia.com/articles/markets/030216/worlds-top-10-telecommunications-companies.asp.

Jonas H. (1974) *Philosophical essays: From ancient creed to technological man.* New York: Atropos Press.

Kahneman D. (2011) *Rápido e devagar: duas formas de pensar.* São Paulo: Objetiva.

Kaminski M. E. (2020) Understanding Transparency in Algorithmic Accountability. *Forthcoming in Cambridge Handbook of the Law of Algorithms, ed. Woodrow Barfield, Cambridge: Cambridge University Press.*

Kang, H. and Mcallister M.P. (2011) Selling You and Your Clicks: Examining the Audience Commodification of Google. Triplec: Communication, Capitalism & Critique. *Open Access Journal for a Global Sustainable Information Society*, [s.l.], v. 9, n. 2:141–153.

Kangal, K., Bastos, M. D. and Bernardi, G. (2020) Discussões marxistas na Economia Digital: uma crítica a Christian Fuchs. *Revista Eptic Online*, 22(2), 67–82.

Kaplan K. (2003). Facemash Creator Survives Ad Board. *The Harvard Crimson*, 19 November. Available (consulted 08 August 2019) at: https://www.thecrimson.com/article/2003/11/19/facemash-creator-survives-ad-board-the/.

Karabell Z. (2020) Alphabet Flirts With $1 Trillion but Needs a Second Act. Wired, 3, February. Available (consulted by 27 September 2020) at: https://www.wired.com/story/alphabet-flirts-1-trillion-needs-second-act/.

Kaspersky Lab (2017) *From digital amnesia to augmented mind.* Kaspersky Lab. Available (consulted 26 July 2018) at: https://media.kaspersky.com/pdf/Kaspersky-Digital-Amnesia-Evolution-report-17-08-16.pdf.

Katz C. (1997) La concepción marxista del cambio tecnológico. *Pensamiento Económico*, n. 1, 155–180.

Katz R. (2012) *The impact of broadband on the economy: Research to date and policy issues.* Broadband Series.

Kaun A. and Stiernstedt, A. (2014) Facebook time: Technological and institutional affordances for media memories. *New Media & Society*, [s.l.], v. 16, n. 7, 1154–1168.

Kaye D. (2018) *Report of the Special Rapporteur on the promotion and protection of the right to freedom of opinion and expression.* Human Rights Council, 38 session, 2018. Available (consulted 03 March 2019) at: https://www.ohchr.org/EN/Issues/FreedomOpinion/Pages/OpinionIndex.aspx.

Keizer, G. (2019) Former Mozilla exec alleges Google torpedoed Firefox with 'oops' excuses. Computerworld, April, 17. Available (consulted by 27 September 2020) at: https://www.computerworld.com/article/3389882/former-mozilla-exec-alleges-google-torpedoed-firefox-with-oops-excuses.html.

Kenney M. and Zysman J. (2016) The rise of the platform economy. *Issues in Science and Technology 32*, n. 3.

Keslassy E. (2019) France's Antitrust Board Slaps Google With $166 Million Fine Over Online Ads. Variety, 20, December. Available (consulted 22 September 2020) at: https://variety.com/2019/digital/global/google-france-antitrust-fine-166-million-dollars-1203449787/.

Kipphan H. (2001) *The handbook of print media.* New York, US: Springer.

Kirkpatrick, D. (2010) *The Facebook effect: The inside story of the company that is connecting the world.* New York: Simon and Schuster.

Kizu T., Kuhn S. and Viegelahn C. (2016) *Linking jobs in the global supply chains of demanda.* Geneva, Switzerland: International Labour Organization.

Klein H.K. and Kleinman D.L. (2002) The social construction of technology: Structural considerations. *Science, Technology, & Human Values*, v. 27, n. 1, 28–52.

Kramer A.D.I., Guillory J.E. and Hancock J.T. (2014) Experimental evidence of massive-scale emotional contagion through social networks. *Proceedings of The National Academy Of Sciences*, [s.l.], v. 111, n. 24, 8788–8790.

Kroes P. (2010) Engineering and the dual nature of technical artefacts. *Cambridge Journal Of Economics*, [s.l.], v. 34, n. 1, 51–62.

Kross E. et al. (2013) Facebook Use Predicts Declines in Subjective Well-Being in Young Adults. *Plos One*, [s.l.], v. 8, n. 8.

Ku M. (2016) Introducing Marketplace: Buy and Sell With Your Local Community. *Facebook Newsroom*, 3 October. Available (consulted 06 January 2019) at: https://newsroom.fb.com/news/2016/10/introducing-marketplace-buy-and-sell-with-your-local-community/.

Kwecka Z. et al. (2014) I am Spartacus: privacy enhancing technologies, collaborative obfuscation and privacy as a public good. *Artificial Intelligence and Law*, v. 22, Issue 2, June.

Lapowsky I. (2018) How Russian Facebook Ads Divided and Targeted US Voters Before the 2016 Election. *Wired*, 16 April. Available (consulted 22 February 2019) at: https://www.wired.com/story/russian-facebook-ads-targeted-us-voters-before-2016-election/.

Lardinois F. and Constine J. (2016) Facebook shatters its Parse Developer Platform. *Techcrunch*, 28 January. Available (consulted 09 February 2019) at: https://techcrunch.com/2016/01/28/facebook-shutters-its-parse-developer-platform/.

Latour B. (1990) Technology is society made durable. *The Sociological Review*, v. 38, n. 1, 103–131.

Latour B. (2000) *Ciência em ação: como seguir cientistas e engenheiros sociedade afora*. São Paulo: Ed. Unesp.

Latour B. (2012) *Reagregando o Social: uma introdução à teoria do Ator-Rede*. Bauru, SP: EDUSC/Salvador, BA: EDUFBA.

Laudon K.C. (1986) *Dossier society: value choices in the design of national information systems*. New York: Columbia University Press.

Lee N. (2014) *Facebook nation. Total information awareness*. New York: Springer.

Lee C. (2017) Facebook declines, Google grows as battle for news audiences continues. Parse.ly blog, 30 november. Available (consulted by 15 march 2019) at: https://blog.parse.ly/facebook-declines-google-grows-news-audiences/

Lee S. S., Lane, D. S. and Kwak, N. (2020) When Social Media Get Political: How Perceptions of Open-Mindedness Influence Political Expression on Facebook. *Social Media+ Society*, 6(2).

Lee, D. (2019) Facebook is trying to entice creators with more monetization options. The Verge, July, 9. Available (consulted 22 September 2020) at: https://www.theverge.com/2019/7/9/20687603/facebook-creators-stars-subscriptions-supporter-groups.

LeGassick C. (2017) *Ai Index Report 2017*. Projeto Artificial Intelligence Index. Available (consulted 05 January 2019) at: https://aiindex.org/.

Lehdonvirta, V., Kässi, O., Hjorth, I., Barnard, H., & Graham, M. (2019). The global platform economy: A new offshoring institution enabling emerging-economy microproviders. *Journal of Management*, 45(2), 567–599.

Leskin P. (2019) Facebook just launched its dating service in the US, and it has a clear advantage that could help it beat out Tinder and Bumble. Business Insider, 5,

September. Available (consulted 22 September 2020) at: https://www.businessinsider.com/facebook-dating-united-states-launch-2019-9.

Lessig L. (2006) *Code V 2.0*. New York: Basic Books.

Lessin S. (2011) Tell your story with timeline. *Facebook Newsroom*, 22 September. Available (consulted 26 December 2018) at: https://newsroom.fb.com/news/2011/09/tell-your-story-with-timeline/.

Levin S. (2018) Facebook documents published by UK – the key takeaways. *The Guardian*, 6 December. Available (consulted 08 February 2019) at: https://www.theguardian.com/technology/2018/dec/05/facebook-documents-uk-parliament-key-facts.

Lev-On, A. (2008) The democratizing effects of search engine use: On chance exposures and organizational hubs. In *Web search*. Berlin: Springer. 135–149.

Lewis M. (2014) *Flash boys: a Wall Street revolt*. New York: ww Norton & Company.

Lievrow L. (2012) Preface. In: Feenberg A., Friesen N. *(Re)Inventing the internet: critical case studies*. Rotterdan, Netherlands: Sense Publishers.

Lima V.A. (2010) *Liberdade de expressão x liberdade de imprensa: direito à comunicação e democracia*. São Paulo: Publisher Brasil.

Lin E. (2016) Why ethics matters for autonomous cars. In: Maurer M., Gerdes J., Lenz B., Winne R. (eds) *Autonomes Fahren*. Heidelberg: Springer.

Lindley G. (2013) Public conversations on Facebook. *Facebook Newsroom*, 12 June. Available (consulted 09 March 2019) at:https://newsroom.fb.com/news/2013/06/public-conversations-on-facebook/.

Liu D. (2018) Marketplace completa dois anos: novos recursos de inteligência artificial e muito mais. *Facebook Newsroom*, 3 October. Available (consulted 05 January 2019) at: https://br.newsroom.fb.com/news/2018/10/marketplace-completa-dois-anos-novos-recursos-de-inteligencia-artificial-e-muito-mais/.

Lomas N. (2018) A brief history of Facebook's privacy hostility ahead of Zuckerberg's testimony. *Techcrunch*, 10 April. Available (consulted 17 January 2019) at: https://techcrunch.com/2018/04/10/a-brief-history-of-facebooks-privacy-hostility-ahead-of-zuckerbergs-testimony/.

Lomas N. (2019) Google fines € 1,49 bin in Europe for antitrust violations in search and brokering. *Techcrunch*, 20 March. Available (consulted 17 February 2019) at: https://techcrunch.com/2019/03/20/google-fined-1-49bn-in-europe-for-antitrust-violations-in-search-ad-brokering/.

Los Angeles Times. (2015) Judge approves settlement in Apple, Google wage case. *Los Angeles Times*, 3 September. Available (consulted 03 February 2019) at: https://www.latimes.com/business/technology/la-fi-tn-tech-jobs-settlement-20150903-story.html.

Lucio A. (2019) Introducing our new company bra.nd. *Facebook Newsroom*, 4, November. Available (consulted 29 September 2020) at: https://about.fb.com/news/2019/11/introducing-our-new-company-brand/.

Lund S., Daruvala T., Dobbs R., Harle Kweck JH. and Falcón, R. (2013) *Financial globalization: Retreat or reSeptember* McKinsey Global Institute.

Lyon D. (1994) *The electronic eye: The rise of surveillance society.* Minnesota, US: University of Minnesota Press.

Lyons T. (2018) Hard Questions: What's Facebook's Strategy for Stopping False News? *Facebook Newsroom*, 23 May. Available (consulted 22 January 2019) at: https://newsroom.fb.com/news/2018/05/hard-questions-false-news/.

Machkovech S. (2017) Report: Facebook helped advertisers target teens who feel "worthless". *ARS Technica*, 10 May. Available (consulted 23 January 2019) at: https://arstechnica.com/information-technology/2017/05/facebook-helped-advertisers-target-teens-who-feel-worthless/.

MacKinnon, R., Hickok, E., Bar A. and Lim, H. (2014) Fostering freedom online: The Roles, challenges and obstacles of internet intermediaries. United Nations Educational.

Mager A. (2016) Search engine imaginary: Visions and values in the co-production of search technology and Europe. *Social Studies of Science*, [s.l.], v. 47, n. 2, 240–262.

Mager, A. (2011). Algorithmic Ideology: How Capitalist Society Shapes Search Engines. *Information, Communication & Society, Forthcoming.*

Mandel E. (1979) *El capitalismo tardío.* Ciudad de Mexico: Era.

Mandel E. (1986) *Las ondas largas del desarrollo capitalista: la interpretación marxista.* Madrid: Siglo XXI.

Marcuse H. (1973) *A ideologia da sociedade industrial: o homem unidimensional.* 4. ed. Rio de Janeiro: Zahar.

Marichal J. (2016) *Facebook democracy: The architecture of disclosure and the threat to public life.* Abongdon: Routledge.

Markets and Markets (2017) *Microprocessor and GPU Markets: global forecast to 2022.* Pune, India: Markets and Markets.

Markets and Markets (2020) Big data Market. Markets and Markets. Available (consulted 22 September 2020) at: https://www.marketsandmarkets.com/Market-Reports/big-data-market-1068.html.

Martin H.J. (1992) La imprenta. In: Williams R. (ed.). *Historia de la comunicación,* Vol. 2: de la imprenta a nuestros dias. Mexico City: Bosch.

Martineau P. (2020) Ad Dollars keep flying into Google and Facebook – for now. Wired, March, 29. Available (consulted 22 September 2020) at: https://www.wired.com/story/ad-dollars-flowing-google-facebook/.

Marx, Karl. (1851) *Cuaderno tecnológico-histórico.* London.

Marx, K. (1980) *Conseqüências sociais do avanço tecnológico.* São Paulo: Edições Populares.

Marx, K. (1982) *Progreso técnico y desarrollo capitalista.* Mexico City: Pasado y presente.

Marx, K. (1984) *Cuaderno tecnológico-histórico.* Puebla: Univ. Aut. De Puebla.

Marx, K. (2008) *Contribuição à crítica da economia política.* São Paulo: Expressão Popular.

Marx, K. (2011a) *Grundrisse*. São Paulo: Boitempo Editorial.
Marx, K. (2011b) *O 18 Brumário de Napoleão Bonaparte*. São Paulo: Boitempo Editorial.
Marx, K. (2013) *O Capital: livro I*. São Paulo: Boitempo Editorial.
Marx, K. (2014) *O Capital: livro II*. São Paulo: Boitempo. E-book.
Marx, K. (2017) *O Capital: Crítica da Economia Política*. O Processo Global da Produção Capitalista – Livro III. São Paulo: Boitempo Editorial. E-book.
Marx, K. (2017). *Miséria da filosofia*. São Paulo: Boitempo Editorial.
Matiuzzo M. (2018) Business models and big data: how google uses your personal information. In: Branco S.; Teffé C. *Privacidade em perspectivas*. Rio de Janeiro; LumenJuris.
Matsakis L. (2019) Larry Page and Sergey Brin Hand Over Alphabet's Reins. Wired, 3, December. Available (consulted 26 September 2020) at: https://www.wired.com/story/larry-page-sergey-brin-step-down/.
Mattelart A. (2000) *A globalização da comunicação*. São Paulo: Edusc.
Mattelart, A. (2002). *História da sociedade da informação*. São Paulo: Loyola.
Mattick A. (2011) *Business as Usual: The Economic Crisis and the Failure of Capitalism*. London: Reaktion.
Maverick J.B. (2019) The Top 6 Shareholders of Facebook. *Investopedia*, 7 February Available (consulted 15 February 2019) at: https://www.investopedia.com/articles/insights/082216/top-9-shareholders-facebook-fb.asp.
McCandless D. (2018) *Diversity in tech: Information is beautiful*. Available (consulted 09 December 2018) at: https://informationisbeautiful.net/visualizations/diversity-in-tech/.
McChesney R.W. (1995) *Telecommunications, mass media, and democracy: The battle for the control of US broadcasting, 1928–1935*. Oxford: Oxford University Press.
McChesney R.W. (2013) *Digital disconect: how capitalism is turning the internet against democracy*. London: The New Press. E-book.
McKinsey. (2016) *Independent work: Choice, necessity, and the gig economy*. London: McKinsey Global Institute.
McKinsey. (2017). *Artificial Intelligence: the next digital frontier?* McKinsey Global Institute. Discussion paper. June, London: McKinsey Global Institute.
Meeker M. (2017) *Internet trends 2017*. Menlo Park, US: Kleiner Perkins.
Meyer C. (2016) Save Time with Quick access in Drive. *Google Drive blog*, 29 September Available (consulted 18 January 2019) at:https://drive.googleblog.com/2016/09/save-time-with-quick-access-in-drive.html
Meyer M. (2011) The power of Google: serving consumers or threatning competition. Hearing Before The Subcommittee On Antitrust, Competition Policy And Consumer Rights Of The Committee On The Judiciary, United States Senate. 21 September.
Micheli M., Ponti M., Craglia M. and Berti Suman, A. (2020) Emerging models of data governance in the age of datafication. *Big Data & Society*, 7(2).

REFERENCES 371

Micheva N. (2020) Introducing Watch together on Messenger. Facebook Newsroom, 14, September. Available (consulted 26 September 2020) at: https://about.fb.com/news/2020/09/introducing-watch-together-on-messenger/.

Miconi A. (2014) Dialectic of Google. In: König R. and Rasch M. *Society of the Query Reader*. Reflections on Web Search. Amsterdam: Institute of Network Cultures, 30–40.

Microfocus. (2018) *Como se preparar para a nova lei de proteção de dados?* Relatório de mesa-redonda. Microfocus.

Miller R. and Shorter G. (2016) *High frequency trading: overview and recent developments*. Washington: Library of Congress. Congressional research service.

Mirani L. (2015) People have no idea they're using the internet. *Quarz*, 9 February. Available (consulted 09 fev 2017) at:https://qz.com/333313/milliions-of-facebook-users-have-no-idea-theyre-using-the-internet/.

Moazed A. and Johnson N.L. (2016) *Modern monopolies: what it takes to dominate the 21st century economy*. New York: St. Martin's Press.

Molla R. (2018) Facebook, Google and Netflix pay a higher median salary than Exxon, Goldman Sachs or Verizon. *Recode*, 30 April. Available (consulted 30 January 2019) at: https://www.recode.net/2018/4/30/17301264/how-much-twitter-google-amazon-highest-paying-salary-tech.

Mollo M.L.R. (2015) The Supremacy of Finance and the Crisis. *Brazilian Keynesian Review*. v. 1, n.1.

Morrisson S. (2020) Facebook's sad summer continues with a $650 million settlement. Recode, 23, July. Available (consulted 30 september 2020) At: https://www.vox.com/recode/2020/7/23/21335806/facebook-settlement-illinois-facial-recognition-photo-tagging.

Mosco, V. (2017) *Becoming digital: Toward a post-internet society*. Bingley, UK: Emerald Group Publishing.

Moss R. (2020) Working from home will be double pre-pandemic levels. Personel Today, 16, July. Available (consulted 23 september 2020) At: https://www.personneltoday.com/hr/working-from-home-will-be-double-pre-pandemic-levels/.

Mosseri A. (2016) Construindo um Feed de Notícias mais relevante para as pessoas. *Facebook Newsroom*, 29 June. Available (consulted 25 January 2017) at: https://br.newsroom.fb.com/news/2016/06/construindo-um-feed-de-noticias-mais-relevante-para-as-pessoas/.

Mosseri A. (2017) Working to Stop Misinformation and False News. *Facebook Newsroom*, 6 April. Available (consulted 09 July 2018) at: https://newsroom.fb.com/news/2017/04/working-to-stop-misinforma-tion-and-false-news/.

Mosseri A. (2018) News Feed Ranking in Three Minutes Flat. *Facebook Newsroom*, 22 May. Available (consulted 30 July 2018) at:https://newsroom.fb.com/news/2018/05/inside-feed-news-feed-ranking/.

Motta M. (2004) *Competition policy: theory and practice*. Cambridge: Cambridge University Press.

Mozur A. (2008) Genocide Incited on Facebook, With Posts From Myanmar's Military. *The New York Times*, 15 October. Available (consulted 17 February 2019) at: https://www.nytimes.com/2018/10/15/technology/myanmar-facebook-genocide.html.

Mozur, P. (2018) A Genocide Incited on Facebook, With Posts From Myanmar's Military. The New York Times, 15 october. Available (consulted by 10 april 2020) at: https://www.nytimes.com/2018/10/15/technology/myanmar-facebook-genocide.html.

Muraleedharan S. (2017) Introducing Snooze to Give You More Control Of Your News Feed. *Facebook Newsroom*, 15 December. Available (consulted 3 February 2018) at: https://newsroom.fb.com/news/2017/12/news-feed-fyi-snooze/.

Musk E. (2015) *Speech on Governments Meeting*. 27 July.

Nadkarni A. and Hofmann S.G. (2012) Why do people use Facebook? *Personality and Individual Differences*, [s.l.], v. 52, n. 3, 243–249.

Negroponte N. (1995) *Ser digital*. Buenos Aires: Editorial Atlántida.

Nellis S. (2018) Apple's user base grows, but analysts probe for more detail. *Business Insider*, 2 February. Available (consulted 30 January 2019) at: https://www.reuters.com/article/us-apple-results-users/apples-user-base-grows-but-analysts-probe-for-more-detail-idUSKBN1FM09R.

Nelson J. (2017) Is 'fake news'a fake problem? *Columbia Journalism Review*, 31 January. Available (consulted 23 February 2019) at: https://www.cjr.org/analysis/fake-news-facebook-audience-drudge-breitbart-study.php.

Nelson R. and Winter S. (1977) In search of a useful theory of innovation. In: Nelson R. and Winter S. *Innovation, economic change and technology policies*. Basel: Birkhäuser. p. 215–245.

Nelson R. and Winter S. (1982) *An evolutionary theory of economic change*. Boston: Harvard University Press..

Newell S. and Marabelli M. (2015) Strategic opportunities (and challenges) of algorithmic decision-making: A call for action on the long-term societal effects of 'datification'. *The Journal of Strategic Information Systems,* [s.l.], v. 24, n. 1, 3–14.

Newman J. M. (2019) Antitrust in Digital Markets. *Vand. L. Rev.*, 72, 1497.

Newman L. (2019) How Incognito Google Maps Protects You – and How It Doesn't. Wired, 2, October. Available (consulted 26 September 2020) at: https://www.wired.com/story/google-maps-incognito-mode/.

Newton C. (2020) Facebook launches Shops to bring more businesses online during the pandemic. The Verge, 19, May. Available (Consulted 2 October) at: https://www.theverge.com/2020/5/19/21263567/facebook-shops-instagram-shopping-e-commerce-small-business-loyalty-program.

Newton C. and Schiffer Z. (2019) Google and Facebook's antitrust problem is getting much more serious. The Verge, 10, September. Available (Consulted 2

October) at: https://www.theverge.com/interface/2019/9/10/20858028/google-antitrust-investigation-state-attorneys-general-facebook.

Nicoletti B. (2017) Fintech Innovation. In: Nicoletti B. *The Future of FinTech 2017*. London: Palgrave Macmillan, p. 81–159.

Nieborg D. B. and Helmond, A. (2019) The political economy of Facebook's platformization in the mobile ecosystem: Facebook Messenger as a platform instance. *Media, Culture & Society*, 41(2), 196–218.

Nielsen. (2016) *Estudo global: vídeo sob demanda*. New York: Nielsen.

Nielsen. (2017) A look at the evolving e-commerce landscape. *Nielsen*, 1 November. Available (consulted 23 December 2018) at:https://www.nielsen.com/eu/en/insights/news/2017/a-look-at-the-evolving-e-commerce-landscape.html.

Noble D.F. (1995) *Progress Without People: New Technology, Unemployment, and the Message of Resistance*. Toronto: Between the Lines Press.

Noble D.F. (2011) *Forces of Production: a social history of industrial automation*. New Brunswick: Transaction Publishers.

Noble, S.U. (2018) *Algorithms of oppression: How search engines reinforce racism*. New York: NYU Press.

Novak M. (2018) Facebok fines just $ 645,000 in UK over Cambridge Analytica scandal, money it makes in less than 10 minutes. *Gizmodo*, 25 October. Available (consulted 17 January 2019) at: https://gizmodo.com/facebook-fined-just-645-000-in-uk-over-cambridge-analy-1829989116>.

Novet J. and Levy A. (2018) Google Cloud CEO Diane Greene is out, to be replaced by former Oracle exec Thomas Kurian. *CNBC*, 16 November. Available (consulted 16 February 2019) at: https://www.cnbc.com/2018/11/16/google-cloud-ceo-greene-being-replaced-by-former-oracle-exec-kurian.html.

NY Attorney General. (2010) Attorney General Cuomo Announces Additional Social Networking Sites Join His Initiative To Eliminate Sharing of Thousands of Images of Child Pornography. *NY Attorney General*, 29 June. Available (consulted 16 February 2019) at: https://ag.ny.gov/press-release/attorney-general-cuomo-announces-additional-social-networking-sites-join-his.

O'Halloran D. (2015) *How technology will change the way we work*. World Economic Forum, August, 2015.

O'Farrell R. and Montagnier P. (2020) Measuring digital platform-mediated workers. *New Technology, Work and Employment*, 35(1), 130–144.

O'Regan G. (2016) *Introduction to the history of computing*. New York: Springer.

Odesk (2014) *Digital Nomads: A Revolution in Work Freedom*. Santa Clara, US: Odesk.

OECD (2017) *Big Data: Bringing Competition Policy to the Digital Era*. Paris: OECD.

OECD (2017) *Key Issues for digital transformation in G20*. Report prepared for a joint G20 German Presidency/OECD conference. Organização para a Cooperação e Desenvolvimento Econômico, jan, 2017, updated 2019. Paris: OECD.

Office of the Privacy Commissioner of Canada (2009) *Report of Findings into the Complaint Filed by the Canadian Internet Policy and Public Interest Clinic (CIPPIC) against Facebook Inc.* Under the Personal Information Protection and Electronic Documents Act. Ottawa: Office of the Privacy Commissioner of Canada.

Ohlheiser A. (2019) The Christchurch mosque shooter, steeped in online culture, knew how to make his massacre go viral. The Washington Post, 15, March. Available (consulted by 30 september 2020) at: https://www.washingtonpost.com/technology/2019/03/15/christchurch-mosque-shooter-steeped-online-culture-knew-how-make-his-massacre-go-viral.

Oliveira A. (2017) *The Digital Mind: How Science is Redefining Humanity*. Cambridge: MIT Press.

Oliveira G.A. (2014) *Indicadores de concorrência: discussão conceitual e testes empíricos*. Brasília: CADE.

Opensignal. (2016) *Global state of mobile networks*. August, 2016. Available (consulted 10 April 2017) at: https://opensignal.com/reports/2016/08/global-state-of-the-mobile-network/.

Oremus W. (2017) Facebook Has Stopped Saying "Fake news". *Slate*, 8 August. Available (consulted 18 January 2019) at: http://www.slate.com/blogs/future_tense/2017/08/08/facebook_has_stopped_saying_fake_news_is_false_news_any_better.html.

Ostry, J.D., Loungani, P. and Furceri, D. (2016). Neoliberalism: oversold. *Finance & development*, 53(2), 38–41.

Ovide S. (2018) Mixing a PC and a Smartphone Is a Great Idea. In Theory. *Bloomberg Gadfly*, 22 February. Available (consulted 27 August 2018) at: https://www.bloomberg.com/gadfly/articles/2018-02-22/mixing-a-pc-and-a-smartphone-is-a-great-idea-in-theory.

Owyang J. and Samuel A. (2015) *The new rules of colaborative economy*. Vancouver, Canada: Vision Critical.

Page L. (2005) *2005 Founders' letter*. Google. Available (consulted 14 January 2019) at: https://abc.xyz/investor/founders-letters/2005/.

Page L. (2007) *2007 Founders' letter*. Google. Available (consulted 14 January 2019) at: https://abc.xyz/investor/founders-letters/2007/.

Page L. (2013) *2013 Founders' letter*. Google. Available (consulted 14 January 2019) at: https://abc.xyz/investor/founders-letters/2013/.

Page L. (2015) *2015 Founders letter*. Alphabet. Available (consulted 14 January 2019) at: https://abc.xyz/investor/founders-letters/2015/.

Page, L. (2004) Founders' letter. Google. Available (consulted 14 jannuary 2019) at: https://abc.xyz/investor/founders-letters/2004/.

Palmer A. (2019) Facebook rejects AG Barr's request to stop encryption plans for messaging apps. CNBC, 10, December. Available (consulted 30 September) at: https://www.cnbc.com/2019/12/10/facebook-rejects-ag-barrs-request-to-stop-messaging-encyrption.html.

Pangrle B. (2011) Power-Efficient Design Challenges. In: Hoefflinger, B. *Chips 2020*. Berlin, Heidelberg: Springer, 189–213.

Paraná E. (2016) *A finança digitalizada: capitalismo financeiro e revolução informacional*. Florianópolis: Editora Insular.

Parikh J. (2016) Introducing Telcom Infra Project. *Facebook Newsroom*, 21 February Available (consulted 18 January 2019) at: https://newsroom.fb.com/news/2016/02/introducing-the-telecom-infra-project/.

Pariser E. (2011) *The filter bubble: What the Internet is hiding from you*. London, UK: Penguin.

Parks M.R. (2010) Social network sites as virtual communities. In: Papacharissi Z. (edi) *A networked self*. Abongdon: Routledge, 113–131.

Pasquale F. (2015) *The black box society*. Boston: Harvard University Press.

Pasquale F. (2016) Two narratives of platform capitalism. *Yale Law & Policy Review*, v. 35, n. 1: 309–319.

Paul K. and Rana A. (2019) U.S. charges Facebook with racial discrimination in targeted housing ads. *Reuters*, 28 March. Available (consulted 15 April 2019) at: https://www.reuters.com/article/us-facebook-advertisers/facebook-charged-with-racial-discrimination-in-targeted-housing-ads-idUSKCN1R91E8.

Peña-López I.(2015) *OECD digital economy outlook*. Paris: OECD.

Pérez C. (1986) Las nuevas tecnologías: una visión de conjunto. *Estudios Internacionales*, v. 19, n. 76, 420–459.

Pérez C. (2002) *Technological revolutions and financial capital: the dynamics of bubbles and golden ages*. Cheltenham, UK: Edward Elgar Publishing.

Pérez C. (2003) *Technological revolutions and financial capital*. Cheltenham, UK: Edward Elgar Publishing.

Pérez C. (2005) *Revoluciones tecnológicas y capital financiero*. La dinámica de las grandes burbujas financieras y las épocas de bonanzas. Buenos Aires, Siglo XXI editores.

Pérez C. (2010) Technological revolutions and techno-economic paradigms. *Cambridge journal of economics*, v. 34, n. 1, 185–202.

Perez J.C. (2007) Facebook's Beacon More Intrusive Than Previously Thought. *IDG News*, 30 November. Available (consulted 25 January 2019) at: https://www.pcworld.com/article/140182/article.html.

Perez S. (2020) Instagram Reels launches globally in over 50 countries, including US. Tech Crunch, 5, August. Available (consulted 30 September) at: https://techcrunch.com/2020/08/05/instagram-reels-launches-globally-in-over-50-countries-including-u-s/.

Pérez, C. (2005). *Revoluciones tecnológicas y capital financiero: la dinámica de las grandes burbujas financieras y las épocas de bonanza*. Ciudad de Mexico: Siglo XXI.

Perry W.J. (2004) Military technology: an historical perspective. *Technology in Society*, Apr 1; 26(2–3), 235–43.

Pesole A., M. Urzí Brancati E. Fernández-Macías F. Biagi and González Vázquez, I. (2018) *Platform Workers in Europe*. Luxembourg: Publications Office of the European Union.

Peters B. (2019) *We Analyzed 43 Million Facebook Posts From the Top 20,000 Brands*. Buffer e Buzz. Available (consulted 20 February 2019) at: https://buffer.com/resources/facebook-marketing-strategy?_ga=2.9742389.1082984056.155378289 8-1045434845.1552924978>.

Pew Research Center. (2016) *Social Media Update 2016*. Pew Research Center. Available (consulted 30 January 2017) at: http://www.pewinternet.org/2016/11/11/social-media-update-2016/.

Pichai S. (2015) *2015's Founders letter*. Google. Available (consulted 14 February 2019) at: https://abc.xyz/investor/founders-letters/2015/.

Pichai S. (2018) *Hearing of the Judiciary Comittee*. U. S. House of Representatives. 11 December 2018.

Pichai, S. (2020) Alphabet's Q1 2020 earnings call. Keyword, 28, April. Available (consulted 30 September) at: https://blog.google/alphabet/alphabets-q1-2020-earnings-call/.

Piper, K. (2019) Exclusive: Google cancels AI ethics board in response to outcry. Vox, april, 4. Available (consulted 2 October) at: https://www.vox.com/future-perfect/2019/4/4/18295933/google-cancels-ai-ethics-board.

Pita M. and Valente J. C. L. (2018) *Monopólios Digitais: concentração e diversidade na Internet*. São Paulo: INTERVOZES. Available (consulted 20 August 2018) at: http://intervozes.org.br/arquivos/interlivo12monodig.pdf.

Polder M. et al. (2009) *Micro and macro indicators of competition: comparison and relation with productivity change*. Statistics Netherlands. MPRA Paper No 18898. Available (consulted 30 September 2019) at: https://mpra.ub.uni-muenchen.de/18898/.

Pon B., Seppälä T. and Kenney M. (2014) Android and the demise of operating system-based power: Firm strategy and platform control in the post-PC world. *Telecommunications Policy*, v. 38, n. 11, 979–991.

Portelli, H. (2002). *Gramsci eo bloco histórico*. São Paulo: Paz e terra.

Poulantzas N. (1981) *O Estado, o Poder, o Socialismo*. São Paulo: Ed. Graal.

Poushter J. (2016) *Smartphone Ownership and Internet Usage Continues to Climb in Emerging Economies*. Pew Research Center. Available at: http://www.pewresearch.org/wp-content/uploads/sites/2/2016/02/pew_research_center_global_technology_report_final_february_22__2016.pdf.

Preskill J. (2019) Why I coined the term "quantum supremacy". Wired, 6, October. Available (consulted 6 October 2020) at: https://www.wired.com/story/why-i-coined-the-term-quantum-supremacy/.

Priotti M. (2020) Final FTC Agreement Represents a New Level of Accountability for Privacy. Facebook Newsoom, 23, April. Available (consulted 30 October 2020) at: https://about.fb.com/news/2020/04/final-ftc-agreement/.

Priotti M. (2020b) Fighting Platform Abuse, Simplifying Privacy in Groups, and Protecting Information While Sharing Data. Facebook Newsoom, 18, June. Available (consulted 30 October 2020) at: https://about.fb.com/news/2020/06/privacy-improvements/.

Qiang C.Z., Rossotto C.M. and Kimura K. (2009) Economic impacts of broadband. *Information and communications for development 2009*, 35–50.

Quattrociocchi W., Scala A. and Sunstein C.R. (2016) Echo Chambers on Facebook. *Ssrn Electronic Journal*, [s.l.].

Quijano A. (2011) Colonialidad del poder y clasificación social. *Contextualizaciones Latinoamericanas*, n. 5.

Quintarelli S. (2015) On Rights and Competition Citizen's Rights and Business' Rights in a Progressively More Immaterial World. *Rivista Italiana di Antitrust / Italian Antitrust Review*, [s.l.], v. 2, n. 3.

Rait Z. (2011) Introducing the subscribe button. *Facebook Newsroom*, 14 September Available (consulted 23 January 2019) at: https://newsroom.fb.com/news/2011/09/introducing-the-subscribe-button/.

Rajwat P. (2020) The evolution of Facebook Watch. Facebook Newsroom, 3, September. Available (consulted 6 October 2020) at: https://about.fb.com/news/2020/09/the-evolution-of-facebook-watch/.

Raley R. (2013) Dataveillance and countervailance. In: Gitelman L. *Raw data'is an oxymoron*. Cambridge: MIT Press, 121–46.

Ranadive A. and Ginsberg D. (2018) New Tools to Manage Your Time on Facebook and Instagram. *Facebook Newsroom*, 1 August. Available (consulted 28 February 2018) at: https://newsroom.fb.com/news/2018/08/manage-your-time/.

Rawls J. (2009) *A theory of justice*. Boston: Harvard University Press.

Read A. (2018) Life After the News Feed: Why Facebook is Shifting to Stories (And Why Your Business Should Too). *Business2community*, 27 November. Available (consulted 20 March 2019) at: https://www.business2community.com/brandviews/buffer/life-after-the-news-feed-why-facebook-is-shifting-to-stories-and-why-your-business-should-too-02145045.

Recuero R. (2012) *A rede é a mensagem: Efeitos da Difusão de Informações nos Sites de Rede Social.* Lo que Mcluhan no previó. 1ed. Buenos Aires: Editorial La Crujía, 205–223.

Reda J. (2019) The text of Article 13 and the EU Copyright Directive has just been finalised. *JuliaReda.Eu*, 13 February. Available (consulted 23 January 2019) at: https://juliareda.eu/2019/02/eu-copyright-final-text/.

Reporters Without Borders. (2018) The Network Enforcement Act apparently leads to excessive blocking of content. *Reporters without borders*, 3 August Available at: https://rsf.org/en/news/network-enforcement-act-apparently-leads-excessive-blocking-content.

Reuters Institute (2018) *Digital news report 2018.* London, UK: Reuters Institute.

Reuters Institute (2020) *Digital News Report 2020.* London UK: Reuters Institute.

Reynolds M. (2017) If you can't build it, buy it: Google's biggest acquisitions mapped. *Wired*, 25 November Available at: https://www.wired.co.uk/article/google-acquisitions-data-visualisation-infoporn-waze-youtube-android.

Ribeiro M. H., Ottoni R., West R., Almeida V. A. and Meira Jr W. (2020, January) Auditing radicalization pathways on youtube. In *Proceedings of the 2020 Conference on Fairness, Accountability, and Transparency* (pp. 131–141).

Riley C. (2019) Google and Facebook run into more trouble over data in Europe. CNN Business, 2, December. Available (consulted 26 September 2020) at: https://edition.cnn.com/2019/12/02/tech/google-facebook-data-europe/index.html.

Rochet J.C., Tirole J. (2003) Platform competition in two-sidded markets. *Journal of the European Economic Association,* n. 1(4), June, 990 –1029.

Rodriguez S. (2019) Facebook acquires the maker of popular 'Beat Saber' VR game. CNBC, november, 26. Available (consulted 30 September) at: https://www.cnbc.com/2019/11/26/facebook-buys-beat-saber-vr-game-maker-beat-games.html.

Roettgers J. (2020) How Google kneecapped Amazon's smart TV efforts. Protocol, 11, March. Available (consulted 21 September 2020) at: https://www.protocol.com/google-android-amazon-fire-tv.

Roland Berger. (2017) *Digitalization for the people: an agenda for more growth, better education and equal opportunities in G20 countries.* Munich, Germany: Roland Berger.

Roland Berger. (2017a) *Mastering the industrial internet of things.* Roland Berger. Available (consulted 29 August 2018) at: www.rolandberger.com/Fpublications/Fpublication_pdf/Froland_berger_industrial_internet_of_things_1.pdf&usg=AOvVaw1VH09VDJIrnK3qTHHkirs6.

Romero E. (2005) *Marx e a técnica: um estudo dos manuscritos de 1861–1863.* São Paulo: Ed. Expressão Popular.

Romm T. and Lerman R. (2020) Facebook acquires Giphy, a popular search engine for viral, animated images. The Washington Post, 15, May. Available (consulted 29 September 2020) at: https://www.washingtonpost.com/technology/2020/05/15/facebook-acquires-giphy/.

Ronayane D. (2018) *Price Comparison website.* Warwick economic research papers, No 1056.

Rosen G. (2020) Investment to fight polarization. Facebook Newsroom, 27, May. Available (consulted 29 September 2020) at: https://about.fb.com/news/2020/05/investments-to-fight-polarization/.

Rosen J. (2012) The right to be forgotten. *Stanford Law Review. Online*; 64:88.

Rosenblat A., Kneese T., and Boyd D. (2014) Algorithmic Accountability. A workshop primer produced for: *The Social, Cultural & Ethical Dimensions of "Big Data"*. New York, March 17.

Rosenblum N. (1997) *A world history of photography*. New York: Abbeville.

Rubin, P. (2019) Google Stadia Lands This Year – If You're Willing to Pony Up. Wired, 6, June. Available (consulted 26 September 2020) at: https://www.wired.com/story/google-stadia-release/?itm_campaign=TechinTwo.

Rule J.B. (2007) *Privacy in peril: How we are sacrificing a fundamental right in exchange for security and convenience*. Oxford: Oxford University Press.

Rushe D. (2013) Facebook and Google insist they did not know of Prism surveillance program. *The Guardian*, 8 June. Available (consulted 20 February 2019) at: https://www.theguardian.com/world/2013/jun/07/google-facebook-prism-surveillance-program.

Russell et al. (2015) *Autonomous weapons: an open letter from AI & Robotics researchers*. Available (consulted 12 February 2020) at: https://futureoflife.org/open-letter-autonomous-weapons/.

Russell S.J. and Norvi G. (2016) *Artificial intelligence: a modern approach*. Malaysia: Pearson Education Limited.

Saad-Filho A. (2015) Neoliberalismo: uma análise marxista. *Marx e o Marxismo – Revista do NIEP*, v. 3 n. 4.

Saad-Filho, A. (2019) Crisis in neoliberalism or crisis of neoliberalism?. In *Value and Crisis: Essays on Labour, Money and Contemporary Capitalism,* Boston: Brill Academica Publishing, 302–318.

Safi M. (2018) 'WhatsApp murders': India struggles to combat crimes linked to messaging service. *The Guardian*, 3 July. Available (consulted 30 December 2018) at: https://www.theguardian.com/world/2018/jul/03/whatsapp-murders-india-struggles-to-combat-crimes-linked-to-messaging-service.

Sánchez-Ocaña A.S. (2012) *Desnudando a Google: la inquietante realidad que no quieren que conozcas*. Madrid, Spain: Grupo Planeta (GBS).

Sandvig C. (2013) *The Internet as Infrastructure*. Oxford: Oxford Handbooks Online.

Santos F. and Cypriano C.P. (2014) Redes sociais, redes de sociabilidade. *Revista Brasileira de Ciências Sociais*, [s.l.], v. 29, n. 85, 63–78, June.

Satariano A. (2020) Facebook Loses Antitrust Decision in Germany Over Data Collection. The New York Times, 23, June. Available (consulted 28 September 2020) at: https://www.nytimes.com/2020/06/23/technology/facebook-antitrust-germany.html.

Schechner S. Grind K. and West, J. (2020) Searching for vídeo? Google pushes YouTube over rivals. The Wall Street Journal, 14, July. Available (consulted 28 September 2020) at: https://www.wsj.com/articles/google-steers-users-to-youtube-over-rivals-11594745232.

Schmidt E. (2007) *Re: WC Docket No. 06-150; PS Docket No. 06-229; WT Docket No. 96-86*. Documento enviado para a Comissão Federal de Comunicações em 20 de julho de 2007. Available (consulted 15 January 2019) at: http://googlepress.blogspot.com/2007/07/google-intends-to-bid-in-spectrum_20.html.

Scholz T. (2016) *Platform cooperativism. Challenging the corporate sharing economy.* New York, NY: Rosa Luxemburg Foundation.

Scholz T. (2017) *Uberworked and underpaid: How workers are disrupting the digital economy.* Hoboken, US: John Wiley & Sons.

Schrage E. (2012) The Facebook site governance vote. *Facebook Newsroom*, 1 June Available (consulted 17 January 2019) at: https://newsroom.fb.com/news/2012/06/the-facebook-site-governance-vote/.

Schroeder R. and Cowls J. (2014) *Big Data, Ethics, and the Social Implications of Knowledge Production.* Apresentado no Workshop Data Ethics. Nova York. 24 August.

Schwab, K. (2019). *A quarta revolução industrial.* São Paulo: Edipro.

Sclove R. (1995) *Democracy and technology.* New York: Guilford Press.

Sclove R. (2009) Strong democracy and technology. In: Kaplan D.M. (ed.). *Readings in the Philosophy of Technology.* Lanham, US: Rowman & Littlefield Publishers.

Searchking vs. Google. (2003) *Case No. Civ-02-1457-M (W.D.).* Okla., 13 January.

Seaver, N. (2019) Knowing algorithms. In: Vertesi J. and Ribes D. *Digitalsts: a field guide for science & technology studies.* Princeton: Princeton University Press.

Seidl T. (2020) The Politics of Platform Capitalism. A Case Study on the Regulation of Uber in New York. Available (consulted by 20 July, 2020) at: https://onlinelibrary.wiley.com/doi/epdf/10.1111/rego.12353.

Sensor Tower. (2017) *Sensor Tower's Q3 2017 report.* San Francisco, US: Sensor Tower.

Shinal J. (2017) Mark Zuckerberg couldn't buy Snapchat years ago, and now he's close to destroying the company. *CNBC Tech*, 12 July. Available (consulted 23 February 2019) at: https://www.cnbc.com/2017/07/12/how-mark-zuckerberg-has-used-instagram-to-crush-evan-spiegels-snap.html.

Shukla S. and Lyons T. (2017) Blocking ads from pages that repeatedly share false news. *Facebook Newsroom*, 28 August. Available (consulted 13 January 2019) at: https://newsroom.fb.com/news/2017/08/blocking-ads-from-pages-that-repeatedly-share-false-news/.

Silicon Valley Rising. (2016) *Tech's invisible workforce.* San Francisco: Silicon Valley Rising.

Silva S.P. (2012) Internet em redes de alta velocidade: concepções e fundamentos sobre banda larga. In: Silva S.P. and Biondi A. *Caminhos para a universalização da Internet banda larga: experiências internacionais e desafios brasileiros.* São Paulo: INTERVOZES, 79–114.

Silveira S. A. (2020). Discursos sobre regulação e governança algorítmica. *Estudos de Sociologia*, 25(48).

Silverman C. (2016) This Analysis Shows How Fake Election News Stories Outperformed Real News on Facebook. *Buzzfeed News*,16 November. Available (consulted 15 February 2019) at: https://www.buzzfeed.com/craigsilverman/viral-fake-election-news-outperformed-real-news-on-facebook.

Simo F. (2020) Paid events online for small business revovery. Facebook Newsroom, 14, August. Available (consulted 25 September 2020) at: https://about.fb.com/news/2020/08/paid-online-events/.

Singh M. (2020) Whatsapp introduces new limit on message forwards to fight spread of misinformation. Tech Crunch, 7, April. Available (consulted 30 September 2020) at: https://techcrunch.com/2020/04/07/whatsapp-rolls-out-new-limit-on-message-forwards/.

Slee T. (2015) *What´s yours is mine: against the sharing economy.* New York: OR Books.

Smith M.R. and Marx L. (Eds.) (1994a) *Does technology drive history?* The dilemma of technological determinism. Cambridge: MIT Press.

Solon O. (2016) Facebook's fake news: Mark Zuckerberg rejects 'crazy idea' that it swayed voters. *The Guardian,* 10 November. Available (consulted 25 January 2019) at: https://www.theguardian.com/technology/2016/nov/10/facebook-fake-news-us-election-mark-zuckerberg-donald-trump.

Solon O. (2017) Underpaid and overburdened: the life of a Facebook moderator. *The Guardian*, 25 May. Available (consulted 27 May 2018) at:https://www.theguardian.com/news/2017/may/25/facebook-moderator-underpaid-overburdened-extreme-content.

Solon O. and Farivar C. (2019) Mark Zuckerberg leveraged Facebook user data to fight rivals and help friends, leaked documents show. NBC News, 16, April. Available (consulted 30 september 2020) at: https://www.nbcnews.com/tech/social-media/mark-zuckerberg-leveraged-facebook-user-data-fight-rivals-help-friends-n994706.

Solon, O (202) Sensitive to claims of bias, Facebook relaxed misinformation rules for conservative pages. NBC News, 7, August. 2020. Available (consulted 30 september 2020) at: https://www.nbcnews.com/tech/tech-news/sensitive-claims-bias-facebook-relaxed-misinformation-rules-conservative-pages-n1236182.

Sophia P. (2018) The history of Google platform. *Linux Academy*, 12 December. Available (consulted 02 January 2019) at: https://linuxacademy.com/blog/gcp/history-google-cloud-platform/.

Sousa Júnior, J.G. and Rampim T.T.D. (2016) Introdução Crítica ao Direito à Informação e à Comunicação na Perspectiva de "O Direito Achado na Rua In: Sousa Junior J.G. et. al (Org), *O Direito Achado na Rua*, v. 8: Introdução crítica ao direito à comunicação e à informação, Brasília: FACUnB.

Spangler T (2019) YouTube Now Has 2 Billion Monthly Users, Who Watch 250 Million Hours on TV Screens Daily. Variety, 3 May. Available (consulted 25 September 2020) at: https://variety.com/2019/digital/news/youtube-2-billion-users-tv-screen-watch-time-hours-1203204267/.

Sparrow B., Liu J. and Wegner D.M. (2011) Google effects on memory: Cognitive consequences of having information at our fingertips. *Science*, n. 333, 776–778.

Spinik A. and Zimmer M. (Eds.) (2008) *Websearch: Mulidisciplinary perspectives*. Berlin, Heidelberg: Springer.

Srnicek N. (2017) *Platform Capitalism*. Cambridge: Polity Press.

Staab, S. and Nachtwey, O. (2016) Market and Labour Control in Digital Capitalism. *Triplec: Communication, Capitalism & Critique*. Open Access Journal for a Global Sustainable Information Society, [s.l.], v. 14, n. 2.

Staff of SEC (2020) Staff Reporto n Algorithmic Trading in U.S. Capital Markets. U.S. Securities and Exchange Comission.

Stallman, R. (2004) *Software libre para una sociedad libre*. Madrid: Traficantes de Sueños, 2004.

Stamos A. (2017) An update on informations operation on Facebook. *Facebook Newsroom*, 06 September. Available (consulted 20 January 2019) at: https://newsroom.fb.com/news/2017/09/information--operations-update/.

Statcounter. (2019) *Search engine Market Share*. Available (consulted 15 February 2019) at: http://gs.statcounter.com/search-engine-market-share#monthly-200901-201902.

Statista. (2018a) *Global market revenue share of leading smartphone applications processor vendors in 2014 and 2017*. Statista. Available (consulted 17 February 2019) at: https://www.statista.com/statistics/233415/global-market-share-of-applications-processor-suppliers/.

Statista. (2018b) *E-commerce market share of leading e-retailers worldwide in 2016, based on GMV.* Statista. Available (consulted 17 February 2019) at: https://www.statista.com/statistics/664814/global-e-commerce-market-share/.

Statista. (2018c) *Global mobile OS market share in sales to end users from 1st quarter 2009 to 2nd quarter 2017*. Statista. Available (consulted 04 March 2019) at: https://www.statista.com/statistics/266136/global-market-share-held-by-smartphone-operating-systems/.

Statista. (2018d) *Share of households with a computer at home worldwide from 2005 to 2017*. Statista.

Statista. (2019a) *Most popular social networks worldwide as of April 2019, ranked by number of active users (in millions)*. Statista. Available (consulted 04 March 2019) at: https://www.statista.com/statistics/272014/global-social-networks-ranked-by-number-of-users/.

Statista. (2019b). *Number of active advertisers on Facebook from 1st quarter 2016 to 1st quarter 2019 (in millions)*. Statista. Available (consulted 27 February 2019) at: https://www.statista.com/statistics/778191/active-facebook-advertisers/.

REFERENCES

Statistic Brain. (2017) *Startup business failure rate by industry.* Los Angeles: Statistic Brain Research Institute.

Stoller M. (2019) Corporate America's Second War With the Rule of Law. Wired, 16, October. Available (consulted 26 September 2020) at: https://www.wired.com/story/corporate-americas-second-war-with-the-rule-of-law/.

Stoy J. (2020) A New Way to Go Live on Facebook From Messenger Rooms. Facebook Newsroom, july, 23. Available (consulted 26 September 2020) at: https://about.fb.com/news/2020/07/go-live-on-facebook-from-messenger-rooms/.

Strecht C. (2013) Global government request report. *Facebook Newsroom,* 27 August. Available (consulted 20 August 2018) at: https://newsroom.fb.com/news/2013/08/global-government-requests-report/.

Struhar C. (2014) Finding Popular Conversations on Facebook. *Facebook Newsroom,* 16 January. Available (consulted 25 January 2019) at: https://newsroom.fb.com/news/2014/01/finding-popular-conversations-on-facebook/.

Stucke M. E. and Ezrachi A. (2020). *Competition Overdose: How Free Market Mythology Transformed Us from Citizen Kings to Market Servants.* HarperCollins.

Su C. (2017) Facebook will dith disputed flags on fake news and display links to trustworthy articles instead. *Techcrunch,* 20 December. Available (consulted 26 February 2018) at: https://techcrunch.com/2017/12/20/facebook-will-ditch-disputed-flags-on-fake-news-and-display-links-to-trustworthy-articles-instead/.

Su S. (2018) An update on MyanMarch *Facebook Newsroom,* 15 August. Available (consulted 14 February 2019) at: https://newsroom.fb.com/news/2018/08/update-on-myanmar/.

Sullivan D. (2011) How Google Instant's Autocomplete Suggestions Work. *Search Engine Land,* 6 April.

Sullivan, J. (2020) Introducing a forwarding limit on messenger. Facebook Blog, 3 september. Available (consulted by 23 april 2021) at: https://about.fb.com/news/2020/09/introducing-a-forwarding-limit-on-messenger/.

Sullivan, J. (2020) Introducing forward limting on Messenger. Facebook Newsroom, september, 3. Available (consulted 29 September 2020) at: https://about.fb.com/news/2020/09/introducing-a-forwarding-limit-on-messenger/.

Sutherland J.R. (1934) "The circulation of newspapers and literary periodicals, 1700–30." *The Library* 4.1, 110–124.

Swierstra T. and Rip A. (2007) Nano-ethics as NEST-ethics: Patterns of Moral Argumentation About New and Emerging Science and Technology. *Nanoethics,* [s.l.], v. 1, n. 1, 3–20.

Taplin J. (2017) *Move fast and break things: How Facebook, Google, and Amazon have cornered culture and what it means for all of us.* London: Palgrave Macmillan.

Taubman P. (2003) *Secret Empire: Eisenhower, The CIA, and the Hidden Story of America's Space Espionage.* New York: Simon and Schuster.

Tavory R. *Teaching iGoogle in East African Universities.* Google Official Blog, 25 July 2008.

Tech Transparency Project (2020) Google is profiting from coronavirus conspiracy sites. Tech Transparency Project, 1st, June. Available (consulted 26 September 2020) at: https://www.techtransparencyproject.org/articles/google-profiting-coronavirus-conspiracy-sites.

Teece D.J. (2010) Business Models, Business Strategy and Innovation. *Long Range Planning*, [s.l.], v. 43, n. 2–3, 172–194.

Tene O. and Polinetsky J. (2012) Privacy in the age of Big Data. *Stanford Law Review Online* 63, 2 February.

Terranova T. (2013) Free labor, in Scholz, T. (ed.) *Digital labor: The internet as playground and factory*. New York: Routledge.

The Economist. (2014) The future of jobs. *The Economist*, 18 January Available (consulted 28 December 2018) at: https://www.economist.com/briefing/2014/01/18/the-onrushing-wave.

The Economist. (2017a) The world's most valuable resource is no longer oil, but data. *The Economist*, 6 May. Available (consulted 24 January 2019) at: https://www.economist.com/leaders/2017/05/06/the-worlds-most-valuable-resource-is-no-longer-oil-but-data.

The Economist. (2017b) Google leads in the race to dominate artificial intelligence. *The Economist*, 7 December. Available (consulted 24 January 2019) at: https://www.economist.com/business/2017/12/07/google-leads-in-the-race-to-dominate-artificial-intelligence.

The Economist. (2018a) How to tame tech titans. *The Economist*, 18 January. Available at: https://www.economist.com/leaders/2018/01/18/how-to-tame-the-tech-titans.

Tiku N. (2018) Google Walkout Is Just the Latest Sign of Tech Worker Unrest. Wired, 1st, November. Available (consulted 26 September 2020) at: https://www.wired.com/story/google-walkout-just-latest-sign-tech-worker-unrest/.

Tiku N. (2019a) Google Walkout Organizers Say They're Facing Retaliation. Wired, 22, April. Available (consulted 26 September 2020) at: https://www.wired.com/story/google-walkout-organizers-say-theyre-facing-retaliation/.

Tiku N. (2019b) Three Years of Misery Inside Google, the Happiest Company in Tech. Wired, August, 13. Available (consulted 26 September) at: https://www.wired.com/story/inside-google-three-years-misery-happiest-company-tech/.

Tivo (2017) *Q4 2017 online video & pay-tv trends report*. San Jose, US: Tivo.

Tivo (2019) Video trends report Q2 2019. Tivo. Available (consulted by 23 march 2020) at: https://blog.tivo.com/news/trends-and-research/tivo-q2-2019-video-trends-report/.

Törpel B. et al. (2009) Participatory design: issues and approaches in dynamic constellations of use, design, and research. In: Voss A. et al (Eds.). *Configuring User-Designer Relations*. London: Springer.

Tosswill C. (2015) How the Reactions Test Will Impact Ranking. *Facebook Newsroom*, 8 October. Available (consulted 23 November 2018) at: https://newsroom.fb.com/news/2015/10/news-feed-fyi-how-the-reactions-test-will-impact-ranking/.

Trefis. (2018) How Discrete GPU Market Growth Can Boost Nvidia's Results. *Forbes*, 12 March Available at: https://www.forbes.com/sites/greatspeculations/2018/03/12/how-discrete-gpu-market-growth-can-boost-nvidias-results/#3391fe301dd8.

Trielli D. and Diakopoulos N. (2019, May). Search as news curator: The role of Google in shaping attention to news information. In *Proceedings of the 2019 CHI Conference on Human Factors in Computing Systems* (pp. 1–15).

Trigueiro M.G.S. (2009) *Sociologia da Tecnologia: bioprospecção e legitimação*. Curitiba: Ed. Centauro.

Tubular Labs. (2017) *Q3 2017 State of Online Video Report*. Mountain View, US: Tubular Labs.

Tufecki Z. (2018) Youtube: the great radicalizer. *The New York Times*, 10 March. Available (consulted 26 February 2019) at: https://www.nytimes.com/2018/03/10/opinion/sunday/youtube-politics-radical.html.

Tugend A. (2014) Its unclearly defined, but telecomutting is on the rise. *The New York Times*, 8 March. Available (consulted 18 August 2018) at: https://www.nytimes.com/2014/03/08/your-money/when-working-in-your-pajamas-is-more-productive.html?_r=1.

Tung, L (2015) Android fragmentation: There are now 24,000 devices from 1,300 brands. ZDNet, 6 august. Available (consulted by 10 february 2019) at: https://www.zdnet.com/article/android-fragmentation-there-are-now-24000-devices-from-1300-brands/.

Tutle B. (2018) All the Celebrities and Companies Cutting Ties With Facebook Because of Privacy Concerns. *Money.com*, 29 March. Available (consulted 24 February 2019) at: http://money.com/money/5220854/delete-facebook-celebrities-companies-cutting-ties-privacy/

Twenge J.M., Martin G.N. and Campbell W.K. (2018) Decreases in psychological well-being among American adolescents after 2012 and links to screen time during the rise of smartphone technology. *Emotion*, [s.l.], v. 18, n. 6, 765–780.

U.S. Bureau of Labor Statistics (2020) Employment by major industry sector. Available (consulted 20 august 2020) at: https://www.bls.gov/emp/tables/employment-by-major-industry-sector.htm.

Uber (2020) Annual Report 2019. San Francisco: Uber.

Unesco. (1983) *Um mundo e muitas vozes: comunicação e informação na nossa época*. Comissão Internacional para o Estudo dos Problemas da Comunicação, Paris: Unesco.

United Nations (1948) *Declaração Universal dos Direitos Humanos*. New York: United Nations.

US Census Bureau. (1999) *Statistical Abstract of the United States: 1999*. Section 31: 20th Century Statistics. Suitland, US: US Census Bureau.

Vaidhyanathan S. (2011) *The Googlization of everything: (and why we should worry)*. Berkley, University of California Press.

Valente J. C. L. (2012) Planos nacionais de banda larga e o papel dos Estados na universalização do serviço. In: Da Silva S.P. and Biondi A. (org.). *Caminhos para a Universalização da banda larga: experiências internacionais e desafios brasileiros*. São Paulo: INTERVOZES.

Valente J. C. L. (2018) Presidente do Facebook admite falha na proteção de dados dos usuários. *Agência Brasil*, 10 April. Available (consulted 23 March 2019) at: http://agenciabrasil.ebc.com.br/internacional/noticia/2018-04/presidente-do-facebook-admite-falha-na-protecao-de-dados-dos-usuarios.

Valente, J.C.L. (2009a). Sistema público de comunicação do Reino Unido. *Sistemas Públicos de Comunicação no Mundo: Experiência de Doze países e o Caso Brasileiro*. São Paulo: Paulus; Intervozes.

Valente, J.C.L. (2009b). Sistema público de comunicação da Alemanha. *Sistemas Públicos de Comunicação no Mundo*. São Paulo: Paulus; Intervozes.

Valente, J.C.L. (2019) MJ abre investigação contra Google por invasão de privacidade. Agência Brasil, 7 February. Available (consulted 23 march 2019) at: https://agenciabrasil.ebc.com.br/geral/noticia/2019-02/mj-abre-investigacao-contra-google-por-violacao-privacidade.

Valinski J. (2020) Google updates Maps to show how bad Covid is in your area. CNN Business, 24, September. Available (consulted 28 September 2020) at: https://edition.cnn.com/2020/09/24/tech/google-maps-coronavirus/index.html.

Vallas S. P. (2019) Platform capitalism: what's at stake for workers?. In *New Labor Forum* (Vol. 28, No. 1, pp. 48–59). Los Angeles, CA: Sage Publications.

Van Couvering E. (2008) The history of the Internet search engine: Navigational media and the traffic commodity. In: Spink A. and Zimmer M. *Web search 2008*. Berlin, Heidelberg: Springer, 177–206.

Van Der Wielen B. (2018) Insights into the 2.3 Billion Android Smartphones in Use Around the World. *Newzoo*, 17 January. Available (consulted 4 March 2018) at: https://newzoo.com/insights/articles/insights-into-the-2-3-billion-android-smartphones-in-use-around-the-world/.

Van Dijck J. (2013) *The culture of connectivity: A critical history of social media*. Oxford: Oxford University Press.

Van Dijck J. (2014) Datafication, dataism and dataveillance: Big Data between scientific paradigm and ideology. *Surveillance & Society*, v. 9, n. 12.

Van Dijck, J. (2020). Seeing the forest for the trees: Visualizing platformization and its governance. *New Media & Society*, 1461444820940293.

Van Dijck, J., Poell, T. and De Waal, M. (2018) *The platform society: Public values in a connective world.* Oxford University Press.

Van Gorp N. and O. Batura. (2015) *Challenges for Competition Policy in a Digitalised Economy, study for the European Parliament.* Available (consulted 02 June 2017) at: http://www.europarl.Europa.eu/RegData/etudes/STUD/2015/542235/IPOL_STU%.

Veblen T. (2001) *The engineers and the price system.* Ontario, CA: Batoche Books.

Veblen T. (2017) *The instinct of workmanship and the state of the industrial arts.* New York: Routledge.

Velasquez, A. and Montgomery, G. (2020) Social Media Expression as a Collective Strategy: How Perceptions of Discrimination and Group Status Shape US Latinos' Online Discussions of Immigration. *Social Media+ Society*, 6(1), 2056305120914009.

Vesnic-Alujevic L. (2012) Political participation and web 2.0 in Europe: A case study of Facebook. *Public Relations Review*, v. 38, n. 3, 466–470.

Video Advertising Bureau (2017) *Be still my viewing heart.* New York: Video advertising Bureau.

Villani C. (2018) *For a meaningful artificial intelligence: towards a French and European strategy.* Paris: Conseil national du numérique.

Vincent J. (2020) Google's $2.1 billion Fitbit acquisition is getting closer scrutiny from EU regulators. The Verge, 3, July. Available (consulted 24 September 2020) at: https://www.theverge.com/2020/7/3/21312383/google-fibit-acquisition-antitrust-data-regulatory-eu-scrutiny.

Vines J. et al. (2013) Configuring participation: on how we involve people in design. In: *Proceedings of the SIGCHI Conference on Human Factors in Computing Systems.* ACM, 429–438.

Viollier. (2017) *El estado de la protección de datos em Chile.* Santiago, Chile: Derechos Digitales.

Vogelstein F. and Knight W. (2020) Wired, 5, May. Available (consulted 26 September, 2020) at: https://www.wired.com/story/health-officials-no-thanks-contact-tracing-tech/.

Wacjman J. (2010) Feminist theories of technology. *Cambridge journal of economics*, v. 34, n. 1.

Wakefield, J. (2020) Facebook staffer sends 'blood on my hands' memo. BBC News, 15, September. Available (consulted 27 September 2020) at: https://www.bbc.com/news/technology-54161344.

Wall M. and El Zahed S. (2011) The Arab Spring|" I'll Be Waiting for You Guys": A YouTube Call to Action in the Egyptian Revolution. *International Journal of Communication.* v. 5, 1333–1343.

Wallach, O. (2021) Wich streaming service has the most subscriptions? World Economic Forum, 10 march. Available (consulted by 15 march 2021) at: https://www.weforum.org/agenda/2021/03/streaming-service-subscriptions-lockdown-demand-netflix-amazon-prime-spotify-disney-plus-apple-music-movie-tv/.

Warzel C. and Mac R. (2018) These Confidential Charts Show Why Facebook Bought WhatsApp. *Buzzfeednews,* 5 December. Available (consulted 3 February 2019) at: https://www.buzzfeednews.com/article/charliewarzel/why-facebook-bought-whatsapp.

Watson F. (2011a) Google's Knol Seems To Be Unit Of Knowledge People Don't Use. *Search Engine Watch*, 20 January Available at: https://searchenginewatch.com/sew/news/2050149/googles-knol-seems-to-be-unit-of-knowledge-people-dont-use.

Watson F. (2011b). Google Shutting Down Knol & 6 More Failed Products. *Search Engine Watch*, 23 November Available at: https://searchenginewatch.com/sew/news/2127299/google-shutting-knol-failed-products.

We Are Social (2020) *Digital 2020.* We Are Social. Available (consulted 20 march 2021) at: https://wearesocial.com/digital-2020.

We Are Social. (2017) *Global Digital Report 2017.* New York: We are social.

We Are Social. (2019) *Global Digital Report 2019.* New York: We are social.

Webb A. (2019) *The big nine: how the tech titans and their thinking machines could warp humanity.* New York: Public Affairs.

Weber M. (1980) *História geral da economia.* 2. ed. São Paulo: Abril Cultural.

Weber M. (1991) *Economia e sociedade.* Fundamentos de economia compreensiva – Volume I. Brasília: UNB.

Weber M. (2004) *A ética protestante e o espírito do capitalismo.* São Paulo: Companhia das Letras.

Weber M. (2005) Remarks on Technology and Culture. *Theory, Culture & Society,* [s.l.], v. 22, n. 4, 23–38.

Webster F. (2014) *Theories of the information society.* New York: Routledge.

Weller T. (2012) The information state An historical perspective on surveillance. In: Lyon D., Ball K. and Haggerty K.D: eds. *Routledge handbook of surveillance studies.* Routledge.

Westin A. (1967) *Privacy and freedom.* New York: Athenaeum.

Whittaker Z. (2019) Facebook failed to download 20% of uploads New Zealand shooter videos. *Techcrunch,* 17 March Available at: https://techcrunch.com/2019/03/17/facebook-new-zealand/. (consulted 22 March 2019.

Wiggins R. (2001) Google acquires deja.com. *Information Today Inc,* 19 February. Available (consulted 18 July 2017) at:http://newsbreaks.infotoday.com/NewsBreaks/Google-Acquires-Dejacom-17652.asp

Williams M. (2014) Building a more diverse Facebook. *Facebook Newsroom,* 25 June. Available (consulted 23 January 2019) at: https://newsroom.fb.com/news/2014/06/building-a-more-diverse-facebook/.

Williams R. (1960) *Culture & society: 1780–1950.* New York: Doubleday Anchor.

Williams R. (1977) *Marxism and literature.* Oxford: Oxford University Press.

Williams R. (2017) *Televisão: tecnologia e forma cultural.* São Paulo: Boitempo Editorial.

Williams, R. (2004). *Television: Technology and cultural form.* London: Routledge.

Winner L. (1980) *Do artifacts have politics?* Cambs, UK: Daedalus.

Winner L. (1986) *The whale and the reactor: A search for limits in an age of high technology.* Chicago: University of Chicago Press.

Winner L. (2016) Decadencia y caída del tecnotriunfalismo. REDES. *Revista de estudios sociales de la ciencia y la tecnologia.* v. 43.

Winters K. (2015) Improving the Experience When Relationships End. *Facebook Newsroom*, 19 November. Available (consulted 30 August 2018) at: https://newsroom.fb.com/news/2015/11/improving-the-experience-when-relationships-end/.

Wired (2020) Google Search Now Reads at a Higher Level. Wired, 25, October. Available (consulted 27 September 2020) at: https://www.wired.com/story/google-search-advancing-grade-reading/.

Wired. (2000) Yahoo goes gaga for Google. *Wired*, 26 June. Available (consulted 13 March 2018) at: https://www.wired.com/2000/06/yahoo-goes-gaga-for-google/.

Wobbe W., Bova E. and Gaina C.D. (2016) *The digital economy and the single market.* Brussels: Foundation for European Progressive Studies.

Woolgar S. and Lezaun J. (2013) The wrong bin bag: A turn to ontology in science and technology studies? *Social studies of science*, v. 43, n. 3, 321–340.

Woollacott W. (2019) Google Tightens Up Privacy Controls For Assistant Voice Recordings. Forbes, September, 23. Available (consulted 28 September 2020) at: https://www.forbes.com/sites/emmawoollacott/2019/09/23/google-tightens-up-privacy-controls-for-assistant-voice-recordings/#40eca9725d2a.

World Bank. (2017) *Annual report.* World bank. Available (consulted 18 September 2018) at: http://documents.worldbank.org/curated/en/143021506909711004/World-Bank-Annual-Report-2017.

World Bank. (2017) *Fixed telephone lines (per 100 people).* Databank, WORLD BANK. Available (consulted 24 July 2017) at:http://data.worldbank.org/indicator/IT.MLT.MAIN.P2.

World Economic Forum. (2016) *Digital enterprises.* World Economic Forum White Paper on Digital Transformation of industries. World Economic Forum.

World Economic Forum. (2018) *Digital Transformation Initiative.* World Economic Forum.

Wu T. (2012) *The master switch: The rise and fall of information empires.* New York: Vintage.

Yeo L. (2020) Uber vs. Lyft: Who's tops in the battle of U.S. rideshare companies. Second Measure, 16, September. Available (consulted 24 September 2020) at: https://secondmeasure.com/datapoints/rideshare-industry-overview/.

Yin R.K. (2001) *Estudo de Caso: Planejamento e métodos.* Porto Alegre: Bookman.

Youtube. (2007) YouTube elevates most popular users to partners. *YouTube Official Blog*, 3 May. Available (consulted 20 March 2018) at: https://youtube.googleblog.com/2007/05/youtube-elevates-most-popular-users-to.html.

Zallo R. (1988) *Economía de la comunicación y la cultura*. Madrid, Spain: Ediciones Akal.

Zarsky T. (2016) The trouble with algorithmic decisions: An analytic road map to examine efficiency and fairness in automated and opaque decision making. *Science, Technology, & Human Values*, v. 41, n. 1.

Zhang Y. and Leung L. (2015) A review of social networking service (SNS) research in communication journals from 2006 to 2011. *New Media & Society*, v. 17, n. 7, 1007–1024.

Zhao, Y., Von Delft, S., Morgan-Thomas, A. and Buck, T. (2020) The evolution of platform business models: Exploring competitive battles in the world of platforms. *Long Range Planning, 53*(4).

Zuboff S. (2015) Big other: surveillance capitalism and the prospects of an information civilization. *Journal of Information Technology*, v. 30, n.1.

Zuboff S. (2019) *The age of surveillance capitalism: The fight for a human future at the new frontier of power*. New York: PublicAffairs.

Zuckerberg M. (2011) Our commitment to the Facebook community. *Facebook Newsroom*, 29 November. Available (consulted 23 October 2018) at: https://newsroom.fb.com/news/2011/11/our-commitment-to-the-facebook-community/

Zuckerberg M. (2013) Personal response from Mark Zuckerberg about PRISM. *Facebook Newsroom*, 8 June. Available (consulted 19 February 2019) at: https://newsroom.fb.com/news/2013/06/personal-response-from-mark-zuckerberg-about-prism/.

Zuckerberg M. (2016) *Blog do autor*. 19 November. Available (consulted 06 March 2019) at: https://www.facebook.com/zuck/posts/10103269806149061.

Zuckerberg M. (2019). The Internet needs new rules. Let's start in these four areas. *Washington Post*, 30 March. Available (consulted 04 April 2019) at: https://www.washingtonpost.com/opinions/mark-zuckerberg-the-internet-needs-new-rules-lets-start-in-these-four-areas/2019/03/29/9e6f0504-521a-11e9-a3f7-78b7525a8d5f_story.html?noredirect=on&utm_term=.a9066640ce43.

Zuckerberg, M. (2017). Author's blog, 1st november. Available (consulted by 12 april 2019) at: https://www.facebook.com/zuck/posts/10104146268321841.

Index

2007–8 crash   1, 105
3D printing   104
4G   122, 129–130, 137n21

accumulation   1–3, 23, 27, 49, 59, 59n3, 61, 64, 64n18, 66, 71, 74, 88, 92–96, 101–102, 106, 109–110, 112, 121, 135, 154, 167, 226, 350
acquisition   146, 179, 179n57, 179n59, 183, 198, 211, 213n48, 216, 221, 224, 235–236, 255, 265, 275, 287, 310–311, 329, 348, 387
acquisition or equity control strategies of competitors or market players   183
active mediation   157, 184, 321
actor–network theory   21n14, 34, 41, 325n1
administrative rules   185, 331, 335
Adorno and Horkheimer   88
AdSense   197, 201n16, 212, 236, 242, 327
Advertisers   208, 248, 272, 342
advertising   3, 16n7, 77, 87–89, 91, 103, 112, 117, 119, 127, 141–142, 149, 158, 161, 163, 164n26, 167–168, 172n38, 172n40, 171–173, 179, 179n57, 183, 196, 197n10, 197–198, 201, 201n16, 201n17, 205, 207, 211, 211n47, 212n48, 212–213, 216, 222, 225, 236–237, 241, 241n94, 247–249, 254–255, 262, 272, 274–276, 276n31, 283, 285–286, 290, 295, 298, 303n57, 303–304, 308, 311, 317–319, 326–328, 330, 332, 353, 387
AdWords   197, 197n10, 211, 331n14
agency process   142
AI   107, 149n31, 145–150, 162, 285, 336, 348, 350, 352–353, 358, 361, 376, 379
algocracy   142
algorithm alienation   143
algorithms   3, 8, 103, 110, 113–115, 118–119, 122, 125, 127–128, 135n17, 139, 141n27, 141n28, 141–146, 149–150, 157n11, 162n25, 164–165, 195, 195n7, 210n42, 218, 242n97, 244, 256, 261, 297, 309, 317, 321, 327–328, 331n14, 335–336, 342, 354
Alphabet   7
Alphabet/Google   4
Althusser   29

Amazon   3–4, 101, 117, 127, 146, 148, 156, 157n11, 160n19, 160–161, 162n24, 164, 164n27, 172n41, 172–173, 175–184, 197, 202, 210n42, 215, 215n53, 235, 245, 250, 255, 304, 327, 330, 330n11, 333n21, 334n24, 378, 383
analytics   225, 248–249, 289, 311
Android   7
Angwin   113
antitrust   114
Antunes   105
app store   221, 286
application programming interface   262
applications   3, 7, 13, 22–23, 42, 110, 115–116, 116n30, 121–122, 129, 133, 134n16, 134–135, 137, 141, 145–147, 151, 157, 158n13, 163–165, 174, 174n46, 178, 180, 183–184, 196, 198–199, 201, 203n26, 203–204, 206, 212, 215, 217, 220–221, 223–225, 228, 235, 240, 240n91, 246, 250, 260, 262n3, 266, 268, 272, 275, 276n30, 279, 280n36, 286–287, 289–290, 299, 303, 304n59, 310n72, 317, 320, 324, 382
appreciation of value   18
appropriation   9, 11, 14, 17, 17n9, 20–21, 24, 40, 43–46, 61n10, 64, 88–90, 108, 122, 135, 144, 167, 191, 231, 234, 252, 254, 257, 290, 294, 296, 316, 319–322, 331n15, 331–332
architecture   9, 16n6, 66, 127, 129, 143, 152–153, 159, 194, 218, 218n61, 220n67, 220–221, 253, 260–261, 281–282, 284, 287–288, 295–297, 304, 318–319, 369
artefact–commodity   16
artefacts   2–3, 13n4, 16n7, 11–19, 21n14, 21–23, 25, 31, 34, 38, 41, 43–47, 49–50, 50n35, 52, 54–56, 59, 63–65, 73, 81, 98, 108, 126, 134, 150, 165, 167n30, 193, 203–204, 207, 209, 211, 216n57, 216–218, 220, 223–224, 227, 230–232, 238, 244–246, 246n104, 256–258, 260, 266n11, 269, 274, 279, 281, 282n41, 309, 324–325, 330, 366
artificial intelligence   3, 8, 104, 113, 118, 122, 125, 128, 134, 134n16, 139, 144–145, 147, 149n31, 162n25, 182, 210, 223, 225, 227, 243, 246n105, 248, 256, 285–286, 310, 313n77, 317, 323–324, 327–328, 330, 334–335, 358–359, 384, 387

asymmetry of information 114
attention economy 3
audience commodity 167
audience network 275, 286
audiences 45
audiovisual 86–87, 171n36, 182, 221–222, 230, 276, 290, 322, 329, 330n11, 333n22, 333–334, 357
autocomplete 242–243
automation 26n17, 31, 36, 100, 104, 106–107, 112, 119, 142, 144, 146–147, 149–150, 227, 311, 326, 349, 373
automaton 65
autonomous' processing 142
autonomy 2, 8, 12, 26, 30, 32, 34–35, 38, 40, 47, 70, 114, 144, 148, 167, 169, 217n60, 258, 335

backbones 129
backhaul 129
Badiou 29
Becerra and Mastrini 117
behaviour modulation 3, 122, 226n71
Bellofiore 92
Benjamin 75
Berger 96
biases 114
Big Data 2, 8, 104, 107, 113, 122, 124–125, 128, 139–140, 143n29, 155, 162n25, 317, 327, 354, 356, 364, 370, 373, 379–380, 384, 386
Bijker and Pinch 15
bits 98, 121, 134n15
Blogger 198
Bolaño 74
Braverman 72
Briggs and Burke 86
broadband 8, 99–100, 125, 128–131, 161, 317, 347, 354, 366, 377
broadband networks 8, 129–130, 317
broadcasting 78
Brown 85
browser 7, 198, 204n29, 204–205, 213n49, 215, 219–220, 234, 245, 256–257, 331n18
bubble filters 305, 321, 333
Bucirossi 52
Bunge 15

business model 16, 86, 88, 103, 134, 155, 162, 165, 171, 172n40, 191, 196, 208, 211–212, 215, 222, 225, 234, 253–254, 272, 275–276, 278, 318–319, 321n85, 328
business models 9
Buzan 81

cable TV 98, 129
Cambridge Analytica 149, 162, 263, 266, 268, 271, 293, 299, 303, 305, 331n18, 348, 365, 373
capital 2–3, 17–18, 23, 26, 28n21, 30, 42, 46, 53, 53n36, 59n3, 62n11, 62n12, 64n18, 64n20, 67n24, 68n25, 59–69, 71, 73, 73n28, 92n2, 93n3, 89–96, 103–104, 109, 118–119, 121–122, 135, 135n17, 146, 167n31, 170, 197, 226, 253, 255, 326, 342–343, 346, 350, 352, 375
Capital 60
capital turnover 67
capital turnover cycle 17
capital's dynamics 59
capitalism 11
capitalist cycles 74
capitalist system 1, 8, 16, 24, 26, 35, 39, 42, 46, 53–54, 59, 70–71, 73, 91, 93, 101, 118, 123, 151, 170, 190, 226, 324
censorship 185, 189
central processing unit 132
centralization 64, 64n18, 72, 103, 135n17, 146, 153n2, 170, 278
Chesnais 92, 95
Chrome 7
Chun 80
civil society 28
Civil society organizations 209, 273
class struggles 37, 303n55
coaxial cables 104, 129
colonies 37, 56, 81, 91
colonization 56
commodity 16, 18, 20, 23, 27, 46, 57, 59n3, 61–63, 75, 84, 91, 111, 167n31, 167–168, 212, 252, 274, 325, 386
communication 18
Community Standards 269, 269n19, 274, 301
competition 3, 17, 20, 20n12, 22–23, 25, 43–46, 52–53, 64n18, 64–66, 72, 86, 94–96, 98, 101, 104, 110–113, 115, 117, 119, 123, 131,

133, 137–138, 151–152, 152n1, 155, 159, 160n19, 161n22, 160–162, 170–171, 178, 183–185, 185n63, 190–191, 201n16, 201–202, 211, 213, 215, 223–224, 235, 238, 244–245, 245n103, 248, 250, 252, 255–256, 269, 271, 275, 278, 286, 288, 296, 298, 309, 311, 317–318, 326, 328, 330, 334n26, 334–336, 355, 370, 376, 378
competition dynamics   111
competitive advantage   115, 159, 162, 171, 288
competitive performance   6, 179
competitive strategies   4, 9, 119, 184, 191, 278
computer   8, 49, 73, 90, 92, 108n24, 129, 132, 133n11, 133–136, 136n20, 141–142, 145, 165, 198–199, 206, 218n61, 225, 237, 247, 251, 289, 310, 382
concentration   64
concentration of ownership   178
connections   7, 126, 137, 153n3, 155, 155n6, 157, 165, 171, 174, 259, 259n1, 261, 266, 275, 281n38, 283n42, 281–284, 311, 318–319, 321, 334
consent   141, 186–187, 189, 200n12, 201n17, 205, 265n8, 265–266, 303–304
conspiracy theories   4, 242
constant capital   17
consumer surplus   114
consumption   11, 16–18, 20, 24, 31, 39n32, 39–40, 45–46, 54, 74, 84–85, 88–89, 94, 96, 108, 122, 134, 134n15, 149, 151, 159, 162, 168, 173, 175, 208, 216n56, 222, 230, 234, 252, 255, 276, 279, 287, 297, 303n55, 314, 314n80, 318, 324
contemporary capitalism   30, 91–92, 100, 123, 157, 196, 230, 324, 344, 350, 353
content   3–4, 9, 11, 13–16, 18, 29n22, 34–35, 38, 46, 49, 54, 87–89, 98, 108, 116, 116n31, 121–122, 126–127, 129n3, 135, 138, 140, 142, 149–150, 152n1, 152–154, 157n11, 157–158, 161–164, 167–168, 168n32, 171, 171n36, 172n40, 175–176, 178–179, 182–185, 188–192, 193n1, 195, 195n6, 197, 197n10, 199, 202n21, 202–204, 204n28, 208, 211, 213n48, 216, 219, 219n64, 222–223, 225, 233–236, 237n87, 237–241, 242n97, 242n98, 243n101, 242–246, 248, 250, 252, 255, 258–265, 265n6, 267n13, 267–269, 269n20, 271–275, 278–279, 280n36, 280–281, 281n37, 285, 290, 293, 294n50, 294n51, 294–298, 301, 304n58, 306n63, 307n64, 304–309, 312n75, 312–313, 313n77, 317–321, 321n85, 322n86, 322–323, 325, 327–328, 330n11, 330–331, 333, 333n23, 335–336, 377
Content circulation   164
content management   186, 265
content provider   153
contextual properties   14, 16–18, 21, 24, 41, 43–44, 135
contradiction   68
control and management structures   9
control and ownership   19
control points   117, 178, 217, 220–221, 256, 285, 331
control structure   6
Copeland   81
COPPA   201
co-production of knowledge   50
copyright   85, 185, 188–189, 201, 203, 247, 250, 261, 265, 267, 331, 335, 346
Coriat   43
cost-per-click   211
COVID-19   107, 200, 212–213, 241–242, 264, 288, 308
crises   32
critical theory of technology   8, 12, 15, 41, 80, 207, 325
cryptocurrency   264, 346
CTT   15, 41, 46–47, 127, 150, 253, 281n39, 320
cultural industries   89
cultural industry   88n47, 87–90, 114, 167, 251
cultural sphere   83
Culture   31
cyber security   149, 227
cycles   37

Dahlgreen   77
Dantas   76
data colonialism   154
data protection   185–187, 192, 200, 230, 238, 240, 257, 265–266, 294, 303, 320, 322–323, 331, 334n26, 334–335
data violation   230
datafication   2, 104, 122, 140, 222n68, 327, 370
data-governance   140

data-intensive activities 183
datapulation 162
dataveillance 162, 183, 240, 240n90, 350, 386
decentralizing production 121
defensive leveraging 179
Delete Facebook 293
democracy 2, 12, 47–49, 127, 193n1, 239, 295, 297, 302, 303n55, 316, 321, 323, 334, 352, 369–370, 380
design 38
determinism 32
developers 6, 106, 143, 150, 157n10, 159n15, 164, 220–221, 225, 228, 231n81, 235, 262, 262n3, 265n7, 268, 271, 286, 294, 294n49, 299, 304, 304n60, 317, 327
digital 1–2, 4–5, 7–11, 55, 91, 97–98, 100, 106, 108, 108n24, 110–113, 115–118, 120–121, 128, 138–142, 151–152, 154–159, 159n14, 167n31, 161–168, 171, 173–174, 176–185, 185n64, 188–191, 198–200, 206n36, 210n42, 213, 213n48, 215n53, 215–216, 221, 222n68, 222–223, 227, 229–232, 236, 244, 246, 249–251, 255–262, 264–266, 268–271, 273–276, 278–279, 285–288, 290–292, 294n52, 294–296, 299–300, 302–303, 307n64, 309, 309n69, 316n84, 316–318, 320, 322–324, 326–330, 330n13, 332–335, 341–342, 347, 352–353, 360, 364, 366, 370, 372–373, 375, 380, 382, 389
digital devices 1, 11, 110
digital divide 100
digital economy 1
digital ecosystem 4–5, 9–10, 138, 327–328, 330, 334
digital media 100
digital monopolies 9–10, 152, 181, 183–184, 230, 287, 329–330, 332, 334–335
digital platforms 4, 9, 152, 154–155, 157, 161–162, 171, 178, 189, 191, 260
Digital platforms 3, 5, 154, 156, 341, 353, 365
digital technologies 116, 227, 257, 260, 324, 326
digital transformation 1–2, 4–5, 110, 118, 155, 324, 326, 334, 373
Digital Transformation 123, 389
digitalization 1, 92, 106, 108, 111–112, 118–119, 121–122, 135n17, 135–136, 139, 147, 324–325, 327

discrimination 114n28, 113–115, 143–144, 148, 150–151, 156, 238, 243, 263, 308–309, 331n17, 333, 334n26, 375
disinformation 1n1, 5, 149, 186, 189, 242, 263, 297, 302, 304, 306, 308, 312, 313n77, 321, 332–333, 335
dissemination 5, 9, 11, 31, 73, 77n33, 83–84, 88, 90, 97, 103, 122, 126, 128, 139, 155, 161, 167, 181, 189, 235, 262n4, 265n6, 269, 272–273, 292–293, 295, 307, 317, 326n3, 326–328, 332–333
diversification of activities 180–183
dominance relations 29
dominant classes 92
dominant position 174, 258, 266
Dosi 21
Dosi and Orsenigo 21
Doubleclick 198, 242, 255
Duménil and Lévy 92
durability 57
Dussel 37

e-commerce 102
economic sphere 70
economic welfare 52
economy 29
efficiency 13–14, 33, 51, 57–58, 85, 88, 324, 390
Ellul 32
engagement 141, 153n4, 153–154, 172, 211n47, 243, 259, 279, 281, 286, 296, 301, 305, 307–308, 312, 315, 319
Engels 28
enhancing value 64
Enlightenment 56
entrance barriers 111
European Commission 128, 130, 153, 163, 179n58, 202, 265, 354
evolutionary economics 21, 36, 70
evolutionary economists 35
expansion cycles 1n1, 37
expansive cycle 106, 118, 248
exploitation of labour 26, 108, 168
extraordinary profits 72
Ezrachi and Stucke 52

Facebook x, 3–9, 16n7, 20, 55, 101, 111, 116, 127, 138–140, 148, 153, 156, 157n10, 159n15, 160n18, 160n19, 159–163, 167,

INDEX   395

172–176, 179n57, 178–183, 190, 198, 202,
 209–210, 215, 223, 228, 231, 235, 237,
 239, 245–246, 249–250, 253, 255, 262n3,
 264n5, 265n6, 265n7, 266n9, 267n14,
 267n16, 269n19, 258–273, 275–276,
 276n31, 284n43, 286n44, 290n46,
 292n48, 294n50, 294n51, 300n53,
 301n54, 303n56, 303n57, 304n58, 278–
 306, 307n64, 308n67, 308n68, 313n76,
 313n77, 313n79, 314n80, 315n82, 315n83,
 321n85, 307–323, 326n5, 328n7, 328n8,
 328n9, 329n10, 330n12, 330n13, 331n14,
 331n15, 331n16, 331n17, 331n18, 332n20,
 326–334, 334n25, 341–383, 385–390
Facebook Ads 262, 367
Facebook Messenger 7, 173–174, 180, 260–
 261, 270, 273, 276, 285–287, 291, 310–311,
 351, 373
Facebook Platform 260, 262, 330n13
Facebook Video 279
factors 6
fake news 5, 149, 186, 189, 274, 293, 295, 297,
 304n60, 307, 307n64, 312–313, 321n85,
 341, 357, 372, 381, 383
false content 297
Feenberg 16
fictitious capital 95
film 86
finance 103
finance-led capitalism 92
financial assets 95
financial capital 20
financial dominance 2, 92
financial market 96, 103, 119, 121, 146, 197,
 205, 206n36, 253, 270, 326
financial markets 93
financial performance 9, 138, 191, 212,
 222, 276
fine 186, 190, 201, 266, 269, 305
Fintech 103
fixed broadband 122
fixed capital 62
flexibilization of labour relations 94
Flichy 85
Forces of production 68
Fordist model 72
Foucault 79
Free Basics 280
free software 135n18, 135–136, 274

freedom of expression 54, 76, 127, 135, 185,
 189, 200n13, 239, 239n88, 241, 280n36,
 294, 302, 309, 334n26, 334–335
Freeman and Louçã 22
frequency spectrum 129, 131
Frey and Osborne 107
FTC 188, 201, 250, 265, 305, 357, 377
functional properties 13–14, 17, 40, 98, 134,
 159, 216, 216n57, 217n58, 223, 232, 236,
 253, 255, 285
functionalities 9, 11, 13, 15, 17n8, 45, 99, 136,
 144–145, 218, 220, 225, 230, 283, 287–
 288, 309, 311

G Suite 208, 211, 218, 225, 228, 257, 326n5,
 329, 332, 360
Garnham 78
gatekeeper 178, 199, 208, 217n59, 249, 255
Gender 243, 343
general intellect 63
general technological trajectory 9, 196
general-use technologies 75
gig economy 155, 168–169, 353, 360, 370
Global Information Technology Report 99
Global Internet Governance Forum 185
Gmail 7, 196n8, 196–197, 208, 211, 212n48,
 218–219, 223, 225, 228, 232, 236, 238,
 240, 243, 245, 254, 328n8, 328n9, 328–
 329, 329n10, 349
Goffman 80
Google x, 4–9, 16n7, 20, 55, 101, 112n25,
 116, 127, 134n16, 138–140, 146–148, 156,
 157n10, 158n13, 160n19, 158–164, 166–167,
 172n41, 174n46, 174–175, 178–179, 179n57,
 181–183, 185–187, 190, 195n5, 197n9,
 201n15, 201n16, 202n18, 202n21, 203n26,
 204n30, 205n31, 210n42, 212n48, 193–
 213, 217n59, 219n64, 219n66, 228n73,
 228n78, 215–234, 237n86, 236–240,
 241n92, 241n94, 243n100, 244n102,
 245n103, 247n106, 241–258, 263,
 266–267, 269, 273, 276n31, 281, 284–
 286, 305n61, 310–311, 317, 322, 326n5,
 328n7, 328n8, 328n9, 329n10, 330n12,
 330n13, 331n14, 331n15, 331n16, 331n17,
 331n18, 332n20, 326–334, 334n25, 343–
 348, 350–354, 356–357, 359–366, 368–
 374, 376, 378–389
Google Ads 211, 331n14

Google Analytics 204
Google Play 174, 174n46, 183, 199, 211, 216, 228
Google Shopping 112n25, 201n15, 217, 219, 333
Google+ 198, 245, 330n13
Googleplex 229
Gramsci 28
great automaton 61
groups of interest 15
Guttmann 92

Habermas 14
Harding 37
Harvey 30
hate speech 1n1, 4–5, 189, 243, 243n101, 281n37, 293, 302, 304n60, 306, 313n77, 321, 333, 336
Heidegger 48
Heilbronner 33
Herscovici 53
Hess et al 50
high-frequency trading 103
historical bloc 28
Hope 98
Horizontal expansion 179
Hughes 19
human right 141
human rights 2, 185–186
Husson and Louçã 97
Huws 107
hyper-connection 261

Ianni 90
ICT technological paradigm 128, 139, 256
ICTs 93
ideological legitimization 88
IGTV 288
impacts on the users' rights 9
incorporation 66, 179, 184, 197, 215–216, 222, 232n84, 263, 278, 287, 296, 322, 329
Industrial Revolution 81
industry 24, 27, 33, 60, 65–66, 72–74, 85–90, 92–93, 96, 99, 101, 105, 105n18, 123, 128, 133, 135, 146–147, 153n3, 159, 166, 177, 206n37, 224, 227, 250, 270, 287, 353, 383, 385
Industry 4.0 100
information and communication technologies 2, 8–9, 70, 75–76, 85, 91, 93, 103, 118, 125, 127, 135, 151, 190, 309, 324–325
information empires 76
information flow 256, 280, 284, 304, 330n12
information networks 53
informational labour 167, 167n30
info-Taylorism 108
initial public offering 197
innovation 15, 20, 20n12, 23, 25, 35, 37, 47, 74, 82, 84, 87, 88n46, 159, 163, 186, 196, 207n38, 268, 360, 372
Instagram 7, 173–175, 179, 179n57, 260–261, 263–264, 266, 270, 275–276, 278, 280, 287–288, 288n45, 291, 296, 300, 300n53, 305, 309, 311, 313n76, 315, 322, 329, 332, 344, 361, 364, 375, 377
integration 31, 74, 93, 113, 122, 180, 198, 217, 220–221, 223–224, 226, 232, 232n84, 234, 240, 256, 260, 263, 279, 285–288, 322, 328, 328n7, 331n17
intellectual labour 6n9, 109, 164–165, 257, 326
intellectual work 164
intelligent processing 3, 128, 142, 157, 327
intermediaries 85, 113, 152, 154, 156, 163, 172, 186, 188, 193, 330
international division of labour 38
internet 3, 5, 7–8, 98–99, 99n11, 102–103, 107, 113, 115, 119, 125–129, 131, 137n22, 137–139, 145, 152–154, 156–157, 160–161, 163, 167n31, 167–168, 175, 181–182, 185, 189, 193n1, 193–196, 199, 200n13, 200–201, 208, 220, 224, 226, 228n77, 228–230, 233, 236, 239, 242, 246, 250, 253–255, 259, 280n36, 290, 292, 294n50, 294–295, 299, 303n55, 313n78, 317, 324, 327–329, 331, 341, 344–345, 349, 354, 368, 370–371, 378, 384
Internet of Things 107, 115, 123–124, 128, 131, 199, 224–225
IoT 124, 128
ITU 99, 129, 131, 185, 364

Jasanoff 35
job security 169
jobless recovery 97
Jonas 48

INDEX   397

Kahneman   113
Katz   36
Kipphan   85
Klein and Kleinmann   50
knowledge stock   21

labour   3–4, 8–9, 14, 17–18, 24, 26–27, 30–31,
      37, 42, 45, 48, 53–54, 59n3, 60n5, 60n7,
      61n10, 61n9, 62n11, 56–63, 63n13, 63n15,
      64n16, 64n17, 64n20, 64–65, 68n25,
      67–69, 71–73, 75, 78–79, 89, 92n2,
      93n3, 91–94, 97, 98n9, 98–99, 101, 104,
      105n20, 105–110, 119, 135n17, 150, 152,
      155n7, 155n9, 158, 164n28, 164–165,
      167n30, 167–168, 168n32, 170, 184, 190–
      191, 209–210, 223, 225–226, 229, 248,
      257, 273–274, 274n28, 311, 324, 326, 333,
      352, 360
labour force   3, 26, 59n3, 58–60, 62n11,
      62–63, 72–73, 79, 89, 91, 107, 109, 119,
      158, 170
labour power   17
last mile   129
Latin America   37
Latour   15
laws   19, 32, 66, 68, 185, 187–188, 210, 250,
      267n16, 267n17, 267–268, 301, 335
leak   187, 264, 293, 304n58, 313
legal, social, and economic aspects   48
legislation   43–44, 77n32, 96, 110, 122, 185n63,
      184–189, 192, 200, 203, 209, 265–266,
      323, 331, 335
Lima   76
Lyon   79

machine   13, 17–18, 32, 59–60, 60n5, 61n8,
      63n15, 63–65, 65n20, 69, 71, 73, 75, 81,
      85, 108, 110, 113, 116, 134, 134n16, 143, 147,
      150, 162n25, 225, 226n71, 256, 308n68,
      310, 334, 353, 362
machinery   15
malicious systems   149
Mandel   36
Maps   197, 211, 212n48, 217, 219, 241, 254,
      372, 386
Marcuse   16
market position   153, 178, 197
market positions   9
market structure   21, 173, 179, 181, 329

Marketplace   264, 276n30, 280, 285–286,
      309, 317, 319, 333, 367–368
Martin   83
Marx   17
mass scale   116
massive data collection   122, 139, 157, 240,
      317, 327
Matchmakers   153, 354
Mattelart   74
McChesney   77
means of labour   17
mediation   3, 17–18, 46, 88n47, 156–157,
      157n11, 179, 183–184, 193, 252, 259, 283,
      283n42, 294–295, 299, 320–321, 336
memory   43, 121, 134, 251, 334, 382
Messenger   260, 275–276, 279–280, 287, 305,
      313n76, 371, 383
microprocessor   132, 132n8, 133n10, 133n12,
      133–134
Microsoft   4, 134n16, 137, 146, 148, 156, 160,
      160n19, 163, 174, 176, 179n58, 179–183,
      213, 215, 219n66, 219–220, 223, 225, 254–
      256, 327, 330, 334n24
microtargeting   149
mills   66
Minimum effort   14
misinformation   5, 242–243, 288, 293, 306,
      308, 381
mobile access   137
mobile devices   81, 107, 114n28, 122, 132–133,
      136–138, 155, 163, 177, 183, 212, 220,
      224, 228, 243, 255, 257, 262n3, 311, 317,
      327–328
Mobile devices   122
mobile operator   138
mode of production   17
Mollo   95
money   62
monopolistic capitalism   72
monopoly   23, 87, 89, 175, 179, 244, 247, 258,
      261, 264, 285, 288, 310, 317, 322–323, 332
Most Valuable Brands   101
multisided markets   158
music industry   86

National Security Agency   249, 263
Nelson and Winter   22
neoliberalism   2, 20, 24, 92, 94–96, 326,
      362, 379

network effects   4, 116–117, 123, 152n1, 152–153, 156–157, 159, 171, 178, 215n55, 317, 327, 334
networks competition   131
neutrality   8
new morphology of labour   108
Newman   117
newsfeed   260, 262, 269, 275, 279–280, 282, 282n41, 286n44, 289, 294n51, 296–297, 305–306, 309, 310n71, 315, 315n82, 315n83, 318–320, 322n86, 328n7, 328n8, 328–329, 332n20
Nightingale   241
Noble   16

O'Halooran   106
Oculus   180, 260, 264, 275, 278, 280, 289–290, 322, 329, 329n10, 356
on-demand service economy   155
online advertising   202, 248, 319
online platforms   153, 156–157
open architecture   221
operating system   7
operation processing system   135
operational systems   138, 174
oppression   12
organic composition of the capital   17
other bets   196, 199, 211, 217–218, 226, 246, 258
over-the-top   185

pages   8, 193, 194n3, 194–195, 197, 203, 205, 205n32, 207, 218, 233, 239, 242n96, 244n102, 254, 259–260, 267n13, 267–268, 275, 279–280, 281n37, 281n38, 281–284, 296, 298, 302, 305, 307, 307n64, 312n75, 312–313, 313n76, 317, 320, 330n12, 332, 350, 380–381
pandemic   107, 200, 212–213, 241, 264, 288, 308, 371–372
Paraná   103
Participatory Design   49
patents   72
Perez   72
periodization   71, 74, 191, 196–197, 263
Perry   82
personal computers   98
personal data   140n25, 153n4, 161, 182, 187–188, 208, 238, 240n90, 266, 299, 303
personal information systems   78
phases   23
phonograph   86
platform   3–6, 8, 111–112, 115–116, 116n30, 138, 146, 153n2, 153n3, 155n5, 152–156, 157n10, 157–159, 160n19, 162–163, 163n26, 164n27, 164–165, 168, 170–171, 172n38, 172n39, 172–173, 175–180, 182–185, 189, 193, 197, 197n10, 199–201, 201n16, 201n17, 202n21, 202–204, 208, 212, 213n49, 215, 215n53, 217, 217n59, 219n63, 219n64, 219–222, 225, 226n71, 228–229, 231n81, 232n83, 231–236, 238–240, 242n97, 244, 247–250, 254–255, 262n2, 262n3, 257–264, 265n6, 265–269, 271–275, 278–279, 279n35, 281n39, 282n41, 281–287, 294n52, 289–295, 304n60, 305n62, 297–306, 308–312, 314n80, 314–315, 317–323, 323n87, 327, 329, 332–333, 341, 354, 356, 358, 362, 366, 373, 375–376, 381
platform capitalism   3, 155, 375
platform politics   155
platform society   156
platforms   3–6, 8–9, 47, 53–55, 91, 97, 111–112, 115, 117, 120, 122, 126, 138–139, 145–147, 149, 153n2, 155n7, 160n17, 160n19, 171n36, 172n40, 151–173, 175–176, 178–185, 188–191, 193, 198–200, 210n42, 215n55, 221, 227, 234, 245–246, 250, 252, 259n1, 258–261, 265–266, 270, 278, 290, 294–295, 299, 301, 309, 310n72, 314, 327–330, 330n13, 332–336, 353–354, 359–360
Platforms   5, 111, 116, 155, 157, 176n50, 188, 351, 354
Play Store   164, 174, 174n46, 178, 183, 208, 213n48, 216, 218, 221, 228, 235, 286, 299
Polder et al   52
political economy of technology   46
political information   259, 302
political–institutional sphere   75, 119, 200, 202, 249, 312, 323, 333
Politics   31
Portelli   28
post-colonial perspectives   37
Poulantzas   36
power relations   11–12, 16, 26, 32, 41–42, 44–46, 50, 52, 135, 135n18, 140, 320, 324–325, 330

precariousness 108
press 76
Price comparison sites 103
price structure 153, 158
privacy 54, 114, 116, 128, 140–141, 141n26, 148, 150, 159n16, 161, 185–186, 192, 198, 201, 230, 238, 240, 240n89, 247, 250, 257, 261–262, 265n8, 265–266, 268, 268n18, 280n36, 294n50, 303, 303n55, 304n60, 304–305, 320, 334n26, 334–335, 345, 347, 356, 367–368
privacy by design 186
private regulation of the connected experience 320
produced productive force 61
production process 6, 11, 13–14, 17n8, 20, 24, 27, 34, 62n12, 61–63, 63n13, 65n20, 73, 94, 105n19, 108, 191, 207, 211, 269, 271, 274, 311
production restructuring 110
production routines 142
productive capital 62
productive forces 35
productive restructuring 2, 93
productivity 1, 1n1, 3, 18, 56–57, 64n17, 64–65, 67, 73–74, 95, 105–106, 110, 118, 124–125, 135n17, 145, 167, 248, 256, 326, 376
productivity gain 64
profiles 140n25, 158n13, 164, 177, 189, 222, 241n92, 259, 262, 267n13, 267–269, 272, 276, 281, 283n42, 283–284, 297, 304n58, 307n64, 318–319, 322, 333, 348
profiling 79
programs 74, 79, 82, 88, 100, 112, 135, 135n18, 140n25, 143, 145, 151–152, 165, 167n31, 180, 217n60, 221, 279, 289, 294, 310
progress 2, 6, 11, 21n13, 23, 25, 29n22, 33, 33n26, 35, 35n27, 37–38, 51–52, 54, 56, 59, 61, 64–67, 71, 75, 81, 84, 150, 197, 199, 223, 230, 253, 316–317, 324
protocols 126–127
public debate 5

qualitative competition 53, 171

R&D 246, 273
radicalization 4, 242, 326, 335, 378
radio 75, 77, 77n32, 85, 87–90, 129–131, 177, 250, 255

rational action 14
rationality 38
regulation 6, 8, 12, 31, 40, 43–46, 52–56, 85n45, 91, 93, 118, 120–121, 126, 131–132, 135n17, 135–136, 138, 149, 151, 159, 161, 184–185, 190, 192, 197, 199–200, 202, 211n46, 216, 216n56, 218n61, 218–219, 221–222, 225, 231, 233, 239, 245n103, 245–247, 251–254, 256, 258, 265, 269, 271–272, 282, 289, 293–294, 296, 301, 310, 310n70, 313, 317–319, 323, 325, 329–330, 332, 334–335
Regulation 12, 43, 186, 200n12, 252, 335, 349, 351, 354, 380
regulation by technology 45
regulation of technology 44
regulation over technology 44
regulatory agent 221, 249, 255, 288, 305, 323, 330
regulatory authorities 44, 202, 208, 265, 320, 331
regulatory bodies 200, 230
relative autonomy 29, 31, 39n32, 38–41, 78n36, 165n28, 258
reproduction cycle 18
right to be forgotten 200, 378
Rights 141n26, 187, 189, 239, 353, 366, 370, 377
Ronayne 103
Rosenblum 86
rotation 62
Rule 78

Saad-Filho 92
scandal 263, 266, 268, 293, 299, 304n58, 304–305, 313, 323, 373
Scholar 197, 251, 254
Science 31
scientific knowledge 19
scientific–technical revolution 36
scientific–technological sphere 43
Sclove 48
SCOT 15, 34, 46, 48, 50, 50n35, 150, 226, 231n81, 253, 281n39
search 3, 5, 7, 13, 25, 49, 50n35, 58, 88, 103–104, 111, 114, 116, 116n30, 121, 127, 139, 142, 145, 156, 159, 162–164, 164n26, 176–179, 181, 188, 195n7, 197n9, 201n15, 193–202, 206–208, 210n42, 211n45, 212n48,

search (cont.)
    210–213, 213n49, 217–220, 220n67, 227, 229, 231–233, 236–237, 239, 241n94, 242n96, 242n98, 241–245, 245n103, 247, 249–251, 253–254, 256–257, 279, 285, 288, 304n58, 307n64, 314n79, 324, 328n8, 328n9, 326–329, 331, 331n15, 343, 346, 350, 362, 364, 368–369, 372, 378, 386, 389
search engine   7, 159, 176–177, 179, 193, 196–198, 200, 207–208, 210–211, 212n48, 212–213, 213n49, 219–220, 220n67, 229, 231, 233, 242, 244, 245n103, 249, 251, 253, 257, 279, 285, 328n9, 346, 378, 386
search engine optimization   233
search engines   142, 145, 164, 164n26, 178, 181, 188, 193, 211n45, 232, 239, 242n96, 244, 250–251, 253, 350, 364
services competition   131
share value   270
simplified tasks   72
smart watch   230
smartphone   20, 133, 137, 181n60, 198–199, 201, 215n52, 235, 257, 290, 304, 328n9, 382, 385
smartphones   105n18, 110, 123, 133, 136, 139, 145, 177, 182, 198–199, 204n30, 220–221, 224, 241, 251, 252n110, 315n82
Smartphones   122, 386
social construction of technology   15, 325
social division of labour   18
social drivers   6
social factors   12
social justice   2, 12, 47
social network   4, 7, 142, 145, 155, 166–167, 179, 182, 191, 197, 231, 233, 254, 258–262, 265–266, 273–275, 278–279, 279n35, 283, 286, 288, 290–292, 296–297, 304n58, 309n69, 313n78, 314n80, 314n81, 315n83, 312–316, 316n84, 318, 322, 344, 354
social networking services   259
social networking sites   153, 259, 307n64
social networks   7, 49, 100, 113, 115–116, 138, 140, 155, 159n14, 163–164, 167n31, 166–168, 173n42, 173–174, 176, 178, 181, 190, 223, 232, 249–250, 255, 259, 269, 274, 276, 276n32, 278, 279n35, 288, 291n47, 302, 314, 327–328, 330n13, 333–334, 366, 382
social plugins   286, 318, 320, 327
social relations of production   11, 27, 30, 35–36, 46, 59, 64, 66, 68–70, 94, 122, 289
sociology of scientific knowledge   35
Soviet Union   82
speculation   95
spheres of activity   6, 9, 39, 43, 70, 184, 192, 325, 332
spheres of society   4–5, 12, 42, 51, 252, 310
stabilization   134, 147, 334
startup   278
startups   101
state   80
State   78n36, 92n2, 201, 206n36, 208, 210, 270n21, 343, 347, 354, 385
steering   114
structures   29
subsumption of intellectual labour   165
subversive rationalization   52, 334
superstructure   28
supply chains   105
surplus value   68
surplus-value   67
surveillance   3, 79n38, 79–80, 110, 128, 140, 149, 155, 212, 222n68, 222–223, 230, 240, 240n91, 246, 249, 263, 274n28, 282, 289, 299–300, 303, 303n55, 309n69, 313, 316, 318, 320, 328, 330, 332, 335, 341, 343, 351, 358, 369, 379, 388, 390
surveillance capitalism   128, 390
Sutherland   76
Swiestra and Rip   48

targeted advertisement   267
TaskRabbit platform   169
Taylorist model   72
technical code   25
technical domains   25
technical progress   65
technical reproducibility   83
technical resources   5–7, 9, 33, 50, 103, 111–112, 146, 164, 191, 218–219, 231, 252, 280, 282–284, 320, 331
technical revolution   58
technique   14, 32, 45, 57, 84, 88
techno-fundamentalism   196

technological basis   5
technological convergence   122
technological design   48
technological determinism   33, 362, 381
technological development   8
technological dimension   12
technological paradigm   6
technological rationality   16, 51, 78, 89, 234, 252
technological solutions   5, 44, 71, 102, 106, 115, 120, 160n19, 209, 221, 227, 284–285, 328
technological style   23
technological system   3, 19–20, 23–24, 43–46, 84, 121, 126, 158, 162, 192, 195, 197, 204, 209, 211, 213n49, 216n57, 217n58, 217–218, 221–222, 229, 231, 231n81, 251–254, 260–262, 267, 269, 271, 273, 275, 278–280, 282, 286, 288–289, 293, 296–297, 303–305, 309, 312, 317–322, 325
technological systems   6, 9, 11–13, 19n11, 19–21, 23, 34, 36, 40–44, 46, 54, 56, 71, 93, 97–98, 102, 121, 126, 139–140, 150–151, 156–157, 184, 191, 194, 195n5, 239, 252, 271, 309, 324, 328, 330–331, 345, 349, 363
technological trajectories   6
technology   1–2, 6–9, 11–12, 14n5, 14–16, 17n9, 17–19, 21n14, 21–23, 25–27, 28n19, 33n26, 44n34, 30–51, 53–54, 56–59, 59n4, 61, 63–64, 69–70, 73, 75–78, 78n35, 80–86, 91n1, 91–93, 98n10, 99n11, 99–104, 106, 108, 111–113, 117, 120–123, 125n2, 125–128, 130, 133, 134n16, 135n17, 134–136, 137n21, 137–140, 140n25, 142, 145–149, 151, 156–157, 159, 161, 166, 168, 183–184, 190–192, 197–199, 202n19, 207–209, 211, 216, 219, 221, 225–227, 230–231, 233, 235, 246, 248, 250, 252–254, 256, 258, 263, 270–271, 271n23, 273, 274n26, 276, 279, 288–289, 292–294, 296, 299, 310, 313, 313n79, 315n82, 315–317, 320, 324–325, 329n10, 331, 334, 336, 343, 345, 347–350, 357–358, 360, 362–363, 366, 369, 372–373, 376, 380–381, 385, 387, 389
technology and society   12, 15, 19, 36, 38, 40, 63–64, 102, 191, 235, 299
technology and society studies   15

technology reform   51
technopolitics   79
telecommunication networks   121
telecommunications   92
tendency of the rate of profit to fall   67
terminals   104, 109, 115, 122, 128
terms and conditions   141
Terms of Service   202, 266, 303
terms of use   141, 186, 189, 299, 332
third-party content   188
timeline   9, 75n29, 260, 263, 280, 282, 285, 315, 319, 347, 368
tools   5, 7, 46, 80, 149n31, 167n30, 167–168, 202, 205n31, 211n47, 217, 222n68, 222–223, 226, 226n71, 234–237, 239, 242, 244, 247–249, 253, 255–259, 262, 264, 267–268, 272, 281, 284–290, 294–295, 298–299, 302–303, 304n60, 307n64, 311, 315, 320, 325, 328, 329n10, 331n14, 331–333
Torpel et al   49
transparency   112, 118, 144, 148, 150, 186, 189, 210, 227, 238, 244, 257, 263, 281, 297, 309, 313, 334n26, 336
Trigueiro   16
TS-commodity   25
TV   75

uberization   170
unbundling rules   131
UNESCO   86

Valente   77
valorization of capital   26
value   62
value bases   12, 45, 47, 53, 334
Values base   47
variable capital   64
Veblen   33
Vertical integration   180
video   7, 129n3, 134, 138, 142, 147, 176–177, 179, 198, 208, 213n49, 215–216, 219, 221–222, 239, 242n97, 244–245, 249, 279, 285, 287–290, 296, 314n80, 330n12, 348, 384
Vines et al   49

Wajcman   50
wealth concentration   326

Web   7
Weber   14
Websites   204, 208
Weller   80
WhatsApp   4, 7, 138, 153, 173–175, 179, 179n57, 182, 235, 260–261, 263–266, 270, 275–276, 278, 280, 287–288, 291, 297, 299, 305, 308–309, 313, 322, 329, 341, 346, 354, 357, 379, 388
Wi-Fi   130–131
Williams   77
Winner   13
winner-takes-all   115
wireless   130, 132
work process   17
workers   106

Workplace   264, 280, 289, 310n71, 310–311, 322, 326n5, 332, 349
World Bank   99
Wu   74

YouTube   4, 7, 157n11, 164, 172n37, 175–176, 178, 183, 198–201, 204n28, 205n32, 208, 211–212, 212n48, 213n49, 215n53, 218n62, 215–219, 219n63, 221–222, 228, 232, 234, 236n85, 236–237, 239–240, 242, 244–245, 249, 251, 255, 264, 279, 288, 327, 328n9, 328–329, 333, 333n23, 345, 347–348, 356, 379, 382, 387, 390

Zallo   89